WITHDRAWN
HARVARD LIBRARY
WITHDRAWN

QUSEIR AL-QADIM 1980

AMERICAN RESEARCH CENTER IN EGYPT REPORTS

Preliminary and Final Reports
of Archaeological Excavations in Egypt
from Prehistoric to Medieval Times

Volume 7

Published under the auspices of
THE AMERICAN RESEARCH CENTER IN EGYPT, INC.

QUSEIR AL-QADIM 1980

Preliminary Report

by

Donald S. Whitcomb

and

Janet H. Johnson

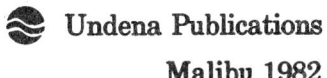 Undena Publications
Malibu 1982

Quseir al-Qadim is the site of a small port on the Egyptian coast of the Red Sea, east of Luxor in Upper Egypt. The site was occupied during the Roman period (first and second centuries of our era, when it was known as Leukos Limen) and again during Islamic times (thirteenth and fourteenth centuries, the Ayyubid and Mamluk periods). This port served as one small link in the international trade network of both these periods, stretching from the Mediterranean through the Indian Ocean.

This volume presents the results of the second season of excavations, during which a Roman merchant's "villa" and part of the central administrative buildings were excavated. A large section of the Islamic town was also cleared, within which were artifacts ranging from China to west Africa. This report presents the excavations and the artifacts recovered; these latter include the pottery, glass, lamps, Roman ostraca and Arabic letters, fauna, flora, shells, and organic materials, the latter including textiles, wood, leather, and basketry. Also included are brief reports on the survey of Bir Kareim, the site of a Roman gold mining settlement and shrine about 20 km. from the port, and a discussion of the old mosques in the modern town of Quseir.

Library of Congress Card Number 81-72088
ISBN 0-89003-112-6 (paper)
0-89003-113-4 (cloth)

© 1982 by Undena Publications

All rights reserved. No part of this publication may be reproduced or transmitted in any form or by any means, electronic or mechanical, including photocopy, recording, or any information storage and retrieval system, without permission in writing from the author or the publisher.

Undena Publications, P.O. Box 97, Malibu, CA 90265, U.S.A.

PREFACE

The excavations of the second season at Quseir al-Qadim began on January 5, 1980 and continued until February 21, 1980, a total of 42 work days. The work force consisted of an average of 25 workmen from Quseir under a Reis (Qa'ud Abd el-Rahman Mohammed) and one other experienced pickman from Quft. The excavations were concentrated in four areas of the ancient site: the area of the Roman villa, Central Building A and the pipeline, Central Building B, and the eastern area. In each of these areas one or more trenches was excavated. The Roman Villa area is one large clearance, mainly in E6b-E7a, which may be subdivided into the Roman villa itself, villa east and villa south (see pl. 2). The second area is a smaller probe into Central Building A (G8b) and a long narrow test trench called the pipeline (see pl. 5). Central Building B was tested with two small trenches (G12c and J14a) (see pl. 7). The eastern area, a counterpart for the horizontal clearance of the Roman villa, was a large exposure of the Islamic occupation, mainly in E18-E19 (see pl. 32), described in terms of northern, southern, and eastern sectors.

The trenches are designated and recorded in terms of a system of squares; a trench may be a portion of a square or multiple squares. The entire site is divided into a grid of 20 x 20 m. units (see pl. 1) designated by a letter and number (e.g., E18). Each of these units is subdivided into four 10 x 10 m. squares; these are given an additional letter (a,b,c,d; a in the northwest, b in the northeast, c in the southwest, d in the southeast). Thus E18a is a 10 x 10 m. square in the northwest of E18. The 10 x 10 m. square is the basic unit of designation for the excavation, subdivided into a theoretically infinite number of loci (e.g., E18a-[4] is the fourth locus excavated in that 10 x 10 m. area). The locus is the basic excavation unit, being a discrete and indivisible volume of soil (or any other material) with a descriptive uniformity. The process of excavation is the removal of each locus while attempting to understand the depositional (and, hence, cultural) history in terms of the surrounding loci. Such excavation relies heavily on the skill and intuition of the individual excavator influenced by a relative scale of care and control, speed and efficiency. In practice, experience at Quseir al-Qadim has led to excavation of 5 x 5 m. areas or smaller in incremental units.

The relative position of each locus may be determined on the trench plans, in the section drawings accompanying those plans, and in the matrix diagram of each trench. This will allow a clear reconstruction of the depositional history and the excavational units; it is not, however, a complete record. The composition, texture and volume will be provided in tabular form in the final report. For the sake of clarity, the plans do not place all the locus numbers, but relative positions may be determined from the matrix diagram.

In distinction from the 1978 report, all walls, whether stone or mud brick, are indicated with hatched lines and identified by a letter. Uncertain walls, wall fragments, or wall faces are indicated by broken hatching. The base of walls is usually estimated unless specifically stated. Only certain key sections are shown and those rendered schematically. As on the plans, ash concentrations are represented by dot patterns and concentrations of organic debris by patterns of broken lines. The exception to these conventions is the eastern area, where such details would have resulted in a cluttered, undecipherable plan. Finally, it should be noted that the plans are always oriented with north toward the top of the illustration.

The illustration of ceramics and other artifacts follows standard archaeological conventions of side view and section (on the right). Patterns of breakage are generally not indicated with the exception that, if a rim fragment is smaller that 1/4 of the diameter, its shape is usually indicated as a warning that orientation, diameter, and shape may be suspect. The painted wares in both Roman and Islamic corpora follow the convention of solid black for black or brown paint, hatched lines for red paint, and dotted areas for yellow. The conventions in the depiction of glazed wares are less consistent; generally black or dark brown is solid, green is diagonal hatching, blue (or, occasionally, brown) is vertical hatching, while yellow is indicated by dots if at all. The description accompanying the drawing should always be consulted as these conventions were kept to a minimum to avoid superfluous lines which would obscure the drawing.

The excavations at Quseir al-Qadim were sponsored by the Oriental Institute of the University of Chicago and by the American Research Center in Egypt. They were funded by the Smithsonian Institution Foreign Currency Program and the National Geographic Society. We gratefully acknowledge this financial assistance. The staff consisted of Donald S. Whitcomb (field director), Janet H. Johnson (co-director), Catharine Valentour (conservator), Wilma Wetterstrom (ethnobotanist), Carol Meyer (draftsman and site supervisor), Patricia Wattenmaker (site supervisor and faunal analyst), Steven Sidebotham (site supervisor and photographer), Jonathan Brookner (site supervisor and registrar), Scott Redford (site supervisor and draftsman), Mona Megalli (site supervisor and draftsman), Hanna B. Tadros (site supervisor and draftsman), Haini el-Zeini (consultant for Islamic mosques), and Rabi'a Ahmad Hamdan (representative of the Egyptian Organization of Antiquities). Especial thanks are due to Rabi'a Hamdan for his untiring helpfulness and his care and concern that ours be a successful field program.

There are many others, especially in Egypt, to whom we owe a debt of thanks and whose help we here most gratefully acknowledge. Many members of the Egyptian Organization of Antiquities went out of their way to help us and to expedite various things for us. The following were especially helpful: Abd el-Qadr Selim, Suleiman Ahmed Suleiman, and Ali el-Khouli at Abbasieh; Dia Abou Ghazi, Mohammed Mohsen, and Mohammed Saleh at the Egyptian Museum; Abd el-Raouf Ali Yusuf at the Islamic Museum; Mohammed Sogheir in Luxor; and Abd el-Monem Shendawili, Husein al-Afyuni, and Rabi'a Hamdan in Qena. We are also indebted to various people in the modern town of Quseir for their interest in our project and their assistance to us on many matters. These include Mitwali Hafez Ragab (director general of administration of the Quseir Phosphate Company, from whom we rented lodgings and work space during our stay in Quseir), Ahmad Nafisi (chief of public relations of the Phosphate Company), and Akid Abou Bakr Dabbous (police commandant) and his assistant Abd el-Bast.

We are also very happy to acknowledge our debt of gratitude to Lanny and Martha Bell, directors of Chicago House, for their continuing interest and support, both moral and practical. From them we obtained living and working accomodations in Luxor, help with purchasing of supplies and equipment, and a continuing interest in the site and the work. We are also grateful to the staff of the American Research Center in Egypt for all their assistance, both helping with preliminaries and helping with supplies and equipment after arrival in Cairo. Especially to be thanked are Paul Walker (American Director), James P. Allen (Cairo Director), Attiya Habachi, and May Trad.

We would also like to thank all those people whose hard work has enabled us to put together this preliminary report within a relatively short time from returning from the field. In addition to the field staff and those who have prepared individual sections of this report, and whose names appear therewith, we also gratefully acknowledge the many hours donated by a series of volunteers. Sally Zimmerman and Lisette Ellis spent innumerable hours labelling all the objects which were granted to the Oriental Institute as a result of the very generous division with the Egyptian Antiquities Organization. David Rosenberg, assisted by Lisette Ellis, spent much of a summer reconstrucing pots, mostly the large storage vessels and amphorae from the Roman villa. Fred Hiebert and Helen Alten both helped in drawing and inking many of the objects which are in Chicago and which appear in the report. An especial note of thanks goes to Carol Meyer, who spent an immense amount of time drawing and inking a very large percentage of the drawings used in this report. Sally Zimmerman, Judy Cottle, and Joan Barghusen spent many long, difficult hours proof-reading this manuscript, for which we are very grateful (Judy Cottle having also provided most of the Munsell numbers given on the pottery legends). Martha Bays is preparing a computer program to handle the materials (so far the pottery) from the 1980 (and, eventually, the 1982) season. Without the efforts of all of these people this report would never have been finished. To all these people, and many others who, for lack of space must remain nameless but not forgotten, we express our thanks.

                                                Donald S. Whitcomb
                                              Janet H. Johnson
                                              December, 1981

TABLE OF CONTENTS

	Preface	iii- vi
	Table of Contents	vii
	List of Plates	ix- x
	List of Figures	xi
	List of Tables	xi
Chapter 1:	Introduction--Donald S. Whitcomb and Janet H. Johnson	1- 20
Chapter 2:	Trench Summaries, Roman Areas--Donald S. Whitcomb	21- 49
Chapter 3:	Roman Ceramics--Donald S. Whitcomb	51-115
Chapter 4:	Trench Summaries, Islamic Areas--Donald S. Whitcomb	117-132
Chapter 5:	Islamic Ceramics--Donald S. Whitcomb	133-192
Chapter 6:	Imported Far Eastern Wares--John Carswell	193-199
Chapter 7:	Large and Small Storerooms of the Roman Villa--Carol Meyer	201-213
Chapter 8:	Roman Glass--Carol Meyer	215-232
Chapter 9:	Islamic Glass--Donald S. Whitcomb	233-241
Chapter 10:	Roman Lamps--Steven Sidebotham	243-256
Chapter 11:	Terra Sigillata Stamps--Steven Sidebotham	257-261
Chapter 12:	Inscriptional Material--Janet H. Johnson	263-266
Chapter 13:	The Red Sea Port of Quseir: Arabic Documents and Narrative Sources--Gladys Frantz-Murphy	267-283
Chapter 14:	Textiles--Gillian Eastwood	285-326
Chapter 15:	Small Objects--Janet H. Johnson	327-346
Chapter 16:	Fauna--Patricia Wattenmaker	347-353
Chapter 17:	Plant Remains--Wilma Wetterstrom	355-377
Chapter 18:	Marine Invertebrates--David S. Reese	379-384
Chapter 19:	Conservation--Catharine Valentour	385-389
Chapter 20:	Bir Kareim--Donald S. Whitcomb	391-396
Chapter 21:	Notes on Some of the Old Mosques in Quseir--Haini el-Zeini	397-406

LIST OF PLATES

1. Quseir al-Qadim Excavations — 6
2. Roman Villa — 22
3. Roman Villa — 24
4. Villa East and Villa South — 33
5. Central Building A and Pipeline — 38
6. Central Building A and Pipeline — 40
7. Central Building B — 45
8. G12c and J14a — 47
9. Roman Villa, Kitchen Wares — 73
10. Roman Villa, Cooking Pots — 75
11. Roman Villa, Bowls — 77
12. Roman Villa, Jars and Bases — 79
13. Roman Villa, Large Vessels — 81
14. Roman Villa, Large Storeroom — 83
15. Roman Villa, Large Storeroom — 85
16. Roman Villa, Large Storeroom — 87
17. Roman Villa, Large Storeroom Oil Jars and Small Storeroom — 89
18. Roman Villa, Small Storeroom Oil Jars — 91
19. Roman Villa, Small Storeroom — 93
20. Roman Villa, Storeroom E6c — 95
21. Roman Villa, Fine Wares — 97
22. Villa East and Villa South, Kitchen and Cooking Pots — 99
23. Villa East and Villa South, Bowls and Bases — 101
24. Villa East and Villa South, Jars and Large Vessels — 103
25. Villa East and Villa South, Fine Wares — 105
26. Central Building A, Roman Ceramics — 107
27. Central Building B, Amphorae from J14a — 109
28. Central Building B — 111
29. Roman Villa and Villa East, Terra Sigillatas — 113
30. Villa South, Pipeline, and Central Building B, Terra Sigillatas — 115
31. Eastern Area — 118
32. Eastern Area — 120
33. Eastern Area, Glazed Cream Wares — 155
34. Eastern Area, Glazed Red Wares — 157
35. Eastern Area, Sgraffiato Wares — 159
36. Eastern Area, Slip-Painted Wares — 161
37. Eastern Area, Mustard Wares — 163
38. Eastern Area, Underglaze Painted Wares, Yellow-Blue Wares, Lamps — 165
39. Eastern Area, Cream Wares — 167
40. Eastern Area, Cream Wares — 169
41. Eastern Area, "African" and Painted Wares — 171
42. Eastern Area, Unglazed Bowls — 173
43. Eastern Area, Large Unglazed Bowls — 175
44. Eastern Area, Glazed Cooking Wares and Storage Jars — 177
45. Eastern Area, Purple Wares — 179
46. Eastern Area, Neckless Jars — 181
47. Eastern Area, Jars and Bottles — 183
48. Eastern Area, Storage Jars — 185

49.	Eastern Area, Bases and Unusual Forms	187
50.	Eastern Area, Kegs and Unusual Forms	189
51.	Central Building A, Islamic Ceramics	191
52.	Imported Far Eastern Wares	197
53.	Large and Small Storerooms	203
54.	Items from Storeroom Floors	205
55.	Roman Villa, Glass	217
56.	Villa East, Villa South, and Pipeline, Glass	219
57.	Quseir Connections with Surrounding Regions (Glass Production Centers)	229
58.	Islamic Glass	235
59.	Figurines, Beads, and Bracelets	239
60.	Roman Lamps	249
61.	Inscriptions	259
62.	1978 Textiles	287
63.	1980 Textiles	291
64.	Embroidery and Batik	295
65.	Hems and Edges	297
66.	Seams	298
67.	Hems, Darts, Etc.; Faults; Loops	299
68.	Faience, Wood, and Stone Vessels	329
69.	Wooden Objects	335
70.	Metal	339
71.	Shoes, etc.	341
72.	Mills, Incense Burner, and Bir Kareim Uraeus	343
73.	Bir Kareim	392
74.	Bir Kareim, Impressionistic Bird's Eye View	396

LIST OF FIGURES

1. View East across Site — 17
2. Looking East across E6c Storeroom — 27
3. Looking West across 1978 Excavations. . .to Roman Villa . . .28
4. Looking East across North End of Large Storeroom — 30
5. Beams and Stringers of Roof of Cellar — 30
6. Altar Found in E7a-14 34
7. G8b looking North — 41
8. J14a looking South — 48
9. Provisional Periodization of Roman Villa Loci 52
10. Looking South across the Eastern Area — 121
11. Keg Amidst Fiber and Ash — 126
12. Looking East across Eastern Area. 128
13. Letter Mentioning Quseir — 268
14. Ms. Quseir 1, RN 592, P8b-18 — 274
15. Ms. Quseir 1, RN 592, P8b-18. 275
16. Ms. Quseir 2, RN 594, P7b-2 — 277
17. Ms. Quseir 2, RN 594, P7b-2 — 278
18. Ost. Quseir 1, RN 634, A22d-1 280
19. Ost. Quseir 2, RN 634, A22d-1 — 281
20. Block Resist and Block Printed Textiles — 292
21. Hats. 293
22. Islamic Wooden Box — 331
23. Houses. . .in Area A, Bir Kareim — 393
24. Temple at Bir Kareim. 395
25. Decoration of Door Lintel of Mosque of Sheikh el-Farran — 398
26. Stela Found in Abd el-Ghaffar Mosque — 401
27. Stela Found in Abd el-Ghaffar Mosque. 401
28. Text of Third Stela Found in Mosque of Abd el-Ghaffar — 402
29. Corner of Mosque of Sheikh Abdullah el-Hindi — 403

LIST OF TABLES

1. Percentage of Late Islamic Caprine Bones Fused — 350
2. Proportion of Sheet to Goat — 352
3. Plant Remains from Fine-Sieve and Flotation Samples--
    Roman Quseir al-Qadim. 357-59
4. Plant Remains from Fine-Sieve and Flotation Samples--
    Islamic Quseir al-Qadim — 360
5. Plant Remains Recovered by Hand During the Excavations — 361-62

CHAPTER 1: INTRODUCTION
Donald Whitcomb and Janet H. Johnson

Quseir is a small modern port located on the Red Sea at the end of the Wadi Hammamat, the shortest wadi system which connects the major cities of Upper Egypt with the Red Sea. Both medieval Arabic texts and Greco-Roman texts refer to a small port in this area. The remains of this earlier port are preserved at Quseir al-Qadim, located on a small natural harbor (or *mirsa*, literally 'anchorage') eight km. north of the modern town. The mound itself is approximately ten hectares in area. The site and region of Quseir have been described by Sandford and Arkell:

> In the vicinity of el-Kusair el-Kadim is a small inlet, behind which is a dry lagoon, probably an elevated part of the purely Pleistocene coral girdle (1939: 36).
> A few hundred yards south of el-Kusair el-Kadim is an embayment of the living reef (the port of the adjacent ruined and long abandoned town). Breaking through the gap with considerable force upon the shore, waves have built up a storm beach, on the landward side of which is a salt marsh, evidently marking a local channel of greater age, that is, of the 25-foot stage.... The 70- and 25-foot platforms dominate the foreshore to el-Kusair and beyond it southward for long distances (1939: 67).

The present mud flats (*sabkha*) behind Quseir al-Qadim might have been a shallow lagoon accessible to small craft in earlier historic times. Within the drainage area of the Wadi Quseir al-Qadim and the smaller tributary from the Bir al-Anz behind the lagoon of the littoral plain are bad-lands formed by terraces and raised beaches, such as described by Sandford and Arkell (1939) and Büdel (1952: 116 and Bd. 2). Despite its proximity to the sea, it is a typical desert landscape with a mean average precipitation which is barely 4 mm. annually (Jackson, 1961). The vegetation of the region was described by Klunzinger (1878), who emphasized its sparcity and xerophytic nature.

The higher elevations of the drainage area are complex hills of Miocene marls, shales, and sandstones with basal igneous and metamorphic rocks to the north and south (Said, 1962: fig. 16). West of the Quseir al-Qadim drainage is the alluvial plain of the Wadi Nakheil. A major fault line runs along the eastern edge of this plain, one of many fault lines which occur in this part of the Red Sea hills and which are often associated with wells and springs (Barron and Hume, 1902: 225 and pl. III).

This ancient and medieval port engaged in trade with the east, including India, in both periods of its occupation and served the pilgrimage route during the Mamluk period. During neither the Roman nor the Mamluk period, however, was Quseir al-Qadim the major Egyptian Red Sea port. But it was the port at the end of the shortest overland route between the Nile valley and the Red Sea. The most important port on the Egyptian coast of the Red Sea during the early Islamic period was Aidhab, located far to the south of Quseir near the modern Suwakin on the Sudanese border. This primacy of the port of Aidhab may have been due to its initial character as the port of Aswan (the first early Islamic center in Upper Egypt), to its proximity to Jedda (the port of Mecca), and to the fact that the monsoon winds reliably carry trading ships only as far north as that latitude (U.S.H.C., 1976). During the 13th and 14th centuries, Quseir al-Qadim also functioned as a port for Qus, the capital of Upper Egypt from the Fatimid period onward. The earliest mention of the name "Quseir" appears in the 13th century under the rule of the Bahri Mamluk sultans. European maps from the 14th century begin to mark Quseir as an important spice port, sometimes confounding it with Qus (Garcin, 1976: 225, n. 2). Qalqashandi, writing in the 14th century, described Quseir's participation in the eastern "spice" trade:

> al-Quseir is on the northern side of Aidhab and some of the ships frequent it; it is near to Qus and Aidhab is far from Qus. The merchandise is carried from Quseir to Qus, then from Qus to the warehouse of al-Karim in Fustat (1913: 463).

Garcin argues that the prosperity of Red Sea trade in the Mamluk period had its roots in the policies of the Ayyubid dynasty (1171-1250 A.D.), when the unity of the Sunni Islamic world was restored and the Red Sea re-opened to commerce.

It was the unity of the eastern Mediterranean following the conquests of Alexander the Great, and especially following the establishment of the Roman Empire, which encouraged the development of trade with the spice lands (in this case southern Arabia, Africa, and India, and, through India, Southeast Asia). The seaborne aspect of this trade, via the Red Sea, involved mostly staples, rather than luxury items, which were more frequently carried overland (Raschke, 1978). One of the Red Sea ports mentioned by the classical geographers as participating in this important element of Egyptian foreign trade was Leucos Limen ('white harbor') (Murray, 1925: 141), located at Quseir al-Qadim. Although it is not the best natural harbor on the western side of the Red Sea, it is, as has been noted, the terminus of the shortest route through the eastern desert. The Wadi Hammamat road has approximately twelve fortified Roman watering stations or *hydreuma* (called *wakala* 'caravanserai' by the Arabs) in the 180 km. between the Red Sea and the Nile valley; a "system of intervisible beacons or signal towers ...may also very probably have been used for signalling to the custom-house at Coptos [i.e., Quft, just north of Qus] the arrival of ships" at Leucos Limen (Murray, 1925: 139, 145).

However, as in the Islamic period, this port was not the major Red Sea port during the Greco-Roman period. Myos Hormos, almost opposite Assiut in Middle Egypt, to which a road led from Qena just north of Quft, was important during the Ptolemaic period (Meredith, 1952: 104). But by the Roman period the major port was Berenice, almost opposite Aswan at the first cataract. Berenice was presumably the preferred port for the same reason that Aidhab flourished in the medieval period: because it was fairly difficult for ships to sail up the Red Sea against the prevailing north wind. The long road (approximately 370 km.) across the eastern desert from Berenice to the terminus at Quft was provided with watering stations similar to those in the Wadi Hammamat, but there were no beacon towers. The Nile valley terminus for both Leucos Limen and Berenice was Quft, whence the goods were shipped up the river to Alexandria for consumption or further shipment across the Mediterranean.

The Wadi Hammamat route into the eastern desert was also used during the Pharaonic period. There are numerous graffiti, in hieroglyphic, hieratic, and demotic Egyptian and in Greek and Latin, at the granite quarries located almost exactly half way through the eastern desert on this road. Most were left by persons connected with quarrying expeditions, but a few were left by people who had gone to the Red Sea to engage in long-distance trade down the African coast. It is possible that there is a Pharaonic port under the modern town of Quseir (blocks decorated in Egyptian hieroglyphs and assumed to come from a Ptolemaic temple were found reused in homes in the modern town [Porter and Moss, 1952: 337-38]); the Middle Kingdom "port" was discovered at Wadi Gawasis, approximately 60 km. north of Quseir. Although no evidence was found of a permanent settlement, a team from the University of Alexandria did discover a number of stelae recording trips to the spice land of Punt, thought to have been on or near the Somali coast, and ostraca mentioning rulers of the early 12th dynasty (Sayed, 1977). It has also been suggested that Quseir and the Wadi Hammamat were possible points for the contact between predynastic Egypt and Mesopotamia which has been credited with spurring the development of Pharaonic civilization (Kantor, 1965: 12). Single Gerzean (late Predynastic of Upper Egypt) burials have been identified on the Red Sea at Ras Samadai (Murray and Derry, 1923) and in the Wadi Hammamat (Debono, 1951: 88). The eastern desert has been exploited during all periods of Egyptian history for its mineral resources and presumably always supported a small tribal population similar to the modern Ababda.

The 1978 Season

The excavation of this small Red Sea port was undertaken to study the international commercial activity of the town, its internal social interaction, and the town as one part of a symbiosis of a port and its urban hinterland, that is, the urban center within the Nile valley to which it transported its merchandise. Each period of mercantile activity in the port of Quseir al-Qadim corresponded to a period of strong, imperial government with mercantile impulses based on an urban center in the Nile valley: Coptos in the Greco-Roman period and Qus in the medieval period, these two cities being in very close proximity to one another. The urban center was responsible for establishing the port and for its maintenance through a constant commitment of urban resources. The mercantile patterns of relationship between ports and their internal urban centers have been explored for modern situations by economic geographers, particularly Vance (1970). This field of inquiry has been studied less often by historical geographers and archaeologists in the Near East, although Whitcomb focused on this problem in his study of medieval southern Iran (1979).

Thus the importance of Quseir al-Qadim stems not only from the value of investigation of the specific historic periods present (medieval Islamic and early Roman) but from the fact that this ancient port offers an opportunity to explore new questions of cultural interaction—patterns of contact between the Nile valley and the Red Sea dealing with long-range trade and patterns of local adaptation and land utilization. Clarification of the economic and political patterns and constraints on these relatively well-documented periods will ultimately provide hypotheses for reconstruction of earlier periods.

A reconnaissance in 1977 indicated that, although there are no structures preserved above ground, the general state of preservation is exceptionally good, even for Egypt with its dry climate and unusually good preservation. It also became clear that any habitation at this site was an artificial one, supported by the constant influx of food-stuffs and all other necessities from the Nile valley, for the site has no agricultural hinterland. Only marine resources are available; even potable water had to be brought in regularly from wells 20 or more km. away. Traces of what were assumed to be the Roman harbor facilities are visible on the surface of the site. The regularity of orientation of the surface walls suggested that the port had been carefully planned according to classical town-planning principles (Ward Perkins, 1974). The spatial organization and associated material culture of a non-Mediterranean classical period harbor would be a useful complement to the recent work on classical Mediterranean ports (e.g., Ward, 1976; Hurst, 1976; Yorke and Little, 1975). Where the classical port was overlaid by the Mamluk port, surface collections revealed a surprisingly sophisticated range of materials. Distinctive glazed ceramics from Syria and porcelains and celadons from China evidenced the international trade imports while some glazed wares, enameled glass, and textile fragments reflected the Egyptian exports (Goitein, 1963: 197-99).

During the first season a contour map of the site was prepared and all surface remains of walls were planned, confirming the initial impression that the town had been laid out in the rectilinear pattern normal for classical cities, with streets defining regular insulae (see pl. 1; note that the modern coast road runs through the site and a strip 80 m. wide has been destroyed). The analysis of the material collected from an intensive surface survey of the undisturbed portion of the city indicated four subdivisions of the site: an Islamic area to the east of the modern road (the eastern area of the 1980 excavations), a mixed Islamic and Roman area along the southern edge of the site west of the modern road, and two slightly different Roman areas north and west of the latter. In order to determine as much as possible of the structural organization, use, and reuse of the western part of the city, a series of small test trenches was excavated in key areas (the areas shown in black in pl. 1).

The remains on the site are generally shallow, between one and two meters in depth; those areas of greatest preserved depth of architecture belong to the large central buildings. Almost all of the site is covered with a hard caliche formation (salt pan) which has acted most severely upon the mud wash and mud bricks, making delineation of walls extremely difficult. Below this caliche seal (which can be from 10 cm. to over one meter thick), preservation is excellent, and a very wide range of artifactual data was discovered, both Roman and Mamluk.

The northwestern area (trenches B4a, C4c, and D4b) was built and occupied in the earliest period of occupation, probably early first century of our era, as is shown by the fact that it is oriented with the rest of the town. However, this whole section was soon abandoned and used as a refuse dump during later Roman occupation. This would seem to indicate a contraction of the size of the town during the Roman period. As a dumping ground, this area provided concentrations of artifacts of all types, the exceeding dryness of the site having preserved a

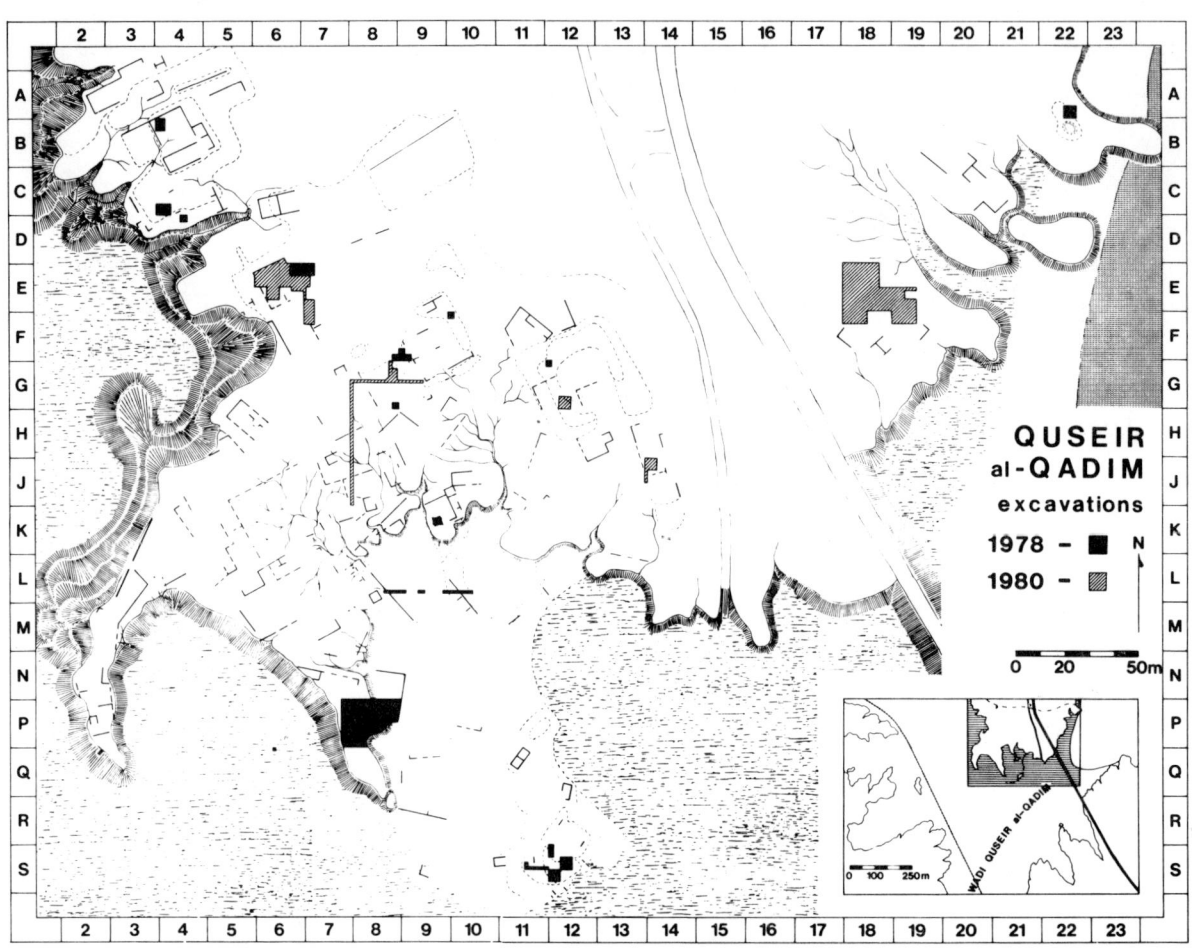

Plate 1: Quseir al-Qadim Excavations

wealth of organic remains (cloth, basketry, matting, wooden objects, seeds, papyrus fragments, and so on) as well as pottery, glass, and metals. These objects reflect both the trade goods vital to the port (glass and cloth were two of the main Egyptian exports to the east during the Roman period) and the materials of daily life of these merchants and sailors (including fish nets, fish hooks, and large numbers of fish bones, fish being the only locally available source of food). Also found in this area were a number of ostraca (in Greek largely, although one was the last line of a tax receipt written in demotic Egyptian and one is in South Arabic, attesting to contact with the Arabian peninsula across the Red Sea) and a few scraps of papyrus (with inscriptions in Latin and Greek). The existence of Latin and of an ostracon mentioning a *chiliarch* (military tribune) suggests the presence of a military unit at Quseir al-Qadim. One Greek ostracon is a dedication made in thanks for safekeeping of the dedicant, written on mica.

The fourth area identified during the surface survey, between the northwest corner of the site and the larger central buildings, may have been an industrial section since a small iron-working furnace and much iron slag were found in this area (E6b-E7a) (this is the area where the Roman villa was cleared during the 1980 season). The pottery found in this trench included imported Roman Arretine wares and local imitations thereof. In addition, one of the amphorae has a short inscription carved on the shoulder. This inscription is in the Brahmi script found at Arikamedu, in Southern India, evidently used to write Tamil, and dating from the first--second century of our era. A comparison of the pottery found at Arikamedu with the materials from Quseir al-Qadim, especially from E6b-E7a, showed that both sites had similar imported first--second century Roman wares and that Quseir al-Qadim has several examples of what the excavator of Arikamedu called native Indian wares (Wheeler, 1946). This is direct confirmation of the trade between Quseir al-Qadim and southern India and may even indicate that there was a small Indian population at Quseir al-Qadim itself. This would certainly be an explanation for the variation observed in the surface collections between this area and the contemporary areas northwest and south of E6-E7.

In 1978, several trenches were sunk in the area of the two large central buildings. Excavations in the more western of the two revealed standing mud-brick walls over a meter in height built in the same header and stretcher construction found, in stone, in the northwest area (C4c). The structure had been reused in the Islamic period, but artifacts below the mud-brick wall fall and resting on floor levels were entirely Roman, first to early third century of our era. In addition to amphora sherds, examples of the plugs used to stop the amphorae were found, stamped with stamps showing Egyptian motifs and inscriptions in Greek. The ones where the inscription is preserved give the names of imperial freedmen, presumably the men in charge of a wine-producing or shipping estate doing business in or with Quseir al-Qadim. The thickness of the walls of this structure certainly fits with the suggestion that these were either government centers or bases of operation for the merchants, but further discussion of the buildings and their functions had to await more extensive clearance of the structures (further trenches in the western central building and areas south of it excavated in 1980 are G8b and the pipeline).

Based on contours it was hypothesized that the rectangular depression straight south of this large Roman building, which is now *sabkha*, was open water in the Roman period and served as the Roman harbor. This possibility was supported by a section cut across the harbor, which revealed the remains of what could have been quay walls on both sides of the depression and little except a few sherds of Roman pottery in the fill. Although what was called the "island" is surrounded by *sabkha* now, it was assumed that it was in open water in Roman times. Therefore, several trenches were put into this "island" in an attempt to discover whether the wall traces on the surface were the remains of a lighthouse or fortification of some sort. However, these wall traces were Mamluk and limited to the immediate surface. Under them was an accumulation of sands and gravels laid down in lenses to a depth of over three meters (these were the only trenches from the 1978 season which did not reach bedrock). There was good first--second century Roman pottery in the lowest levels dug. The hypothesis which seems most probable is that this "island" is the spoil heap from successive Roman dredging operations, attempts to keep the harbor open.

It was thus suggested that this small port was laid out as a unit but soon began to shrink in size. The occupation lasted from perhaps early in the first century of our era into the early third century at the latest. All datable evidence (pottery, glass, coins, ostraca) confirms a first and second century occupation. These dates include the active period of trade between the Roman Empire and India attested in written documents. Both Greek and Egyptian speaking Egyptians seem to have lived at Quseir al-Qadim, and they had contact with people in the Arabian peninsula and India; indeed, there may even have been a small Indian colony living at the site. Note also that a Nabataean graffito was found during the regional survey, perhaps indicating the presence of Nabataean traders at Quseir al-Qadim. Artificial efforts to maintain the harbor facilities seem to have been undertaken.

Nevertheless, perhaps early in the third century, Quseir al-Qadim was abandoned. It was not until approximately 1000 years later that it was again selected as a small center for trade with the east--East Africa and India, and, through the latter, with the Far East. By this time the Roman harbor had completely silted up and the shoreline had receded at least beyond the "island." Islamic buildings were scattered upon the *sabkha*, but more important ones were located on the higher parts of the city, often reusing or modifying older Roman structures. The Islamic occupation does not seem to have been as large as the Roman occupation at its largest since no Islamic materials were found in the northwestern part of the site.

Work in 1978 on the Islamic occupation was concentrated on the area of the old Roman harbor. One small trench was put in at the northeast corner of the old harbor (K9b), which revealed a small room with two distinct occupations. A tradition of unglazed painted wares was noted as well as glazed materials. But work on the Islamic occupation concentrated on a series of houses on top of and running down the eastern side of the peninsula forming the western side of the old harbor (P7-P8). There must have been an earlier Roman occupation of this area since a large amount of Roman material had been carefully swept down the slope and plastered over, where it served as floor for rooms part way down the slope. Some of the walls may, indeed, have been reused Roman walls. The excavations revealed a series of regular domestic units including courtyards, sitting rooms, and storerooms opening off a series of streets and lanes. Such features as *mastabas* and floor mats were found *in situ*. A wide range of artifactual material was discovered, including imported Chinese porcelains and celadons and a large corpus of cloth, mostly assorted checks and stripes but including one elaborately embroidered piece, all datable to the 13th to 15th centuries.

On the eastern part of the site, a small trench was sunk to clarify the situation of a group of disturbed Islamic burials. In this trench were found imported Syrian Mamluk blue and white glazed wares, East African paddle-stamped wares, and scraps of printed cloth of a type called "Fustat" cloth, made in India and dated between the 12th and 15th centuries. This collection is duplicated in the 1980 season eastern area excavations.

Also found was a very large corpus of letters, written in Arabic in black ink on paper. They had been crumpled, torn up, and thrown away by the original writer or by the recipient after they had been read. They are scattered throughout the site in Islamic levels, almost 100 fragments coming from the large house complex in P7-P8. They are largely private letters or religious spells and charms; one bears the date 615 A.H. [=1214 A.D.]. In addition, a series of inscribed pieces of ostrich eggshell was found with the Muslim burials in the northeast corner of the site. Again the collection is greatly augmented by finds from the 1980 season (see chapter 13 on the Arabic documents).

Thus, although the Islamic occupation of the site may have been small and short-lived, it has left evidence of its organization (reuse of the large central Roman buildings, house structures near the harbor), its extensive overseas trade connections (East African, Indian, and Chinese imports), and a corpus of written materials which potentially could reveal an amazing amount of detail about the town and its times.

While the mapping and excavation were going on on the mound, the area within twenty km. of the site was subjected to an intensive survey. Despite the seemingly desolate character of the environs of the port, this survey revealed a wealth of attestations of human presence. Most immediate were the caravan routes, marked by guard posts and caravanserais. A caravanserai was found at Nakheil, near a Roman mining settlement. This settlement was mapped and extensive pottery collections were made for comparison with Quseir al-Qadim. These comparisons have shown that the Nakheil material is late Roman, dating after the abandonment of Quseir al-Qadim. South of the modern road, at Bir Kareim, were found a well and gold mines contemporary with the Roman occupation of Quseir al-Qadim. The temple and site were restudied in 1980 (see chapter 20). Numerous small footpaths were also found. Evidence of mining operations for iron, manganese, and gold were discovered, as were carnelian and limestone quarries, the latter presumably the source of the limestone used to build the walls at Quseir al-Qadim which gave it the ancient name Leucos Limen "white harbor." Numerous rock drawings were found in areas of Nubian sandstone depicting such animals as ostriches, gazelles, and camels. Others showed mounted hunters or enigmatic symbols commonly called tribal signs or are inscriptions of travellers.

Thus, although no evidence of direct support activities for the port was found, the mining of the desert's resources and its function as a conduit between the Nile valley and the Red Sea were well attested, as was nomad use, presumably from prehistoric times.

Thus the 1978 season in and near Quseir al-Qadim provided evidence of trade and daily life of a small port during the two periods of intensive economic activity on the Red Sea, provided direct confirmation of assumed trade patterns (to India, East Africa) and trade goods (e.g., glass, cloth), and produced the first evidence for the spatial organization of such a small Red Sea port. The wealth of material preserved because of the extreme dryness of the site produced a large corpus of artifactual evidence, much of it of types which have been little studied and will help in the clarification of the social, economic, and political patterns and constraints involving such a port.

The 1980 Season

The second season of excavations at Quseir al-Qadim continued to focus on the economic organization of the port, introducing a resource base model. Since the regional survey around Quseir al-Qadim had indicated the absence of any possibility of agricultural hinterland and the results from the excavations had pointed to a considerable capital investment in the foundation and maintenance of the port (e.g., Roman dredging operations to keep the harbor open), Quseir al-Qadim was seen to take its locational rationale not from the existence of a market supply system of location based on settlement patterns and retail demands (as in locational models such as the Central Place model) but rather as a focus of communications located by convenience of external contacts, in this case propinquity to riverine urban centers and other Red Sea centers (e.g., Leuke Kome, Jedda, Aden). (See Hodder, 1965: 99-100 [quoted in Adams, 1974: 243], on traditional African markets as foci of communication, not nuclei of settlement, the markets having been introduced from outside contacts, not developed naturally within an existing socio-economic framework.) As more information is available (especially documentary evidence, both internal, from excavations, and external, especially from the Nile valley), more sophisticated analyses of investment in production and transportation as comparative costs, or input-output models such as those utilized in locational geography, may be possible.

Attendant upon using a resource base model for the economic analysis of Quseir al-Qadim are the factors of uncertainty and risk. Following the mode of analysis of Sinclair,

> ...the success, welfare, and vitality of a port, as reflected in the volume and nature of its imports, and exports, is dependent upon the nature of (a) the port's *hinterland*, described as the developed land space, connected with the port by means of transport lines, which receives or ships goods through the port; (b) its *foreland*, the overseas land areas shipping goods to or receiving goods from the port by means of ocean carriers; (c) the *maritime space*, the water body between the port and the foreland which is organized and patterned by man to facilitate commerce; and (d) the *port* itself, including the physical site and situation, wealth and variety of facilities, and the character of its entrepreneurs and citizens (1967: 356, emphasis added).

In the specific case of Quseir al-Qadim, there must have been a constant uncertainty as to reception in the foreland (whether India, South Arabia, or some other region), availability of trade goods, and acceptability of exports. Likewise the maritime space held constant dangers of natural catastrophes and possible piracy. After the discovery of the monsoon, the limited sailing seasons put temporal strictures on maritime ventures pinning the hopes of a full year on one sailing season, and this with a length turn-around time in between.

The hinterland was, as mentioned above, a city of the Nile valley connected to the port by a relatively short, but nevertheless tenuous, link, the caravan route, which was secured by watchtowers and manned by patrols against desert tribes and robbers (Bagnall, 1977). The valley itself endured periods of famine and political disturbances which could threaten the supply to the port of virtually all foodstuffs and manpower; these are extremes of fluctuation of prices and official concern which would have been vital concerns for Quseir al-Qadim's inhabitants.

Finally the port itself was dependent on a presumably daily supply of water brought from a distance (most likely from Bir Kareim), a constant expense and concern. The masses of amphora fragments may represent a compensatory strategy in this regard.

Bearing these and other such risks in mind, it was hypothesized (following Arrow, 1974) that the commercial enterprise at Quseir al-Qadim would have been organized to allow alternative strategies, fall-back positions, necessary features of risk aversion. Such alternatives which would show up in the archaeological record include maintenance of minimal standards of living in the port, utilization of numerous storage facilities, and development of alternative resources (such as mining and local light industry). Seasonal migration of part or all of the population was also considered possible. This hypothesis also assumes an entrepreneurial group, that is, a risk-taking group, whose social organization and institutions were geared to long-term patterns of economic efficiency. This economic efficiency derived from an efficiency in information gathering and dissemination (thus, including a well-developed communications system) as well as incorporation of general expectations derived from past experience. This view of these commercial practices emphasizes the primacy of tradition, a complex set of behaviors and expectations--of adaptations--necessary for such a sustained commercial venture. This was a pattern implanted and sustained from external resources, one of which was inherited knowledge of feasibilities. For the Romans, these derived from the Ptolemaic and South Arabian practices, modified by the discovery of the monsoon navigation system, and a multiplication from examples of successful ports. This same respect for tradition may have led the Ayyubids to settle on the remains of this ancient port rather than choosing an alternate bay for their port.

Quseir al-Qadim did not develop into a large and important port as a result of either attempt at settlement there. These failures may be linked to one specific historic cause, a fatal disruption of the patterns of supply, trade, or social organization; more likely, historic factors accentuated a long-term adjustment problem, a gradual realization of entrepreneurial overextension without the development of compensatory commercial or social advantage. Similar speculative ventures could be multiplied in modern examples. Even in recent times, settlement on the littoral of the Red Sea has been an economically precarious situation. One of the main contributions of archaeological research in the Near East has been to document the progress in human settlement in inhospitable areas, often with unexpected social and technological complexity and success, even when temporary. The research at Quseir al-Qadim explores such historic patterns of adaptation, not without parallels in contemporary enterprise, a pattern in commercial practice abstracted from larger cultural patterns.

Given the resource base model with the ramifications noted above, a reconstruction of the urban structure of Quseir al-Qadim for the early Roman and medieval Islamic periods was hypothesized. Although the organization of Roman ports does not seem to have been determined according to explicit principles, general patterns have been identified (Sauvaget, 1934) for the configuration of classical ports, both riverine and maritime. Relative to the body of water on which it sits, the city is laid out broadly facing the water, the orientation of the streets generally parallel to the coastline. The *decumanus maximus* stretches roughly parallel to the harbor and coastline; the *cardo maximus* crosses this avenue and invariably ends in the center of the harbor area. This makes the *cardo* the main connecting link between the harbor and the forum and other markets which are generally located in the vicinity of the crossing of these two main avenues.

Considerations of planning for the major ports of the Roman world are a different order of magnitude to those for this small port of Quseir al-Qadim. As a successful urban entity, Quseir al-Qadim must be confessed to have failed. Archaeologically, the absence of long, continuous rebuilding and alterations of urban space are an asset for determining the intended organization and short-term functions of the site. But Quseir al-Qadim's failure makes archaeological and historic comparisons even more difficult since most urban and port studies have naturally dealt with the most successful and long-lived examples. Nevertheless, even merchant depots, so-called *stationes* (which seem equivalent to the later medieval *funduq*) seem to have been established with the optimistic prospect of development into full urban size and complexity, if not status. [Note that, in Roman Egypt, most cities were such in social and economic rather than administrative (legal) terms (Rostovtseff, 1957: 297); even Alexandria was not a city in the latter sense until 199 A.D.] Thus, some influence from this tradition was to be expected even at a small, non-Mediterranean port. The orthogonal plan of the city was clearly indicated, as noted above, from which it was suggested that the *decumanus* at Quseir al-Qadim was located at the widest portion of the site free from erosional surfaces, probably south of the western central building and north of the eastern central building (see pl. 1), while the *cardo* would have stretched from the harbor area through the length of the built up area. These survey lines may or may not have been realized as major avenues at Quseir al-Qadim, given the small size of this port, but the proposed building areas thus defined would have been further subdivided into units known as the *actus*, adapted as necessary to the natural contours of the coral ridge. (Although variant sizes are attested, squares 35.5 m. seem the most common; Dilke, 1971: 70.)

Since the fundamental division within Roman town plans was the distinction between public and private sectors, with areas in the public sector left empty anticipating future growth, it was suggested that the public sector at Quseir al-Qadim consisted of Central Buildings A and B, the flat, undeveloped (?) area north of these buildings, and the harbor to the south of Central Building A, while the residential (and industrial) areas were confined to the western periphery of the site (see pl. 1). Because of the centrality of Central Building A, its well-built walls (as determined by one of the tests in the first season), its nearness to the harbor, and the fact that it is surrounded by open, flat areas, it was suggested that this building was the center for the collection, storage, and redistribution of trade goods and subsistence supplies. Thus the building was postulated to be an *horrea* or storage depot and the open spaces to have functioned as a *forum*, or *fora*, where the loading and unloading of ships or smaller lighters, the display and trading of import and export goods, storage and processing of these same trade wares, and their repacking for land shipment would have taken place. To judge by the finds of the first season, light industry undertaken while waiting for shipments or sailing times might have included iron working, glass making, weaving and other cloth manufactures, as well as ship repairs and preparation of naval stores (rigging, sails, tar, etc.).

For the medieval port, the excavations in the first season had illustrated some standardization in house plans but a marked absence of concern for orientation. Thus all surface features departing from Roman cadastral orientation were suggested to be medieval. Islamic artifacts are generally confined to a crescent beginning northeast of Central Building A, crossing that building, filling the open ground south of it, and ending in the spur in the southwestern part of the site where the Mamluk houses had been cleared in the first season, with flimsy architectural features and artifacts stretching into the Roman harbor and eastward to the modern coastline. Some Roman structures, including Central Building A, had been reused in medieval times, but the Roman harbor had silted up before the medieval reoccupation and it was suggested that the bluffs on the east, adjoining the modern coastline, where concentrations of imported ceramics were found in the surface collection, were the commercial center of the medieval town, which had grown organically rather than being orthogonically planned, as the Roman had been.

The areas to be excavated during the second season were chosen to test these hypothesized reconstructions of the port in the two periods. The residential aspect of the Roman town would be studied by the complete excavation of the building in the northwestern part of the site where the first season's excavations had found an iron forge and Indian materials (the Roman villa). The nature of Central Building A, the focus for the mediating institutions around which the city was organized, would be studied by extending the first season's trenches which had been put into that building (G8b and the pipeline). The investigation of the medieval occupation would concentrate on the eastern area, the suggested center of the maritime, commercial aspect of the medieval port. Although both Roman and medieval materials would be found in the excavations in Central Building A, because of the medieval reuse of the mound of the Roman building, the other two major areas of excavation would contain materials from only one of the two periods of occupation--the northwest only Roman, since the medieval occupation never extended that far north, the eastern only Islamic because the Roman occupation apparently had never extended so far to the east.

Just as the focus of questions asked about the organization of the port of Quseir al-Qadim had sharpened in the research design for the second season as a result of the first season's work, so the regional survey, whose first season goal had been the general delineation of the immediate hinterland of the port, concentrated during the second season on the function of and relationship to Roman Quseir of the apparently contemporary settlement at Bir Kareim, 25 km. to the southwest and the source of sweet water of reliable quality nearest to Quseir al-Qadim. In addition to its wells, Bir Kareim was a large mining encampment and surface features indicated what appears to have been a small temple. Thus, Bir Kareim may have represented for Quseir al-Qadim both a vital daily resource and a seasonal secondary economic asset.

The direct archaeological evidence for trade found in the excavations at Quseir al-Qadim, such as the Tamil inscriptions for Roman trade with India or Chinese ceramics for the Islamic contacts across the Indian Ocean, supplements documentary evidence, both internal to the site and external historical and geographical narratives of both periods. The evidence obtained through these excavations, when pieced together, will furnish a broad characterization of the commercial functions of a small commercial establishment on the Red Sea and a paradigm of possibilities for port facilities. The two very different cultural periods represented at Quseir al-Qadim present two solutions to similar problems of social relationships, with communities undergoing the stresses of uncertain essential supply lines and the vagaries inherent in maritime commerce. The overt archaeological responses to these inherent stresses are found in the architectural layout of the ports of these two periods and the subsequent patterns of areal usage and development. The results of the first two seasons show a pattern of orthogonal growth, retraction of fortunes, and secondary adherence to fundamental Roman principles of settlement patterns. In the Islamic port, the patterned residential units of the 13th century gave way, by the 14th century, to organic growth patterns, more on the order of village types of spatial utilization.

In both instances the stresses--and, ultimately, the artificial economic underpinning of these settlements, prompted out of a set of larger imperialistic policies--led to the collapse of settlement and failure of these ports. The developmental history of Quseir al-Qadim must be cast in terms of the character of the initial optimistic establishment of these facilities. Therefore, the excavations in the third season will be directed toward the earliest and most central aspects of the Roman and Islamic ports: the storehouse and associated buildings in the area of Central Building A and an Islamic knoll south of this building tested in the first season and found to contain at least two identifiable periods of Islamic occupation.

The primary goals will remain both historical and theoretical, the historical aspects devoted to the explication of archaeological materials--ceramics, glass, textiles, etc.--diagnostic for the Roman and Islamic periods, the study of artifacts introduced into the site as evidence of the commercial functions of the port, the architectural elements through which the port was spatially organized, and the internal literary evidence documenting the functions and culture of ancient Quseir. The theoretical framework seeks to use the archaeology of the Roman and Islamic priods for an understanding of the problems of economic development and urban organization.

Fig. 1: View East across Site with Red Sea in Background and Modern Road through Site Visible in Front of Excavators Working in Eastern Area

The present report, like the first preliminary report (1979), is intended as a first presentation of the results of the 1980 excavations. The intention of these preliminary reports is descriptive, an adequate outline of the results: the trenches excavated, the artifacts recovered, and specific studies of artifactual categories. Although there is never an absolute separation of description and interpretation, the broad assessment of the results, interpretations and explanations in terms of the history and archaeology of Roman and Islamic Egypt, is reserved for the final report. The above discussion provides background and presents the guiding hypotheses for the 1980 field season. We have avoided drawing conclusions in this report in the belief that meaningful conclusions must be based on analysis of the excavations with quantitative and qualitative correlations (both internal and external), all of which will form the subject of the final report.

Bibliography for Introduction

Adams, R. McC.
    1974   "Anthropological Perspectives on Ancient Trade," *Current Anthropology* 15: 239-58

Arrow, K. J.
    1974   "Limited Knowledge and Economic Analysis," *The American Economic Review* 64: 1-10

Bagnall, R. S.
    1977   "Army and Police in Roman Upper Egypt," *Journal of the American Research Center in Egypt* 14: 67-86

Barron, T., and W. F. Hume
    1902   *Topography and Geography of the Eastern Desert of Egypt*, Cairo

Büdel, J.
    1952   "Berich uber klimä-morphologische und Eiszeitforschungen in Niederafrika," *Erdkunde* 6: 104-32

Debono, F.
    1951   "Expédition archéologique royale au désert oriental (Keft-Kosseir). Rapport préliminaire sur la campagne 1949," *ASAE* 51: 59-91

Dilke, O. A. W.
    1971   *The Roman Land Surveyors: An Introduction to the* Agrimensores

Garcin, J.-C.
    1976   *Un centre musulman de la haute-égypte médièvale: Qūs*, Cairo

Goitein, S. D.
    1963   "Letters and Documents on the India Trade in Medieval Times," *Islamic Culture* 27: 188-205

Hodder, B. W.
   1965   "Some Comments on the Origins of Traditional Markets in Africa South of the Sahara," *Institute of British Geographers, Transactions* 36: 97-105

Hurst, H.
   1976   "Carthage, the North Harbor in the Roman Period. Temple and Commercial Activity," paper given at Ports of Call in the Ancient Mediterranean, AIA Colloquium, Chicago

Jackson, S. P., ed.
   1961   *Climatological Atlas of Africa*, Pretoria

Kantor, H. J.
   1965   "The Relative Chronology of Egypt and Its Foreign Correlations before the Late Bronze Age," in *Chronologies in Old World Archaeology* ed. by R. W. Ehrich, pp. 1-46

Klunzinger, C. B.
   1878   "Die Vegetation der egyptisch-arabischen Wüste bei Kosseir," *Zeitschrift der Gesellschaft für Erdkunde zu Berlin* 13: 432-62

Meredith, D.
   1952-53   "The Roman Remains in the Eastern Desert of Egypt," *Journal of Egyptian Archaeology* 38: 94-111; 39: 95-106

Murray, G. W.
   1925   "The Roman Roads and Stations in the Eastern Desert of Egypt," *Journal of Egyptian Archaeology* 11: 138-50

Murray, G. W., and D. E. Derry
   1923   "A Pre-Dynastic Burial on the Red Sea Coast of Egypt," *Man* 23: 129-31

Porter, B., and R. L. B. Moss
   1952   *Topographical Bibliography of Ancient Egyptian Hieroglyphic Texts, Reliefs, and Paintings*, Vol. 7: "Nubia, the Deserts, and Outside Egypt," Oxford

Qalqashandi
   1913   *Subh al-A'sha*, Vol. 3

Raschke, M. G.
   1978   "New Studies in Roman Commerce with the East," *Aufstieg und Niedergang der römischen Welt* 9,2: 604-1361

Rostovtseff, M.
   1957   *The Social and Economic History of the Roman Empire*, 2 vols., 2nd rev. ed.

Said, R.
   1962   *The Geology of Egypt*, Cairo

Sandford, K. S., and W. J. Arkell
   1939   *Palaeolithic Man and the Nile Valley in Lower Egypt*, Oriental Institute Publications, Vol. 46, Chicago

Sauvaget, J.
   1934   "Le plan de Laodicée-sur-Mer," *Bulletin d'Etudes Orientales* 4: 81-114

Sayed, A. M. A. H.
    1977   "Discovery of the Site of the 12th Dynasty Port at Wady Gawasis on the Red Sea Shore," *Revue d'Egyptologie* 29: 139-78

Sinclair, R.
    1967   "Port-Hinterland-Foreland-Maritime Space Relationships of the Port of Detroit," *Festschrift Leopold G. Scheidl* 2: 356-76

United States Hydrographic Center
    1976   *Sailing Directions for the Red Sea and Gulf of Aden*, Washington

Vance, J. E.
    1970   *The Merchant's World: The Geography of Wholesaling*, Englewood Cliffs, New Jersey

Ward, V.
    1976   "Piraeus, Commercial, Secular and Religious Establishments," paper presented at Ports of Call in the Ancient Mediterranean, AIA Colloquium, Chicago

Ward-Perkins, J. B.
    1974   *Cities of Ancient Greece and Italy: Planning in Classical Antiquity*,

Wheeler, R. E. M.
    1946   "Arikamedu: An Indo-Roman Trading Station on the East Coast of India," *Ancient India* 2: 17-124

Whitcomb, D. S.
    1979   "Trade and Tradition in Medieval Southern Iran," unpubl. Ph.D. diss., University of Chicago

Yorke, R. A., and J. H. Little
    1975   "Offshore survey at Carthage, Tunisia, 1973," *International Journal for Nautical Archaeology and Underwater Exploration* 4: 85-101

CHAPTER 2: TRENCH SUMMARIES, ROMAN AREAS

Donald Whitcomb

The investigation of the Roman occupation at Quseir al-Qadim during the 1980 season concentrated on an horizontal exposure in E6 and E7 as an extension of the E6b-E7a trench of 1978 (Whitcomb and Johnson, 1979: 25-27); see pl. 1. This resulted in a total exposure of 310 sq.m., including the 50 sq.m. excavated in 1978. The trench delineated one full building, called, with an ironic grandiloquence, the "Roman villa," and partial buildings to its east and south, called villa east and villa south respectively; see pl. 2. The second area of Roman excavations was a continuation of the trenches in Central Building A, which had been explored in trenches F8d, F9c, and F10a in 1978 (Whitcomb and Johnson, 1979: 28-34); see pl. 1. This clearance delineated portions of the central building and an adjacent "white building" in G8b; see pl. 5. A long, thin trial trench was conducted to the west and south to the harbor area, called the "pipeline;" this was intended to sample quickly the character of occupational debris across this potentially important section of the Roman town. Both the central building and the pipeline encountered Islamic materials in the upper levels, both associated with architectural details and as refuse materials. In a third area, two small trenches (G12c and J14a) continued the exploration of Central Building B; see pl. 7.

The results of these excavations in these three areas have greatly amplified our understanding of the Roman occupation at Quseir al-Qadim. The Roman villa offers an example of the residential areas of the northwestern part of the site. Central Building A is confirmed as an important center of the town and will be the focus of the 1982 excavations. The efforts on Central Building B repeated the intractability of this structure, although the excavation in J14a produced very interesting materials in ancillary structures. In general, the excavation of Roman strata involves very different and far more difficult excavation techniques than those needed in the Islamic occupation. This is due to the extensive use of salt-impregnated mud-brick which has produced masses of rock hard detritus, severely hampering excavation and delineation of these buildings.

Roman Villa

The difficulties in actual excavation of this structure were more than compensated by the excellent preservation of materials within this building. Three storerooms were found intact with many of their original vessels and other artifacts *in situ*; these are called the "large storeroom," the "small storeroom," and "E6c storeroom." The first two of these storerooms form the eastern side of the villa; the large storeroom leads onto a large courtyard; see pl. 2. The entrance to the

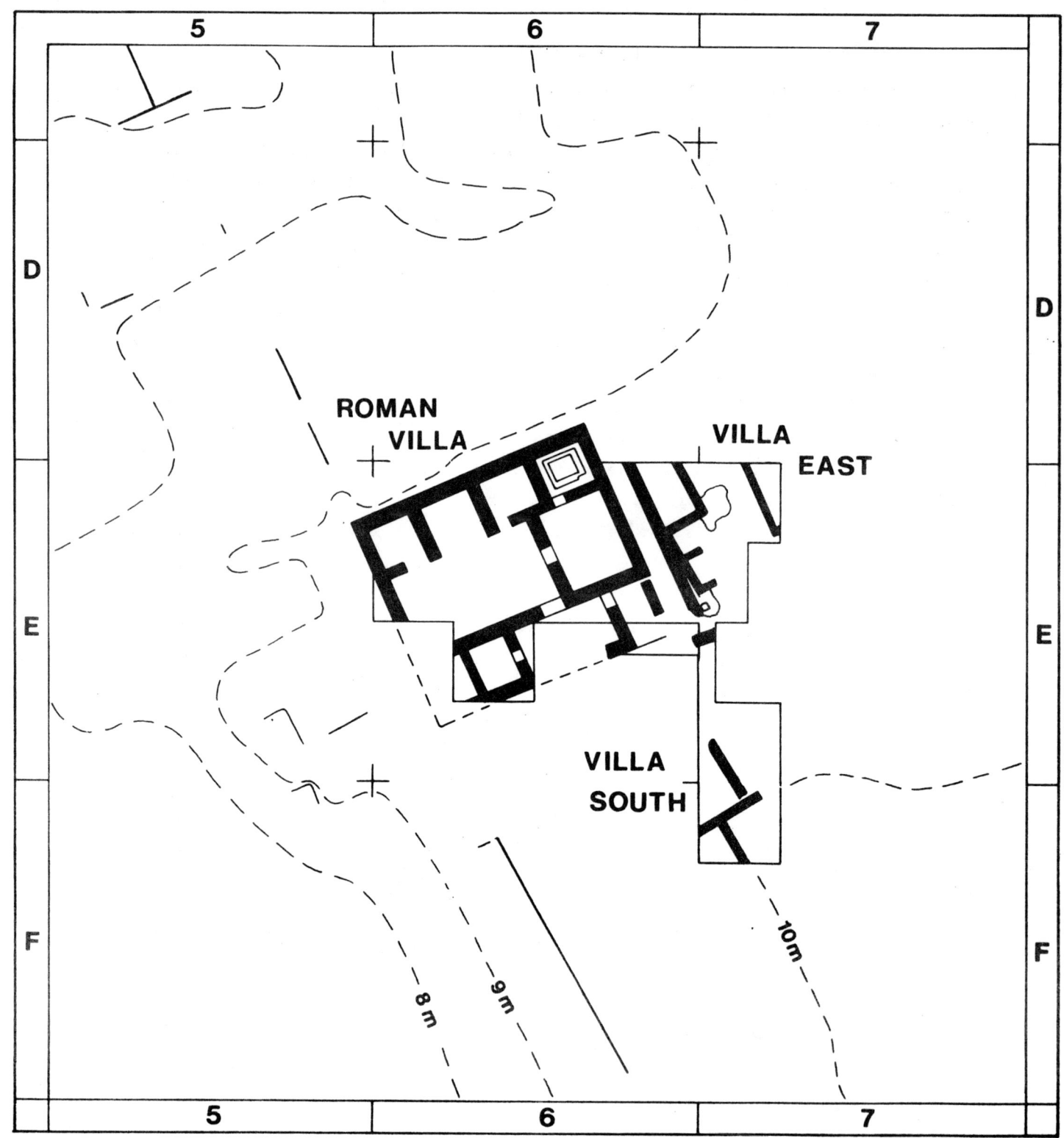

Plate 2: Roman Villa

courtyard and hence the building is from the south, through what appears to have been an anteroom. Storeroom E6c also opens onto this room; it remains uncertain whether this room and the anteroom were part of the original structure or additions.

East of the villa was a narrow street. This street extended to the north would lead directly in front of the northwest building tested in 1978 (B4a); extended to the south the street would pass beside the white building and end in a corner of the harbor area. Although the pipeline failed to detect evidence of this street, the excavation of the white building in 1982 hopefully will confirm this extension. East of the street is the yard cleared in 1978 (E6b-E7a) in which was found an iron-working furnace and where a series of small rooms was excavated this year facing this yard (villa east, see below). South of the villa were fragmentary walls of other structures, unfortunately poorly defined due to massive caliche formation. Surface features in this area indicate that the west wall of the villa aligns with longer sections of walls (see pl. 1), suggesting that this line was a major cadastral boundary. From surface contours before excavation it is likely that the Roman villa is the focal building but that further structures extend around this building on each side.

The Roman villa is located in squares E6a, E6b, E6c, and D6d; see pl. 2. E6a comprises the main courtyard and three rooms on the north side. The portion of E6a beyond the north wall of the villa was not excavated. E6b takes in the large and small storerooms and a corner of the anteroom. The excavation of the small storeroom necessitated opening a portion of D6d. Finally, E6c holds another corner of the anteroom, a side room, and the E6c storeroom, of which only a part was excavated.

The northern rooms off the large courtyard in E6a were excavated following the northern exterior wall (B) (see pl. 3), which was visible on the surface before excavation (Whitcomb and Johnson, 1979: fig. 3). Three rooms were excavated, beginning with that nearest the small storeroom. The interior face of the northern wall was very badly eroded through salt action; the thinner partition walls (G,F) were in very poor condition to the extent that toward the center of the building virtually no matrix of the wall was left. Rather, an homogeneous salt mud layer or caliche (hard pan) spread over the area where the wall and fallen wall fragments once had been. (This phenomenon is somewhat analogous to the complete mineralization of a bronze coin, where the metal core has been transferred to two layers of metallic salts; likewise the substance of these mud brick walls has shifted to masses of collapse and melt to form a substance as hard as or harder than the wall itself.)

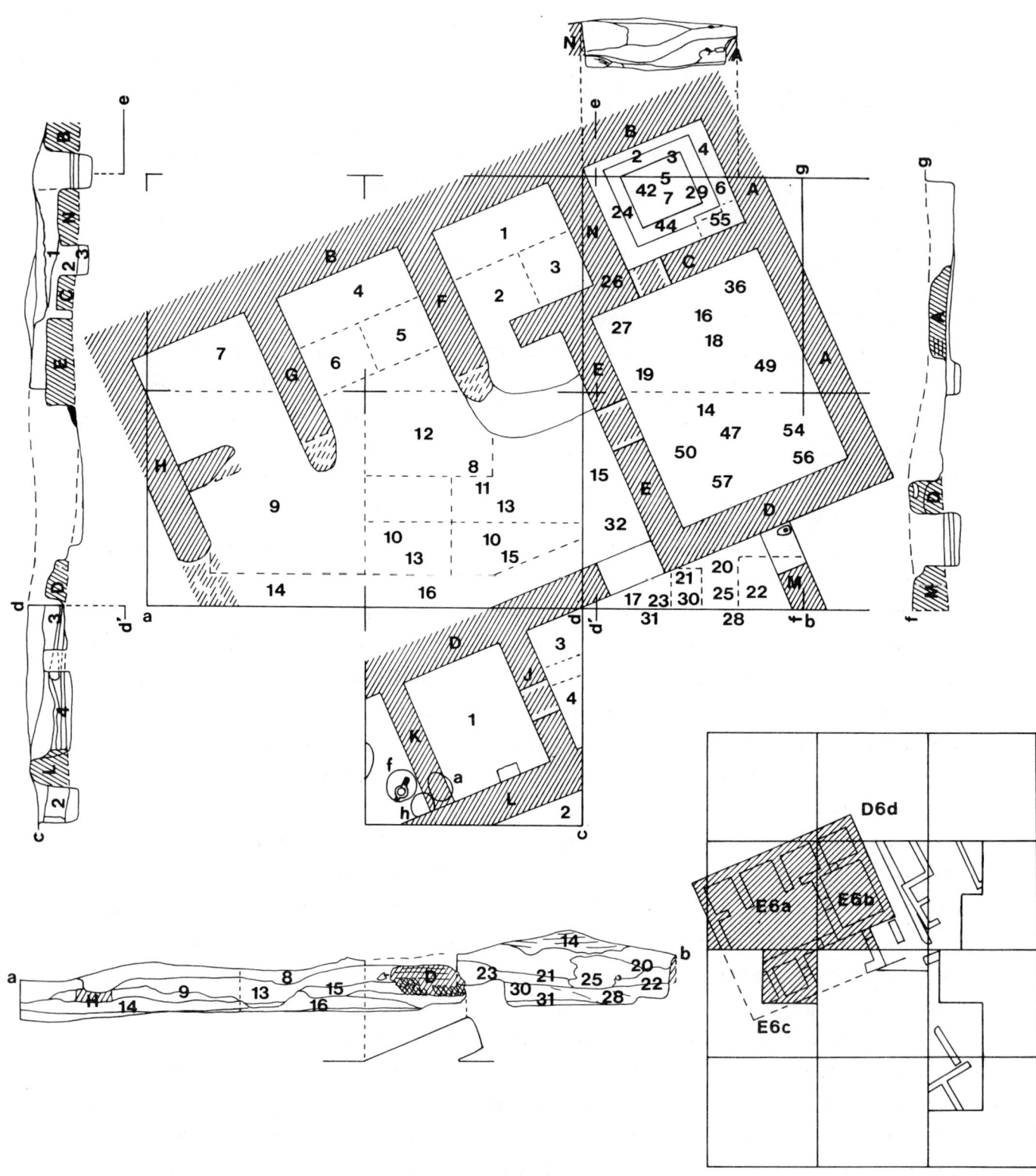

Plate 3: Roman Villa

The caliche was mixed with wind blown sand which had settled into rain soaked pockets. This natural decomposition was augmented by piled trash, containing ceramics, glass, and organic debris, well after the building had ceased to function for habitation.

The upper layers of each of these three rooms (E6a-[1],[4],[7]) were mixtures of caliche with soft sandy deposit and thick accumulations of sherds and other artifacts (with the exception of E6a-[7], which had relatively few sherds). Below this were further layers of the combination of soft brown sand and sherdy trash between the caliche cores of the walls (E6a-[2],[5],[6]). Pockets of ash occurred in E6a-[5], but no indication of a prepared floor was encountered. A deeper test (E6a-[3]) probed similar brown sandy soil which ran beneath the adjacent walls (C,N). These areas were not continued down to bedrock. The total deposition, as seen in section d'-e, was approximately 1.25 m.

The courtyard is defined by walls H,D,E and the three north rooms. The specific architectural details of the doorways to these rooms were unfortunately lost to the caliche. At one time there seemed to be some evidence for a wall connecting F with E, but this was most likely a mass of hardened wall fall. The surface layers (E6a-[8],[9]) were mainly hard accumulations of caliche mixed with soft sand with little in the way of artifacts (sherds, shells, organics). Beneath this were soil deposits (E6a-[11]) which held pockets of ash with some shell and bone in the eastern portions (near wall E, and E6a-[10], where the caliche was mixed with gravel and some gypsum traces and the ceramics were mostly amphora fragments. The layers below this caliche were a darker brown with heavy concentrations of sherds, glass, and shells (E6a-[12],[13],[15],[16],[14]). This layer runs beneath the adjacent walls and would appear to represent a land-fill prior to construction of this building. E6a-[15] contained both ash and pieces of bitumen. A corner of the courtyard was within E6b, where the caliche layer ([15]) led down to a surface with a large mass of bitumen melted against wall E; E6b-[32] was a seep hole within the caliche. It should be noted that the layers E6a-[9],[14] on the western side of the courtyard appeared to have a limited amount of Islamic contamination; otherwise all loci contained only Roman materials.

The stratigraphy of the courtyard is seen in section a-d. Wall H was found in the south baulk but conscious efforts during the excavation failed to confirm the extension of this wall just north of that baulk. Wall D, on the other hand, was relatively well preserved and gave us a first indication of construction techniques. The lowest two courses of mud brick were laid almost vertically; such diagonal lower courses were frequently seen in the 1978 excavations (Whitcomb and Johnson, 1979: fig. 6, pl. 6, walls A,B,D). Above this were vague indications of horizontal coursing but no details indicating whether the usual header--stretcher technique was used here or not. The doorway is implied from the presence of a number of large stones suggesting a threshold; the area is, however, badly disturbed by the seep hole. The stratification for the courtyard and northern rooms is:

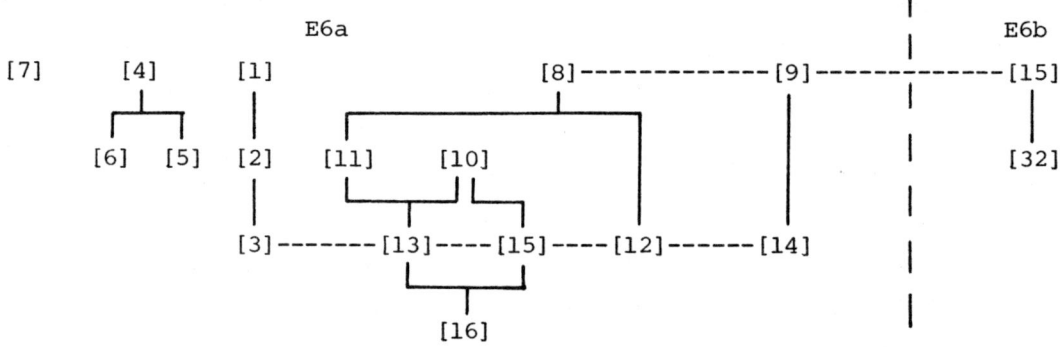

South of the courtyard are rooms excavated in E6c, which may or may not have been part of the original villa (as mentioned above). The south face of wall D was badly eroded and appeared to have two faces, although this may have been one line of bricks (the height of this wall above the floor in E6c-[1] was less than 10 cm. in height). This locus (E6c-[1]) is defined by walls D,J,L and was comprised of caliche and sand accumulations 80 cm. thick lying upon a smooth floor. A bowl, a pulley made of wood, and an amphora were found on this floor as well as a square stone base (against wall L); see pl. 3. In the course of clearing this floor, the line of wall K, only a few centimeters in preserved height, was found. This wall K seems to have been pulled down during the use of the building, since storage jars a and h were found lying upon this wall. Other storage jars, f and one appearing in the west baulk, indicate that this was another small storeroom; see pl. 20 for drawings of these vessels. See fig. 2.

The south face of wall L was traced in E6c-[2], which was mainly a soft brown deposit with the very edge of a small pit. At the base of wall L a lower layer, a darker brown sherdy fill, was encountered. There is some evidence of a limited amount of Islamic mixture in E6c-[1],[2]. Wall J had a long thin stone set in a fashion suggesting a possible threshold, although this remains extremely dubious.

Fig. 2: Looking East across E6c Storeroom with Pots f and h over Wall K and Stone Base Visible on Floor Adjacent to Wall L

East of wall J was a corner of the anteroom; this was excavated in two loci (E6c-[3],[4]) separated by a narrow baulk; see section c-d. Both of these loci were composed of brown soil mixed with thick layers of ash and organic debris; this deposit was piled up higher in E6c-[3], where fragments of broken bricks, burnt red, were found. Depth of this deposit was approximately 40 cm. to the surface of the brown sherdy layer.

The remainder of that part of the anteroom which was cleared was in square E6b; this was the first area of the villa to be excavated and it proved to be frustratingly difficult. The deposit was capped with a Roman trash pile composed mainly of sherds, glass, etc. (E6b-[14]). Below this was a thick layer of caliche from the fallen portions of the surrounding walls (E6b-[21],[22]), the latter of which held a large seep hole, part of which was an open cavity. Below, but still mixed with this caliche, was brown soil with sherds which seemed in small spots to rest upon a yellow surface; this was locus E6b-[25], which had one Islamic sherd, perhaps acquired from the seep hole above, and E6b-[23], which contained some white plaster and mortar chunks. The same layer also contained locus E6b-[17] in the angle in front of the doorway to the courtyard; this locus continued the ash and burnt materials with some amphora sherds found in E6c-[3],[4]. At the other end of the room was E6b-[20], which was a small accumulation of similar material including wood fragments. Finally, below these loci was the brown fill with sherds which seems to have made up the pre-construction surface (E6b-[28], [30],[31]). Locus E6b-[28] was taken down to a surface of reddish pebbles which may be the bedrock. It should be emphasized that inexperience and complex erosion make the stratigraphy in this area particularly suspect. The anteroom was bounded by wall M, where a number of stones were found, together with a door pivot, marking a possible doorway.

The stratigraphy of this area may be provisionally suggested as follows:

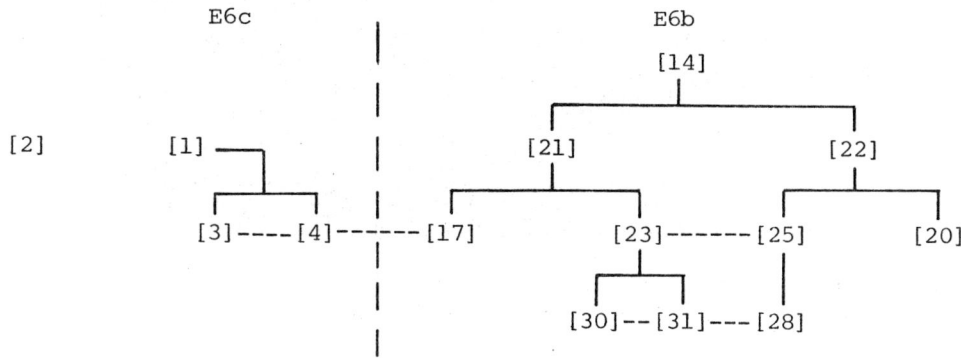

The remainder of the Roman villa was devoted to the two storerooms, the large storeroom and the small storeroom. These rooms both fronted on the small street with wall A; see fig. 3. This wall was one of the best constructed of the

Fig. 3: Looking West across 1978 Excavations and Street Running South toward Harbor to Roman Villa. Large Storeroom and Cellar on East Side of Villa in Middle Ground; Central Courtyard beyond Large Storeroom; Walls of Northern Rooms Visible behind Large Storeroom. Mud-flats beyond Site Visible in Background.

building, being made of red bricks laid in horizontal courses upon a yellow mud foundation; preserved height ranged from 40-50 cm. The large storeroom was bounded by walls A,C,D,E. Several large stones in wall E suggest the location of the doorway into this room, in this case marking the strengthening of the jambs of the doorway. Against wall C, especially, there were fragments of wood or the stains thereof. At first this was assumed to be accidental deposition; however, repeated occurrence suggests the occasional use of a wooden framework to buttress these walls, analogous to the technique seen in buildings at Karanis (Husselman, 1979: 34 and pl. 14). Within the small storeroom, limited by walls A,D,C,N and entered by a doorway marked by threshold stones, was a cellar with its roofing intact. The cellar was cut into the bedrock and then its walls were built up with well laid angular limestones. Embedded in the upper courses of the cellar walls were similar wooden reinforcements; see pl. 53 in chapter 7.

The large storeroom was covered with later Roman trash dumps (with some Islamic fragments) mixed with the upper caliche formation; these loci were E6b-[14],[15],[16],[18],[19], the last of which was larger than usual with soft reddish brown soil, either a pit or, more likely, a hollow within the caliche (a seep hole?). It was in E6b-[18] that the first pot (FN 9) was encountered. Thereafter, the excavation was a process of removing the hard yellow caliche and soft brown soil down to a floor level, a trampled, unprepared surface, upon which were scattered small whole vessels and the sherds of larger vessels broken *in situ*. Loci were assigned to arbitrary areas in an effort to separate the location of the sherds; nevertheless, several vessels had widely scattered sherds. These loci were E6b-[49],[27],[36] in the northern half of the room (see fig. 4) and E6b-[47],[50], [54],[57] in the southern half where the caliche was much thicker and the artifactual debris less. During the excavation a partition wall seemed to emerge from wall A between loci E6b-[49] and [54]; eventually it was decided that this was rather a thick caliche of fall from wall A.

The small storeroom was covered with a thick accumulation of caliche (E6b-[16],[18]). The lines of walls C and N were uncovered with locus E6b-[26]. Below the caliche mass were yellow sand, patches of white gypsum, and lumps of caliche amidst a concentration of whole artifacts lying upon a floor; this was loci E6b-[24],[29]. Some of the artifacts seemed to be lying within the matrix of the floor directly upon a roof structure; these were uncovered with the removal of the floor as E6b-[44],[42], an orange pebbly material. Below this flooring was a woven

Fig. 4: Looking East across North End of Large Storeroom with Roman Amphora in Corner of Walls C (to Left) and A, Rim of Basket near Wall C, Several Small Oil Jars, and Sherds of Broken Large Storage Vessels. Beyond Wall A is Street Running North and South across the Site.

matting, wood stringers, and three strong beams making the roof of the cellar; see fig. 5.

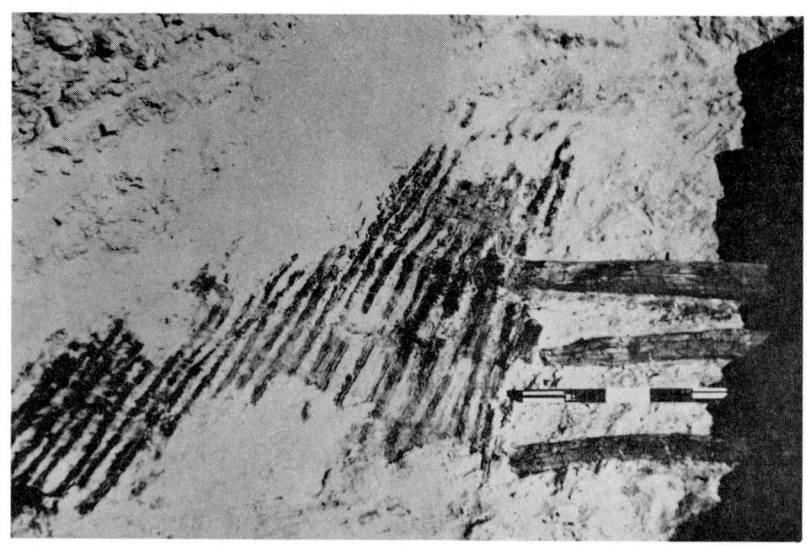

Fig. 5: Beams and Stringers of Roof of Cellar

At this point the northern section of the small storeroom was excavated following the levels seen in the section between walls N and A (see pl. 3). D6d-[1] was a mass of caliche 50-60 cm. thick. Below this was brick fall mixed with soft brown soil and ash layers to the floor surface (D6d-[2],[3]). Other than a few artifacts within the baulk almost no artifacts were found on the northern section of this floor. After the removal of the cellar roof, the D6d numbering was used for loci within this room. The exterior of the cellar wall was traced with loci D6d-[4],[6] after having been examined in a small test pit (E6b-[55]). This soil was the dark brown fill with abundant sherds which elsewhere marked the pre-construction phase and indeed it appeared to go beneath these walls as well. The collection from D6d-[4] will provide a controlled sample of artifacts from this phase. The interior of the cellar was excavated in two layers (D6d-[5],[7]), the upper of which was a very soft sandy brown deposit in which fragments of the broken trap-door were found. Below this was the lowest deposit, yellow-orange sand with some fibrous content which ran down to the floor carved out of the bedrock. Other than several rocks and a fragment of a brick, nothing was found within the cellar. The contents of the cellar had been carefully removed, whereas the artifacts scattered about the floors of the large and small storerooms represent property which was abandoned just before the villa ceased to be utilized (see chapter 7 on the large and small storerooms).

The stratigraphy of these storerooms may be summarized:

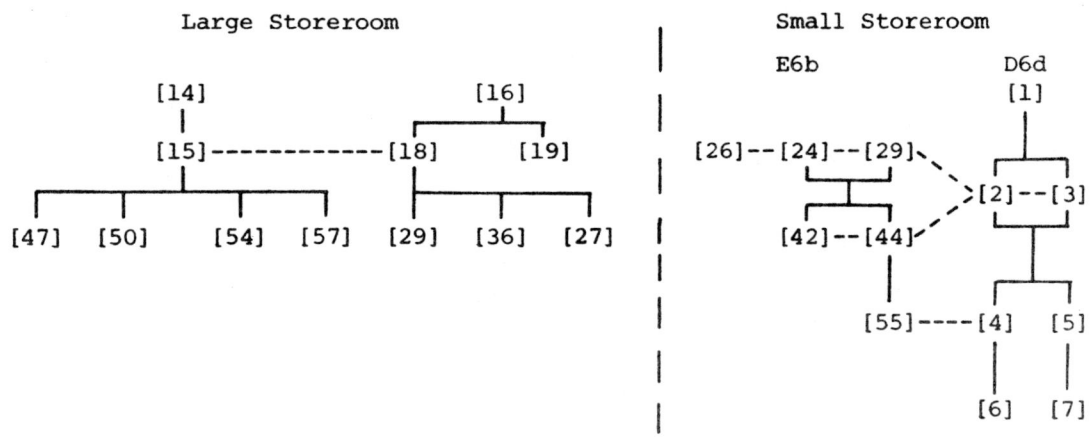

Villa East

The excavations peripheral to the Roman villa have been divided into two arbitrary sections: villa east, comprising the remainder of E6b, E7a, E6d, and a 1x5 m. trench in E7c, and villa south, comprising two 5x5 m. squares in E7c and F7a; see pl. 4. Villa east is a southward expansion of trench E6b-E7a excavated in 1978; this trench included the room with an iron-working furnace (within walls B,E,F) (in the right foreground of fig. 3), an open yard east of this room divided by wall J, and the street (the nature of which was not understood in 1978 since much of the section of wall A was cut away and not recognized in the baulks). The 1980 excavations found the continuation of this street, a room south of the villa, and east of the street, a continuation of the open yard (in the left foreground in fig. 3).

South of wall D of the villa was an area blocked off from the street by wall C. This wall appears to have been a late addition of well-laid horizontal yellow bricks in header-stretcher fashion. As it did not continue to the baulk, there might have been a doorway giving an indirect access to the villa through the door in wall M. A vague line in the caliche suggests a wall abutting the south end of wall M, enclosing the area as a small room. If this was the case, the room was almost completely destroyed. Within this area, beneath the general surface clearance (E6b-[33]), were loci E6b-[43],[48], composed of fine brown soil with pebbles and quantities of sherds. In the south was a yellow caliche; the center had an area of burning with ashes and scorch marks on a clay base suggesting a small hearth (E6b-[48]). A slightly deeper test trench (E6b-[52]) was placed against the south baulk in a futile attempt to ascertain the continuation of wall C. This produced yellow caliche lying over a dark brown sherdy fill (the possible wall line visible in section a-b remained too ambiguous to be certain). This test was continued across the room as E6b-[52].

The street runs between walls A and B; the upper layer (E6b-[34]) was a loose light brown soil with organic debris down to yellow melt from wall B. Below this was locus E6b-[37], layers of yellow melt from wall B. Below this was locus E6b-[37], layers of yellow melt mixed with sherds. A test trench was placed across the street (E6b-[46]) measuring 1x1.5 m.; this produced the familiar dark brown sherdy fill mixed with pebbles. The eastern wall lining the street, wall B, proved to be a composite with an overlying section of wall D placed at a slightly different orientation. Both walls B and D were made of irregular stones, often

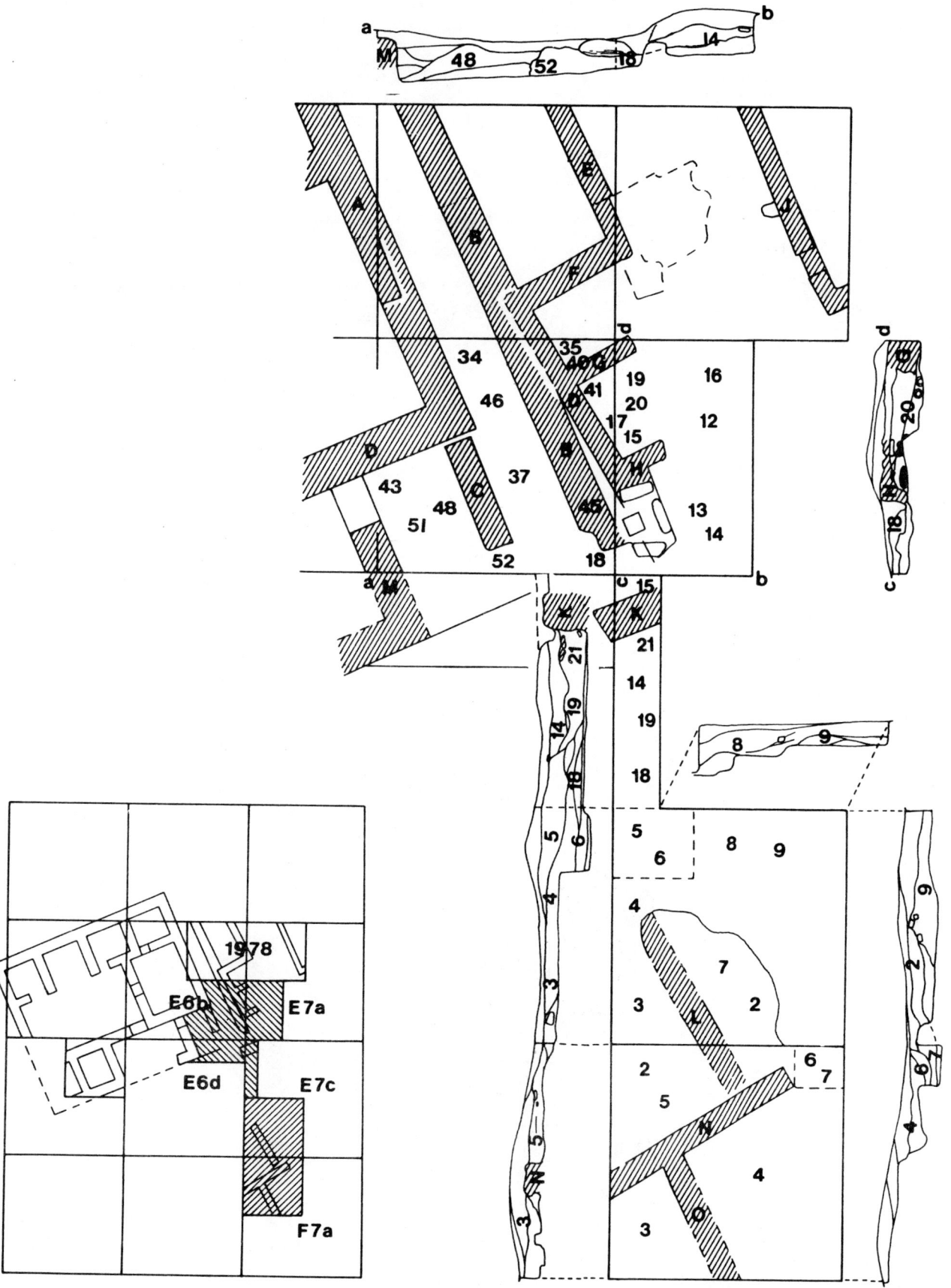

Plate 4: Villa East and Villa South

set vertically (as in the northern section; see Whitcomb and Johnson, 1979: 25); caliche above and around these stones shows that they served as a foundation for the walls. E6b-[45] was a section of this caliche over wall B, as were E6b-[35] (a continuation of E6b-[11] [see Whitcomb and Johnson, 1979: 27]) and [41]. E6b-[41] began to encounter numerous amphora sherds.

East of wall D, beneath the caliche, was a fine reddish brown soil (E6b-[38]) within which was a burnt area of ash and bones (E6b-[39]), perhaps a hearth in the northern angle of walls D and G. Beneath the hearth this soil continued as locus E6b-[40]. At this point a 3x5 m. trench was opened in E7a in order to elucidate the superimposed walls B and D. The upper layer was a brown caliche with sand, pebbles, and some organic material (E7a-[11],[12], equivalent to E7a-[7],[8], Whitcomb and Johnson, 1979: 27). The lower locus (E7a-[12]) was excavated as E7a-[15] on the western half of the trench where the hard yellow caliche and stones were encountered. In the southeast corner, a red-brown soil with pebbles was found (E7a-[13]), which appeared to be a possible Islamic pit although no outlines were found. Below this was E7a-[14], with yellow caliche mixed with fragments of plaster and white mortar. In the western section of this locus was isolated a solid mass of caliche within which were embedded four larger stones; three rectangular stones seemed grouped around the base of the fourth, which was an altar, upright and somewhat battered; see fig. 6. It remains unclear

Fig. 6: Altar Found in E7a-14

whether these stones were a continuation of the foundation of wall D and the altar was incorporated into the wall or, on the other hand, the stones formed a base for the altar which was left open and facing the street. Neither wall B nor wall D appears to reach the south baulk; locus E7a-[18] was a small test to clarify this point and produced only yellow caliche.

North of the stones and altar was a mass of caliche and random stones which are described as wall H. Wall H, with walls D,G, forms an open room or stall, parallel to that bounded by walls G,D,F. Within this room was a fine brown soil mixed with lumps of caliche (E7a-[16],[17]); beneath this layer was a red-brown soil with many sherds (equivalent to E6b-[38]). Numerous fragments of brown amphora necks such as that used for the iron-working furnace (Whitcomb and Johnson, 1979: 25-27) were found in this area. This overlay a burn layer mixed with sherds (E7a-[20]), equivalent to E6b-[39] and running beneath wall G. It would thus seem that, sometime after the construction of wall B, the eastern area was divided into a large room with the iron-working furnace and two stalls facing onto a large yard. The altar complex may have been part of this later walling or may have been a small shrine along the street. Little may be said concerning the function of the stalls except that the burning and the amphora parts in association with the furnace suggest storage units as part of an industrial area. In E7a-[16] a further graffito in Tamil was found (see chapter 12 on inscriptions).

The stratigraphy for this area is:

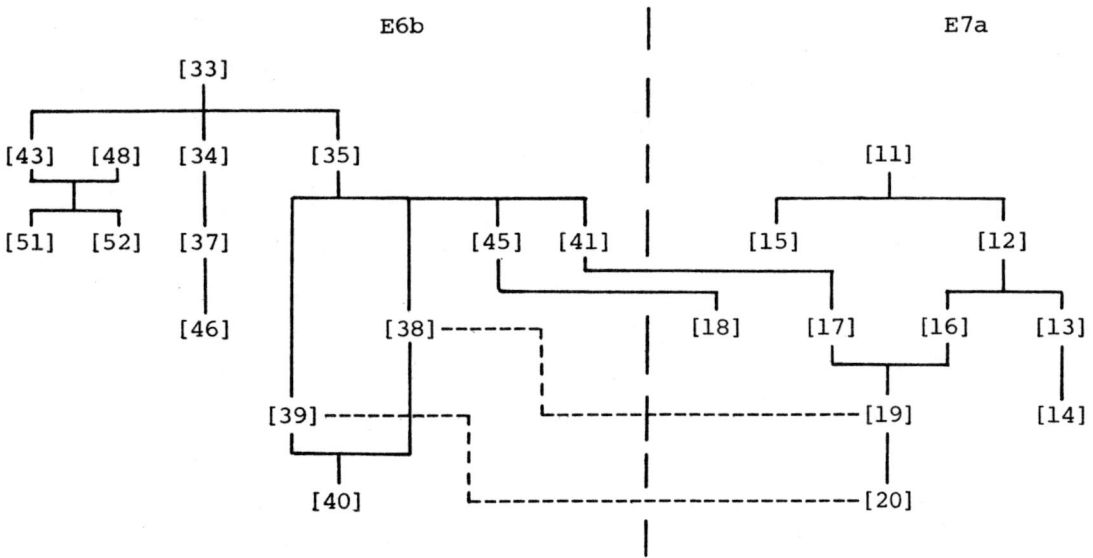

The small (1x5 m.) trench connecting this area with villa south presented further complexities. Rather than finding the continuation of wall B, as anticipated, there appeared a short stub of a cross-wall, wall K, which did not reach the north baulk (section a-b). A deposit of soft brown soil north of this wall was locus E7c-[15]. The surface of this trench was a light brown sand (E7c-[10]); beneath this were further sand layers (E7c-[11],[14]) dipping east to west, suggesting that the sand is piled against mounding or a wall further to the east. In the south of the trench, below E7c-[11], was a layer of dark brown soil with sherds (E7c-[12]) dipping in the same manner. Beneath this was E7c-[13], a hard brown sand alternating with thin lenses of lighter and darker hues. This overlay a brown-black deposit with some charcoal (E7c-[17]) with a pocket of ash on the west side of the trench (E7c-[16]) and a mass of yellow caliche on the east side (E7c-[20]), possibly fall from the wall posited on that side. These layers rested upon a gravelly orange-brown material which is probably the bedrock in this area (E7c-[18]). In the northern part of the trench, beneath E7c-[14], was another layer of brown sand and sherds (E7c-[19]) and a hard brown deposit of brick fall (E7c-[21]), probably from wall K. Distinctive to this area south of wall K is the series of wind blown sand layers which suggests an open area between structural remains, in this case the villa on the north and the constructions to the south.

Villa South

Villa south comprises two 5x5 m. trenches in E7c and F7a, where traces of walls were found amidst a particularly unrelenting mass of caliche. Walls L, N, O are thus not completely certain; wall N is the best preserved. The surface layers of the northern trench were brown sand and pebbles mixed with sherds (E7c-[1],[2]). These sand layers continued throughout most of the trench (E7c-[4],[5],[6],[8],[9]), only the last of which had an appreciable quantity of sherds. The central area was a different story, where E7c-[7] encountered a very hard mass of caliche, presumably fall from wall L. West of this wall, E7c-[3] was a layer of organic debris mixed with ashes and stones; this continued in the angle of walls L and N as loci F7a-[1],[2],[5]. Organic debris here was almost a peat-like mass with "grass bundles" often appearing; this appeared to go beneath the footing of wall N. South of wall N was a solid mass of caliche with pockets of softer brown soil (F7a-[3],[4]). An attempt was made to utilize a portable drill (pavement breaker) borrowed from the local mining company to remove this caliche; unfortunately, the instrument succeeded only in poking round holes into this rock salt. A small test trench was forceably opened (F7a-[6],[7]), which succeeded in showing that wall N did not continue across the entire trench and that ash and occupational debris were to be found beneath this rock mantle. At this point the trench was reluctantly abandonned.

The stratigraphy in villa south and the 1x5 m. trench are

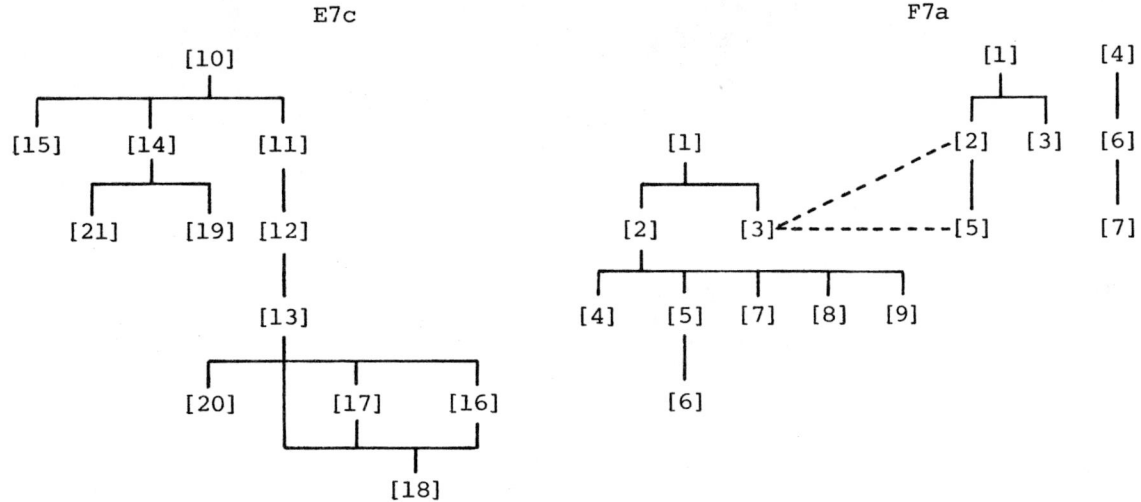

Central Building

The examination of Central Building A was limited to a trench in G8b; see pl. 5; previous understanding of this important structure was confined to the results of F8d-F9c and a northern test pit, F10a (Whitcomb and Johnson, 1979: 28-34). F8d-F9c had shown that the western side of Central Building A was probably a series of rooms with doorways facing onto a central courtyard; this trench had not discovered the depth of these rooms or the exterior wall and possible adjacent structures hypothesized to be lining the main street running between the harbor and the Roman villa. Therefore, a long east-west trench (30x1 m.) was set out incorporating the southern 1 m. of the G8b trench and designed to confirm the existence of further rooms on the east and, hopefully, to cut across the street on the west. This trench was then turned south as a long cut across the surface of the site to the edge of the harbor; the whole 50x1 m. trench is referred to as the pipeline; see pl. 6. The purpose of the pipeline was to sample quickly the stratification and architectural remains across this important section of the town and to gain an impression of the Roman and Islamic occupational patterns.

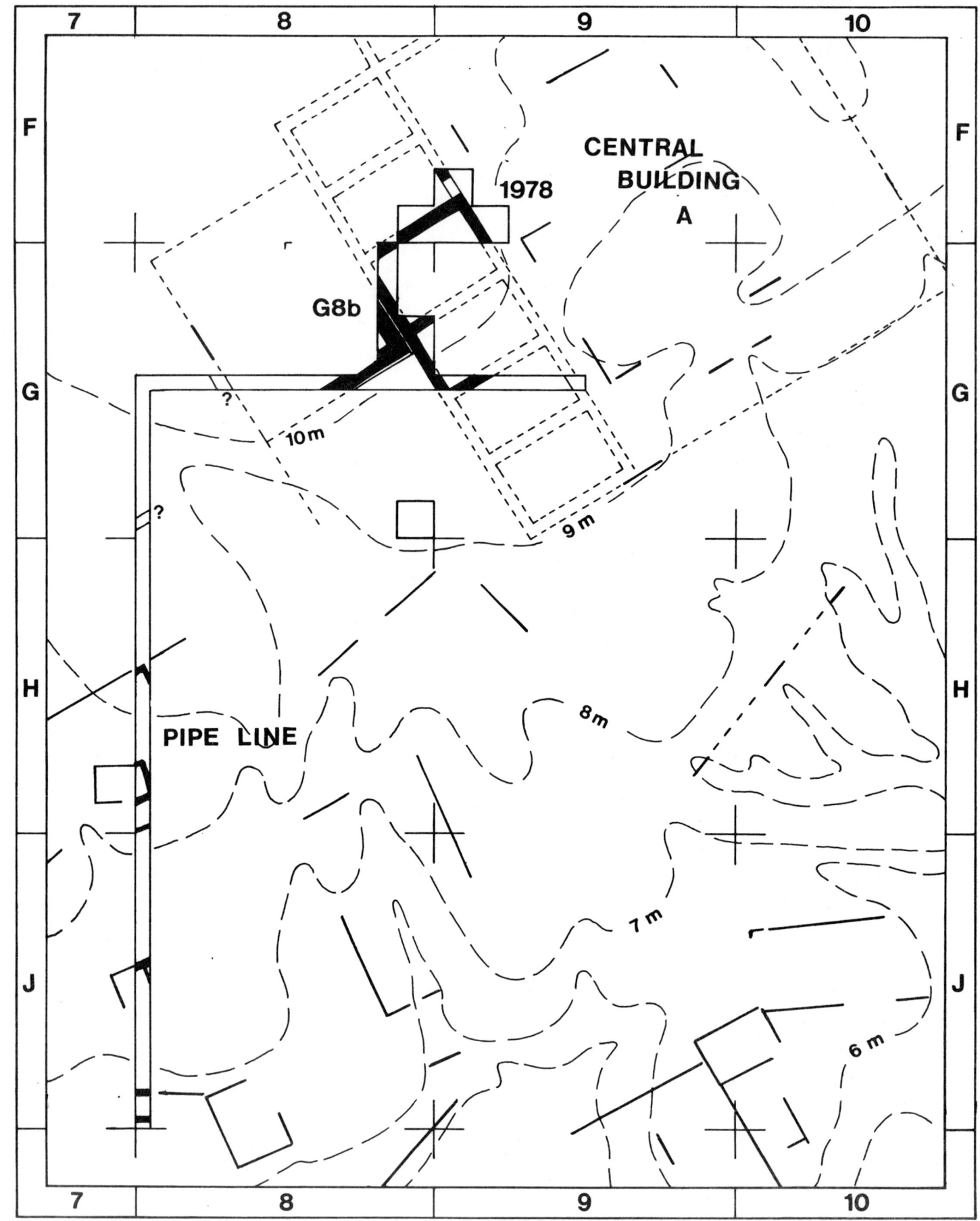

Plate 5: Central Building A and Pipeline

The 1978 excavations in F8d-F9c had encountered Islamic remains in the upper layers before reaching the Roman architecture. The excavations in G8b also uncovered 20-50 cm. of Islamic occupational debris, including architectural fragments, shown on pl. 6 as "upper level." The trench began as a 1x10 m. east-west trench, in which the surface layer (G8b-[1]) soon uncovered wall A and a few stones aligned to form wall J. The Islamic layer between these walls (G8b-[2], soft brown soil with organic debris and fallen bricks measuring 31x21x5 cm.) was expanded northward to wall H as G8b-[7] after an overburden (G8b-[5]) was removed. This light brown soil was expanded further as G8b-[17],[18], but the very fragmentary stone walls became very uncertain. Between walls G and H was an Islamic period room, the deposit being G8b-[9] down to the floor. In this floor were found three pot hearths (G8b-[8],[13],[14]), broken sections of jars which were filled with ashes and evidently used as ovens, presumably for baking bread and other foodstuffs (see the eastern area, chapter 4, for numerous examples of this type of feature). Associated with these pot hearths was a shallow pit (G8b-[15]) filled with ash. North of wall G the same features recurred with one pot hearth (G8b-[10]) and a thick lens of ash (G8b-[11]).

All of these Islamic remains were placed upon a pebbly red-brown fill with mixed artifacts of both Roman and Islamic occupations (G8b-[12]) within which the lines of the Roman architecture were first delineated. A wall (C) running diagonally across the trench appears to be the western wall of the central building. Small portions of two of the rooms lining this side of the central building were excavated. The room bounded by walls D,C,D is part of that excavated in 1978 (Whitcomb and Johnson, 1979: 31); the floor level in this room (G8b-[16]) was below a hard bricky wall fall and was soft and peat-like organic material (equivalent to the matting found in 1978, F9c-[10]) resting upon the bedrock. The upper floor was not discerned in the cramped space of this trench.

The second room, defined by walls E,C,F, likewise contained hard bricky wall fall above a soft organic occupational debris (G8b-[19]). The bricks in this building measured approximately 35x22x8 or 35x17x10 cm. The continuation of this room in G9a was disrupted by a large Islamic pit (G9a-[2]) which continued down to the bedrock. South of wall F was undoubtedly a third room; unfortunately the wall fall here became an impenetrable mass of caliche and it was only in the eastern section (G9a-[3]) that any depth of excavation was achieved. In this area the hard brick fall rested upon a thin, soft brown deposit, probably covering

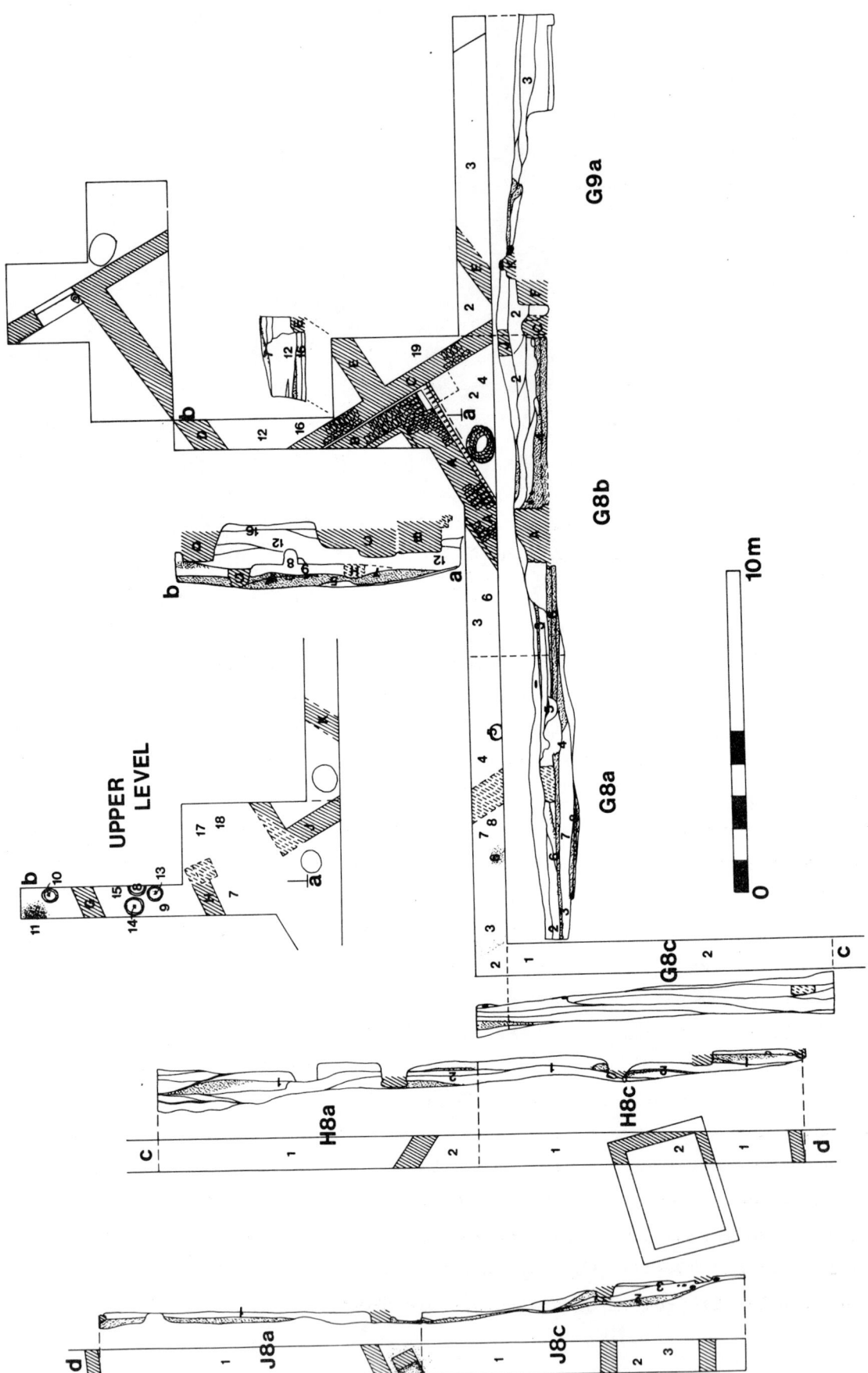

Plate 6: Central Building A and Pipeline

the bedrock "floor;" an ambiguous line was found, possibly marking the eastern end of the room. The eastern wall of this room may have been completely knocked down or the trench inadvertently passed directly through the doorway. A third possibility remains that there was no wall here but an open extension of the courtyard, which would account for the increased formation of caliche in G9a-[3]. These two rooms are visible in the top right half of fig. 7.

Fig. 7: G8b Looking North with Two Rooms of Central Building A in the Top Right and the White Building to the Left

With the excavation of wall C, a second wall, wall B, was found, wall B forming a corner with wall A. The inner face of this corner was coated with a thick mud plaster; see pl. 6 and fig. 7. The parallel bricks of walls B and C showed dramatically the different clay sources for the bricks of these two structures. Wall C (and the other walls of Central Building B) was a pebbly red-brown material while walls A and B were a light yellow in color, a contrast which gave this structure its name: the white building. The bricks in the white building measure 35x16x10 cm. Wall A was preserved 5-8 courses high; the fall within the area of this wall and wall C was a brown pebbly deposit (G8b-[4]). A large coil of heavy rope (cable) was found lying next to wall A within this locus and upon the bedrock. Delineation of wall A showed that it was constructed upon a wide footing of vertical bricks, two courses high, one of which was sunk into the bedrock; wall C was constructed directly upon the bedrock. Both of these walls were constructed of bricks laid in header-stretcher fashion; see fig. 7.

West of wall A were brick fall and Islamic surface layers (G8b-[3]); these were extended in a further western 1x10 m. trench as G8a-[1]. At the western end of this trench was a deposit of soft light brown organic debris (G8a-[2]) which continued south as G8c-[1]. Beneath this was a layer of dark brown soil with ash lenses (G8a-[3]) which moved eastward beneath a mass of caliche which possibly incorporates a wall; east of this the dark brown deposit, mixed with fragments of matting and cloth, is G8a-[4]. Within this layer was a small pit (G8a-[5]), cut from the upper Islamic level, and an area of burning, with stones, charcoal, and ashes (G8a-[6]). This dark brown soil with organic debris continued up to the footing of wall A (G8b-[6]). Beneath this layer was a deposit (G8a-[7]) which was slightly harder, of a light brown bricky consistency but still mixed with organic material. At the base of this layer, lying on the bedrock, was again a darker brown layer (G8a-[8]) mixed with dark grey ash and charcoal.

The description of the white building remains elusive. The structure was the most carefully constructed yet found at Quseir al-Qadim and the plaster facing suggests an inner orientation to the north. The mounding of the surface of the site suggests that the white building may be a large rectangular structure and, if a single building, one of central importance for the town, perhaps even a small chapel. The discovery of several figurine fragments in this area, the only ones from the site until now, gives a very indirect, and somewhat dubious, reinforcement to this hypothesis. Yet no western limit can be seen other than the possible wall in G8a built upon loose debris. The depression of ground surface (although this is always questionable due to the hard caliche formations) might suggest the passage of the main north-south street, filled with accumulated debris. Could then the white building be some sort of stall, shop, or official building placed along this street? This question will be the foremost goal during the 1982 season.

The stratigraphic summary for the areas excavated in 1980 is

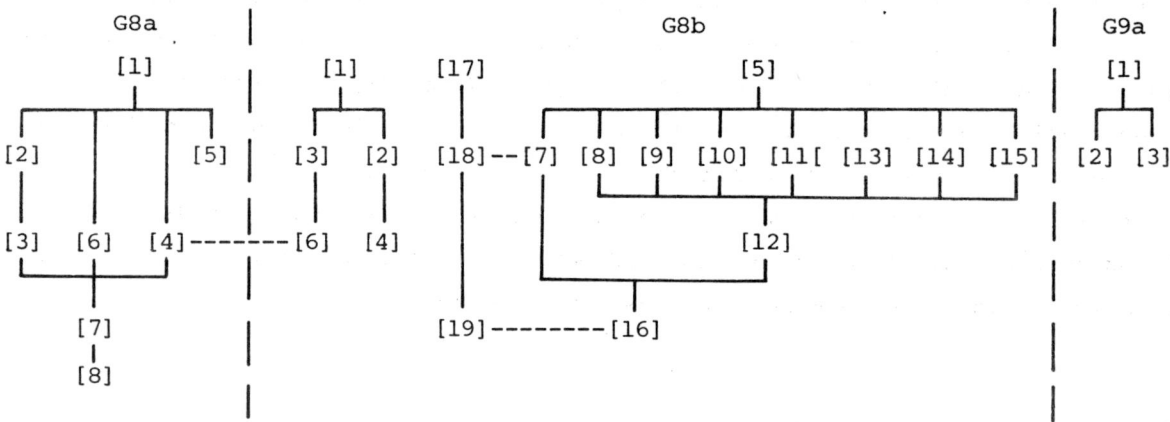

The Pipeline

The pipeline begins at the western end of G8a and stretches south for 50 m. through squares G8c, H8a, H8c, J8a, and J8c. Both the pipeline, divided into segments, and its sections are given on pl. 6. The northernmost trench was G8c, where G8c-[1] continued the excavation of light brown organic Islamic trash deposit lying upon a thick mass of caliche stretching the length of the trench. In section a possible wall appeared which might account for this caliche deposit; interestingly, if this wall does indeed exist, it is in alignment with wall A of G8b (the white building). Below this caliche was a thin layer of soft brown soil with numerous ungulate bones.

The second segment of the pipeline has mixed Islamic-Roman debris in H8a-[1]) north of a stone wall with caliche accretions around it visible on the surface. This wall was only one stone deep and presumably Islamic; the trench north of the wall was taken to bedrock. South of this wall was H8a-[2], which was marked by a varied collection of Roman artifacts including the gladiator lamp (pl. 60:b), two ostraca, two plaster plugs, and a large glass base. This layer continued as H8c-[1], containing few sherds of mixed periods down to gravels of the eroded bedrock. Within this trench was a portion of a room, the limestone walls of which were visible on the surface. Within the room (H8c-[2]) were many pieces of amphorae. Judging from the orientation, this room probably belongs to the Roman period. At the southern end of the trench in H8c was a much decayed wall, most of which had collapsed northward (near "d" on the plan).

The final segment of the pipeline begins with J8a on the north. This trench held only shallow deposits of Islamic remains (J8a-[1]) intersected by a small drainage cut revealing the bedrock gravels. At the southern end of this trench was a 50 cm. wide mud-brick wall crossing the trench. Against the south face of this wall was a fire-box with ashy soil lined with burnt bricks; the fire-box continued into the west baulk. Again, from the orientation one may suggest that this is a Roman installation, although few sherds were found. South of this the deposit was very shallow in J8c-[1], containing Islamic cloth and matting. Two walls of a room cut directly across the trench; they are composed of yellow mud brick on a stone foundation. Fall from these walls filled the room (J8c-[2]), beneath which was a greenish clay floor upon which was a variety of debris (J8c-[3]), including animal bones, leather, pottery, and a wooden stake protruding up through the debris and wall fall.

The discoveries along the pipeline confirm one's general expectations for this area between the central buildings and the harbor area. The deposition is, on the whole, very thin, due to the increased erosion on this slope. The fragments of Roman structures are mixed with Islamic materials, and therefore ambiguous, as a result of the Islamic utilization of this same area. Islamic occupational remains seem confined to poorly preserved wall fragments and trash accumulations; the situation seems very analogous to that uncovered in the eastern area (see chapter 4) and on the "island" (Whitcomb and Johnson, 1979: 40-44).

Central Building B

This large structure is indicated by surface mounding to have been a second central building comprising, with Central Building A, the major architectural features of the Roman occupation at Quseir al-Qadim; see pl. 1 and 7. The stratigraphic evidence from this building repeats the characteristics of the eastern central building, A. Below a thin Islamic occupation is a thick capping of caliche and hardened brickfall deriving from very substantial walls, no doubt constructed from bricks made of the lagoonal mud with a very high salt content. Building B (G12c) has proven more intractable than A toward revealing walls among the masses of brickfall. The few walls discovered confirm the orientation of the mounding of the building, but they do little to confirm the architectural character of this structure.

Surface indications of specific walls were more evident on a terrace south of the main mounding. The slopes of this terrace have concentrations of Islamic debris and therefore a trench (J14a) was placed to determine whether Islamic structures might be found built with the same orientation or reusing Roman structures. The resulting materials suggest that this later occupation had little to do with these wall fragments and that this terrace was an architectural extension, a long row of rooms and courtyards south of the main building, constructed and used during the Roman period. The quantities of terra sigillata in J14a suggest a relative importance of Central Building B and its extension.

J14a

This trench set out to examine the surface features of a broad terrace south of Central Building B. While most of these features were oriented with the remains of the Roman town, the presence of considerable dumps of Islamic remains suggested a reuse during this later period. The architectural remains excavated in this trench dramatically reinforced the general validity of the map of surface

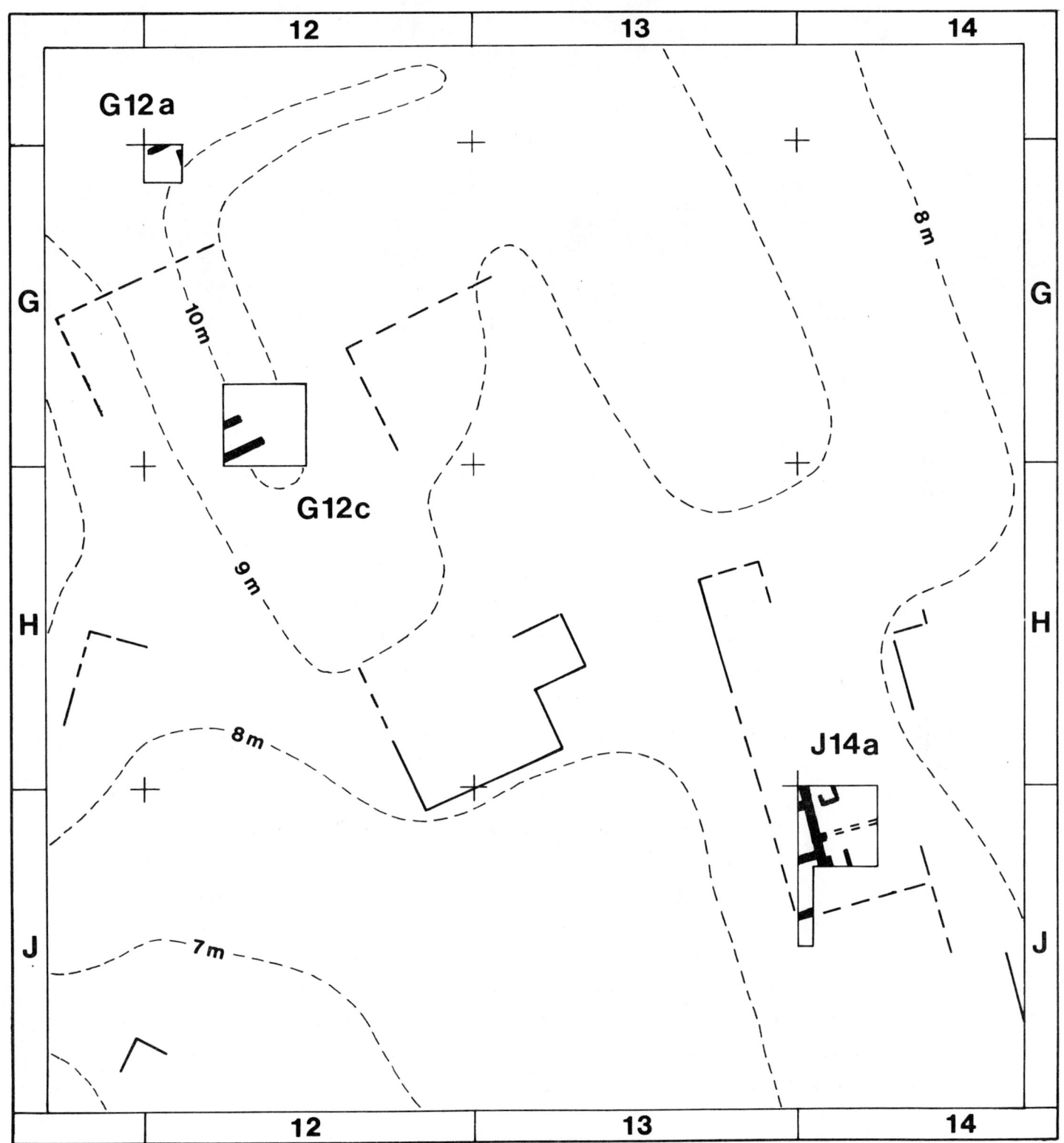

Plate 7: Central Building B

features. Other than mixed debris in the upper layers, no specific Islamic occupation was encountered.

The trench J14a began as a long pipeline 1x10 m., within which was a yellowish soil either soft or hard caliche ([1]), a combination of wind-blown sand and bricky detritus; see pl. 8. A series of walls was encountered near the surface; wall A was a major north-south wall with cross walls built onto its western side, presumably a series of rooms. These walls were constructed in a header-stretcher method. The northernmost of these rooms was the best preserved. In this an accumulation of organic debris was piled against the north wall (see section) above and next to brick detritus. This was lying upon a thick white plaster floor, which rested on a soft ashy grey-brown fill ([2]). The plaster floor extended to a brick footing or wider and earlier wall (more likely the former). By way of contrast, a probe into the room to the south of wall B showed the brick fall resting on multiple layers of brown fill without a plaster floor intervening ([9]).

The northern trench was expanded into a 5x5 m. trench, the surface layers being a mixture of organic debris, sand, and caliche ([3]). Abutting wall A was the stub of a substantial cross-wall, D, attached but not bonded; at lower levels the fragmentary remains of this wall were found directly on the virgin soil (bedrock), indicating that this wall had been removed during the Roman period. North of wall D was a mounded accumulation of debris, some organic (matting, rope, etc.) but mainly sherds. The upper layers may have received additions from the Islamic period, but the lower was purely Roman. This Roman trash was contained within a rather scrappy wall made of mud and stones, which seemed to form a small bin ([4]); see fig. 8. A similar bin was found south of wall D ([5]), again filled with Roman pottery, including the upper half of an amphora with its plaster plug intact over pieces of cork. It is tempting to see this complex as a long series of rooms with courtyards, each with its bin for trash. Between these bins was a yellow bricky debris but no structural remains ([6]). Deep soundings on the eastern side of the trench encountered deposits of yellow-brown soil which was almost sterile down to bedrock ([7],[8]). Bin [4] and probably all of the walls of this complex were constructed on this bedrock, which was rarely more than 1 m. below present ground surface.

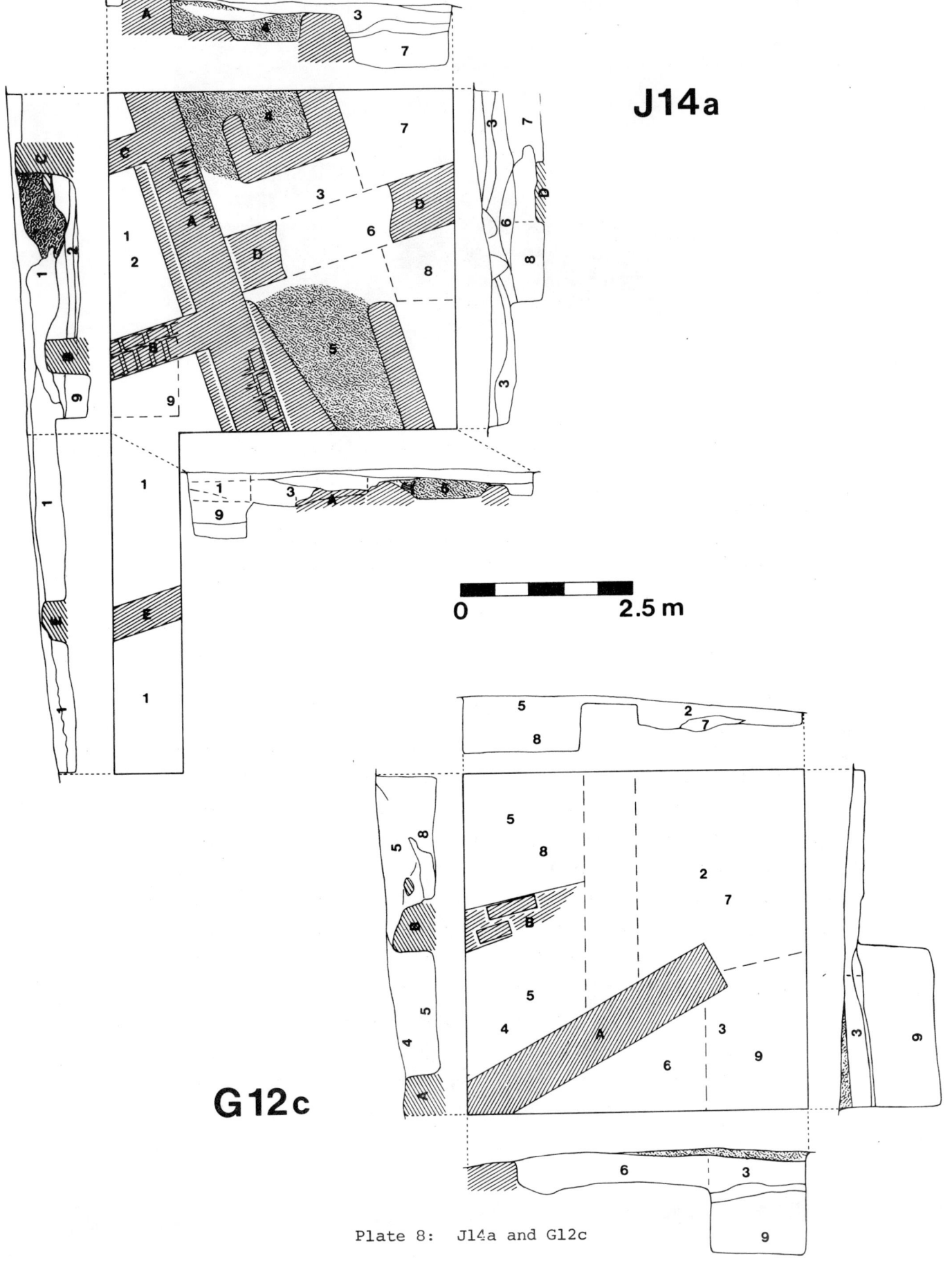

Plate 8: J14a and G12c

Fig. 8: J14a Looking South with Bin [4] in the Middle Ground to the Left of Wall A

The stratigraphy for J14a is:

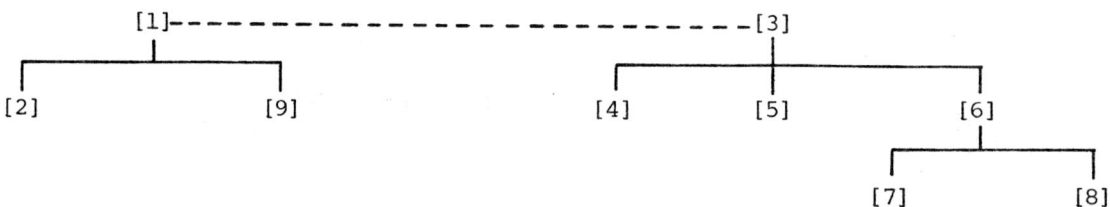

G12c

This trench was a second attempt to examine directly the nature of the large central building, Building B. Again its nature proved to be difficult; excavation from one to two meters in depth moved painfully through caliche and a hardened compact mass of mud brick fall. Only fragments of two walls were delineated within this hard amorphous mass. The deepest probe began to encounter softer soils more amenable to controlled excavation, but the burden of removing the dense overburden was quite beyond the time and man-power available. Regretfully, the effort was abandoned without obtaining a satisfactory delineation of the architecture and stratigraphy and without reaching bedrock.

The surface layers ([1],[2],[7],[8]) were deceptively soft soils made up of sand and pebbles with organic debris. Several small pits with ash and a tether rope were found, but no architectural fragments were encountered among these Islamic remains. Two small test pits in the southern corners ([3],[4]) encountered the same organic debris (rope, fibers, cloth, etc.) down to the surface of the caliche. The western test pit revealed wall A running diagonally across it. North of this wall a 2 m. wide trench ([5]) revealed a second, thinner wall B which had collapsed toward the south. Bricks within both of these walls measured ca. 32x16x8 cm. The southern face of wall A was followed from the section of [4], where tip lines of caliche and more sandy brick were clearly observed ([6]). Wall A abruptly ended two-thirds of the way across the trench in a large hole, although the placement of the hole might be coincidental if it derives from the upper Islamic layers.

In the southeast corner, test pit [3] was continued down to a depth of 2 m. ([9]). Within this lower layer were burnt bricks and a suggestion of the burnt face of wall A. Pockets of ash were mixed with softer clay and two possible floor layers (uncertain due to the limited workspace). A number of amphora bases were found within this debris; these and other Roman artifacts made more difficult the abandonment of this trench before completion.

The stratigraphy for this area is

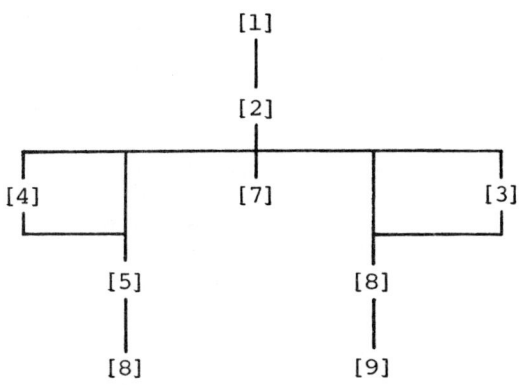

Bibliography for Roman Trench Summaries

Husselman, E. M.
    1979   *Karanis: Topography and Architecture*, Ann Arbor, Michigan

Whitcomb, D., and J. H. Johnson
    1979   *Quseir al-Qadim 1978: Preliminary Report*, Cairo

CHAPTER 3: ROMAN CERAMICS

Donald Whitcomb

The following corpus of ceramics is a selection from the loci of the areas of Roman occupation excavated during the 1980 season. The ceramics of the Roman villa are presented as a typological corpus, followed by ceramics of villa east and villa south, the central building, and building B (J14a and G12c), loosely organized along the same typological lines. This procedure departs from that used in the report of the 1978 season, which took as its unit of study the individual locus. The former approach allowed the presentation of primary evidence of assemblages in stratigraphic units; the limitations of this approach are excessive duplication of drawings of similar artifacts and possible distortions given the greater number of loci excavated in 1980. Further, the ceramics arranged in this manner are difficult to compare internally and with other sites, making the report cumbersome for archaeologists. Neither system of presentation, typologically or by loci, is very satisfactory--the number of loci or types selected and drawn remains limited; hopefully it is not so limited as to distort the full artifactual range.

The Roman Villa (Plates 9-21)

The Roman villa, as a discrete architectural unit, has been used as the source of the main ceramic corpus. This corpus is enhanced by numerous whole and almost complete storage vessels and other artifacts found on the floors of the large storeroom, the small storeroom, and the E6c storeroom. These artifacts may be considered as approximating a typical inventory at the time of departure and therefore during the occupation of the building. Stratigraphic indications suggest that the surrounding deposits present both pre-villa and post-villa artifactual assemblages.

In several areas specific loci of the lowest strata, generally dark brown sherdy soil, were apparently land-fill made up of early refuse and antecedent to the construction of the villa and surrounding buildings. This pre-occupation phase of the villa may be separated from the occupation of the villa. Likewise, after the abandonment of the villa and collapse of many of its walls, mounding of sherdy refuse was deposited over sections of the villa. This deposition signifies a post-villa phase of deposition. The danger of mixture with deposits partially contemporary or immediately after the main occupation of the villa has required an overly cautious selection of loci belonging to this third phase.

The significance of this periodization lies in the chronological limits of the Roman occupation in this area and in Quseir al-Qadim in general. The evidence collected to present uniformly indicates an occupation beginning around the turn of the millennium and continuing no later than the very beginning of the third century, a period of approximately 200 years. The stratigraphic evidence from the Roman villa, allowing for a length of time for accumulation of the pre- and post-villa refuse, suggests that a close refinement of the chronological range of these artifacts may be possible here. One must emphasize that this ceramic corpus is only a tentative first step toward distinctions which in the end may prove more amenable to statistical than formal analysis. The sample presented here is still far too limited to reflect functional or socio-cultural distinctions, which likewise will be considered in further analyses.

	E6a	E6c	E6b	D6d
Post-Villa	1,4,7,8,9	---	14,15,16	---
Villa	2,5,6,10,11 12,13,14	1,2,3,4	17,20,21,22,23,25,32 (large storeroom) 18,19,26,27,36,47, 49,50,54,56,57 (small storeroom) 24,29,42,44	(small storeroom) 1,2,3,5,7
Pre-Villa	3,15,16	---	28,30,31,55	4,6

(Loci with drawn ceramics underlined.)

Figure 9: Provisional Periodization of Roman Villa Loci

Plate 9: Kitchen Wares

The term "kitchen wares" refers to a grouping of relatively crude pots and bowls, most of which show evidence of repeated exposure to fire. Most are blackened or "purple" in color (a red or red-brown fabric darkened), while others are buff to orange with fire-blackening only on the exterior surface. This blackening of the exterior is often a thick layer of caked soot. The tempering is generally common to abundant sand of a coarse size range, as one might expect in vessels used for cooking. Several of the pot forms have burnished rims and interiors, a technique which is fairly rare in the Roman pottery at Quseir al-Qadim.

The forms of the kitchen wares are relatively limited. There are a limited number of bowl forms: heavy open vessels (a-c); close-mouthed bowls, one with a ledge or lug handle (d,e, and perhaps f); and forms which reproduce common bowls in a heavier or larger manner (g,h). The forms of the pots are most interesting. The first series has an outward flaring rim sharply attached to a sloping shoulder; thereafter one may suggest a sharp carination (k) and a smoothly rounded base (i-m). This type of pot is often burnished on the rim and interior. The form represents an earlier version of carinated pots found in the Islamic eastern area and may signify a continuity of exposure to an Indian tradition. Two examples (n,o) of lids which seem to fit the above described carinated pots are illustrated (although they might as well have been bowls).

A second type of pot has a horizontal ledge rim, often with grooves for resting the lid, a gently curving wall and, presumably, a round base (p-s, possibly excepting q). This type of pot is usually orange or orange-brown; one illustrated example was burnished (s). The last type of pot has a rounded body and a thick flaring rim (u-w). An example of this type with handles on the shoulder is u; a further example of the handle form is t. The heavy pots (v,w) are distinctive for their abundant chaff tempering agent; they are also burnished on the rim and interior.

Plate 10: Cooking Pots

The Roman "cooking pots" are related to the above discussed kitchen wares in wares, predominantly red and red-brown (purple), and in external fire-blackening. The cooking pots are lighter (with moderate medium sized sand temper) and appear to have more attention to finish (slips). Characteristic of the cooking pot is the presence of two handles, large and functional or symbolic vestiges (b); vessel forms illustrated without handles have been reconstructed from rim sherds and may have had handles at other points on their circumference. Bases were rarely identifiable but may be presumed to have been generally rounded, as on the whole vessel b.

The first grouping of cooking pot forms includes vessels with vertical necks (a-h). Most have slightly thickened rims which become an external beveled rim on larger examples (e,f). The neck can be somewhat curved as in g and h. This type of cooking pot is occasionally made in cream ware or covered with a cream slip (d-g). A second type of cooking pot (i,j) has no neck but a concave sloping shoulder forming the rim, which has an internal beveled surface. The varieties of internally beveled (or curved) rims are shown in k-p; this feature, like the ledge rims of the kitchen wares, seems designed to hold lids securely (two of which are depicted, s,t). The last four cooking pots show the varieties of more complex rims: external beveled surfaces with lid bevels or ledges (q,r) and ledge rims with grooves or lid ledges (u,v). These last two are larger than average and tempered with coarse sand.

Plate 11: Bowls

The forms of Roman bowls are relatively limited. Their wares tend to be finer than the forms discussed so far and most commonly orange in color with both cream and red slips applied selectively to the interior and exterior surfaces. Cream wares are represented by only two examples, a and c. Bases were rarely identifiable but are most likely to be either flat or low ring bases. Vessel walls are almost always incurving.

The first type of bowl has slightly incurving sides above a slight carination above the base (a-c). Simple black painted decoration is occasionally found on such bowls. Similar carinated bowls (d-f) have a slightly flaring rim. (The heavier example, f, may be a different type.) A further variation shows the rim folded over or flattened as a ledge (g-i). This type is generally orange with a darker orange or cream slip; only the variants d-f have a coarse sized sand temper. The large, deep bowl (j) may be a variant of this type.

Bowls with incurving sides, often thickened at the rim, are depicted in examples k and l. More common is the type of bowl with a higher, accentuated carination just below the rim; this type of bowl seems influenced by terra sigillata forms (m,n, with interior red slips) or forms of faience bowls (see below) (o). A fusion of these influences is seen in the series p-r, where the vessels are covered with a cream slip on the exterior.

Simple, almost hemispherical bowls are shown in examples s and t, the latter of which was recovered with a chunk of caliche (rock salt) inside and holding the badly fragmented bowl together. Finally, there are three "bowl" forms (u-w) which could well be lids, two of which are blackened on the exterior and may be misplaced kitchen wares.

Plate 12: Jars and Bases

Jars from the Roman villa are usually a red or orange fabric, often with a cream or, more rarely, red slip and coarse sand temper. Two of the jars have chaff tempering, which is very rare at Quseir al-Qadim. Jars with a narrow aperture at the neck may more properly be considered bottles when the full form is discovered. Within this type is the oil jar found in the storerooms with a variant neck depicted here (b). A few wide-mouth jars are finer wares (c,d) and may be associated with a rounded body (n; this example is a distinct and unusual piece).

Most of the jars have one or, more often, two handles with sizes ranging from small (a) to large (p). One example shows a rim form typical of the pilgrim flask (l). Other features of these jars include pouring lips (g,i), strainers (o, the forerunner of the Islamic filter neck) and shoulder spouts (f). One example (e) has been transformed by the insertion of a fired ceramic plug in the neck, perhaps for use as a rattle.

Two examples of rim forms for Roman kegs are depicted here (j,k). These rims are readily distinguishable from the rim types of Islamic kegs. The kegs found in the large storeroom each had had this rim (or spout) broken off and, as evidenced by the wear along the broken edges, continued to be used.

The bases grouped on this plate may have belonged to either jars or bowls, although in many cases more complete examples will allow an identification as to the precise forms. As with the jar forms, the ware is usually red or orange (two cream examples are shown here, y, aa) and the heavier forms (v,cc,dd) tend to have coarse sand temper. The grouping here gives an idea of the formal range involved. There is a series (q-t) which features the splaying ring foot of varying elaboration. Most common, however, is the simple ring foot which may be rounded in section or have a flat or beveled outer face (u-aa). Jar bases often have nearly vertical sides and a low ring base (dd-ff). Two unusual types are the simple string-cut base (cc) and a rounded base (bb).

Plate 13: Large Vessels

With the discovery of numerous abandoned vessels on the floor of the large storeroom, the character of many of the large vessels used in Roman Quseir al-Qadim may be determined. A number of larger forms are still known only partially. One is a large jar or pitcher with a pouring lip and one handle (a); another is a large pot, similar to the cooking pots (c) with a lid (b). Otherwise there are rim forms for large storage vessels, especially with splayed rims (e,f, with d). Two forms of large globular jars are shown here (g, with a slightly ridged body, and h, distinctive for its heavy cream ware tempered with abundant chaff). An unusual ribbed strap handle is also depicted (i).

The bases for large storage vessels are especially important in that, very unfortunately, the bases of very few of the vessels from the storerooms could be reconstructed with certainty. The range of these bases is from hollow pointed forms (j,k) to solid knobs (l,m). These last types may have become detached before the vessel was discarded. In any case, the lower portion of these vessels was usually badly spalled, making even tentative joins impossible.

Plate 14: Storage Vessels, Amphorae and Kegs

The ceramic vessels found on the floor of the large storeroom provide an interesting assemblage of storage vessels utilized immediately before the abandonment of this building. The first two vessels (a,b) are somewhat unusual at Quseir al-Qadim in that their ware is a soft brown, the larger with a grey core and tempered with abundant coarse white grit. The forms are analogous, being more or less barrel shaped. The smaller (b) has a very thick rim, while the larger (a) has a simple outcurved rim on a vertical neck. The juncture of the neck with the body is decorated with a raised band incised with cross-hatching.

Two of the three kegs (also called water-bottles) which were found are illustrated (c,d). Both are of red ware. The first has two indentations accidentally produced before firing. The second (d) has an incised mark near the spout (a "crowsfoot" or perhaps *psi*). Neither keg was found with a spout and both showed wear marks around the broken edges to suggest utilization after the spouts had been broken off. The spout depicted here (e) was found on the floor of the small storeroom.

The most common type of amphora, to judge from sherd counts, is the long, thin type (f,g) made of red-brown ware with sand and some chaff tempering. The two slightly differing rims fit very closely with the plaster plugs recovered from the excavations. After the discovery of innumerable fragments, the recovery of a whole vessel was particularly welcome, enabling an appreciation (however limited) of this amphora form. As suspected, the shoulder is only slightly rounded and the neck disproportionally wide in relation to the body. The foot is long and heavy and rarely distinguished from the line of the body. The handles, attached high on the neck, often break off from the neck.

Plate 15: Large Storage Vessels

A common type of storage vessel or amphora (a) is characterized by an almost horizontal shoulder and high vertical neck with simple widened rim. The handle, attached to the shoulder and neck, is pinched in a way to form a deep ridge on the exterior. This example has painted loops (or festoons) on the shoulder in black paint. A number of examples were also found in storeroom E6c, all broken at the shoulder; not one certain example of a base for these vessels was recovered.

A second form of amphora (b,d) was typified by the shoulder section, which was nearly vertical and set off from the neck and body by ridges often emphasized by painted lines. The handles were double and square sectioned. Wear marks at the base of the neck show that both vessels were used after their tops had been broken off (the tops are reconstructed from examples found in 1978). The absence of bases is more difficult to explain; the base shown here (c) likely belonged to this type although no join was possible. The painting was in red and poorly preserved.

The third type of storage vessel depicted here is larger, widening slightly near the base. The first example (e) has two short handles on the sloping shoulder and a thick out-curving rim. The second has a short solid foot and red painted letters. Both vessels are distinguished by vertical scraping of the exterior surfaces; otherwise the identity of these vessels as a single type is open to question. The fabric of each of these three vessel types is a red-orange shading to buff in the smaller types. All have a cream slip on the exterior.

Plate 16: Large Storage Vessels

One of the largest and best preserved of the storage vessels had a bag-like body (widening toward the base), with shallow ridging on the exterior and interior base (a). The neck thickens to the rim and a slight groove marks the top of the rim and the neck. The handles attach to the shoulder and the neck and bear two grooves giving a tripartite section. An incised inscription in Greek letters appears on the shoulder. The base was very badly spalled and may have been punctured by a cut hole. Such holes appear on the lower third of the body, one freshly cut and a second stopped up with plaster. Whatever the use of these holes, it would appear that the operation was repeated after the first hole had been closed.

Another type of amphora (c,f) has an ovoid body and is distinguished by large handles with oval sections joining the shoulder and the rim itself. The rim is wide and rather triangular in section with an interior groove. The first vessel (c) has an inscription (?) in red paint on the shoulder. The base (f) is badly preserved and does not join either vessel. Two additional, badly preserved bases were also found (d,e).

Finally, a section of the body of a storage vessel was reconstructed from badly salt damaged sherds. It varies from the usual orange-buff with cream slip; rather, it is a grey-brown grading to orange near the exterior surface. Nothing similar was found and it is possible that this heavy fragment had some use in its broken state.

Plate 17: Oil Jars and Other Forms

The large storeroom also produced a series of six small oil jars. The largest oil jar (a) was orange with a red slip (and a cream slip on the lower one-third of the exterior). This jar is within the size range of the oil jars from the small storeroom. The remaining jars belong to a smaller series not found in the small storeroom. These usually had a string cut base but were otherwise identical to the larger jars.

The small storeroom of the Roman villa contained a wide range of ceramic vessels in addition to other categories of artifacts. One may see here types already discussed: large and small two handled jars (g,k=12:a,p), a pilgrim flask (h=12:l), and two small bowls (i,j=11:t).

Plate 18: Oil Jars

The most characteristic feature of the small storeroom was the numerous small jars with a very constricted neck, a pouring lip and single handle. These features (as well as their presence in the small storeroom) suggest a valuable liquid, most probably an oil. The forms and size are closely standardized, although the bases differ slightly (rounded or vertical ring bases, flat bases). Two vessels with flattened sides (e,f) also bear inscriptions in black ink. Several of these oil jars appear to have had a small hole cut into the side, possibly to facilitate quickly emptying the oil into larger vessels for shipment. This practice is corroborated by a similar jar in the Cairo Museum (from Jebel Adda) where a small hole was cut and subsequently filled with plaster for reuse.

Plate 19: Amphorae and Other Forms

The small storeroom also contained the broken fragments of an amphora, a type not encountered in the other storerooms or in the villa in general. The body is ribbed and sharply tapering below a rather flat shoulder; the neck is narrow and tall and the handles heavy with a single groove on the exterior face. Red painted decoration covers the body, which is a red-brown with a buff surface. Two jars were also found: one with a wide neck (b) and one a small pitcher (c) with handle and pouring lip and an unusual indented base. Both of these vessels had small holes cut into their sides. Finally, an isolated base (d) of a large storage vessel suggests that this part of broken vessels may have had some use; this would help to explain the absence of bases from so many large storage vessels found in the other rooms.

Plate 20: Storage Vessels

The third storeroom was in square E6c, a room not completely excavated (and, indeed, some portions of vessels were left within the west baulk). The range of types of storage vessels recapitulates the types found in the large storeroom. The first vessel is a large, heavy jar (a) without handles; although the ware is very different (here an orange-buff with cream slip), the vessel seems similar to two examples in the large storeroom (14:a,b). Three broken rims found here (b,c,d) correspond to the type illustrated in 15:a. Likewise, the long thin amphora body (e) is an example of the common amphora type (14:f,g), here with an inscription in black ink on the upper shoulder. A third type of storage vessel (f,g) is represented in the large storeroom by two examples (16:c,f), and the bases are likened to one example here (i). Finally, sherds of a massive vessel (h), orange in ware with a shaved cream slip, seem variants on those depicted on 15:e,f.

The reproduction of this typological range within different storerooms has implications for storage practices and the functions of the vessel types.

Plate 21: Fine Ware Forms

The category of fine wares found in the Roman villa includes fine, thinly potted vessels, painted, and glazed wares. The wares are usually a light orange or cream fabric with little or no tempering agent. The most common fine wares are thin walled deep bowls or small jars (a,b,c), often with a light grey exterior slip (this is also known as brittle ware). Bases for this type of ceramic have either a shallow ring (f,g,h) or a flat disk base (i-l). Two painted wares fall

into this grouping. The first (d) is an incurving rim with feathery decoration in
a red paint; this will be immediately recognized as an archetypical Nabataean
product. The second is a basal fragment (e) with a broad stroke of purple paint,
perhaps related to 26:d, found in the central building.

Two heavier vessels are included here, a base with interior ridging (m) and
a rim with interior comb decoration on a black burnished ware (o). One further
painted fragment (p) with brown paint on a cream ware is also included. The
most unusual painted ware, however, is the shoulder and neck of a jar (q). The
ware is orange with a white slip on the exterior; upon this is painted decoration
in red and black. Similar painted sherds were found in 1978, when contextual
periodization was uncertain (Whitcomb and Johnson, 1979: 28:g; 38:d).

Roman glazed wares were also found. The rim of a deep bowl (or jar) (n)
has a green glaze over a crenellated incised pattern also found on unglazed fine
wares. A glazed base and curved sides of bowls (or perhaps a jar shoulder)
were found (r,s) with yellow glaze on one side and green glaze on the other over
a moulded design of grape leaves and bunches of grapes.

Villa East and Villa South (Plates 22-25)

The Roman ceramics from villa east and villa south have been combined into
one typological series as a test and amplification of the categories of the Roman
villa. As is true of the ceramics from the villa, this ceramic corpus is not
meant as a final summation of the ceramics collected but only a preliminary
systemization. Quantitative and areal distributions are obviously missing. The
collections illustrated come from a variety of loci: the possible room bounded
by walls C,D,M is represented by E6b-[43],[48],[51]; the street by E6b-[34],[37];
east of the street by E6b-[35],[40], E7a-[15],[16],[18]; and the connecting trench
by E7c-[11],[19]. From villa south ceramics were selected from E7c-[1],[2],[5],
[7],[9] and F7a-[1],[3],[4].

Plate 22: Kitchen Wares and Cooking Pots

The kitchen wares show a broadly similar range of types to those of the villa.
Ledge rim pots (a,b) correspond with 9:p,s, respectively; carinated pots (e,f)
with 9:m,i; and round pot g with 9:v. Several of these vessels have an orange
ware, rather than the more common purple, perhaps as the result of varying exposure
to fires. Two of the forms presented here as kitchen wares (c,d) seem to find
parallels among the cooking pots (10:u,v). Likewise the large bowl (j) is also
illustrated as a bowl (9:c). The bowl form (i) might be variously interpreted

as a lid (9:n) or as a bowl (11:u). Two pieces illustrated here do not find parallels within the Roman villa, the bowl with sharply beveled rim (h) and the horizontal pierced lug handle (k).

The cooking pots show a much tighter grouping with most of the Roman villa types also occurring outside that building. Most common are the cooking pots, often with two handles, with an internally beveled rim (l-o) which are illustrated on 10:i-k. Variants of this form with a curving rim (q,r) correspond to 10:n,o. Pots with a high vertical neck (s,t,v, the latter of which did not have handles) are also found (10:a,c). The variant of the high vertical neck with a beveled rim (p) is also represented (10:f). Finally, a form with a more complex rim (u) seems to be similar to 10:v. The wares of each of these formal types correspond very closely.

Plate 23: Bowls and Bases

Bowl forms, while falling into corresponding categories as those in the villa, show somewhat greater latitude in variability. The first type is the carinated bowl, often with a red slip; there are both straight rims (d=11:c, g=11:b) and folded over rims (a=11:g; b and h are loosely related to 11:e and i, respectively). The folded over rim of a hole-mouth form (c) is unparalleled in the villa corpus. Forms with a high emphasized carination (or rounded ridge) (e,) correspond loosely with 11:p,q. Two large examples of inward curving rims (k,l) take a general similarity to 11:k.

The crude hemispherical bowl (j) would seem to be a large version of 11:s. Lids are represented in m corresponding to that over a cooking pot (10:s). Two other unusual bowl forms (i,n) may also actually be lids, or indeed belong with the kitchen wares (9:g,o). Finally, there is a fine bowl (o) with a burnished red slip which is unique at Quseir al-Qadim. It has a beaded rim and a short band of applied decoration on the body with a chain ridge design.

The bases present several new forms: an internal indented form (p) and a shallow ring with an external ridge (q), both of which seem to derive from terra sigillata forms. Parallels may be found for the remaining forms in the villa (r-t=12:u,ee,z,v).

Plate 24: Jars and Large Vessel Forms

Jar forms from outside the villa duplicate the range found within that building. Out-curving necks (a-c) are present (12:c,d) as well as oil jars (d,e) (12:b), two handled jars (g=12:a, although larger; k,l=necks of 12:p), strainers (h=12:o), and pilgrim flasks (i=12:l). No examples of kegs were found in this area.

The neck of a somewhat larger vessel (j) may belong to a storage jar of the type found in the E6c storeroom (20:b). Another rim (m) may in fact not be a jar but rather a large bowl and be better placed among the kitchen wares. Other fragments of large vessels appear to introduce forms not encountered in the villa. Only the heavy rim (n) appears to be similar to 13:d. The folded rim in red-brown ware is quite unusual. Two handles depicted here (p,q) are a short strap handle and a round sectioned handle with multiple grooves. Two body sherds show unusual techniques, the use of appliqué with a red slip (r) and grooved and incised patterns (s). The occurrence of variance in the category of large vessels may be an accident of sampling or may point to a functional differentiation between the villa and its surrounding structures.

Plate 25: Fine Ware Forms

Fine wares found outside the Roman villa both duplicate the forms within the villa and, such is the nature of these small special wares, greatly amplify this category. Forms of jars and bowls (a-d) are additions with techniques such as crenellated (seen on the glazed fragment, 21:n) and an example of barbotine (d). There is an incurving rim of a bowl (e), a heavier version of 21:d. Bases are similar with both ring (g,h) and flat disk forms (f,i,j,k).

Distinctive pieces are, first, the small moulded orange ware (l), an example of the classical Megarion ware. A deep bowl or jar (n) has black and orange painted decoration on a cream ware recalling the 1978 bowl (Whitcomb and Johnson, 1979: 26:e) and one from the central building (26:d). A somewhat similar form has the base but not the foot, accentuated by a trace of brown paint. A small handle (m) and a lid in fine ware (p) were also found.

Central Building A (Plate 26)

The pipeline contained, in general, very few Roman loci, the majority being Islamic overburden. The loci in and near central building A utilized here are G8b-[3], immediately west of wall A, seemingly post-dating the collapse of that wall, G8a-[4], west and below the previous locus, seemingly contemporaneous with the use of the white building, and G8b-[18], a deposit wthin a room (walls C,E,F) of the central building.

The selection of ceramics presented here illustrates the presence of many, but not all, the ceramic categories identified in the villa. Kitchen wares (l, m,n) are typical forms (9:r,s,c, the latter of which is very approximate). Cooking pots (j,k) are also common forms (10:j,m). Bowls are limited to two carinated and one round form (a=11:c; b≃11:j; e=11:k). The bases illustrated here (g,h,i) are variants of 12:ee and perhaps v. No jar forms were selected from these loci. The larger vessels are storage jar rims which do not precisely parallel those of the Roman villa; rims o,p may be variants of the storage jars in the E6c storeroom (20:b-d) and rims q,r may have belonged to amphorae of the type found in the small storeroom (19:a). The fragment of a shoulder illustrated here (s) has a deeply incised inscription (?). Finally, two fine wares are shown: rim c, which approximates 21:h, and a painted base which closely parallels a bowl found in 1978 (Whitcomb and Johnson, 1979: 26:e) and the decorative schema of 25:n.

Central Building B (Plates 27-28)

The ceramics from J14 have been selected mainly from the two bins [4] and [5] and the intervening locus [3]. This debris contained a large number of amphora fragments, the most important of which (27:a) contained the original plaster plug still in place. The inscription on the top of the plug had been effaced, but below the plaster, which contained broken bits of pottery, were numerous fragments of cork. This amphora and that illustrated in 27:h seem to be variants of the type seen in the large storeroom of the villa (15:b,d), although here the shoulders are more nearly horizontal. A fragment of a shoulder of this type had monograms in red paint.

A second type of amphora (b) is a variant of the typical Egyptian amphora, although the cream slip is unusual (14:f,g). A shoulder fragment bore an inscription in black paint (20:e, E6c storeroom). Bases (e,f) could belong to either type of amphora (15:c,f, both in the large storeroom). It is very likely that base g attached to amphora h.

In addition to the amphorae, J14a produced an interesting but limited range of ceramic forms. The rim of a bowl (28:a) corresponds to 11:1, but here in brown ware with a purple burnished slip. Bases range from a fine ware (b=21:1) to an oil jar (c=17:e in the large storeroom) and a ring base (12:ee). Jar forms are somewhat variant (e, new to the corpus and reminiscent of large vessel 13:g; and f=24:j in villa east). Four examples of cooking pots are presented here (h= 10:k; i=10:u; and j=10:j); the fourth example (g) is very large and may be a variant of 10:u. Kitchen wares would seem to be absent from the assemblages considered.

Trench G12c produced very little in the way of Roman ceramics. The selections are from loci of building collapse. A bowl rim with an unusual beaded rim (k) may be related to the bowl from villa east (23:o). Another unusual fragment (l) is folded over and may be a lid. This may belong to the kitchen wares, as should the horizontal loop handle (n). Finally, the lowest test pit, G12c-[9], produced the slightly ribbed body of a small jar, unfortunately without its rim (o) and without precise parallel in the corpus.

Sigillata Wares (Plates 29-30)

The terra sigillata wares (a fine red ware with highly polished red slip) found in the Roman areas form an interesting and important corpus for determining the date and external connections of this ancient port. The general observations made here result from discussions with Dr. John Hayes, who generously "read" a large selection of these sherds for us.

The terra sigillata wares which occur at Quseir al-Qadim may be divided into four categories: Eastern Sigillata A, Eastern Sigillata B, Arretine, and Cypriot. These different wares suggest a diverse distribution pattern for these widespread, highly valued ceramics. Of particular interest is the occurrence at Quseir al-Qadim of examples parallel to ones found in other Red Sea ports (e.g., Clysma), Petra, India (Arikamedu), and within Egypt (Coptos, Alexandria, etc.).

The eastern sigillata A wares (ESA) were presumably a product of the Levantine coast. The ware is usually a light cream to buff with a thin red slip which flakes away easily. Within the 1980 excavation areas they form approximately 50% of the terra sigillata collection. All forms are datable to the first century of our era; there is nothing pre-Augustan and nothing post 100 A.D. Most seem to fall into the earlier half of this century. Within the Roman villa, eastern sigillata A wares make up 2/3 of the collection and, although the actual count is too small for statistical validity, only this type of terra sigillata is found in pre-villa and villa occupations, suggesting that the occupation of the villa belongs to the first half of the first century of our era.

Eastern sigillata B, which comes, seemingly, from Asia Minor, forms only 10% of the 1980 collection from Quseir al-Qadim. This is an orange ware with micaceous inclusions, a soapy feel, and flaking red slip. Dating of the forms discovered is generally the same as the eastern sigillata A. The ware seems evenly distributed throughout the excavated areas.

The Arretine wares are Italian products although the "crudeness" suggests a Campanian source rather than Arezzo itself. The Arretine ware is pink-red; it is well bonded to the slip, which is highly polished. The collection, which is entirely datable from 0 to 50 A.D., would be typical for Alexandria, but not for cities in the Nile valley. Preliminary counts suggest a very high concentration of this ware near Central Building B (in J14a).

A small percentage (about 10%) of the sigillata wares from Quseir al-Qadim in 1980 come from Cyprus. The Cypriot ware is orange with an orange-red slip, well bonded but not highly burnished. It is normal to find this ware in association with Arretine and all the forms found here are also datable to the first century of our era. No examples are identified as coming from the villa.

The presentation of the forms begins with those from the Roman villa. While this is the largest corpus, there is significantly little duplication of the forms found in other Roman areas. Pl. 29:a,b,f,g,h,o shows a series of plates with curved sides and beaded or overhanging rims. There is often interior scoring and one example of an impressed decoration (h), the only example found at Quseir al-Qadim in either season. It can be dated approximately 100 A.D. A second series of plates (29:i,j,k,l) has vertical sides which are scored or faceted, attaching to a horizontal base. One example shows rouletting on the exterior rim (l). Fitting in neither of these categories is plate 29:d. Bowls vary from a hemispherical form with beaded rim (29:q) to the more common carinated bowl (29:e,m,n). Bases for such bowls are illustrated in 29:u,v,w. Finally, small cups made of eastern sigillata A have been found (29:s,t) with incised monograms on the base. Stamps have been found on the interior of the base of these cups and other bowl forms (29:v)(see chapter 11 on stamps). The only "oddity" in this corpus is the heavy rolled rim (29:c), perhaps from a jug or flagon.

The terra sigillata forms from villa east expand this corpus with a plate with inward curving sides (29:y) and a heavy beaded-rim Cypriot plate (29:z). Vertical sided plates are found (29:aa,bb) and a carinated bowl form (29:cc, comparable to 29:n). Small bowls or cups are also comparable to those in the villa (29:dd,ee) with both stamps and incised monograms. A shallow curved-in rim (29:x) is an unusual form from this area.

South of the villa there appear a number of new forms for the bases of plates (30:a,b,c,e) with central rouletted decoration on the interior surface. The small ESA cup again appears (30:f), as does a new rim form of Cypriot ware (30:d).

Along the length of the pipeline sherds of terra sigillata wares present the same range of forms: curved sided plates (30:g), vertical sided plates (30:h,j), and carinated bowls (30:k-n). Again the unusual is reserved for the Cypriot ware (30:i).

Finally, the forms from J14a represent variations of the same categories; plates (30:o-r) include a large over-hanging Arretine rim (30:p). Bowls are seen in carinated forms (30:s,t) and in smaller cups (30:v,w).

The forms, then, fall into a relatively few categories at this level of analysis, a level which will no doubt shock the serious devotees of this art. The purpose of the presentation is to show both the pattern of overall formal categories, which may reflect functional categories as well, and to present the enormous variation of formal detail which characterizes this highly complex medium. Consideration of the expanded corpus of terra sigillata from the full three seasons of excavation, all of which pieces are individually saved and recorded, will allow the final report to combine data on wares and forms into a meaningful analysis of distribution patterns. The same will, of course, be done for all the Roman and Islamic ceramics.

Discussion

The ceramics of the Roman period at Quseir al-Qadim, as those of the Islamic period, present a complex picture of local Egyptian industries set in a wide-ranging interregional style with an admixture of specific regional products from outside Egypt. There seems little likelihood that there was any ceramic production at Quseir al-Qadim itself; nevertheless, the lack of information on products of Upper Egypt, specifically Coptos (Quft, as Qus in the Islamic period) as the natural resource area necessitates far-ranging, imprecise comparisons for the Egyptian component. Part of this problem may be corrected with increased attention to the wares of these ceramics (Adams, n.d.). Recent preliminary studies by Matson (1974) indicate the potential for technological studies of Egyptian pottery. In this article Matson compares Helwan, Qena, and Ballas clays, of which the Nile muds at Qena (not far from Coptos) appear quite similar to the Quseir al-Qadim corpus (1974: 136). Matson also notes that the Ballas white surface ware might be the result of deposition of soluble salts on the surface of the pottery; this points to a caution in the accuracy of our "cream slipped red wares."

Stylistic analysis of the Roman ceramics indicates that forms current in the empire were utilized (or copied) and that products in regional styles were imported and transported through this port. The separation of these possibilities is rarely simple nor is the conjunction of separate formal developments to be ruled out. A case in point is found in the "kitchen wares" (pl. 9), where pots with similar forms may be seen in the Athenian agora and at Arikamedu. For instance, pot 9:j,k occurs in 2nd-3rd century contexts in Athens (Robinson, 1959: Pl. 11: J57, Pl. 13: K55) and at Arikamedu (Wheeler, 1946: Type 24, fig. 19, 20; Casal, 1949: fig. 15: 35a). Likewise, another pot form (9:r) is seen at Athens (Robinson, 1959: Pl. 14: K96, Pl. 3: F80, Pl. 8: H13; 1st-3rd centuries) and in India (Wheeler, 1946: Type 93, fig. 32).

While these similarities may be coincidental, the parallels of Quseir al-Qadim ceramics with materials from Arikamedu (noted in Johnson, 1979: 67) are striking. Wheeler's types may be compared with the present corpus: 6 = 22:i; 8 = 9:g; 24 = 9:j,k,l,m, 22:e; 28 = 28:1; 30 = 9:h; 33 = 11:u; 43 = 13:g; 93 = 9:u. As Wheeler describes these ceramics as local Indian wares, the Quseir al-Qadim examples are either imported pieces or local imitations; in either case, the fact that most of these are kitchen wares strongly suggests the presence of Indians using and/or making these forms in Egypt. Further delineation of this problem will necessitate comparison of actual artifacts; the 1982 season hopes to have an Indian archaeologist as part of the excavation to assist with this identification.

The discovery of a small sherd of a Nabataean painted bowl (21:d) points toward another range of external comparisons. The presence of Nabataeans had been noted in an inscription near Quseir (Hammond, 1979: 245-47) but the extent of their involvement in ports on the Egyptian coast is unknown. The ceramics from Nabataean sites include the painted wares, eastern sigillata A, and megarion bowls (cf. 25:1) (Negev, 1974; Murray and Ellis, 1940). Other ceramics of less distinguished type are more difficult to determine, although a recent ceramic sequence from Petra offers numerous putative parallels (Parr, 1970: 9:q = 4:48, 5:59 [VIII-IX]; 10:c = 6:81, 8:126, 138 [XI, XVII-XVIII]; 10:f = 3:40 [VII]; 10:q = 3:34, 40 [VI-VII]; 11:m = 5:99 [X-XII]; 11:w = 8:129 [XVIII]; 15:e,f = 4:41 [VIII]; 21:f = 2:6 [IV]; 22:h = 4:43 [VIII]; 22:p = 3:32 [VI]; 24:d = 5:61 [IX]; 25:p = 2:22 [V]). The majority of these comparisons are found in Parr's middle levels (VII-XI; 1st century B.C.--1st century of our era). What proportion of these ceramics are specifically Nabataean, as opposed to Roman, must remain for further analysis.

Roman ceramic forms, such as the cooking pots (pl. 10), have a wide geographical range, occurring for instance in Palestine (Lapp, 1961: 184A), in the Sinai (Rothenberg, 1972: fig. 72:1), and in Nubia (Adams, n.d.: fig. 7,8; cf. Hayes, 1976: 249, 1st--2nd centuries). The same range of comparisons might be made for bowl forms, jars and juglets, pilgrim flasks, oil jars (pl. 18), thin wares (Barbotine) and glazed wares. The commonality of ceramic forms during the Roman period throughout the eastern Mediterranean does not mean that specific Egyptian traditions may not be separated out (an excellent beginning is found in Hayes, 1976). Fieldwork such as the Dakhleh Oasis project (Hope, 1981) will greatly clarify this problem (one should note that the "Roman" ceramics from Dakhleh suggest a very different regional tradition when compared with Quseir al-Qadim, with an important exception being the distinctively Egyptian kegs, 14:c,d,e; Hope, 1981: 235-37).

It is with the amphorae that the question of Egyptian and imported ceramics becomes most explicit. The distinctive Egyptian amphora form is a red-brown ware, long and narrow, with two handles attached to the neck. Accentuated forms (Hayes, 1976: 364; Bruyere, 1966: pl. XXIV) seem to be somewhat later developments of this type (Kelley, 1976: pl. 97:32). Hayes shows an example with an intact seal very similar to those from Quseir al-Qadim (27:a = 1976: 362). Ribbing is usually very indistinct and undeveloped on this type of amphora. A slightly more accentuated ribbing occurs on the small amphora from the small storeroom (19:a), which appears to be an imitation(?) of a Chian type of amphora (Zemer, 1978: pl. 10: 30,31). A vessel with similar painted decoration was found in Athens (Robinson, 1959: pl. 19: M54; middle of 2nd century).

Also from Athens is a very close parallel to the bag-shaped amphora (16:a) (Robinson, 1959: pl 29: M273; this is dated to the 4th century but occurs in a refuse pit containing first century materials). The type may be related to Dressel 20 (Beltran Lloris, 1970: fig. 188:7). Zemer also illustrates an example which may be related, depending on the nature of the foot (1978: pl. 15:42); this example has a hole cut into the side, as does the Quseir al-Qadim example (see Zemer, 1978: 116, for a discussion of such holes; the explanation as a tap seems the most convincing; Callender, 1965: 43). Such amphorae seem to have come from North Africa, although Spanish sources are not impossible. The numerous amphorae with handles attached to the rim (16:c,f; 20:f,g) are likewise North African or Spanish (Parker, 1977: fig. 7); such piriform vessels may be related to Dressel 30. The rim form is noted in Beltran Lloris (1970: fig. 189:12) and in Lusuardi Siena (1977: fig. 25).

The amphora type 15:a, 20:b,c,d was found in late first-early second century context in Athens (Robinson, 1959: pl. 8: G199) and is dated by Zemer to second to third centuries (1978: pl. 15: 41, described as a North African type). The largest amphorae also appear to be a North African type (15:e, 20:h), corresponding to Dressel 26 (datable to the first and second centuries; Callender, 1965). Other examples are in Parr (1971: 4:41) and in Beltran Lloris (1977: fig. 153:10 and 154:14); Zemer illustrates an amphora with handles in differing positions (1978: pl. 13:37).

The remaining amphorae seem to be variants of Dressel 2-4, a very common form of wine amphora in the Mediterranean (Callender, 1965). These are characterized by long vertical double handles. The example from J14a (27:a) has wide-ranging parallels: Jaffa (Kaplan, 1964: fig. 2:3; 50 B.C.--150 A.D.), Athens (Robinson, 1959: Pl. 3: F93), Qasr Ibrim (Adams, n.d.: fig. 18:Am4), and Arikamedu (Wheeler, 1946: fig. 9:46,55). Likewise, 27:h has parallels from Luni (Lusuardi Siena, 1977: fig. 16) and Carthage (Hayes, 1978: 51; first century). Another variant of this type of amphora (15:b,d) conforms to Group 4 of the Dressel 2-4 amphorae at Pompeii (Panella, 1977: fig. 27-32). This type is also present in India at Arikamedu (Wheeler, 1946: fig. 9:53).

It is interesting that the amphorae found at Arikamedu, like the terra sigillatas, have parallels at Quseir al-Qadim, supporting the hypothesis that these wares may have been traded through this port. The types of amphorae are those current in the Mediterranean during the first and second centuries, and several would seem to be North African types. These vessels, specialized containers for transport, were by their very nature distributed widely (and perhaps repeatedly).

The contents may only be speculated, although the predominant use would seem to have been for wine (especially those with resinous inner sealing). Oil and olives were other common products, while some of the forms with wider mouths may have been used for fish-sauce (*garum*, still an Egyptian delicacy under the name *fisikh*). Callender cites instances of a great variety of other contents attested (e.g., nuts, pepper, grains and flour, lentils, beans), all of which are found at Quseir al-Qadim (see chapter 17) and could have been transported in these amphorae (1965: 39-40). The amphorae in the storerooms of the villa show clearly that these vessels continued to be used to store goods after their original contents were emptied (e.g., the two holes in 16:a or the well-worn broken necks of 15:b,d).

While the possible comparisons for the Roman ceramics at Quseir al-Qadim might be multiplied, the above suggestions are intended to outline the utility of this evidence. As in most archaeolgoical situations, the study of the pottery provides a basis for chronology and evidence for contact with surrounding regions. Its functional interpretation provides suggestions for the pattern of life, in this case the trade and domestic activities of the inhabitants of this port.

Bibliography for Roman Pottery

Adams, W. Y.
    n.d.   "Pottery Wares of the Ptolemaic and Roman Periods at Qasr Ibrim: Preliminary Ware Descriptions"

Beltran Lloris, M.
    1970   *Las anforas romanas en espana*, Zaragoza

Bruyère, B.
    1966   *Fouilles de Clysma-Qolzoum (Suez) 1930-1932*, Cairo

Callender, M. H.
    1965   *Roman Amphorae*, London

Casal, J. M.
    1949   *Fouilles de Virampatnam--Arikamedu*, Paris

Hayes, J. W.
    1976   *Roman Pottery in the Royal Ontario Museum*, Toronto
    1978   "Pottery Report--1976," in J. H. Humphries, ed., *Excavations at Carthage 1976*, pp. 23-98

Hope, C. L.
    1981   "Dakhleh Oasis Project: Report on the Study of the Pottery and Kilns; Third Season--1980," *The Society for the Study of Egyptian Antiquities Journal* 11: 233-41

Johnson, W. R.
    1979   "Pottery," in D. S. Whitcomb and J. H. Johnson, *Quseir al-Qadim 1978: Preliminary Report*, Cairo, pp. 67-103

Kaplan, J.
　1964　　*Two Groups of Pottery of the First Century A.D. from Jaffa and its Vicinity*, Tel Aviv

Kelley, A. L.
　1976　　*The Pottery of Ancient Egypt*, Toronto

Lapp, P. W.
　1961　　*Palestinian Ceramic Chronology 200 B.C.--A.D. 70*, New Haven

Lusuardi Siena, S.
　1977　　"Appunti su alcuni tipi di enfore lunensi," in G. Vallet, ed., *Methods classiques et methods formuelles dans l'étude des amphores*, Rome, pp. 207-30

Matson, F. R.
　1974　　"Technological Studies of Egyptian Pottery--Modern and Ancient," in A. Bishay, ed., *Recent Advances in Science and Technology of Materials*, vol. 3, New York, pp. 129-40

Murray, M. A., and J. C. Ellis
　1940　　*A Street in Petra*, London

Panella, C., and M. Fano
　1977　　"Le anfore con anse bifide conservate a Pompeii: contributo ad una loro classificazione," in G. Vallet, ed., *Methods classiques et methods formuelles dans l'étude des amphores*, Rome, pp. 133-77

Parker, A. J.
　1977　　"Lusitanian amphorae," in G. Vallet, ed., *Methods classiques et methods formuelles dans l'étude des amphores*, Rome, pp. 33-46

Parr, P. J.
　1970　　"A Sequence of Pottery from Petra," in J. A. Sanders, ed., *Essays in Honor of Nelson Glueck*, Garden City, New York, pp. 348-81

Robinson, H. S.
　1959　　*The Athenian Agora*, Vol. 5: *Pottery of the Roman Period*, Princeton

Rothenberg, B.
　1972　　*Timna: Valley of the Biblical Copper Mines*, London

Wheeler, R. E. M.
　1946　　"Arikamedu: An Indo-Roman Trading-Station on the East Coast of India," *Ancient India* 2: 17-124

Zemer, A.
　1978　　*Storage Jars in Ancient Sea Trade*, Haifa

Plate 9: Roman Villa Kitchen Wares

	Locus	RN	Description	Munsell
a	E6a-9	397	brown-black; fire blackened out; abundant coarse sand	5YR 2.5/2
b	E6a-1	396	black; fire blackened out; abundant coarse sand	10YR 3/1, 3/2
c	E6b-16	367	black; fire blackened out; abundant coarse sand	10YR 3/1
d	E6b-30	367	orange; fire blackened out; common coarse sand	5YR 2.5/1 out 5YR 4/6 in
e	E6c-4	332	buff; fire blackened out; moderate coarse sand	5YR 5/1, 5/2 out 5YR 5/4 in
f	E6a-2	396	black; hole in side; common coarse sand	10YR 3/1 out 10YR 4/2, 3/1 in
g	E6c-3	332	purple (i.e., red-brown); fire blackened out; common medium sand	7.5YR 3/2, 2/0 out 7.5YR 5/4, 4/2 in
h	E6c-3	336	purple; fire blackened out; common coarse sand	
i	E6a-1	396	brown; fire blackened out; moderate medium sand	5YR 2.5/1 out 5YR 4/6 in
j	E6c-4	332	purple; burnished; fire blackened out; moderate medium sand	2.5YR 3.2 out 2.5YR 4/4 in
k	E6b-44	367	brown; fire blackened out; abundant coarse white sand	7.5YR 2/0
l	E6a-15	397	purple; burnished rim; fire blackened out; abundant coarse white sand	7.5YR 2/0 out 7.5YR 3/2 in
m	E6b-16	367	purple; burnished rim and in; fire blackened out; abundant coarse white sand	2.5YR 5/6, 4/4 out 2.5YR 3/2 in
n	E6a-1	396	buff; light brown slip in; fire blackened out; abundant chaff	7.5YR 6/4, 4/2 out 5YR 5/6 in
o	E6a-1	396	purple, black core; fire blackened out; moderate medium	10YR 3/1 out 5YR 3/3 in
p	E6a-2	396	purple; fire blackened out; common coarse red sand	7.5YR 2/0 out 5YR 5/3 in
q	E6a-1	396	orange-brown; fire blackened out; common coarse red sand	5YR 3/1, 7/6 out 5YR 7/4, 5/3 in
r	E6a-15 E6a-4	397 396	orange-brown; common medium sand	5YR 4/4
s	E6b-16	367	orange; burnished; fire blackened out; moderate coarse	5YR 3/1, 3/2 out 5YR 5/6 in
t	E6b-30	367	purple; fire blackened out; moderate medium	2.5YR 3/4, 2.5/0 out 2.5YR 4/4 in
u	E6a-4	396	purple; fire blackened out; abundant coarse white sand	5YR 3/1 out 5YR 4/4 in
v	E6a-15	397	black-brown; burnished rim and in; abundant chaff	7.5YR 3/2, 2/0 out 7.5YR 3/2, 3/4 in
w	E6a-1	396	black; burnished rim and in; fire blackened out; abundant chaff	5Y 2.5/1

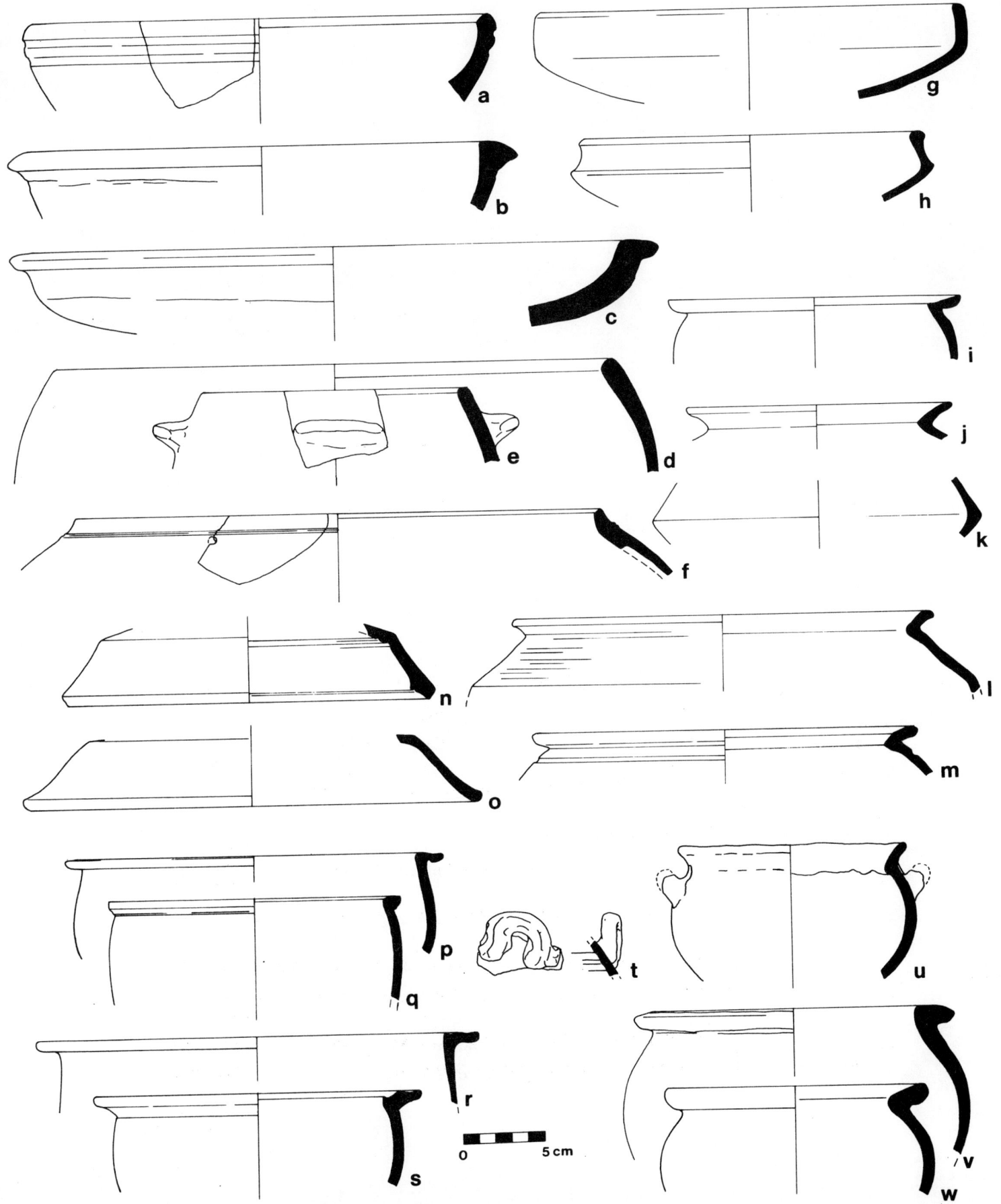

Plate 9: Roman Villa Kitchen Wares

Plate 10:   Roman Villa Cooking Pots

	Locus	RN	Description	Munsell
a	E6a-2	396	red; dark red slip; moderate medium sand	2.5YR 3/6
b	E6c-3	418	red-brown; resin in, pool of residue at bottom; fire blackened out; moderate medium sand	
c	E6a-15	397	red; orange slip; moderate medium sand	5YR 6/6 out 5YR 4/6 in
d	E6a-9	397	red-grey; cream slip out; moderate medium sand	5YR 7/3, 6/4 out 2.5YR 6/6 in
e	E6c-4	332	cream; buff slip out; moderate medium sand	5YR 6/6 out 7.5YR 7/6 in
f	E6a-1	396	brown; cream slip out; common medium sand	10YR 7/4 out 7.5YR 5/4 in
g	E6a-4	396	orange; cream slip out; moderate coarse sand	10YR 7/4 out 2.5YR 5/6 in
h	E6a-15	397	red; dark red slip; fire blackened out; moderate medium sand	2.5YR 2.5/0, 2.5/4 out 2.5YR 4/4 in
i	E6a-1	396	brown; fire blackened out; moderate medium sand	5YR 3/1 out 5YR 3/4 in
j	E6a-2	396	red-brown; fire blackened out; moderate medium sand	
k	E6a-3	396	red; orange slip out and rim; moderate medium sand	2.5YR 6/8 out 10YR 8/4, 5/4 in
l	E6b-24	366	red; red slip; moderate medium sand	2.5YR 6/6
m	E6c-4	332	cream-orange; moderate medium sand	5YR 6/6
n	E6a-5	396	red; fire blackened out; moderate medium sand	7.5YR 2/0 out 5YR 4/6 in
o	E6a-3	396	red; orange slip; fire blackened out; moderate medium sand	2.5YR 5/6
p	E6b-55	366	red-brown; moderate coarse sand	5YR 6/4
q	E6a-3	396	red; orange slip out and rim; moderate medium sand	2.5YR 6/8 out 2.5YR 5/6 in
r	E6a-4	396	red-brown; fire blackened out; moderate medium sand	2.5YR 4/4
s	E6a-9	397	dark orange; red-orange slip; abundant coarse sand	2.5YR 5/8
t	E6a-3	396	red, grey core; dark red slip; moderate coarse sand	2.5YR 5/4 out 2.5YR 4/4 in
u	E6a-15	397	dark orange; brown slip; abundant coarse sand	2.5YR 6/6
v	E6a-15	397	red; dark red slip; moderate coarse sand	2.5YR 4/6

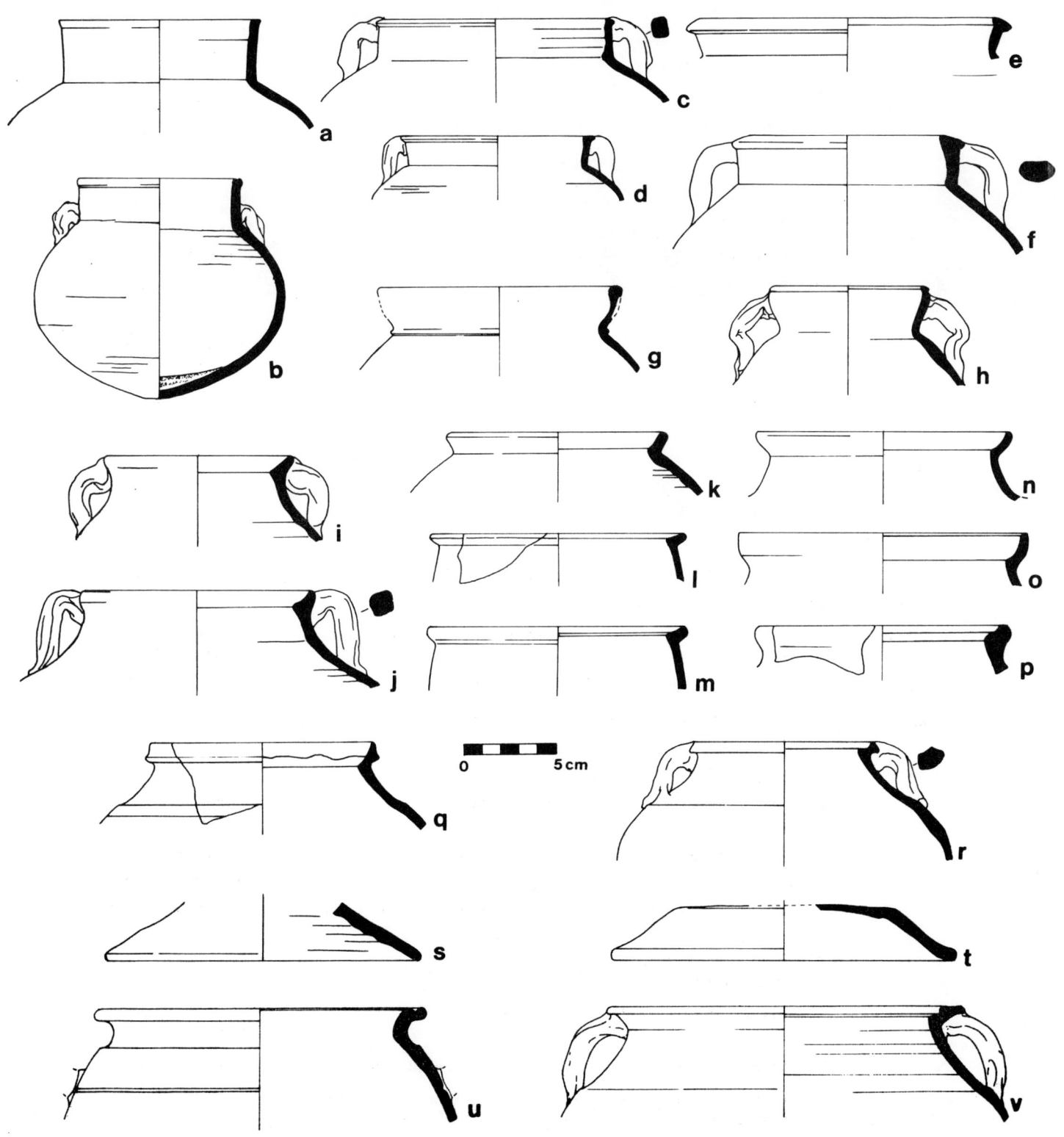

Plate 10: Roman Villa Cooking Pots

Plate 11: Roman Villa Bowls

	Locus	RN	Description	Munsell
a	E6a-1	396	cream; brown slip; common medium sand	5YR 6/4, 5/4 out 5YR 7/4 in
b	E6a-4	396	red; orange surface out, silvery lustre in; fine	5YR 6/6, 5/6 out 5GY 6/1, 5G 6/1 in
c	D6d-6	366	light orange; dark orange slip out; black paint; abundant medium sand	2.5YR 5/6 out 5YR 7/6 in
d	E6b-36	446	light orange; moderate coarse sand	5YR 7/6 out 5YR 7/4 in
e	E6b-36	367	brown; cream slip; abundant coarse sand	2.5Y 8/4, 7/4
f	D6d-6	366	dark orange; cream slip; moderate coarse sand	2.5YR 6/6
g	E6c-4	332	light orange; dark orange slip; abundant medium sand	2.5YR 6/8
h	E6a-15	397	light orange; orange slip; moderate medium red sand	2.5YR 6/8
i	E6a-1	396	orange; red slip out; abundant medium sand	2.5YR 4/8
j	E6a-1	396	red; red slip out; moderate medium sand	2.5YR 4/8
k	E6a-9	397	light orange; orange slip; common medium sand	5YR 7/6, 6/6
l	E6a-15	397	red; common medium sand	2.5YR 5/6
m	E6b-30	367	red; dark red slip in; moderate medium sand	2.5YR 5/8 out 2.5YR 5/8 in
n	E6a-2	396	red; dark red slip in; moderate medium sand	2.5YR 6/6
o	E6b-16	367	buff-orange; red-orange slip out; moderate coarse sand	5YR 6/6
p	E6c-1	332	cream; fine	7.5YR 8/6, 7/6
q	E6a-1	396	red; cream slip out; common medium sand	10YR 7/4 out 5YR 6/6 in
r	E6a-2	396	red; cream slip out; moderate medium sand	2.5YR 6/6, 5/6 out 2.5YR 5/8 in
s	E6a-1	396	orange; cream slip out; abundant medium sand	2.5YR 6/6 out 2.5YR 5/6 in
t	E6a-9	434	red; cream slip out; moderate coarse sand; filled with salt	7.5YR 7/4
u	E6b-55	366	brown; blackened out; common medium sand; lid?	5YR 3/2 out 5YR 6/6 in
v	E6b-30	367	orange; cream slip out; common medium sand	10YR 6/4
w	E6a-4	396	orange-red; burnished; blackened out; common medium sand	2.5YR 5/8, 4/8

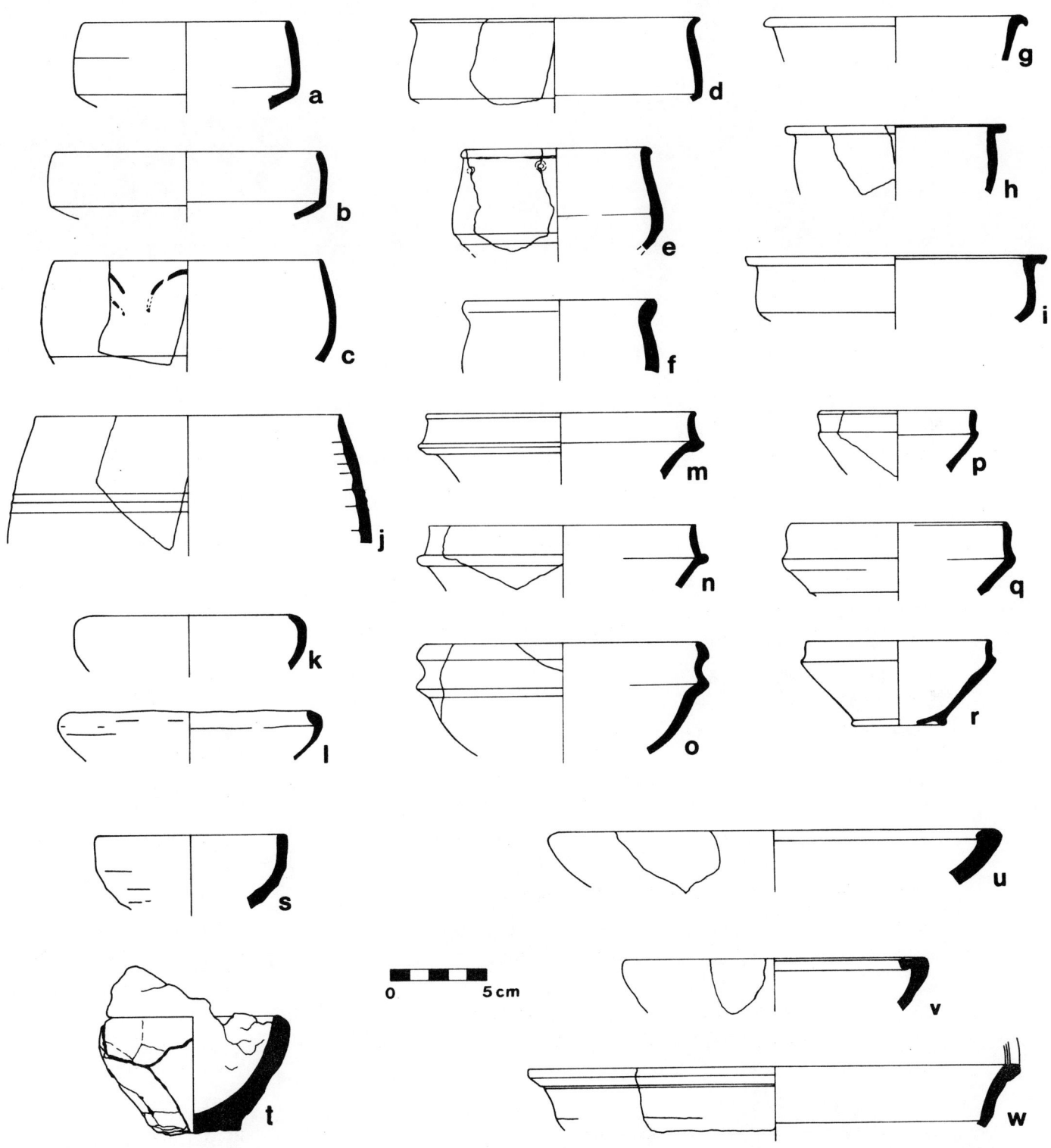

Plate 11: Roman Villa Bowls

Plate 12: Roman Villa Jars and Bases

	Locus	RN	Description	Munsell
a	E6a-9	397	red; cream slip; abundant coarse sand	10YR 7/4 out, 10R 6/8 in
b	E6b-16	367	buff; brown slip; common medium sand	5YR 7/4, 6/4
c	E6a-2	396	red; cream slip out; fine sand	10YR 8/4 out, 5YR 5/6 in
d	E6a-2	396	light red-brown; burnished red slip; moderate medium sand	2.5YR 6/6
e	E6a-9	397	orange; cream slip; abundant coarse sand; ceramic plug in top	7.5YR 7/4 out, 5YR 7/6 in
f	E6a-1	396	red; cream slip; abundant coarse sand	2.5Y 7/2 out, 2.5YR 5/6 in
g	E6b-29	309	orange; light grey slip out; common medium sand; pouring lip	5YR 7/6
h	E6a-15	397	red-brown; buff slip; common medium sand	7.5YR 5/4
i	E6b-44	366	red; cream slip out; abundant coarse sand	10YR 7/3 out, 2.5YR 6/8 in
j	E6b-44	366	red-brown, grey core; abundant coarse sand	5YR 5/4, 4/1
k	E6b-29	366	red; abundant coarse white sand	2.5YR 6/6
l	E6b-29	366	orange; red slip; abundant coarse sand	2.5YR 6/6
m	E6b-44	366	orange; common medium sand	2.5YR 6/6
n	E6b-49	474, 476	light red; red slip out, cream slip in; chaff	2.5YR 5/6 out, 5YR 7/4 in
o	E6a-3	396	red; cream slip; abundant coarse sand	10YR 8/3 out, 2.5YR 6/6 in
p	E6b-55	366	brown; cream slip; moderate coarse sand and chaff	5Y 8/2 out, 7.5YR 6/4 in
q	E6c-1	283	red; dark red slip out; black paint; moderate medium sand	2.5YR 4/6, 7.5YR 6/4 out, 5YR 5/8 in
r	E6a-4	396	red-orange, grey core; fine	
s	E6a-1	396	orange-buff; moderate medium sand	5YR 7/6
t	E6a-15	397	red-brown; buff surface out; moderate medium sand	7.5YR 7/6 out, 5YR 6/6 in
u	D6d-6	366	light orange; abundant medium sand	5YR 7/6
v	E6a-2	396	red-brown; cream slip; common coarse sand and chaff	10YR 6/4 out, 7.5YR 6/4 in
w	E6a-15	397	orange; fine	2.5YR 5/8
x	E6a-1	396	red-orange; red slip; common coarse sand	2.5YR 5/8
y	E6a-9	397	cream; abundant medium sand	7.5YR 5/2, 7/6, 7/4
z	E6a-1	396	orange-buff; cream slip; abundant medium sand	5YR 7/6 out, 7.5YR 6/4 in

Continued on Plate 13

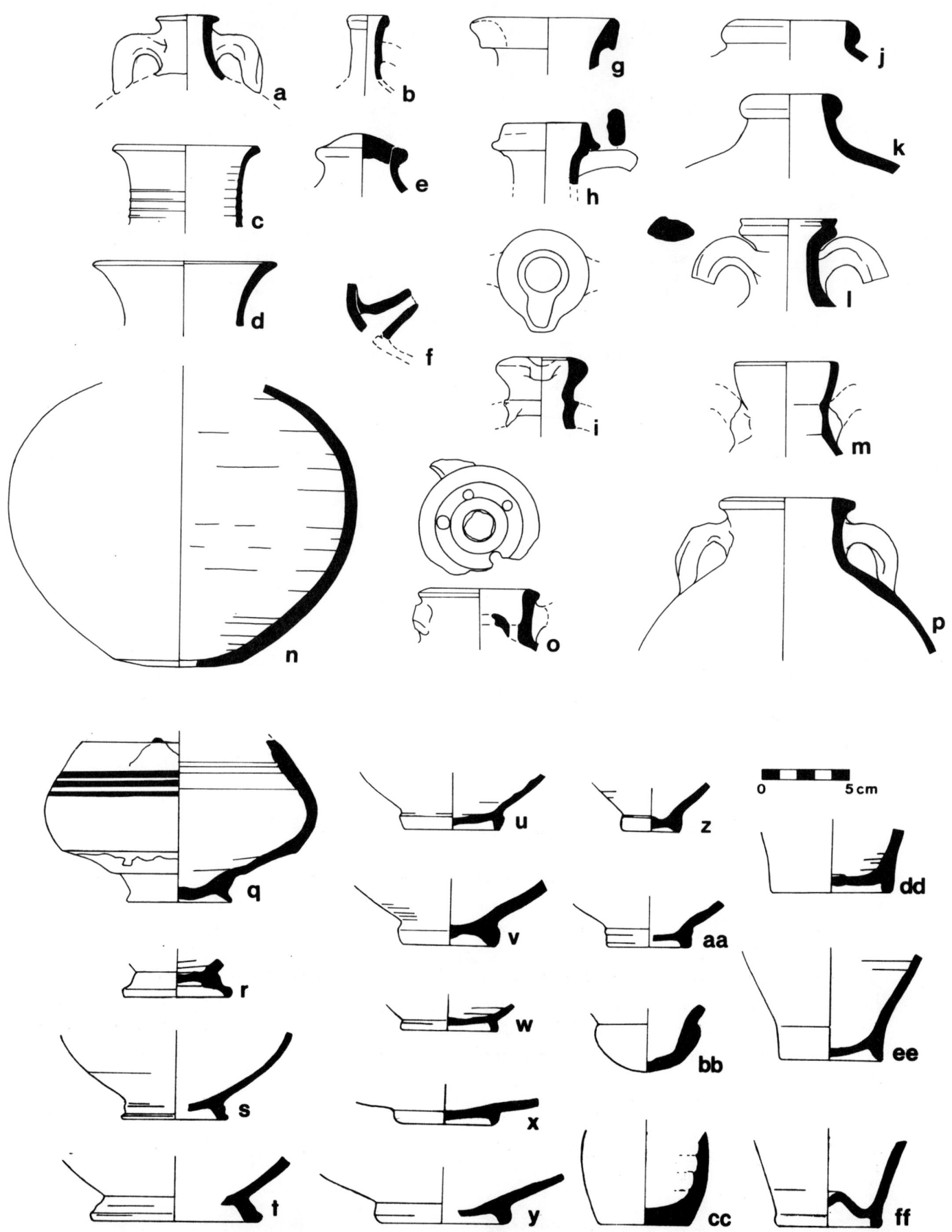

Plate 12: Roman Villa Jars and Bases

Plate 13:   Roman Villa Large Vessels

	Locus	RN	Description	Munsell
a	E6a-2	396	orange-red; grey-brown slip; moderate medium sand	2.5YR 6/8 core 2.5YR 5/2, 5/6 slip
b	E6b	367	brown; red surface; cream slip out; red slip in; common coarse sand	7.5YR 7/6 out 2.5YR 4/6 in
c	E6a-3	396	red, brown core; cream slip; abundant coarse sand and chaff	2.5YR 6/6 out 7.5YR 7/4 in
d	E6a-1	396	grey; abundant coarse white sand	10YR 5/1, 5/2
e	E6a-9	397	orange-red; red slip; common coarse sand	2.5YR 5/8
f	E6b-55	366	red, grey core; common coarse sand	2.5YR 6/6 out 5YR 5/4, 6/4 in
g	E6a-13	397	red; orange surface; moderate coarse sand	5YR 6/6, 2.5YR 6/6, 7.5YR 7/4
h	E6a-4	396	cream; abundant chaff	2.5YR 8/2, 7/4
i	E6a-15	397	brown; red slip; abundant medium sand	2.5YR 6/6 out 5YR 5/4 in
j	E6b-16	367	orange; brown surface out; burnished	5YR 5/4 out 5YR 6/6 in
k	E6a-10	397	cream; abundant medium sand	10YR 7/3
l	E6b-49	366	cream; moderate medium sand	10YR 7/4
m	E6c-1	332	red; common medium sand	2.5YR 6/6

Plate 12 Continued

	Locus	RN	Description	Munsell
aa	E6a-9	397	cream; light buff slip; abundant medium sand	5YR 7/4 out 7.5YR 7/4 in
bb	E6b-30	367	grey; red slip out; common medium sand	2.5YR 5/6 out 10YR 5/1 in
cc	E6a-9	397	red-brown; cream slip out; abundant coarse sand	10YR 7/4 out 2.5YR 6/6 in
dd	E6a-1	396	dark orange; grey-brown slip; abundant coarse sand	2.5YR 6/8
ee	E6b-29	366	red-brown; moderate medium sand	5YR 6/4, 6/6 out 2.5YR 5/6 in
ff	E6a-15	397	red; moderate medium sand	2.5YR 5/6

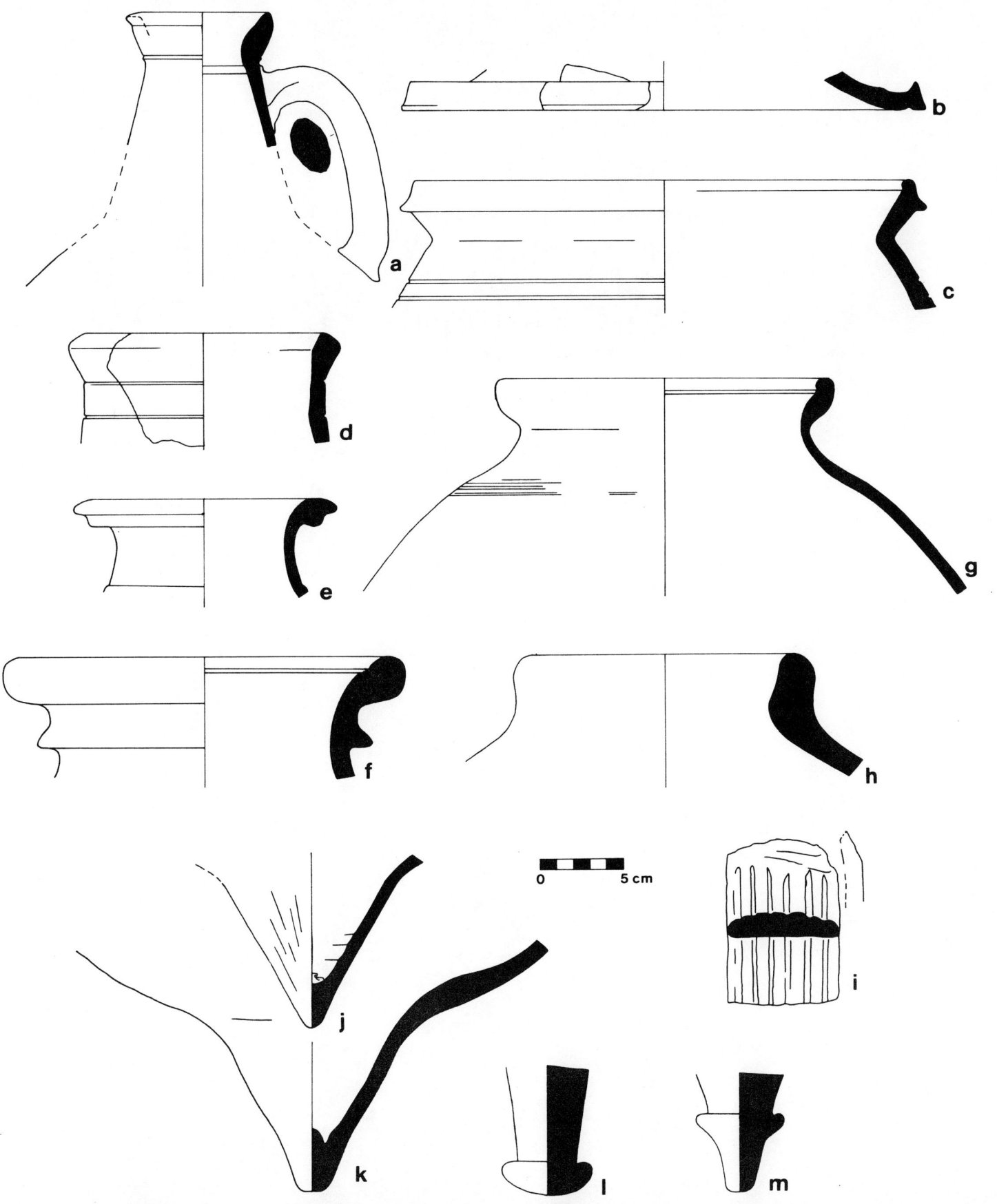

Plate 13: Roman Villa Large Vessels

Plate 14: Roman Villa, Large Storeroom

	Locus	RN	Description	Munsell
a	E6b-36	446	brown-red, dark grey core; abundant coarse white sand and chaff; pot Q; FN 8	5YR 6/6
b	E6b-49	473	brown; abundant coarse white sand; pot E; FN 10	5YR 5/4
c	E6b-49	474	light red-orange, light grey core; cream slip?; abundant medium sand; pot O; FN 19	2.5YR 5/6
d	E6b-49	447	red-brown; abundant medium sand; pot P; FN 20	5YR 5/6
e	E6b-29	366	red-brown; abundant medium sand; from small storeroom	
f	E6b-27	472	brown; common medium sand and chaff; pot T; FN 22	2.5YR 4/2
g	E6b-36	453	brown-red; common medium sand and chaff; pot S; FN 6	5YR 6/3

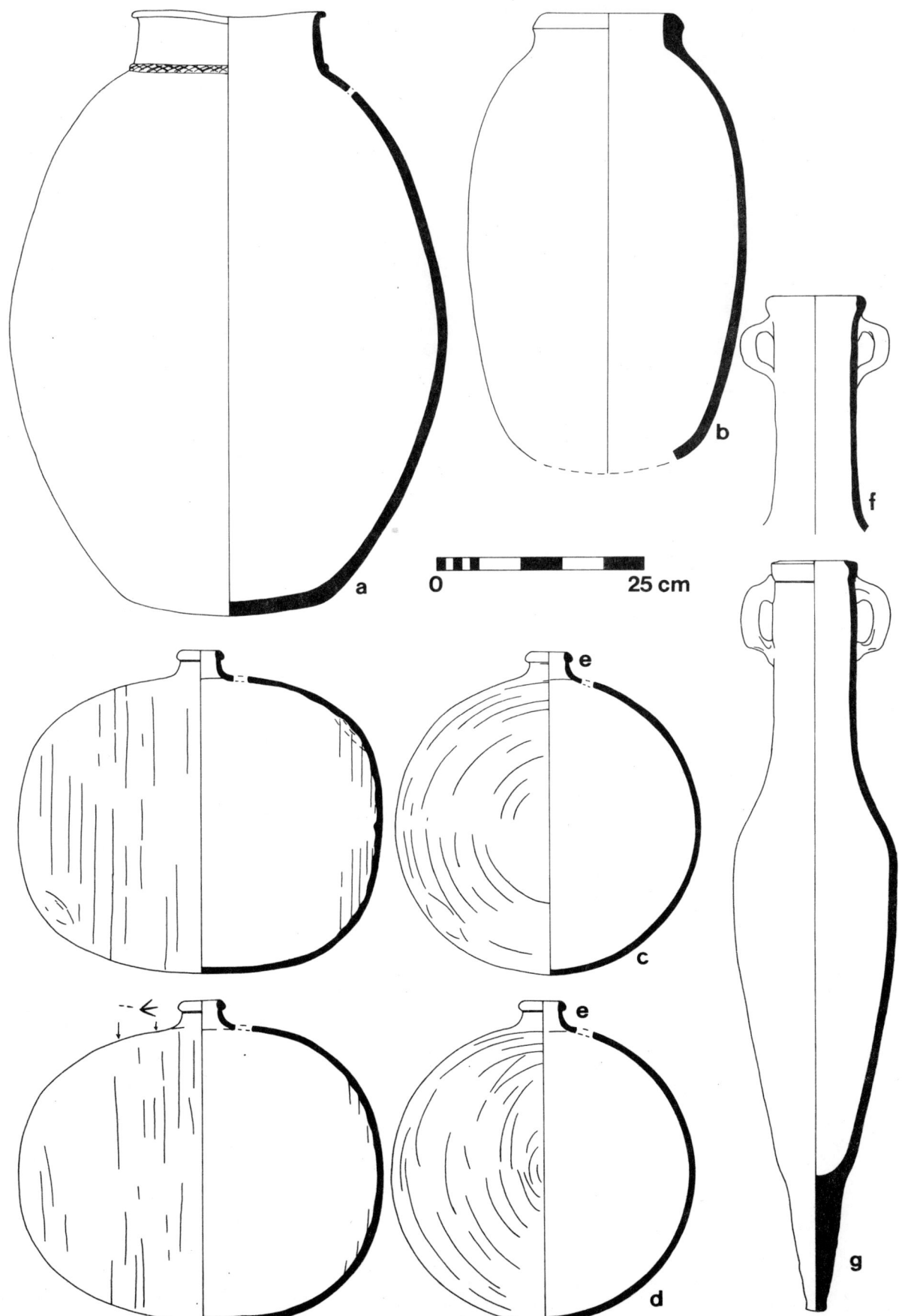

Plate 14: Roman Villa, Large Storeroom

Plate 15: Roman Villa, Large Storeroom

	Locus	RN	Description	Munsell
a	E6b-49	464, 470	buff; cream slip; black paint; common coarse sand; pot B and C; FN 7 and 8	7.5YR 7/6 10YR 8/2 slip
b	E6b-49	475	red-brown; cream slip; red paint; common coarse sand; pot M; FN 17	5YR 6/6 10YR 8/4 slip
c	E6b-49	475	same as b	
d	E6b-49	467	buff-orange; cream slip; red paint; common coarse sand; pot K; FN 15	5YR 7/6 10 YR 8/3, 7/4 slip 2.5YR 4/6 paint
e	E6b-49	440, 474	red; cream slip; moderate medium sand; pot A; FN 4	2.5YR 6/6 10YR 7/3 slip
f	E6b-54	441	orange; cream-grey slip; abundant medium white sand	2.5YR 5/8 10YR 7/2 slip

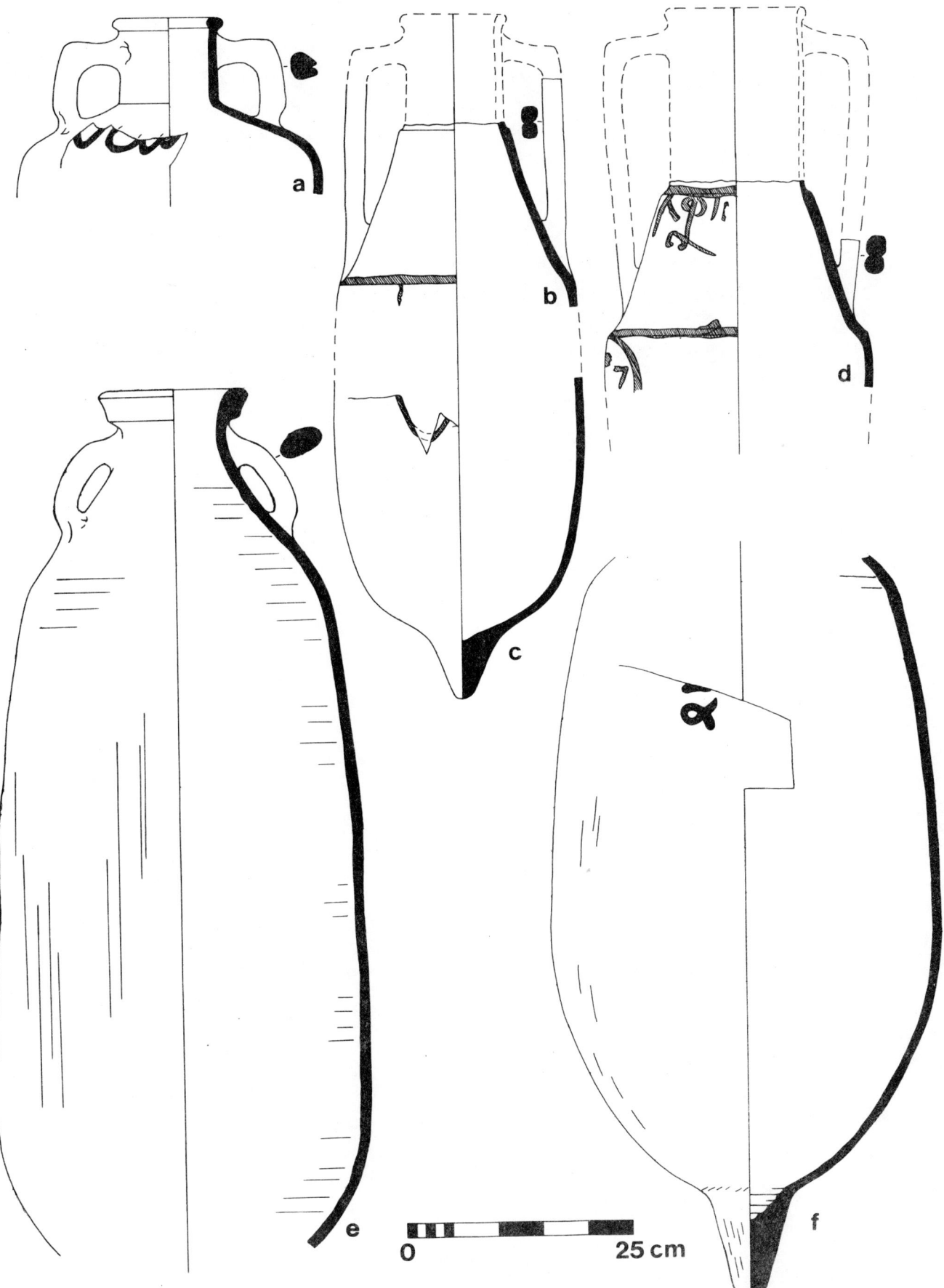

Plate 15: Roman Villa, Large Storeroom

Plate 16: Roman Villa, Large Storeroom

	Locus	RN	Description	Munsell
a	E6b-49	468, 476	light orange; cream surface out; incised inscription; cut hole on side, second hole plastered closed; moderate medium sand; pot N; FN 18	5YR 7/3; 10YR 7/3
b	E6b-49	473, 475	light grey-cream; abundant coarse sand; pot F; FN 11	
c	E6b-49	442, 614	buff-light orange; cream surface out; red paint; abundant coarse sand; pot H; FN 13	2.5YR 8/2 out; 5YR 7/4
d	E6b-49	471	orange-buff; abundant coarse sand	
e	E6b-49	476	grey-brown; orange surface; abundant coarse sand	
f	E6b-49	457, 471	orange; cream surface; abundant coarse sand; pot J; FN 14	5YR 7/6; 10YR 8/3 surface

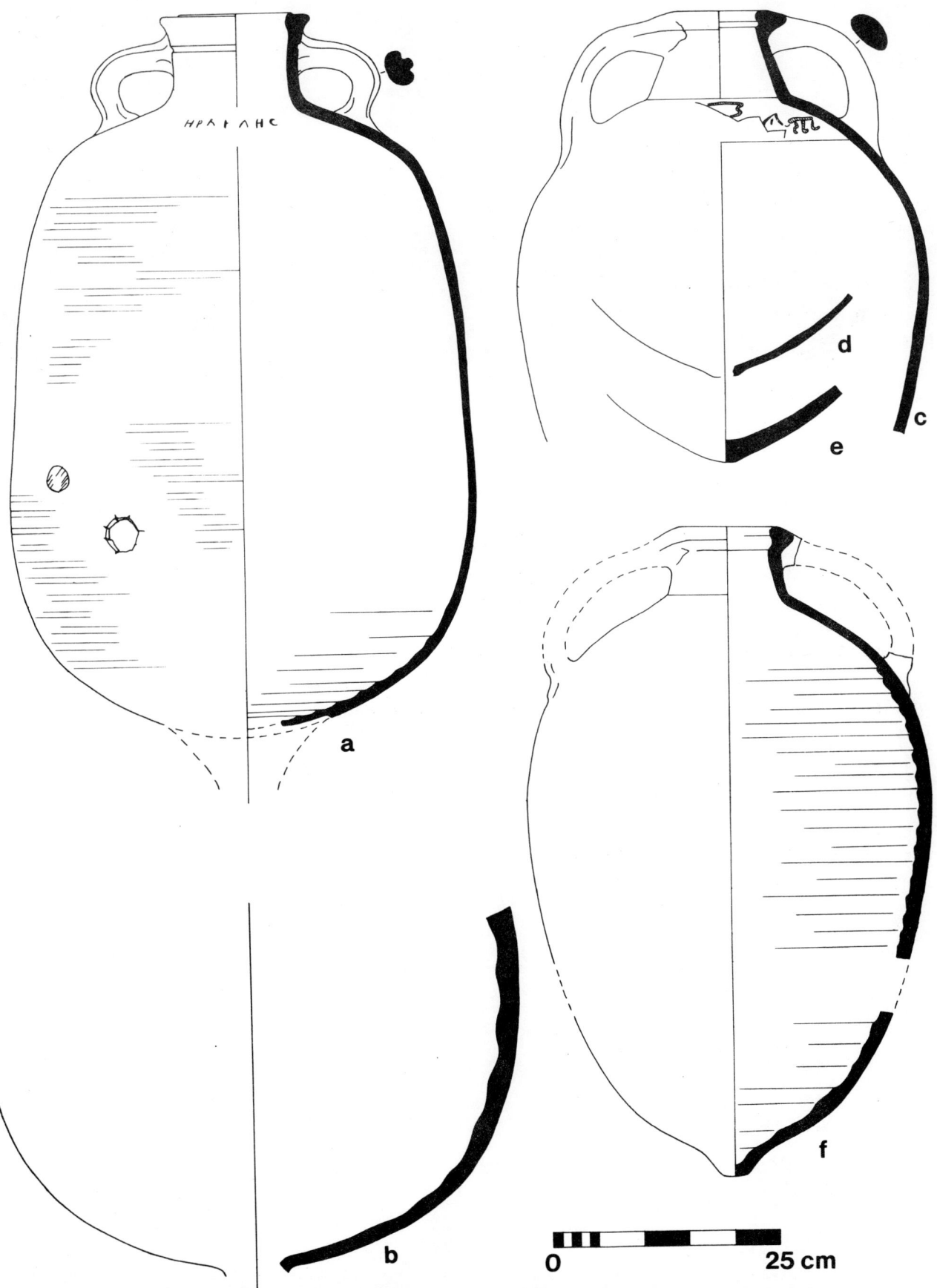

Plate 16: Roman Villa, Large Storeroom

Plate 17:   Roman Villa, Large Storeroom Oil Jars

	Locus	RN	Description	Munsell
a	E6b-49	429	orange; red slip; cream slip base; common medium sand	5YR 7/6 2.5YR 4/8 r slip 10YR 7/3 c slip
*b	E6b-36	361	red; red slip; FN 1	
*c	E6b-36	354	red; FN 3; Pot D	
d	E6b-36	362	orange-red; cream and red slip; moderate medium sand; FN 2; Pot B	2.5YR 5/6; 2.5Y 8/2
*e	E6b-36	360	red; FN 5	
f	E6b-36	359	red-brown; FN 4; Pot A	5YR 4/4

Plate 17:   Roman Villa, Small Storeroom

	Locus	RN	Description	Munsell
g	E6b-29	437	brown; cream slip; blackened interior and rim; common coarse sand	
h	E6b-24	420 366	orange-red; red slip; moderate coarse sand; FN 9	2.5YR 6/6 out 5YR 6/4 in
i	E6b-24	422	orange; cream slip out; moderate coarse sand; FN 17	10YR 7/3 out 5YR 7/6 in
*j	E6b-24	423	buff; cream slip out; FN 18	
k	E6b-44	355	red; cream slip; moderate coarse sand; FN 10	2.5YR 5/6 5Y 8/3 slip

*sherd not available to check drawing

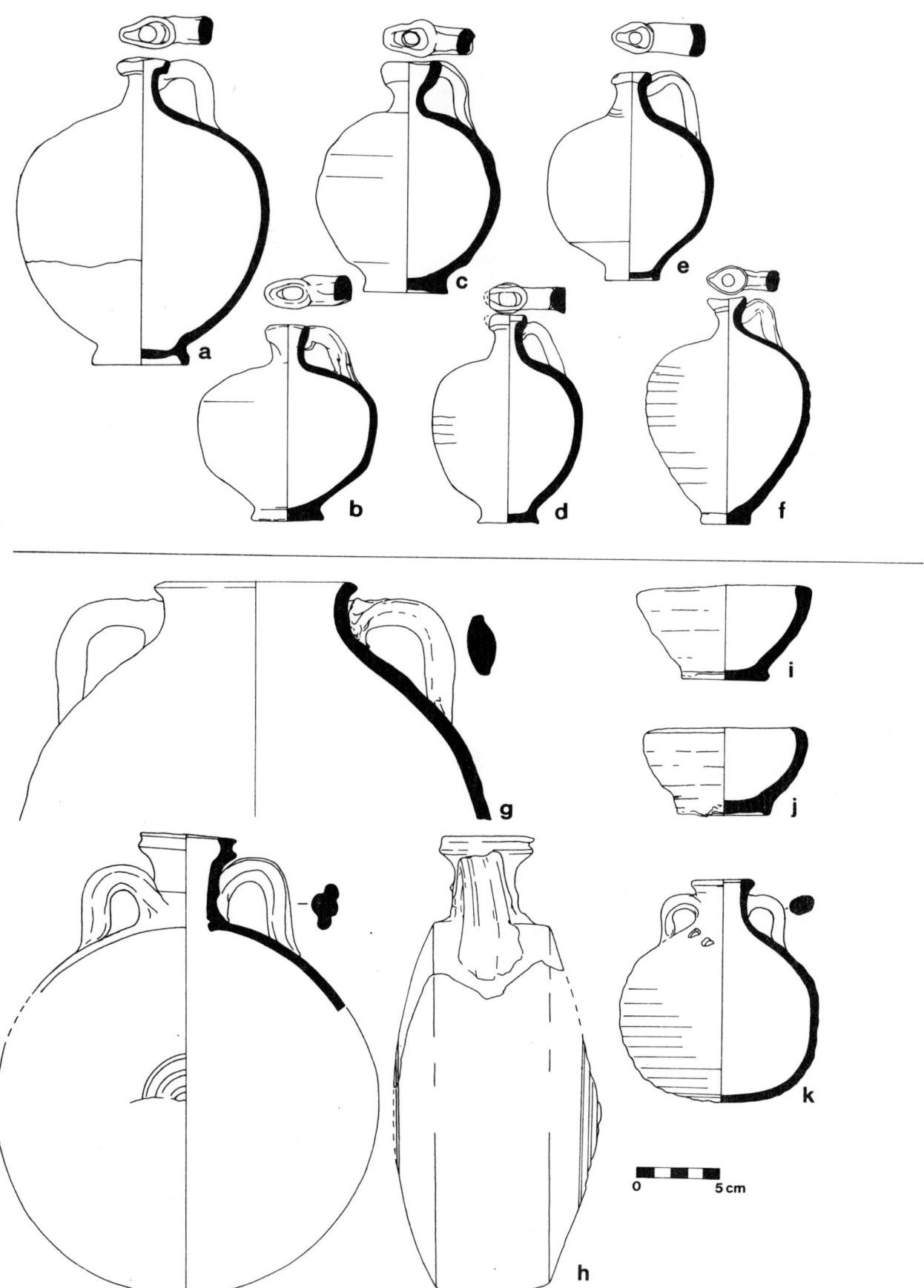

Plate 17: Roman Villa, Large Storeroom Oil Jars and Small Storeroom

Plate 18: Roman Villa Small Storeroom Oil Jars

	Locus	RN	Description	Munsell
a	E6b-29	364	buff; orange slip; blackened base; moderate medium sand; FN 1	5YR 7/3 5YR 6/8 slip
b	E6b-44	353	orange; light red slip; moderate medium sand; FN 11	2.5YR 6/6, 6/8
c	E6b-44	298	light orange; orange slip; common medium sand FN 7	5YR 7/4 5YR 6/6 slip
*d	E6b-24	357	light red; orange slip; FN 8	
e	E6b-24	425	brown-orange; red slip; black paint; moderate coarse; FN 10	5YR 4/6 2.5YR 5/8 slip
f	E6b-29	358	orange-red; cream slip on base; black paint; red slip on upper out; moderate medium sand; FN 6	2.5YR 6/8 10YR 7/3
g	E6b-44	428	orange; red slip; common medium sand; FN 6	5YR 6/6 2.5YR 6/6 slip
*h	E6b-24	351	orange-red; cream slip on base; FN 5	
i	E6b-44	350	orange-red; moderate medium sand; FN 12	2.5YR 6/6 7.5YR 7/4
*j	E6b-24	352	red; red slip; cream slip on base; FN 7	

* indicates unchecked field drawing

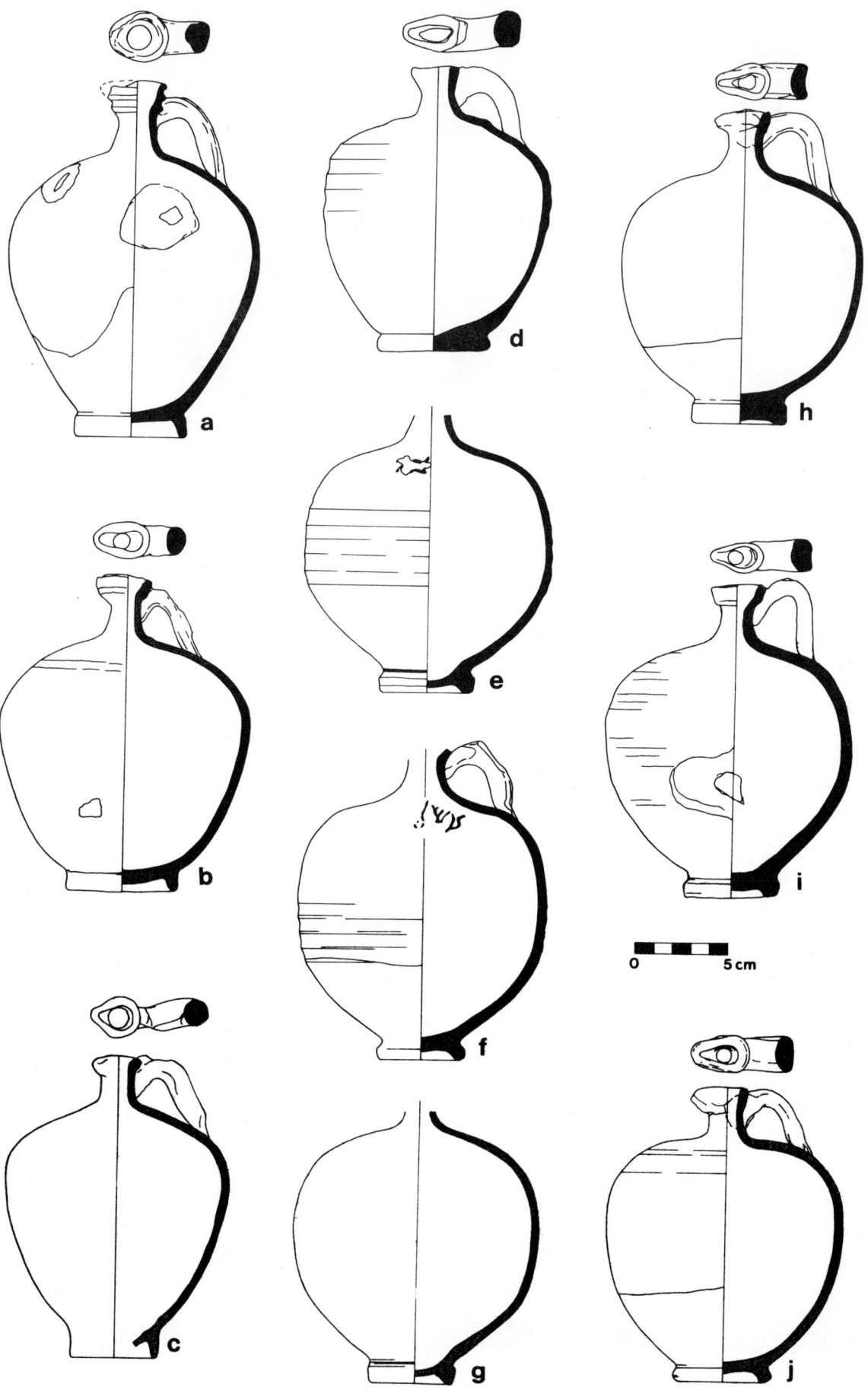

Plate 18: Roman Villa Small Storeroom Oil Jars

Plate 19: Roman Villa, Small Storeroom

	Locus	RN	Description	Munsell
a	E6b-29	436	red-brown, buff surface; red paint; moderate coarse sand; FN 2	2.5YR 5/6 2.5YR 6/4 surf 10R 6/4 paint
b	E6b-24	365	orange-red; moderate medium sand; FN 4	5YR 7/6
c	E6b-24	363	brown; common coarse sand; FN 6	5YR 4/4
d	E6b-44		red, cream surface; resin in; abundant coarse sand; FN 7, 9	

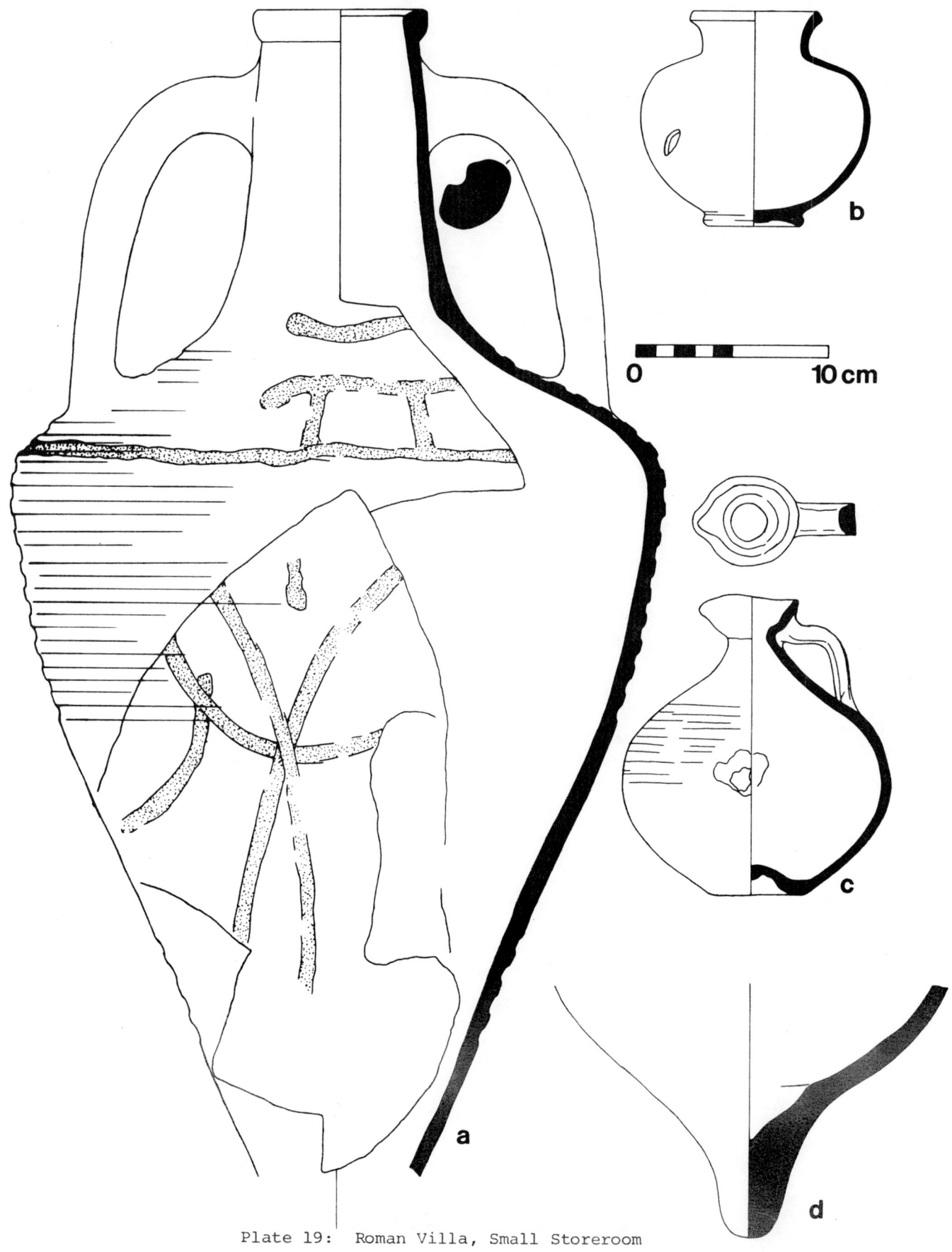

Plate 19: Roman Villa, Small Storeroom

Plate 20: Roman Villa, Storeroom E6c

	Locus	RN	Description	Munsell
a	E6c-1	445 449 450 451	orange-buff; cream slip; common coarse white sand	5YR 6/6 7.5YR 7/2 slip
b	E6c-1	458	orange-buff; abundant coarse sand	
c	E6c-1	458	cream, cream-buff core; abundant coarse sand	
d	E6c-1	443 451	cream; abundant coarse sand	
e	E6c-1	443 449 451	brown; black paint; common medium sand	5YR 6/4
f	E6c-1	443 445 450 451	orange-buff; cream slip; abundant coarse sand	5YR 7/6 7.5YR 8/2 slip
g	E6c-1	449	orange; cream slip; black paint; abundant coarse sand	2.5YR 6/6 10YR 7/3 slip
h	E6c-1	443 445 449 450 451	orange; shaved cream slip; abundant coarse sand	2.5YR 6/6 10YR 8/2 slip
i	E6c-1	449	buff-orange; abundant coarse sand	

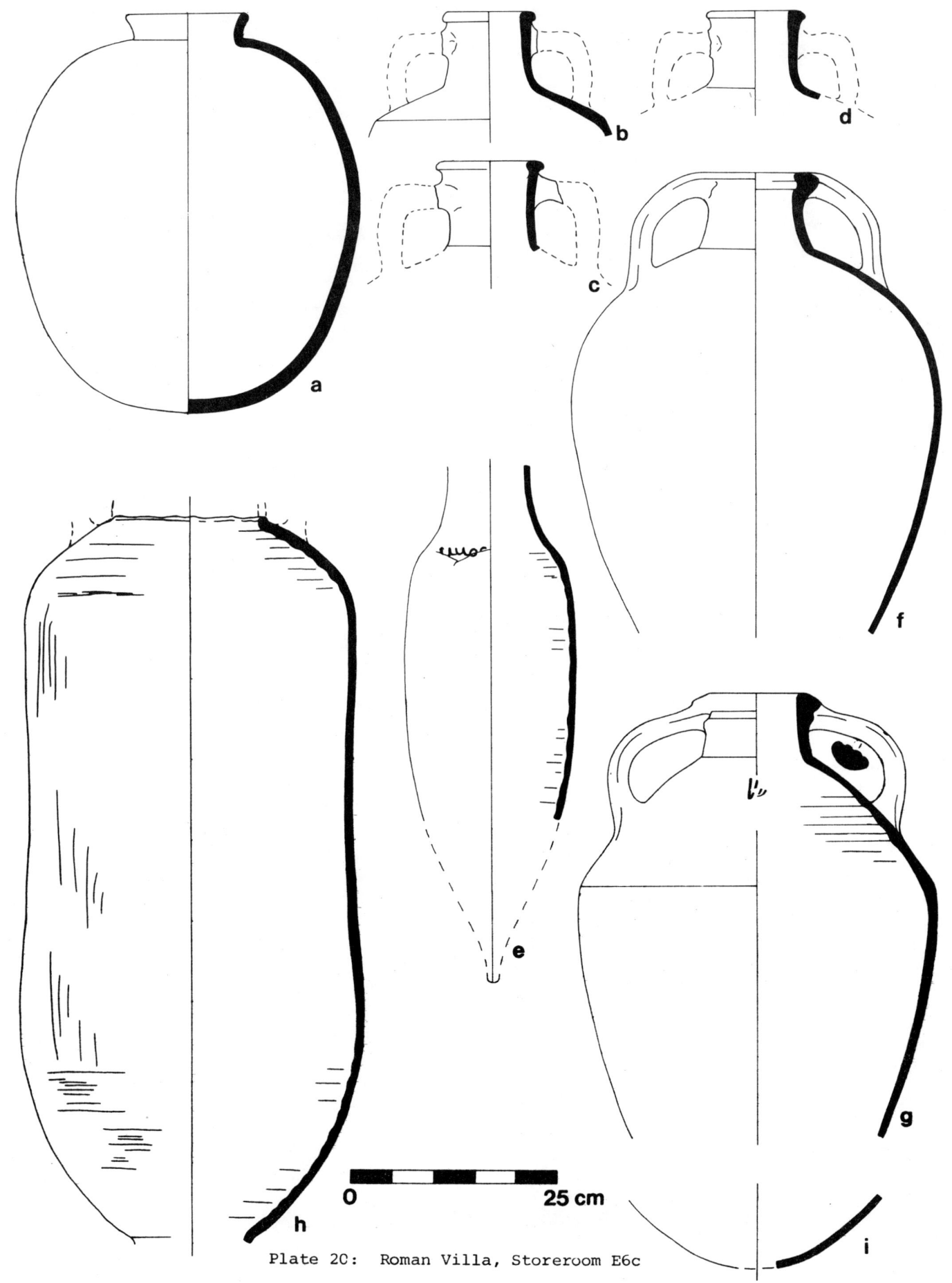

Plate 20: Roman Villa, Storeroom E6c

Plate 21: Roman Villa Fine Wares

	Locus	RN	Description	Munsell
a	E6b-49	367	light orange; grey slip out; fine	10YR 5/2 out 5YR 7/6 in
b	E6a-4	396	orange; grey slip out; fine	2.5Y 5/2 out 5YR 5/6 in
c	E6a-3	369	light orange; grey slip out; fine	5YR 4/1 out 5YR 6/6 in
d	E6a-9	397	orange; red paint; fine	2.5YR 6/8 10R 5/6 paint
e	E6b-16	367	buff; purple paint; fine	
f	E6b-31	367	orange; fine	2.5YR 5/8
g	E6a-15	397	orange; purple surfaces; burnished; fine	2.5YR 6/6 2.5YR 3/0, 3/4 surface
h	E6a-1	396	light orange; cream slip out; common medium sand	5YR 6/6
i	E6a-1	396	cream; fine	7.5YR 8/4
j	E6b-55	366	cream; light orange surfaces; fine	7.5YR 8/2 core 5YR 6/6, 4/1 out 5YR 7/6 in
k	E6a-2	396	cream; fine	7.5YR 7/4
l	E6a-3	396	orange; fine	2.5YR 6/8
m	E6a-1	396	orange, grey core; dark brown slip out; moderate medium sand	7.5YR 3/0 core 7.5YR 3/2 out 5YR 6/6 in
n	E6b-16	367	orange-brown; green glaze in and out; fine	
o	E6b-29	366	grey; black burnished, incised lines in; moderate medium sand	
p	E6b-44	366	cream; brown paint; fine	
q	E6b-49	285	orange; white slip out; red and black paint; moderate medium sand	2.5Y 8/2, 2.5YR 5/8, 2.5YR 6/6 2.5/0 out
r	E6b-25	367	cream; yellow glaze out; light green glaze in; moderate medium sand	
s	E6a-2	312	cream; green glaze out; yellow glaze in; fine	

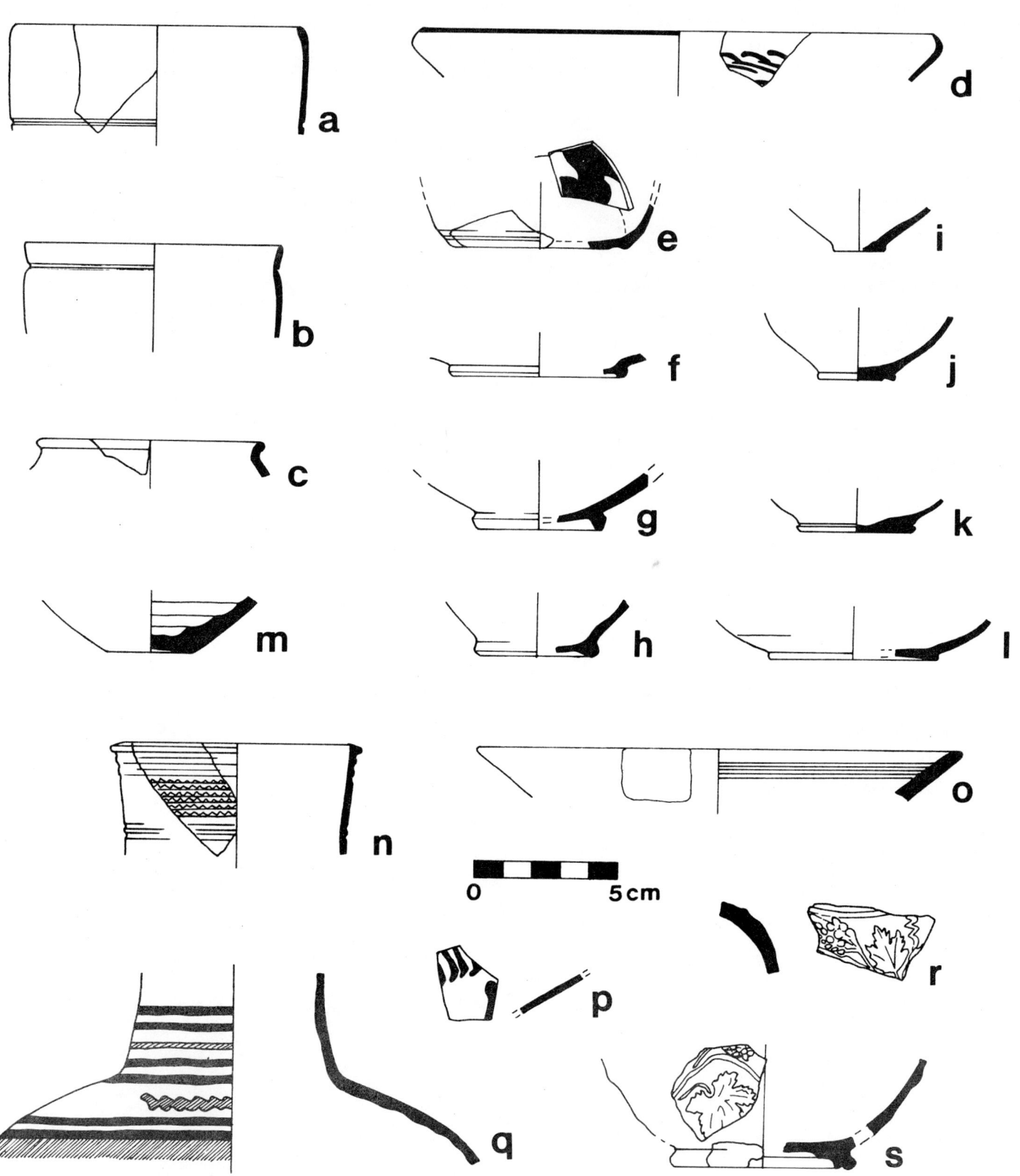

Plate 21: Roman Villa Fine Wares

Plate 22: Villa East and Villa South, Kitchen and Cooking Pots

	Locus	RN	Description
a	E7c-7	335	orange; brown slip; rim fire blackened; common medium sand
b	E6b-51	367	purple; fire blackened out; moderate medium sand
c	E7c-1	335	purple, grey core; moderate medium sand
d	E7a-15	334	orange; common medium sand; diameter unknown
e	E6b-51	367	orange, grey core; blackened out; common medium sand
f	E7c-1	335	purple, black core; blackened out; burnished rim; abundant coarse
g	E6b-48	367	black; blackened out; burnished rim; abundant coarse
h	E7c-1	335	orange; red slip; blackened out; common coarse sand
i	F7a-1	337	purple; blackened out; common coarse sand
j	F7a-1	337	brown; blackened out; burnished rim and in; abundant coarse sand
k	E6b-51	367	brown; burnished in; blackened out; abundant coarse sand
l	E6b-48	367	orange; red slip; moderate coarse sand
m	E6b-51	367	orange-red; moderate medium sand
n	E6b-51	367	orange-red; red slip; moderate medium sand
o	F7a-1	337	orange; black slip out and rim; common coarse sand
p	E7c-7	335	red-brown; cream slip; common medium sand
q	E7c-7	335	red; abundant medium sand
r	E6b-51	367	red-brown; blackened out; moderate medium sand
s	E7c-1	335	red; blackened out; moderate medium sand
t	E6b-48	367	red; moderate medium sand
u	E7c-1	335	orange; moderate medium sand
v	F7a-1	337	red, grey core; common medium sand

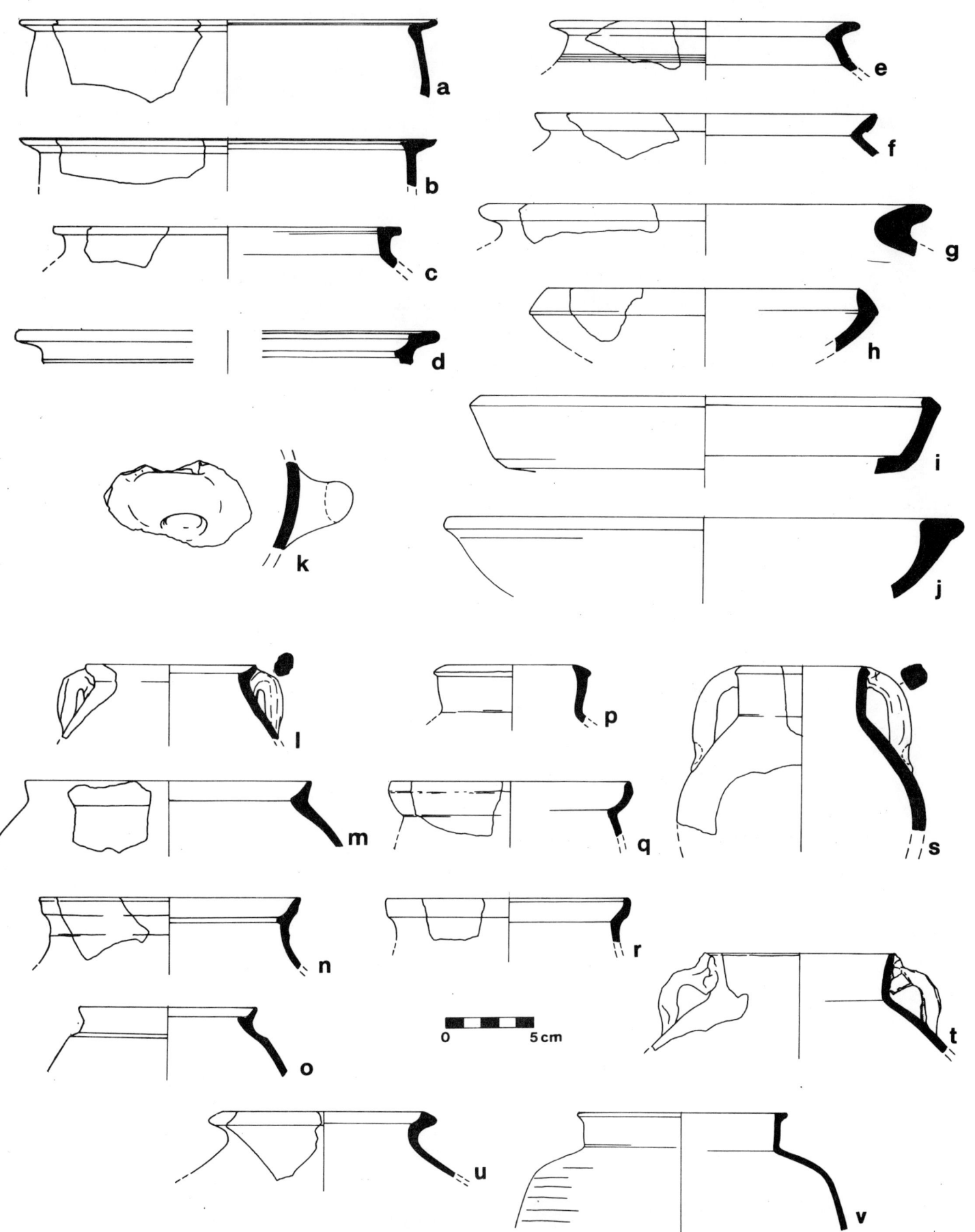
Plate 22: Villa East and Villa South, Kitchen and Cooking Pots

Plate 23: Villa East and Villa South, Bowls and Bases

	Locus	RN	Description
*a	E7c-2	335	orange
b	E7c-1	335	red; red slip; moderate medium sand
c	E6b-43	367	red-orange; common coarse sand
*d	E7c-14	334	cream; red-brown slip; black paint
e	E6b-35	367	buff; dark red slip out and rim; moderate medium sand
f	E7a-16	334	cream; moderate coarse sand
g	E6b-43	367	red-orange; cream slip?, moderate medium sand
h	E7c-7	335	red; red slip; blackened; common coarse sand
*i	E7c-20	334	dark brown
j	E6b-37	367	red; cream slip; abundant coarse sand
k	E6b-43	367	buff-light orange; common medium sand
*l	E7c-7	335	red; coarse
m	E6b-51	367	buff-orange; abundant coarse sand
*n	E7c-2	335	grey; blackened
o	F7a-1	294	orange-red; red slip; burnished; moderate medium sand
p	E7c-7	335	orange; moderate medium sand
q	E6b-48	367	orange; black slip out; moderate medium sand
r	E6b-51	367	grey; brown slip; moderate medium sand
s	E6b-51	367	orange; dark orange slip; moderate coarse sand
t	E7a-16	334	buff; moderate medium sand
u	E6b-51	367	red-orange; abundant coarse white sand

*sherd not available to check drawing

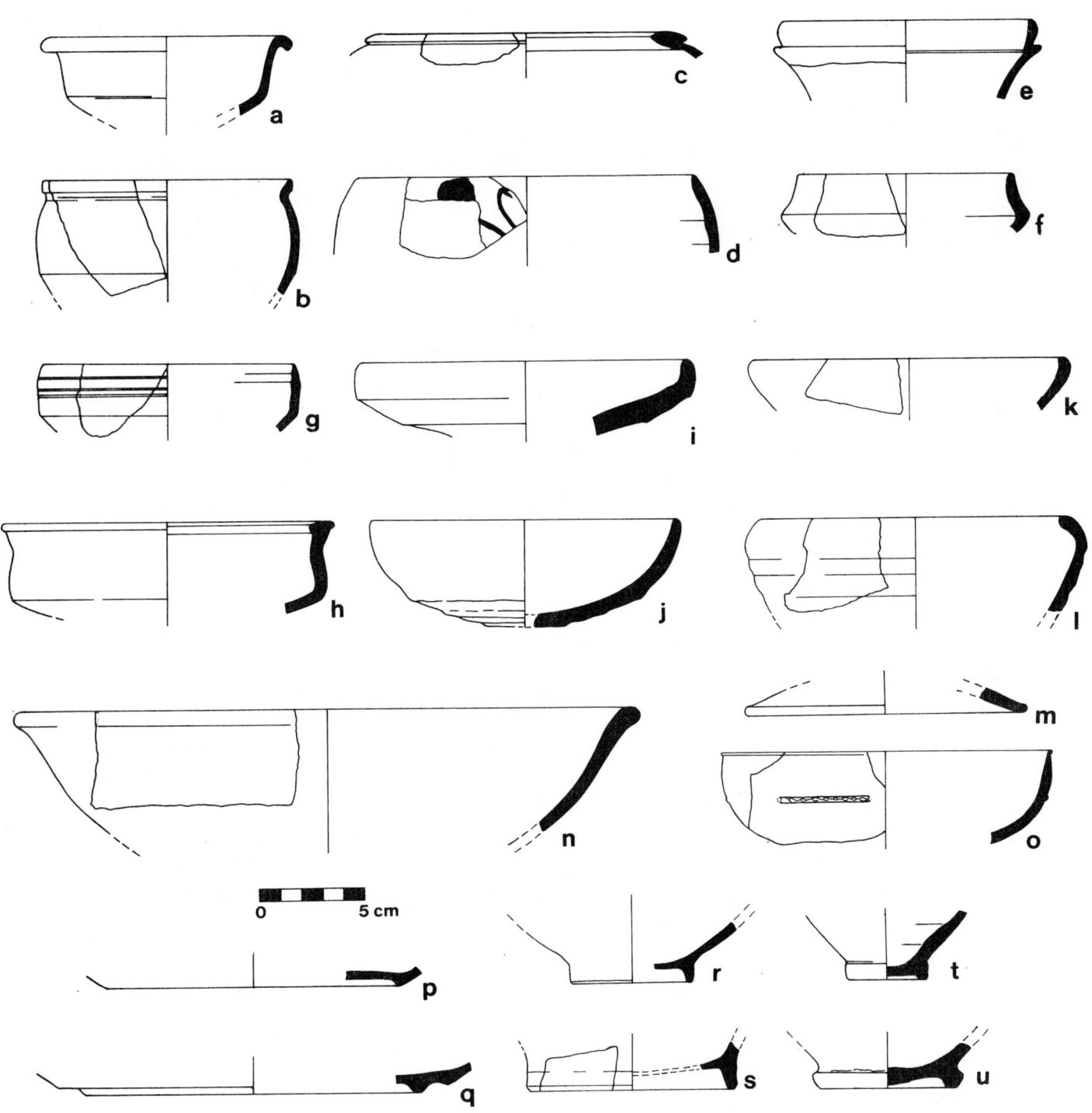

Plate 23: Villa East and Villa South, Bowls and Bases

Plate 24: Villa East and Villa South, Jars and Large Vessels

	Locus	RN	Description	Munsell
a	E7a-16	334	orange-red; cream slip; moderate medium sand	5YR 7/4 2.5Y 8/2 slip
b	E6b-51	367	grey; moderate medium sand	2.5Y 4/0, 6/2
c	F7a-4	330	red; dark red slip; black paint; moderate medium sand	2.5YR 6/6 2.5YR 5/4 slip 2.5YR 3/0 paint
d	E6b-48	367	red-orange; common coarse sand	2.5YR 5/8
e	E6b-43	357	buff; light brown slip; moderate medium sand	5YR 7/4 5YR 6/4 slip
f	E7a-18	334	red-orange; red slip; moderate medium sand	2.5YR 6/8
g	E7a-16	334	red-orange; cream slip; moderate medium sand	2.5YR 6/6
h	F7a-1	337	red-brown; cream slip; common coarse sand	2.5YR 5/6 2.5Y 7/4 slip
i	E7a-16	334	orange; red slip; moderate coarse sand	2.5YR 6/8
j	E7c-7	335	red; light cream-brown slip; moderate medium sand	2.5YR 5/6 5YR 6/4 slip
k	E6b-48	367	cream; common coarse sand	2.5Y 7/4
l	E6b-51	367	orange; common coarse sand	5YR 5/4
m	E6b-51	367	orange; moderate medium sand	2.5YR 6/6
n	E6b-34	367	brown; common coarse sand	7.5YR 5/4 core 5YR 5/4 slip
o	E7c-7	335	red-brown; blackened in and out; moderate coarse sand	2.5YR 5/6
p	E7c-7	335	orange; cream slip; moderate medium sand	2.5YR 6/8 7.5YR 7/4 slip
q	E7c-7	335	cream; moderate coarse sand	10YR 7/4
r	E6b-51	367	orange, grey core; red slip out; abundant coarse sand	10YR 5/1 core 2.5YR 5/8
s	E7c-1	355	grey; blunt grooves and incised lines; abundant coarse white sand	10YR 4/1

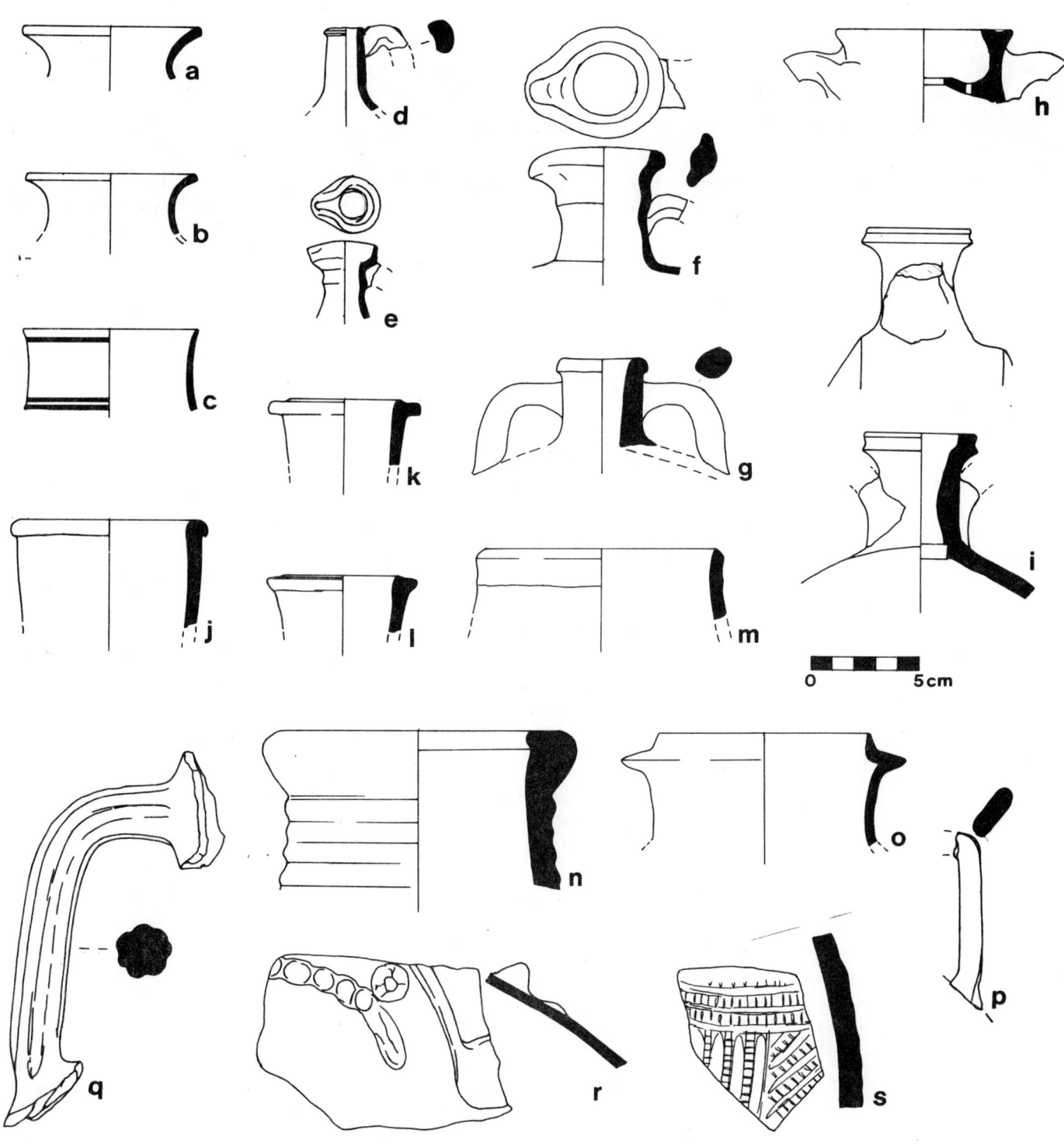

Plate 24: Villa East and Villa South, Jars and Large Vessels

Plate 25: Villa East and Villa South Fine Wares

	Locus	RN	Description	Munsell
a	E7c-7	335	grey; dark grey slip; fine	7.5YR 5/2 core 10YR 4/2 slip
b	E7c-5	355	cream; fine	7.5YR 7/6
c	E6b-40	367	cream; brown surface out; fine	10YR 4/2, 5/6, 8/6 out 10YR 8/3
d	E7c-7	335	buff; brown slip; cream prunts; fine	5YR 7/6 7.5YR 6/2 paint 10YR 8/3 prunts
e	E7a-15	334	brown; red slip; moderate medium sand	
f	E6b-51	367	cream; fine	7.5YR 7/4
g	E7c-19	334	grey; cream slip out; fine	10YR 8/4 out 10YR 5/1
h	E7a-15	334	grey; red surfaces; cream slip out; fine	
i	E7c-5	355	orange; fine	5YR 6/6
j	E7c-19	334	buff; fine	5YR 7/6
k	E7c-5	355	red-grey; cream slip?; fine	7.5YR 5/4 out 2.5Y 4/2 in
l	E7c-7	299	orange; fine	
m	E7a-15	334	cream; grey slip; fine	5YR 8/2 core 5Y 6/1 out
n	F7a-3	337	cream; orange and black paint; fine	7.5YR 8/6 2.5YR 6/8, 4/2 paint
o	E7c-9	335	orange; brown paint; fine	5YR 6/6
p	F7a-3	337	cream; brown-grey slip; fine	7.5YR 8/4 5Y 5/1 slip

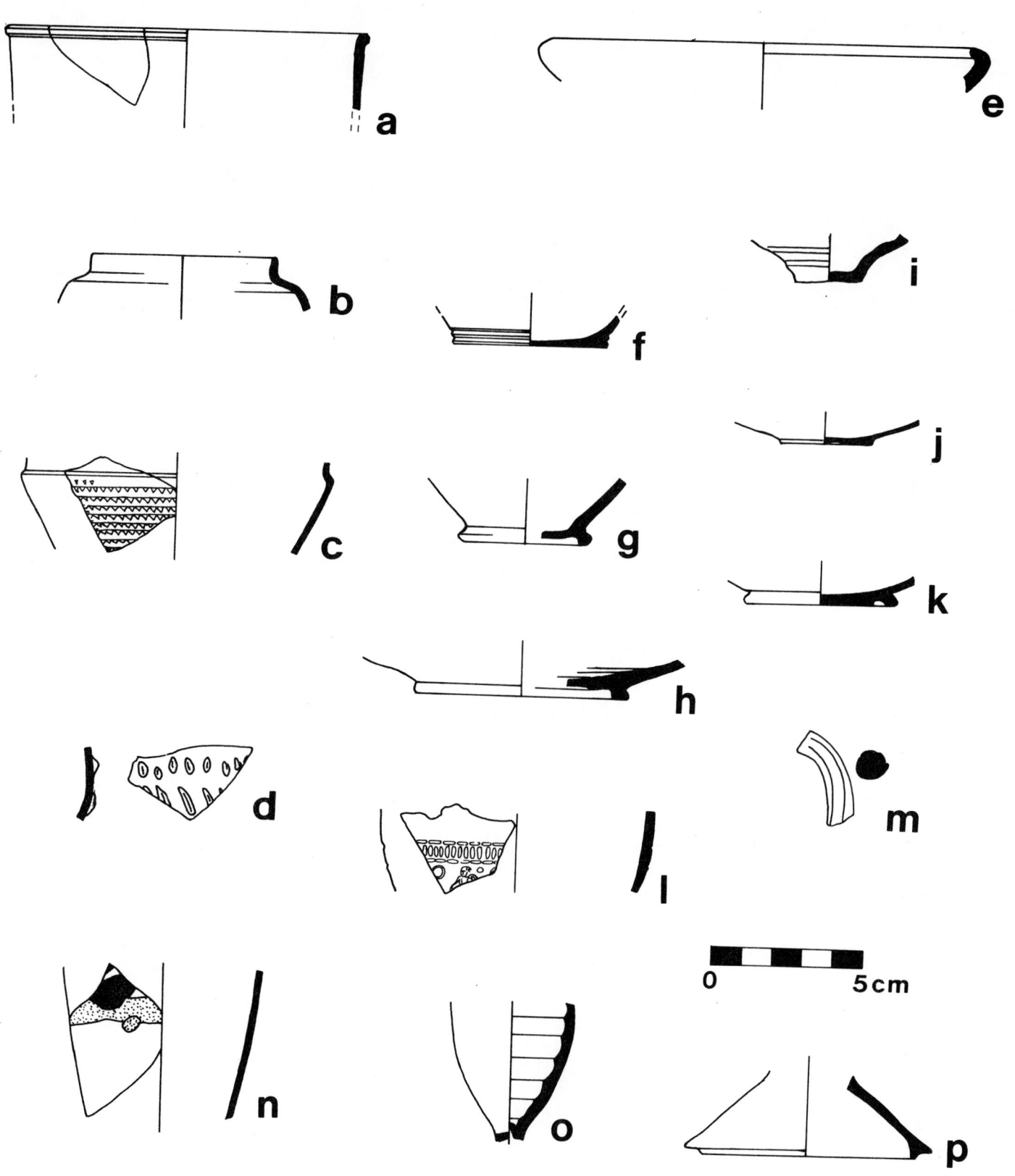

Plate 25: Villa East and Villa South Fine Wares

Plate 26: Central Building A, Roman Ceramics

	Locus	RN	Description	Munsell
a	G8b-3	328	light orange; dark orange slip out; black paint; moderate medium sand	2.5YR 6/6, 4/0 out 5YR 7/4
b	G8b-3	328	red-orange; dark red slip out; moderate medium sand	10YR 5/3 out 5YR 7/4
c	G8b-3	328	cream; brown slip out; moderate medium sand	
d	G8b-18	328	cream; orange and black paint; fine	7YR 8/4 7YR 8/4, 5YR 6/8, 4/3 in
e	G8a-4		orange; moderate medium sand	
f	G8b-3	328	buff-pink; orange slip in; moderate medium sand	5YR 8/4 2.5YR 6/8 in
g	G8b-3	328	red-brown; moderate medium sand	
h	G8b-3	328	red; cream slip out; common coarse sand	10YR 7/4 out 2.5YR 5/8
i	G8a-4		red; cream slip out; common coarse sand	
j	G8a-4		brown; red slip; common medium sand	
k	G8a-4		light orange; blackened out; common medium sand	
l	G8b-3	328	purple; moderate coarse sand	2.5YR 5/6
m	G8b-3	328	purple; blackened out; moderate medium sand	5YR 5/4 core 10YR 6/4, 3/1 out
n	G8a-4		black; blackened out; abundant coarse sand	
o	G8b-3	328	light orange-buff; common coarse sand	5YR 8/4
p	G8a-4		orange; abundant coarse sand	
q	G8a-4		red; cream surfaces; common coarse sand	
r	G8a-4		red; cream surface out; common coarse sand	
s	G8b-18	91	orange; cream slip out; common coarse sand	10YR 8/4 out 5YR 6/8

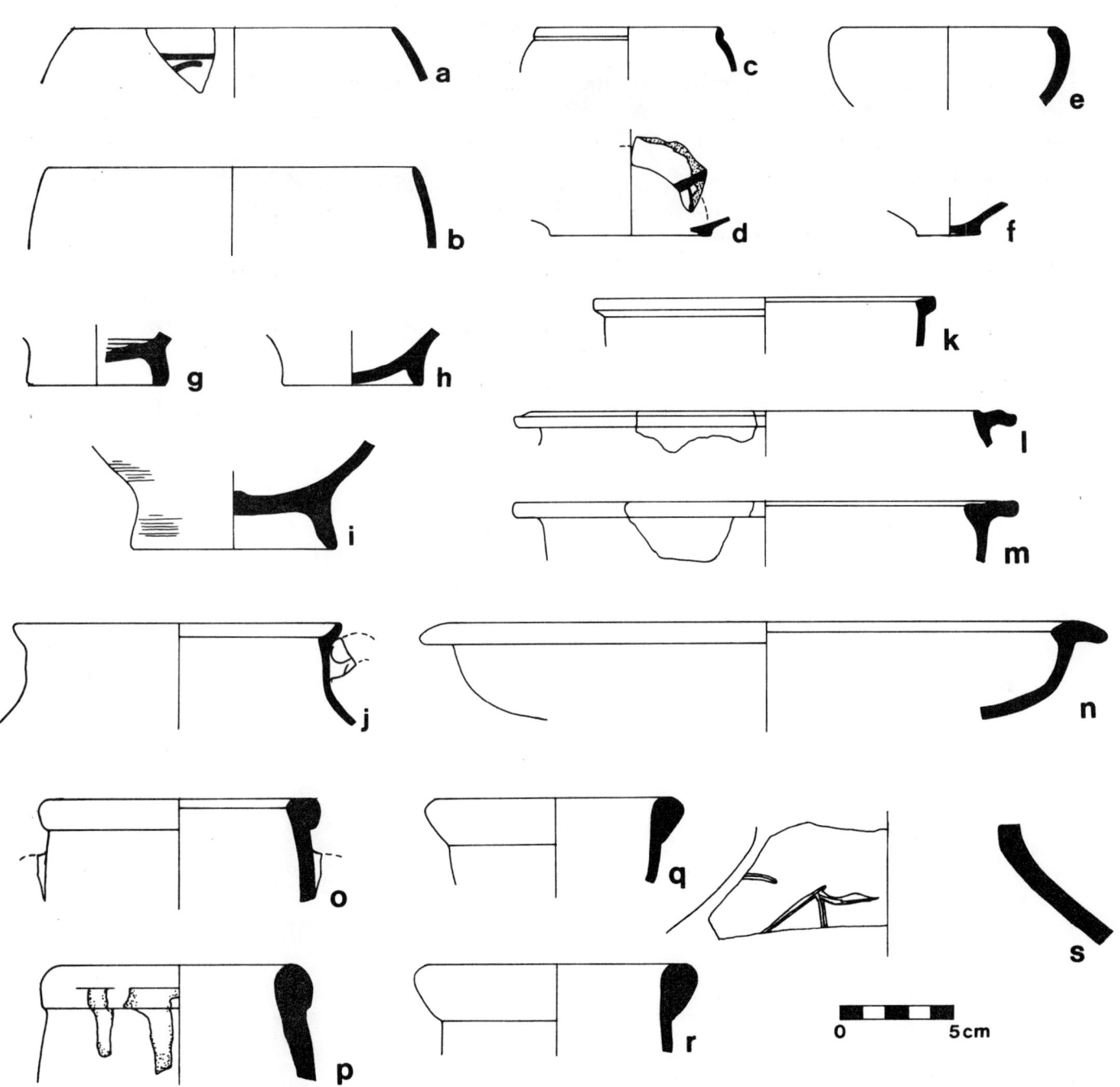

Plate 26: Central Building A, Roman Ceramics

Plate 27: Central Building B, Amphorae from J14a

	Locus	RN	Description	Munsell
a	J14a-5	438	light orange; cream slip out; resin in; abundant medium sand	
b	J14a-4	331	coarse red; cream slip out; resin in; abundant medium sand	2.5YR 6/6
c	J14a-5	103	buff; cream slip; red paint	
d	J14a-5	101	brown; black paint	
e	J14a-5	436	orange-red; grey interior surface; cream slip out; moderate medium sand	5YR 7/6 out 10YR 6/4, 4/2 in
f	J14a-4	331	coarse red; common medium sand	2.5YR 5/6 out 7.5YR 7/4 in
g	J14a-3	329	orange-buff; resin in; abundant medium sand	5YR 7/6, 7/8 out 7.5YR 3/2, 8/6 in
h	J14a-3	329	orange-buff; resin in; abundant medium red sand	10YR 6/4 out 2.5YR 6/6 in

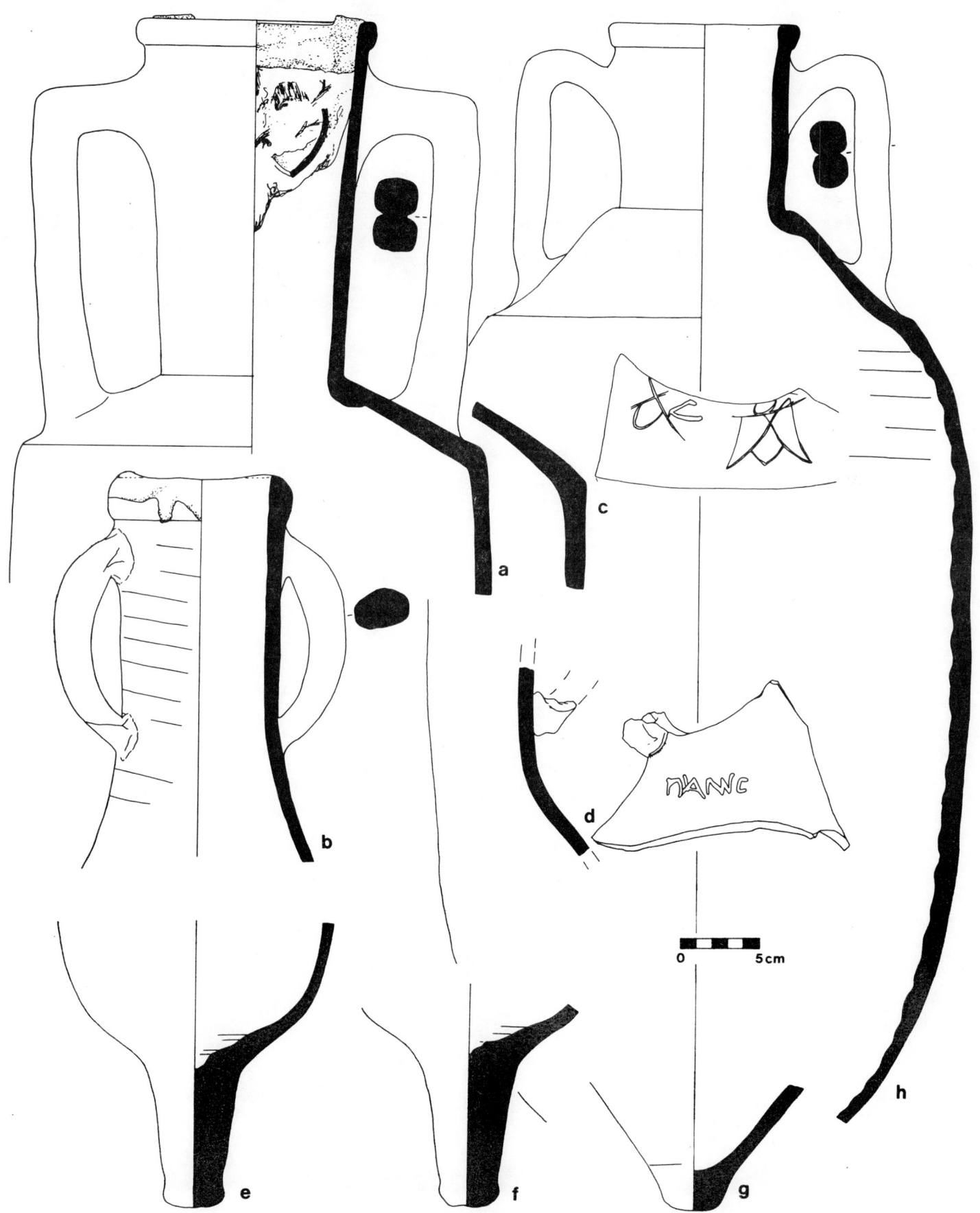

Plate 27: Central Building B, Amphorae from J14a

Plate 28: Central Building B

	Locus	RN	Description	Munsell
a	J14a-1	329	brown; purple burnished slip out; moderate medium sand	10R 3/4 out 10R 3/6 in
b	J14a-3	329	grey-brown; cream surface in; very fine sand	
c	J14a-5	331	red-brown; moderate fine sand	5YR 5/6 out 5YR 5/4 in
d	J14a-5	331	buff; greenish cream surfaces; abundant medium sand	10YR 8/4, 6/4
e	J14a-5	331	buff-cream; resin in and rim; common medium sand	10YR 8/4, 6/4 out 10YR 5/4 in
f	J14a-3	329	dark brown; cream slip out; moderate medium sand	7.5YR 6/4, 3/2 out 10YR 6/3, 2/2 in
g	J14a-4	331	red-tan; abundant medium sand; diameter ca. 40 cm.	2.5YR 6/6
h	J14a-5	331	red-brown; buff slip; blackened in; moderate medium sand	5YR 5/4, 5/6 out 5YR 3/2 in
i	J14a-3	329	buff; cream slip; common medium sand	7.5YR 7/4
j	J14a-5	331	red, grey core; moderate fine sand	2.5YR 5/6
k	G12c-8	330	red, grey core; sparse fine sand	7.5YR 3/2 out 2.5YR 6/6 in
l	G12c-8	330	red; burnished in; blackened out; abundant coarse sand; lid?	2.5YR 3/6, 2.5/0
m	G12c-5	330	orange; common medium sand	7.5YR 6/6
n	G12c-8	330	dark brown; common medium sand	5YR 4/6
o	G12c-9	330	light red; cream slip; common medium sand	7.5YR 7/4 out 5 YR 7/4 in

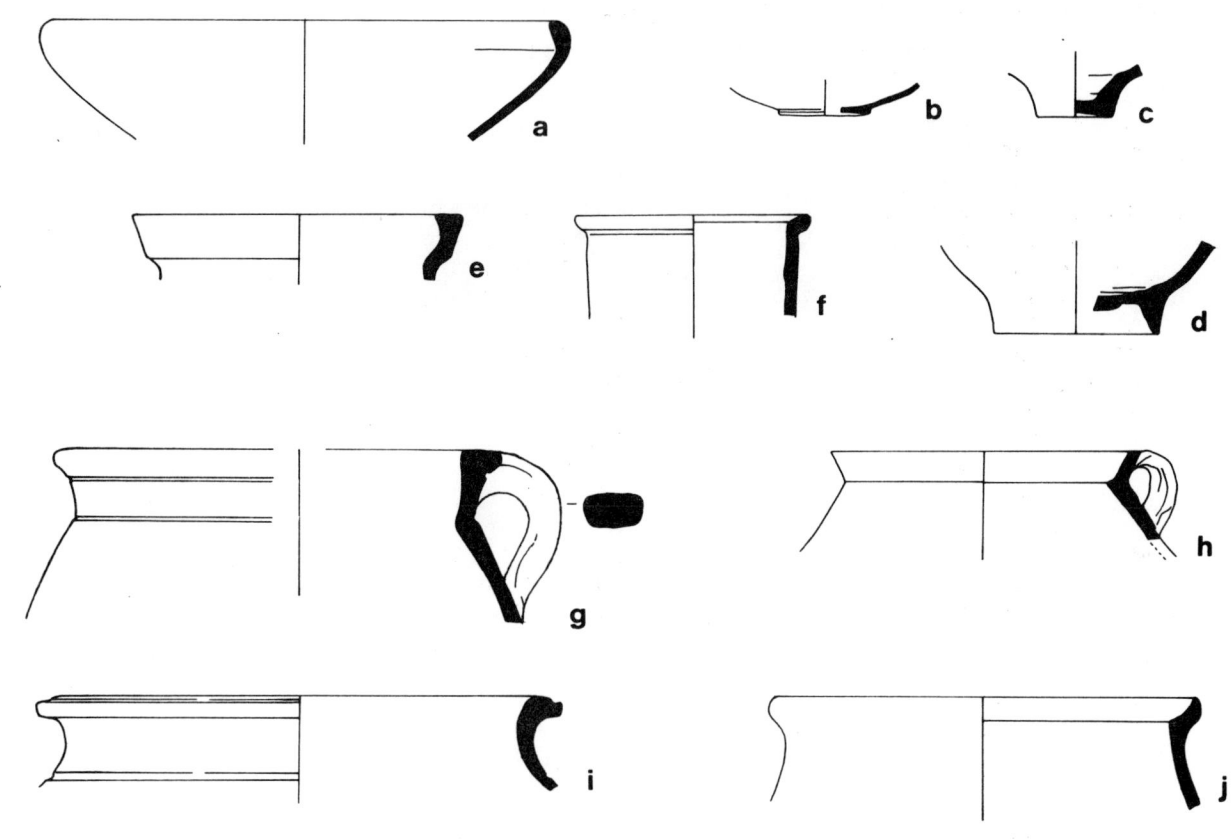
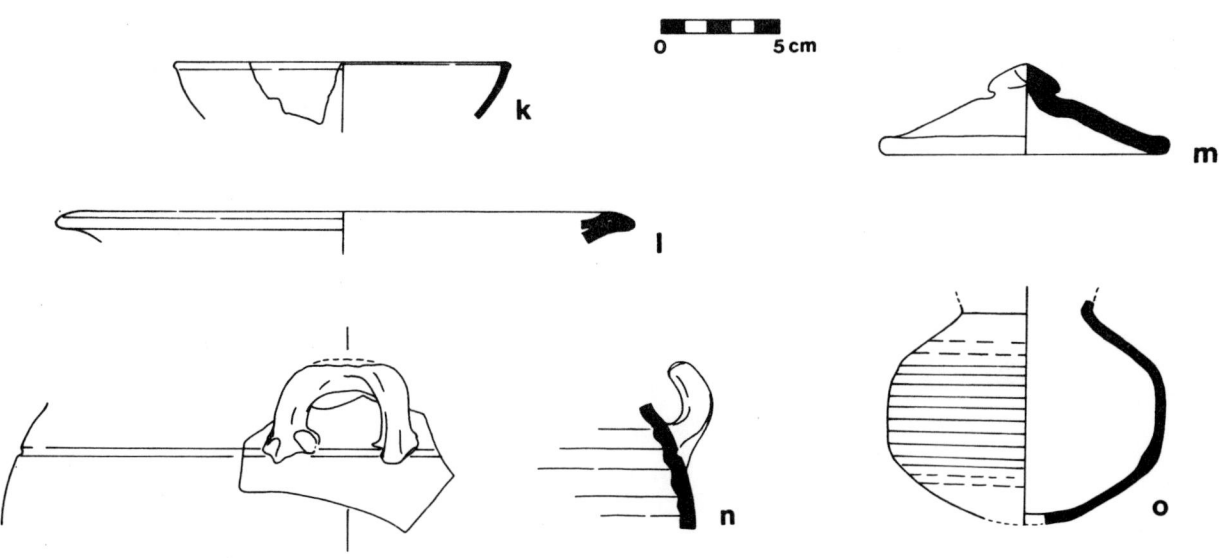

Plate 28: Central Building B

Plate 29: Roman Villa and Villa East Terra Sigillatas

	Locus	RN	Description	Munsell
a	E6a-2	396	ESA	10R 4/8
b	E6a-4	396	ESA	2.5YR 6/6
c	E6a-1	396		
d	E6a-1	396	ESB	2.5YR 4/8
e	E6a-1	396	ESA	10R 4/6 out; 5YR 6/6 in
f	E6a-8	396	ESB	2.5YR 4/6, 4/8
g	E6b-44	366	ESA	2.5YR 4/4, 3/6
h	D6d-6	301	ESA	10R 5/8, 4/8
i	E6b-51	367	ESA	5YR 6/6
j	E6a-1	396	Arr	2.5YR 6/6
k	Eb6-51	367	Arr	10R 5/6, 4/6
l	E6b	367		10R 4/8
m	E6a-4	396	ESA	10R 4/8
n	E6a-4	396	ESB	2.5YR 4/8
o	E6b	367	ESA	10R 4/6, 3/6 out; 10R 4/6, 4/8 in
p	E6b-48	367	Arr	
q	E6a-5	396	ESA	10R 5/6, 4/8
r	E6a-4	396	ESA	10R 3/4 out; 2.5YR 6/6, 5/6 in
s	E6a-4	396	ESA	2.5YR 4/6, 3/6
t	E6a-2	396	ESA	
u	E6a-4	396	ESA	10R 4/6
v	E6a-7	108		
w	E6b	367	ESA	10R 5/6
x	E7a-15	334		10R 5/6, 4/6
y	E7c-19	354	ESA	10R 4/8 out; 5YR 6/6 in
z	E7a-15	334	Cypriot	5YR 6/6
aa	E7c-19	334	Arr	2.5YR 4/8
bb	E6b-40	367	ESB	10R 4/6, 4/8
cc	E6b-40	367	ESB	2.5YR 5/8, 4/8
dd	E6b-40	107	Arr	
ee	E7a-20	110	Arr	10R 4/8

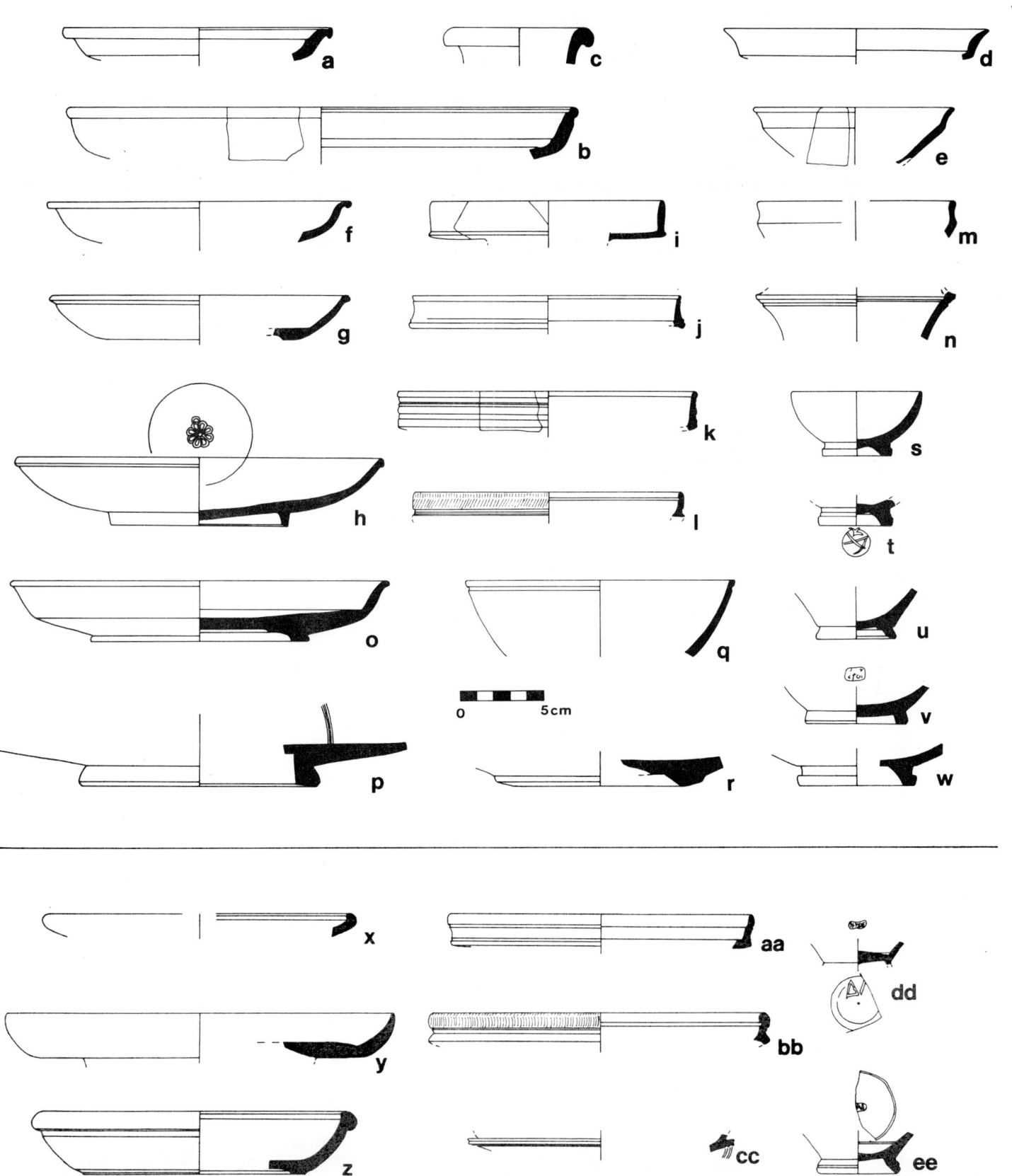

Plate 29: Roman Villa and Villa East Terra Sigillatas

Plate 30: Villa South, Pipeline, and Central Building B Terra Sigillatas

	Locus	RN	Description	Munsell
a	E7c-7	335	ESB?	10R 4/6
b	E7c-1	335	Cypriot	10R 4/6
c	E7c-7	335	ESA	10R 5/6, 4/6, 3/6 out; 10YR 7/4, 7/6 in
d	E7c-7	335	Cypriot	10R 5/8
e	E7c-1	335	Arr	10R 4/8
f	E7c-1	335	ESA	10R 5/8
g	H8a-1			
h	H8a-1		Arr	
i	H8c-1	333	Cypriot	10R 5/8
j	G8a-7		ESA	
k	H8c-1	333	Arr	2.5YR 4/8
l	H8a-2	333	Arr	10R 5/8
m	H8a-1		ESA	
n	H8c-1	333	ESA	10R 4/8
o	J14a-5	331	ESA or Arr	10R 4/8
p	J14a-4	331	Arr	2.5YR 4/8
q	J14a-5	331	Arr	
r	J14a-5	331	Arr	10R 4/8
s	J14a-5	331	Arr	2.5YR 4/8
t	J14a-5	331	ESB	2.5YR 4/6, 3/6
u	J14a-5	331	ESA	
v	J14a-3	329	ESB	
w	J14a-4	111	Arr	

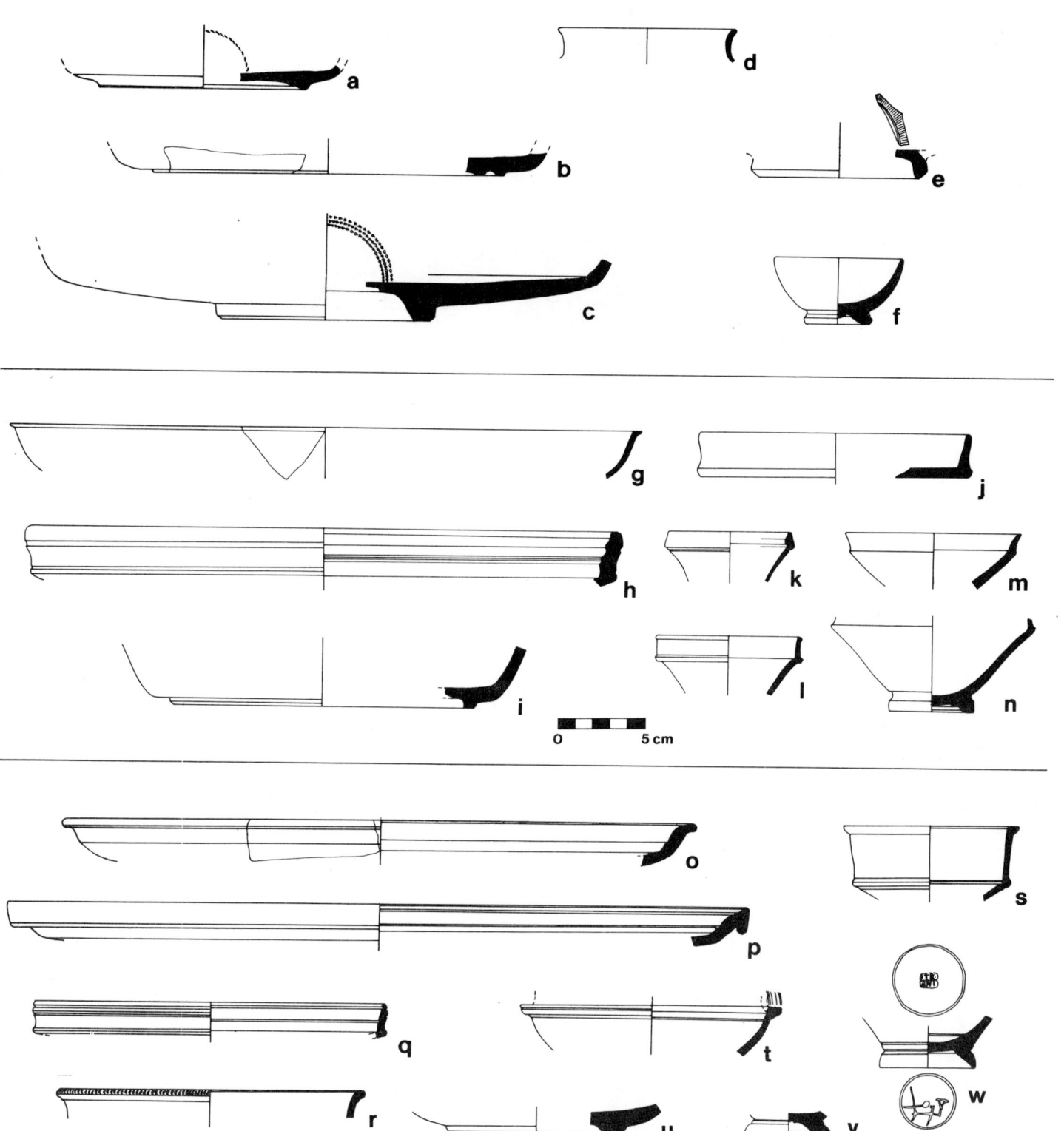

Plate 30: Villa South, Pipeline, and Central Building B Terra Sigillatas

CHAPTER 4: TRENCH SUMMARIES, ISLAMIC AREAS
Donald Whitcomb

The existence of ruins on the eastern side of the modern asphalt coastal road was noted during the 1968 excavations. These remains were concentrated on bluffs directly above the beach; it is likely that a few of these ruins were destroyed with the building of the road. Thus a line of occupational remains stretched from the island, south of J14, through E18 to A22; see pl. 1. This easternmost point had been the location of previous clearance and was the site for one of our 1978 trenches (Whitcomb and Johnson, 1979: 57-59). This excavation in A22d revealed a number of Muslim burials and fragmentary stone walls of structures which may have been funerary or may have post-dated the use of this area as a cemetery. Little was found in the way of occupational debris other than some ceramics (which included both blue and white porcelains and crude, paddle-stamped pottery; Whitcomb and Johnson, 1979: pl. 49).

This combination of medieval ceramics with the absence of Roman materials indicated that the eastern area would be a useful location for a broad exposure for the Islamic period. Interest was further increased by observation, through surface collections, of relative concentrations of celadon and porcelain sherds in this area as well as pieces of enameled glass. It was hypothesized that the occurrence here of these imported sherds might have resulted from discard of broken remains during inspection and repacking, possibly during customs inspection. Specialized trading facilities, such as the *furḍa* (warehouse), the port equivalent of the urban *wakala*s and *funduq*s, might have existed on a limited scale in medieval Quseir. But the physical character of the settlement uncovered was far from the image of urban institutions we had contemplated and was far closer to a small fishing village. The paradox of the "rich" artifactual contents in a "poor" architectural setting suggests that the functional character of these remains is more complex than one might have assumed from the architecture alone.

The surface remains indicated buildings along two ridges. The eastern was the more confined in space (mostly at C20), with far less associated debris scattered on the slopes of the bluff. The western ridge, located on E18, E19, F18, F19, and extending toward the road (see pl. 31), presented a wide area of settlement with masses of debris on the steep slopes of the wadi and beach. The ridge is rather flat and rises toward the northwest and the road. On the center of this ridge a broad area of excavation was carried out, approximately 530 sq.m. in extent. The excavations revealed a relatively shallow deposit of occupational debris and architectural foundations. The majority of this exposure was a building

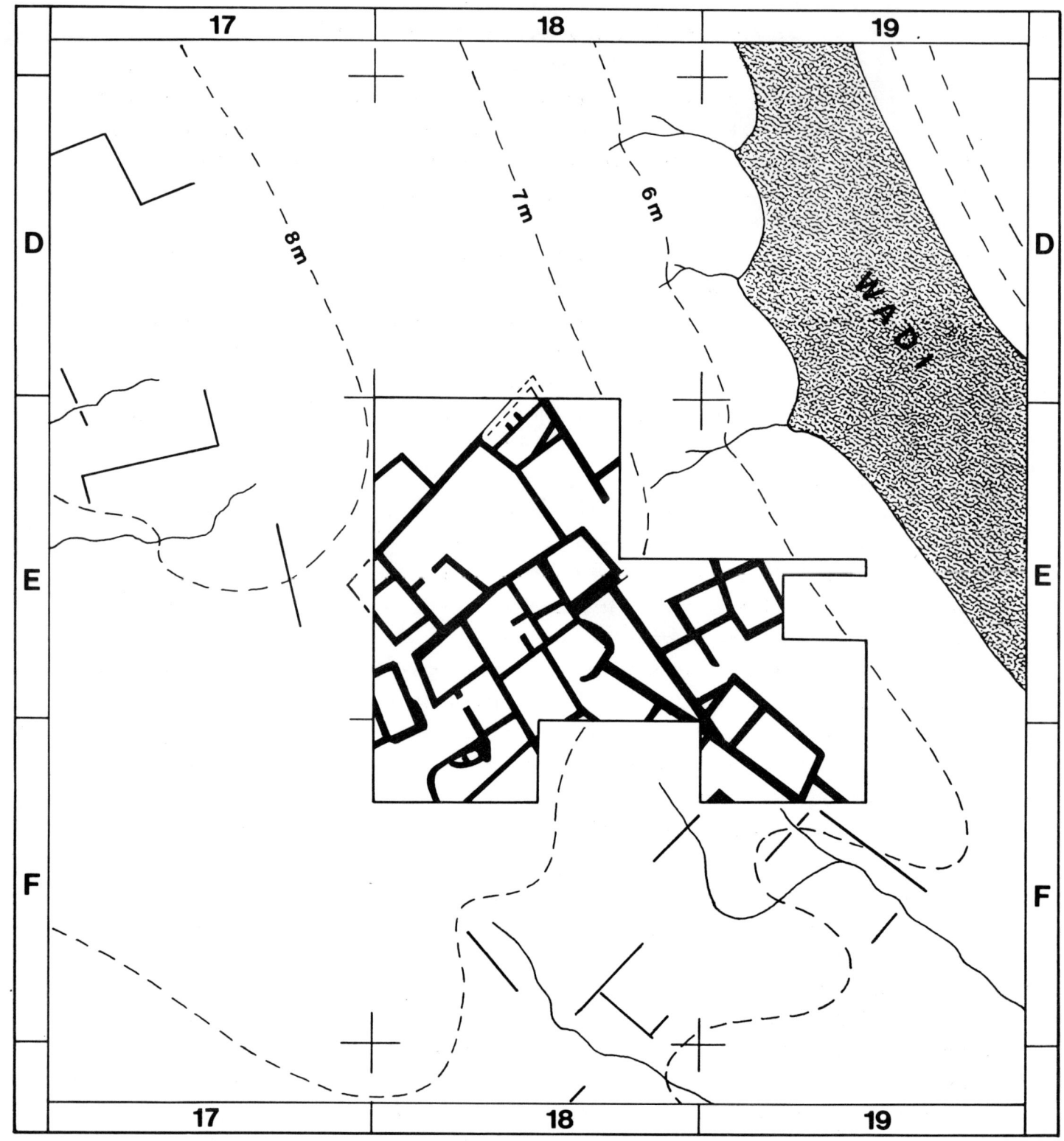

Plate 31: Eastern Area

complex in E18a (north sector, see below). The southeastern part of the excavations held buildings with an orientation suggesting a separate complex on the southern part of the ridge. Indeed, surface indications of walls indicate that architectural units with this orientation occupied F18 and F19. A third building complex may be seen in the surface indications in D17 and E17 with an orientation similar to that of room corners in E18c, the small portion of this third complex included in the excavations. Thus the 1980 excavations have delineated the central of three separate but interlocking building complexes along this ridge.

Little can be said about the probable nature of these complexes, since it is very difficult to interpret the architecture which has been excavated. Due to the shallow depth of the occupational deposit (usually less than 50 cm.) and the nature of the construction techniques, phasing of walls and sequential utilization of rooms, courtyards, etc., is problematic. Almost certainly the overall plan represents several different occupational phases with little evidence available to sort out the phases. In general one might observe a notable lack of symmetry and architectural centralization, as well as the frequent neglect of the right angle. There is, in the present limited sample, no suggestion of a recurring architectural pattern, as was seen in the residences in P8a,b (Whitcomb and Johnson, 1979: pl. 17). Nor is there any clear evidence for functional specialization of the rooms, other than the courtyards. Finally, there is no indication of defensive structures within the settlement. There is a suggestion of concentration, of compact utilization of this space over a period of time. How long the occupation here continued is difficult to estimate, due to the strong likelihood of periodic or even seasonal abandonment. Architectural investment was minimal, there being not the slightest suggestion of embellishment beyond rudimentary shelters. Within the excavated area slightly over 33% was probably roofed space; another 25% was enclosed space (yards, courtyards). At present this settlement might be viewed as an ancillary, "slum" area to the more substantial Islamic residences on the western part of the site. Dating indications suggest, however, that this portion of Islamic Quseir al-Qadim may be dated to the late 14th--early 15th century, and thus post-date the P8 buildings which seem to belong to the 13th--14th centuries. The role of the eastern area will be clarified during the 1982 season, subsequent to which a synthesis of all the data on the Islamic occupation at Quseir al-Qadim will be undertaken.

Plate 32: Eastern Area

This eastern area is a complex situation where shallow occupational debris averaging 20-50 cm. in depth is associated with stubs of mud, mud brick and stone walls. Very little in the way of stratigraphic evidence could be found to assist in the difficult task of isolating building phases and depositional sequences. The confusion of building units of doubtful contemporaneity makes even the basic description a complex undertaking. Initial distributional studies in the field of artifact categories strongly indicated three sectors: a northern sector (E18a, E18b and parts of E18c and d), a southern sector (F18a and parts of E18c and d), and an eastern sector (E19c, F19a, and part of E18d). This division is at present somewhat arbitrary and will be adjusted on the basis of a full analysis of artifactual contents and functional implications.

North Sector

The northern sector comprises an open area leading toward the north, a large enclosed courtyard and a series of rooms on the eastern and southern sides of this court; see pl. 32 and fig. 10.

Fig. 10: Looking South across the Eastern Area from the Northwest corner of the North Sector with Modern Road and Red Sea Visible in Background; Notice shallowness of Occupational Deposit, Pits and Stakes Found in Courtyards

The northern squares of E18a are the northwestern limit of the excavations in the eastern area; they are also the highest in elevation. In the course of excavation part of the reason for this height was readily apparent--surface clearance in levels of approximately 10 cm. (in the northeast 5x5 m. square E18a-[2], in the northwest square E18a-[1],[3]) revealed thick layers of trash, i.e., accumulations of organic debris in the form of rope, matting, reeds, and other fibers, cloth, and wood (twigs, branches, stakes, etc.). These layers were interspersed with pockets and irregular layers of sand and pebbles, although rarely consistent and large enough to follow and use for stratigraphic separation. As this was one of the earliest excavated areas of this ubiquitous trash, an effort was made to record and analyze its composition; later the recording had to be limited to individual objects and to cloth for this organic mass of material.

The northern open area, which may have been a second large courtyard, is limited on the south by a long substantial wall made of white limestone (A). Traces of decomposed or robbed out stones were found in a northwestern extension; thus wall A diagonally bisects E18a as a major property division. A room was added on the north of this wall, a part of which was excavated (E18a-[4], walls B,C). This room was bounded by a thin wall (10 cm. wide) made of mud bricks set vertically. Collapse of these walls, as well as wall A, was toward the north. Room E18a-[4]) was filled with organic debris (matting, rope, etc.) mixed with brown soil; this was interspersed with yellow pebbly layers near the walls. Accumulation of debris was thicker near the western baulk where thick lenses of ash were found. This ash was the result of two pot hearths found in the room. Pot hearths of this type were ubiquitous in the northern sector and may be described in general as a round plastered hole (30-60 cm. wide) usually lined with a section of a ceramic vessel such as the inverted top of a storage jar. These hearths were found filled with ash and partially burnt fuel surrounded by heavy accumulations of ash; they probably functioned as ovens for baking bread in the midst of hot ashes, a common Arab bedouin practice, or for other types of cooking. Pot hearths are often associated with shallow pits, large and small, which may have held fuel, food, or cooking vessels, and are now found filled with ash.

The occupational debris of this room was not particularly different from the open area to the north. The loci there (E18a-[5],[6],[10],[13]) lay beneath almost purely organic debris (E18a-[3]) and were characterized by relatively "clean" sand and pebbles and, in the south, brick fall from the walls. Locus [6] had, in addition to this brick fall, thick accumulations of ash resulting from a pot hearth located in the angle of the large stone wall A and smaller mud brick wall B. On the sand in this area an incense burner was found. Near wall C was a similar accumulation of ash ([5]). Below these loci was a sand layer taken to have been an undisturbed stratum lying on the bedrock; toward the east, however, this pre-occupational stratum had a plastered or bricky quality suggesting landfill or a platform (under [10]).

The northeast square of E18a is an extremely complicated affair with mud brick structures much decayed and much eroded. Beginning from the north, locus [10] was a trash layer mixed with yellowish brick material and ash down to a prepared bricky platform, in which alignments but not individual bricks could be delineated. The platform was in turn placed on a layer of ash and ended in a line running northeast-southwest as an extension of the north face of the large stone wall. It was expected that this stone wall would indeed continue further northeast, but the trash layers ([9]) led down to a red-brown soil with fine sand and pebbles, strongly suggesting that the stones of this wall may have been robbed out. The southern part of this locus revealed a thin mud brick wall D (bricks 6x25 cm.) or partition composed of bricks set vertically parallel to the supposed wall and at right angles in a way to suggest cribbing, whether for structural units (storage bins?) or as facing for a mastaba or bench (see a similar structure from P8a-[8], with the same size bricks, in Whitcomb and Johnson, 1979: 53). South of this brick structure was an area of trash with much brick fall ([8]) resting on a hard packed red fine sand, a rare instance of a believable floor. An area of burn marks on the bricks and black ash suggest a small fire next to the mud brick structure. In the center of the room was a large shallow pit of white sand, shell, and coral with no artifacts. A small corner of this room was excavated as E18b-[1]. Walls limiting this area (E,F) are all thin, scrappy mud brick or mud with a few small stones. Beneath wall F was a short fragment of an earlier wall with a slightly different orientation.

With the clearance of trash debris from walls E and F (E18a-[7]), the northern corner of the large courtyard was defined. This courtyard is a rectangular area 9x6-7 m., with a secondary room in the southern corner. The loci for this courtyard are E18a-[11],[14],[15],[16], E18b-[4], E18c-[3],[9],[11],[12]. Seven pot hearths were found in this court, all near the northern walls; at least 4 pits were associated with these hearths. In addition, a number of wooden stakes were found in the courtyard; the tops of these stakes, which protruded 10-20 cm. through the trash debris, were uniformly burnt black. The occupational debris was from 20 to over 60 cm. in depth and composed of thick layers of organic trash interspersed with lenses of yellow sand and pebbles, brown soil, and grey ash accumulations.

In section these layers have a horizontal varve-like alternation which might suggest a seasonal or at least periodic pattern of deposition. In excavation these varves proved impossible to follow as individual reed mats would undulate through supposedly discrete layers. More precise, "tea-spoon" archaeology, techniques were reluctantly ignored in view of the over-all information desired.

The northern corner of the courtyard (E18a-[11]) revealed, amidst the trash, extensive mud brick fall from walls A and E over a pot hearth and, in the angle of these walls, a large pit. Accumulations of ash and charcoal were found and some of the bricks were burnt red. A niche in wall E held three wooden stakes, presumably the remains of longer sticks used as a rack or as part of the wall. Near this northern corner were two pot hearths, one partially superimposed upon the other; they were again surrounded by ash and near a pit against wall A. Another pot hearth was found against the southern portion of wall E, not far from a broken grinding stone (in E18b-[4]). Four wooden stakes were placed in the yard parallel to wall E (in E18a-[15]); three additional stakes were found near wall G (in E18c-[3]). The placement of these stakes suggests the vertical supports for light roofing (of matting) or perhaps drying racks for fish nets (which nets were occasionally found in the debris, complete with floats and weights).

In the western corner of the courtyard (E18a-[14]) was a corner pit with a possible mud brick lining next to a pot hearth; a broken rotary grindstone was found near this hearth. Ash accumulations often over 20 cm. thick predominated in this area and into E18c-[12]. Next to wall A were two more pot hearths separated by a shallow pit. This pit contained two overturned wooden bowls and, partially hidden beneath the wall, a wooden cosmetic box (see pl. 68). Directly in front of these hearths and pit were four stakes arranged in a square, presumably for a rack or support. Locus E18a-[14] was taken down well below the apparent occupational surface of the courtyard. Ashy lenses at a depth of 30 cm. below this floor indicate that an occupation preceding the architectural configuration visible on the surface is likely. The bedrock had been cut to even the floor of this courtyard.

A corner of the courtyard was separated from the yard by mud brick walls (G,H) with a doorway, partially blocked, in wall H. This room was filled with organic trash identical to the remainder of the courtyard (E18c-[9],[11]) to a depth of 20-30 cm. Ash layers were particularly noticeable near the brown soil of the floor. A single row of wooden stakes bisects the room as the remnant of poles for racks or, more likely, supports for an awning or roofing. The western wall of the courtyard (J) is substantial (20 cm. wide) and connected to a peripheral room defined by walls K,L,M. This room is distinctive for its symmetry with wall J and the careful right angles of its walls; more importantly, the deposits from within this room (E18c-[14]) were composed of sterile brown soil without the usual organic debris. The narrow corridor south of wall L seems to have had a platform at its eastern end, somewhat reminiscent of the platforms in P8a (Whitcomb and Johnson, 1979: pl. 17).

The rooms discovered south of the large courtyard are very problematic in that there seems to be no clear sequence of construction or architectural phasing. Whether these rooms should be considered part of the courtyard complex or as a separate, central architectural unit is quite uncertain. The decision to group them with the northern sector is arbitrary at this point and may need to be reconsidered for the final report when all the data has been systematically analyzed. Four rooms are here considered: E18c-[6],[10], E18c-[13], E18d-[15], and E18d-[13], E18b-[5]. The root of the problem is in the complex nature of wall N, which has a stone central stretch and thereafter is composed of bricks set vertically.

The stone portion of wall N is north of a rectangular room (E18c-[13]) filled with dark organic debris down to an ash layer (walls N,O,P,Q). Wall Q separates this room from a small "anteroom," (E18d-[15]) which has a doorway opening to the south (in wall R). Here the deposit held less organic debris and more dark brown soil mixed with ash and charcoal. A doorway led from the northern room into room E18c-[6],[10]. This room contained brick fall from wall N mixed with a deep accumulation of dark ash, charcoal, and coral sand (upon which this debris was lying). Two short partition walls or low platforms extended into the room and may have defined the firing area (no effects were found on the low wall stubs). Near the partition walls were found intact, in heavy ash and fiber, a jar and a bottle (more properly a small keg); see fig. 11. While wall R seems contemporaneous with the first two rooms discussed, wall S may be a later addition. Finally, the eastern room (E18d-[13] and E18b-[5]) was filled with mounds of donkey dung (a fuel?) mixed with brown pebbly soil and brick fall from wall N. The walls of this room (N,P,T,U) suggest more than one building phase with both P and T having earlier inner walls.

Fig. 11: Keg Amidst Fiber and Ash near Partition Wall in E18c-[10]

East of the large courtyard is a large room (E18b-[3],[4], E18a-[12]) bounded by walls E,F,V. This last wall is a substantial wall 25 cm. wide made of white limestone and similar to wall A; as such it would seem to have formed a major property boundary. Beyond this wall (V) to the east seems to have been an open area with a stone wall (W) abutting it. The southern portion of wall V has been eroded away, leaving only white traces of the wall alignment. It is possible that this wall originally continued in walls with the same alignment found in the eastern sector (see below).

The room west of wall V had very little organic debris but was composed mainly of brown soil mixed with yellow sand. Two wooden stakes marked the central line of this room, between which was a small pit filled with hair and bones (goat?). Two other pits were found in the southern part of the room and a fourth pit cut across and below (i.e., antecedent to) wall V. On the east of wall V was a deposit 20 cm. deep mixed with brick fall near wall V and tapering off to a thin surface cover in the northeastern corner of the excavations, following the downward sloping contours of the bedrock. An alignment of five wooden stakes ran parallel to wall W, as if they were an extension of wall F. These stakes were first interpreted as tether posts for animals and indeed this interpretation, rather than a structural one, might be suggested for other stakes. The occupational surface here showed three burnt areas and a shallow pit with coral sand. Otherwise the deposit (E18b-[2]) was a dark brown soil with organic trash.

South Sector

The eastern boundary of the south sector is arbitrarily chosen as wall A, a 20 cm. wide stone and mud brick wall which continues the orientation of the courtyard walls. Between wall A and wall F are a series of walls (B,C,D,E) with an entirely new orientation, extensions of buildings from the southeast excavation area (F19a). In this latter trench there was clear evidence that wall B is constructed over wall A; wall A was antecedent and may have gone out of use when wall B (and walls C,D,E) were constructed. The northern portion of wall A was significantly lower, although this may be a product of erosion.

The triangular area between walls A and B was composed of heavy accumulations of trash, organic debris mixed with dark brown soil and some ash (in the northern portion) (E18d-[4],[5]). This continued north to wall T as locus E18d-[16]; here were found five wooden stakes and, indeed, one stake was found set into the northern end of wall A. Wall B was made of stone and mud brick, 35 cm. wide, and ended in a cross wall (D) and stub of wall E, both made of stone. Walls D and E were replaced by a semi-circular walling of scrappy mud brick closing off locus E18d-[10], a trash deposit distinguished by the occurrence of both crude paddle stamped pottery and sophisticated Syrian moulded wares. South of wall B was a room (with walls D,H,C) which had an accumulation of organic debris some 40 cm. in depth. This room may be considered the northernmost of a series beginning in the southeast (F19a).

West of wall F is a large rectangular room (E18d-[9], E18c-[4]) within walls F,G,R,S. The debris within this room was almost sterile in the north, mainly fallen mud bricks from wall R (which was made of vertically set bricks at this point). The southern part had about 25 cm. of organic debris. West of this room was a small "anteroom" with a doorway leading onto a winding alley. This room, within walls S,P,O,H (E18c-[2]), was filled with organic trash in a dark brown soil with an admixture of coral sand. It is possible that this room led into that to the north (E18c-[8]) which is a small enclosed courtyard, as suggested by the presence of two pot hearths, four wooden stakes (for racks?) and the usual ash accumulations with organic trash and brick fall. This court is defined by walls S,P,Q, and N, the last of which presents a very confused jumble of rebuildings.

The alley was not distinguished from the scrappy mud brick walls U,V,W,X until after the removal of about 20 cm. of almost purely organic debris (E18c-[5]). The alley opened in the south into a wider area (F18a-[4]) which had a shallow trash deposit marked by quantities of unglazed sherds. The scrappy nature of the mud walls west of the alley is repeated in the walls to the south (J,K,L). These walls, usually only 5 cm. wide, are made of mud bricks set vertically. Locus F18a-[1]) contained ash and debris mixed with wall fall from walls H and S. In the adjacent locus (F18a-[2]) were two mud brick bins and quantities of donkey(?) dung, suggesting a small stable area. A long thin wall J separated this area from F18a-[3], which held a thick accumulation, 25 cm. deep, of organic trash; see fig. 12.

Fig. 12: Looking East across Eastern Area from Southwest Corner of South Sector with Red Sea Visible in Background

East Sector

East of wall A was a slight rise or knoll before the steep slope into the wadi leading to the beach; surface collections indicated a concentration of Far Eastern ceramics here. The area east of the north end of wall A was a sandy open area with very little debris and some ash (E19c-[1],[2],[8]). The ash was the product of two pot hearths, each associated with at least one stake. Wall D abutted wall A, suggesting that this complex may have been a later addition. The room defined by walls C,D,E,G was found to contain very little debris mixed with fallen mud brick (E19c-[5], E18d[3]). This was in sharp contrast to the room immediately to the east (within walls E,F,G,H), which contained a deposit over 55 cm. in depth made up of organic debris including much leather and parts of fish (bones, fins, skin) mixed with brown soil and ash (E19c-[3],[4]). This deposit lay upon sterile sand and pebbles; a layer of coral pebbles was found near the base of the walls. Wall H, composed of small stones approximately 5x10x15-20 cm., is preserved 7 courses high; 2-3 courses is more common throughout this area. North of this room may have been a further room with similar trash debris (E19c-[1]). A test trench was extended down the slope to the east; debris which was 25 cm. deep near wall H gradually thinned to a surface scatter down the slope (E19c-[2]).

South of these rooms was a room adjoining wall A (with walls D,C,J) within which were two superimposed trash layers. The upper deposit (E18d-[6]) was mixed with brick fall from walls C and D. This was separated by a sandy layer from a lower trash deposit (E18d-[7]), a thick accumulation of organic remains and ash which ran beneath walls C and D. East of this room was an open area with thick accumulations of organic trash, characterized by the unusual mixture of fish remains and Far Eastern celadons and porcelains (E19c-[6],[7],[9]). The southeastern 5x5 m. area was only partially excavated as it became apparent it was a homogeneous mass of matting, rope, cloth, fish bones, etc.

South of this open area two rooms were excavated which were associated with wall B. The smaller of these rooms was within walls B,K,L,M; wall K was poorly preserved but clearly was superimposed over wall J. The different orientations of walls J and K reflect the differing directions of walls A and B. This room held a thin layer of organic debris below which was clean fill (E19c-[8],[10]). The larger room, walls B,L,M,N, contained a layer of trash within a dark brown soil (F19a-[2]), below which was a deep deposit of dark brown soil with little organic material, some 35 cm. deep (F19a-[3]). This lower deposit contained a number of Roman sherds which, with the dark coloration not unlike the lowest fill of the villa area, suggests a possible earlier occupation in this area.

South of wall B was an open area, probably a courtyard limited by wall stub P on the north and a corner of walling Q. This courtyard contained two pot hearths, a wooden stake, and a pit full of ash ranged against wall B. These features, with a broken grinding stone, were associated with an upper deposit of ash and sand mixed with organic debris (F19a-[4]). Below this was a deposit of dark brown soil 35 cm. in depth. Finally, east of these rooms was a wall (O) and thick organic debris (F19a-[5]).

Summary

It may be seen from the above descriptions that the interpretation of the occupations in the eastern area must be very tentative. The great mass of organic debris which covers most of the excavated areas has many implications. First, it should be borne in mind that the extent of preservation is somewhat atypical, even in Egypt. Had the organic elements disintegrated, the shallow scatter of sherds would give a very different impression of occupation here. The extensive use of reed matting and fibrous materials, including rope, may indicate that roofing and perhaps the upper portions of walls may have been constructed of this material. The ubiquity of this trash poses a problem in terms of occupational patterns. Almost certainly particular areas of this excavation were occupied sequentially, with other abandoned or ruined plots gathering refuse. Alternatively, it is very likely that periodic abandonment of the entire settlement, perhaps seasonally, allowed a slow accumulation of debris which would have been covered with new matting upon reoccupation. Settlements of this type are depicted by Kammerer (1929-35) on the Abyssinian coast and by Van der Meulen and Wissman at Mukalla (1964: 13).

The fluidity or adaptability of such architecture, compounded with its shallow preservation, makes the identification of residential units very problematic. Individual rooms range from 2-3 m. in width to 3-5 m. in length, though a middle range of 2.5x3 m. is as close to a standard as seems likely. There is a slight suggestion of paired rooms in the east sector, but nowhere does a symmetrical or recurring pattern seem to emerge.

Beginning with the periphery of the excavated buildings, one sees rather differing situations. On the eastern edges there are exceptionally thick mounds of trash lining the slopes of the wadi. By contrast, the southwestern corner of the excavations revealed shallow deposits with little organic matter. And on the northern periphery there are again thick deposits overlying a utilized area of pot hearths, pits, and wooden stakes.

The occurrence of pot hearths is in itself interesting. There are far too many to suggest anything but a sequential use over the period of occupation. The very nature of this firing indicates areas of pot hearths were probably open courtyards, perhaps protected by awnings. Most of the pot hearths were placed near the southern face of substantial walls (although there seem to be exceptions), probably to protect the fires from the strong north wind. Most of the pot hearths occur in the large courtyard and north of this yard in E18a; others were found in the eastern open area (E19c-[11]), in the small court (E18c-[8]), and in court F19a-[4].

The impression is left that the northern area, the north sector, represents one functional unit with a large courtyard and subsidiary rooms on the south. The southwest is peripheral to this and may be loosely associated with the architectural units in F19a, which may be the northern edge of a second building or residential complex. The eastern buildings in E19c seem to represent a separate and later addition, perhaps associated with fish processing.

The stratigraphy for these sectors is given on the next page.

Bibliography for Islamic Trench Summaries

Kammerer, A.
    1929-35   *La Mer Rouge*, Cairo

Van der Meulen, D., and H. von Wissmann
    1964   *Hadramaut: Some of its Mysteries Unveiled*, Leiden

Whitcomb, D., and J. H. Johnson
    1979   *Quseir al-Qadim 1978: Preliminary Report*, Cairo

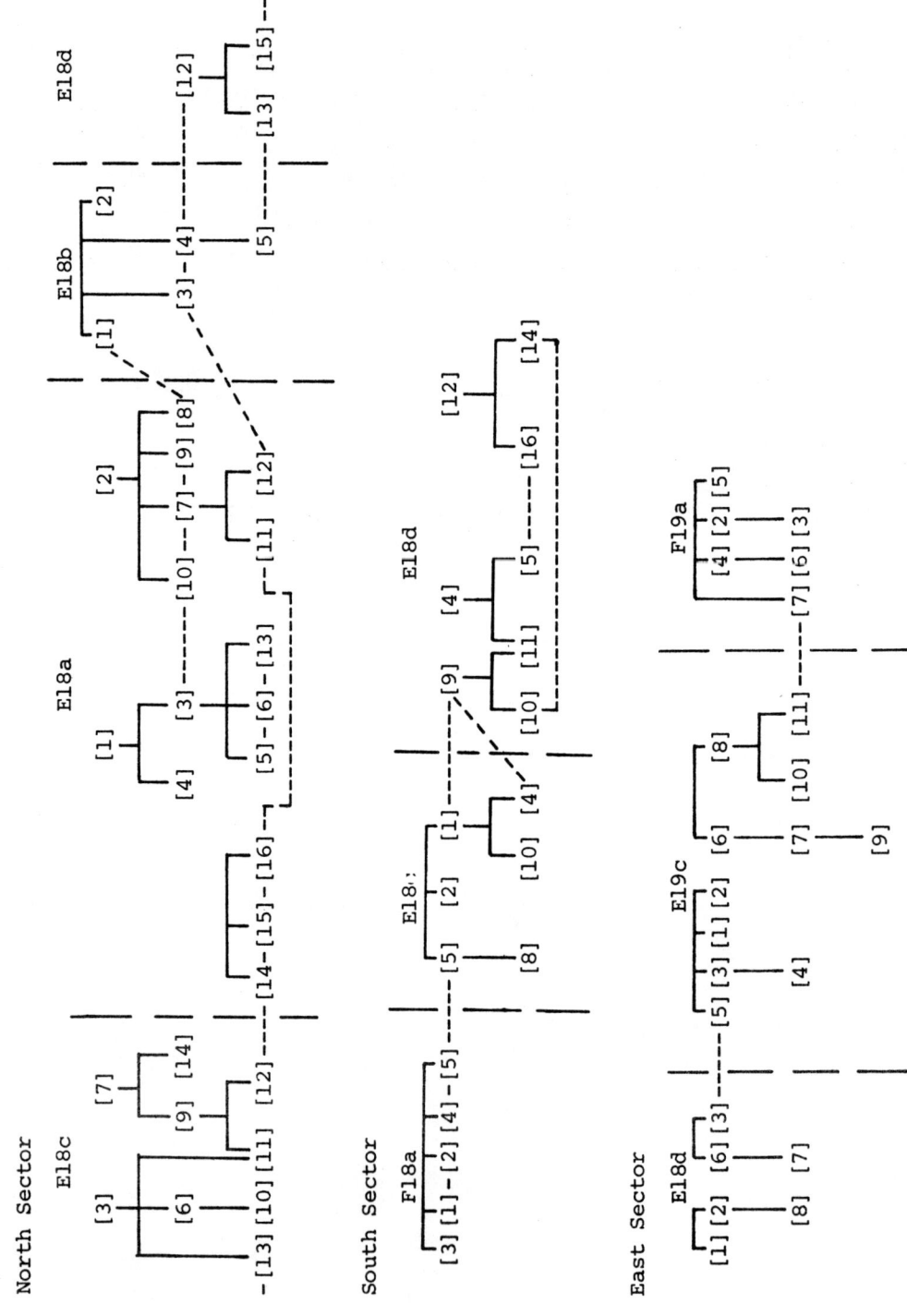

CHAPTER 5: ISLAMIC CERAMICS
Donald Whitcomb

The organization of the ceramics from the Islamic areas, mainly the eastern area, presents formidable problems due to the great diversity of forms and decorative techniques. As one will quickly note, the range of ceramic forms is no larger than that of the Roman corpus, perhaps smaller. The range of forms also cuts across distinctions in color and type of fabric. The formal element which was to be followed in the creation of this preliminary typology was, thus, defeated by the overwhelming element of decorative distinctions. This is a common tendency for all who have studied Islamic ceramics and, indeed, it is realized that an abandonment of a decorative typology would possibly make the corpus more difficult for specialists to utilize. It should also be noted that use of decorative techniques in setting out a typology based on sherds, not whole vessels, means that occasionally a sherd lacking a given technique will be classed in a different category than would the full vessel from which the sherd came. Which method, formal or decorative analysis, will be the more beneficial for archaeological study in the future is not completely clear. A preliminary typology of formal types, with decoration as a secondary feature, has also been prepared and will be tested during the 1982 field season.

The organization of the Islamic ceramics begins with the glazed wares, mostly bowls and a few jars, divided initially by cream and red fabrics. Following this are decorative techniques of incising (sgraffiato) and slip-painting. It should be noted that most of the red wares have a light colored slip added before glazing to bring out the color of the glaze. The mustard wares and yellow-blue wares depart from this principle in using an opaque glaze directly over the red body. Finally there are fine underglaze painted wares in a variety of styles and a few glazed lamps.

Unglazed ceramics are separated into red and cream wares, the latter with distinctive moulded and punctate decoration. Punctate and paddle-stamped vessels are grouped as "African" wares (see below); unglazed painted wares, not unlike much earlier Nubian wares, are also attested. The remainder of the corpus consists of unglazed bowls, jars, and other forms with the exception of certain cooking pots and storage jars which have a functional glaze added.

The ceramics from the eastern area were, for the most part, mixed with the trash debris which covered the site. Within such a context very few whole or reconstructable vessels were discovered. Nevertheless it has often been possible to make probable joins on the basis of decorative elements, glaze colors and quality, etc. The distribution of individual types of ceramics was not uniform over the whole of the eastern area and area (locus) concentrations were noted during the course of the excavations. There thus remains a potentially informative study of patterns of associations among the glazed and unglazed ceramics and between ceramics and other types of artifacts which will yield both functional and chronological (and ultimately social) distinctions. This must necessarily comprise a second phase of analysis (just as for the Roman villa), after the refinement of the comparative elements under consideration.

Plate 33: Glazed Cream Wares

The presence of a glaze on a cream body is relatively rare at Quseir al-Qadim. It should be noted that the potential distinction between a cream clay and a frit body has not been made here since the difference is often of a chemical nature and visual criteria do not seem sufficient to the author. The color range of the glaze is turquoise, light to dark blue, light to dark purple, green, and, rarely, white. The bowl forms begin with a small bowl with out-flaring sides and a thin ring base (a-g). These are covered with turquoise, blue, purple, or white glaze. Larger bowls (m-r) are almost exclusively green glazed and have out-flaring or hemispherical sides. Bases are small, heavier rings; further base forms are illustrated in ff-mm. Decoration includes scalloping on the rims and light incising with a blunt instrument (sgraffiato). Other bowl forms include ledge rims (aa,bb) occurring in the same color glaze as the small bowls. Such a rim appears on a deep bowl or pot (ee) with a low carination and at least one handle. Other less common rim forms are illustrated in cc,dd,y,z, the last of which (z) is glazed yellow and may be a misfired red ware.

A limited range of glazed jar forms was found with the color range of turquoise, purple, and white for the smaller forms (h-k) and green (rarely blue or turquoise) for the larger forms (l-v). Generally the neck is wide and vertical with a sharp angle at the shoulder. Decorative techniques used on the body are vertical ribbing (l), shallow incising (u,t), diaper pattern (s), and carving or moulding (v). Handles are attested on the body (w) and neck (x; this sherd had a string tied to it after it was broken [as a weight or plaything?]). The cream glazed wares thus form a corpus of relatively limited shapes: three distinct types of bowls, with some less well defined forms, and one general jar form, with a range of decorative devices.

Plate 34: Glazed Red Wares

The glazed ceramics with a red (or red-brown) body display an analogous range of forms, although there is an obvious tendency to larger, heavier, and not as finely potted forms. One sees again the small bowl with out-flaring side (a-e) and the hemispherical bowl (f,g); some light scalloping on the rim is present but incising seems to be absent. The color range is white, green, and blue-green or dark turquoise. It should be noted from the outset that glazed red wares strongly pick up the coloration of the fabric, given the translucency of the glaze. Thus, for example, the in-curving sided bowls (l,m) are described as having a brown glaze when the situation is more likely a clear glaze picking up the body coloration. This translucency is a relative factor depending on thickness, chemical nature, and preservation. The descriptions remain the visual impression, although these factors should be borne in mind. This is particularly important in regard to the use of a white slip, an effective method of hiding the dark fabric. Where a white slip is described, it was visible where the glaze had flaked off or along the break. A light green glaze *may* be presumed to have a very thin slip (verifiable only under a microscope) and, conversely, a dark blue-green glaze is likely to have been placed directly on the red body. This imprecision may be shocking and will certainly be replaced by more technical study in the future; nevertheless, the visual impression is the usual criterion in the field and when confronted with museum or published pieces.

The larger bowls (h-k,n) often have squared off rims, incised exterior bands, and small ring bases (n is an unusual form). Here the colors are green and a yellow-brown, the result of the thin irregular slip under a yellow glaze. Bowls with a ledge rim are present (o,p,q), the last of which has a low carination. The bases (s-y) show three contrasting tendencies: a high, slightly splayed ring base (t,u), a very small ring becoming almost a knob (v,w), and a wide flat ring becoming almost a disk base. Jar forms are present but, in contrast to the glazed cream ware examples, they are larger, seemingly with decoration on the body and with curving necks smoothly joining the shoulder. The coloration ranges from dark turquoise to yellow-green and an olive green (occasionally found on bowl fragments). It seems accurate to say that, based on this corpus, glazed red wares without decorative features duplicate the forms established in the glazed cream corpus. We will next turn to the changes in form of glazed red wares when decorative techniques are employed.

Plate 35: Sgraffiato Wares

The ceramics with sgraffiato (incised) decoration occur normally on a red ware, very often with a thick white slip. The incising was made with a sharp instrument cutting through the slip and producing a dark brown line. The glaze is either green or yellow and the yellow, where it thickens into drops (f) or pools (x base), becomes a darker honey color or brownish (this effect also occurs where the slip is thin or not present).

The bowl forms with sgraffiato decoration begin with a group having straight sides (in effect a conical bowl) with occasionally a slight in-turning at the rim (a-g, the latter of which has a rare, out-turning rim). The decoration may be divided into two styles, an epigraphic (a,b,d,e) and a floral style (f,g). Within the epigraphic style the lettering is brightened with a thicker slip. Colors of glazes are often combined, generally a yellow interior with a green rim and exterior (c,e,f).

The remainder of the bowls are roughly hemispherical (i.e., with curving sides). Little attention is paid to the rims, with the exception of a beveled rim (u) which may be compared with a cream ware (33:cc). An exterior horizontal ridge is occasionally present near the base (l,q) and on the jar shoulder (h). Bases are either small, knob-like rings (v; 34:w) or high simple out-flaring rings (q,r,w,x; 34:u). Decoration is confined to the interior (excepting i) with horizontal bands near the rim, sometimes embellished with incised scalloping (i, q), and careless circular strokes. (More careful examples [k] approximate the sgraffiato on the glazed cream wares [33:n,o].) In general the forms of these bowls correspond to the yellow and green glazed red ware bowls (34:i).

The single example (h) of a jar with sgraffiato decoration has a poorly preserved epigraphic motif on a yellow glaze. The over-all form would seem closest to a glazed red ware form (34:z). An unique artifact with yellow-brown glaze and traces of sgraffiato decoration (s) may be a "leg" of a large object or, conversely, a sort of finial. In comparison with the foregoing group of glazed ceramics, it would seem that, while some rim forms (g,u) and decorative motifs (k) approximate glazed cream wares, the general affinity is with the forms of the glazed red wares. More interesting is the fact that there would seem to be an inverse relationship between the range of different forms and the utilization of surface decoration.

Plate 36: Slip-Painted Wares

It is a short step from the enhancement of epigraphic decoration with a slip to the use of the slip as a decorative element. Generally the slip is painted on before the translucent glaze is added; occasionally an over-all slip is cut away revealing the dark fabric (b,e). The result is a light and dark green or a yellow and brown (which may be further decorated with spots of green glaze). One rare example (d) shows this technique under a blue glaze. Slip-painting never occurs in combination with sgraffiato excepting the epigraphic examples.

The bowls may be divided into three groups. The first has hemispherical forms on high ring bases (a-e); the rims of this group sometimes turn outward (e). Decoration is confined to horizontal bands and radiating lines. The second group is distinctive in that the slip-painting occurs under a green glaze on a cream-buff body (h,i). The rim forms are straight or slightly out-flaring and somewhat finer than the red wares. The deocration is epigraphic or patterns of dots and lines of the slip. The same decorative range occurs in the third group where dots and swirls of lines (here truly pseudo-epigraphic) predominate (j-r). The decoration is often enhanced by additions of green glaze to the usual yellow glaze. The form of these bowls is again hemispherical on a high ring foot or base.

Jars are represented by two examples, a yellow glazed red ware with epigraphic decoration on the shoulder (f; the rim is somewhat similar to the cream ware 34:aa). The second example is again a green glazed cream ware (g) with dots and an epigraphic decoration on the shoulder. The slip-painted wares confirm an impression of finer, more delicate forms in the cream ware and heavier forms in the red ware. The attention to decoration again seems to have displaced variety and embellishment of the ceramic forms. Formal variety is more restricted than the range in vessels with sgraffiato decoration.

Plate 37: Mustard Wares

This glazed ceramic ware is a type commonly found during the 1978 excavations, especially in P8 (Whitcomb and Johnson, 1979: pl. 37, 41-44, 46, 48). This ware may be defined as an opaque, poor quality yellow glaze (or opaque light green glaze, l,m) on a red body (cream bodies occasionally appear as a variant). Decoration, when present, is painted in brown (darkening to almost black) and green and is predominantly hanging semi-circles or festoons.

Bowl forms range from simple hemispherical (b,h) to heavy in-turned rims (i,j); the most common form has a ledge rim ornamented with festoons (f,g). An extremely unusual rim is a pie-shaped (crinkled) rim (a). Bases are always low, wide rings (m,n,p) or flat, disk bases (o,q,r). New motifs encountered this season include a loose guilloche on the rim (d,e) and a radiating "chain" (k). The one jar form, a shoulder, is possibly a bowl fragment (c).

The mustard wares fit loosely into the range of forms found in the glazed red wares (34:g,o-q,x). The unusual opaque glaze, as well as the ledge rim and disk base, set this ware apart from the tradition of the sgraffiato and slip-painted wares.

Plate 38: Underglaze Painted Wares, Yellow-Blue Ware, Lamps

This last assemblage of the glazed ceramics is the most complex. We may begin with the yellow-blue ware (v-aa). This ware can be associated with the mustard wares in that the glaze is opaque and ledge rims (w) and in-turning rims (x) occur. The basic glaze is yellow, to which broad radiating sections of opaque blue glaze have been added. Where the glazes have mixed there is usually a green glaze, the thickness depending on the amount of glaze used. Very few sherds of this ware were found.

A small minority of sherds from the Islamic areas of Quseir al-Qadim exemplify the fine glazed ceramics of the Islamic period. These wares usually are on a cream or buff-orange body which may often actually be a frit ware. The decoration is painted on the vessel in black or blue and the surface then covered with a clear or turquoise (green) glaze. Vessels tend to be small and well-potted, generally bowls with simple or out-turning rims and jars. The forms are comparable to the glazed cream wares (pl. 33).

Five groups may be separated tentatively on the basis of the few sherds found. The first is characterized by black or blue and black paint under a clear glaze with a variety of decorative schemes (a,b,d,j,n). The second is blue painted in imitation of Chinese blue and white porcelains, often with floral motifs (e-i). Another tentative type has black paint under turquoise or dark green glaze (k,l,m,s). These latter with a green glaze may properly belong rather to another type which has black paint under a clear glaze (c,p,q). Connective links between these two groups may be seen in spots of green used in the decorative pattern (c) or in use of a pale green and darker green in a complex radiating design (q). Significantly, the ware of this last group colors from buff to orange. A similar ware is present in one of two examples of jar bodies (r,t) which have brown painted designs under a clear to light green glaze.

One painted sherd belongs to an entirely different ceramic tradition (o). This cream-pink ware with an opaque white glaze painted with manganese and light blue is a majolica ware, the first found in the excavations (a few others have been found on the surface).

Finally, the glazed ceramics include lamps, although these were very rare (bb,cc). One is a long spout, probably for a jar form; the other is an open bowl form with a bent over rim making the spout and with the broken stump of an interior handle. In both cases the ware is red-brown and the glaze an olive or light green. (Bowl u is a red ware with white slip and green glaze. A broad section of the slip has been removed--and not painted; this example should have been considered with the slip-painted wares.)

Plate 39: Cream Wares

The unglazed Islamic ceramics are introduced by two plates of cream wares. Ceramics with this color fabric form a corpus of relatively few general forms and, as such, represent a distinct type. Other than one bowl with incurving sides and an incised decoration (d), all examples illustrated here are jars. The three necks shown (a,b,c) have small loop handles above which is a ridge and slightly bulbous neck constricting at the rim. The form is that of a gudulia or water jar; unfortunately no examples were found which clearly associate this neck with a body form. It thus remains possible that they were part of pilgrim flasks, the moulded sides of which were occasionally found (e-i). The decoration of the sides of these vessels with moulded patterns clearly points to the Syrian industry described by Sauvaget (1932; see below).

A more common form of decoration was the use of incised and punctate patterns. These occur on wide-mouth jars (with a high neck and simple rim)(j,q,r,s). One of these has a filter with simple radiating perforations (r). Narrow jar necks were also found (k,n). Comb incising is occasionally present (k,l), especially on the few fine red wares (k,l,m). Incising, like the punctate decoration, is found principally on the neck and shoulder. One example (t) indicates that pilgrim flasks were also made with this decorative technique. Otherwise the bodies seem to have been globular. A few spouts made of this cream ware were found (u). The bases for these vessels cannot be determined with certainty but may include examples found on the following plate.

Plate 40: Cream Wares

Further examples of jar necks include the filter necks found in the eastern area (a-e); these are usually perforated with random holes, although one has punctate decoration as well (d). Two examples of long, relatively narrow necks are shown here (e,f). A series of rim forms (g-j,o) shows a variety of shapes in this cream ware (h has an uncomfortable resemblance to Roman filter necks and may be suspect; see 12:o). Two examples of a heavy crude type of vessel (m,n) with a buff ware are included here. The range of bases begins with a high, gracefully flaring ring base (k,l,p,q,r) and a high ring base (t) one might expect on a glazed vessel (34:u). The remaining forms of bases are low wide ring bases, often folded in appearance (s-w), which most likely belonged to the globular jars above mentioned. With the exception of various rims and two crude vessels (g-j,m-o), the cream wares seem limited to jar forms, i.e., water (or, at least, liquid) carriers.

Plate 41: "African" and Painted Wares

This selection of ceramics may seem an odd and rather subjective one, especially in the classification "African." This is a provisional characterization referring to the unusual aspects of the fragments selected (a-f), all of which bear some similarity to ceramics outside the main sphere of Islamic pottery production (in geographical terms) and associated with either the Sudan or East Africa (see below). The painted ceramics likewise form a distinctive regional tradition, perhaps best associated with Nubia (excepting p,q, which are Syro-Palestinian; see below). In formal terms there is no overlap with the glazed Islamic forms, although analogies will be seen with unglazed ceramics. The importance of this classification is the clear archaeological association of these ceramic traditions with the glazed Islamic traditions.

The "African" ceramics have three distinguishing types based on decorative techniques. The first is a red or brown ware with incised lines (a,b,d,g); the latter two seem to have the lines filled with a white paste. One example (a) has a sort of rocker pattern and circular punctates near the rim; it may thus be associated with the second type, a black ware bowl with punctate decoration (c). Burnishing is occasionally applied to the surfaces. The third type has impressions of paddle stamping on the exterior of a buff-cream ware covered with an orange-red slip. The patterns may be either simple parallel grooves (f) or crossed grooves (e) (the decoration carved on the stamping implement). All of these wares are very rare within the collections.

The painted wares include a series of bowls with thick out-curving sides and often a grooved rim (h-j); the base may approximate that known from one preserved example (k). The ware is orange or buff with an orange slip; the painted decoration is in red and black (rarely cream). Horizontal bands and a variety of loosely painted black motifs are added. The same decorative scheme is present on jars and deep globular bowls (o,r-y; v may be misfired or an exception). Here the ware is either an orange or red with an orange or, more commonly, a cream slip. The decoration is red and black bands within which are zones of decorative motifs, usually in black. Both these forms and the bowls are occasionally burnished.

Several painted wares do not fall into the above described type. A small cup (l) is a red ware with dark brown paint. A distinctive type, of which only sherds m,n were found, is either red or cream ware with painted decoration in black and green. The paint is very thick and flakes off easily; at least the green may actually be a glaze. The two final examples (p,q) are globular jars with loop handles on the sides. They are cream wares with brown paint (p is black but seems to have been overfired or smoked). The painting is very different from the previous styles and is comparable to the "Arab geometric" of the Syria-Palestine area, as is the form of the handle.

Plate 42: Unglazed bowls

The description of unglazed bowls presents a special problem of artifactual style and functional analysis. Given the large corpus of glazed bowl forms, these plain ceramics introduce a formal redundancy suggesting specialized functions or socio-economic explanations. Functional analysis is unfortunately guesswork at this point; more important are the stylistic attributes which link these more humble vessels with the glazed and painted traditions. Rather than ignoring such wares as essentially amorphous constants, the study of unglazed wares may eventually add an increasing sensitivity to the artifactual record. Unglazed pottery should not be considered a "ceramic underworld of Islam" (Lane, 1947) but as an integral part of the ceramic tradition with (undefined) functional and even aesthetic aspects.

Unglazed ceramics are not, however, easy to classify; there are suggestive features in common with types already described. A heavy bowl (a) with punctate decoration may be related to the "African" bowl (41:a). The distinctive rim form of b bears an uncomfortable resemblance to a Roman bowl type (9:h). This form and other bowl forms (e-i,u,t) may be formally too minimal in features to be validly comparative, but they have an importance in the structure of the entire corpus of Islamic ceramics and should not be ignored. Other bowls seem to have comparisons with glazed forms: the in-curved sided bowls (c,d=34:1,m), simple rims with a single incised band around the exterior (l,m=33:y), and other rim forms (q=37:l; r=34:o; s=33:cc, 35:u). Unpainted examples with forms seen in painted bowls also occur (o,p=41:h). Most of the wares are orange-red in color and the forms compare more closely with the glazed red corpus. One distinctive type of unglazed bowl (j,k) features heavy straight sides with a cut off rim and a band of comb-incised decoration near the rim. The two examples are brown with a tan slip and buff with a cream slip. Bases are not ascertainable for each type, but the range is depicted on pl. 49.

Plate 43: Large Unglazed Bowls

The larger unglazed bowls present a consistent range of forms with curving sides and heavy club rims, often forming a flat, external bevel. Occasionally the body and rim are marked with rope impressions (h,i). Most of these are orange wares, although red and brown variants occur. A variant of this form has an interior indentation on the rim (a,b) and comb and punctate decoration. A feature of this form is the inclusion of micaceous and vegetable tempering agents (which also occur in other unglazed forms). The ware is a pink-buff in color. The bases for these bowls seem to be heavy low ring bases. A very wide rim (m) also has comb incising and seems similar to the heavy club rim (l). This last vessel was used as the lining for an oven, although this may not have been its original function since broken jars were employed for the same purpose. The smaller rim fragment (e) may not be appropriate within this grouping. Overhanging rims on heavy bowls are found within the Roman kitchen wares (9:b), but in general this form seems to be distinctively Islamic in the Quseir al-Qadim context.

Plate 44: Glazed Cooking Wares and Storage Vessels

Although these wares should properly belong in the glazed ware typology, the glaze is used here on the interior (presumably to reduce porosity) of the pot and not as a decorative element. The ware coloration ranges from grey-orange to buff and the glaze an olive green darkening to a green-brown.

The forms in this ware include straight sided bowls (a,b,c) of which one (c) is identical to a glazed red ware (34:o), suggesting that differences in coloration may be a product of repeated exposure to fire. A small loop handle was attached to one of these bowls (a). Jar rims were also present in both glazed and roughly analogous unglazed versions (d,e), again comparable to glazed red ware forms (34:cc). Small jars with folded rims, both unglazed (f,g), may be related to a glazed jar (34:r).

The major form within this ware is a round pot, presumably a cooking pot analogous to the Roman cooking pots. The rim is folded over, a form already seen in the unglazed painted wares (41:r); small loop handles, often degenerated into dabs of clay, are attached near the rim; the sides are often ribbed and the base, on the evidence of one example (r), seems to have been rounded. These pots are glazed on the interior only and unglazed versions occasionally occur (h,i,k). The only decorative element attested is a short appliqué of chain-ridging with oblique orientation to the rim (q).

These cooking pots were often very hard and well-fired (especially n,q); superficially the sherds are very similar to those of large storage vessels s,t,u, except that the latter are glazed on the outside, rather than the inside. These storage vessels are classic Far Eastern forms, the rims, loop handles on the shoulders, and flat bases recalling the brown glazed stonewares generally known as Martaban jars. These storage jars, which should be included in the Far Eastern corpus, have been illustrated here in view of their possible influence over this category of cooking wares. The analogy should not, however, be overdrawn.

Plate 45: Purple Wares

These wares, like the cooking pots, are often blackened with soot and were primarily cooking vessels. As such they are related to the "kitchen wares" of the Roman ceramic corpus in function and in form; the comparison is repeated and close enough that an homologous rather than analogous explanation may be advanced (see below). The wares are often burnt completely black; where coloration may be seen it ranges from red to red-brown (here described as purple); both interior and exterior surfaces are burnished.

The forms are generally rim and neck fragments of large jars or pots. While the variations in form might be seen as almost continuous, some types or groupings may be suggested. First there are sinuous sided vessels with overhanging (and often ridged) rims (a-d; cf. 9:r, 22:c, 26:1, 28:i). A similar rim form has an in-curving inner surface (e,j). Other forms have a more pronounced neck with a groove (for a lid) on the rim (f,g,h,l,n) or an interior ridge (g,h,i) (h=22:d; k=9:i; l=22:u [kitchen wares]; and n=10:u [cooking pot]). Rims with smaller diameters and vertical grooves on the exterior do not seem to be paralleled (p,q).

A small pot with folded out rim (r) may be compared with Roman examples (10:l,m) of cooking pots. Perhaps most striking, however, are the similarities in form of pots with a sharply out-turned rim and carinated side (s,t,u-9:l,m, 22:e; also on Islamic cooking pots, 44:k). A subtle distinction lies in the comparison of the carination (9:k) where the Islamic type produced a ridge on the upper surface (u-w,y). The bases are most likely to have been rounded although examples of flat bases in this ware have been found (z,aa).

Plate 46: Neckless Jars

The most common form of unglazed jar has rounded or inward sloping sides and a rolled out rim. The ware varies from a brown to orange. The heavy round sided jars (a-d) occasionally have two handles on the shoulder. Smaller versions of the same shape (e-g) seem to lack these handles and are cream to orange in color. The sloping sided jars have an out-turned rim (h,i) or a rim almost triangular in section (j,k). These vessels have a wavy comb-incised band on the shoulder and a manufacturing join on the interior of the shoulder. Another form of these sloping sided jars (l-p) has a single ridge on the exterior of the rim and tends toward a red or red-orange color (r may be a variant of this type). Finally there is a large sloping sided jar (q) which has a disturbing parallel in the ceramics from the Roman villa (13:g); at present it would be more satisfactory to see this as an errant Roman type than to admit mixture of E6a-[13]. The identification of this type will become evident with the discovery of further examples.

Plate 47: Jars and Bottles

A further series of jar forms may begin with shapes close to the sloping sided neckless forms (d,f,g), ranging from curved necks (e) to sharply defined junctures (especially a). A wide range of wares is evident. Jars with two handles are found (b,c), which form is analogous to Roman jars (12:p, 17:g); handles in the Islamic types seem to form more complete loops, with both ends on the shoulder, rather than neck to shoulder. Such loop handles are found on one example (h) where the interior is coated with a green glaze. An unusual rim belonging to a large jar (i) has wavy comb incising and a hole on the rim.

A series of jars with narrow necks, i.e., bottles, may be judged against a complete form (m) with a flat bottom and two small loop handles on the curving shoulders. Sherd n duplicates this neck and rim (also 41:v). A larger neck had two handles attached (k) and its bulbous central section recalls the cream ware jar necks (39:a). This neck may be compared with the partially preserved necks and shoulders of two examples (j,l). These are suggested to have been bottles although the pattern of breakage suggests subsequent use as funnels.

Plate 48: Storage Jars

The larger jars begin with an unique vessel (a) which is brown with a black lustrous slip with patterned burnishing; both the ware and form are unparalleled on the site. More numerous are red sherds with ridged sides (c,d), of which only a shoulder and rounded base forms are known (the former was used as an oven). Other storage jar forms are characterized by features such as relatively narrow necks, long arching handles usually faceted by grooves (f,g,h; g has an incised inscription which seems to be the name Salim), an impressed finger mark at the join of the handle with the shoulder (b,h), and one example of wavy comb incision (i). Only the rim form b might be confused with Roman forms (26:r). Wares are usually red with a cream slip or, rarely, cream. One example of a pointed base (e) is vaguely analogous with Roman forms. Hopefully further examples will define this range of Islamic storage vessels more precisely.

Plate 49: Bases and Unusual Forms

Illustrated here are various forms of bases (m-z) related to unglazed forms. Most are wide ring bases analogous to those found among glazed red wares. Also present are flat disk bases (p,s,t), which form was also encountered in the mustard wares as well as the cream wares. Two unusual small bases (q,r) were also found. One example (x) illustrates the rounded base for a small jar or bottle (cf. 34:z). Also noteworthy is the relationship of base with body form (m,n) where the position of maximal width is contrasted. Two very heavy bases (y,z) are illustrated, the latter being the more common form.

The remainder of the plate illustrates unusual forms which do not fit comfortably within the above described groupings. Two rims (a,b) may be related to 34:aa (a red glazed jar) or 47:g (another jar form). Two spouts are illustrated, the first without parallel and the second similar to the spout in cream ware (39:u). The two small bowls are special in that the first is covered with bitumen (c) while the second (d) is hard-fired and would seem to have been a crucible. An unusual lid form (e) was found as well as a heavy based vessel with triangular pinched rim (f; from blackened deposits this would appear to have been a lamp).

Plate 50: Kegs and Unusual Forms

The kegs of the Islamic priod are analogous and perhaps homologous with kegs of the Roman period (14:c,d). The rims are completely distinctive, the Roman having a rounded lip (12:j,k) and the Islamic a simple straight rim, often with a pouring lip (o,p). A small form is known through an almost complete example (n), much fire blackened. A second form of Islamic keg is known only from its spout or opening (i,l,m), which is relatively wide with a short neck often beveled on the interior face.

The remainder of the plate is more difficult to assess. Two unusual rim forms, each with paint on the rim (a,b), might properly belong with the painted wares. Two examples of heavy pots (e,g) are similar to those already illustrated with the cream wares (40:m,n), although here with a red-orange fabric. Rim d may belong to such a vessel; rim f, on the other hand, is a ribbed red ware without immediate parallel. Finally there are rim forms analogous to the Roman cooking pot (k=10:k). The heaviest of these (h) may belong to the Islamic purple wares. The handles on another (c) are without precise parallel in the Roman corpus and bear a similarity to the horizontal loops of Martaban jars; the rim and execution of the handles strongly suggest an affinity with the glazed cooking pots. In sum, these cooking pot forms would seem to be Islamic variants of the more diverse Roman cooking pot.

Plate 51: Islamic Ceramics from Central Building A

The test of a typology is its applicability and the examination of Islamic ceramics from the central portion of the site provides both confirmation and disconformities. The glazed cream wares are represented by a fine bowl (f,g) and a jar shoulder with sgraffiato decoration (j). The style of this piece conforms more with the glazed cream than the sgraffiato wares. A handle similar to 33:w is in a red ware (m). Otherwise, the glazed red wares seem to be absent except for the mustard wares, of which there are numerous examples (a-e). Rim d is what might be considered a classic type (37:f,g) with brown paint; likewise rim e has green painted decoration (37:b). The overhanging rim (a) poses a problem and it is tempting to see the base (37:m) as the same type of cream ware variant.

The cream wares are represented by a jar with a narrow neck (r) similar to 39:n but without punctate decoration. Two filter necks (n,o) were found which are similar to but more elaborate than 40:d. An extremely unusual fragment (l) seems to be painted in red and green glaze on a cream fabric; the technique bears some similarity to 41:m,n. The only other painted ware was an unusual painted base (t) in a red ware with a white painted design. The effect is rather as if a slip-painted glazed ware were left without its glaze; the relation of this piece within the corpus is not certain. A small crude bowl in a red-brown ware (h) is likewise without parallel in the corpus. More easily recognized is the shoulder of a Far Eastern storage jar (k=44:s) and an example of purple ware (q=45:d). A fine example of a neckless jar (s) has an out-turned rim, handles, and low carination; it is thus similar to 46:h,i, but without the comb incised decoration. A large rim for a storage jar (p) is paralleled by 48:f. Finally, there is a glazed red rim fragment (i) which seems similar to the unusual rim form 49:a,b.

The Islamic ceramics from the central building substantially reproduce the majority of wares within the corpus. In such a small sample the absence of certain wares is probably not significant. The preponderance of mustard wares is not an anomaly but corresponds to the frequency of its occurrence in the areas excavated during the 1978 season. The distinction between the two seasons may be seen by comparing these wares with those reported in the 1978 preliminary report (Whitcomb and Johnson, 1979). The 1978 season recovered Islamic wares mainly from the central and southwestern parts of the site (P8) and it is a working hypothesis (to be tested during the third season) that the eastern and western areas show differences in wares and in relative quantities of these wares and that this difference may be chronological. If this proves to be true, refinement of the temporal range of this Islamic pottery will result from the final full analysis of all the pottery following the third and final season.

Discussion

The plain glazed Islamic ceramics from the eastern area of Quseir al-Qadim may be initially divided into the two groups distinguished above--the glazed cream wares and the glazed red wares. While most of the forms are analogous between the two fabrics, there are important differences in formal characteristics and glazes; this may be an indication of contemporaneous production in two or more industrial areas or traditions. The glazed cream ware is generally a superior product in fineness of form and quality of glaze. Glazes have a larger variety of colors (turquoise, purple, white, light green). By contrast, the glazed red wares show heavier potting, less attention to detail and decoration with colors usually ranging from blue-green and green to yellow.

Little work has been done on these generally undecorated glazed wares and the possibility of detailed analysis of these ceramic forms is largely unexplored. One exception is the so-called pseudo-celadon wares (33:m,n,o,q), which may be compared to examples from Fustat (Scanlon, 1971: pl. 5b). The notched rims of these bowls (degraded petals) may also be seen in white glazed red ware bowls (34:a,b,d), no doubt also inspired by Far Eastern ceramics.

The glazed red wares are the predominant tradition at Quseir and may be subdivided according to decorative style. As noted above, the increased attention to surface decoration with the sgraffiato wares corresponds to a less varied formal repertoire (within the red ware tradition). The sgraffiato designs are characteristic Mamluk ceramic products, well represented at Fustat (*ibid.*: pl. 1h,2a,4d,e, p. 224 bottom). Though the external ridge occurs (35:1,q), the characteristic Fustat carinated goblet is not present, hemispherical bowls being more typical; these forms are currently being studied on the basis of the extensive collections from Fustat (Scanlon, pers. comm.).

The slip-painted wares are normally grouped together with the sgraffiato and indeed there is a strong overlap in vessel form and decorative schema. The two techniques are never combined at Quseir al-Qadim. The distinctive green glazed ware with slip painted decoration (36:g,h,i) is a cream ware, and thus a special category. This ware is common at Fustat (Scanlon, 1971: 6h, p. 229) and occurs in Nubia (for Kom el-Dikka, see Lane, 1949; Marzouk, 1959; and Abd er-Raziq, 1967, 1970). Both sgraffiato and slip painted wares have been reported recently from the Dakhleh oasis, where they are taken as diagnostics of Mamluk occupation (Keall, 1981: fig. 1; comparisons to his site 33/390 are 35:d,q; 36:h,o and to site 32/390 are 37:f?; 38:j,s). Keall (*ibid.*: 216) notes in his discussion the relative sparcity of "classic Mamluk" wares (i.e., sgraffiato and slip-painted types) at Quseir al-Qadim as presented in the report of the 1978 season. The 1978 excavations at Quseir al-Qadim encountered Islamic remains generally in the central and western periphery (P7-8) of the site (see pl. 1), while the corpus under discussion for 1980 is mainly from the eastern area. This has lead to the hypothesis (which will be tested in the 1982 season) that there is a chronological difference between the occupations of these two areas of the site. The evidence suggests that the 1978 (western) areas are Ayyubid/Mamluk datable to 1200-1300 while the 1980 (eastern) areas are strictly Mamluk datable to 1300-1400. There does not seem to have been a break in the occupation nor a segregation of occupation areas. One of the primary aims of the third season will be to find stratigraphic situations where this chronological progression may be more carefully delineated.

A close parallel for the slip-painted wares occurs near Aden, reported by Lankester Harding (1964: pl.V:11 = 36:k). Another type of glazed red ware is the mustard ware (pl. 37), discussed in the 1978 report (Whitcomb and Johnson, 1979: 105-6), where various speculations were offered on the origin of this ceramic type. The references to occurrences in Aden (Lane, 1948; Doe, 1963: 153) are corroborated by the depiction of an example from Khanfar, near Aden (Lankester Harding, 1964: Pl. V:10). This sherd is almost identical to 37:g. The ceramic context at Khanfar is interesting in that several examples of mustard wares are found with slip-painted ware; an example of this technique with blue glaze on red ware (*ibid.*: 11) is comparable to 36:d at Quseir al-Qadim. Likewise unglazed incised wares may compare with Quseir al-Qadim 41:b,d. The site of Khanfar is provisionally dated between the 13th and 15th centuries; a large collection of the ceramics from Khanfar (and other sites in southern Arabia) at the Smithsonian Institution are currently being studied by the author. As for the mustard wares, there remains the strong likelihood that this style emanates from Yemen, where recent but unpublished surveys use this yellow glazed ware as an index fossil for medieval occupation.

If the sgraffiato and slip-painted wares may be thought of as decorated glazed red wares, the classical decorated style of glazed cream wares may be considered the underglaze painted wares (pl. 38). These ceramics are well-known and published; numerous parallels may be cited with Fustat (38:a = Scanlon, 1971: pl. 3c; 38:c = 6f; 38:e = 5g; 38:g = 5f; 38:j = 3d; 38:k = 3g; 38:n = 3k; 38: = 6b)). These fine decorated ceramics belong to a stylistic universe which includes both Egypt (Fustat) and Syria, where this tradition is manifest in the Raqqa wares.[1]

Vessel forms for bowls in Raqqa wares have been drawn as a type series by Porter (1981: fig. 1-10, in a style which recalls those of Lane for al-Mina, 1937; Riis and Poulsen, 1957; and Touier, 1973). The rim forms at Quseir al-Qadim are simple out-flaring (fig. 5), in-curving (fig. 8) or ledges (fig. 4, 10), while wide plate rims and thickened forms (fig. 7, 9) are absent. The bases follow the same pattern with fig. 5 and 8 (highrings) most common and fig. 4 and

---

[1] Several of the Syrian and Egyptian connections mentioned here were called to my attention by Scott Redford.

10 present (wide rings). Jar forms such as Pl. VIII are also represented at Quseir al-Qadim. The stylistic wares which Porter identifies may be represented at Quseir al-Qadim only in the blue and black under a clear or turquoise glaze (38:a,b,j-n), which sherds reproduce a number of isolate motifs (the three balls rim, floral elements, a bird). The most interesting parallel is the panel decorative scheme of her Pl. XXXIII which compares closely with 38:q. Her blue and white bowl (pl. XXXIV) compares with 38:e-g as imitations of Chinese wares. The comparisons with Raqqa ware do not, of course, necessitate the identification of Syria as the source for the Quseir al-Qadim examples as the contemporary Egyptian industry produced much the same repertoire.

A more definite Syrian connection may be seen in the moulded flasks (pl. 39). The five examples of cream ware with moulded decoration (39:e-i) compare very closely with the large corpus of moulded pilgrim flasks published by Sauvaget (1932; Sarre, 1925). These flasks were discovered in Damascus in an apparent workshop datable to the 14th century (Sauvaget, 1932: 2-5). The flasks had both flat and convex sides, the former usually in a "white" fabric (cream?), and the latter varying from reddish to grey as well as white. In addition, numerous decorated filter necks and double-handled spouts for the flasks were included in the collection but unfortunately not published.

Both the style and decorative elements are closely duplicated at Quseir al-Qadim. Given the amazing variety and innovation within the collection, the absence of precise parallels is not surprising. Sauvaget's stylistic grouping begins with abstract decorative fields of arabesque designs. 39:e is such a geometric design, a hexagonal pattern of six stars (each with six points) around a seventh central star. The stars are formed by a double intertwining line. Damascus no. 59 shows a very similar star design. The circling rope is a common motif in the Damascus collection. Two small fragments (39:f,g) belong to an epigraphic type, with a central field holding the inscription below an arc with floral motifs; this is comparable to Damascus no. 83, and others. The last two are more difficult to compare. The first (39:h) seems to be a circling floral motif around a central hexagon (Damascus no. 96, et al.) and the second (39:i) may have been similar to Damascus no. 61.

Sauvaget discussed the origin of these decorations and, while noting similarities with blazoned and encrusted metalwork in Egypt, felt that this ceramic tradition must look more toward northern Mesopotamia as its source. It should be

noted that the encircling floral motifs and inscription are very close in style
to the wooden bowl and lid from Quseir al-Qadim (Whitcomb and Johnson, 1979:
fig. 25,26). It would seem likely that the moulded flasks at Quseir al-Qadim
may be from this Damascene atelier. Their presence at Quseir al-Qadim does not,
however, imply a use in the pilgrimage; as Sauvaget notes, the inscriptions and
blazons suggest *une clientèle profane*, mostly military (1932: 2).

A second cream ware style may be seen in the incised and punctate decorated
vessels (39:d,k-v). This tradition would seem to be more African (Sudanese),
though only a few examples were found at Kilwa (Chittick, 1974: pl. 116c, fig.
150: M30). This black ware with punctate decoration, taken in context of incising
and roulette decoration (41:a), would seem to be a continuation of a very long
African tradition. Likewise the paddle-stamped pottery (noted in A22d, 1978,
Whitcomb and Johnson, 1979: 49:a,b, p. 57) is a technique common to African wares
(pan-Sudan, from West Africa to the east); examples very similar to 41:e have been
reported from Chad.

A comparison between Quseir al-Qadim and Kilwa (Period IIIa) reveals a very
similar range of ceramics within the glazed wares (Chittick, 1974). The Kilwa
"late sgraffiato" is similar to Quseir al-Qadim examples, although the Mamluk
sgraffiato and slip-painted wares seem to be absent from Kilwa. The black on
yellow ware is compared to Khanfar and seems related to Quseir al-Qadim mustard
wares. Likewise the Islamic monochrome wares seem similar to the glazed red
wares, although with a more limited range of forms. Finally, the underglazed
painted occur in similar proportions during the comparable period. Most striking
is the range of Far Eastern wares at Kilwa during period IIIa (Lung Chu'an celadons,
rare blue and white, Tehua [Marco Polo ware], Tz'u Chou; see chapter 6, below).
Preliminary comparison of the non-glazed ceramics at the site of Hafun suggests
that careful analysis of this archaeological material will greatly enhance an
understanding of the relationship between the Red Sea and East African coasts
during this time period (Chittick, pers. comm.).

One may look toward the south for parallels with the painted wares at Quseir
al-Qadim (41:h-o,r-y). Both in decorative style and in motif similarities may
be seen with the painted ceramic tradition of Nubia. The classification of Nubian
painted pottery (Adams, 1962; 1967-68) chronologically overlaps the occupation
at Quseir al-Qadim during the late or terminal Christian period (ca. 1100-1500).
The distribution of this ceramic tradition is less well known in Upper Egypt

where, as was pointed out in the 1978 report (Whitcomb and Johnson, 1979: 104, 45:f,g), the generic label of "Coptic" pottery is applied. The forms of this pottery occur also as unpainted ceramics at Quseir al-Qadim (and are distinct from the Nubian forms), suggesting a local adaptation of this southern tradition. A second painted ceramic tradition points again toward Syria-Palestine (41:p,q), where examples of "Arab geometric" are present (cf. *ibid.*: 104, 50:n).

The unglazed ceramics, as noted above, will ultimately prove at least as important as the glazed styles for the study of medieval archaeology. Resemblances of forms with glazed ware forms give a preliminary indication of the Egyptian elements within these assemblages. External influences and actual artifacts are more difficult to determine, due to the lack of published comparanda. A preliminary indication may be offered with comparisons to Kilwa (e.g., Chittick, 1974: fig. 116 = 42:g; fig. 141a = 45:a; fig. 140c = 45:t; fig. 141a = 46:a; fig. 140i = 48:b) and to Khanfar (e.g., Lankester Harding, 1964: pl. IV,V:7 = 42:j; pl. IV:8 = 43:b; pl. V:3 = 43:f; pl. V = 48:i; pl. V = 49:h). This latter connection with Aden and Yemen may become clearer with an analysis of comb decorations and use of chaff (and mica?) tempering materials, implying the importation of not only vessels containing trade commodities but also vessels for domestic use.

Particularly interesting in this context is the type of jars or pots called purple wares (pl. 45). These forms, also found at Kilwa and in southern Arabia, seem to originate as part of an Indian tradition (and indeed may be a continuation of the kitchen wares of the Roman period; see above). Identical vessels have been collected in Ceylon (Sri Lanka; Carswell, pers. comm.) and occur on the coast of Oman (at Ras al-Hadd; Whitcomb, 1975: fig. 9:i-o), both of which would seem to be contemporary or slightly earlier than the Quseir al-Qadim context.

This concentration on identification of exotica, while an important aspect of the functional interpretation of this port, should not displace the importance of this collection for the Islamic archaeology of Egypt. The publication of the unglazed wares from the excavations at Fustat will be crucial for the correction of this perspective (e.g., Scanlon, 1976: fig. 13 would seem an early example of 46:i). Likewise the recent publication of Islamic wares from the Dakhleh oasis (with the important association of kilns) exemplifies this potential. The distinctive Islamic kegs (Hope, 1981: XXVIII:n) are identical to those of Quseir al-Qadim (50:o,p; 1979: 36:i; other comparisons are *ibid.*: XXVIII:m = 43:1; XXVIII:k = 46:i).

Bibliography for Islamic Pottery

Abd ar-Raziq, A.
    1967   "Documents sur la Poterie d'Epoque Mamelouke Sharaf al-Abawani," *Annales Islamologiques*
    1970   "Notes on Islamic Graffito Ware of the Near East," *Annales Islamologiques*

Adams, W. Y.
    1962   "An Introductory Classification of Christian Nubian Pottery," *Kush* 10: 245-88
    1967-68   "Progress Report on Nubian Pottery I: The Native Wares," *Kush* 15: 1-50

Chittick, N.
    1974   *Kilwa, an Islamic Trading City on the East African Coast*, 2 vols.

Doe, D. B.
    1963   "Pottery Sites near Aden," *Journal of the Royal Asiatic Society*, pp. 150-62

Hope, C. L.
    1981   "Dakhleh Oasis Project: Report on the Study of the Pottery and Kilns, Third Season--1980," *The Society for the Study of Egyptian Antiquities Journal* 11: 233-41

Keall, E. J.
    1981   "Some Observations on the Islamic Remains of the Dakhleh Oasis," *The Society for the Study of Egyptian Antiquities Journal* 11: 213-23

Lankester Harding, G.
    1964   *Archaeology in the Aden Protectorates*, London

Lane, A.
    1937   "Medieval Finds at Al Mina in North Syria," *Archaeologia* 87: 19-78
    1947   *Early Islamic Pottery: Mesopotamia, Egypt and Persia*
    1949   "Archaeological Excavation at Kom-el-Dik: a preliminary report on the Medieval Pottery," *Bulletin of the Faculty of Arts, University of Alexandria* 5: 143-47

Marzouk, M. A.
    1959   "Egyptian Sgraffito Ware Excavated at Kom ed-Dikka in Alexandria," *Bulletin of the Faculty of Arts, University of Alexandria* 12

Porter, V.
    1981   *Medieval Syrian Pottery*, Oxford

Riis, P. J., and Vagn Poulsen
    1957   *Hama--Les Verreries et Poteries Medievales*, Copenhagen

Sarre, F.
    1925   *Ba'albek*, vol. 3, Leipzig

Sauvaget, J.
    1932   *Poteries syro-mesopotamiennes du XIVe siècle*, Paris

Scanlon, G. T.
    1971   "The Fustat Mounds, A Shard Count, 1968," *Archaeology* 24: 220-33
    1976   "Fustat Expedition: Preliminary Report, 1968, Part II," *Journal of the American Research Center in Egypt* 13: 69-89

Touier, K.
    1973   "Ceramiques Mameloukes a Damas," *Bulletin d'Etudes Orientales* 26

Plate 33: Eastern Area Glazed Cream Wares

	Locus	RN	Description	Munsell
a	E18d-7	398	cream; turquoise glaze in and out	2.5Y 8/4
b	E18d-10	398	cream; light turquoise glaze in and out	2.5Y 8/4
c	E19c-6	412	cream; turquoise glaze in and lip out	10YR 7/4
d	E19c-9	407	cream; deep blue glaze in and out	7.5YR 6/6
e	E18d-12	399	cream; purple glaze in and out	7.5YR 5/4
	E18a-5	413		2.5Y 8/4
f	E18d-2	405	top: cream; dark purple glaze in and out	10YR 7/4
	E18c-7	417	bottom: cream; purple glaze in; light green glaze out	
g	E18d-3	405	cream; dark purple glaze in	2.5Y 8/4, 7/4
h	E18d-7	398	cream; turquoise glaze in and out	10YR 8/6
i	E18b-3	401	cream; purple glaze in and out	10YR 8/6
j	E18c-13	402	cream; turquoise glaze in and out	5Y 7/3
k	E18a-10	411	cream; purple glaze in and out, vertical streaks	7.5YR 5/8
l	E19c-5	411	cream; green glaze in and out	
	E18c-13	402		
m	E18a-10	414	cream; light green glaze in and out	10YR 8/3
n	F19a-2	404	top: cream; light green glaze, sgraffiato	5YR 6/6
	E19c-10	411	bottom: cream; thick, glossy green glaze in and out, not on base; shallow sgraffiato	
o	E18a-10	414	top: cream; thick, light green glaze, sgraffiato	5YR 6/8
	E18b-3	401	bottom: cream; dark green glaze; sgraffiato	2.5Y 7/4
p	E18c-1	417	cream; thin, light blue glaze	10YR 7/4, 7.5YR 6/4
q	E19c-6	412	cream; green glaze; sgraffiato	7.5YR 7/6
r	F19a-4	404	cream; thick, glossy green glaze in and out, streaks toward center; moderate medium	
	E18c-11	416		
s	E18d-7	398	cream; turquoise glaze in and out	10YR 7/6
t	E19c-6	412	cream; thin, light blue glaze in and out; common medium	2.5Y 7/4
u	E18b-3	401	cream; green glaze; sgraffiato	
v	E18a-3	408	cream; turquoise glaze in and out	2.5Y 8/4
w	E18a-14	410	cream; green glaze in and out	10YR 8/4
x	E18a-4	409	cream; turquoise glaze in and out; twine knotted to neck	2.5Y 7/4
y	E18a-14	410	cream; turquoise glaze in and out; moderate coarse	10YR 7/3
z	F19a-7	404	cream-pink; yellow glaze with brown splotches in	
aa	E18a-5	413	cream; turquoise glaze in and out	5YR 5/8
bb	E18c-2	417	cream; turquoise glaze in and out	7.5YR 6/6
cc	E19c-1	411	cream; green glaze	5YR 6/6 core, 10YR 7/4, 3/1 out, 7.5YR 7/4 in
dd	E18d	398	cream; green glaze in and rim	
ee	E19c-2	411	cream; turquoise glaze in and out	7.5YR 7/6
ff	E18b-3	401	cream; green glaze with red spots in and out, not base	2.5Y 8/2
gg	E18c-2	402	cream; thin, green glaze out; clear and green glaze in	7.5YR 6/6, 2.5Y 7/4
hh	E19c-9	407	cream; thick, green glaze	
ii	E18a-13	413	cream; whitish-green glaze in and out, not base	2.5Y 8/2, 8/4
jj	E18a-14	410	cream; blue glaze in; green glaze out, oxidized red near base	2.5Y 6/2
kk	F19a-4	404	cream; green glaze out; greenish turquoise glaze in	2.5Y 7/4
ll	E18a-14	410	cream; whitish glaze, greenish hue	10YR 8/4
mm	E18a-7	415	cream-red; green glaze, red streaks; moderate medium	5YR 6/6

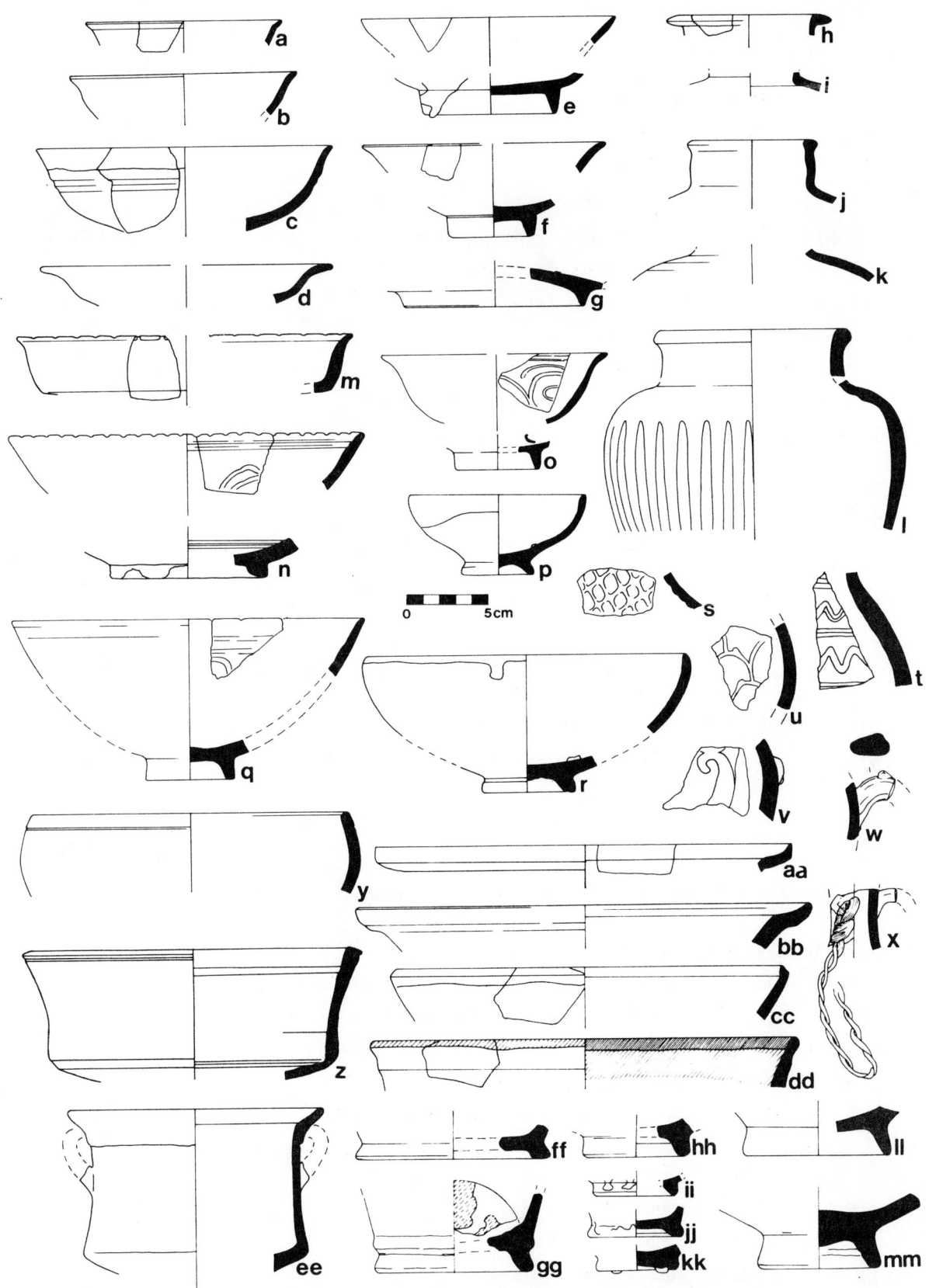

Plate 33: Eastern Area Glazed Cream Wares

Plate 34:   Eastern Area, Glazed Red Wares

	Locus	RN	Description	Munsell
a	E18d-4	398	red; white glaze	5YR 5/6
b	E18d-3	405	light brown; white glaze with greenish hue	7.5YR 6/6
c	E18a-10	414	red; green glaze, red splotches	7.5YR 5/4
d	E19c-9	407	red; white slip; green glaze in and rim	
e	E18a-4	409	brown; dark blue-green glaze	
f	E18d-14	399	red; green glaze in and out	5YR 5/8
g	E18a-14	410	red-brown; dark turquoise glaze; moderate coarse	5YR 5/6
h	F19a-6	404	red; white slip; yellow-brown glaze	
i	E18a-4 E19c-4	409 top 411 bottom	brown-red; yellow and brown glaze; base not glazed	
j	E19c-9 E18b-3	411 top 401 bottom	red; yellow glaze	
k	E19c-3 E18a-3	411 top 408 bottom	red; white slip; green glaze splotches; common medium	
l	E18a-3	408	red; brown glaze; vertical streaks	
m	E19c-3	411	red; brown glaze in and out	
n	E18c-2	417	red; white slip; green glaze in and out; base not glazed; moderate coarse	5YR 6/6
o	E19c-9	407	red-brown; yellow-green glaze	
p	E18a-6 E18a-13 E18a-3	400 413 408	red; white slip; light green glaze, thick, glossy; common medium	7.5YR 5/8
q	E18a-4	409	orange; dark turquoise glaze	5Y 5/6 core 5Y 4/3 out
r	E18a-4	409	red; white slip; yellow-green glaze; bitumen out; moderate medium	
s	E18a-10	414	red; green glaze; coarse	
t	F19a-6	404	red; red slip; light green and light brown glaze	
u	E19c-3	411	red and grey; brown glaze; moderate medium	
v	E18a-16	413	red; yellow, brown, and green glaze	
w	F19a-2	404	red; pink slip; yellow-pink glaze	
x	E18a-10	414	red; white slip; thin blue glaze; moderate coarse	5YR 5/6
y	E18a-14	410	grey-red; dark olive glaze in and out, center in not glazed	
z	E19c-6	412	red-brown; turquoise glaze	5YR 4/6
aa	E18a-13	413	red; light olive green glaze, glossy	
bb	E18a-4	409	red; yellow-green glaze	
cc	F19a-4 E18b-3	404 top 401 bottom	cream-pink; light olive green glaze	

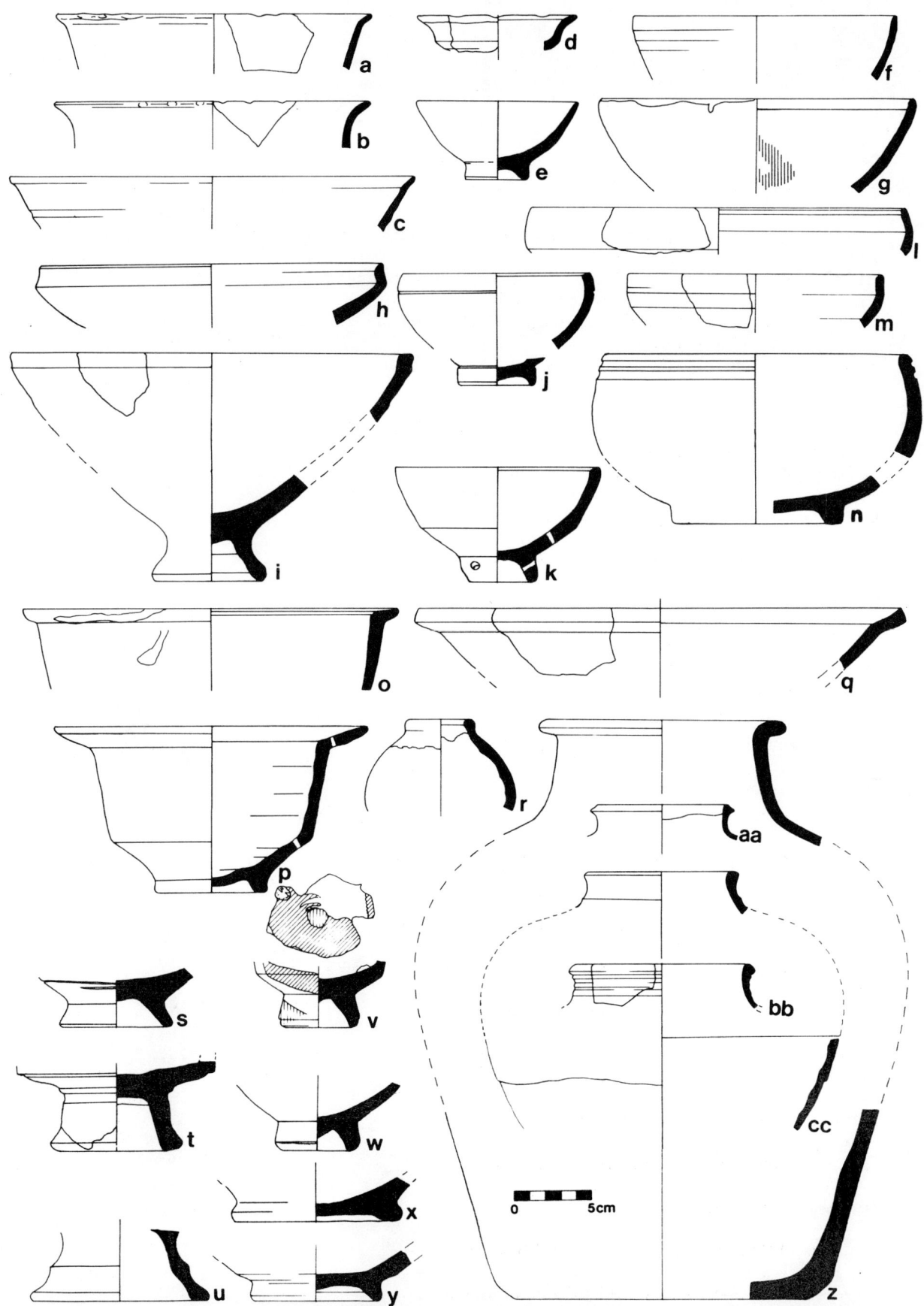

Plate 34: Eastern Area, Glazed Red Wares

Plate 35: Eastern Area, Sgraffiato Wares

	Locus	RN	Description	Munsell
a	E18c-11	416	red; white slip; yellow glaze in and out, brown streaks in	5YR 5/3 2.5Y 6/6 glaze
b	E19c-3 E18d-2	411 405	red; white slip; yellow glaze out; yellow-brown glaze in	2.5YR 6/6, 4/6 10YR 5/8 out
c	E18a-14	410	red; green glaze in; dark green glaze on rim; yellow glaze out	
d	E18c-13	402	red-brown; white slip; yellow glaze in; green glaze out	
e	E19c-3	411	red; yellow-brown glaze in and out	5YR 4/4 5Y 7/6 out 10YR 4/6 in
f	E18d-7 E19c-10	398 411	red; white slip; yellow glaze, greenish on rim, brown spots	5YR 4/4, 5/3 5Y 7/6 glaze
g	E18d-3	405	red; green glaze in and out	
h	E18d-6	398 top	red; white slip; yellow glaze in and out; moderate medium	5YR 5/4 10YR 3/6, 4/6 out 10YR 7/4 in
	D18d-10	414 bottom	dark red; yellow glaze; sandy	5YR 4/4 2.5Y 6/6 glaze
i	F19a-6	404	red; light green glaze with darker green glaze	5YR 4/6 5Y 7/4, 2.5Y 7/6 glaze
j	F19a-6 E18c-11	404 416	red; white slip; yellow glaze out; green glaze in	2.5YR 4/8 2.5Y 7/4 out
*k	E18c-3	417	dark red; yellow glaze	
l	E18a-13	413	red; yellow glaze	5YR 4/4 2.5Y 6/6 glaze
m	F19a-6	404	red; yellow glaze	2.5YR 4/8 2.5Y 7/6 glaze
n	E18a-4	409	orange; green glaze	
o	E18a-14	410	red; yellow glaze with green spots in and out; moderate medium	5YR 4/6 2.5Y 6/6 glaze
p	E19c-1	411	red; white slip; yellow glaze out; brownish glaze in	2.5YR 4/6 2.5Y 6/6 out 2.5Y 2/0, 6/6
q	E18c-11 E19c-5	416 411	red; white slip; green glaze, thin, glossy, splotchy	
r	F19a-2 E18a-3	404 408	red; white slip; yellow glaze out; green splotchy glaze in; common medium	
s	E18a-4	409	red-brown; yellow-brown glaze out	5YR 5/4 10YR 6/8 glaze
t	E19c-6	412	red; white slip; yellow glaze out and in, green and brown spots in	2.5YR 4/8 5Y 7/6 glaze 5YR 8/4 slip
u	F18a-4	403	red; yellow glaze	5YR 3/3 10YR 4/4 glaze
v	E18d-7	398	red; yellow glaze in and out	5YR 4/6 2.5Y 7/6 glaze
w	E18a-14	410	red; yellow glaze	5YR 4/6 10YR 6/8, 2.5Y 6/6 glaze
x	E18a-3	408	red; white slip; yellow glaze	5YR 4/6 10YR 10/8 glaze
	F19a-6	409	red; white slip; brown glaze	5YR 4/6 2.5Y 7/8 glaze

*Sherd not available to check drawing

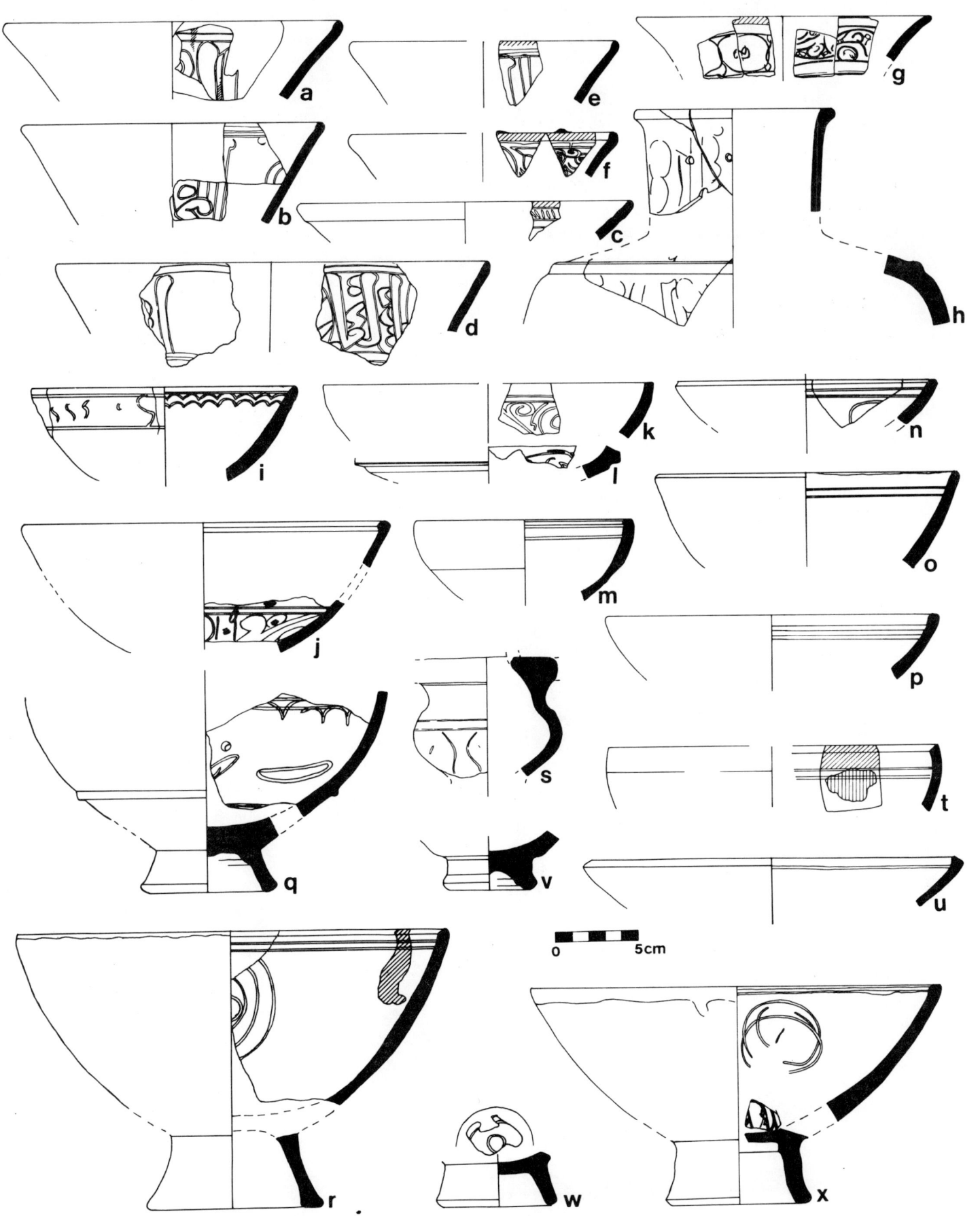

Plate 35: Eastern Area, Sgraffiato Wares

Plate 36: Eastern Area, Slip-Painted Wares

	Locus	RN	Description	Munsell
a	E18a-7 E19c-	413 411	red; white slip; green glaze, glossy, splotchy; common medium	
b	E18a-3	408	dark red; yellow glaze	5YR 4/4 2.5Y 7/6 glaze
c	E18c-13 E18a-3	402 408	red; yellow and yellow-brown glaze	2.5YR 5/6 5Y 6/6 glaze
d	F19a-4	404	red; white slip; thin blue glaze; medium coarse	5YR 5/6
e	E18a-7	415	red; yellow and brown glaze; coarse	
f	E18a-3	408	red; clear yellow glaze; moderate medium	5YR 4/6 10YR 6/6 glaze
g	E18d-	398	cream; green glaze	
h	E18d-10	398	red-buff; white slip; green glaze	
i	E19c-3 E19c-6	411 412	cream-buff; green glaze	
j	E18d-10	398	red; green, brown, and yellowish clear glaze	2.5YR 4/6 2.5Y 6/6 green 5Y 8/6 yellow 7.5YR 3/4 brown
k	E18d-12	399	orange; green glaze out; white slip, brown and transparent green glaze in	
l	E18a-2	417	red; green, brown, and yellowish clear glaze	5YR 5/6 7.5YR 3/4 brown 10YR 7/4 yellow
m	E18d-12	399	brown; yellow glaze out; brown glaze in with cream and black-green design	7.5YR 7/4 2.5Y 7/8 out 2.5Y 8/4 in, cream
n	E18a-7	415	red-brown; light yellow glaze	2.5YR 4/4
o	E18d-15	399	red; yellow glaze out; dark brown with light brown glaze in, streaks and blobs	
p	E18c-10	417	red; yellow glaze	5YR 5/3 10YR 6/6 glaze
q	F18a-3	403	red; yellow glaze out; yellow and green glaze in	
r	E19c-6	412	red; yellow glaze	2.5YR 4/8 2.5Y 6/6 yellow 7.5YR 3/4 brown 10YR 7/4 beige

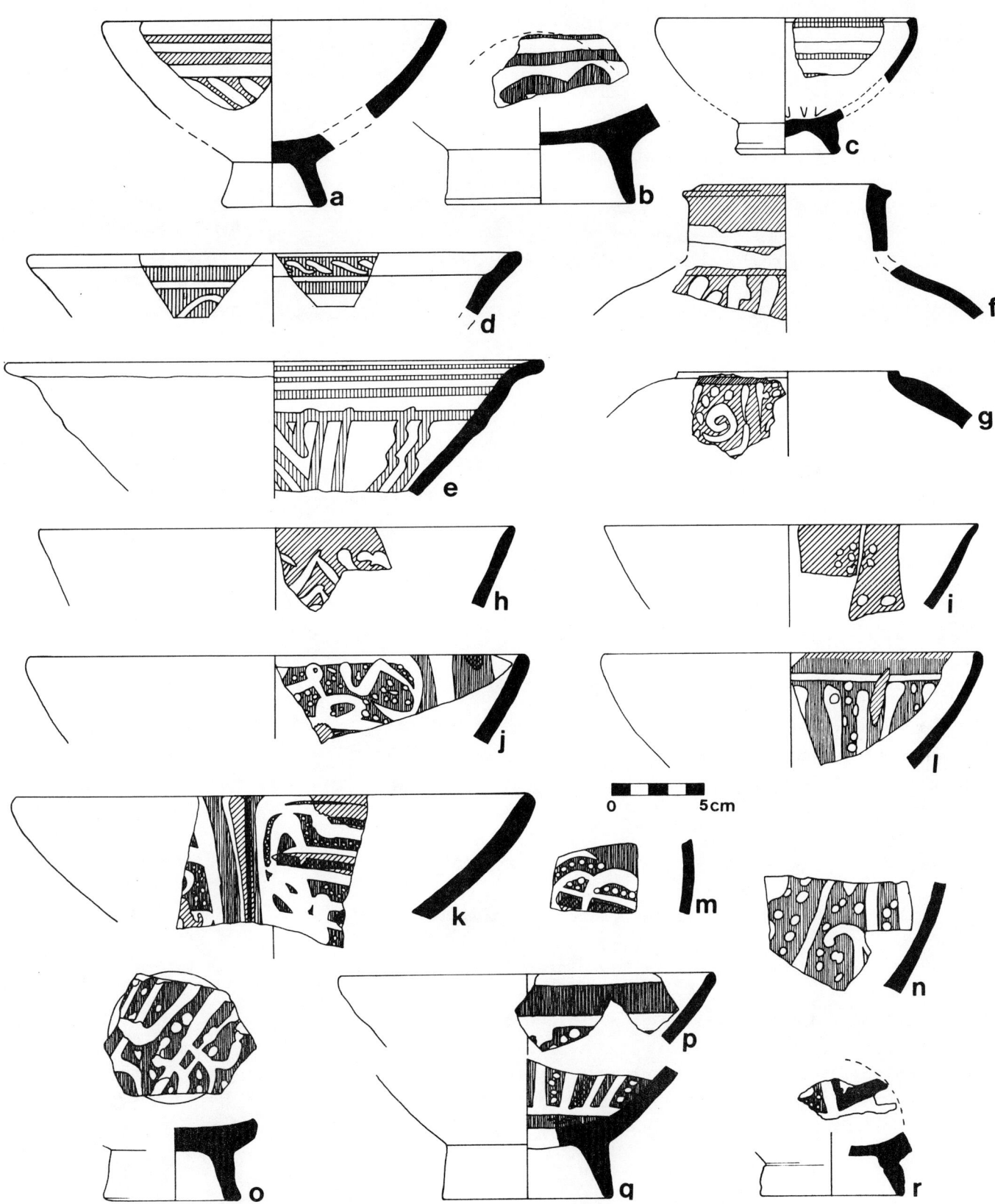

Plate 36: Eastern Area, Slip-Painted Wares

Plate 37: Eastern Area Mustard Wares

	Locus	RN	Description	Munsell
a	E18a-11	413	red; yellow glaze, green and brown paint	7.5YR 6/4 out 5Y 8/6 glaze
b	F19a-2	404	red; yellow glaze	7.5YR 6/4 out 5Y 8/6 glaze
c	E18a-6	400	red; yellow glaze, spot of green	5YR 5/6 core 5Y 6/6 glaze
d	E19c-6	412	red-brown; yellow glaze, green lines	5YR 5/6 out 5Y 6/6 glaze
e	E18d-12	399	orange; yellow glaze, green design in and out	5YR 6/6 core 5Y 6/6 glaze
f	E18a-14	410	red-brown; yellow glaze, brown and green paint	5YR 6/6 out 5Y 6/6 glaze
g	E18a-7	415	red; yellow glaze, brown paint	5YR 5/6, 6/4 out 5Y 7/4 in
h	E18a-13	413	red; yellow glaze	7.5YR 6/4 out 5Y 7/6 glaze
i	E18a-14	410	red; yellow glaze	5YR 4/4 out 5Y 8/6, 6/6 glaze
j	E19c-5	411	red; yellow glaze	2.5YR 4/8 out 5Y 8/6 glaze
k	E18d-8	398	red; yellow glaze, brown paint	5YR 5/6 core 7.5YR 6/4 out 5Y 6/6 glaze
l	E18d-10	398	red; green glaze; abundant coarse	2.5YR 4/8
m	E18d-7	398	cream; light green glaze, brown paint	2.5Y 7/4 core 5Y 8/2 out 5Y 6/3 in
n	E18a-14	410	brown; yellow glaze, brown paint	5YR 4/3 out 5Y 7/6 glaze
o	E18c-11	416	orange; yellow glaze, brown paint	5YR 4/6, 3/2 out 5Y 7/6 in
p	E18d-7	398	red-brown; yellow glaze, brown paint	5YR 5/6 out 5Y 8/6, 2.5Y 7/6 glaze
q	E18b-4	401	red; yellow glaze, brown paint	7.5YR 5/4 out 2.5Y 5/4 glaze
r	E18c-13	402	red-brown; yellow glaze, brown paint	5YR 4/6 out 5Y 6/4 glaze

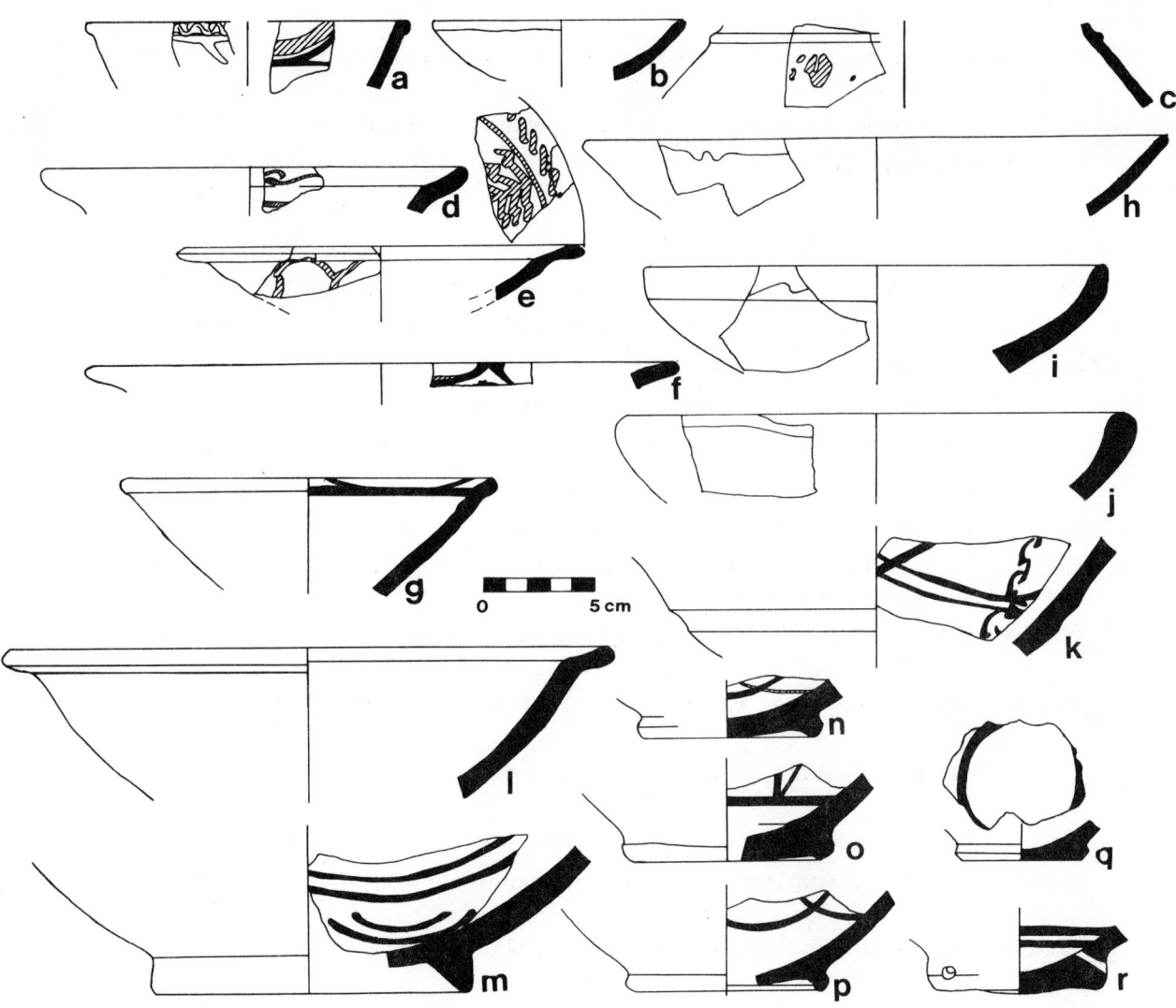

Plate 37: Eastern Area Mustard Wares

Plate 38: Eastern Area, Underglaze Painted Wares, Yellow-Blue Wares, Lamps

	Locus	RN	Description	Munsell
*a	F19a-7	404	red?; black under turquoise glaze	
b	F19a-4	404	cream; black paint under clear glaze in, blue glaze out	10YR 8/2, 7/3
c	E18a-14	410	orange; white slip in and out; purple-black paint under clear glaze with green glaze in	5YR 6/6
d	F19a-5	404	cream; blue and black paint under clear glaze	2.5Y 8/4
e	F19a-4	404	red; white slip; blue paint under clear glaze out	10R 4/8
f	E18d-2	405	red; white slip; blue paint under clear glaze out	10R 4/8
g	E19c-6	412	cream; white slip; blue paint under clear glaze	2.5Y 8/2
h	F19a-4	404	red; white slip; blue paint under clear glaze	10R 4/8
i	F19a-4	404	red; white slip; blue paint under clear glaze	10R 4/8
j	E19c-6	412	cream; black paint under clear glaze	2.5Y 7/4
k	E19c-8	411	cream; black paint under green glaze	2.5Y 8/4
l	E18d-10	398	cream; black paint under turquoise glaze	7.5YR 8/4
m	E18a-14	410	cream; black paint under turquoise glaze	
*n	E18a-10	414	cream; black and blue paint under clear glaze	
o	E18a-10	414	cream-pink; manganese and light blue paint on opaque white glaze	
p	F19a-4	404	buff-red; white slip; black paint under clear glaze	7.5YR 6/6
q	E18c-13	402	buff-orange; white slip; black paint under light and dark green glaze	5YR 5/8
	E18d-12	399		
r	E18a-14	410	cream; dark brown paint under greenish clear glaze out	10YR 8/4
s	E18a-10	414	buff-orange; black paint under dark green glaze out	
t	F19a-4	404	orange; white slip; red-brown paint under clear glaze out	7.5YR 7/4
u	E18d-7	398	red-brown; white slip (partially removed); green glaze	
v	E19c-6	412	red-orange; yellow, blue and green (where mixed) glaze in; common medium and mica	5YR 5/6
w	F19a-4	404	red-orange; yellow, blue and green glaze in; common medium and mica	5YR 5/6
x	E18c-3	417	red; yellow and blue glaze	2.5YR 5/8
y	E19c-7	406	red; yellow, blue and green glaze in	5YR 6/6
z	E18d-12	399	orange; blackened exterior; yellow and mixed blue/green glaze in	5YR 6/4, 6/6
aa	E18c-1	417	red; yellow, blue and green glaze in	5YR 5/8
bb	E18a-3	408	red-brown; light olive green glaze on spout	
cc	F19a-2	124	brown; light green glaze in and out	

*sherd not available to check drawing

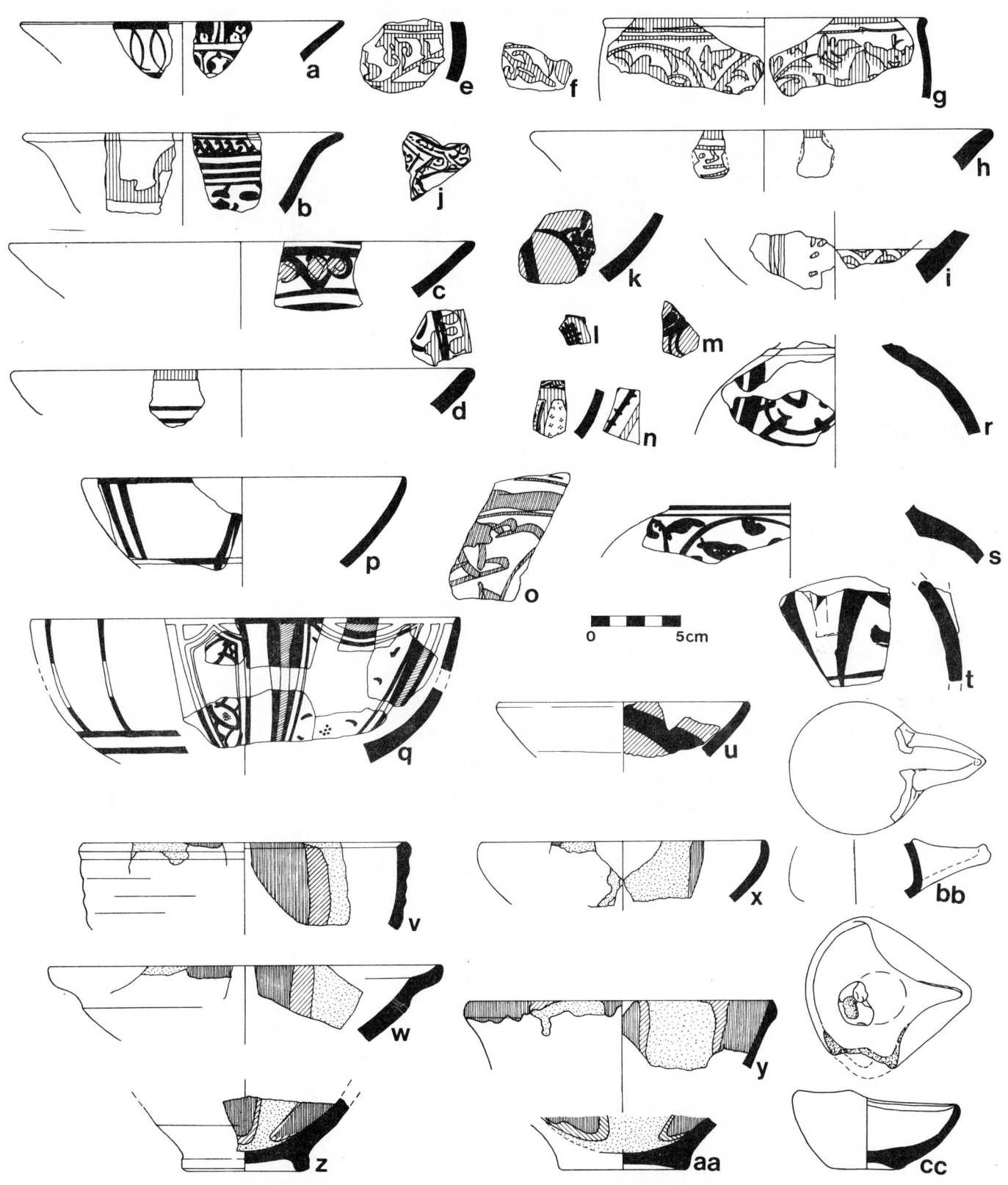

Plate 38: Eastern Area, Underglaze Painted Wares, Yellow-Blue Wares, Lamps

Plate 39: Eastern Area Cream Wares

	Locus	RN	Description	Munsell
a	E19c-7	406	cream	2.5Y 8/2
b	E18c-13	402	cream	2.5Y 8/2
c	E18d	398	cream	5Y 8/2
d	F19a-6	404	cream; incised	10YR 7/3, 6/3 out; 10YR 7/3 in
e	E18c-1	287	cream; moulded	2.5Y 8/2 out; 10YR 7/4 in
f	E18d-10	287	cream; moulded	2.5Y 7/2 out; 7.5YR 5/4 in
g	E18d	287	cream; moulded	2.5Y 7/4 out; 7.5YR 6/4 in
h	E18d	287	cream; moulded	2.5Y 7/2 out; 7.5YR 6/4 in
i	F18a-4	290	cream; moulded	5Y 8/2 out; 10YR 7/2 in
j	E19c-4	411	cream	10YR 8/4 core; 2.5Y 8/2 out and in
k	E18a-3	403	red; cream slip	5YR 6/4 core; 2.5Y 7/4 slip
l	F19a-7	404	red; cream slip	7.5YR 6/4 core; 10YR 7/3 out
m	E18c-1	417	red; cream slip	7.5YR 7/6 core; 7.5YR 7/4 out
n	E18d-8	398	cream; punctate	10YR 8/3
o	E18d-7	398	cream; punctate	5Y 8/2
p	E19c-9	407	cream; punctate	10YR 8/1
q	E18d-11	399	cream; punctate	2.5Y 8/2
r	E18d-4 E18a-3	409 408	cream; punctate	10YR 8/3, 2.5Y 8/2
s	E18d-10	398	cream; incised	2.5Y 8/2
t	E19c-9	407	cream; punctate	2.5Y 8/2 out; 7.5YR 8/4 in
u	E18c-13	402	cream; punctate	10YR 8/2
v	E18d-12	399	cream; punctate	2.5Y 7/2

Plate 39: Eastern Area Cream Wares

Plate 40:   Eastern Area Cream Wares

	Locus	RN	Description	Munsell
a	E18d-3	405	cream-buff; red slip; abundant medium	10YR 7/4 core; 2.5YR 5/6 slip
b	E18a-3	408	buff	2.5Y 7/2
c	E18c-11	416	cream	5Y 8/3
d	E18c-13	402	cream	5Y 8/2
e	E18c-13	402	cream	5YR 7/4 core; 2.5Y 8/2 out
f	E19c-6	412	pink; cream slip; some mica	5YR 7/6; 2.5Y 8/2 slip
g	E18a-4	409	greenish cream	5Y 7/3
h	F18a-4	403	cream	10YR 8/2 out; 2.5Y 8/2 in
i	E18c-11	416	cream	2.5Y 8/2
j	E19c-9	407	light buff	2.5Y 8/2
k	E18a-10	414	cream	2.5Y 8/2
l	E18d-3	405	cream	2.5Y 8/2
m	E19c-4	411	buff	7.5YR 8/6 core; 10YR 8/2, 7/4, 6/4 out
n	E18c-13	462	buff	
o	E18a-14	410	buff; cream slip	2.5Y 8/4 out; 7.5YR 7/6 in
p	E18c-13	402	light buff	2.5Y 8/2
q	E19c-9	407	cream	5Y 8/2
r	E19c-4	411	cream	2.5Y 8/2
s	E18a-5	418	cream	10YR 7/4 core; 10YR 7/3 out and in
t	E19c-7	406	cream	2.5Y 6/4, 7/4, 8/2; 2.5Y 3/2 inner part
u	E18b-4	401	cream; coarse	2.5Y 7/2
v	E19c-4	411	buff	10YR 8/3
w	E19c-3	411	cream	2.5Y 8/2

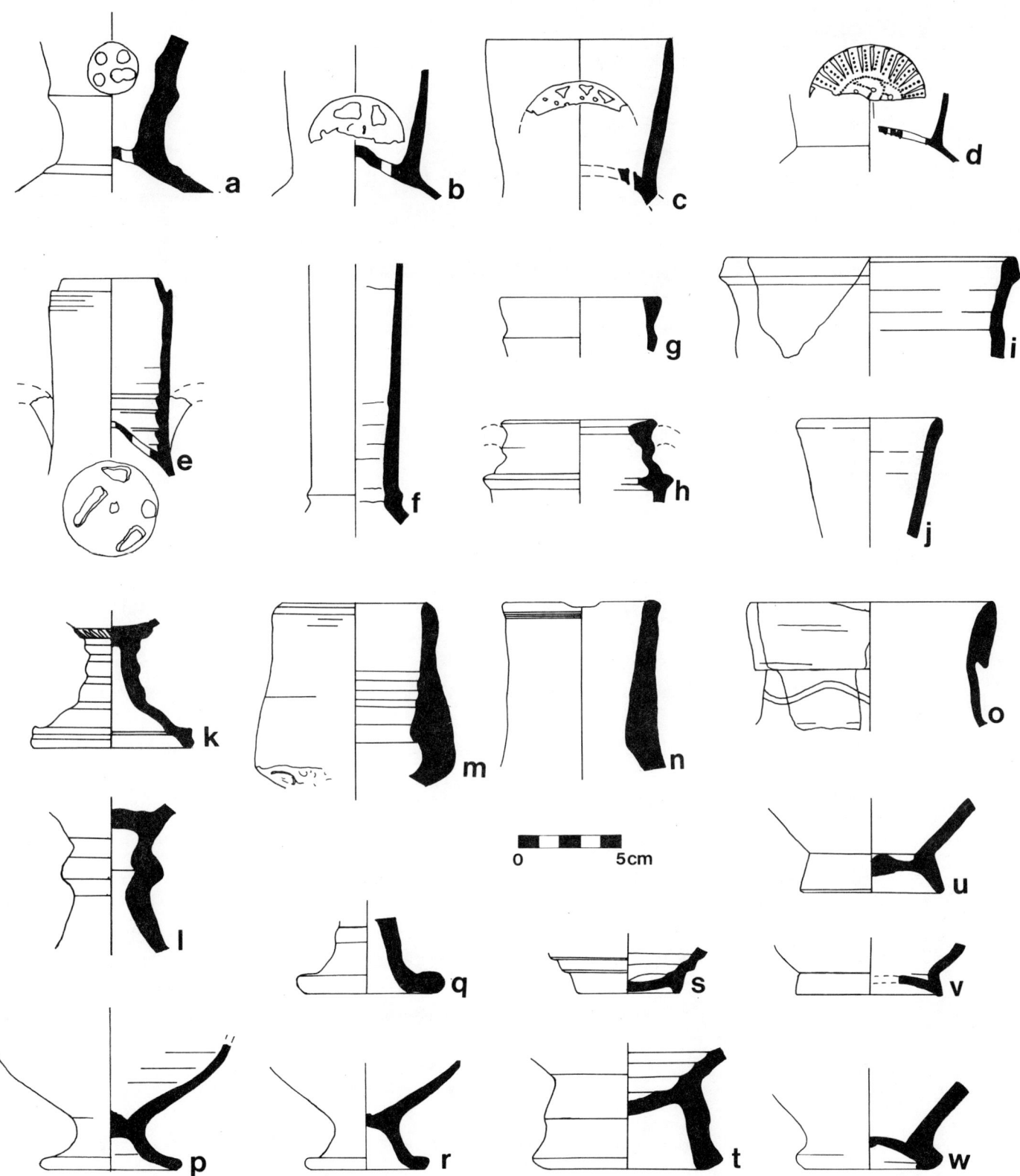

Plate 40: Eastern Area Cream Wares

Plate 41: Eastern Area "African" and Painted Wares

	Locus	RN	Description	Munsell
a	E18a-14	410	brown; rocker and punctate; common coarse	5YR 6/4 core 5YR 6/4, 6/6, 3/2 out 5YR 6/4, 4/4 in
b	E18a-2 E18a-15	413 413	brown-black; abundant coarse white	5YR 5/3 core 5YR 4/1, 4/4 out 5YR 4/1, 4/2 in
c	E18a-4	409	black; burnished; incised and punched design; medium coarse white	2.5Y 2/0, 10YR 5/2 out 2.5Y 2/0 in
d	E18c-1	417	dark red; incised; white paste; mica	
e	E18d-14	399	cream; red-orange slip out; paddle-stamped; common coarse	5YR 7/4 core 5YR 5/4 out 5YR 6/4 in
f	E18a-10	414	buff-cream; red-orange slip out; paddle-stamped; common coarse	7.5YR 8/4 core 2.5YR 6/6, 2.5/0 out 2.5YR 6/6 in
g	E18c-1	417	dark red; vertical burnish; white paste in incising; common coarse	10R 5/6 core 7.5YR 6/2; 10YR 5/6 out 5YR 5/3 in
h	E18d-12	399	buff-cream; orange slip out; bands of brown and red-brown paint in; abundant coarse	7.5YR 7/8; 10YR 8/4 out 5YR 5/8, 3/3; 10YR 7/4 in
i	E18a-5	413	orange; red and black paint; common coarse	5YR 6/6; 2.5YR 4/6, 4/0 5YR 6/6 out
j	E18c-13	402	buff; orange slip; black and red paint; common coarse	5YR 7/6, 6/6, 4/1
*k	E18a-6 E18a-13	400 413	buff; burnished; red, black and cream paint; common medium	7.5YR 6/4 core 5YR 3/2, 3/3, 6/3 out, in
l	E18a-3	408	orange-red; dark brown paint; chaff	2.5YR 5/6 core 2.5YR 5/6; 5YR 3/2 out 2.5YR 5/6 in
*m	E19c-3	411	red-brown; cream slip; black and green paint	
n	E18a-8	413	cream; thick caustic black paint, some traces green paint; fine	2.5Y 7/4, 3/0 out 10YR 8/4 in
o	E18a-3	408	orange-red; red and black paint; common medium	5YR 4/6; 2.5YR 5/6, 3/0 5YR 5/6, 4/6 in out
p	F19a-7	404	cream; grey slip; black paint; common coarse	10YR 8/6 core 10YR 5/1, 5/2, 4/1 out 5YR 5/6, 4/2 in
q	E18a-7	302	cream; brown paint; burnished; abundant coarse	10YR 8/6, 7/4; 10R 3/2 7.5YR 7/6 in out
r	F19a-6	404	red; cream slip; red and dark brown paint; moderate medium	5YR 6/6 core 5YR 7/6, 4/2; 10R 5/6 out 5YR 7/6 in
s	E18b-5	284	red; orange slip out; burnished; red and black paint	5YR 6/4 core, in 5YR 6/6; 10R 5/6; 5YR 3/1 out

continued on plate 43

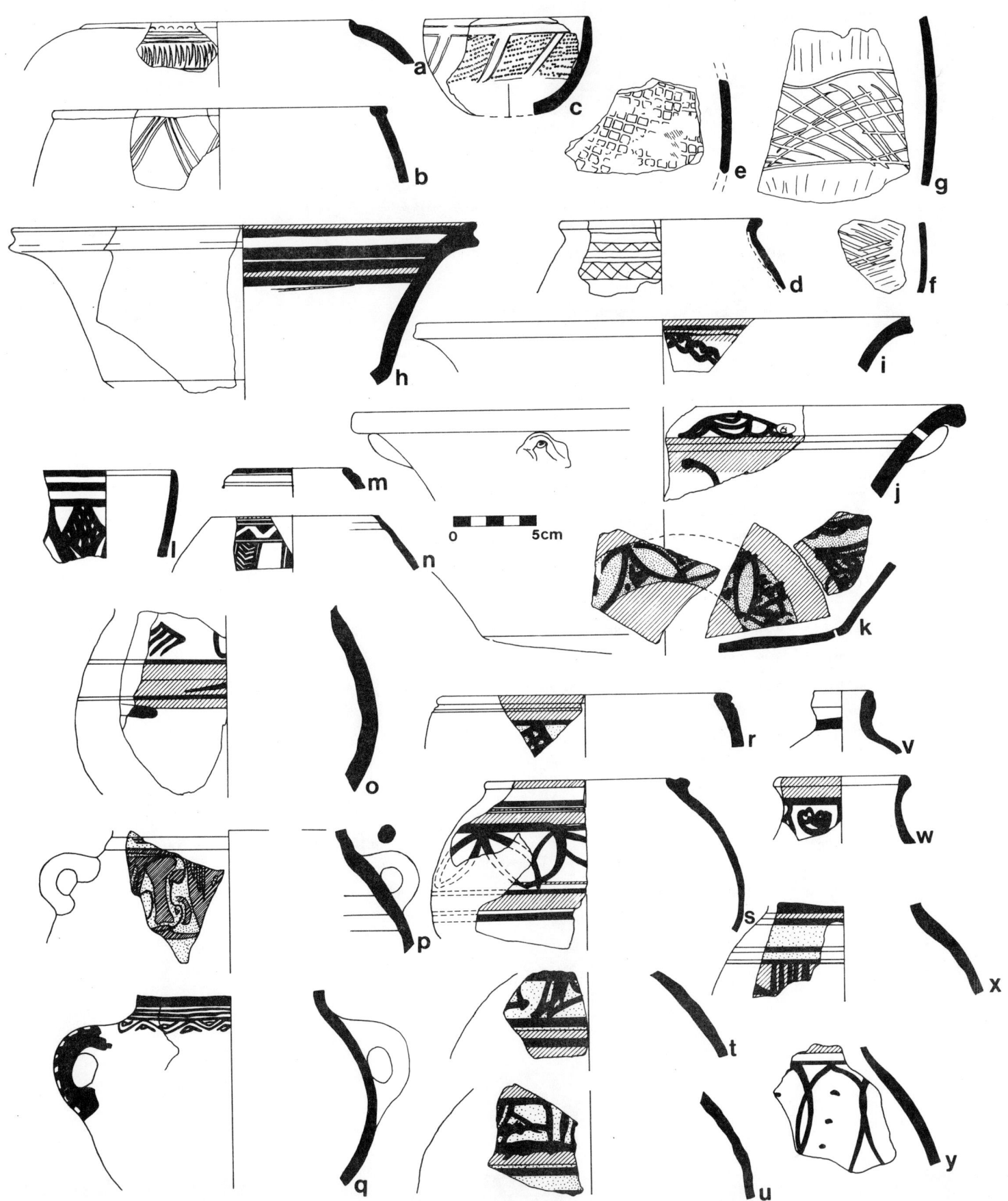

Plate 41: Eastern Area "African" and Painted Wares

Plate 42:   Eastern Area, Unglazed Bowls

	Locus	RN	Description	Munsell
a	E19c-3	411	buff; burned black in and out; black residue in; very shallow indentations; rim warped; coarse, chaff; diameter approximate	
b	F18a-4	403	red; red-brown slip; burnished	
c	E19c-6	412	red-orange; white grits	
d	E18a-14	410	red-orange; moderate medium	
e	E19c-3	411	brown; blackened in and out; moderate medium	
f	E19c-3	411	brown; smudged in and out; common coarse	
g	E18a-1	413	red-brown; moderate medium	
h	E18c-13	402	red-orange; coarse, porous, chaff	
i	E18a-14	410	red-brown; moderate medium	
j	E19c-6	412	brown; beige slip, slightly striated; chaff and mica	10YR 7/3, 6/2, 6/3
k	E18d-1	405	buff; cream slip; moderate medium and chaff	
l	E18a-5	413	orange; moderate medium and mica	
m	E18a-5	413	orange-red; moderate medium	
n	E18d-3	405	red-brown; abundant medium	
o	F19a-7	404	red-brown; abundant medium and mica	
p	E18a-16	413	orange-brown; mottled burnish on rim; abundant medium	
q	E18a-10	414	orange; rim warped; mica; diameter varies from 30-34 cm.	5YR 6/4, 5/4
r	E18c-11	416	buff; chaff and some sand	10YR 7/3, 7/4
s	E18a-3	408	red-orange; common coarse and chaff	
t	E19c-9	407	brown, dark core; organic residue in and out; cut hole in base; soft, crumbly	5YR 4/6
u	E19c-4	411	red-brown; cream slip out; medium coarse	

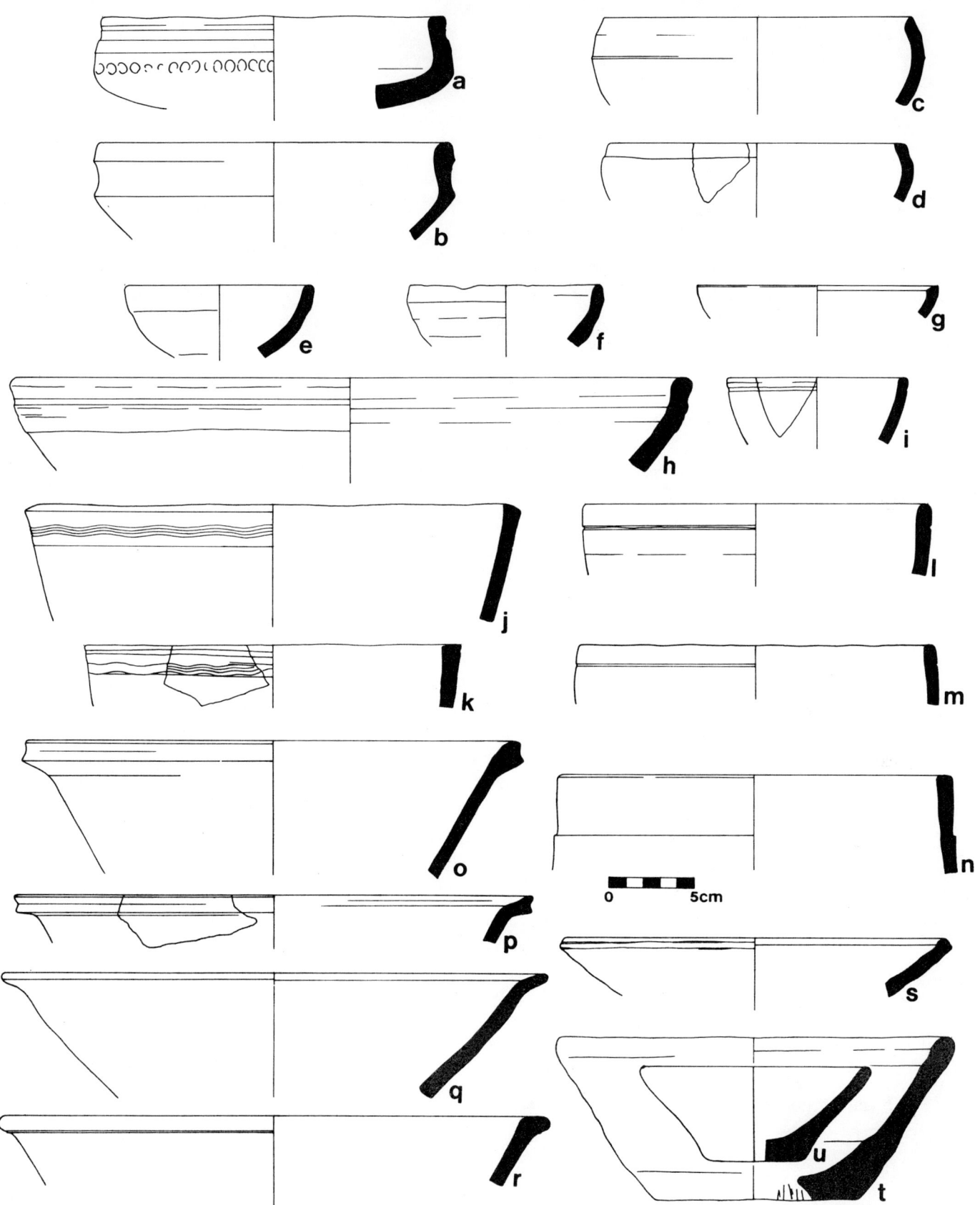

Plate 42: Eastern Area, Unglazed Bowls

Plate 43: Eastern Area Large Unglazed Bowls

	Locus	RN	Description	Munsell
a	E19c-6	412	pinkish; shallow combing; mica and chaff	7.5YR 6/4
b	E18c-11	416	pinkish buff; cream slip in and out; comb punched and lightly dragged in; mica and chaff	7.5YR 7/4, 6/4
*c	F19a-7	404	brown; light brown slip	
d	F19a-4	456	dark red; pot 3	2.5YR 5/8
e	E18a-7	419	red; orange slip out; chaff	2.5YR 5/6, 5/8
f	E19c-3	411	orange; cream slip in and out; grit	10YR 8/3, 8/4, 7/3, 7/4
g	E18d-15	310	orange; red slip in; coarse, chaff	5YR 7/6, 6/6, 6/8
h	E18a-7	415	orange; cord marks; coarse, porous, chaff	2.5YR 5/6, 5/8
i	E19c-3	411	orange, light grey core; cord-impressed design; rim uneven, drill/mend holes; chaff	5YR 5/2 core 5YR 4/6 out 5YR 5/3 in
j	E18a-4	409	brown	7.5YR 5/4, 6/4
k	E18d-14	399	brown; black smudges in and out; coarse	
l	E18a-4	452	red-brown; purple-brown slip out; used as oven; pot A, 44 cm. diameter	
m	E18a-14	410	light brown; chaff and some sand	5YR 6/3

* sherd not available to check drawing

Plate 41: Continued

	Locus	RN	Description	Munsell
t	E18a-16	413	red-brown; cream slip; red and black paint; moderate medium	5YR 6/6 core 2.5YR 4/6, 6/6, 2.5/2 out 2.5YR 4/0 in
u	F19a-7	404	orange; cream slip; red and dark brown paint	5YR 6/6, 3/2 out 5YR 5/6 in
*v	E19c-3	411	red; purple paint	
w	E18a-3	408	tan-brown; red, cream, and black paint; moderate medium	5YR 7/6 core 5YR 4/3, 6/6, 3/1 out 5YR 5/3 in
x	E18a-3	408	tan and red; cream slip; red and black paint; common medium	
y	E18d-8	398	red-brown; orange slip; red and black paint; burnished; common medium	5YR 7/6, 6/4, 3/1 out 5YR 5/3, 2.5/2 in

* sherd not available to check drawing

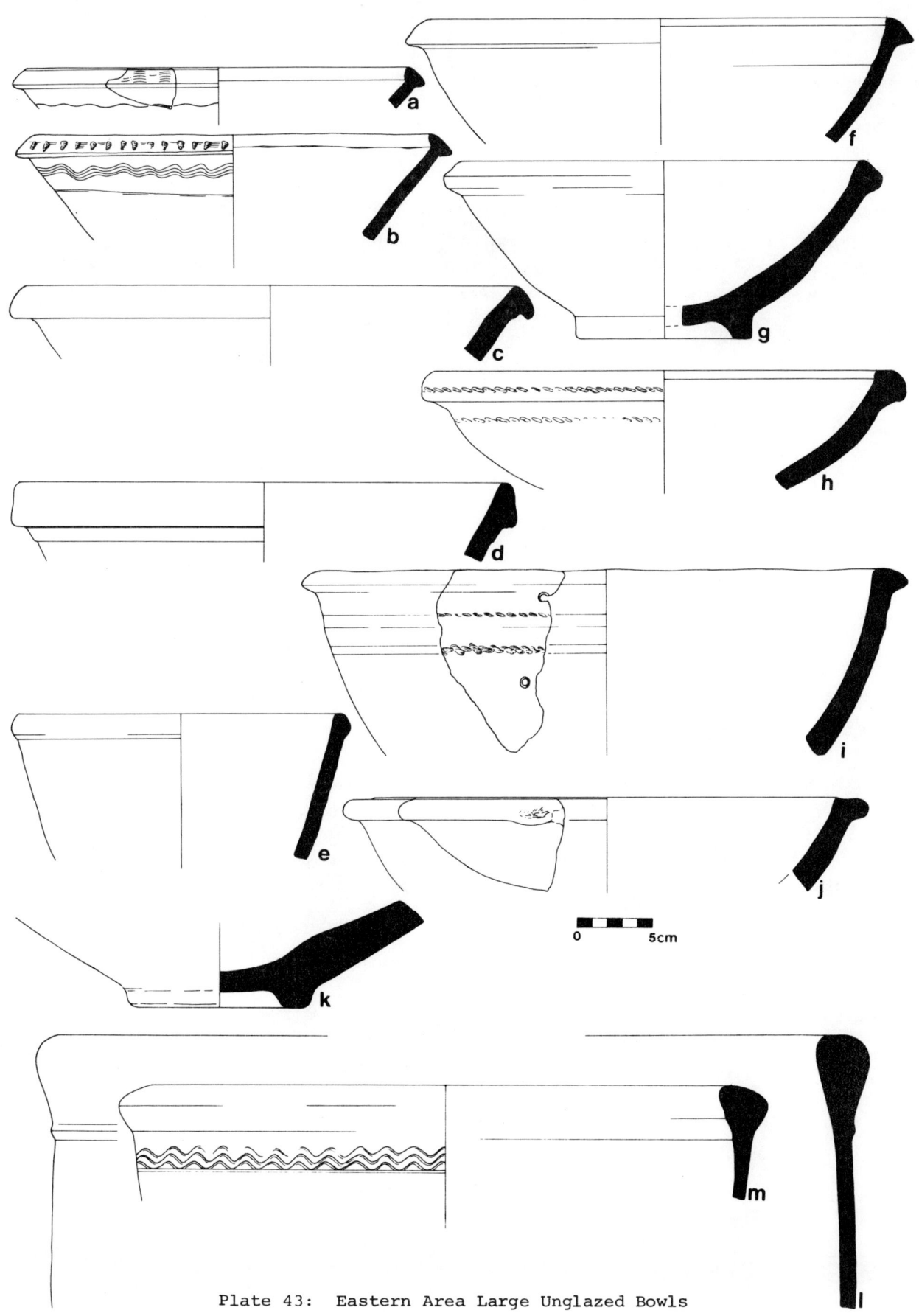

Plate 43: Eastern Area Large Unglazed Bowls

Plate 44: Eastern Area Glazed Cooking Wares and Storage Jars

	Locus	RN	Description	Munsell	
a	E18c-11	416	grey-buff; olive glaze in; black residue out, some in	10YR 3/1 10YR 4/6 glaze	
b	E18a-14	410	pink; olive glaze in and lip; blackened out; hard-fired	7.5R 2.5/0 10YR 3/4 glaze	
c	E19c-9	403	orange and grey; olive glaze in and slopped over rim, brown speckles; blackened out; rim mashed down; hard-fired	7.5YR 2/0 2.5Y 5/4 glaze	
d	E18a-10	414	orange-brown; olive glaze out and over lip; hard-fired	2.5Y 4/4	
e	E18b-5	401	orange; common medium		
f	E19c-5	411	cream; moderate medium		
g	E18a-13	413	red-orange; moderate medium		
h	E18a-3	408	orange; brown slip out		
i	F19a-7	404	buff; red slip out and slopped in; sand and chaff		
j	E18a-7	415	red-brown; olive glaze in; moderate medium		
k	E18a-16	413	buff; blackened; moderate medium		
l	E19c-3	411	light grey; olive glaze in, over rim, dribbles; sand	7.5YR 6/2 10YR 3/2 glaze	
m	E18a-7	415	orange; olive glaze in and lip; hard-fired	5YR 6/4	
n	E18a-11	418	grey stoneware; olive glaze in, spot on rim; blackened out	5YR 3/1 7.5YR 4/6 glaze	
o	E19c-6 F19a-6	412 404	grey-orange; olive glaze in, brown speckles; grey to blackish out; hard-fired	10YR 4/1 2.5Y 4/4 glaze	
p	E18a-5 E18a-13	413 413	buff; olive glaze in, very thin towards bottom, splashes over rim; blackened out	5Y 2.5/1 2.5Y 4/4 glaze	
q	E18a-3	408	orange-grey; olive glaze in, very thin towards bottom, slops over rim and down side, splash on scalloped decoration; blackened out; hard-fired	5YR 3/1 7.5YR 4/6 glaze	
r	E18a-13	414	buff; olive glaze in; brown out, blackened in spots	10YR 3/2 2.5Y 4/4 glaze	
s	E18a-3	408	grey stoneware; olive glaze out; grit; plaster plug sealed with very sandy bitumen	10YR 3/2 10YR 3/3, 3/4, 3/6 glaze	
t	E19c-7	406	grey stoneware; olive glaze out, brown and streaky in	2.5Y 3/2	
u	E18c-7	417	grey stoneware; olive glaze out, blackened; grit	10YR 3/2	

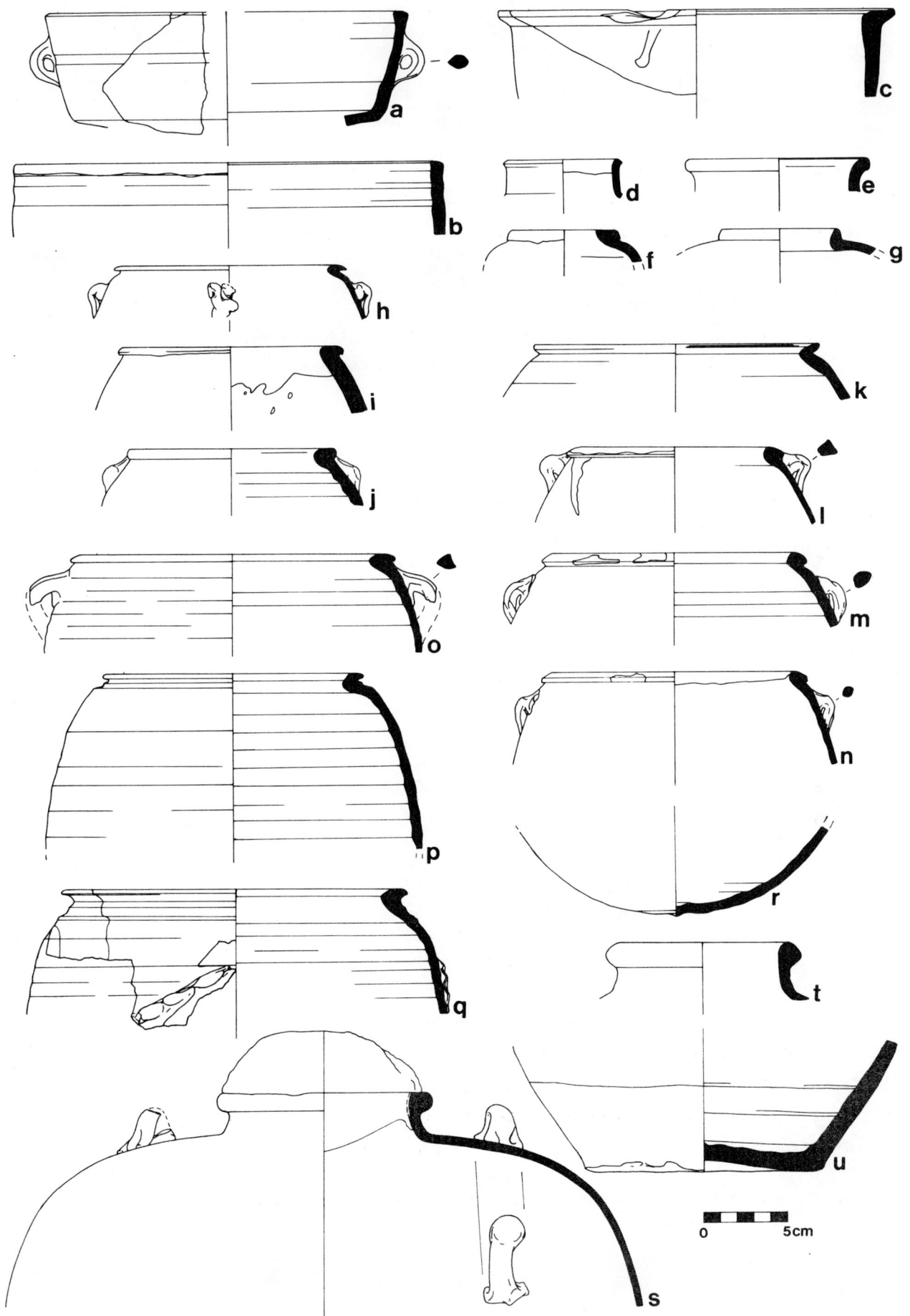

Plate 44: Eastern Area Glazed Cooking Wares and Storage Jars

Plate 45: Eastern Area Purple Wares

	Locus	RN	Description	Munsell
a	E18c-2	417	brown-black; burnished out; moderate coarse	7.5YR 4/4 core 2.5YR 2.5/0 out 2.5YR 3/4 in
b	E18a-10	414	black-brown; burnished	
c	E19c-7	406	grey-brown; blackened in and out; burnished	
d	E18a-15	413	cream; red-brown wash; moderate medium	10YR 8/2 2.5YR 4/8 wash
e	E19c-4	407	grey-brown; abundant coarse	
f	E18a-3	408	red; light burnish, blackened out; common coarse	7.5YR 5/4 core 5YR 5/4, 3/1, 7/3
g	E18a-11	416	grey; blackened, burnished body and rim	
h	E18a-7	415	black	7.5YR 2/0, 3/0
i	E19c-6	412	black	7.5YR 2/0
j	E19c-6	412	red-brown; blackened out; light burnish; moderate medium	
k	E19c-2	411	red-brown; blackened in and out; moderate medium	5YR 5/3, 5/4
l	E18a-4	409	black; burnished; moderate medium	2.5Y 3/2 core 2.5Y 2/0, 10YR 3/1
m	E19c-6	412	black	
n	E18c-13	402	black; burnished	2.5Y 2/0
o	E18d-7	398	brown	5YR 6/3
p	E18a-2	413	red-brown; common coarse	2.5YR 4/6
q	E18c-13	402	black	7.5R 3/0
r	E18d-11	399	buff; blackened out; moderate medium	2.5YR 2/0 out 7.5YR 6/4
s	E18a-1	413	red, grey core; abundant medium	
t	E18c-5	417	black; burnished; moderate medium	7.5YR 2/0, 3/0
u	E18d-10	398	black; mica and chaff(?)	
v	E18d-14	399	red; common medium and chaff	
w	E18d-14	399	red-brown; blackened in	2.5YR 4/6
x	E18c-5	417	black; burnished on ridges; coarse	
y	E18d-7	398	black; partly burnished; mica	
z	E18d-3	405	grey; buff slip out)?); blackened in	10YR 5/3 out 10YR 4/2 in
aa	E18a-4	400	red-brown; blackened out; burnished in; common medium	

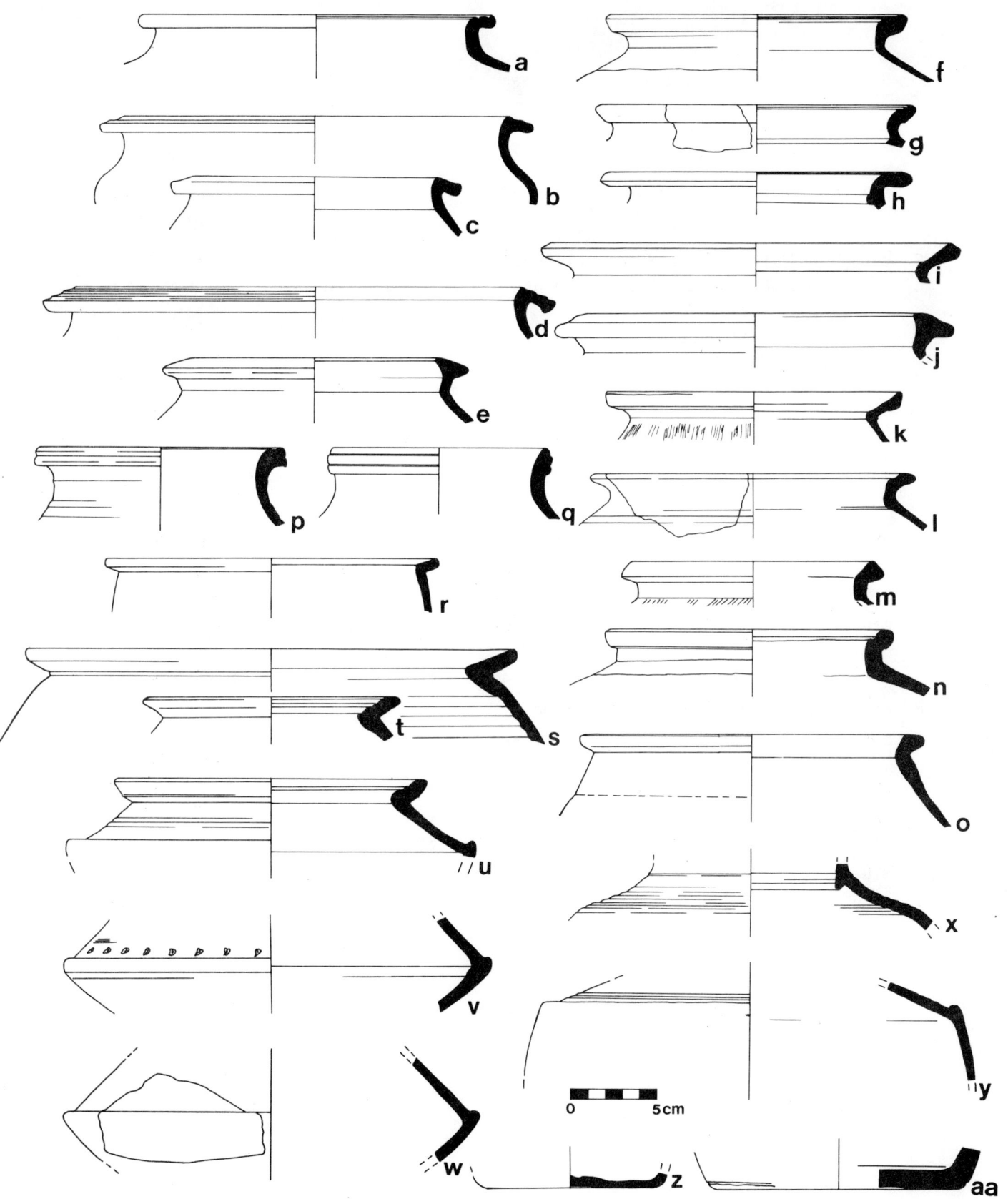

Plate 45: Eastern Area Purple Wares

Plate 46:   Eastern Area, Neckless Jars

	Locus	RN	Description	Munsell
a	E19c-4	411	brown; blackened in and out; chaff	2.5YR 4/6, 3/6
b	E18a-15	413	orange; sand	2.5YR 5/6; 7.5YR 6/4
c	E18a-4	409	red-brown; red slip in and out; coarse	2.5YR 5/6
d	E19c-3	407	orange out; red-brown and black in; grit and chaff; coarse	5YR 4/6, 5/6
e	E18a-1	416	buff; traces of orange-red slip out; moderate medium	7.5YR 6/4 core, in 5YR 7/6, 10YR 8/3 out
f	E18a-2 E18a-16	413 413	cream; brown slip in and out; common medium	10YR 6/4 core 7.5YR 4/2 slip
g	E18c-11	416	orange; cream slip out; moderate medium	5YR 5/6 7.5YR 7/4 slip
h	E19c-6	412	brown; chaff	10YR 6/4 out 5YR 5/4
i	E18a-4	409	tan-brown; moderate medium and chaff	7.5YR 6/4
j	E19c-3	411	buff; cream slip out; common medium and chaff	7.5YR 6/4 10YR 7/4 slip
k	E18c-11	410	light brown; cream slip out; mica and chaff	5YR 6/4 10YR 7/3, 7/4 slip
l	E18d-7	398	red-brown; common coarse and chaff	2.5YR 4/8 core
m	E18d-7	398	orange; moderate medium	5YR 7/6
n	E19c-6	412	orange; buff out; chaff and mica	5YR 6/6 core, in 7.5YR 7/4 out
o	F19a-7	404	red	2.5YR 5/8 5YR 5/6 in, out
p	E19c-6	412	red-orange; common coarse and chaff	5YR 5/6
q	E18a-4	452	red-grey surface out; grit; pot 2	
r	E18c-11	416	red-orange; chaff	2.5YR 5/6, 5/8

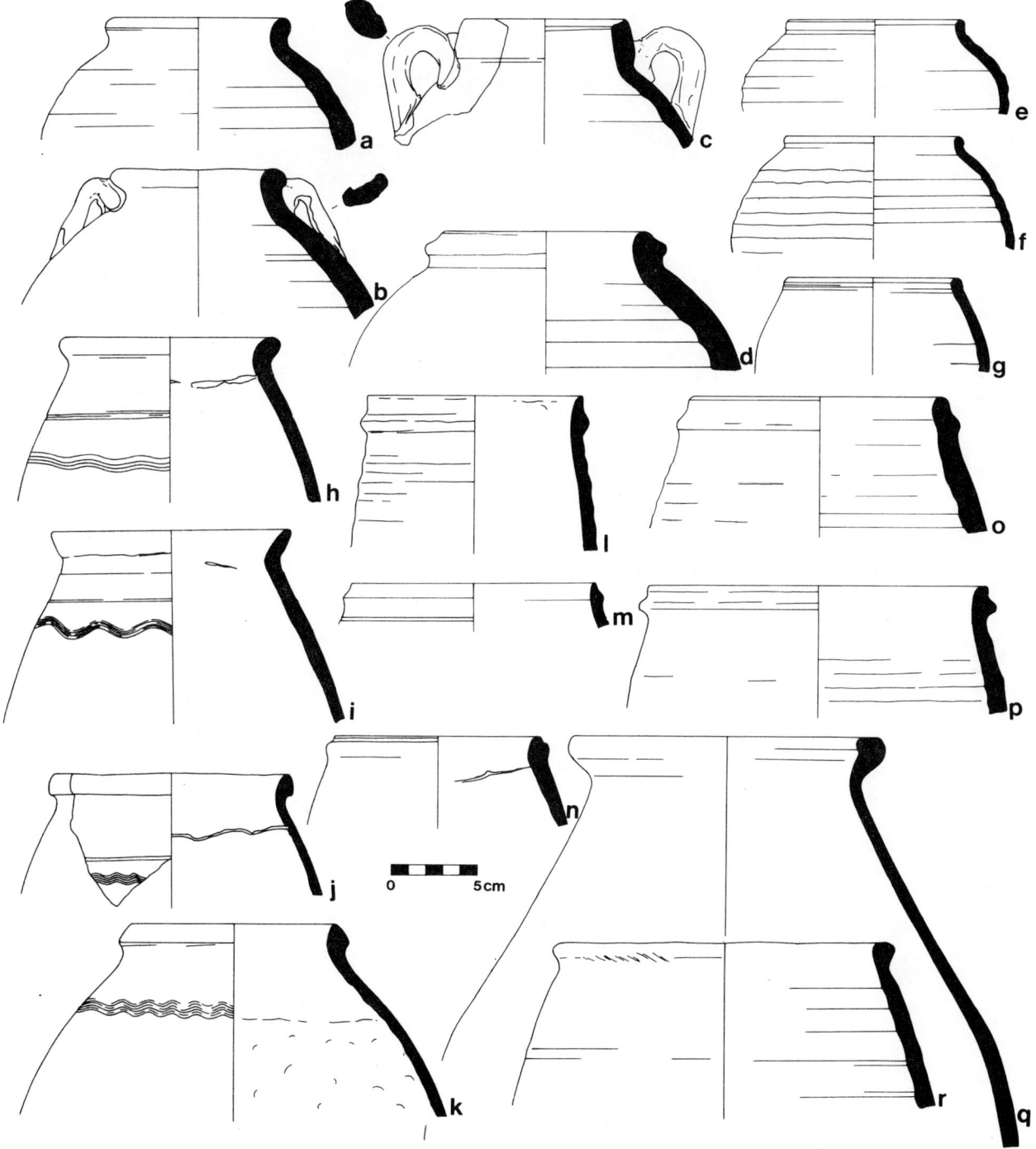

Plate 46: Eastern Area, Neckless Jars

Plate 47: Eastern Area, Jars and Bottles

	Locus	RN	Description	Munsell
a	E18c-11	416	orange; blackened in; coarse	5YR 5/4
b	E18a-14	410	light buff	10YR 7/4
c	E18c-9	469	red; cream slip out; abundant medium; warped and irregular	
d	E18c-2	411	brown; common coarse and chaff	5YR 3/2, 3/3
e	E18a-10	414	dark grey, brown top layer; black in, brown out; hard-fired	10YR 4/2
f	E18d-7	398	orange; cream slip; moderate coarse	2.5YR 5/6 core 7.5YR 7/4, 7/6 slip
g	E19c-2	411	cream; red-brown slip in and out; common medium	7.5YR 7/6 core 7.5YR 4/2 out 5YR 6/6 in
h	E19c-6	412	cream-buff; green glaze in	
i	E18c-13	402	greyish buff; bitumen stain out; chaff	10YR 7/3, 6/3 out 10YR 6/4 in
j	E18d-14	399	orange; traces cream slip out; bitumen in; blotches out rim and shoulder	
k	E18a-14	410	red-brown	2.5YR 5/6, 6/6
l	E18d-8	424	orange; bitumen in	
m	E18c-6	433	brown; red-brown slip; blackened out; FN 2	
n	E19c-3	411	red-brown; organic and soot smears in and out; large white grits; crudely made	2.5YR 4/4
o	E18a-14	439	buff; cream slip in; sand and some mica	2.5Y 8/2 out 10YR 7/4 in

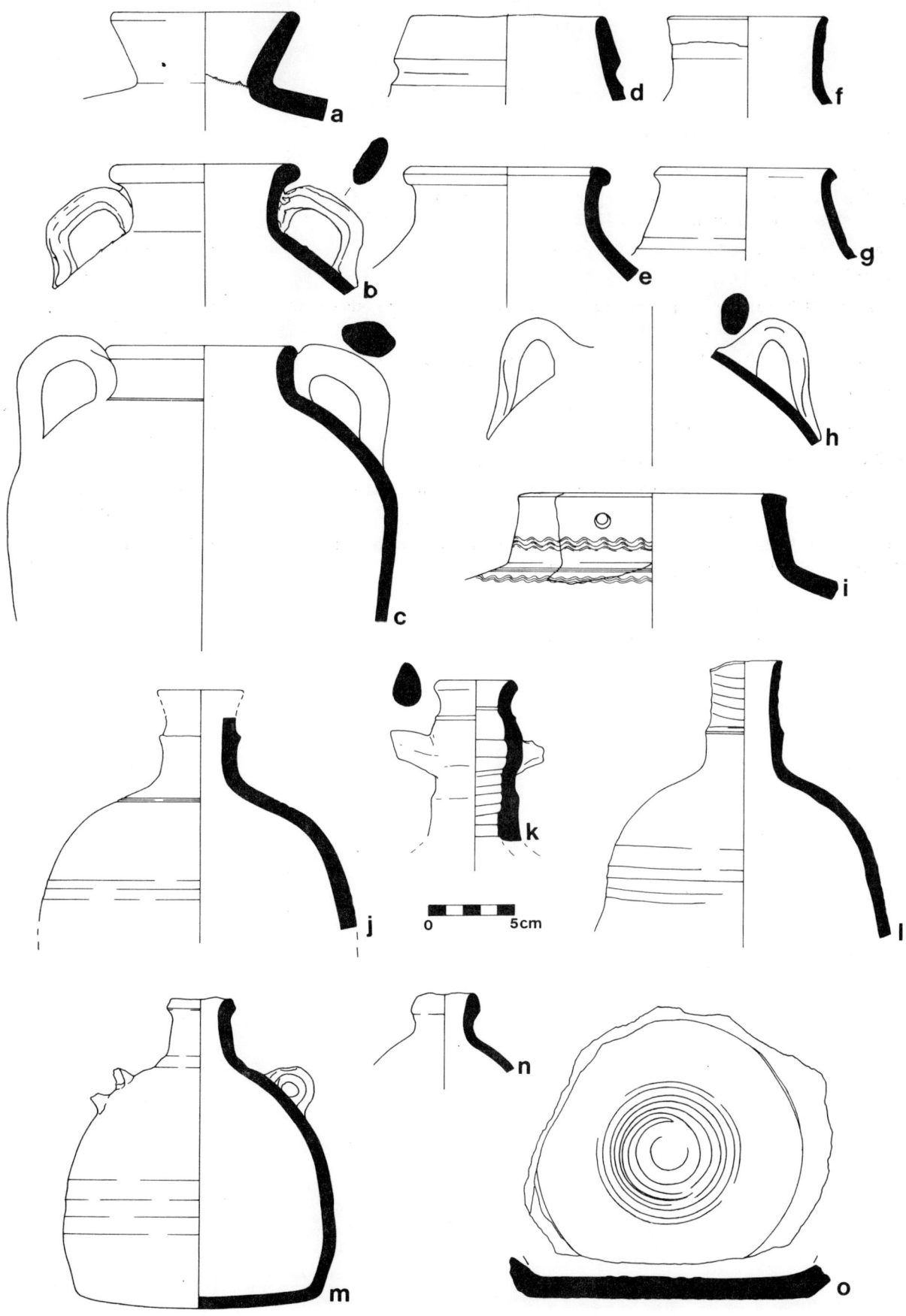

Plate 47: Eastern Area, Jars and Bottles

Plate 48: Eastern Area, Storage Jars

	Locus	RN	Description	Munsell
a	E18d-8	430	brown; black slip out; streak-burnished out; medium sand and chaff	
b	F18a-5	403	red-brown; cream slip	7.5YR 7/4, 7/6 core
	F18a-3	403		10YR 7/4, 6/4, 6/2 out
c	E18a-3	462	red-brown; abundant medium and chaff; used as hearth, burnt lower edge	5YR 3/4
d	E18a-4	409	red-orange; sandy, friable; pot B	
e	E18a-6	400	red	2.5YR 5/6
f	E18a-4	452	cream; pot 2	10YR 6/4
*g	F19a-5	404	red; cream slip	
h	E18c-6	417	red; cream slip out; black residue out; blackened in	2.5YR 5/6 core 7.5YR 6/4 slip
i	E18a-7	415	red-brown; mica and chaff; neck varies in thickness; finger indentations in	2.5YR 4/2
	E18a-7/11	461		

*sherd not available to check drawing

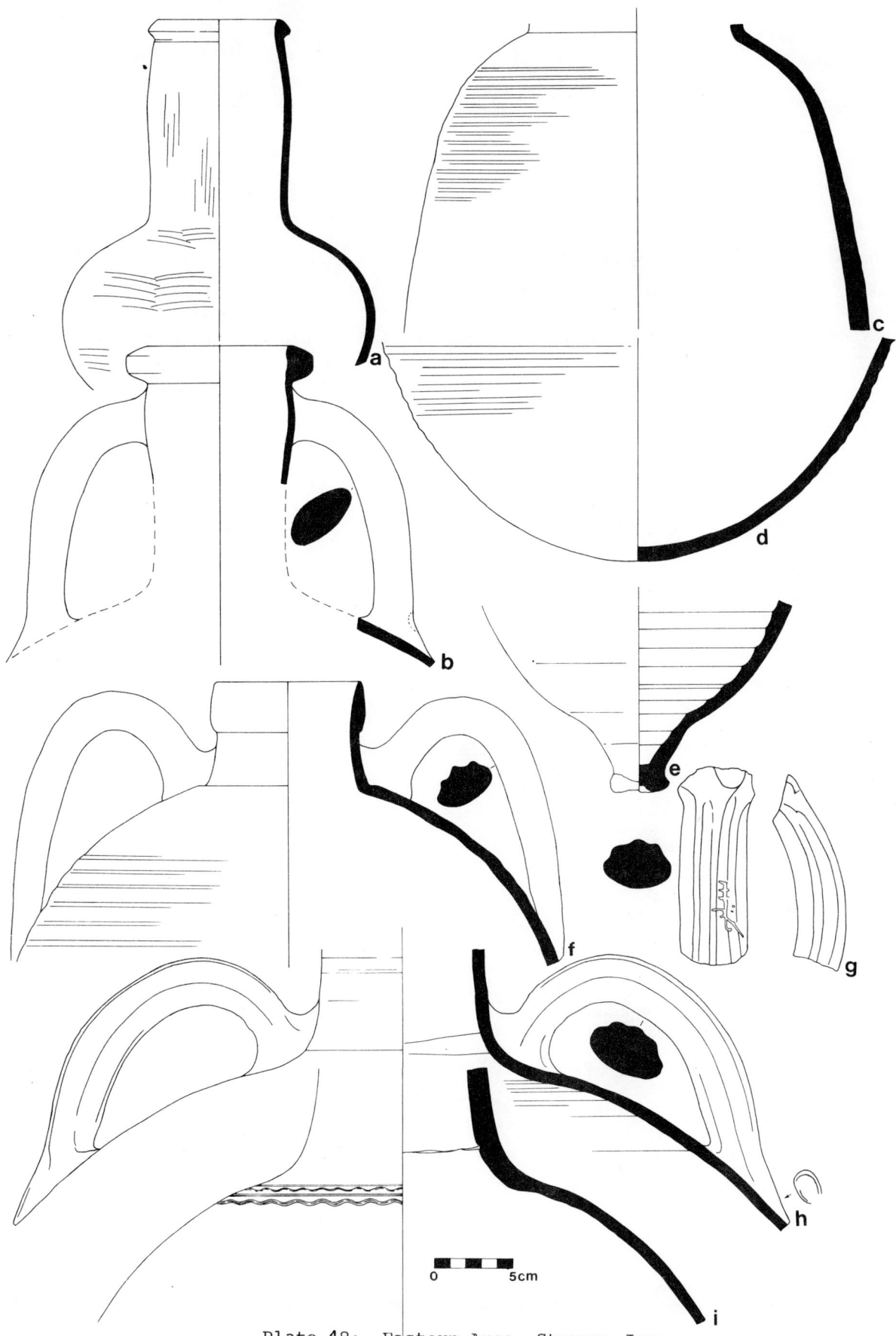

Plate 48: Eastern Area, Storage Jars

Plate 49: Eastern Area, Bases and Unusual Forms

	Locus	RN	Description	Munsell
a	E18a-2	413	orange; moderate medium	2.5YR 5/6
b	E18b-3	401	brownish cream	10YR 6/4
c	E18b-3	401	buff; bitumen coating in	5YR 6/6 core 7.5YR 4/6 out 7.5YR 4/4 in
d	surf	663	red; blackened; common coarse and chaff	7.5YR 4/2 out 5YR 4/4, 3/1
e	E18d-6	398	red	2.5YR 4/6
f	E18a-14	276	black	
g	E18d-14	399	brown; black in and out	10YR 6/3 out 10YR 3/2 in
h	F18a-5	403	orange-pink; yellowish surface; black paint on tip; black smudges	5YR 7/4 core 10YR 8/6, 7.5YR 7/8 surf 2.5YR 3/2 paint
i	E18d-7	398	grey-black stoneware	
j	E18a-3	295	buff; grey slip out; punctate	
k	E18c-13	402		
l	E18b-2	401	grey; dark purple glaze out; dense	
m	E18d-12	421	orange; traces cream slip out; brown glaze in	5YR 4/4
n	F18a-5	403	red-brown; bitumen residue in	
o	E19c-7	406	red-brown; blackened out; coarse sandy?	
p	E18a-3	408	brown; blackened in; coarse	
q	E18c-13	402	buff to light orange; much sand	5YR 7/6, 6/6
r	E18a-14	410	red-brown	2.5YR 6/6
s	E18a-8	408	orange; bitumen in	
t	E18b-3	401	light brown; cream slip out; black (burn?) spot in	
u	E18a-3	408	buff; mica and sand	
v	E19c-9	407	light pinkish buff; cream slip out; black on base in; sand and some mica	
w	E18d-14	399	buff; blackened in	
x	E18a-4	409	brown; cream slip out; thick encrustation yellow-brown glaze in; black residue in	
y	E18a-13	413	brown; blackened in and half of out; coarse	
z	E18a-3	408	brown; coarse; chaff	

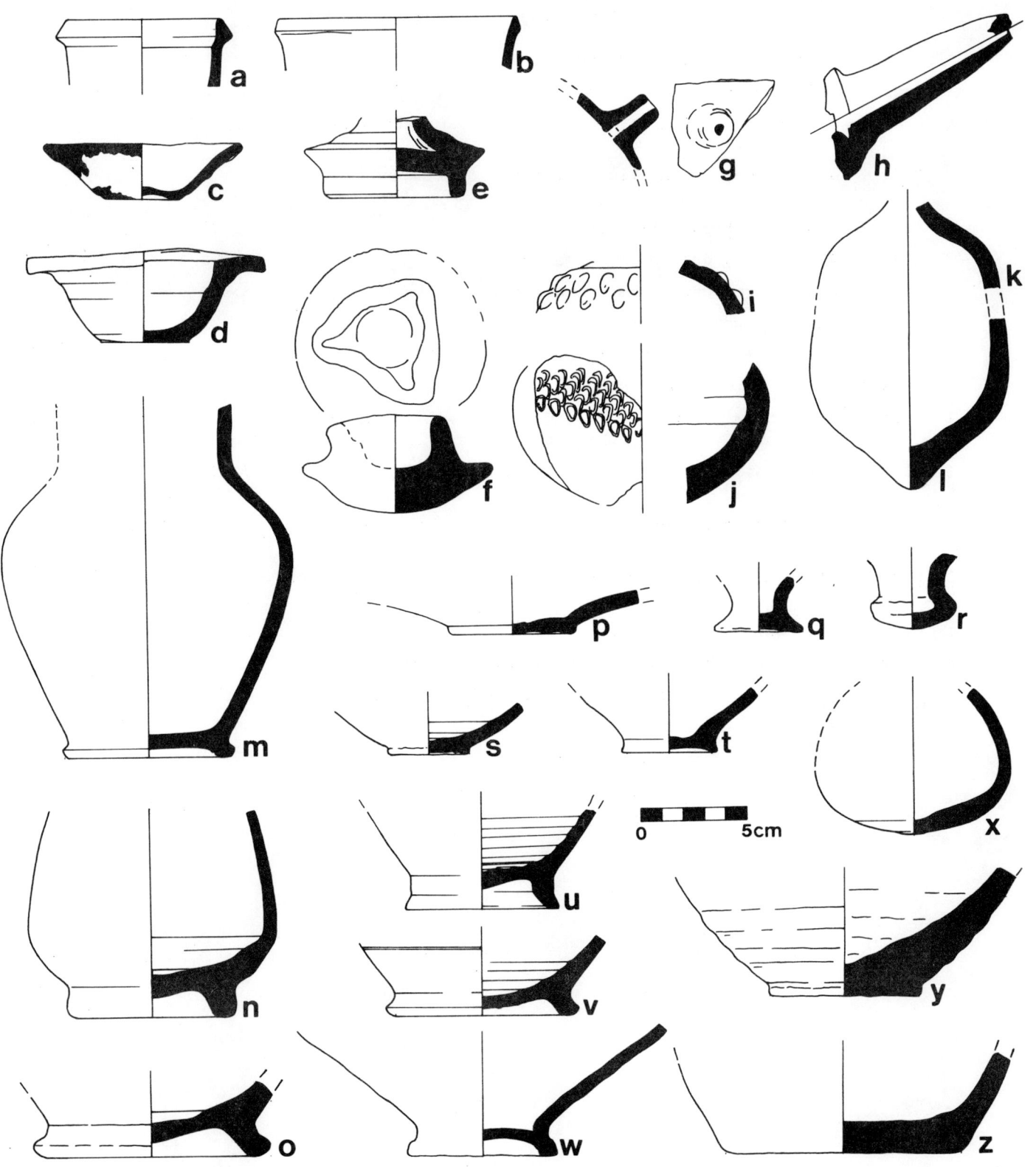

Plate 49: Eastern Area, Bases and Unusual Forms

Plate 50:   Eastern Area Kegs and Unusual Forms

	Locus	RN	Description	Munsell
a	E18d-2 E18c-5	405 411	cream; buff slip; red paint on rim; abundant medium	10YR 7/3, 8/4
b	E18a-4	409	orange; cream slip out; black on rim and dot below	
c	E18d-7	398	buff; brown slip out; gritty	7.5YR 5/4
d	E18a-4	409	orange, grey core; cream slip out	5YR 6/3, 6/4
e	E18a-2	413	orange, grey core; common medium	2.5YR 5/4, 5/6
f	E18a-10	416	red; common coarse	2.5YR 4/8
g	E19c-3	411	red-orange; burnt in and out; crumbly	2.5YR 4/8
h	E18a-4	409	red-brown; blackened in	
i	E18c-13	407	brown; brown slip in and out; rim blackened; coarse, crumbly, white grits	
j	E19c-8	411	cream; grey slip out; abundant medium	7.5YR 8/4 2.5Y 5/2 slip
k	E18d-7	398	buff-tan; orange slip out (now brown); sand; fine	
l	E19c-6	412	orange, grey core; buff slip out; gouges in neck	5YR 5/3 10YR 7/4 slip
m	F18a-3	403	red; cream slip out	10YR 7/4
n	E18c-3	432	brown; bitumen encrustation and blackened out	
o	E18a-4	409	orange; cream slip; very crudely finished; small spout	7.5YR 6/4 7.5YR 7/4 slip
p	E18d-11	399	orange; sand	5YR 6/6

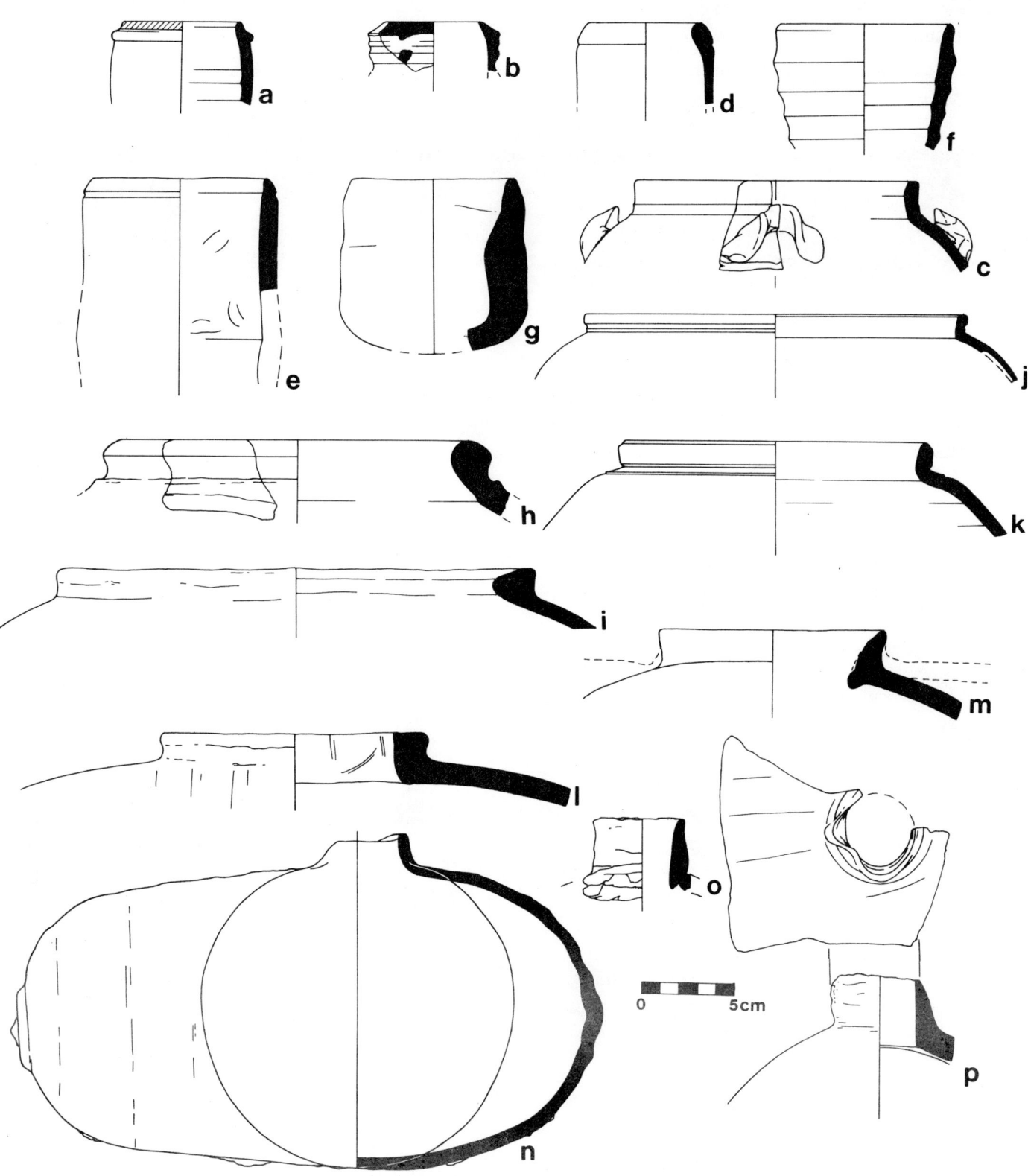

Plate 50: Eastern Area Kegs and Unusual Forms

Plate 51: Central Building A, Islamic Ceramics

	Locus	RN	Description	Munsell
a	G8b-1	328	cream; olive green glaze, brown paint on rim; common coarse sand	10YR 7/4
b	G8b-5	328	red; yellow glaze, green traces; moderate coarse sand	5YR 5/6
c	G8b-18	328	light red-buff; yellowish green glaze in and out; moderate medium sand	5YR 6/6
d	G9a-1	333	red; light yellow glaze, brown paint; moderate medium sand	5YR 6/6 core 2.5Y 6/4 glaze 2.5YR 2.5/4 paint
e	G8b-18	328	red; yellow glaze, green paint; moderate medium sand	7.5YR 6/4 core 10YR 7/3 out
f	G8b-5	328	cream; light bluish white glaze out and in; frit	10YR 8/6
g	G8b-5	328	cream; light bluish white glaze in and out; frit	
h	G8b-5	328	red-purple; blackened in; abundant coarse sand	2.5YR 5/6 out 2.5YR 2.5/0, 3/4 in
i	G8b-5	328	red; clear glaze out and rim; moderate medium sand	2.5YR 4/8 5YR 7/3 glaze
j	G9a-1	333	cream; green glaze, sgraffiato; frit	2.5Y 8/4
k	G9a-1	333	grey-brown; chocolate brown glaze out; common coarse white sand	7.5YR 6/4 core 7.5YR 3/0 out 2.5Y 5/2 in
l	G8b-5	328	cream; green and red glaze; moderate medium sand	10YR 7/4
m	G8b-5	328	red; dark olive green glaze in and out; moderate medium sand	7.5YR 7/4, 7/6 5Y 4/4 glaze
n	G9a-1	333	cream; common coarse sand	2.5Y 8/2
o	G8b-5	328	cream; common coarse sand	2.5Y 8/2
p	G8b-5	328	cream; resin in and rim; moderate coarse sand	2.5Y 8/2
q	G8b-5	328	grey, black core; red slip shoulder, rim, neck in; common coarse white sand	2.5YR 2.5/0 core 2.5YR 4/2, 4/4 out 2.5YR 3/6, 5/4 in
r	G8b-5	289	greenish cream; moderate coarse sand	5Y 8/3
s	G8b-19	328	red-orange; cream slip out; resin in and rim; moderate medium sand	2.5YR 6/6 core 10YR 7/4 out 5YR 2.5/1 in
t	G9a-1	286	red; white paint; common medium sand	5YR 6/6, 7.5YR 8/4 out 2.5YR 5/6 in

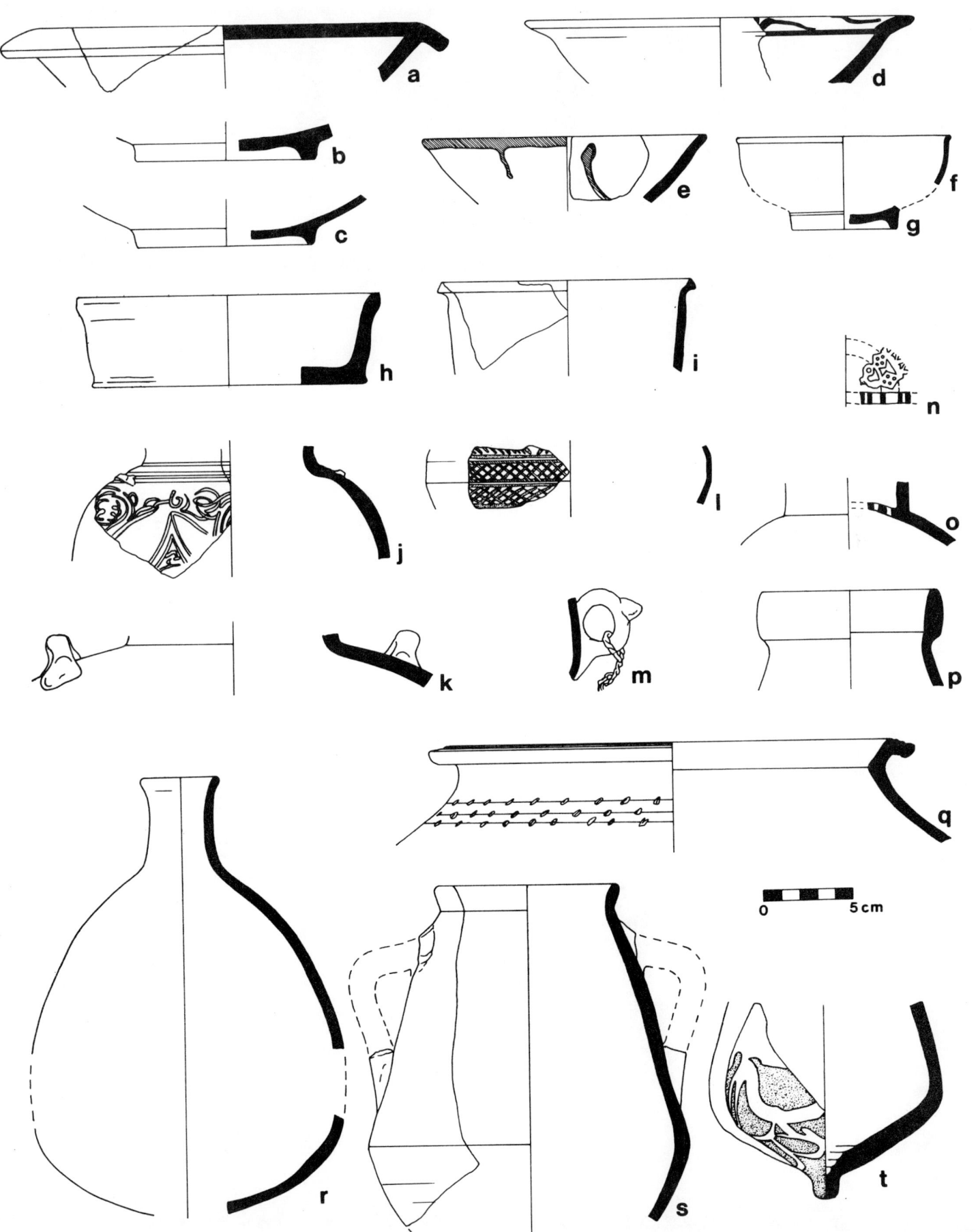

Plate 51: Central Building A, Islamic Ceramics

Whitcomb, D. S.
    1975   "The Archaeology of Oman: A Preliminary Discussion of the Islamic Periods," *Journal of Oman Studies* 1: 123-57

Whitcomb, D. S., and J. H. Johnson
    1979   *Quseir al-Qadim 1978: Preliminary Report*, Cairo

CHAPTER 6: IMPORTED FAR EASTERN WARES
John Carswell

Among identifiable Chinese fragments from Quseir al-Qadim are three pieces of a bowl of Têhua ware (52:a). Like many Ting ware bowls, the rim was left unglazed so that the bowl could be fired upside-down in the kiln. The bowl was impressed in a mould, and the raised pattern of lotus-petals on the outside is here reduced to a ring of elongated chevrons. Related examples of this type of ware and decoration from kiln sites in China, at Putain in Fukien province, have recently been published; Putain is on the coast about 60 km. east of Têhua. Chinese scholars date the Putain kilns to the Yüan dynasty (1280-1386 A.D.) (Hughes-Stanton and Kerr, 1981: X, 34-36, nos. 185, 186, 187).

A famous example of Têhua ware is a jar in St. Mark's Treasury in Venice, said to have been brought back from China by Marco Polo and remaining in the hands of the same Venetian family until being presented to the Treasury half a century ago. This piece has a moulded chevron pattern on the lower part of the body, like the Quseir al-Qadim bowl (Donnelly, 1969: 42-43, pl. 1a). A smaller similar jar was excavated at Kota Cina in North Sumatra; this site yielded a C^{14} date of 1200±75 A.D. (McKinnon, 1977: 65, pl. 35). A fragment of a Têhua bowl identical to the Quseir al-Qadim bowl was found on Male in the Maldive Islands (Carswell, 1977: 152, no. 499, pl. 60c). Têhua ware has been found in Borneo and elsewhere in the Far East (Harrisson, 1959: 48-49; Sullivan, 1963: 61-77).

Regarding Ting ware in general, to which Têhua ware is closely related, it is relatively scarce at Fustat, where no more than ten pieces were identified among the more than 4,000 sherds examined by Gyllensvärd (Gray, 1977: 233). This relative paucity is echoed at Quseir al-Qadim, where the imported material is also dominated by a preponderance of celadon.

Three sherds of porcelain from Quseir al-Qadim include two fragments of small bowls painted in underglaze cobalt blue and part of a base ring (52:b,c,d). They may be compared with fragments of three bowls from Fustat, one of which has similar lotus-panels with thick and thin borders and a similarly sharply-cut foot, fired iron red on the unglazed portion. The Fustat bowls are indisputably of 14th century date, closely related to the David vases of 1357 A.D. (Carswell, 1967: 44, pl. 4b, fig. 1b; 1981: 31). The second bowl fragment from Quseir al-Qadim (52:d) is painted with blue rings inside and out, and a single vertical stroke on the outside; there is no reason to doubt that it is also 14th century.

Three fragments of a small celadon bowl with slightly everted rim and dark olive crackled glaze (52:e) have a moulded pattern on the inside, of two rings of radiating petals. This moulded petal pattern is to be found on a plain Ying ch'ing porcelain bowl in the Ashmolean Museum, which is in turn related to one of the three bowl fragments from Fustat. The Fustat bowl is painted in cobalt blue with a floral design at the centre, superimposed on similar moulded rings; using an earlier plain prototype like the Ashmolean bowl as a base, this bowl may be among the earliest known examples of blue-and-white, an attribution further reinforced by the pattern of breaking serpentine waves on the exterior (Carswell, 1967: pl. 4d, fig. 1d). A further example of this type of moulded design is in the British Museum, an Annamese bowl with a green glaze. The Quseir al-Qadim moulded bowl may also be of provincial Far Eastern origin.

Two fragments of Yüeh ware from Quseir al-Qadim (possibly from the same bowl) (52:f,g) have a hard grey body and glossy grey glaze. The base sherd is unglazed on the lower body and base, and the base bears traces of two iron-red kiln spurs; in the cavetto is a carved ring, in typically Sung style. The rolled rim (52:f) has been noted at Fustat, in a group of imported ware assigned to the T'ang period (Gyllensvärd, 1973: 105-6, pl. 13). But it should be noted that rolled rim bowls also occur, in various sizes, in a collection of Chinese vessels excavated in Ceylon which can be dated to ca. 1100 A.D. (Carswell, 1979: 37-42; pl. 3, no. 200; fig. 11, nos. 326, 200, 201, 202, 240). The type may well have persisted for several centuries.

The Lung-ch'üan celadon sherds are mostly too small to be classified, even allowing for the present imprecision in the dating of celadon as a whole. Two sherds (52:h,i) sharply carved on the exterior with pointed lotus petals fit into the Fustat group dated to the Northern Sung (960-1127 A.D.) (Gyllensvärd, 1975: 99-100, pl. 7, nos. 1, 2). A bowl fragment (52:j) with more smoothly carved petals belongs to the later Fustat group, of Southern Sung (1128-1279 A.D.); and a base fragment (52:k) is typical, fired iron-red on the unglazed area (Gyllensvärd, 1975: 101-2, pls. 10, 11). Bowls with smoothly carved lotus-petals have been found on the Sinan wreck off the coast of South Korea, dated between 1310-1331 A.D. (Choi, 1977: pls. 31, 32). One Quseir al-Qadim sherd (52:l) has a close parallel with a Yüan bowl, also from the Sinan wreck (Choi, 1977: no. 138).

Three celadon sherds (52:m,n,o) with finely moulded designs are probably Yüan or early Ming. Similarly moulded sherds have been collected from the Maldives (Carswell, 1977: pl. 61c, fig. 8, nos. 341, 71). A celadon rim sherd is incised on the outside with a key-fret band (52:p).

Among remaining fragments, a large dish with flat rim, of grey ware with a crackled orange-brown glaze (52:q) is loosely decorated in the cavetto with a swirling carved and combed design, similar to a celadon dish from the Korean shipwreck (Choi, 1977: pl. 20). A small sherd of (Ying ch'ing?) white ware with a pale grey glaze (52:r) incised with triangular tick-like motifs is of similar type to another group of Fustat material (Gyllensvärd, 1973: pl. 22, nos. 4, 5, 6; pl. 23, no. 1). The shoulder of a grey stoneware jar (52:s) is glazed on the upper half in lustrous dark brown, with a single incised ring, and resembles Tz'u Chou ware. A fragment of a large storage vessel (52:t) of orange ware is glazed a degraded orange-brown.

The neck and rim of a "Martabani" storage jar (44:s) has survived with its plaster stopping intact; dating of "Martabani" ware is problematical, but in all probability its manufacture continued over several centuries. A large storage jar of similar form with a black glaze was found on the Sinan wreck (Choi, 1977). "Martabani" jars are still in everyday use in the Maldive Islands, both for storage in the market and on shipboard, where they are used to carry fresh water (Carswell, 1977).

Bibliography for Far Eastern Wares*

Carswell, J.
    1967   "A Fourteenth Century Chinese Porcelain Dish from Damascus," *American University of Beirut Festival Book (Festschrift)*, pp. 38-58
    1977   "China and Islam in the Maldive Islands," *Transactions of the Oriental Ceramic Society* 41: 121-98
    1979   "China and Islam: A Survey of the coasts of India and Ceylon," *Transactions of the Oriental Ceramic Society* 42: 24-58
    1981   "Cities Lost and Found," *Splendors of the Past--Lost Cities of the Ancient World*, National Geographic Society, pp. 10-33

Choi, S., and Y. Chung
    1977   *Special Exhibition of Cultural Relics found off Sinan coast*, Seoul

Donnelley, P. J.
    1969   *Blanc de Chine, The Porcelain of Têhua in Fukien*

Gray, B.
    1977   "The Export of Chinese Porcelain to the Islamic World: Some reflections on its significance for Islamic Art before 1400," *Transactions of the Oriental Ceramic Society* 41: 231-62

Plate 52: Imported Far Eastern Wares

	Locus	RN	Description	Munsell
a	E18a-7 E18a-9 E18a-15	415 413 419	cream-coloured ware with fine grey grits; coarsely crackled opaque white glaze; rim unglazed in and out; moulded decoration out	7.5YR 8/2 10YR 8/4 2.5Y 8/4 10YR 8/1 glaze
b	E19c-6	412	light grey porcelain; off-white glaze with blue-grey underglaze painting	5B 7/1
c	E18a-3	408	light grey porcelain fired orange on unglazed base; heavy viscous blue-grey crackled glaze	2.5Y 8/0 core 5G 7/1 glaze 5YR 7/4 back
d	E19c-9	407	light grey porcelain; off-white glaze with blue-grey underglaze painting	5G 7/1
e	E18a-3 E19c-2	408 411	grey ware; light olive crackled glaze; moulded decoration in	5Y 5/3
f	E18b-3	410	light grey ware; sparkling grey glaze	5GY 7/1
g	E18d-12	399	light grey ware; pale grey glaze; scored ring in	5GY 7/1
h	E18c-3	417	grey ware; grey-green celadon glaze; carved decoration out	5GY 6/1
i	E18a-4	409	off-white ware; pale green crackled celadon glaze; carved decoration out	5GY 7/1
j	E18a-14	410	grey ware; thick dimpled grey-green celadon glaze; moulded decoration out	5GY 7/1
k	E18a-1	413	grey ware, fired red on unglazed base; light green celadon glaze	5GY 7/1
l	E18d-11	399	light grey ware; grey-green celadon glaze; scored decoration in and out	5GY 7/1
m	E19c-7	406	grey ware; grey-green celadon glaze; moulded decoration in	5GY 6/1
n	F19a-6	404	light grey ware; pale green celadon glaze; moulded decoration in	5Y 8/1
o	F19a-7	313	light grey ware; pale green celadon glaze; moulded decoration in and out	5GY 6/1
p	West of Island	369	ochre ware; grey-green celadon glaze; carved decoration out	2.5Y 7/4 5GY 6/1 glaze
q	E19c-6	412	grey-buff ware; heavily crackled olive-brown glaze; carved and combed decoration in	2.5Y 6/4
r	E18d-4	398	off-white ware; pale grey glaze; incised decoration in	5GY 7/1
s	F18a-3	403	gritty grey-brown ware; lustrous dark brown glaze on shoulder with splashes of glaze in; incised ring out	10YR 6/3 10YR 2/2 glaze
t	West of Island	369	ochre ware; fine grey grits inner surface, orange-brown slip out	7.5YR 6/6 7.5YR 5/8 slip

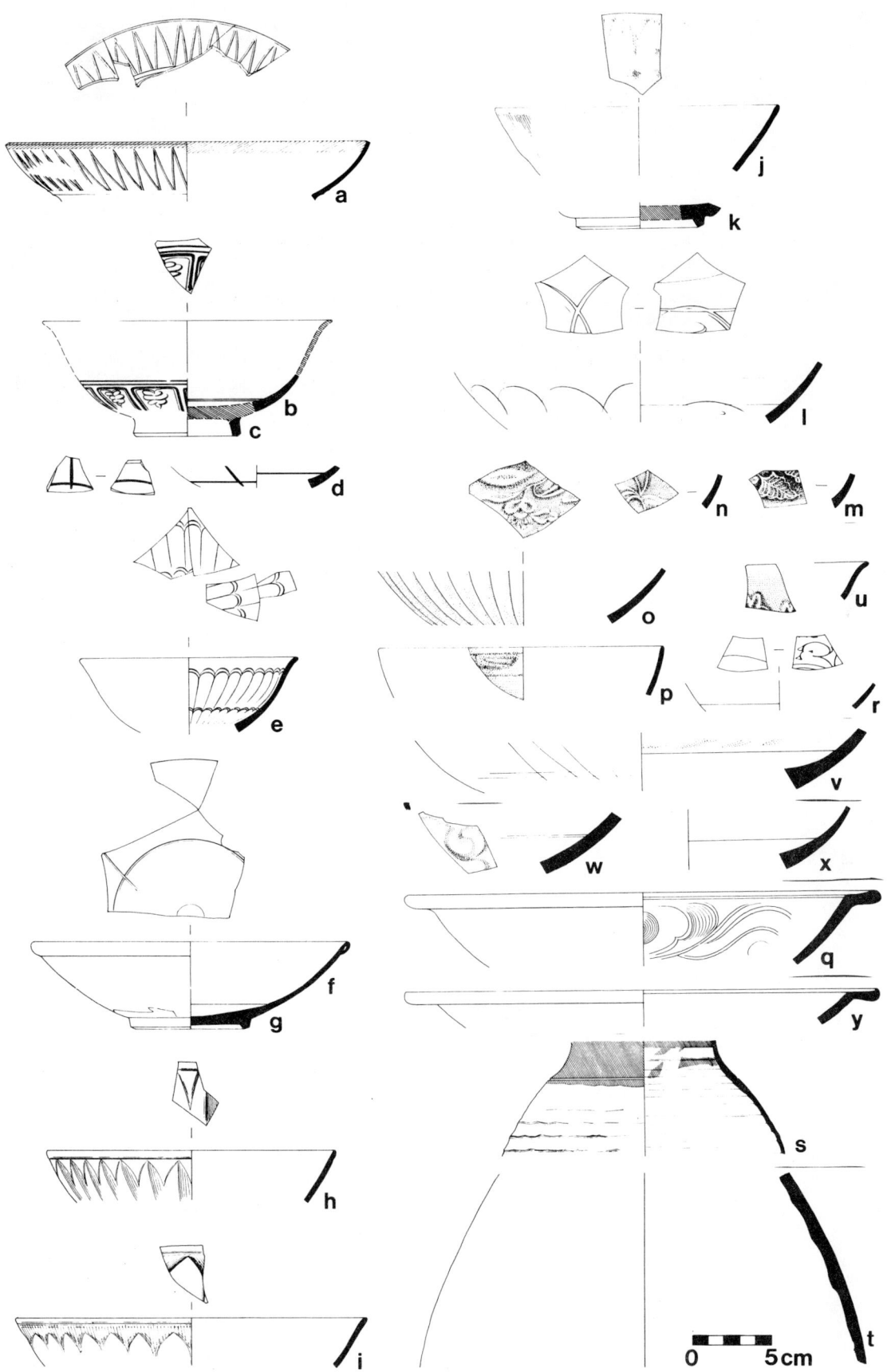

Plate 52: Imported Far Eastern Wares

Plate 52 continued

	Locus	RN	Description	Munsell
u	E18d-10	398	grey ware; olive-grey celadon glaze; moulded decoration in	7.5YR 7/0
v	E19c-6	412	grey ware; grey-green celadon glaze; moulded decoration in	5Y 7/1
w	West of Island	369	light grey ware with orange deposits; grey-green glaze; carved decoration in and out	5Y 7/1 5GY 6/1 glaze
x	E18d-7	398	grey ware; dull olive celadon glaze; scored ring in	
y	West of Island	369	olive-grey ware; dull olive glaze	2.5Y 6/2 5Y 6/3 glaze

Gyllensvärd, B.
    1973   "Recent Finds of Chinese Ceramics at Fostat. I," *Bulletin of the Museum of Far Eastern Antiquities* 45: 91-119

    1975   "Recent Finds of Chinese Ceramics at Fostat. II," *Bulletin of the Museum of Far Eastern Antiquities* 47: 93-117

Harrisson, T.
    1959   "Export Wares found in West Borneo,"

Hughes-Stanton, P., and R. Kerr
    1981   *Kiln Sites of Ancient China, An Exhibition lent by the People's Republic of China*, London

McKinnon, E. P. E.
    1977   "Oriental Ceramics Excavated in North Sumatra," *Transactions of the Oriental Ceramic Society* 41: 59-120

Sullivan, M.
    1963   "Notes on Chinese Export Wares in Southeast Asia," *Transactions of the Oriental Ceramic Society* 33: 61-77

*to which may be added works cited in Whitcomb and Johnson, *Quseir al-Qadim 1978: Preliminary Report*, pp. 109-11

CHAPTER 7: LARGE AND SMALL STOREROOMS OF THE ROMAN VILLA

Carol Meyer

The western portion of E6b was excavated in 1980 as an extension of the 1978 exposure which had revealed a small iron-working installation (Whitcomb and Johnson, 1979: 25-27). The 1980 operations discovered a narrow lane and a large house, the Roman villa, two storerooms of which contained numerous pottery vessels and other artifacts *in situ*. The small storeroom, here called the cellar room from its most unusual feature, and the large storeroom deserve particular attention because a) all of their artifacts were in use contemporaneously and b) intact working floors with associated finds are quite uncommon among Roman period Egyptian excavations (cf. Husselman, 1979). Such an assemblage *in situ* should provide some clues as to what vessels or objects were used or stored together.

Cellar Room, Post-Villa Levels

The top layers (E6b-[16], [18] and D6d-[1]) represent fill and debris deposited on top of the collapsed villa and the natural reworking of the fill to produce a rock-hard cap of varying thickness. The uppermost layer, the topsoil, is generally loose earth and may contain an admixture of Islamic materials. The bulk of the fill, however, contains only Roman material and results from post-villa Roman occupation elsewhere on the site. The fill varies from a loose brown or yellowish soil with more or less sand, gravel, or sherds to large or small pockets of melted brick and rock salt caliche. The strata may be seen, for example, on the E6b north profile (pl. 3), which cut across the cellar room.

Cellar Room Construction

Only the bottom few centimeters represent the floor and associated items, although the wall stubs projected as much as 60 cm. high. The walls are made of regularly laid mud brick and are about 90 cm. thick; the interior floor space is approximately 2.5x3.0 m., not a particularly large room. The north and east walls continued into square D6d and appear to have formed the northeast corner of the building.

The entrance to the room was never discovered. There was no trace of a door in either the north or east wall, and it is unlikely that a small storeroom full of goods would have opened directly to the outside. Furthermore, the position of the trapdoor within the room would have made a north or east entrance difficult. The west and south walls, unfortunately, were reduced to stumps only one to two bricks high. It is possible that the door lay in the west wall, but given the positions of the artifacts and the presence of a wooden beam (=threshold?) in the large storeroom, plus the possible functional relationship of these two rooms, the door is reconstructed as penetrating the south wall (pl. 3).

The room was probably roofed. The width, ca. 2.5 m., could have been covered without difficulty by a beam-stringer-mat-clay roof, and the value and condition of the finds, especially the wood, suggests that they were protected.

A satisfactory floor was never traced, probably because of the unusual subfloor construction, which sagged in places. A thin layer of yellowish clay or mud (cf. pl. 3) is the most likely floor level. The layer immediately over the clay and in which the artifacts were embedded was generally a soft, uniform brown soil readily distinguishable from the hardpan or fill above. Loci E6b-[24], [29], [42], [44] and D6d-[2], [3], and [4] and their finds constitute the floor level.

Cellar Room Finds

The finds in the cellar room are mapped on pl. 53 and listed below starting from the west corner (E6b-[24]) and running along the south wall (E6b-[44] to E6b-[29]). The first number corresponds to the object number on the plate; the find number, registration number, and plate reference are listed after the description of the object.

```
20   Shell with purplish powder, E6b-[24], FN 25, RN 172
18   Oil juglet, E6b-[24], FN 6, RN 363, pl. 19:c
 4   Pottery cup/bowl, E6b-[24], FN 18, RN 423, pl. 17:j
 3   Pottery cup/bowl, E6b-[24], FN 17, RN 422, pl. 17:i
21   Black stone (weight?), E6b-[24], FN 13, RN 139
13   Oil juglet, E6b-[24], FN 5, RN 351, pl. 18:h
 9   Oil juglet, E6b-[24], FN 8, RN 357, pl. 18:d
22   Wooden block, E6b-[24], FN 14
 2   Pilgrim flask, E6b-[24], FN 9, RN 420+366, pl. 17:h
15   Oil juglet, E6b-[24], FN 7, RN 352, pl. 18:j
10   Oil juglet, E6b-[24], FN 10, RN 425, pl. 18:e
23   Top of rotary mill, E6b-[24], FN 15, RN 150
```

A tun shell and numerous fragments of wood were found around this cluster of oil juglets. Some of the juglets had small, flat slabs of gypsum (E6b-[24], RN 140) underneath, like coasters, as if to provide a level base or to catch fluid seepage or drip. The doorway as reconstructed would have entered this point near the southwest corner, between the top and bottom of the rotary mill.

```
24   Bottom of rotary mill, E6b-[24], FN 16, RN 150, pl. 54:f
25   Wooden block with two spools, E6b-[24]
26   Smooth oval stone slab, E6b-[24], FN 12
27   Smooth round stone slab, E6b-[44], FN 13
     (Detectable, but fragile, traces of rope were found under stone slabs
     26 and 27.)
28   Wooden bar with two holes and a groove, E6b-[44]
```

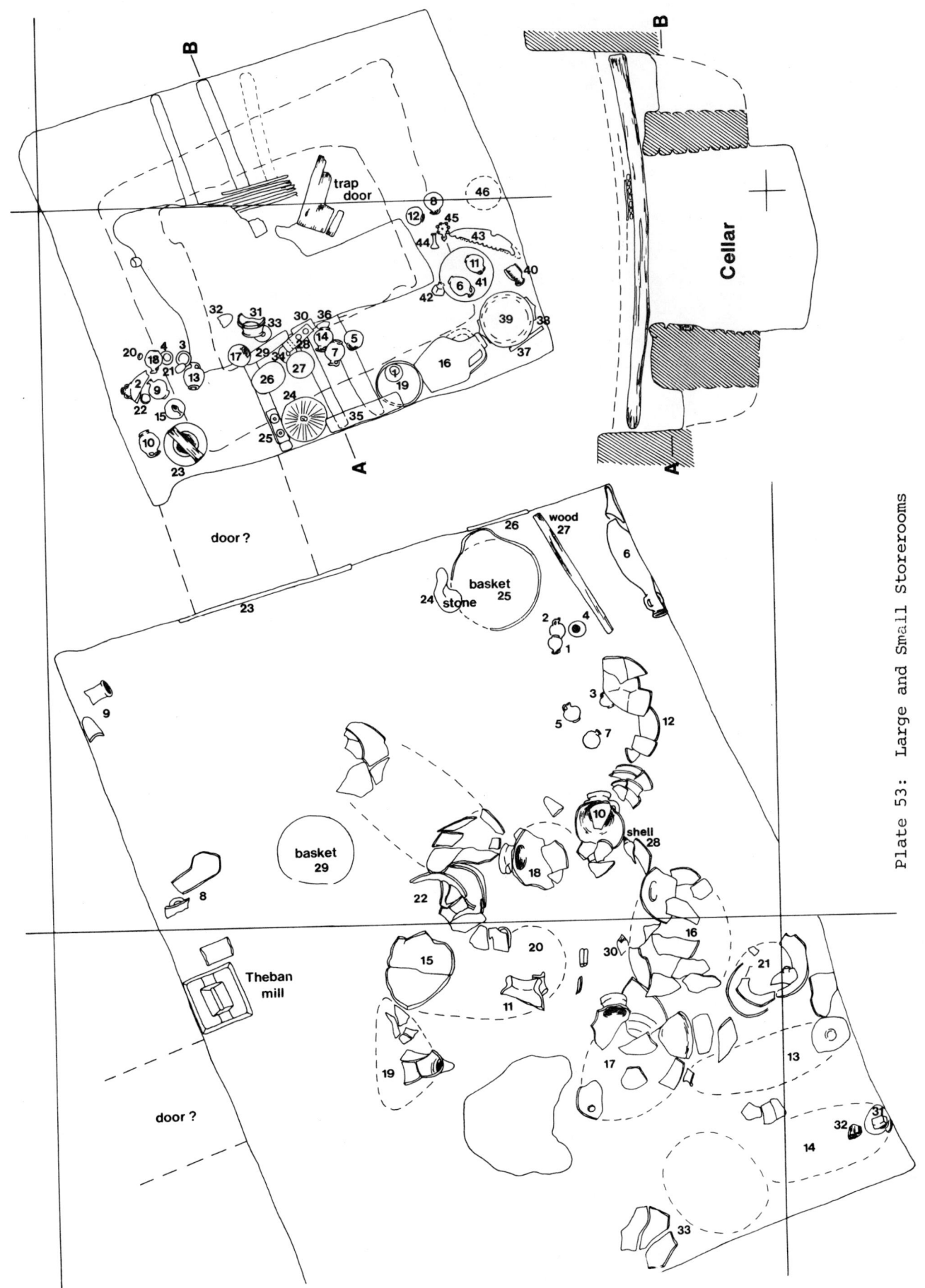

Plate 53: Large and Small Storerooms

Plate 54:   Items from Storeroom Floors

	Locus	RN	Description
a	E6b-29	122	lamp; FN 3
b	E6b-29	68	glass; FN 4
c	E6b-44	356	frit; 3 spur marks; FN 14
d	E6b-29	142	stone jar; FN 7
e	E6b-29	641	wooden bowl; FN 8
f	E6b-24	150	basalt mill; lead plug in center; FN 16
g	E6b-50	151	basalt mill; FN 1

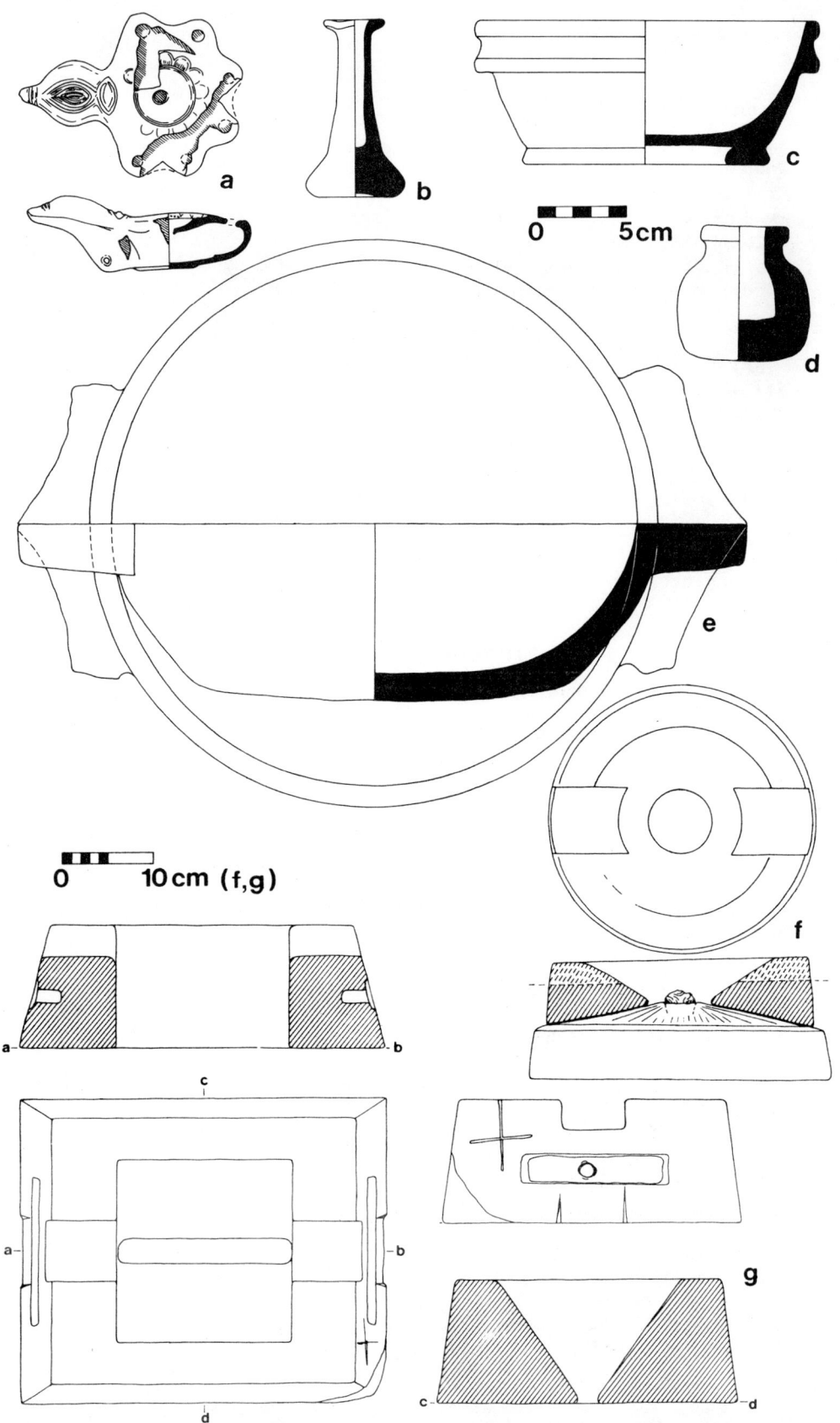

Plate 54: Items from Storeroom Floors

17	Small jar, E6b-[24], FN 4, RN 365, pl. 19:b	
29	Wooden beam, E6b-[24]	
30	Wooden block, E6b-[24]	
31	Frit bowl, E6b-[44], FN 14, RN 356, pl. 54:c	
32	Oval wooden object, E6b-[44]	
33	Wooden disk, E6b-[44], FN 15	
34	Wooden disk, E6b-[44], FN 16	
35	Wooden beam along south wall	

Also found in E6b-[24] but not shown on the floor plan were:

> A patch of carbonized wood and bitumen near beam 35 (sample = RN 280)
> Nail, E6b-[24], FN 19, RN 324
> Wooden stake
> Dentalium shell, E6b-[24], RN 177
> 7 coins, E6b-[24], FN 1, 2, 3, 11, 20, 23, 24, RN 524, 535, 557, 559

E6b-[44] lay slightly lower than E6b-[24]; here were found:

14	Oil juglet, E6b-[44], FN 12, RN 350, pl. 18:i
36	Piece of wood, E6b-[44]
7	Oil juglet, E6b-[44], FN 11, RN 353, pl. 18:b
5	Two-handled juglet, E6b-[44], FN 10, RN 355, pl. 17:k
12	Oil juglet, E6b-[44], FN 6, RN 428, pl. 18:g
8	Oil juglet, E6b-[44], FN 7, RN 298, pl. 18:c

Fiber or grass (=padding?) and wood fragments were detected under the locus [44] juglets. Also recovered from E6b-[44] but not shown on the floor plan were:

> 4 coins, E6b-[44], FN 1, 2, 3, 4; RN 520
> Iron loop, E6b-[44], FN 5, RN 371

E6b-[29] at the eastern half of the room included:

1	Crude cup, E6b-[44], FN 8, RN 455, which was inside
19	Lower half of large jar, E6b-[44], FN 9a, RN 419; pl. 19:d
16	Large jar with red paint, E6b-[29], FN 2, RN 436, pl. 19:a
37	Wooden stick (1 of 2 found), E6b-[29]
38	Large jar, E6b-[29], RN 437, pl. 17:g
39	Wooden bowl, E6b-[29], FN 8, RN 641, pl. 54:e
	Fishnet under bowl
40	Badly shattered pottery jar, E6b-[29], FN 10, RN 309
6	Oil juglet, E6b-[29], FN 1, RN 364, pl. 18:a; this and
11	Oil juglet, E6b-[29], FN 6, RN 358, pl. 18:f were found inside
41	Large jar, E6b-[29], RN 459
42	Small calcite jar, rectangular, E6b-[29], FN 7, RN 142, pl. 54:d
	Quartz crystal, E6b-[29], RN 134
	Patch of red pigment

More grass or fiber (padding?) was detected under the locus [29] vessels.

43	Wooden "rake," E6b-[29], FN 9
44	Glass perfume flask, E6b-[29], FN 4, RN 68, pl. 54:b
	Glass rim and neck, E6b-[29], FN 5, RN 76, pl. 55:o
45	Six-wick oil lamp, E6b-[29], FN 3, RN 122, pl. 54:a
	2 coins, E6b-[29], FN 7, 13, RN 563, 564

A few more items were recovered from D6d:

    46   Pilgrim flask, D6d-[2], FN 3, RN 455
         5 coins, D6d-[2], FN 1, 2, 4, 5, 6, RN 539, 544, 546
         1 coin, D6d-[3], FN 1, RN 521

The artifacts in the cellar room obviously pertain to a variety of activities from personal grooming (perfume flasks), food preparation (mill), food service (frit bowl? and cups), commerce (coins), to subsistence (fishnet), but this point will be treated in more detail in the discussion of the function of the room.

Floor and Cellar

The initial difficulty in locating a reasonably level floor was eventually explained when it was found that the floor was also a cellar roof, which had sagged. The cellar was dug in the middle of the room through the pre-villa Roman sherd and rubble fill (E6b-[55]) and the gravelly bedrock to a maximum depth of approximately 1.6 m., scarcely high enough to stand in. The internal dimensions were only 1.4x1.2 m. The lower part of the cellar walls consisted of bedrock, then six courses of small cut stones, then three courses of larger stones laid in two rows (cf. pl. 53). Two wooden bars or beams remained stuck in the mud plaster (?) on the south and west walls about two-thirds of the way up.

Two wooden beams stretching from the south to north walls of the room, but not quite touching them, covered the cellar. The third and heaviest beam started parallel to the other two at the south wall but did not reach all the way across; it ended half way over the cellar in a confused patch of wood fragments, ash, and carbon, so it is impossible to tell how or whether it was supported. Across the beams in the middle of the room lay some 24 to 33 thin stringers, about 2 cm. wide on the average, which did not reach any of the walls. A mat of regular weave covered the stringers and over that was spread the layer of yellowish clay. The area covered by the stringers and matting is indicated in outline with a few stringers drawn in on the floor plan of the cellar room (pl. 53; see also fig. 5 in chapter 2). The northeast corner is not covered. The cellar was entered here by a wooden trap door, which was found where it had fallen into the soft cellar fill. Whether the trap door was hinged or lifted off remains unclear; fragments of iron and bronze were found in the area, but not enough for one, much less two, hinges; leather could conceivably have been used. Apart from two coins, however, the cellar was completely empty.

Large Storeroom

The large storeroom, so designated to distinguish it from the large courtyard to the west, adjoins the cellar room on the south, and they share the same eastern outer wall (pl. 3, 53). A large number of vessels and artifacts were found *in situ* in this storeroom, although quite different from the finds in the cellar room.

The fill overlying the storeroom (loci E6b-[14], [15], [16], [32], and [57]) was similar to that over the cellar room. The uppermost layers of debris (E6b-[16]) had some Islamic admixture. Some of the soil was fine yellowish or reddish sandy fill; some, the rock-hard caliche. E6b-[57] was an especially large seephole in the southwest corner of the courtyard that all but obliterated the floor and wall angle there.

Large Storeroom Construction

The large storeroom was bounded by four thick mud brick walls, in most places preserved 40-50 cm. high. The enclosed floor space was about 5x4 m.

There is no evidence that the area was roofed, and the minimum width, 4 m., would have required long and sturdy beams, costly items in the desert. Furthermore, the contents of the large storeroom, large amphorae and jars, may not have required as much protection as the contents of the cellar room, e.g., perfume flasks or wooden equipment.

The suggested door in the north wall, apparently provided with a wooden sill (#23 on pl. 53), leading to the cellar room has already been mentioned. There was no indication of a door in the eastern wall; the gap on the plan is the result of an early trial trench. Also, if the numerous vessels lined up against the eastern wall are in fact in place, they would make an entrance there awkward. A door might have pierced the south wall, leading to one of the small rooms on the south side of the villa. There is a gap in the south wall, but the whole corner was badly damaged by hardpan. The main access to the large storeroom is therefore reconstructed near the middle of the west wall, which has been denuded to only a few centimeters height. Such an entrance would have allowed convenient communication with the large courtyard immediately west and convenient access to the jars as they now lie; many of the vessels would have been difficult to move, especially when full.

The floor seems to have been fairly uneven, perhaps not too surprising in an open working yard. The north end of the floor was marked by a whitish layer; the center, mainly by the bottoms of the pots; and the south, heavily damaged by caliche.

The fill varied from soft, brownish or yellowish soil in the north and center to hardpan in the south. The loci that yielded the finds attributable to the large storeroom floor are E6b-[36], [49], and [50]; E6b-[18], [19], [27], [47], and [54] may be room fill of the same period; E6b-[56] is the very soft, ashy sub-floor fill.

Large Storeroom Finds

The finds are listed for convenience clockwise from the square stone Theban mill, next to the suggested door in the west wall. By no means all the sherds were or could have been plotted *in situ*. Only rims, bases, and the largest pieces are indicated; dotted lines enclose the areas of sherd scatter of some of the pots. All sherds were bagged in the field according to the vessels to which they belonged, based on the ware and position on the floor. The reconstructed vessels are shown on plates 14-17.

	Theban mill, basalt, E6b-[50], FN 1, RN 151, pl. 54:g
8	Wine amphora, E6b-[49], FN 22, RN 472, pot T, pl. 14:f
9	Wine amphora, E6b-[49], FN 21, RN 475, pot R
23	Wooden bar (=threshold?), E6b-[36]
24	Smooth, irregular stone, E6b-[36]
25	Basket, rim mashed down, E6b-[36]
26	Wooden bar against wall, E6b-[36]
27	Wooden beam, E6b-[36]
6	Wine amphora, E6b-[36], FN 6, RN 453, pot S, pl. 14:g
	(For a view of these items *in situ*, see fig. 4, chapter 2.)
2	Oil juglet, E6b-[36], FN 2, RN 362, pl. 17:d
1	Oil juglet, E6b-[36], FN 1, RN 361, pl. 17:b
4	Oil juglet, E6b-[36], FN 4, RN 359, pl. 17:f
5	Oil juglet, E6b-[36], FN 5, RN 360, pl. 17:e
7	Oil juglet, E6b-[36], FN 7, RN 427, pl. 17:a
3	Oil juglet, E6b-[36], FN 3, RN 354, pl. 17:c
12	Large jar, E6b-[36], FN 8, RN 446, pot Q, pl. 14:a
10	Large jar, E6b-[49], FN 4, RN 440+474, pot A, pl. 15:e
28	Triton shell, E6b-[49], FN 5
18	Large jar, E6b-[49], FN 7+8, RN 470 464, pot B+C, pl. 15:a
22	Large jar, E6b-[49], FN 9+12, RN 466, pot D+G
29	Basket, traces only
11	Large jar, E6b-[49], FN 10, RN 473, pot E, pl. 14:b
15	Large jar, E6b-[49], FN 11, RN 473+475, pot F, pl. 16:b
19	Large jar, E6b-[49], FN 17, RN 475, pot M, pl. 15:b+c
20	Large jar, E6b-[49], FN 15, RN 467, pot K, pl. 15:d
30	Tun shell, E6b-[49], FN 6
16	Large jar, E6b-[49], FN 13, RN 614+442, pot H, pl. 16:c
17	Large jar, E6b-[49], FN 14, RN 457+471, pot J, pl. 16:f
21	Large jar, E6b-[49], FN 18, RN 468+476, pot N, pl. 16:a (enlargement of inscription on neck, see pl. 61:n)

```
13    Water jar, E6b-[49], FN 19, RN 474, pot O, pl. 14:c
14    Water jar, E6b-[49], FN 20, RN 447, pot P, pl. 14:d
31    Brick
32    Wooden block
33    Fragments of large jar, E6b-[54], RN 441, pl. 15:f
```

The top of the last-named jar (33) was found early in the excavation, before it had been ascertained that the area was a storeroom. Thus only the lower sherds were mapped *in situ*, enough however to show their position. Also found in the large storeroom, but not shown on the floor plan, were:

```
Glass bottle fragment, E6b-[49], FN 1, RN 76, pl. 55:z
2 coins, E6b-[49], FN 2, 3; RN 517
```

Only the three long, skinny, rather friable amphorae (6, 8, and 9 on the plan) are called "wine amphorae." The two "water jars" (13 and 14 on the plan) are barrel-like vessels of hard-fired orange clay. They have tiny mouths and are designed to be slung horizontally one on either side of a donkey. Inasmuch as good drinking water came from a day's journey away, water would probably have been a constant concern, and carefully conserved.

The uses of the other large jars are not known so specifically. Some must have held grain, grist for the rotary and Theban mills. Conceivably some were used in brewing beer, long an Egyptian staple. Onions, vegetables, fruits or dried fruits, vinegar, and perhaps honey, garum, pickles, relishes or other condiments must have been brought to the town, although the latter would probably not have been kept in an open court. The oil juglets bespeak a supply of olive oil, assuming that that is what they were actually used for. None of the soil samples from the bottoms of the jars has yet been analyzed. No animal or fish bones were noted, although fish scales were recovered from the ashy sub-floor fill below vessel 22.

Interpretation

Part of the interpretation of these two areas has been implicit up to this point: storage. The sheer abundance of finds in them makes this a reasonable assertion. It is possible, however, to go a little further.

In addition to containing an array of vessels for wine, water, grain, and other commodities, the large storeroom was probably used for a certain amount of domestic activity, notably grain grinding. The Theban mill could not have been used where it now lies, flat on the floor, but must have been raised on a frame or cradle (Forbes, 1965: 146-48). A bowl or basket would have been placed underneath to catch the flour from the slot. Also, the upper part of the mill is missing. If the mill were properly raised into position, the large storeroom would be a reasonable place to grind grain. The grain was presumably kept in one of the jars; the court wall would have sheltered the grain and flour from the wind, and even today a great many domestic activities in the Middle East are carried out in the open air. The two parts of the rotary mill could easily have been carried by one person from the cellar room outdoors into the large storeroom. It must have been placed on a mat, basket (#25?), cloth, or something to catch the flour. There are, however, neither ovens nor stoves in the large storeroom or its near vicinity, nor soot-blackened cooking pots, so presumably the later stages of food preparation were carried out elsewhere (probably in the large courtyard to the west). The baskets could have been used for storing, sorting, or carrying items such as raisins, dates, or beans, for drying things like fish or conch, etc.

Stepping into the cellar room would have been a contrast, thanks to the shade and clutter. The room seems to have served as a back room for all sorts of household items. Most apparently rested on the floor, viz. the padding or coasters under the juglets, but the two pilgrim flasks or canteens might have hung from wall pegs. Both were badly broken, both lay near a wall, and neither could have stood easily by itself.

A few items pertain to personal grooming, particularly the perfume flasks and shell with paint. The flasks might have been expected in the living quarters rather than a storeroom, unless they were extras or empties.

Other artifacts would have served in food preparation. The wooden bowl could have been used for kneading dough or any of a number of other purposes. The turquoise blue frit bowl would have made a presentable serving dish; certainly the other vessels are quite plain. The rotary hand mill, as mentioned, was used for grinding grain. The numerous oil juglets would have held olive oil, the best quality of which was Mediterranean, or other fluids such as vinegar, honey, or sauces. The contents of the large jars remain unknown. The large (reused?) jar bottom (#19) with the cup inside could have served as bin and scoop, perhaps for grain or flour, or even water for washing. The simple little cups or bowls could have served any of a number of purposes.

Most of the wooden objects remain unexplained. The series of disks, spools, and bars with circular holes are especially tantalizing; they might have been pulleys or block and tackle devices, but how they were mounted and used is unknown.

Rope, however, was noted near them. The arched board with notches on the long edge and one notch on top has been tentatively called a rake.

The only local resource available to the Roman inhabitants was fish. Carried out for sport or necessity, fishing could have been a useful supply of fresh food. The fishnet stored in the cellar was perhaps an extra. Shells such as the tuns and tritons found in these two areas are washed up on the beach after storms. What functional value they might have had is uncertain. The quartz crystal would seem another casual "find." The mountains not far away are known to contain masses of pure quartz.

The coins point to formal commercial activity. Unfortunately all are bronze and too corroded to provide much more information. It may be noted, though, that far more coins (15) were recovered from the cellar room than from the large storeroom (2).

The most intriguing feature, of course, is the cellar itself. The six-wick lamp was conveniently placed near the trapdoor and could have lit the cellar. The cellar was found quite empty. If it had served to cool jars of water or wine, a few sherds, at least, might have been expected. Nor is there any indication that it was a root cellar. Given that the only reason for the existence of Roman Quseir was the trade with Africa and India, the master of the house was presumably involved in commerce, either directly or indirectly. Conceivably he might have kept some of his valuables in this most inner, inaccessible little room, in a private hole underground. If so, the items were not bulky. The cellar is tiny, hardly big enough to stand and move around in, especially if there were much in it. Many import goods were not bulky, however, such as silk bales, pearls, cinnamon, and spices; pepper sacks, on the other hand, would probably have filled the whole cellar. Whatever the case, this of all spots in the cellar room and large storeroom had been meticulously cleaned out when the villa was abandoned.

This highlights the question of the relationship of the cellar and large storeroom to the rest of the villa. Although badly eroded in parts, enough walls could be followed to trace the plan of a sizable building, large enough for a fairly large household. The two areas under discussion would have been a back region behind the living quarters and public areas. Given the remoteness of the port, the household may well have had to be more self-sufficient than usual in terms of provisions stocked and range of activities undertaken. There is, however, nothing in the finds from either storeroom to indicate that this was a merchant's main warehouse. A limited amount of goods could have been kept in the cellar, but the normal export goods, with the possible exception of specie, could not. Wine, perfume, and glass were important export goods, but the evidence for these commodities from the villa does not suggest sufficient quantity for a merchant's trading stock, or even wastage from his stock. There were large, public buildings nearer the center of town and closer to the harbor that would have been more suited for warehouses.

Finally, the villa seems to have been abandoned leaving many useful or even valuable articles in place. Due to the difficulty of provisioning Roman Leucos Limen year-round and to the presence in the "home port" only twice a year of ships which sailed with the monsoon winds, many of the inhabitants may have retreated to the Nile valley between trading seasons. If the master of this villa did so, he might reasonably be expected to remove his most valuable possessions (from the cellar?) and leave what he expected to use the next season, especially awkward items such as water jars or grinding mills. The items were not left tidily; e.g., the large jar set squarely on top of the upside down wooden bowl on top of a fishnet. For one reason or another, he did not return and those who did did not disturb his possessions much, if at all. The handful of odd coins, the perfume flasks, canteens and dishes were still worth owning, if not worth sending an emissary from the Nile to reclaim. Unbroken jars, the mills, and even the beams roofing the cellar could easily have been put to use in town. But all the objects seem to have been left in place long enough for sand and silt to filter into the cellar and corners of the room. Finally, roof and walls collapsed, covering whatever the silt had not, and still no one looted what was clearly an abandoned building. It would be easy to explain the relatively untouched condition of the cellar room and large storeroom if the entire port had been abandoned at the same time or within a few years of the villa, but this was probably not the case, as witness the layers of later Roman trash covering the building.

Bibliography for Storerooms

Forbes, R. J.
    1965   *Studies in Ancient Technology*, Vol. 3, 2nd ed., Leiden

Husselman, E. M.
    1979   *Karanis: Topography and Architecture*, Kelsey Museum of Archaeology 5, Ann Arbor

Whitcomb, D. S., and J. H. Johnson
    1979   *Quseir al-Qadim 1978: Preliminary Report*, Cairo

CHAPTER 8: ROMAN GLASS
Carol Meyer

A large corpus of glass from the first and second centuries of our era was recovered during the 1980 excavations at Quseir al-Qadim. The sherds included in this report were found in the Roman villa, areas and dumps adjoining the villa, the pipeline (for these designations, see Chapter 2, Roman Trench Summaries), and surface collections. About 390 diagnostic glass sherds, e.g., rims, bases, and decorated fragments, were registered, and a representative sample of about 100 is illustrated on plates 55 and 56. The non-diagnostic sherds were counted, recorded, and discarded. The counts have been entered in the computer files, although the non-diagnostic sherds will not be analyzed until later. A preliminary typology for the diagnostic sherds is presented below, but it will have to be checked against the results of the 1982 season before it can be finalized.

The Roman glass from Quseir al-Qadim is of interest in three respects. It is, first, datable to a relatively short period of time. No chronological distinctions in the glass from different loci have yet been detected; this will be sought in the more detailed final analysis. Secondly, the glass, although shattered, represents an *excavated* corpus that includes a wide variety of vessels. Most of the Roman glass in museums or publications lacks good provenience or does not include the full range of types from everyday storage jars to luxury ware. Finally, glass was one of the goods traded by the Roman period merchants to Africa and India, trade that was carried through Red Sea ports. Some discussion of the glass trade is therefore included at the end of the report.

The corpus of diagnostic glass sherds is grouped under six main headings: Bowls and Dishes, Jars and Beakers, Bases, Unguentaria and Flagons, Decorative Techniques, and Amulets and Beads. The headings are further subdivided into types labelled with small letters, a, b, c, ... z. A definition or clarification of each type name is given where needed, as well as the plate illustration numbers. Exact square and locus numbers are presented on the plate labels. For certain types of vessels some further discussion is given, but this is not meant to be exhaustive, only to present some idea of the vessels' use, possible place of manufacture, and distribution.

Harden in his report on the Karanis glass grouped it into nine fabrics or types of glass. Fabrics 1, 2, 8, and 9 were predominant up to about A.D. 200, and possibly a little later (Harden, 1936: 32). The other fabrics were typical of later periods and do not need to be discussed here. Fabric 1 was a colorless ware that was used for the most symmetrical and best-finished vessels; it has a milky weathering surface, if any. Fabric 2 is also colorless but tends to be

Plate 55: Roman Villa Glass

	Locus	RN	Description
a	E6a-9	64	green-blue
b	E6a-13	64	dark blue
c	E6b-14	76	clear
d	E6a-5	64	clear, cut decoration
e	E6a-1	64	clear
f	D6d-1	71	clear
g	D6d-1	71	clear
h	E6b-18	71	clear, sides pinched
i	D6d-1	71	clear
j	E6a-12	64	clear, blue prunts
k	E6a-13	64	green, with red, white, yellow, black millefiore
l	E6a-1	64	clear, cut decoration
m	E6a-1	64	clear, red, purple, yellow, green paint
n	E6a-1	64	green
o	E6b-29	76	clear, FN 5
p	E6c-3	67	blue-green
q	E6c-2	67	green
r	E6a-9	64	green
s	E6a-10	64	dark blue-green
t	E6b-49	76	clear
u	E6b-29	68	light green, FN 4
v	E6c-1	67	dark green
w	E6c-1	67	light blue-green
x	E6b-22	76	black
y	E6c-1	67	dark blue
z	E6b-25	76	black
aa	E6b-49	76	black
bb	E6a-15	76	dark green
cc	E6a-1	64	clear
dd	E6a-9	64	clear
ee	E6a-9	64	clear
ff	E6a-13	64	clear, greyish
gg	E6a-1	64	light blue
hh	E6a-9	64	light yellow
ii	E6b-14	76	clear, sides pinched
jj	E6a-9	76	light yellow-green
kk	E6a-9	64	green
ll	E6c-1	67	green

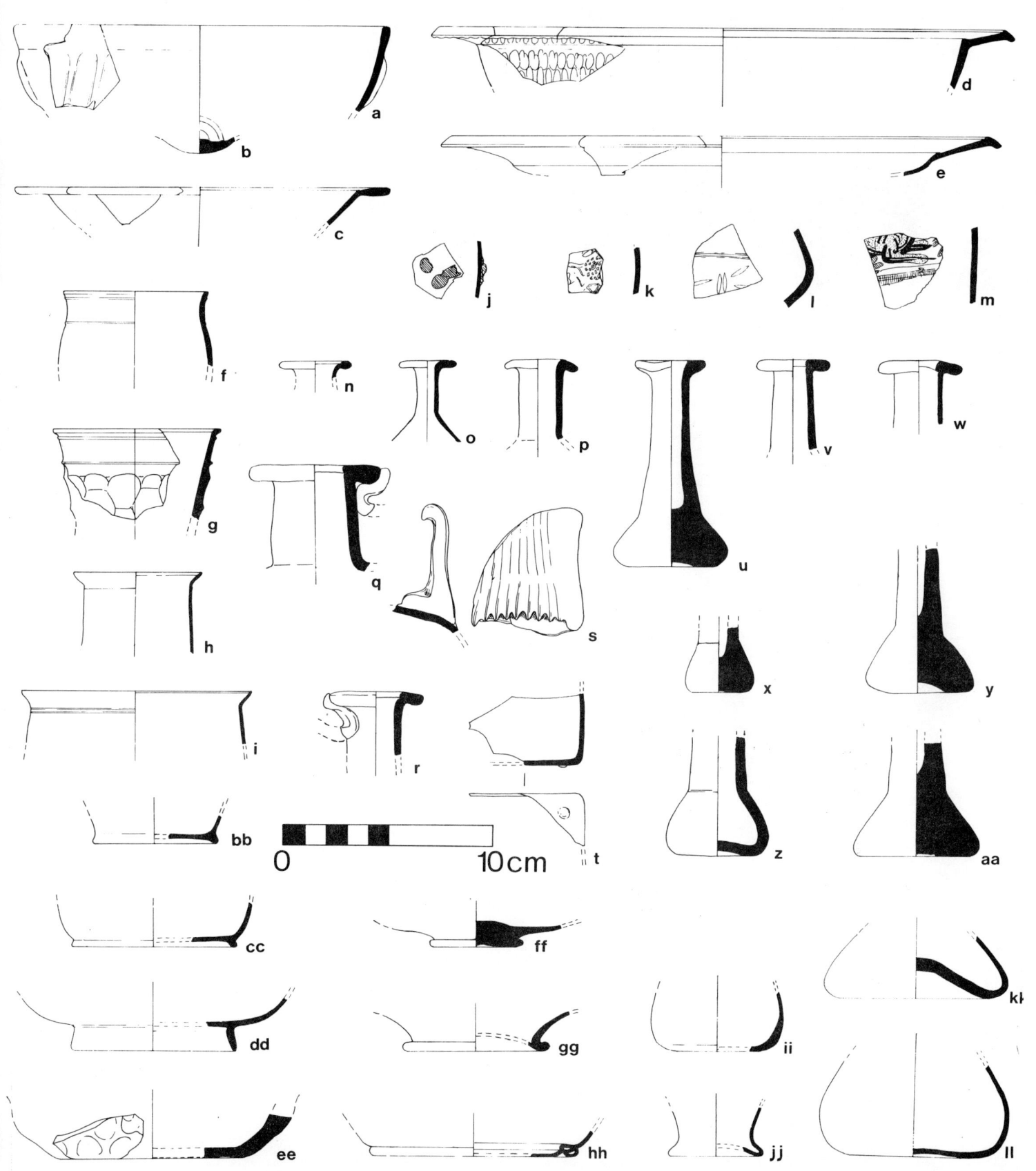

Plate 55: Roman Villa Glass

Plate 56: Villa East, Villa South, and Pipeline Glass

	Locus	RN	Description
a	E7a-5	55	yellowish clear
b	E7a-20	55	clear
c	E7a-12	55	clear
d	E7a-11	55	clear
e	E7a-5	55	light blue, bubbles
f	E7a-12	55	clear, bubbles, sides pinched
g	E7a-5	55	light green
h	E7a-2	55	green
i	E6b-35	76	light blue-green
j	E7a-1	55	clear
k	E7a-20	55	clear
l	E7a-16	55	dark green
m	F7a-6	65	blue
n	F7a-1	65	clear
o	F7a-2	65	green and yellow millefiore
p	E7c-7	56	clear
q	F7a-3	65	clear
r	F7a-1	65	clear
s	F7a-3	65	clear
t	F7a-1	65	clear
u	E7c-5	56	clear
v	F7a-1	65	clear
w	F7a-2	65	light green, yellow strings
x	E7c-5	56	light yellow-green
y	E7c-2	56	light green
z	F7a-3	65	clear
aa	E7c-1	56	black
bb	G8a-4	73	brown
cc	G8b-5	73	light green
dd	H8a-1	69	clear
ee	G8a-4	73	clear
ff	H8a-1	69	dark green
gg	H8a-1	69	green
hh	G8a-4	73	clear
ii	G8a-4	73	clear
jj	G8b-3	73	clear
kk	G8a-4	73	light green
ll	H8a-1	69	light green
mm	G8b-5	73	light green
nn	G8b-5	73	light brown

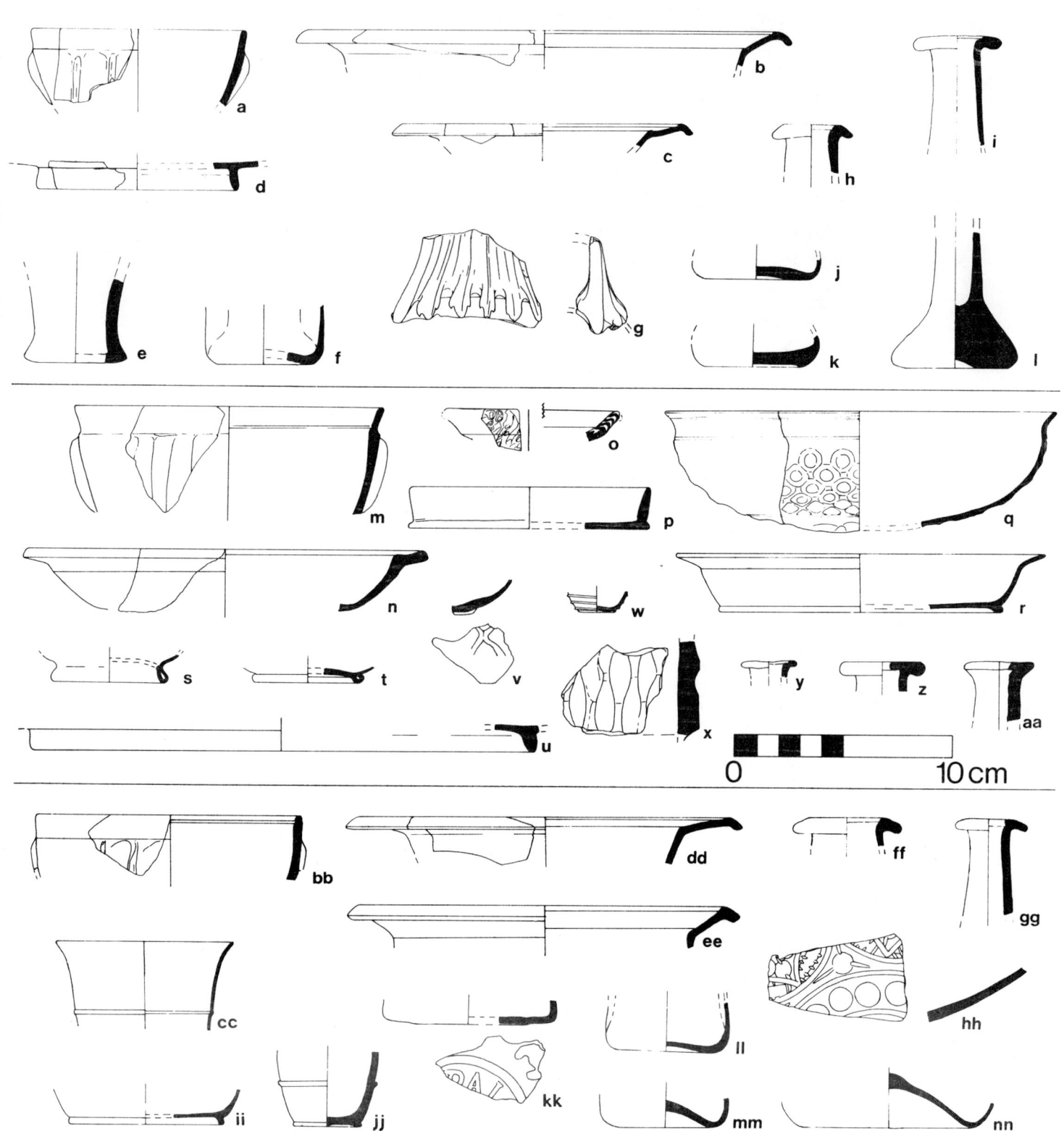

Plate 56: Villa East, Villa South, and Pipeline Glass

thicker and to acquire a more frosted patination. Fabric 8 is often bubbly and ranges from pale to true green or blue-green. Fabric 9 is the poor quality green bottleware that contains many bubbles and impurities; it was used especially for the rectangular flagons and toilet bottles (Harden, 1936: 22-24). The early glasses were usually richly colored and opaque; clear glass, which required the addition of antimony or manganese to decolor it, did not start to replace colored glass until late in the first century of our era (Harden, 1969: 60-62). Harden's classification of glass fabrics seems applicable and useful for the Quseir al-Qadim corpus. Although none of the following types are designated "Fabric 1" or "Fabric 9," etc., in general the colorless glass was used for the finer vessels and the bubbly green for the coarser ones.

Bowls and Dishes

(a) Bowls. The most distinctive group of bowls are the "pillar-molded bowls." Most of the sherds are rims that preserve some of the slightly angled ridges or "pillars" on the outside and incised lines on the inside (55:a; 56:a, m, bb); b, however, shows a molded base. The bowls were made in a variety of colors, including yellowish green, reddish amber, green, blue, and purple. Colors of ancient glass do decay and alter, but these samples at least seem relatively stable.

The bowls were carefully made and were probably relatively valuable. They are thought to have been manufactured in Syria, a center of the glass industry where they are fairly common, and in Cyprus and the Crimea (Harden, 1936: 99-100). Some may even have been made in Aquilea (Calvi, 1968: 70-71), possibly by emigrant Syrian glassworkers. In Egypt, however, examples of pillar-molded bowls have hitherto been rare, with one fragment at Karanis and one at Armant (Harden, 1936: 99-100). Harden considers the pillar-molded bowls an early style (Harden, 1969: 47), but Hayes would date them to the middle-late first century of our era, up to ca. A.D. 100 (Hayes, 1975: 16-17).

(b) Bowls. The illustrated bowl is hemispherical, but the type is actually defined by its rim, which flares out slightly. The base of this example (56:g) is round (h Base), the fabric clear, and the exterior ornamented with cut grooves and cell pattern (u Decoration). Isings dates such round bottomed bowls as early as the first century, although more common after the second century (Isings, 1957: 104).

(d) Plates/Bowls. This is a group of plates or bowls distinguished by wide, flat, flaring rims, usually overhung (55:e; 56 :b, c, dd). They are typically made of clear glass. The uncertainty in the label "Plate/Bowl" arises from the fact that in some cases not enough of the rim and body are left to determine whether the vessel was a flat dish or whether the wall turned abruptly down to form a bowl. This type of vessel originated in the second or early third century of our era (Isings, 1957: 116), but went out of fashion after the third century in favor of oval dishes (Harden, 1936: 49), none of which have been found to date at Quseir al-Qadim. Circular dishes are said to have been rare in Egypt, but both they and oval dishes were even less popular outside Egypt (Harden, 1936: 51).

56:p shows an unusual shallow bowl. Enough of the smooth basal flange is left to indicate that it was not a broken-off High Base (i).

(e) Deep Bowls. Most of these, like the "Plate/Bowl" category, have wide, flaring rims but also preserve enough of the body or even the base to prove that they are indeed bowls and not plates (55:c, d; 56:n, r, ee). They are typically made of transparent glass. One has a ring base (Base g) and one was ornamented with shallow cut ovals, even below the overhung part of the rim (55:d).

Jars and Beakers

(a) Jars. Jars are not particularly common, and only one example (55:f) is illustrated. It is of clear glass with a carefully worked rim.

(b) Beaker. Only one of these beakers is illustrated here (55:g), but some of the honeycomb cut glass discussed under Decorative Techniques (u) may well have come from beakers. They are characteristically made of clear or almost colorless glass, rather thick, and deeply cut with circles or ovals that overlap to produce the honeycomb effect. Such beakers were made from the end of the first to the second centuries of our era and have been found all over the Roman Empire. Their distribution, however, suggests that they came from Egypt, or perhaps Syria (Isings, 1957: 37-38). Some indication of the value of the beakers may be seen in two intact ones from Karanis that had been sealed in a niche in a wall during the late third or early fourth century. Harden considered them heirlooms made in the second or early third century (Harden, 1936: 137).

(c) Beaker. These are thinner, less elaborate vessels (56:cc), usually of transparent glass. The rims are simple and vertical or slightly flaring. Decoration, if any, is limited to incised lines or a raised ridge. The cheaper type of beaker is reported to have been more common at Karanis than the fancy cut-work beakers (Harden, 1936: 135).

(d) Beaker. The distinguishing feature of this group of beakers is the short but sharply outflaring rim (55:h, i). The fabric is usually whitish or clear glass and decoration consists of incised lines only. One example (55:h) may have had sides that were pinched in to make a squarish body. If so, then the pinched bases (Base a) would be the lower part of the (d) Beakers. Beakers with pinched sides and loop bases, usually blue-green, were widely distributed in the Roman Empire in the first century of our era, especially in the Mediterranean basin. They have been reported at Pompeii, which was destroyed in A.D. 79, Cyprus, Thera, Corinth, Lucerne, and Vindonissa (Calvi, 1968: 54).

Bases

A wide variety of bases was found. Some clearly pertain to one kind of vessel, e.g., the pinched-sided pieces, but others could have been broken off vessels of different shapes and sizes.

(a) Pinched-Sided Bases. The vessels were blown and the bases are concave, as might be expected from the attachment of the working iron. The distinctive feature is the indentations made on four sides while the glass was still soft (55:ii; 56:f, 11). The pinched bases are fairly common at Quseir al-Qadim and may belong with Beaker (d) rims, as noted above. The base fragments represented here are usually clear or light green. Hayes states that "indented beakers" are common in both the east and west and date to the second half of the first century to the first half of the third century of our era (Hayes, 1975: 41).

(c) Loop Bases. The loop bases were formed by kicking up the base of a still soft vessel to make in effect a hollow ring base in only one step (55:gg, hh; 56:s, t). Judging from the examples here, loop bases were made on a variety of vessel forms and fabrics, clear, blue, and light amber. Calvi reports a pinch-sided beaker with a loop base (Calvi, 1968: 112-13). Isings dated such bases very broadly to the first to fourth centuries (Isings, 1957: 48-49).

(d) False Foot Base. The one example illustrated (55:jj) has a kicked up base that did not join the inside of the vessel to make a loop base.

(d) Disk Base. This is a miscellaneous category of rather fine vessel bases. One (55:ff) is a thick, translucent, molded base of an apparently shallow vessel. The gray color is most unusual. Another (56:jj) is almost crystal clear, thick glass with sharply raised ridges. Yet another (56:w) is the bottom of a small, thin green vessel with raised yellow threads trailed on. This is a fairly uncommon mode of decoration although Harden notes one example at Karanis (Harden,

1936: pl. XVII, #557). The final "disk base" (56:v) is by no means clear and the drawing cannot be checked because the sherd was retained in Cairo.

(f) Flat Base. This refers to a thick base that does not actually rest flat; the bottom was molded or cut in slightly (56:k).

(g) Ring Bases. Ring, unlike Loop Bases, are solid (55:bb, cc; 56:ii). Judging from the quality of the fabric, transparent, the bases may represent the lower portions of Bowls/Plates (d) or Deeper Bowls (e). One of the bases has cut decoration, like at least one of the Deeper Bowls (e).

(i) High Bases. The High Bases are similar to but taller than the Ring Bases (55:dd; 56:d, u). Most of the High Bases are of the transparent glass used for some types of luxury vessels.

(j) Concave Bases. These are one of the most common base types (55:kk, ll; 56:j, mm, nn). They come from medium to small blown bottles, the base having been kicked in, sometimes quite deeply, by the working iron attached to the bottom of the hot vessel. A number of the bases still preserve the scar where the iron was snapped away. Most of the examples here are green or greenish glass, although one (56:nn) is light yellow-brown.

(k) Miscellaneous Bases. The remaining base (56:e) fits into none of the above groups. It is completely flat on the bottom, unlike the (f) Flat Base. The fabric is also unusual, a pale blue translucent bubbly glass.

Unguentaria and Flagons

Both unguentaria and flagons are relatively common forms, both at Quseir al-Qadim and throughout the Roman Empire. They were generally used for the practial purposes of holding perfumes, other liquids, or even pickles. Most were blown or blown into molds, and the glass is usually the common green ware, often bubbly.

(a) Unguentaria. The (a) and (b) Unguentaria are differentiated by the rim treatment. The (a) rims are turned out, or out and slightly down, or out and slightly rolled up along the outer rim (55:o, p, u; 56:y). The (b) rims seem to be folded all the way back into the neck of the vessel, often forming a groove around the inside of the mouth (55:n, v, w; 56:h, i, aa, ff, gg). It is difficult to make the distinction sometimes, especially if the glass is well fused, and the (a) and (b) categories may have to be lumped. Most of the (a) Unguentaria are made of green glass, including the only intact example, found on a room floor (RN 68, 55:u) in the villa. One unusually delicate "perfume jar" (55:o) seems to have been white or clear but is now heavily patinated. The (a) Unguentaria, as exemplified by RN 68, correspond to Harden's A type. Such vessels were most common in the second century, although known earlier and later (Harden, 1936: 38). Harden A type vessels are said to have been predominant among Egyptian export shapes, especially to southern Russia (Harden, 1936: 265).

(b) Unguentaria. As noted above, (b) Unguentaria have rims that were formed by folding back on themselves, leaving a groove inside the neck (55:n, v, w; 56:h, i, aa, ff, gg). Almost all examples here are green, although one (56:aa) is black and one, not illustrated, clear. The red stripes down the inside of the necks of two are said to be accidental (Goldstein, pers. comm.). The (b) Unguentaria are even more abundant in this corpus than the (a) type.

(c) Solid Unguentaria Bases. Except for RN 68, none of the unguentaria are complete, so bases and rims have been given separate labels. The (c) Unguentaria Bases (55:x, y, aa; 56:i) are almost entirely solid and so thick that they could have contained only small amounts of perfume. Most unguentaria bases look opaque black but are actually dark green, the glass being so thick at the base as to transmit almost no light. The small body capacity, certainly a feature of the majority of the Quseir al-Qadim unguentaria, is eastern; such flasks probably date to ca. A.D. 100-150 (Hayes, 1975: 42-45).

(d) Hollow Unguentaria Bases. The Hollow Unguentaria Bases also correspond to the Harden A type (triangular bodies), but are much less common than (c) Unguentaria Bases. The one shown (56:z) is opaque black, heavily patinated.

(e) Flagons. Flagons are represented in this corpus by two necks with handle attachments (55:g, r), two broad handles (55:s; 56:g), and two square or rectangular bases (55:t). Flagons or "hydria" were one of the most common types of glass vessels in the first and second centuries of our era. They might have cylindrical, round (Calvi, 1968: 80-81), or hexagonal bodies (Isings, 1957: 63-66); the only identifiable flagon bases at Quseir al-Qadim were square or rectangular. Flagons were either free-blown and flattened on a slab or mold-blown (Isings, 1957: 63-66), although it is difficult to tell from the examples here. The two reeded handles, possibly preformed in molds, are said to be typically eastern (Hayes, 1957: 45). The base with nubbin feet (55:t), however, must have been mold-made; it is an unusually thin, translucent pale blue. The fragment with a molded inscription (56:kk) may have come from a flagon or a beaker. The inscription consists of parts of three letters only and has not yet been matched with a more complete example from elsewhere. The flagons could have been used for holding or shipping liquids, pickles, preserves (Auth, 1976: 137), etc.; the square shape would have been easy to pack (Isings, 1957: 63-66).

Decorative Techniques

Obviously, the "Decorative Techniques" described below were applied to Bowls, Beakers, or other vessels, usually the finer types, but the following collection of glass sherds, although interesting in themselves, cannot be securely matched with a particular vessel form. Almost all methods of glass decoration are represented.

(t) Millefiore. Millefiore is an exceedingly laborious and surprisingly ancient method of making a glass vessel. Rods of different colored glass are assembled into larger rods and fused in a furnace. The large rods, which now have a design in cross-section, are cut into disks and the disks stacked inside a mold. The inside of the assembled unit may be packed with some filler material to keep the disks from slipping. The whole is fired again until the disks fuse to make a whole vessel with complex designs that pass all the way from interior to exterior of the walls. The surface and rim usually require grinding and polishing. Two pieces of millefiore with flower designs were recovered in the 1980 season. One is 55:k; there is a close parallel for the second in the Brussels museum, except that the flowers have blue, not pink, centers. The Belgian bowl is dated to the first century of our era and is thought to be Alexandrine (Brussels, n.d.: #32). Hayes, however, calls the rather common flower millefiore Syrian and would date it more narrowly to the first half of the first century of our era (Hayes, 1975: 23). Another fragment of Quseir al-Qadim millefiore (56:o) has only green and yellow swirls but resembled a bowl said to have been found near Homs and dated to the first century of our era (Auth, 1976: 55). The swirled millefiore may be what the ancients called "murrhine glass," an imitation of the even more costly agate vessels (*Periplus*, p. 68).

(u) Cut. Two main techniques are represented here, thick transparent glass deeply carved with ovals or circles to make a honeycomb pattern and more shallow wheel-engraving. The first has been discussed with the Beaker (b) type, and another fragment is shown on 56:x. The fine, often elaborate wheel-engraved designs have been mentioned as applied to Bowl (b), Bowl (e), and Ring Base (g) types. Two further examples may be seen on 55:l; 56:hh. In addition, simple lines were sometimes incised around the bodies of vessels, or just below the mouths, or on the insides.

(v) Molded. A variety of vessels, from plates to flagons, were formed in molds, but here "Molded" refers to molded decoration. One type, a thick, transparent bowl base with smooth indentations (as opposed to the sharp edges of a cut honeycomb design), is shown in 55:ee. The inscribed fragment (56:kk) was also mold-made.

(w) Painted. One fine painted sherd was recovered (55:m). It shows the forequarters of an animal in yellow, purple, and red-brown glossy paint, some yellow-green floral matter below, and a yellow and red-brown ground line. There is an excellent parallel for the animal design in the Victoria and Albert Museum, on a bowl recovered from Oxyrhynchus (Harden, 1936: 100). Harden states that most of the enamel painted glass came from Egypt (Harden, 1936: 59), and Hayes would attibute it to the second century of our era (Hayes, 1975: 132).

(x) Prunted. This refers to objects of clear glass decorated with applied blue blobs. Only one example was recovered in 1980 (55:j), but there were several from the first season, although not all clear-and-blue (Roth, 1979: pls. 58, 62-64). Harden refers to bowls, beakers, and cone lamps decorated with blue blobs, found in Syria and Egypt (Harden, 1936: 59). The Syrian glass had blue blobs, either singly or in triangular groups, as here. All of the Karanis pieces were late (Harden, 1936: 156-57).

Beads and Amulets

Only one amulet was recovered (59:g), and it probably represents the headdress of a Bes figure. It is turquoise blue with applied lime green dots.

One large millefiore bead was found (59:f). It has black and white bull's eyes on a green ground. A string (59:e) of six red alternating with six yellow beads and terminating in a larger blue bead came from G8b-2 and was assigned to the Roman assemblage. It is unusual in preserving the original string. The remaining beads are shown on plate 59. Some of the larger ones are striated as if made by trailing threads of glass around a rod or pin. One bead was hexagonal but most of the others were round, cylindrical, or disk-shaped. Excluding the string of beads, blue was the most popular color (6), then yellow (3), black (2), and red (1).

Glass as a Trade Good

Glass had been manufactured since the second millennium B.C., but it was usually cast, ground, and polished; the amount of time and effort involved made it definitely a luxury item. Glass-blowing may have been discovered as early as the second or first century B.C. (Isings, 1957: 1); the invention certainly revolutionized the industry by making rapid production possible. The technique may or may not have been discovered in Syria, but in any case it was a major center of the glass-blowing industry by the first century of our era (Harden, 1969: 46-47). Alexandria is a less likely site for the invention; the glassworkers there continued to favor the older methods of millefiore, engraving designs, or casting and then grinding and polishing (Harden, 1969: 47-48).

In the Augustan period (30 B.C.--A.D. 14), glass was still a luxury, but became more common in Claudian times (Isings, 1957: 163-64). The industry spread quickly; the glassmakers themselves may have emigrated from the Levant to Italy and beyond (Isingers, 1957: 49). Setting up a glass house might well have been easier than shipping masses of fragile glass. By the late first century of our era, then, there were a number of glass-making centers in the eastern Mediterranean, in Cyprus, Asia Minor, notably at Tyre and Sidon (Harden, 1969: 51-52), certainly at Alexandria, and the *Periplus* mentions glass from Diospolis (*Periplus*, §6). As glass, particularly blown glass, became more common there was a concomitant trend towards making more and more colorless glass instead of the older style richly colored fabrics. Natural greens were still used for unguentaria, jars, and cheap tableware (Harden, 1969: 61-62).

Three centers of glass-working seem to have supplied the glass for the Roman period settlement at Quseir al-Qadim: Syria, Alexandria, and possibly Diospolis. Out of the glass inventory discussed above, perhaps three types may be attributed to Syrian workshops: the "pillar-molded" bowls, the mold-decorated vessels, and the blue-blob decorated sherd.

To Alexandria may be attributed some of the fancy types, the cut and engraved vessels, the painted pieces, the clear molded dishes and plates, the millefiore and probably the swirling imitation agate or murrhine glass, and the perfume unguentaria. The last are not especially elegant vessels, but as perfumes were manufactured at Alexandria, it would be reasonable to make the flasks there as well (Charlesworth, 1924: 29). The *Periplus* mentions murrhine glass made at Diospolis, presumably Diospolis Magna below Thebes. There is no information yet about the place of manufacture of the cruder glass, the pinch-sided beakers, flagons, etc. It is worth noting that--in addition to the all-important grain trade (Charlesworth, 1924: 30)--glass was one of the imperial monopolies (Charlesworth, 1924: 26).

There are two likely routes by which the glass from the above-mentioned production centers could have been transported to Quseir al-Qadim: down the Red Sea or up the Nile and through the Wadi Hammamat. Plate 57 shows the cities and sites under discussion. Glass is fragile and could be more safely carried by ship than overland because pack animals would have to be reloaded and off-loaded every day. Glass is known to have been shipped on the Mediterranean from Alexandria to the western provinces, and even beyond to Britain, during the first and second centuries of our era (Harden, 1936: 45).

Syrian glassware could have been carried in the boats that regularly coasted to Alexandria. From there, both Syrian and Alexandrine glass could have been shipped on the great canal from an eastern branch of the Nile to Arsinoë at the head of the Gulf of Suez. The canal was 150' wide, sufficient to take the largest ships (Charlesworth, 1924: 18-20). South of Suez on the western side of the Red Sea lay important ports at Myos Hormos (near present-day Safaga), Leucos Limen (Quseir al-Qadim), Berenice, and others down to the Bab el-Mandeb straits. Evidence for the use of the Red Sea route to Quseir al-Qadim lies partly in the numbers of pillar-molded bowls, which are reported to be rare at Karanis (Harden, 1936: 99-100). Charlesworth (1924: 27) states that there would have been little use for imported Sidonian glass or western pottery at Alexandria, but both are definitely present at Quseir al-Qadim. One advantage of the Red Sea route would have been that the cargo, including glass, could sit in its padding and containers and would not have to be loaded daily on and off animals, whether donkeys or camels (Raschke, 1978: 884). Furthermore, in ancient times shipping was usually cheaper and faster than land transport. On the other hand, a storm could destroy an entire cargo and the ship as well.

Shipping glass up the Nile would avoid the sea-storm danger but would mean that the glass would have to be packed overland through the Wadi Hammamat. The journey from Coptos, which served as "the major entrepôt directly in touch with the India trade" (Raschke, 1978: 644), to Myos Hormos took seven days (Charlesworth, 1924: 21) and presumably the one to Leucos Limen would have been comparable. Wagons are known to have supplied the Wadi Hammamat mines, which are about half way along the Coptos-Leucos Limen route (Raschke, 1978: 884, n. 943). Raschke's statement that "there is no evidence that Leucos Limen...[was] used for trade with the East in the Roman Period" (1978: 901, n. 993) is not supported by the results of the Quseir al-Qadim excavations. There is no evidence that any route besides

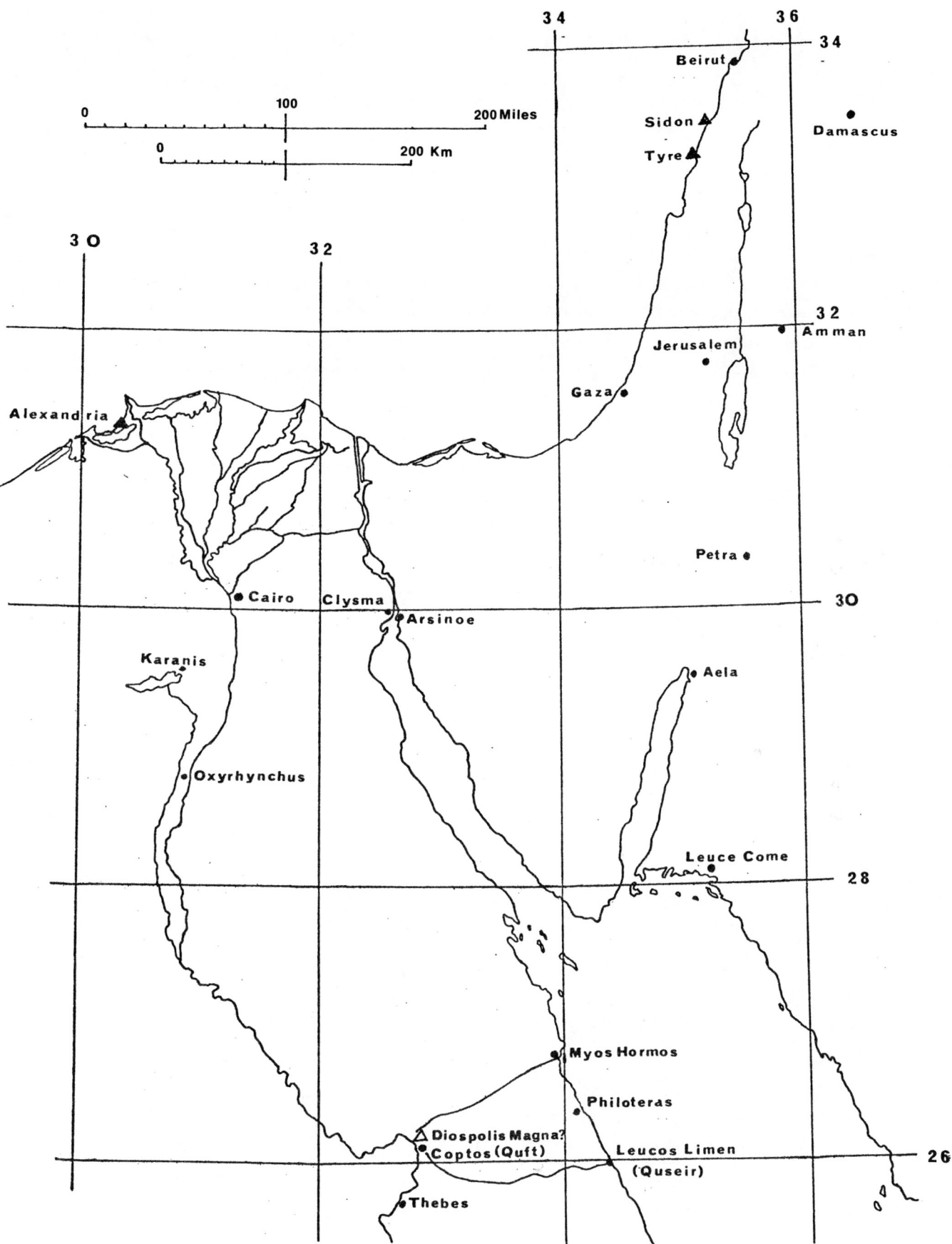

Plate 57: Quseir Connections with Surrounding Regions
(Glass Production Centers)

these two, the Red Sea and the Nile, played an important role in the shipment of glass to Leucos Limen, although there is as yet no way to choose between them. Both may have been used.

Finally, glass was one of the items exported from Egypt and the Roman Empire to Africa and India. It is quite possible that the glass at Quseir al-Qadim was intended for the residents' use only, but the *Periplus of the Erythrean Sea*, which may have been written in the middle of the first century of our era (Warmington, 1928: 47; Raschke, 1978: 649, although the date is still debatable), records glass, among many other items, as an export good. Specifically it is reported that glass was exported to: Adulis on the south end of the Red Sea (Charlesworth, 1924: 65); the "Berbers" in what is now Ethiopia (both "flint" and "murrhine" glass [*Periplus*, §6]); Avalites, present-day Djibouti (*Periplus*, §7); Mosyllum, now Somali (*Periplus*, §10); and ultimately to Barygaza (*Periplus*, §48-49) and Nelcynda (*Periplus*, §56) in India.

Actual finds of Roman glass in India are as yet rare. The treasure hoard at Begram, far up the Indus river, includes glass vessels that are probably Alexandrine, although the dates are so vague they could range from first to fourth centuries of our era (Raschke, 1978: 632-34). A pillar-molded bowl, a blue bowl "doubtless also of Mediterranean origin," (Wheeler, 1946: 102) and glass beads are reported from Arikamedu on the east coast of India (Wheeler, 1946: 95-101).

If Leucos Limen was playing a role in the India trade, and there is evidence for this in some Indian pottery and a peppercorn, then the port would have been busiest at the seasonal departure and arrival of the ships. A navigator, Hippalos, is said to have discovered the use of the monsoons in the early first century of our era (Warmington, 1928: 47) to sail to India and back in one year. The ships bound for India left about July (Warmington, 1928: 49), sailed to the Yemen or Guardafui and thence to the Malabar coast in about 40 days (Warmington, 1928: 46). The ships would restock in the Indian ports and start back about November, reaching Alexandria about February (Charlesworth, 1924: 60). Apart from July and January, then, only a skeleton occupancy of Leucos Limen need have been maintained. Given the harshness of the Red Sea coast, many merchants may well have retreated to the Nile Valley in the off seasons, unless carrying on trade not dependent on the monsoons.

The Roman period Red Sea ports managed to survive for only a relatively short time, when exceptionally favorable conditions existed. Augustus imposed the Pax Romana on the provinces and cleared the Red Sea of pirates (Charlesworth, 1924: 60). The discovery of the monsoons was probably made during the reign of Claudius (Warmington, 1928: 38), A.D. 41-54, and the trade to India burgeoned thereafter. The Roman rulers, with few lapses, fostered the trade, and it continued until the time of Marcus Aurelius, A.D. 161-80 (Charlesworth, 1924: 71), when internal disruptions preoccupied the government to the detriment of foreign luxury trade.

Nothing in the corpus of Roman glass presented here would be out of line with a first to second century date. Whether or not the glass at Quseir al-Qadim was intended for use there or for export abroad, it certainly represents a variety of types, from ordinary beakers to perfume flasks, perhaps valued mainly for their contents, to some of the finest products of the Alexandrian and Syrian workshops. Bleak as the site may now be, the ancient glass indicates cosmopolitan contacts for the port of Leucos Limen during its heyday.

Bibliography for Roman Glass

Auth, S.
   1976   *Ancient Glass from the Newark Museum*, Newark, New Jersey

Brussels, Musees Royaux d'Art et d'Histoire
   n.d.   *Florilege de la Verrerie ancienne*, Brussels

Calvi, M. C.
   1968   *I Vetri Romani del Museo di Aquileia*, Aquileia

Charlesworth, M. P.
   1924   *Trade-Routes and Commerce of the Roman Empire*, Cambridge
   1951   "Roman Trade with India: A Resurvey," in *Studies in Roman Economic and Social History*, ed. by P. R. Coleman-Morton, Princeton

Harden, D. B.
   1936   *Roman Glass from Karanis*, Ann Arbor, Michigan
   1969   "Ancient Glass, II: Roman," *Archaeological Journal* 126

Hayes, J. W.
   1975   *Roman and Pre-Roman Glass in the Royal Ontario Museum*, Toronto

Isings, C.
   1957   *Roman Glass from Dated Finds*, Groningen

Raschke, M. G.
   1978   "New Studies in Roman Commerce with the East," in *Aufstieg und Niedergang der Romischen Welt*, Vol. 9, part 9:2, ed. by H. Temporini, New York

Roth, A.
   1979   "Glass," in *Quseir al-Qadim 1978: Preliminary Report*, by D. S. Whitcomb and J. H. Johnson, Cairo

Schoff, W. H., trans.
   1974   *The Periplus of the Erythrean Sea*, New Delhi, India, reprint

Warmington, E. H.
   1928   *The Commerce between the Roman Empire and India*, Cambridge

Wheeler, R. E. M., A. Ghosh, and K. Deva
   1946   "Arikamedu: an Indo-Roman Trading-station on the East Coast of India," *Ancient India* 2

CHAPTER 9: ISLAMIC GLASS
Donald Whitcomb

The glass from the eastern area (see pl. 58) forms an important assemblage of glass of the Islamic period in which the probability of Roman admixture is minimal. Needless to say, this very fragile material has yielded few entire forms, although parallels from other collections allow many reconstructions.

The two examples of bowl forms illustrate the two major "wares" in which the glass is shaped. The first (a) is an open bowl of clear translucent glass, here with a blue band of glass on the rim. The prevalent colors of other clear glass are translucent light green, dark green, amber, dark brown, and dark blue. The second type is illustrated by a bowl with incurving sides (b) in which the glass is an opaque white and purple. This white glass is also found combined with a dark purple ranging to black, brown, and green in a marvering technique not unlike that employed during the Roman period. The marvering technique occurs on one other large rim (dd); otherwise, it is confined to small vials (cc,ee, mm-pp). This form usually has a straight rim (cc), rounded shoulder (mm), and narrow foot, square in section (nn). Sherd oo shows the distinctive neck bulge. The marvering technique is also employed in some of the Islamic bangles.

Very few bowl forms are present (relative to the Roman corpus), no doubt due to the functional duplication of impervious glass vessels in glazed ceramics. Deep bowls or beakers are found, however. The straight rims, often with a folded ridge, seem most common (c-e). The beaker form introduces two decorative techniques into the corpus. The first is appliqué dots (prunts), often in a contrasting color (here blue on clear, h), or appliqué zigzags or spiraling bands (i). The second type of decoration is painting or enameling of the glass. The painting is most often gold bands outlined with thin red lines (r,s). This is further elaborated with inscriptions against a blue background (p,q) or with fine scroll or floral motifs in which green and red colors are added (m,n,o; m may be the neck of a small jar).

A third decorative technique uses cut designs and seems mainly to have been employed on small jars or vials; the glass is either clear (t,u) or dark blue (ff, gg). One example of moulded decoration was found (qq), the base of a vial with a rounded foot. The jar forms include very small forms, both simple spherical forms (k+l) and a more complex shape (j) with a folded over base (not unlike the closed form of base ss or large base rr). Rim forms, probably for jars, are varied but tend to be rolled inward (v,w). Simple forms tend to curve outward (hh, a long neck of a jar or vase, jj, kk); rolled over rim ii is exceptional. Another

Plate 58: Islamic Glass

	Locus	RN	Description
a	E18b-2	77	clear, blue rim
b	F18a-1	74	purple, white marvered
c	F18a-6	77	amber
d	E18a-3	78	light green
e	E18c-2	78	green
f	F18a-4	74	green
g	E18c-2	77	clear
h	E18d-7	77	clear, two clear and one blue prunt
i	E18d-8	78	clear
j	E18d-12	77	green
k	E18c-2	78	green-brown
l	E18a-5	77	green
m	E18a-15	77	clear; gold, blue, with red outline
n	E18a-13	77	clear; gold, white, red, with red outline
o	E18a-13	77	clear; gold, yellow, green, with red outline
p	E18a-11	77	clear; gold, blue, with red outline
q	E18b-4	77	clear; gold, blue, with red outline
r	E18d-10	78	clear; gold with red outline
s	E18b-4	77	clear; gold with red outline
t	E18d-8	78	clear, cut decoration
u	E18d-8	78	clear, cut decoration
v	E18c-13	621	dark brown
w	E18a-15	77	clear, pale grey
x	E19c-3	74	dark brown
y	E18a-16	78	clear
z	E18d-14	77	green
aa	E18c-3	78	light green
bb	E18c-3	78	black
cc	E18a-13	77	green, white marvered
dd	E18a-3	77	purple, white marvered
ee	E18a-3	78	brown, white marvered
ff	E18b-4	77	dark blue, cut decoration
gg	E18d-7	77	blue, cut decoration
hh	E18b-2	77	light yellow-green
ii	E18a-14	78	green
jj	E18a-14	77	yellow-green
kk	E18a-14	78	green
ll	F18a-1	617	green
mm	E18d-5	77	green, white marvered
nn	E18c-8	77	black, white marvered
oo	E18b-2	77	brown, white marvered
pp	E18a-3	78	brown, white marvered
qq	E19c-10	79	dark brown, moulded, squared body
rr	E18d-7	77	amber
ss	E19c-6	79	dark green
tt	E18d-14	77	green
uu	E18d-11	78	clear
vv	E18c-2	77	clear
ww	E18a-16	78	brown
xx	E18b-4	77	green

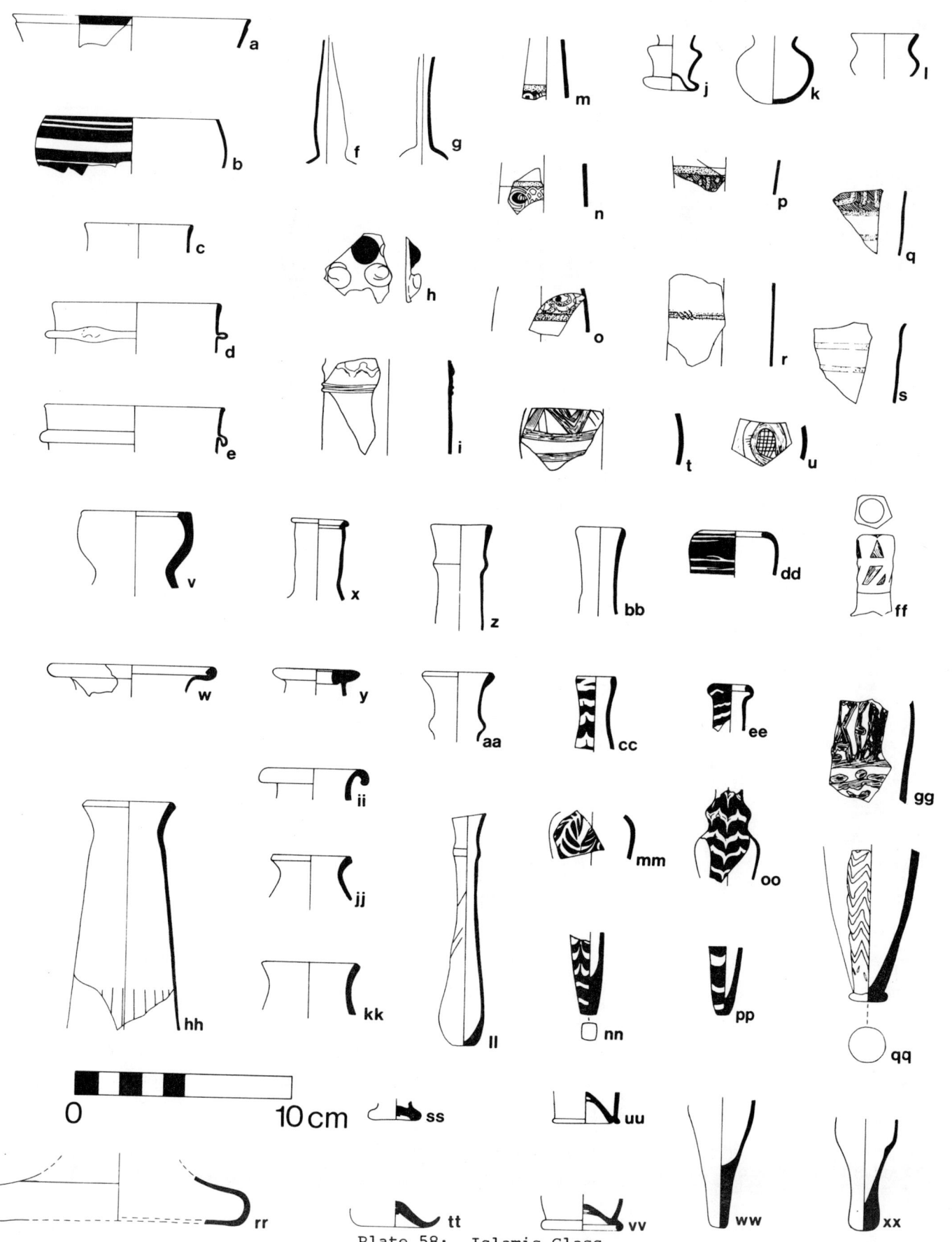

Plate 58: Islamic Glass

rim form (x,y) has a folded over, flat form which is uncomfortably similar to the common rim on Roman vases. The bases for jars or vases seem most often to have been common blown forms with a kick-up in the center (tt); a ring was occasionally added around the exterior of this base (uu,vv).

The most common glass form is the small vial. The rim is usually simple and slightly flaring (bb), often with a bulge in the neck (z,aa,ll). The base may have been bulbous, as in the complete example (ll), but was probably more often a solid foot (ww,xx). The complete form was probably similar to that posited for the marvered vials (cc+mm+nn). Two exceptionally thin examples of drawn glass may be necks for vials or dropper spouts (f,g).

Discussion

During the Ayyubid-Mamluk period, the glass industry produced an important export product of Egypt, much as it had during the Roman period. The industry was centered on Alexandria (Kom el-Dikka; Dabrowski, 1960; Lane, 1949) and at Fustat (although this material is somewhat earlier; Scanlon, 1967: 73ff.; Pinder-Wilson and Scanlon, 1973). As in the Roman period, a parallel industry was current in Syria (Riis and Poulsen, 1957; Salam-Liebich, 1978).[1] While some of the glass vessels found at Quseir al-Qadim may have been in use at the port, the majority were probably intended as export products.

The glass inventory reported at Soba and, more importantly, at the Red Sea port of Aidhab offer instructive comparisons on the distribution of these products (Shinnie and Harden, 1955). Beakers with a folded ridge are present (*ibid.*: fig. 43 = 58:c,d,e), bulbous jar rims (fig. 37:16 = 58:v), flaring jar rims (fig. 43 = 58:ii,jj,kk) and base forms, including beaker bases with an external ring (fig. 45 = 58:ss-vv). The same range of forms has also been reported for the East African coast at Kilwa (Chittick, 1974: fig. 160d,e; 155n; 157a; 156e; 157l,n). While moulded vessels occur at Aidhab (similar to 58:qq) and cut decorations occur (Shinnie and Harden, 1955: fig. 41b = 58:u), marvered glass and enameled glass appear to be absent. An important decorative technique at both Quseir al-Qadim and Aidhab is the use of prunts, presumably to decorate beakers (*ibid.*: fig. 40 = 58:h).

The use of prunts on glass vessels points to developments in this industry which are common to the development of Mediterranean, and specifically Venetian,

---

[1] Several of the Egyptian and Syrian connections mentioned here were called to my attention by Scott Redford.

glass wares during this time period (Gasparetto, 1979). The glass from the excavations at Corinth illustrate this form and the characteristic neck-bulge (Davidson, 1952: 742-44, 780). Medieval glass from Heshbon illustrates a similar range of forms, as well as marvering decoration (Goldstein, pers. comm.), suggesting an interrelationship between Mediterranean and Egyptian influences. The Egyptian products may be seen in the collection of the Benaki, most of which seems to come from Fustat/Cairo (Clairmont, 1977; this includes close parallels with the Quseir al-Qadim corpus, including enameled and marvered wares). This interrelationship has been graphically demonstrated in the glassware from the Serge Limen wreck, which seems to have been of Egyptian origin. The series of bottles from this wreck finds an intriguing parallel in the wide bottle rim found at Quseir in 1978 (Whitcomb and Johnson, 1979: 63:f). A number of other forms and cut decorations also find parallels; however, the wreck, which is currently dated to the early 11th century, is somewhat earlier than the remains at Quseir al-Qadim (Bass, pers. comm.).

The glass from Quseir al-Qadim stands thus between developments in the Mediterranean and the trading patterns of the Red Sea, a pattern which one also sees in the ceramics and other artifacts from this port. While the small vials and the bottles may have served as containers for perfumes and other valuable products, it is likely that most of the glass vessels were trade goods being shipped for their own sake.

The glass bangles at Quseir al-Qadim are probably imported into Egypt as a product of Aden (especially Khanfar; Lankester Harding, 1964), where wasters have been found amid extensive glass slag. This Aden glass industry was probably not confined to these bangles, which raises the possibility of other imported Aden glass wares at Quseir al-Qadim. Bracelets have also been found in India (Sankalia, 1960), where local production is also claimed. This widespread craft is also a feature in Syrian sites (Salam-Liebich, 1978: 145; Riis and Poulsen, 1957: 60).

Much of the quandry as to dating and regional production will be clarified with technical descriptions and analyses. The bracelets found in the eastern area of Quseir al-Qadim are usually either 4.5 or 6.0 cm. interior diameter. The majority of fragments are plain glass, usually black (or very dark blue) or light blue or green, and they are triangular in section (59:o,p). A second type is twisted glass, either a solid color or threads of alternating colors; these twisted bracelets have a circular section (59:q,r).

Plate 59: Figurines, Beads, and Bracelets

	Locus	RN	Description
a	G8a-4	297	red ware; grey core; FN 2
b	E6a-7	291	red-orange ware; grey core
c	F7a-1	292	red ware; grey core
d	E6d-2	61	glass weight, 1.7 gm.
e	G8b-2	81	red, yellow, and blue glass beads; 2:1
f	D6d-7	71	green, black, and white glass; 2:1
g	G8b-3	80	turquoise glass with yellow dots; 2:1
h	E18d-8	77	black glass with yellow trails; 2:1
i	G12c-1	58	2:1
j	F7a-5	65	black glass; 2:1
k	G8b-5	73	agate; 2:1
l	E7a-1	55	turquoise glass; 2:1
m	G8b-9	73	orange brown glass; 2:1
n	E18d-10	77	turquoise; diameter 4.7 cm.
o	E18c-1	77	dark turquoise; diameter 4.8 cm.
p	E18d-10	77	yellow and blue green; diameter 6 cm.
q	F18a-1	74	white, yellow, and red; diameter 6 cm.
r	F19a-4	74	blue, white and red band; diameter 6 cm.
s	E18d-5	77	yellow, green, yellow, light blue, red stripes
t	E18d-17	77	blue, yellow, red, and white
u	E19c-7	79	green, brown stripes; diameter 6 cm.
v	E18a-6	77	yellow, red dots; diameter 6 cm.
w	E19c-9	79	green, yellow, white, red, black; diameter 6 cm.
x	E18d-4	78	black, yellow-brown stripes, yellow, brown, turquoise dots
y	E18c-3	77	dark blue, yellow, brown, white stripes and dots; diameter 5 cm.

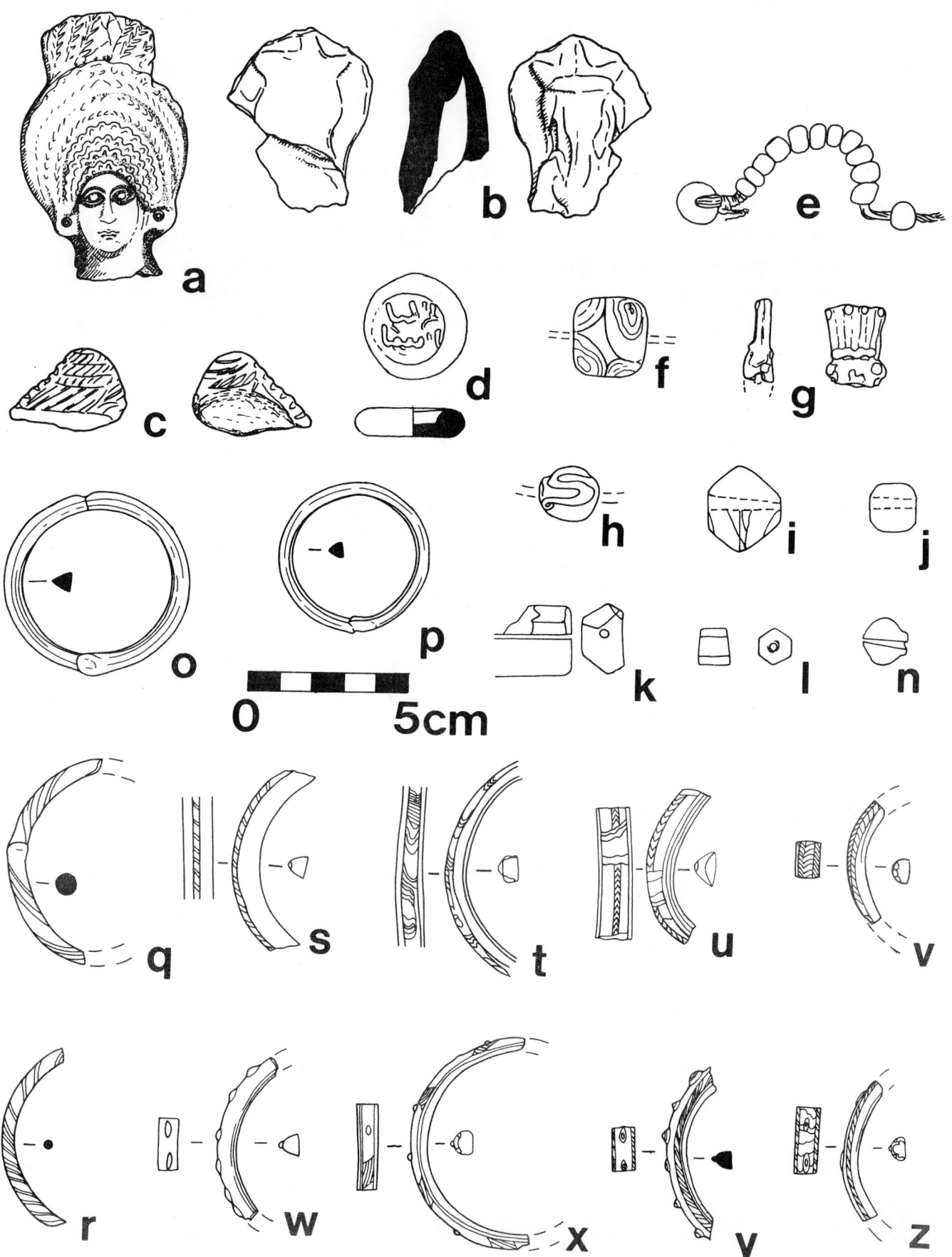

Plate 59: Figurines, Beads, and Bracelets

Fancier bracelets have a variety of colored glass decorations added to the dorsal (exterior) edge of a dark green or dark blue base, either triangular or semi-circular in section. In addition to blue and green, glass colored red, white, yellow, and light blue is used. These additions are: twisted bands (59:s), marvered bands (59:t,v) or combinations, i.e., twisted bands with marvered stripes (59:u). More elaborate bracelets have a series of prunts added dorsally to simple bracelets (59:w), on marvered stripes (59:x), with twisted bands (59:y), or on top of combinations (59:z). These last two examples have prunts which are built up of concentric colors. The decoration on bracelets may thus be considered additive in complexity, the most elaborate being extremely colorful. While the technique of marvering and use of prunts fits in well with techniques found in the glass vessels, the correlation of these glass products and their regional sources must await further publication and detailed analyses.

As a final note on the glass artifacts from Quseir al-Qadim, one Islamic glass weight was found in the 1980 season; this glass weight is epigraphic, unlike the excavated weight from 1978 (Whitcomb and Johnson, 1979: 74:j). These glass weights (and several from surface finds in 1978) will be studied separately; in view of the current discussion of the purpose of these artifacts (Bates, 1981; Balog, 1981), their presence in these excavations (with a barrel weight and coins) may yield information on the commercial use of these artifacts. This weight is 1.7 gm., a very rare "denomination" in Bates' system (1981: 92).

Bibliography for Islamic Glass

Balog, P.
1981 "Fatimid Glass Jetons: Token Currency or Coin-Weights?," *Journal of the Economic and Social History of the Orient* 24: 93-109

Bates, M. L.
1981 "The Function of Fatimid and Ayyubid Glass Weights," *Journal of the Economic and Social History of the Orient* 24: 63-92

Chittick, N.
1974 *Kilwa, an Islamic Trading City on the East African Coast*, 2 vols.

Clairmont, C. W.
1977 *Catalogue of Ancient and Islamic Glass, Benaki Museum*, Athens

Dabrowski, L.
1960 "Resumé des recherches archéologiques faites autour du Fort Kom El Dikka en Alexandrie," *Alexandria University Bulletin* 14

Davidson, G. R.
1952 *Corinth*, vol. 12: *The Minor Objects*, Princeton

Gasparetto, A.
    1979   "Matrici e aspetti della vetraria veneziana e veneta medievale," *Journal of Glass Studies* 21: 76-

Lane, A.
    1949   "Archaeological Excavation at Kom el-Dik, A Preliminary Report on the Medieval Pottery," *Bulletin of the Faculty of Arts, University of Alexandria* 5: 143-47

Lankester Harding, G.
    1964   *Archaeology in the Aden Protectorates*, London

Pinder-Wilson, R. H., and G. T. Scanlon
    1973   "Glass Finds from Fustat: 1964-1971," *Journal of Glass Studies* 15: 12-30

Riis, P. J., and V. Poulsen
    1957   *Les Fouilles de Hama*, Copenhagen

Salam-Liebich, H.
    1978   "Glass," chapter 7 in O. Grabar, *City in the Desert: Qasr al-Hayr East*, Cambridge

Sankalia, B.
    1960   *From History to Pre-history, Nevasa*, Poona

Scanlon, G. T.
    1967   "Preliminary Report 1965, Part II, Fustat Expedition," *Journal of the American Research Center in Egypt* 6: 65-86

Shinnie, P. L., and D. B. Harden
    1955   *Excavations at Soba*, Sudan Antiquities Service, Occasional Papers, No. 3, Khartoum

Whitcomb, D. S., and J. H. Johnson
    1979   *Quseir al-Qadim 1978: Preliminary Report*, Cairo

CHAPTER 10: ROMAN LAMPS

Steven Sidebotham

Thirty-five Roman lamps or lamp fragments were discovered at Quseir al-Qadim in the 1980 season: Fifteen had been manufactured in Egypt, twenty had been imported from elsewhere in the Roman world. The distribution figures of lamps found at Quseir al-Qadim in 1978 and 1980 are:

	1978	1980	Total
Roman imports	4	20	24
Egyptian made, Roman period	11	15	26
Total	15	35	50

The distribution of Roman imports compared to the total number of lamps found in each of the two seasons contrasts sharply: Imports comprise over 26% of the total for the 1978 season and over 57% of the total for the 1980 season. However, it is more meaningful to contrast the totals of the categories for both years. The distribution of these fifty securely attributed Roman period lamps shows that slightly more than 50% (26) were manufactured in Egypt, slightly less than 50% (24) were imported. It is not surprising to find Roman import lamps at Quseir al-Qadim, but the high percentage is unusual for an Egyptian site. That Quseir al-Qadim was a Roman port engaged in international trade, handling many products from throughout the empire for export abroad, may explain the availability of imported lamps at an otherwise desolate place.

Most of the imports discovered at Quseir al-Qadim were made in Italy, although catalogue nos. 1, 10, 14, 15, and 19 may be of eastern Mediterranean provenance and no. 6 may not be a lamp fragment at all, but part of another type of coroplastic decoration. Other sites in Egypt have produced a number of lamps imported from elsewhere in the Roman world, especially Italy. It seems that imported lamps must have been readily available and of reasonable price; indeed, a private letter from Heraclides to his father Horion at Oxyrhynchus (P. Oxy. I. 188) during Hadrian's reign (A.D. 117-38) deals with the purchase of a slave and a pair of Italian lamps.

In general, the imported lamps found at Quseir al-Qadim are better preserved than the Egyptian made ones. This seems due to the finer, sturdier fabric of the imports compared to the more friable clays of the Egyptian products.

There are two problems confronting the study of Roman lamps made in Egypt: their chronology and place of manufacture. The excavations at Quseir al-Qadim shed some light on the former problem, but none on the latter. With few exceptions, publications on Roman lamps made in Egypt do not inspire confidence with regard to dating. This is a problem which stems, for the most part, from lack of strict stratigraphic controls on excavations in Egypt. Most of the parallels cited for the Quseir al-Qadim specimens made in Egypt show a 3rd-4th century date while practically all the Roman imports are securely dated to the 1st-2nd centuries. Is one to conclude from this that the two categories, imports and Egyptian made lamps, were not used simultaneously at the port? This is doubtful as several of the imported lamps have been found in the same loci as Egyptian lamps. For example, catalogue no. 1 (RN 126c) and nos. 26 (RN 126a) and 27 (RN 126b) are from the same locus, E6a-1. RN 126c is an import from Italy closely dated to Augustus-Tiberius (c. 30 B.C.--A.D. 37). Yet parallels cited for RN 126a and 126b vary from the 2nd to the 4th century. Clearly, based on the date of RN 126c, the dates for RN 126a and 126b also must be Augustan-Tiberian. Throughout the catalogue, Egyptian made lamps of the Roman period from Quseir al-Qadim have been left undated unless dated imports were found with them in the same locus or the Egyptian made lamps have parallels with other Egyptian made lamps dated by imports from the same locus.

Egyptian made lamps from the Roman period have been found at a variety of sites in Egypt and it is difficult, given their wide geographic distribution, to ascertain their place of manufacture. The fabric and slip of the Egyptian made lamps is fairly uniform: Shades of brown and red fabric predominate while slips tend to be slightly darker tones of browns and reds. In general, the clays are finer textured in the lamps with more realistic, detailed decoration and coarser in the more schematically decorated ones. The finer textured Egyptian lamps are also usually larger in size than the coarser textured specimens. Undoubtedly several widely scattered centers of manufacture existed in the Nile Valley to supply such a wide market, but the location of these factories remains unknown.

All the lamps described in the catalogue are mould made in two halves--top and bottom. All dates in the catalogue are A.D. Although the fuel used in the Quseir al-Qadim examples is unknown, a number of classical sources note that the Egyptians favored kiki (castor) oil[1] and it may be suggested tentatively that kiki oil was also used at Quseir al-Qadim.

---

[1] Herodotus 2.94; Diodorus Siculus 1.34.11; Strabo 17.2.5; Pliny, *NH* 15.7.25; see also W. L. Westermann, "Account of Lamp Oil from the Estate of Apollonius," *CP* 19, 3 (1923) 229-60, and A. E. Samuel, "Illumination by Castor Oil--P. Cornell 1," *BASP* 1 (1963-1964) 32-38.

Bibliography for Roman Lamps

Bailey, D. M.
    1980   *A Catalogue of the Lamps in the British Museum*, Vol. 2, *The Roman Lamps Made in Italy*, London

Bernhard, M. L.
    1955   *Lampki starożytne*, Warsaw

Bovon, A.
    1966   *Lampes d'Argos, Ecole française d'Athènes, Etudes Péloponnésiennes 5*, Paris

Brants, J.
    1913   *Antieke terra-cotta lampen uit het Rijksmuseum van oudheden te Leiden*, Leiden

Breccia, E.
    1914   *Alexandrea ad Aegyptum*, Bergamo

Bresciani, E.
    1968   *Missione di scavo a Medinet Madi (Fayum), Rapporto preliminare delle campagne di scavo 1966 e 1967*, Milan

Broneer, O.
    1930   *Corinth*, Vol. 4, part 2, *Terracotta Lamps*, Cambridge, Massachusetts

Bruneau, P.
    1965   *Exploration archéologique de Délos faite par l'Ecole française d'Athènes*, Vol. 26, *Les Lampes*, Paris

Bruyère, B.
    1966   *Fouilles IFAO*, Vol. 27, *Fouilles de Clysma-Qolzoum (Suez) 1930-1932*, Cairo

Cahn-Klaiber, E.-M.
    1977   *Die antiken Tonlampen des Archäologischen Instituts der Universität Tübingen*, Tübingen

Deneauve, J.
    1969   *Lampes de Carthage*, Paris

(Ephesos)
    1937   *Forschungen in Ephesos*, Vol. 4, part 2, *Das Cömeterium der Sieben Schläfer (Österreichisches Archäologisches Institut)*, Vienna

Farka, C.
    1977   *Die römischen Lampen vom Magdalensberg (Kärtner Museumsschriften 61)*, Klagenfurt

Heres, G.
    1972   *Die römischen Bildlampen der Berliner Antikensammlung*, Berlin

Kaufmann, C. M.
    1915   *Graeco-ägyptische Koroplastik; Terrakotten der griechisch-römischen und koptischen Epoche aus der Faijûm-Oase und anderen Fundstätten*, Leipzig--Cairo

Lerat, L.
    1954   *Catalogue des collections archéologiques de Besançon: Les lampes antiques (Annales littéraires de l'Université de Besançon*, 2nd ser., Vol. 1, part 1), Paris

Loeschcke, S.
    1919   *Lampen aus Vindonissa*, Zurich

Michałowski, K., et al.
    1950   *Fouilles franco-polonaises rapports III Tell Edfou 1939*, Cairo

Michelucci, M.
    1975   *La collezione di lucerne del Museo egizio di Firenze*, Florence

Oziol, T. J.
    1977   *Les lampes du Musée de Chypre (Salamine de Chypre 7)*, Paris

Perlzweig, J.
    1961   *The Athenian Agora*, Vol. 7, *Lamps of the Roman Period First to Seventh Century after Christ*, Princeton

Petrie, W. M. F.
    1904-   *Roman Ehnasya (Herakleopolis Magna)*
    1905   *Plates and Text Supplementary to Ehnasya*, London

Ponsich, M.
    1961   *Les lampes romaines en terre cuite de la Maurétanie tingitane (Publications du Service des Antiquités du Maroc*, fasc. 15), Rabat
    1963   "Les lampes romaines de la Collection Ingres (Musée du Montauban)," *Revue Archéologique du Centre* 2, pp. 100-32

Robins, F. W.
    1939a   "Graeco-Roman Lamps from Egypt," *JEA* 25, pp. 48-51
    1939b   *The Story of the Lamp (and the Candle)*, London-New York

Rosenthal, R., and R. Sivan
    1978   *Ancient Lamps in the Schloessinger Collection (QEDEM Monograph 8 of the Institute of Archaeology, The Hebrew University of Jerusalem)*, Jerusalem

Shier, L. A.
    1978   *Terracotta Lamps from Karanis, Egypt, Excavations of the University of Michigan (The University of Michigan Kelsey Museum of Archaeology Studies* 3), Ann Arbor, Michigan

Szentléleky, T.
    1969   *Ancient Lamps*, Amsterdam

Whitcomb, D. S., and J. H. Johnson
    1979   *Quseir al-Qadim 1978: Preliminary Report*, Cairo

Catalogue of Roman Lamps

The catalogue adopts the following format: 1) brief description of state of preservation: If a fragment, what remains is described; if nearly complete, the missing parts are specified. 2) measurements (maximum, including handles, in cm.) 3) color of fabric and slip (based on the *Munsell Soil Color Charts*

[Baltimore, 1954] 4) Quseir al-Qadim 1980 registration number (RN) and locus designation 5) detailed description of lamp 6) date, if ascertainable 7) type, if ascertainable 8) parallels, if ascertainable. The following abbreviations are used: fr fragment, l left, r right, no(s) number(s), fig figure, stg standing, C century, pl plate, p(p) page(s) L length, W width, H height, Th thickness, P preserved.

Imports

1) fr, parts of discus, rim; PL/PW 4.6; yellow (10YR 7/6) fabric; very dark greyish-brown (10YR 3/2) slip
    RN 126c/E6a-1
    discus: part of shell with 7 ribs
    rim: 4 raised bands and 4 grooves separate discus from narrow undecorated rim
    Augustan-Tiberian
    Loeschcke, 1919: type IV
    Loeschcke, 1919: nos 570-74; Bruneau, 1965: no 4609 (seems to be Cnidian or could be Italian import)

2) fr, parts of discus, rim, body wall; PL/PW 4.7; PH 2.55; very pale brown (10YR 7/4) fabric; brown/dark brown (10YR 4/3) slip
    RN 123/H8a-2
    discus: 2 gladiators fighting (only 1 visible and part of shield of 2nd), gladiator advancing r armed as a Thrax wears helmet, holds sword in r hand, shield in l, part of fill hole
    rim: 3 raised bands and 3 grooves separate discus from narrow undecorated rim
    Augustan-Tiberian
    Deneauve, 1969: type IVA; Cahn-Klaiber, 1977: type 5.2.1.5; Broneer, 1930: type XXII; Loeschcke, 1919: type I
    Cahn-Klaiber, 1977: no 244 (from Kom-esh-Shufaga in Alexandria, late Augustan--early Tiberian); Rosenthal, 1978: no 61 (1st C); Farka, 1977: no 817 (only 1 gladiator, Augustan--Tiberian)

3) fr, parts of discus, rim, volute nozzle; PL 3.75; PW 2.0; PH 1.05; yellow (2.5Y 8/6) fabric; very worn yellow (2.5Y 7/6) slip
    RN 396b/E6a-4
    discus: too fragmentary to determine decoration
    rim: discus defined from narrow undecorated rim by 3 raised bands and 3 grooves, parts of volute nozzle
    1st C
    Michelucci, 1975: type 20; Bailey, 1980: type A; Loeschcke, 1919: type I
    Shier, 1978: nos 320, 431 (early 2nd-early 3rd C); Michelucci, 1975: nos 48-49 (second half 1st C); Oziol, 1977: nos 174 (similar volutes), 176 (similar discus/rim division, these lamps imported to Cyprus perhaps from Italy, 1st C); Bailey, 1980: nos Q765EA, Q766-769 (Augustan--Tiberian)

4) fr, part of volute nozzle, wick hole; PL 3.75; PW 1.65; PH 1.8; reddish-yellow (7.5YR 7/6) fabric; red (2.5YR 5/6) slip
    RN 396a/E6a-7
    volute nozzle and wick hole, evidence of burning

Plate 60: Roman Lamps

	Locus	RN	Description
a	E6a-1	126c	yellow (10YR 7/6) fabric; very dark greyish-brown (10YR 3/2) slip
b	H8a-2	123	very pale brown (10YR 7/4) fabric; brown/dark brown (10YR 4/3) slip
c	E6a-4	396b	yellow (2.5Y 8/6) fabric; very worn yellow (2.5Y 7/6) slip
d	E6a-7	396a	reddish-yellow (7.5YR 7/6) fabric; red (2.5YR 5/6) slip
e	E7c-1	335b	red (2.5YR 5/8) fabric; red (2.5YR 4/8) slip
f	E7c-1	335a	very pale brown (10YR 8/4) fabric; dark reddish-brown (5YR 3/2) slip
g	E6b-29	122	red (2.5YR 5/6) fabric; red (2.5YR 4/8) slip
h	E6b-16	367a	reddish-yellow (7.5YR 6/6) fabric; red (2.5YR 4/8) slip
i	E6b-14	367b	pale yellow (2.5YR 7/4) fabric; pale yellow (2.5YR 7/4) slip
j	E6b-16	367c	dark grey (7.5YR 4/0) fabric; very dark grey (7.5YR 3/0) slip
k	E7a-5	115	reddish-yellow (7.5YR 7/6) fabric; brown (7.5YR 5/4) slip
l	E7a-14	112	reddish-yellow (7.5YR 7/6) fabric; red (2.5YR 4/8) slip
m	surf	662	pink (5YR 8/3) fabric; light red (2.5YR 6/8) worn slip
n	E7a-16	118	light red (2.5YR 6/6) fabric; red (2.5YR 5/6) slip
o	E7a-16	334a	reddish-yellow (7.5YR 7/6) fabric; red (2.5YR 5/6) slip
p	E7a-16	334b	light red (7.5R 6/8) fabric; weak red (7.5R 4/4) slip
q	E7a-16	334c	light brown (7.5YR 6/4) fabric; red (2.5YR 5/8) slip
r	E7a-16	334d	light red (2.5YR 6/6) fabric; red (2.5YR 5/6) slip
s	surf	662	light red (2.5YR 6/6) to grey (7.5R 6/0) fabric; red (2.5YR 5/6) slip
t	surf	662	reddish-yellow (7.5YR 8/6) fabric; red (2.5YR 5/8) slip
u	E6b-33	367f	red (2.5YR 5/8) fabric; red (2.5YR 5/6) slip
v	F7a-1	119	yellowish-red (5YR 4/6) coarse fabric; red (2.5YR 5/6) slip
w	E7c-7	117	light red (2.5YR 6/6) fabric; very pale brown (10YR 7/3) slip
x	E6b-14	121	red (2.5YR 5/6) fabric; light red (2.5YR 6/6) slip
y	E6a-1	126a	red (2.5YR 5/6) coarse fabric; light yellowish-brown (10YR 6/4) slip
z	E6a-1	126b	reddish-yellow (5YR 7/6) coarse fabric; light red (10R 6/8) slip
aa	E7c-1	335c	reddish-brown (5YR 5/4) to very pale brown (10YR 7/4) fabric; very pale brown (10YR 7/3) slip
bb	E6a-13	113	reddish-yellow (5YR 6/6) fabric; dark reddish-brown (5YR 3/3) slip
cc	E6a-13	114	reddish-yellow (5YR 6/6) fabric; red (2.5YR 4/6) slip
dd	E7a-8	116	very pale brown (10YR 7/4) fabric; olive brown (2.5YR 4/4) slip
ee	surf	662	red (2.5YR 4/8) fabric; reddish-brown (2.5YR 5/4) slip
ff	E6b-38	120	very dark grey (2.5YR 3/0) fabric
gg	surf	662	light reddish-brown (5YR 6/4) fabric; reddish-brown (5YR 4/4) slip
hh	E6b-16	367e	red (2.5YR 4/6) fabric; red (2.5YR 4/6) slip

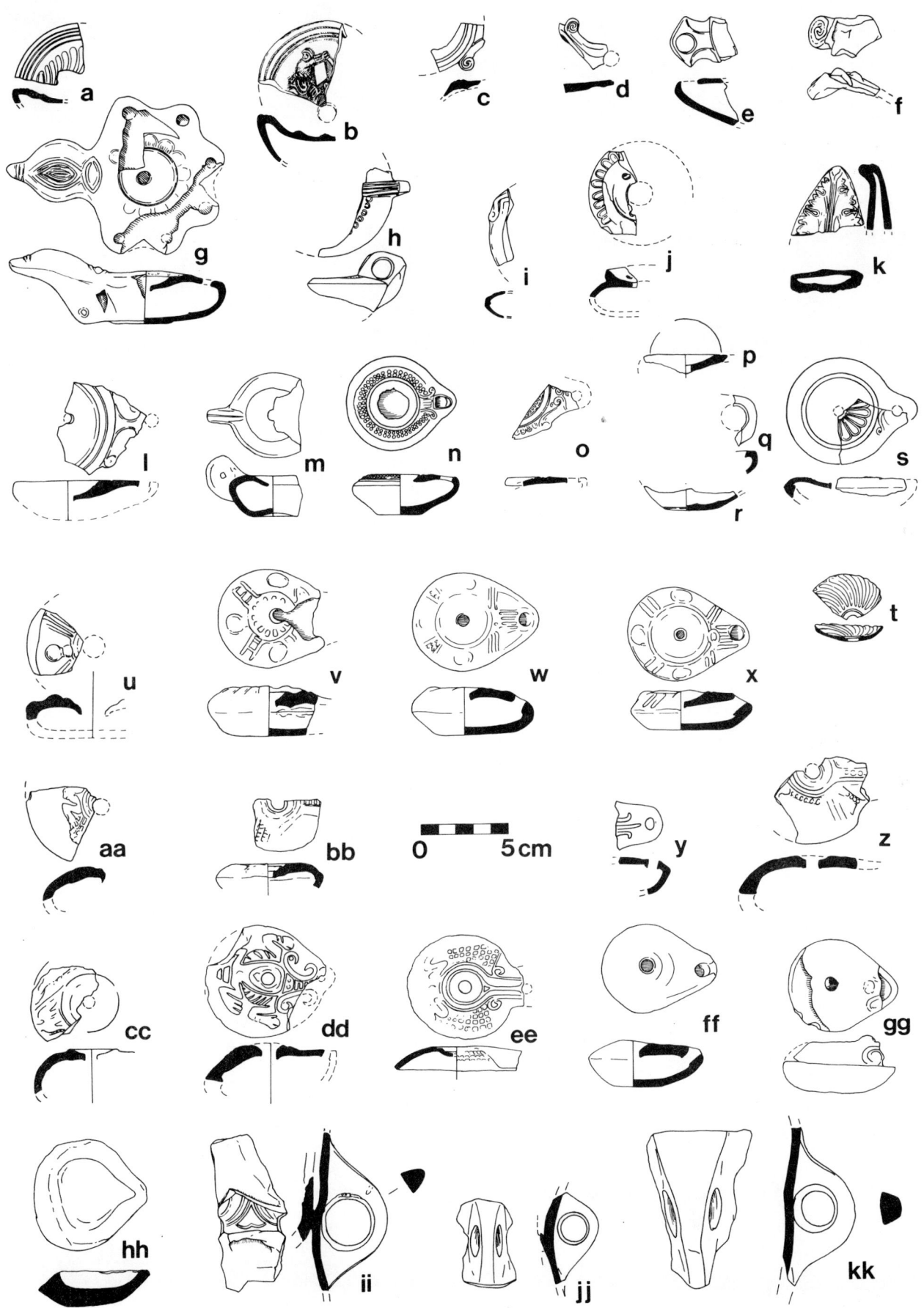

Plate 60: Roman Lamps

Plate 60 continued

ii G8b-18 328   buff; red-brown slip; moulded decoration; ESA
jj E6a-15 397   cream
kk J14a-5 331   buff; red slip; ESA

5) fr, part of nozzle; PL 3.4; PW 3.25; PH 3.8; red (2.5YR 5/8) fabric; red (2.5YR 4/8) slip
RN 335b/E7c-1
triangular shaped volute nozzle, evidence of burning
Augustan-Flavian
Deneauve, 1969: type IVA; Cahn-Klaiber, 1977: type L.I; Bailey, 1980: type AII or AIII (Augustan-Flavian); Loeschcke, 1919: type I or IB
Petrie, 1905: pl LIII, nos 6, 67g (similar nozzles), possibly pl LIII, no 75i, pl LVI, no 12, no 88 (on r) (all similar nozzles); Breccia, 1914: p 237, fig 91 (similar nozzle, from Alexandria); Deneauve, 1969: nos 278-369; Cahn-Klaiber, 1977: nos 160-69 (perhaps from Alexandria, Tiberian-second half 1st C)

6) fr, part of volute nozzle and body wall (?) (may not be lamp); PH 4.15; very pale brown (10YR 8/4) fabric; dark reddish-brown (5YR 3/2) slip
RN 335a/E7c-1
elaborate volute

7) nearly complete; parts of discus, rim, nozzle, body walls and base missing; L 12.5; W 9.55; H 4.3; red (2.5YR 5/6) fabric; red (2.5YR 4/8) slip
RN 122/E6b-29
discus: undecorated with off-center fill hole
rim: discus defined from undecorated rim by single groove, 1 complete nozzle, parts of 5 others, pierced almond-shaped reflector handle decorated with grooves and bands following shape of handle, body walls slope to slightly raised base defined by incised line, evidence of burning
Augustan-late 1st C
Bailey, 1980: type D; Broneer, 1930: type XXI
Kaufmann, 1915: fig 128 bottom row, 3rd from l (handle similar); Petrie, 1905: pl LV, no 95 top row 5th from l, 2nd row 1st on l (similar handles); Shier, 1978: no 321 (handle similar, late 1st C); Farka, 1977: no 620 (handle similar, Augustan-Tiberian); Bailey, 1980: no Q1025 (handle similar, late Augustan-early Flavian)

8) fr, handle, parts of rim, body wall; PL 5.9; PW 5.25; PH 3.55; reddish-yellow (7.5YR 6/6) fabric; red (2.5YR 4/8) slip
RN 367a/E6b-16
rim: decorated with 5 incised dots and part of 6th, complete pierced handle decorated with 3 grooves and 4 ridges
second quarter 1st-first half second C
Michelucci, 1975: type 22 or 23
Michelucci, 1975: no 71 or 72 (seem to be imports)

9) fr, parts of discus, rim, volute nozzle, body wall; PL 4.5; PW 1.2; PH 1.65; pale yellow (2.5YR 7/4) fabric; pale yellow (2.5YR 7/4) slip
RN 367b/E6b-14
discus: too fragmentary to determine decoration
rim: discus defined from undecorated rim by single groove, volute protrudes onto rim

10) fr, parts of discus, rim, nozzle; PL 4.95; PW 1.7; PH 3.1; dark grey (7.5YR 4/0) fabric; very dark grey (7.5YR 3/0) slip
RN 367c/E6b-16
discus: deep, undecorated with 1 complete air hole, part of 2nd, part of fill hole
rim: discus defined from rim by thick raised ridge, 8 tongue patterns and part of 9th, ridge defines part of nozzle from rim and discus
possibly Bernhard, 1955: no. 333 (3rd C)

11) fr, part of reflector handle; PL 3.95; PW 4.0; Th 1.4; reddish-yellow (7.5YR 7/6) fabric; brown (7.5YR 5/4) slip
RN 115/E7a-5
triangular shaped reflector handle broken at base, reflector decorated with stem and leaf design
Augustan-Trajanic
Bailey, 1980: type D; Brants, 1913: type IX; Broneer, 1930: type XXI
Brants, 1913: no 262a (handle similar, Tiberian-2nd C); Farka, 1977: no 616 (first half 1st C); Bailey, 1980: nos Q1023 (late Augustan-early Flavian), Q1044 (Augustan-early Trajanic); Shier, 1978: no 329 (early 2nd C)

12) fr, parts of discus, fill hole, rim, volute nozzle, wick hole and body wall; PL 5.0; PW 5.45; PTh 1.3; reddish-yellow (7.5YR 7/6) fabric; red (2.5YR 4/8) slip
RN 112/E7a-14
discus: undecorated with part of central fill hole
rim: discus defined from undecorated rim by 3 grooves, parts of double volute nozzle and wick hole
mid 1st-2nd C
Cahn-Klaiber, 1977: type L.IV; Michelucci, 1975: type 21
Petrie, 1905: pl LIII, no 33 (volutes similar), no 25a (volutes only); Michelucci, 1975: no 63 (similar, but decorated, second half 1st-2nd C); Cahn-Klaiber, 1977: no 175 (nozzle similar, unknown findspot, mid 1st C, Italian import); Ponsich, 1963: no 108

13) nearly complete; parts of discus, rim, nozzle, body walls, and base missing; PL 5.65; W 5.05; H 3.5; pink (5YR 8/3) fabric; light red (2.5YR 6/8) worn slip
RN 662/surface
discus: deep undecorated with broken central fill hole
rim: discus defined from undecorated rim by worn raised ridge, single groove decorates pierced handle, body walls curve to very worn concave base defined by worn raised band, lamp covered with patchy bituminous substance
1st-2nd C
Ponsich, 1963: type III BI; Loeschcke, 1919: type VIII; Broneer, 1930: type XXV; Lerat, 1954: 3rd series B; (Ephesos), 1937: type VIII; Bailey, 1980: type P, group I
Bernhard, 1955: nos 258-60 (similar, 1st C, no 258 from Cherchell, Algeria); Ponsich, 1963: no 62 (similar, Claudian/Neronian-Hadrianic); Perlzweig, 1961: nos 126, 176 (similar, mid 1st-2nd C); (Ephesos), 1937: nos 94, 96 (similar, could be as late as second half 2nd C); Szentléleky, 1969: nos 141a-b (similar), 155a-b (similar, 161a-b (similar) (all second/third quarter 1st-2nd C); Bailey, 1980: nos Q1255, Q1258 (Flavian-early Antonine)

14) nearly complete; part of discus missing; L 6.0; W 5.3; H 2.0; light red
    (2.5YR 6/6) fabric; red (2.5YR 5/6) slip
    RN 118/E7a-16
    discus: two rows of raised dots
    rim: discus defined from rim by 2 raised bands, rim defined from body walls by
    2 raised bands, double volute nozzle with large wick hole protrudes onto
    rim, body walls chipped, slope to raised foot separated from body walls by
    incised band
    Broneer, 1930: type XVIII (?)
    Broneer, 1930: p 103, fig 48, no 20 (similar rim decoration, but 3 rows of
    dots)

15) fr, parts of discus, rim, body wall; PL 4.25; PW 2.8; PH 1.65; reddish-yellow
    (7.5YR 7/6) fabric; red (2.5YR 5/6) slip
    RN 334a/E7a-16
    discus: decorated with indented lines radiating from center of discus (?)
    rim: discus defined from rim by 2 widely separated grooves, rim decorated
    with 4 tongue/dart patterns, volute nozzle with wick hole, incised dots above
    volutes and at top of nozzle, evidence of burning
    1st-2nd C

16) fr, parts of discus, rim; PL/PW 4.75; light red (7.5R 6/8) fabric; weak red
    (7.5R 4/4) slip, from a worn mould
    RN 334b/E7a-16
    discus: undecorated with single off-center fill hole
    rim: discus defined from undecorated rim by 2 widely separated grooves
    1st-2nd C (?)
    Bovon, 1966: no 231 (similar, 1st-2nd C)

17) fr, part of nozzle; PL 1.4; PW 2.95; PH 1.7; light brown (7.5YR 6/4) fabric;
    red (2.5YR 5/8) slip
    RN 334c/E7a-16
    end of nozzle
    1st-2nd C (?)

18) fr, base, parts of body walls, base of nozzle; PL 5.7: PW 5.15; PH 2.15;
    light red (2.5YR 6/6) fabric; red (2.5YR 5/6) slip
    RN 334d/E7a-16
    slightly convex base defined from body walls by incised line
    1st-2nd C (?)

19) fr, parts of discus, rim, nozzle, body wall; PL 4.8: PW 3.9; PH 1.15; light
    red (2.5YR 6/6) to grey (7.5R 6/0) fabric; red (2.5YR 5/6) slip
    RN 662/surface
    discus: 5 petals and part of 6th
    rim: discus defined from undecorated rim by 2 widely separated grooves,
    heart-shaped volute (?) nozzle
    late 1st-2nd C
    Cahn-Klaiber, 1977: type L.IV; Ponsich, 1961: type II B1
    Heres, 1972: no 405 (petals similar, 2nd C); Cahn-Klaiber, 1977: no 179
    (petals similar, second half 1st C, from Cos); Ponsich, 1961: no 39 (late
    1st-early 2nd C); Farka, 1977: no 1271 (petals similar, Tiberian-Claudian)

20) fr, part of discus; PL/PW 4.0; reddish-yellow (7.5YR 8/6) fabric; red (2.5YR 5/8) slip
    RN 662/surface
    top: 10 elements of fan/leaf pattern, fill hole defined by raised band
    1st-2nd C
    Brants, 1913: type 9; Heres, 1972: type C; Loeschcke, 1919: type I; Broneer, 1930: type XXII
    Brants, 1913: no 309 (similar, Tiberian-2nd C); Farka, 1977: no 1363 (Augustan); Heres, 1972: 198 (discus similar, end 1st-2nd C); Lerat, 1954: no 27 (discus similar)

Egyptian

"Boss" lamps

21) fr, parts of discus, fill hole, rim; PL/PW 3.9; PH 1.5; red (2.5YR 5/8) fabric, red (2.5YR 5/6) slip
    RN 367f/E6b-33
    discus: concave, undecorated with central fill hole (?)
    rim: discus defined from rim by raised band and groove, 2 bosses joined, 2 parallel grooves across rim

22) nearly complete; parts of discus, fill hole, rim, nozzle, body walls and base missing; PL 6.25; W 5.7; H 2.95; yellowish-red (5YR 4/6) coarse fabric; red (2.5YR 5/6) slip
    RN 119/F7a-1
    discus: concave with central fill hole, edge of discus near rim decorated with incised dots
    rim: discus defined from rim by raised band and groove, rim with 3 raised bosses alternating with 2 ladder patterns across each side of rim, body walls curve to flat base
    Shier, 1978: nos 187-90 (late 3rd-early 4th C); Petrie, 1905: pl LXVII, nos 8-10, 34 (similar, discus smaller and undecorated); Bernhard, 1955: no 540 (from Deir el-Medineh, 3rd-4th C); Whitcomb and Johnson, 1979: pp 102-3 j, k (similar types); RN 117 (catalogue no 23), RN 121 (catalogue no 24 similar type)

23) complete; L 7.3; W 5.8; H 2.8; light red (2.5YR 6/6) fabric; very pale brown (10YR 7/3) slip
    RN 117/E7c-7
    discus: as RN 119 (catalogue no 22), but smaller
    rim: discus defined from rim by raised band and groove, rim with 3 raised bosses alternating with 2 pairs of parallel grooves across each rim, 2 other pairs of parallel grooves define rim from nozzle, 4 parallel grooves between wick hole and discus-rim boundary, body walls slope to flat base, evidence of burning
    Shier, 1978: nos 187-90 (late 3rd-early 4th C); Bernhard, 1955: no 540 (from Deir el-Medineh, 3rd-4th C); Whitcomb and Johnson, 1979: pp 102-3 j, k; RN 119 (catalogue no 22); RN 121 (catalogue no 24)

24) Complete; L 7.05; W 5.4; H 2.35; red (2.5YR 5/6) fabric; light red (2.5YR 6/6) slip
    RN 121/E6b-14
    discus: concave with slightly off-center fill hole
    rim: as RN 117 (catalogue no 23), but slightly narrower and circular band at nozzle-discus boundary, evidence of burning
    same parallels as RN 117 (catalogue no 23); RN 119 (catalogue no 22)

Egyptian of uncertain type

25) fr, wick hole and part of nozzle; PL 2.95; PW 3.1; PH 2.1; red (2.5YR 5/6) coarse fabric; light yellowish-brown (10YR 6/4) slip; from a worn mould
RN 126a/E6a-1
wick hole and part of nozzle with indistinct decoration, evidence of burning
Augustan-Tiberian

"Frog" lamps

26) fr, parts of fill hole, top and nozzle; PL 5.7; PW 4.9; PH 1.85; reddish-yellow (5YR 7/6) coarse fabric; light red (10R 6/8) slip
RN 126b/E6a-1
part of top half of lamp with schematic frog decoration, broken concave fill hole on back of frog separated from frog by groove, frog decoration extends onto nozzle, evidence of burning
Augustan-Tiberian
Michelucci, 1975: type 29
Bruyère, 1966: pl XXXIV bottom row, 3rd from l (similar?); Petrie, 1905: pl LXIV, no. 29; Shier, 1978: nos 77-86 (similar, late 3rd-early 4th C), 92 (early 2nd-early 3rd C), 93 (late 3rd C); Michelucci, 1975: nos 151-63 (similar, nos 155-57 2nd C); Bernhard, 1955: no 484 (similar, from Edfu, 2nd C, photo too poor for close comparison)

27) fr, part of top and fill hole; PL/PW 4.45; reddish-brown (5YR 5/4) to very pale brown (10YR 7/4) fabric; very pale brown (10YR 7/3) slip
RN 335c/E7c-1
top quarter of lamp decorated with schematic frog, broken fill hole on back of frog
Augustan-Flavian
Bruyère, 1966: pl XVIII, 3rd row, 1st on l (similar?)

28) fr, parts of top and fill hole; PL/PW 4.55; reddish-yellow (5YR 6/6) fabric; dark reddish-brown (5YR 3/3) slip
RN 113/E6a-13
part of top and concave fill hole, most decoration worn off
perhaps same type as RN 126b (catalogue no 26)
perhaps same parallels as RN 126b (catalogue no 26)

29) fr, part of top and fill hole; PL/PW 5.1; PH 1.85; reddish-yellow (5YR 6/6) fabric; red (2.5YR 4/6) slip
RN 114/E6a-13
part of top and concave fill hole, most decoration worn off

30) fr, fill hole, part of top; PL 7.0; PW 6.6; PH 1.85; very pale brown (10YR 7/4) fabric; olive brown (2.5YR 4/4) slip
RN 116/E7a-8
top half of lamp decorated with schematic frog, concave fill hole on back of frog, part of nozzle and wick hole, evidence of burning
Petrie, 1905: pl LXIII no 25 (similar); Shier, 1978: nos 108 (late 3rd C), 109 (late 3rd-early 4th C); Robins, 1939a: no 9, pl XI (3rd C); Robins, 1939b: p 68k (similar); Bresciani, 1968: no 20 (from Medinet Madi, 3rd C)

31) fr, fill hole, part of top; PL 6.75; PW 6.05; PH 1.85; red (2.5YR 4/8) fabric; reddish-brown (2.5YR 5/4) slip
RN 662/surface
most of top half of lamp decorated with schematic frog, concave fill hole on back of frog and defined from frog by deep groove which extends to broken nozzle as 2 parallel grooves, evidence of burning
Michelucci, 1975: type 29; Cahn-Klaiber, 1977: type 3.1.12
Shier, 1978: nos 77-93 (similar, late 3rd-early 4th C, nos 82, 87, 92 might be 2nd C); Cahn-Klaiber, 1977: no 129 (vaguely similar, from Alexandria, 4th C?); Michałowski, 1950: pl 32, nos 32, 579 (photograph too small for good comparison); Tell Douch no 401 (unpublished from 1979 IFAO season; I wish to thank the director of the French excavations at Tell Douch for allowing me access to material discovered in the course of his 1979 season)

32) complete; L 6.7; W 5.2; H 2.8; very dark grey (2.5YR 3/0) fabric; slip difficult to determine
RN 120/E6b-38
all decoration worn off

33) nearly complete; parts of top and nozzle missing; L 6.45; W 5.6; H 3.1; light reddish-brown (5YR 6/4) fabric; reddish-brown (5YR 4/4) slip
RN 662/surface
all decoration worn off

34) fr, bottom half of lamp; PL 6.45; PW 6.2; PH 2.65; red (2.5YR 4/6) fabric; red (2.5YR 4/6) slip
RN 367e/E6b-16
body walls curve to wide flat base, interior of lamp covered with bituminous substance, evidence of burning at base of nozzle

35) fr, bottom half of lamp; PL 6.3; W 6.0; PH 2.0; light red (7.5YR 6/6) fabric; very worn red (10YR 5/6) slip
RN 662/surface
body walls curve to wide flat base, base of nozzle

CHAPTER 11: TERRA SIGILLATA STAMPS

Steven Sidebotham

Among the substantial quantity of terra sigillata sherds found at Quseir al-Qadim in the 1980 season, seven bases stamped with makers' marks were discovered, six of which bore letters allowing tentative identification. All but one (RN 108) seem to be of Italian manufacture. RN 108 has a duller, brownish-red fabric and more orange slip than the Italian pieces; this, together with a Greek signature, points to an eastern Mediterranean provenance for this vessel.

Two of the Italian sherds with makers' marks also have graffiti, in Greek, on the bases. A Δ and the slash of a second letter are evident on RN 107 while a more complex graffito, which includes a Δ, appears on RN 111. Δ, the fourth letter of the Greek alphabet, was used in documents and on coinage of the Roman period in Egypt to represent the number four. Perhaps the Δ on both these vessels signifies the value of each (4 obols?). The graffiti may also be the initials of the owners of the vessels.[1] Alternatively, the graffiti may have been inscribed after the vessels had been broken; if so, in each case, these "ostraca" may have served as records of account or receipts of some sort.

Dr. Howard Comfort provided invaluable help by tentatively identifying most of the makers' marks[2] and to him I owe many thanks.

As in the case of the lamps, the quantities of terra sigillata sherds, especially of Italian manufacture, discovered at Quseir al-Qadim, should cause no surprise; Quseir al-Qadim was a port through which goods from foreign lands and from elsewhere in the Roman Empire passed in Rome's maritime commerce with South Arabia, South India, and other lands of the Erythraean Sea littoral.[3]

The catalogue has the following format: Quseir al-Qadim 1980 registration number (RN) and locus designation, description of the stamp, identification of the maker (if possible), parallels (if ascertainable), vessel form (if discernible), and date (all dates are A.D. unless otherwise indicated).

---

[1] For parallels for owners' names on vessels, see Robinson, 1959: 49, no. H33, a dipinto on a vessel of the first half of the second century.

[2] Letter from H. Comfort to the author, February 25, 1981. Unfortunately, two basic works pertaining to vessel identification, Dragendorff, 1895, and Loeschcke, 1909, were unavailable to me. Therefore, vessel identification has been made using Oxé and Comfort, 1968, and Oswald and Pryce, 1920. Although Oswald and Pryce deal mainly with Gallic workshops, they frequently cite Arretine prototypes.

[3] The Erythraean Sea here designates three bodies of water: the Red Sea, the Indian Ocean, and the Arabian Gulf.

Plate 61: Inscriptions

	Locus	RN	Description
a	J14a-4	111	TS stamp
b	E7a-20	110	TS stamp
c	E6b-40	107	TS stamp
d	E6a-7	108	TS stamp
e	E7a-5	625	TS stamp
f	G12c-6	109	TS stamp
g	E6b-14	87	ostracon; ink
h	E6a-1	93	ostracon; ink
i	E6b-25	90	ostracon; ink
j	E6b-32	82	ostracon; ink
k	J14a-5	438	plaster plug
l	G9a-3	106	plaster plug; red top
m	E6a-9	41	plaster plug; red top
n	E6b-49	476, 468	graffiti; incised
o	E7a-16	102	graffito; incised

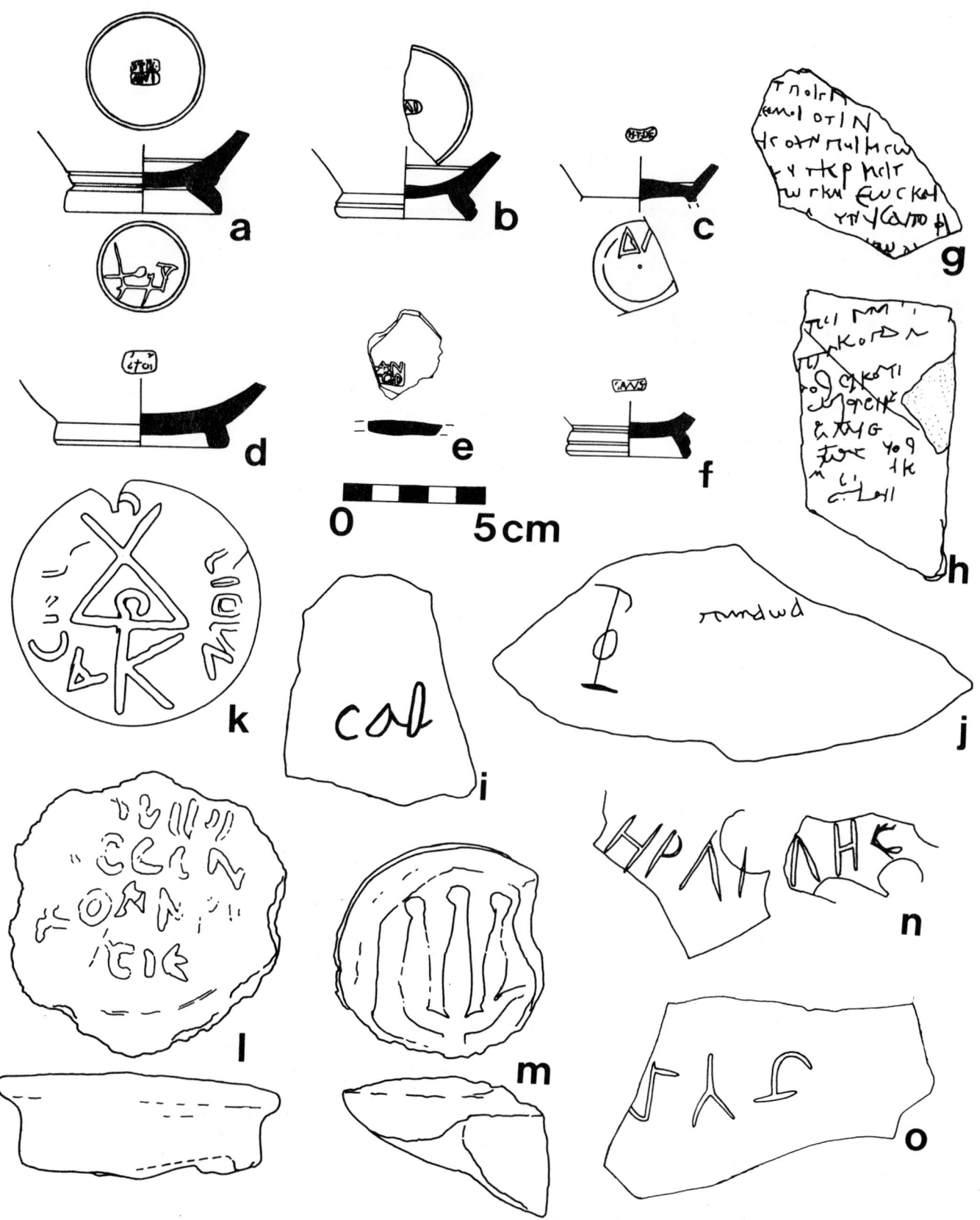

Plate 61: Inscriptions

Bibliography: Terra Sigillata Stamps

Dragendorff, H.
    1895   "Terra Sigillata," *Bonner Jahrbücher* 96, pp. 18-155

Loeschcke, S.
    1909   "Keramische Funde in Haltern," *Mitteilungen der Altertumskommission für Westfalen* 5, "Einleitung" and "Terra Sigillata," pp. 101-90

Oswald, F., and T. D. Pryce
    1920   *An Introduction to the Study of Terra Sigillata*, London

Oxé, A.
    1927   "Terra Sigillata aus dem Kerameikos," *Mitteilungen des Deutschen Archäologischen Instituts Athenische Abteilung* 52, pp. 211-24

Oxé, A., and H. Comfort
    1968   *Corpus Vasorum Arretinorum*, Bonn

Reinach, A. J.
    1911   "Rapport sur les fouilles de Koptos, Deuxième campagne, janvier-fevrier 1911," *Bulletin de la Société française de fouilles archéologiques* 3,2, pp. 47-82

Robinson, H. S.
    1959   *The Athenian Agora*, Vol. 5, *Pottery of the Roman Period*, Princeton

Waagé, F. O., ed.
    1948   *Antioch on-the-Orontes*, Vol. IV, 1, *Ceramics and Islamic Coins*, Princeton

Whitcomb, D. S., and J. H. Johnson
    1979   *Quseir al-Qadim 1978: Preliminary Report*, Cairo

Catalogue: Terra Sigillata Stamps

1) RN 107/E6b-40   H·Γ·L· *in planta pedis* = HY·L·TI (ligatured)
                  Hy. L. Titus had a wide distribution: central Italy, Tarragona, Athens
    Maker: Oxé and Comfort, 1968: 489, nos. 2106; 2108; 2109
    Vessel form: Oswald and Pryce, 1920: 170-71; Dragendorff, 1895: form 8; Loeschcke in Oxé and Comfort, 1968: type 8a, 8b, 15a, or 15b
             graffito Δ/ on base
    Date: Augustan-Tiberian

2) RN 108/E6a-7 ----- rectangular stamp in two lines, very worn, in Greek
              --ΤΟΥ
    Maker: perhaps Waagé, 1948: 35, P2305, fig. 20: ΔΗΜΕ "Pergamene" stamp
                                                    TPIQY in divided square
           or Waagé, 1948: 38, P2305, fig. 21: KOIP "Samian" stamp in
                                                     ANOY rectangle
    Vessel form: Robinson, 1959: 11, profile F7, last three quarters of the first century B.C. or, more likely, p. 24, profile G13 or G14, first half of the first century, "Pergamene" ware
    Date: first half first century (?)

3) RN 109/G12c-6   C·A͡N·S   narrow rectangular stamp = G͡A͡M͡U͡S (ligatured)
   Gamus of Pozzuoli had a wide distribution: Gaul, Germany, Spain, Northern Italy
   Maker: Oxé and Comfort, 1968: 204, no. 725c. 1 is closest
   Vessel form: similar to Oxé, 1927: 215, Abb. 2, no. 17, and p. 221; Loeschcke in Oxé and Comfort, 1968: type 11; and Oswald and Pryce, 1920: 186-88; Dragendorff, 1895: form 27
   Date: Augustan and later (?)

4) RN 110/E7a-20   IV[--?   *in planta pedis*
   Maker: possibly Oxé and Comfort, 1968: 234, no. 856, Iunius (?) of Pozzuoli (?) or pp. 230-31, nos. 838, 839 for Iulius; less possible p. 230, no. 834, Iucundus of the Po Valley, or no. 835, Iucundus of Italy; cf. Whitcomb and Johnson, 1979: 100-1 k (IVCV) from E7a-10 (RN 365); Reinach, 1911: 82, n. 1, also found stamps of Iucundus at Coptos
   Vessel form: Loeschcke in Oxé and Comfort, 1968: type 8Ab
   Date: ?

5) RN 111/J14a-4   STEP   rectangular stamp = STEPHANUS
                   ANI   Stephanus had a wide distribution: Rome, Ampurias, Tarragona, Cherchel
   Maker: Oxé and Comfort, 1968: 113, no. 305c
   Vessel form: Loeschcke in Oxé and Comfort, 1968: type 8a, 8b, or 15b
                graffito on base:
   Date: ?

6) RN 625/E7a-5   A-N ?   rectangular stamp
                  CID
   Maker: Howard Comfort (see n. 2, above) had no suggestions for this stamp
   Vessel form: not extant
   Date: ?

CHAPTER 12: INSCRIPTIONAL MATERIAL

Janet H. Johnson

The majority of the inscribed materials from Roman loci were ostraca, written in Greek; some were fragments of private letters or accounts (61:g,h). One consisted of the personal name Psenosiris son of Petronius (RN 95, G9a-1, FN 2). There are a few scraps of papyrus, mostly with fragmentary inscriptions in Greek. The rest would seem to have been identificational devices carved on fairly large pots (61:i,j); similar names or monograms are found on the large reconstructed vessels from the large storeroom of the Roman villa (61:n). It is assumed that these were names or monograms indicating the owner of the vessel. Similar monograms are occasionally found on the plaster plugs with which the large amphorae were sealed (61:k). Other plugs contained inscriptions (61:l) or distinctive designs (61:m) stamped into the wet plaster. One amphora top was found with the plaster plug still intact (27:a); the vessel had evidently been opened by cutting off the neck below the level of the plug rather than by removing the plug. Terra sigillata bowls were also occasionally stamped to indicate the maker of the bowl or had a graffito scratched on the base or outside of the bowl, presumably indicating the owner (see chapter 11 on Terra Sigillata stamps).

The graffito which had been carved into the side of one large storage vessel found in the area called villa east, near where the iron-working furnace had been found in 1978, is written in the Tamil-Brāhmī script and in the Tamil language (61:o). Another graffito in this script and language had been found in 1978 in this same area (Whitcomb and Johnson, 1979: pl 27:j) and identified by I. Mahadevan as a masculine proper name datable to the first or second century of our era. A drawing and photograph of this second inscription, from the 1980 season, were sent to Mahadevan who commented as follows:

"The inscription found on a potsherd is in the Tamil-Brāhmī script and in the Tamil language. The occurrence of ∩ (_n_) in the script and the pronominal ending -_an_ in the language are conclusive evidence.

"The text consisting of 3 extant letters is incomplete. The first extant character at the left is also fragmentary. It is most probably _cā_. (The only other possibilities are _hā_ or _lā_; but both are extremely unlikely in the present context. Tamil does not have _h_ and Tamil names do not begin with _l_.) The text may be read as:]_cā(?) ta n_.

"This is a well-attested male personal name in old Tamil. The name (_cātan_, var. _cāttan_) occurs in the Tamil-Brāhmī inscriptions (Mahadevan, 1966: No. 17, 51, 53, 69).

"The literary form is *cattan̲*, a very popular name especially among the Tamil mercantile community (e.g., *Pur̲am*, verses 178, 242, 395; also frequently in *Cilappatikāram* and *Man̲imēkalai*).

"The inscription can be dated on palaeographical grounds to about the second century of the modern era. The letter *ca* with the open loop (occurring in the bi-lingual Satavahana silver coins of the second century) indicates a later date for the present inscription than for Arikamedu graffiti or the even earlier Tamil-Brāhmī cave inscriptions. (For a bi-lingual coin of a Satavahana, see Nagaswami, 1966: 200 and facing plate.)" (pers. comm., 1980)

The Greek ostraca and papyrus fragments will be published in full by Roger Bagnall in the report on all the inscribed material to be included in the final report. During Bagnall's visit to Cairo in March, 1980 (made possible by a grant from the American Philosophical Society, from its Penrose Fund), he was able to work on the originals of several of the written documents from the first season. As a result of this work, he prepared the following notes for inclusion in this preliminary report:

"The letter of Maximus to his brother (J. 93632) makes requests for wine, pease, beans, vinegar, and pepper, among other items. In J. 93633 we get Λευκ((i.e., Leukos Limen), evidently as the destination of the jar on which it was written.

"A mention of hunger occurs in J. 93621. Another Latin fragment has been identified in the ostrakon J. 93662. The papyrus letter J. 93660 begins with the well-known *proskynema* formula (on which, see Geraci, 1971: especially p. 11 for examples in the Wadi Fawakir ostraka) and speaks of 'descending', i.e., travelling to the Nile valley." (pers. comm., 1980)

In the Islamic loci were found numerous fragments of paper, some blank but most bearing inscriptions in Arabic written in black ink. Numerous such fragments were also found during the 1978 season (Whitcomb and Johnson, 1979: 247-48). Occasionally, a complete text has been preserved (e.g., RN 15, E18b-2, a long, thin piece of paper with writing on both sides which had been folded in thirds the long way and then folded into a small packet by folding this strip 11 times). One piece of cloth bearing an inscription in Arabic was also found. Proper study of these documents requires personal inspection of many of the pieces and the full study of the entire corpus must await study of them in Cairo. They will be published, and their contribution to understanding of the Islamic presence at

Quseir al-Qadim will be studied, in conjunction with the final report following the third season of excavations (Winter, 1982). A preliminary notice, based on the documents found in 1978 and including the publication of four of those documents, appears below, chapter 13. A few wooden objects, especially combs, also bore Arabic inscriptions; see chapter 15.

Eighty Roman coins were found during the 1980 excavations; none were part of hoards. Most of them are very badly eroded due to the action of salt on the metal; only 17 were at all identifiable. A preliminary report on the coins was prepared using the limited facilities of the library at Chicago House, in Luxor, by Steven Sidebotham. The comments cited below are from his report, submitted in March, 1980. The identifications are to be considered tentative since many of the basic reference works were unavailable to him. He will prepare a final report on these coins, based on the study of the cleaned coins which were given to Chicago during the division of finds following the 1980 season and the casts made of all the coins in the field. This report will appear in the final report following the third season of excavations.

All but three of the Roman coins were aes (copper alloy); the other three were billon (debased silver) tetradrachmas from the Alexandria mint. Neither silver nor gold coins were found. All the coins which could be identified were minted in Alexandria or in Egyptian nome mints; none had been minted outside of Egypt. This coincides with the regulation that, upon entry to Egypt or Alexandria, imperial issues and coinage from elsewhere in the empire had to be exchanged for issues minted in Egypt (Milne, 1930: 169-70). The identifiable coins date from the first or second century of our era. The only later coin (RN 510) was found not in the Roman section of the site but across the modern road in the Islamic area and may well have been a later, surface deposit, picked up and re-deposited during the Islamic occupation.

The following coins were tentatively identified by Sidebotham (the format consists of registration number; locus; diameter in millimeters; weight in grams; die positions; obverse and reverse descriptions; mint; denomination; identification; and year):

a) RN 509; E7a-15; 25mm.; 4.8g.; ↑↑ ; obv: bare head right, legend lost/faint ---NAV--; rev: eagle standing right, wings folded, LA in field to right; Æ 25; first regnal year Tiberius to Nero or Otho (A.D. 14-68)

b) RN 510; F19a-2; 23mm.; 9.7g.; ↑↖ ; obv: laureat crowned head right, legend faint; rev: eagle sitting left, head turned right, A in field to right(?); Alexandria mint; billon tetradrachma, last third of the third century

c) RN 511; E7c-7; 25.5mm.; 8.6g.; ↑↗ ; obv: laureate head right, legend faint; rev: laureate bust of bearded deity right; Æ 25.5; portrait of Julio-Claudian, most probably Claudius (41-54 A.D.)

d) RN 513; F7a-3; 24mm.; 4.9g.; ↑↑ ; obv: laureate bust right, legend faint; rev: eagle sitting right, legend faint; Æ 24; portrait is Flavian (69-96 A.D.), especially Domitian (81-96)

e) RN 514; G8a-4; 25.5mm.; 10.4g.; obv: head bare right, legend lost; counterstamp (x across face; rev: lost; Æ 25.5mm.; Julio-Claudian portrait(?)

f) RN 515; D6d-7; 25mm.; 7.2g.; ↑↗ ; obv: laureate head right, legend lost; rev: young head right, legend lost; Alexandria mint; billon tetradrachma; third quarter of first century

g) RN 516; E6c-1; 28mm.; 3.9g.; ↑↑ ; obv: laureate(?) head left, legend faint/lost; rev: personification(?) head right, ETOYC to left; Æ 28; portrait looks Flavian or possibly Tiberius

h) RN 518; surface; 25mm.; 12.7g.; ↑↘ ; obv: laureate bust right wears poludanentum, AVTKAITPAIAΔPIACEB or AVTKAICTPAIANAΔPIANOCCEB; rev: Nilus reclining left, holds cornucopia or wheat sheath, crocodile beneath right, LIZ above; Alexandria mint; billon tetradrachma; Hadrian (117-38), 17th regnal year=A.D. 133/4

i) RN 520d; E6b-44; 23mm.; 3.6g.; obv: head, legend faint/lost; rev: figure standing, legend faint/lost; Alexandria mint; billon tetradrachma; late first, early second century of our era

Numerous Islamic coins were also found; they will be published by Michael Bates together with those from the third season in a full study of all the Islamic coins from Quseir al-Qadim to appear in the final report.

Bibliography for Inscriptional Material

Geraci, G.
    1971   "Ricerche sul Proskynema," *Aegyptus* 51: 3-211

Mahadevan, I.
    1966   *Corpus of the Tamil-Brāhmī Inscriptions*

Milne, J. G.
    1930   "The Roman Regulation of Exchange Values in Egypt: A Note," *Journal of Egyptian Archaeology* 16: 169-70

Nagaswami, R.
    1966   *Seminar on Inscriptions*, Madras

Whitcomb, D. S., and J. H. Johnson
    1979   *Quseir al-Qadim 1978: Preliminary Report*, Cairo

CHAPTER 13: THE RED SEA PORT OF QUSEIR
ARABIC DOCUMENTS AND NARRATIVE SOURCES
Gladys Frantz-Murphy

The Arabic documents referred to in this study were selected on the criteria of their legibility from slides taken in the field of approximately 200 documents unearthed in the first season. Thirty of those documents were partially or wholly read. Pending inspection of the originals, provisional editions and translations of several documents are included. Narrative sources which provide relevant information include geographical surveys (Ibn Hawqal [d. post 367/977], 1938-39; Yāqūt [d. 626/1229], 1866-70), travelogues (Ibn Jubayr [539-614/1144-1217], 1964; Ibn Baṭṭūṭa, 1975), treatises (Ibn Mammātī [d. 606/1209], 1943; al-Nābulusī [d. 660/1261], n.d.; Qalqashandī [d. 821/1418], 1972), and historical narratives (al-Musabbiḥī [d. 420/1029], 1978; Maqrīzī [d. 845/1442], 1934-58; Ibn Taghrī Birdī [d. 874/1470], 1929-56) written by government officials.

Dates for the Use of the Port in the Islamic Period

Though a place named Quseir was known in the eighth century, it is doubtful that this is identical with the later port.[1] A passage in an eleventh century history of Egypt refers ambiguously to a "Quseir" in Egypt (Musabbiḥī, 1978: 97). In another account a Christian pilgrim, who has been dated to about 1017, refers to the route between Qūṣ and Quseir and to Quseir's role in the spice trade (Thietmar, Bishop of Merseburg, cited by Kammerer, 1929: 80).

Beginning in the late 12th century Quseir would have taken on strategic importance because of the Crusades. Egypt's northern ports on the Mediterranean and on the Sinai, as well as sites along overland routes in the North, were under attack, cutting off supplies from the North. Additionally, the overland route between the southern port of ᶜAydhāb and the inland city of Qūṣ was under attack (Kammerer, 1929: 61-62; Leiser, 1977: 87-100; Yāqūt, 1866-70: vol. 2, pp. 604-5; Ibn Wāṣil, n.d.: vol. 3, pp. 316-18, quoting Salāh al-Dīn as reported by Abu Shama).

---

[1] Yāqūt (1866-70: vol. 4, p. 127) records the opinions of Ibn Lahīᶜa [d. 174/791], Mufaḍḍal ibn Fuḍḍāla [d. 181/798] and Ibn ᶜAbd al-Ḥakam [d. 257/871] as to whether or not there is a harbor at Quseir. The varied opinions seem to result from the confusion of two different places by the same name in Egypt. Qalqashandī citing ᶜUmarī refers to a "Quseir" which seems to have been on the route leading from Cairo to the Syrian frontier (1972: vol. 14, p. 377).

I can find no basis for the statement by Plessner (n.d.: 1158) that the port flourished in ᶜAbbāsid times. By the same token, Plessner's dismissal (*ibid.*: 1157) of Yāqūt as unreliable is probably based on a misunderstanding of Yāqūt's statement that, "Quseir is near ᶜAydhāb. Between it (i.e., Quseir) and Qūṣ are five days (i.e., by land) and between it (i.e., Quseir) and ᶜAydhāb are eight days (i.e., by sea)," (1866-70: vol. 1, p. 127). Elsewhere (*ibid.*: vol. 4, p. 159) Yāqūt accurately states that Quseir is half way from Qulzum to ᶜAydhāb.

Thus Quseir would have been vital as a source of supplies shipped in from the South. Ibn Jubayr reports arms shipments from India which arrived at Yemen from where they were shipped to ᶜAydhāb (1964: 43). Thereafter, Quseir would have retained its importance through the Ayyūbid period (564-650/1169-1250) due to that dynasty's interests in the Red Sea and control of the Yemen. Quseir was displaced by the port of al-Ṭur, located 150 miles to the North, in the late 14th century.

Documents: Incoming Correspondence

The overwhelming majority of documents read were personal and business correspondence which had been sent into Quseir from the interior of Egypt. Quseir is referred to by name in one fragment (from S12c-7, RN 593); see fig. 13. Therefore, these documents are more informative about affairs in the interior than about the port city itself. Most of the letters touch solely on personal matters; e.g., wishing health and blessings on family members, notification of a death in the family, etc.

Fig. 13: Letter Mentioning Quseir

Two business letters (one whole, one partial with addressee missing) indicate that the receiver(s) had major business interests in the interior. In one letter, a nephew writes to his Uncle Jaᶜfar that he is having difficulty in selling grain because the price is falling and the mamluk has arrived to collect his rent. The implication is that the nephew is managing an estate on behalf of his uncle and that the drop in grain prices is making it difficult to raise enough money to meet his obligations.

The partial letter is a report from an agent to his employer. The agent reports that a shipload of grain en route on the Nile from Aswan to Cairo has sunk and that his employer has suffered a loss. He also reports that he has collected 1000 ardabbs of grain and that a second agent has received grain which had been paid for at Edfū.

Documents: Business Activities in Quseir

Two of the documents read deal specifically with shipping transactions at Quseir. As with the incoming correspondence, these also involve transactions dealing with grain. Ms. Quseir 2 is a letter informing the receiver that a shipment of flour has been dispatched to him and instructing him to arrange to dispatch the flour to some further destination. Ms. Quseir 1 is an official receipt for grain that had arrived on a government ship, been stored temporarily, and then released to a group of pilgrims and transferred, presumably, to their ship.

This concentration of documents relating to trade in grain suggests that many of the documents found in the first season may represent the archive of a particular grain exporting agent or agency.

Quseir and Southbound Traffic

Ms. Quseir 1 clearly substantiates that Quseir was a stage en route to the pilgrimage. Sources tell us that pilgrims preferred to travel inland, specifically up the Nile or along the Arabian coast (Hourani, 1951: 82). The pilgrims mentioned in Ms. Qusier 1, therefore, most likely had travelled South up the Nile to Qūṣ, then overland to Quseir.

In contrast to the southbound Nile route of travellers, narrative sources all specify a southbound Red Sea route for cargo. Taking advantage of prevailing northerly winds, cargo ships sailed South on the Red Sea to Quseir. Narrative sources list the itinerary of Suez (Yāqūt, 1866-70: vol. 4, p. 160)[2] to Quseir to ᶜAydhāb and thence South and East (Qalqashandī, 1972: vol. 5, pp. 17, 86; Yāqūt 1866-70: vol. 4, p. 160). Yāqūt lists Quseir as a port for traffic moving South and East from Cairo and Syria (*ibid.*: vol. 3, p. 198). Ms. Quseir 1 also substantiates this southbound Red Sea cargo route in its reference to the arrival of grain on a government ship. The ship had to have come from the North via the Red Sea as no source suggests that grain grown along the Nile was transported overland and shipped North on the Red Sea.

Quseir and Northbound Cargo

Northbound cargo travelled North on the Red Sea, but only so far as Quseir. Prevailing northerly winds rendered sailing further North than Quseir difficult. "The northward passage was especially hard to early seafarers, because northerly

---

[2] The port at Suez had replaced Qulzum already in the 5th/11th century; see editorial notes by M. Ramzī in Ibn Taghrī Birdī (1929-56: vol. 8, pp. 151-52).

winds blow down this part of the Sea the whole year round" (Hourani, 1951: 5, citing *The Red Sea and Gulf of Aden Pilot*, 9th ed., London, 1944). In modern times it has been noted that "Monsoon winds will reliably carry trading ships (presumably large sailing ships) only as far North as the latitude of Aydhab" (U.S.H.C., 1976, cited from Whitcomb and Johnson, 1979: 3). Yet some kind of trading ships did occasionally sail 300 miles farther North to Quseir and Yāqūt specifies that Quseir was a port for Yemeni ships (1886-70: vol. 4, p. 127). According to Qalqashandī, prior to the 15th century:

> Some ships used to come to Quseir because of its proximity to Qūṣ and distance from ᶜAydhāb.... But the frequency of arrivals there does not approach the extent at ᶜAydhāb. (1972: vol. 3, pp. 464-65)

No narrative source intimates that trading ships sailed further North than Quseir on the Red Sea prior to the late 14th century.

While documents read provide no evidence of international commerce at Quseir, as noted above, those documents are almost exclusively in reference to commerce in grain. They may represent an archive of a grain agent and as such would not be representative of the scope of commercial activities at Quseir. Other evidence indicates that international commerce did arrive at the Port of Quseir, e.g., the fragments of fine pottery imported from China. It has been suggested that crates which had originated in China may have been opened at the port when unloaded for overland transport to Qūṣ and broken pieces discarded at Quseir. Further, Qalqashandī specifically writes of the international role of Quseir. Quseir was one of four Red Sea ports at which customs duties were levied, and it was used by the Kārimī merchants (Qalqashandī, 1972: vol. 3, pp. 464-65; Labib, n.d.: 640-43). What appear to be two partial folios from a treatise on levying the tax lends support to Qalqashandī's statement.

From Quseir, two northbound routes would have been possible. Qalqashandī details one: "Merchandise is carried from Quseir to Qūṣ, then from Qūṣ to the *fundūq* of the Kārim in Fusṭāṭ" (1972: vol. 3, p. 465). Cargo was transported inland from Quseir to Qūṣ. From Qūṣ cargo was safely and efficiently transported North down the Nile by the River's current. This was the route of international cargo imported into Egypt by the Kārimī merchants who dominated Red Sea commerce in Egypt from the 13th into the 15th century.

The alternative route was coastal sailing North on the Red Sea. International merchants such as the Kārimī would have arrived at Quseir with their valuable cargo on large ships, which, as stated above, went no farther North than Quseir, probably because of prevailing northerly winds. Cargo shipped farther North on the Red Sea would have been shipped in small coastal vessels. Coastal shipping northward is reported, but along the Arabian coast, not the Egyptian (Yāqūt, 1866-70: vol. 2, pp. 4, 77; vol. 1, p. 503; Qalqashandī, 1972: vol. 3, pp. 239, 465; Ibn Hawqal, 1938-39: vol. 1, pp. 38-39; Arabic, p. 40). Nevertheless, sailing North on the Red Sea was and is hazardous. Small ships had to sail for hundreds of miles against violent winds hugging a barren coast lined with coral reefs. Because of coral islands along the coasts, sailing was at great risk and could only be done by daylight. The difficulties and insecurities detailed by successive Arab writers suggest that valuable cargo originating from India and China would not have been risked in coastal sailing given these conditions (Yāqūt, 1866-70: vol. 4, p. 160; Hourani, 1951: 80, 82; Villiers, n.d.: 44).

Quseir and the Rise of al-Ṭūr

After 780/1380 Quseir and ᶜAydhāb were both displaced by the international Egyptian port of al-Ṭūr, a port 450 miles to the North of ᶜAydhāb, 150 miles North of Quseir. Qalqashandī explains that this was a result of the port of al-Ṭūr having been actively promoted by the Chief Customs Inspector of Egypt[3] (1972: vol. 3, p. 465). Other narrative sources specify two additional causes. Writing somewhat later, Maqrīzī states that Quseir was abandoned in favor of al-Ṭūr because of the rapacious tax policies of the Governor of Qūṣ, which caused the fisc of the central government to suffer. Additionally, he cites insecurity along the overland route from the port of ᶜAydhāb (Garcin, 1976: 405-6, citing Maqrīzī). The Chief Customs Inspector may have developed and promoted the new northern port in order to secure Egypt's international trade in the Red Sea and the revenue which it generated, as the government had earlier organized convoys to protect Kārimī merchants from pirates in the southern Red Sea (Labib, n.d.: 642).

However, as indicated above, it does not seem to have been possible for large vessels to sail North of Quseir in the Red Sea until the time of the pre-eminence of al-Ṭūr. And it is unlikely that international trade would have been consigned to coastal shipping for the reasons outlined above. Therefore, some change in shipping technology must have taken place in order for al-Ṭūr to become an international port. The Chief Customs Inspector who effected the shift to the northern port of al-Ṭūr had long been the customs official of the port of Alexandria, by

---

[3] the Amīr Salāḥ al-Dīn, Khalīl ibn ᶜArrām, ḥājib al-ḥujjāb of Egypt.

all accounts the largest and most important Egyptian port.[4] He was, therefore, familiar with Mediterranean naval technology. Is it possible that he promoted a change in Red Sea shipping technology incorporating Mediterranean technology?

According to Qalqashandī the port of al-Ṭūr had formerly been important in northbound coastal shipping along the Arabian shore. More recently al-Ṭūr had been avoided because of coastal pirates preying on shipping in its vicinity.

> This situation continued until the Chief Customs Inspector constructed a ship and had it journey in the Red Sea. This was followed by another ship, after which other travelers did likewise. Then ships from the Yemen arrived with their merchandise, while ᶜAydhāb and Quseir declined. (Qalqashandī, 1972: vol. 3, p. 465)

The sequence of events outlined by Qalqashandī is ambiguous. It could be conjectured, however, that the customs inspector had inaugurated a shipyard at al-Ṭūr and had effected some change in naval construction which enabled ships to sail clear of the coast, thus avoiding pirates. His example was followed by others who themselves then constructed similar ships. Finally, ships of the Yemen arrived carrying merchandise. No earlier source states that Yemeni ships had sailed due North to al-Ṭūr. The customs inspector's successful ship building efforts, followed by those of others, and concluded by the remark that in turn Yemeni ships arrived, suggests that those ship-building efforts were somehow related to the subsequent arrival of Yemeni ships.

In 1429, the Egyptian government displaced the Kārimī merchants and established a monopoly of trade in the Red Sea. The fact that the spice trade became a government monopoly supports the conjecture that the government had initiated some technological change. It could have afforded and would have benefited by a change which secured al-Ṭūr as the international Red Sea port of Egypt.[5]

Finally, the eclipse of the two southern ports at the end of the 14th century would have entailed the eclipse of the overland routes from those two cities to Qūṣ. In turn, the Nile would have lost its pre-eminence as a highway for international trade, with significant repercussions on the local economy of Middle and Upper Egypt. (Garcin, 1976: part 3).

---

[4] He had held many official positions and had formerly been several times customs agent at Alexandria (Ibn Taghrī Birdī, 1929-56: vol. 11, pp. 183-87, 203).

[5] From a different perspective Garcin (1976: 406, 420-25) discusses the problematical decline of ᶜAydhāb as it related to the sudden rise of al-Ṭūr.

Editions and Translations

Ms. Quseir 1

Ms. Quseir 1 is an official receipt dated 615/1218, just prior to the pilgrimage and some four or five months after the Fifth Crusade had launched its attack on the Mediterranean port of Damietta, and just after al-Kāmil Muḥammad had become the Ayyūbid ruler of Egypt. The document substantiates that the port was open at that early date, as well as the fact that the port was a stage en route to the Ḥijāz for the pilgrimage.

The receipt refers to arrangements for the pilgrimage and states that wheat had arrived earlier on a government ship, that the grain had been delayed in Quseir, and during the interim the wheat had been deposited with the ᶜArīf/Inspector. The grain in question in this document had arrived on a government ship, i.e., it had come South via the Red Sea, not overland from Qūṣ. Two official witnesses assigned to the Rīf (i.e., the coast) and the Ḥijāz testify that the grain had subsequently been put on board a ship.

The receipt, however, does not specify the amount of grain in question. Why would the Inspector and witnesses have executed an official document without specifying the amount of grain being released? A possible explanation is provided by a contemporary in the Ayyūbid administration. Al-Nābulusī was an official in the highest levels of financial administration at the time this document was executed (between 615-635/1214-1238). From 627-634 he traveled throughout Egypt inspecting provincial administration. In his discussion of regulations in force in the Egyptian provinces al-Nābulusī details administrative abuses. Among those which he brought to the attention of the ruler was one involving the transport of grain to the government warehouse in Fusṭāṭ.

Al-Nābulusī inveighs against the abuses of ship captains and provincial officials who colluded in selling grain destined for the government warehouse in Fusṭāṭ while en route from Upper Egypt. Despite the fact that all grain was loaded in the presence of witnesses, who attested to the quantities originally loaded in the presence of witnesses, the boats always arrived at the dock with a lesser amount than that recorded in the receipts. So many officials were involved that each blamed the other and no one could be held accountable. The continual shortfalls were simply carried forward on the books. In this instance the potential for abuses would have been greater, since grain was presumably being dispensed from the warehouse (al-Nābulusī, n.d.: tr. Cahen, pp. 112-13, Torrey, pp. 74-75).

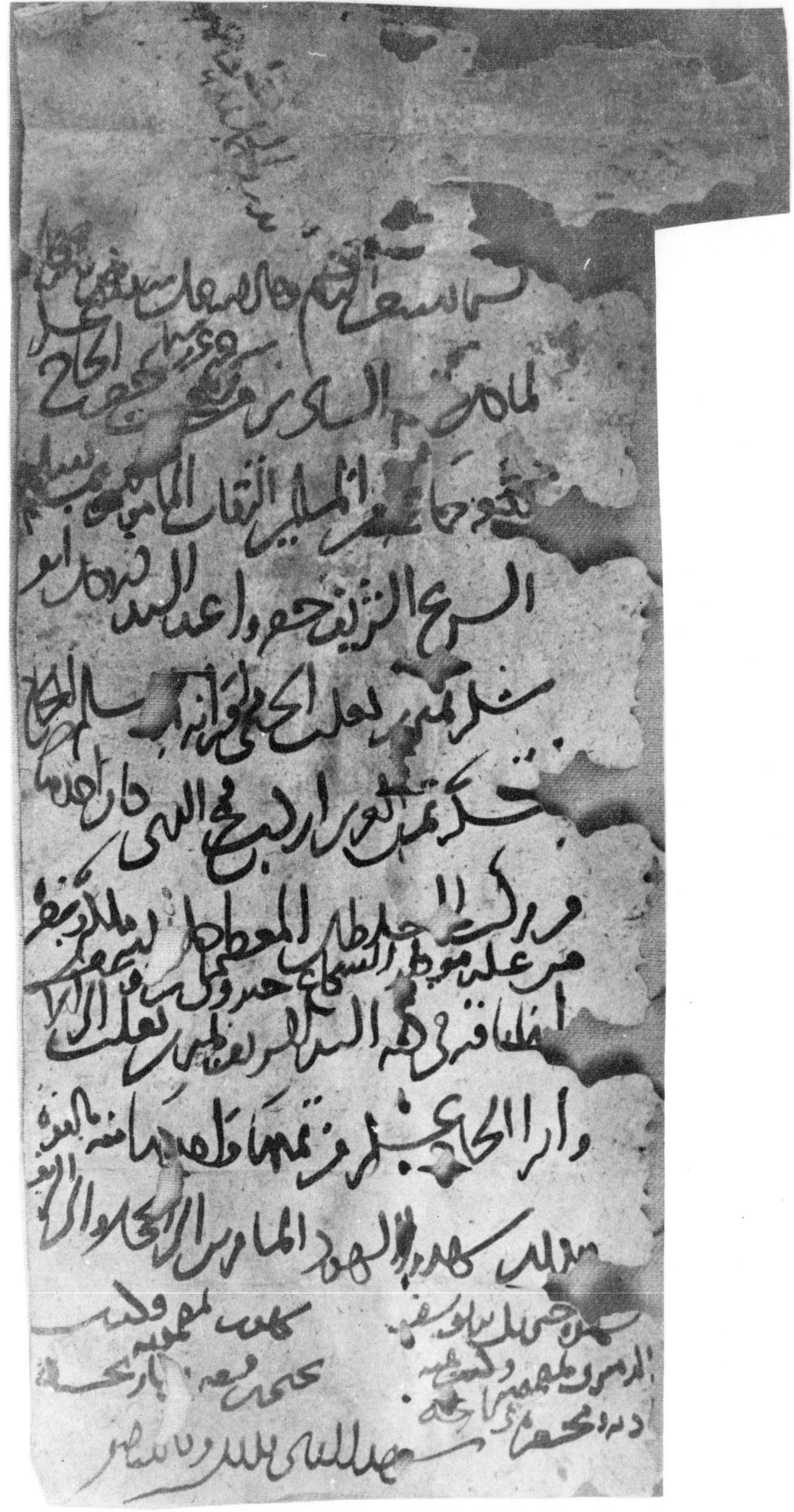

Fig. 14: Ms. Quseir 1, RN 592, P8b-18

١. بسم الله (الرحمن الرحيم) وصلى الله على سيد (نا) محمد نبيه ( )   ( ) و الحمد الله ( )
٢. لما (كان اليو)م السا(ى) سنة خمس عشرة وستماية على ( ) حضر الحاج
٣. (ثقته) جما(عات) من المسلمين الثقات المامونين ممن يسلم
٤. الشريع الشريف حضروا عند الاجل ابو
٥. شكر تميم بن تغلب الحيى واقر انه ( ) سلم لالحاج
٦. [ابو] شكر تميم العريف اركب قمح التى كان اخذها
٧. من مركب السلطان المعطمى ( ) ملكه وضع
٩. من غلة موجلة الشجاع جيرون بن (ي)وسف
٨. لنا باقيه فى كنز السيد العريف تميم بن تغلب الى الان
١٠. وابرا الحا(ج) غلة فى تمها فلقبضها منه بالقوة
١١. هذين شهد الشهود العامرين الى الحجاز والى الريف
١٢. شهد جبريل بن يوسف   شهدت بمضمونة وكتبت
١٣. الدميرى بمضمونة وكتب عنه يحيى بن معز (فى) تاريخه
١٤. اذنه ومحضرة فى تاريخه
١٥.   شهد للناس بذلك وبالامضو

٣ المأمونين ٩ موجَّلة ١٠ أبرأ ، تامها ١١ مأمورين ١٥ الامضاء

Fig. 15: Ms. Quseir 1, RN 592, P8b-18

Ms. Quseir 1

Paper   615 AH/ca. 1218 AD

1. In the name of God the Compassionate, the Merciful. And God bless ⟨our⟩ lord Muḥammad (the Prophet   )
2.   in year fifteen and six hundred (When it was the exalted day   ) the pilgrims arrived
3. (relying on) groups of trustworthy faithful Muslims from among those who preserve
4. the sacred law. They presented themselves to the most great lord, the father of
5. Shakr Tamīm the son of Taghlib al-Hayyī. And he affirmed that [   ] delivered to the pilgrims.

6. [The father of] Shakr Tamīm the Inspector put on board wheat which had been taken
7. from the ship of the August Sovereign. his possession
9. from the crops delayed by the Courageous Jayrūn son of Yūsuf.
8. the remainder of which had been placed in the treasury of the lord the Inspector Tamīm son of Taghlib until now,
10. He released grain in its entirety to the pil(grims). Thereupon it has been taken by the authority
11. of these two. The official witnesses of the Ḥijāz and the Rīf testified.
12. (2nd hand) Jabrayal son of Yūsuf   (3rd hand) I testified to the warranted and I wrote
13. al-Damiyri testified to the warranted   Yaḥya ibn Muᶜizz on its date. and he wrote
14. his authorization for it and he was present on its date.
15. (4th hand) Testimony was given to the people and the execution.
(at the top) (thanks be to God   )

    2. The reading of line two might be, "When it was the exalted day on which it was decreed;" confirmation of this reading is, however, dependent upon examination of the original document. For *ḥajj* as a plural form of *ḥajj*, viz. Lane (1863-93: s.v.).

    4. The title *al-ajall*, "most great," is associated with the Fāṭimid dynasty and was their highest honorific title. The combination *al-sayyid al-ajall* became a commonly used honorific thereafter (Qalqashandī, 1972: vol. 6, p. 6).

    5. Taghlib was a well-known Arab tribe; however, the reading Thaᶜlab is also possible. A village in the Eastern province (*al-sharqiyya*) was known as *ḥawḍah al-thaᶜlab* (Ibn Mammātī, 1943: 128). The *nisbah* (place of origin) of the person in question is tentatively read as *al-Ḥayyī*, also the name of a village in the Eastern province (Ibn Ḥawqal, 1938-39: 131, no. 16). Ibn Mammātī lists *al-ḥayy al-khānāfis*, "The Quarter of the Scarabs," as a village in Sharqiyya province (1943: 128).

    6. The Inspector (*ᶜarīf*, lit., "knower") was an official responsible for keeping census records, regulating and warranting comestibles, markets and prices (Qalqashandī, 1972: vol. 13, p. 362). The honorific "August Sovereign" was the highest title associated with government in Egypt (*ibid.*: vol. 6, p. 9).

    9. The "Courageous" (*al-shajāᶜ*) was an unofficial honorific.

11. In Egypt the *rīf* referred to Egypt South of Cairo. *Rīf* can also indicate specifically "the coast." In conjunction with the Ḥijāz and Quseir the *rīf* must refer to the Red Sea Coast on the Egyptian side, opposite the Red Sea coast on the Arabian side, the Ḥijāz.

12. The *maḍmūna*, "object warranted," i.e., the grain. For the role of official witnesses in warranting grain shipments see al-Nābulusī (n.d.). The first official witness, Jabrayal son of Yūsuf, may have been the brother of Jayrūn son of Yūsuf mentioned in line 9, i.e., the person who had delayed the grain earlier (cf., al-Nābulusī, n.d.). For the vocalization of Jayrūn see al-Dhahabī (1962: vol. 1, pp. 41, 287).

13. Damīrah, a village in Sammanūd province, in the central delta (Ibn Ḥawqal, 1938-39: p. 131, no. 72). Ibn Mammātī lists a North and a South Damīrah, both in Sammanūd province (1943: 135) and a dam of South Damīrah in Gharbiyya (the Western) province (1943: 214).

Ms. Quseir 2

Ms. Quseir 2, the only letter which relates to affairs at Quseir, is in regard to a shipment of flour, seemingly for forwarding elsewhere.

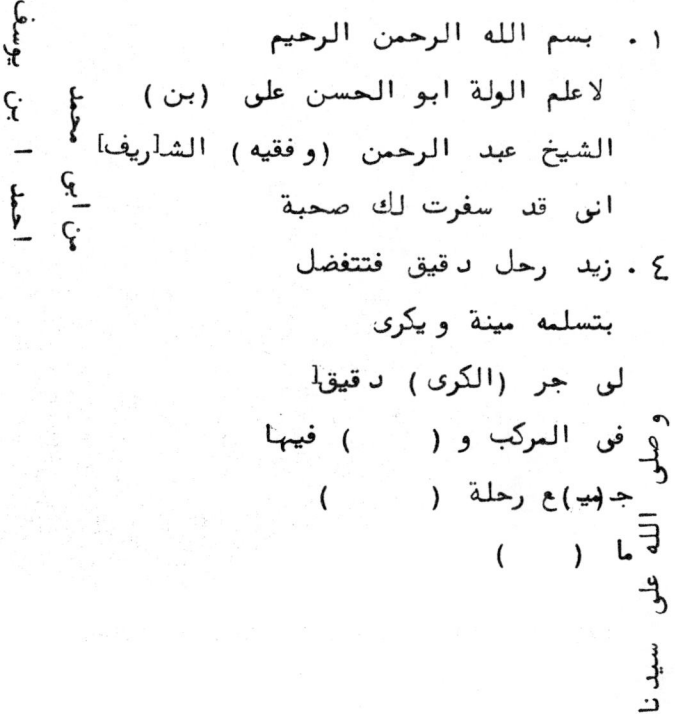

Fig. 16 : Ms. Quseir 2, RN 594, P7b-2

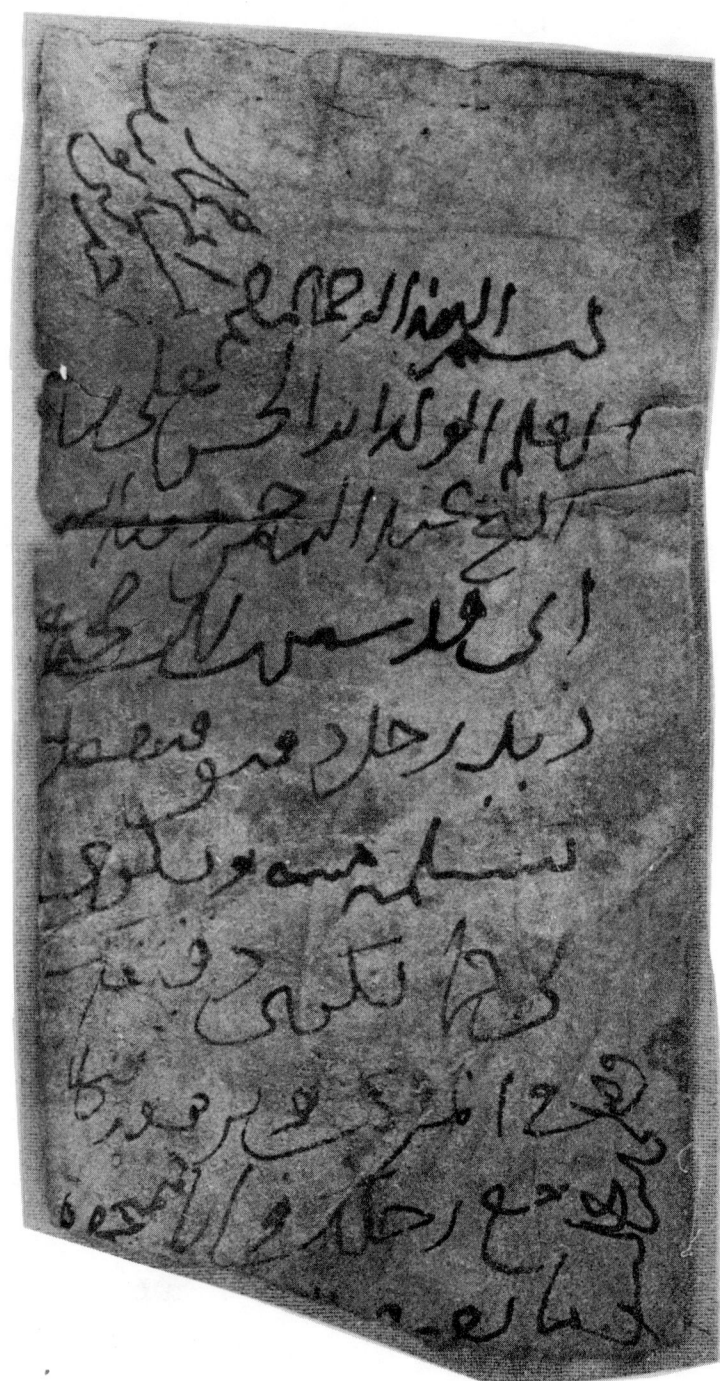

Fig. 17: Ms. Quseir 2, RN 594, P7b-2

Ms. Quseir 2

Paper

1. In the name of God the Compassionate, the Merciful.
2. To the leader of the most learned, the father of al-Hasan ᶜAli (the son of)
3. the Sh(aykh and honored religious scholar) ᶜAbd al-Raḥman.
4. Verily I have dispatched to you in the care of
5. Zayd a shipment of flour. Be so kind as
6. to deliver it to the port and to rent
7. for me (haulage   for flour)
8. in the ship and (   ) in it
9. (for the whole journey   )

right side: And God bless our lord /Muḥammad/

left side: From the father of Muḥammad, Aḥmad the son of Yūsuf.

9. *Riḥla* could also be read *raḥlihi*, "for the whole of its shipment." The correct reading is dependent upon the context which may be possible to determine from the original document.

Ost. Quseir 1 and 2

Ostrich eggs served and still serve as containers for transporting and storing liquids and in areas lacking pottery they are used as canteens.[6] This would explain the abundance in which they were found at Quseir, a site devoid of an immediate fresh water supply (Prickett, 1979). Ibn Baṭṭūṭa records drinking from ostrich egg shells at a roadside stop between ᶜAydhāb and Sawākīn (1975: vol. 1, p. 269; tr., vol. 2, p. 362). However, shells found at Quseir bear written inscriptions. In view of the expense, it seems unlikely that inscribed shells were simple canteens used by primitive people lacking pottery. The medieval range of the ostrich included Egypt and Arabia as well as East Africa. Ostriches became extinct on the Red Sea coast only in the 1890's and in Arabia only in 1941 (Couyat, 1910: 139). At Quseir the inscribed egg shell fragments were found concentrated in an ambiguous context but related to a funerary site (Whitcomb and Johnson, 1979: 57, 59). One tentatively read, partial inscription (Ost. Quseir 1) reinforces their contextual occurrence as having been funerary. It and a second fragment (Ost. Quseir 2) are dated.

---

[6] For information on the uses of ostrich egg shells, I am grateful to William Cherf. See *Encyclopaedia Britannica, Micropaedia* (1974) 7: 618; *Encyclopaedia Americana* (1976) 21: 36.

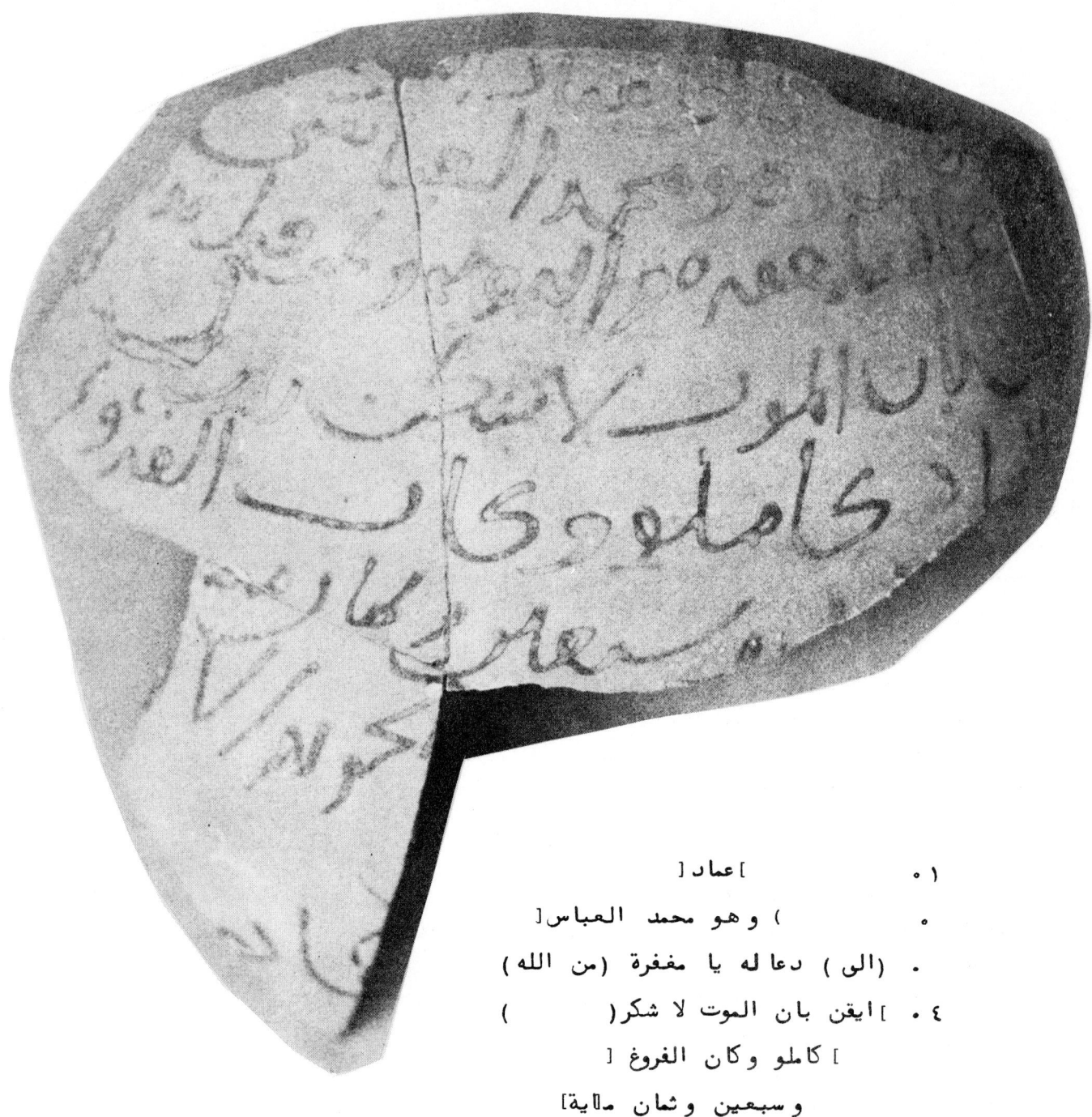

1. [عماد]
2.) وهو محمد العباس[
3. (الى) دعا له يا مغفرة (من الله)
4.]ايقن بان الموت لا شكر( )
5. [كاملو وكان الفروغ]
6. وسبعين وثمان م]اية[

Fig. 18: Ost. Quseir 1, RN 634, A22d-1

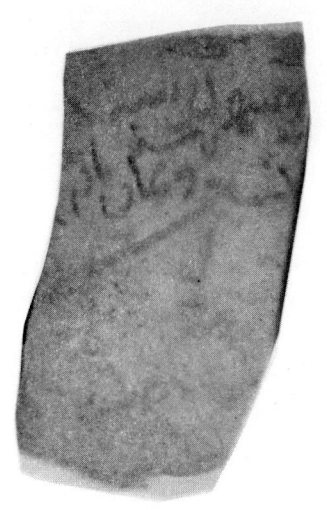

١٠ شهر الحجة سنة
[تسعين وثمان ماية

Fig. 19: Ost. Quseir 2, RN 634, A22d-1

Ost. Quseir 1

Ostrich egg shell   87X AH/1465-1475 AD

1. support
2. and he is Muhammad al‑^{c}Abbās
3. (to) a call for him, oh forgiveness (from God   )
4. it is certain that death without doubt
5. they completed and the expiration was
6. seventy and eight hundred

Ost. Quseir 2

Ostrich egg shell   89X AH/1485-1495 AD

1.
2. in the month of the pilgrimage of year
3. ninety and eight hundred

Bibliography for Arabic Documents

Couyat, J.
1910 "Les routes d'aidhab," *Bulletin de l'Institut Francais d'Archéologie Orientale* 8: 135-43

al-Dhahabī
1962 *al-mustabih fī al-rijāl*, ed. A. M. al-Bajāwī, Cairo

Garcin, J.-C.
1976 *Un centre musulman de la Haute-Egypte medievale: Qūṣ*, Cairo

Hourani, G.
1951 *Arab Seafaring*, Princeton

Ibn Baṭṭūṭa
1975 *riḥla*, 2 vols., ed. A. M. al-Kittānī, Beirut; tr. H. A. R. Gibb, *The Travels of Ibn Battuta AD 1325-1354*, 3 vols., Cambridge, 1962

Ibn Hawqal
1938-39 *kitāb sīrat al-arḍ*, ed. J. H. Kramers, BGA 2, Leiden; tr. Wiet and Kramers, *Configuration de la Terre*, Beirut, 1965

Ibn Jubayr
1964 *riḥla*, Beirut

Ibn Mammātī
1943 *kitāb qawānīn al-dawāwīn*, ed. A. S. ᶜAṭīya, Cairo

Ibn Taghrī Birdī
1929-56 *al-nujum al-zāhira fi mulūk miṣr wa al-qāhira*, 12 vols., Cairo

Ibn Wāṣil
n.d. *muffarij al-kurūb*, Cairo

Kammerer, A.
1929 *La Mer Rouge*, Cairo

Labib,
n.d. "Kārimī," *Encyclopedia of Islam*², 1: 640-43

Lane, E. W.
1863-93 *An Arabic-English Lexicon*, London

Leiser, G. L.
1977 "The Crusader Raid in the Red Sea in 578/1182-83," *Journal of the American Research Center in Egypt* 14: 87-100

Maqrīzī
1934-58 *kitāb al-sulūk*, ed. Ziada, 2 vols., Cairo

al-Musabbiḥī
1978 *akhbār miṣr*, ed. Sayyid and Bianquis, Cairo

al-Nābulusī
n.d. tr. Ç. Cahen, "Quelques aspects de l'administration égyptienne médiévale vus par un de ses fonctionnaires," *Bulletin de la Faculté des Lettres de Strasbourg* 26,4 (1948) 97-118; C. C. Torrey, "Scandal in the Egyptian Treasury: A Portion of the *Lumaᶜ al-Qawānīn* of ᶜUthmān ibn Ibrāhīm al-Nābulusī," *Journal of Near Eastern Studies* 14 (1955) 70-80

Plessner, M.
- n.d. "Qusayr," *Encyclopedia of Islam*[1], 2: 1157-58

Prickett, M. E.
- 1979 "Quseir Regional Survey," in Whitcomb and Johnson, *Quseir al-Qadim 1978: Preliminary Report*, pp. 257-352

Qalqashandī
- 1972 ṣubḥ al-aʿshā, ed. Al-Baqlī and ʿAshūr, 14 vols., Cairo

Villiers, A.
- n.d. *Men, Ships and the Sea*, Washington, D. C.

Whitcomb, D. S., and J. H. Johnson
- 1979 *Quseir al-Qadim 1978: Preliminary Report*, Cairo

Yāqūt
- 1866-70 muʿjam al-buldān, ed. Wüstenfeld, 6 vols., Leipzig

CHAPTER 14: TEXTILES

Gillian Eastwood

1978 Season

The 318 pieces from the 1978 season represent an unusual collection of textiles, especially as they come from a site excavated under controlled conditions with well-defined dates. Many of the textiles come from rubbish tips and are not obviously "museum worthy" examples: There are no elaborate hangings or silks. Instead they represent a wide cross-section of ordinary textiles which provide useful information about the range of fibres, dyes, weaves, and designs available during the Roman and Mamluk periods. Due to the climatic conditions at the site, there has been no differential survival of fibres which is the common problem with textiles from northern European sites.

Textiles from the Roman Levels

The textiles from the Roman period come from the following loci: B4a-1, 3, 4; C4c-3, 4, 7; D4b-1; F8c-7; F8d-2, 8; P8b-7; and S11b-3. Nos. 57, 138, 207, 218, 219, and 286 are probably of Roman origin.

The majority of the Roman textiles are made from sheep's wool of various qualities; from the fibres which have been examined, generalised medium to coarse wool appears to be more common than true fine or shortwools. Surprisingly, cotton (*Gossypium*) is more common than flax (*Linum usitatissimum L*). Nos. 24-36 were found together in a tight bundle (locus D4b-1). In this group there are 7 examples of cotton to 5 of flax; the 13th piece is possibly palm. The woollens tend to be S-spun while the cottons and flaxes are Z-spun.

The colour range is limited. Most of the pieces are undyed, although there are examples of red, blues, and greens. The greens were double-dyed, yellow on blue; the red is probably madder (*Rubia tinctorum*) and the blue an *Indigofera*. This does not mean that the Romans had a narrow range of colours. There are two small fragments of shaded band (no. 19) in orange, green, red, purple, yellow, and brown wool. Such bands are typically Roman and have been found on sites as far apart as the Crimea, Palmyra, and Qasr Ibrim in Nubia. An apparent reference to this type of cloth is found in the first century *Periplus of the Erythraean Sea*, XXIV, 15. There is a description of the imports into the town of Muza, which includes ζωναι σκιωται 'shadowed' or 'shaded belts'. The reference in the Oxyrhynchus papyrus, no. 921, σινδόνια σκιωτὰ is to 'shaded linens' (perhaps with self bands woven in). The Quseir al-Qadim pieces were woven in weft-faced tabby whereas most of the Roman textiles from this site were woven in balanced tabby which varies from a very coarse example (no. 36) with a count of 4 x 5 to a very fine one with a count of 28 x 28 (no. 29). There are also examples of narrow 'pyjama cord' (which are also considered to be typically Roman) woven in a warp-faced 2/1 basket weave. Examples of this type have been found at Ibrim, although only one Quseir al-Qadim example (no. 28) has the pink stripes near the selvage. No. 22 has the single example of a corded edge which is very similar to the edge type B2 from Nubia (Bergman, 1975: 33). All the examples found there, however, are S-twisted, while the Quseir al-Qadim one is Z-twisted. Most of the selvages are plain/simple; but there is one example of a circular or hollow selvage (no. 12, 65:5,5a), which is most unusual in the eastern Roman world; in the western provinces it is associated with 2/2 twills. Wild (1970: 56) suggests that this type of selvage was woven using tablets on a warp-weighted loom. (Other evidence for this type of loom at Quseir al-Qadim is a section of possible starting cord [no. 4] and a woollen tabby with a single wedge [no. 148] [see Bergman, 1975: 16-21].) No. 12 was woven in a coarse 2/2 twill, with yarn of blended naturally pigmented fibres. Other 2/2 twills include a "hound's-tooth" twill in dark blue and natural wool (no. 147, 62:2).

The most interesting of the Roman textiles is an example of a 1/3 diamond twill with displacement in brick red wool (no. 54, 62:3). No other examples of this type are known from this period.

Textiles from the Islamic Levels

The majority of the textiles come from the Islamic period, although there are several pieces (nos. 112, 157, 162) which could easily be of nomadic tribal origin. Most of the textiles are checked flax. There are two qualities of flax present: The first is a degenerate form associated with poor quality dyeing and loose weaving while the second is a good quality which, when dyed blue, produced a deep strong colour. The flax tended to be Z-spun, but this is not a firm rule, as there are examples of both S-spun and Z-spun yarns in the same textile. The predominanace of Z-spin is interesting because at Ibrim flax tends to be S-spun (E. Crowfoot, pers. comm.). In the fustian examples from Quseir al-Qadim the flax is always S-spun, whilst the cotton is Z-spun. Raw cotton has been used in all the quilted and padded textiles. Various bast fibres including jute (*Corchorus capsularis* or *C. olitorius*) have been used but generally for sewing thread rather than for the actual textiles. Silk is unspun and double stranded rather than plyed. Other animal fibres identified include goat, camel, and mohair.

Plate 62: 1978 Textiles

As in the Roman textiles, the colour range in the Islamic material is basically undyed, blue, and red, with an emphasis on blue. In a few examples (nos. 262, 289, 295) it is possible that the red is not a madder in origin, but an insect dye. (Samples are being examined by Prof. Mark Whiting of Bristol University.)

All the checks and most of the striped textiles are tabby woven, although some of the stripes are warp-faced tabbies, usually in blue and natural with blue wefts (e.g., nos. 44b, 216, 220). The fragments of coarse goat and wool girth-bands are also warp-faced tabbies, but with weft-faced inlays which do not appear on the reverse of the textile. They are similar in construction and appearance to the camel girths described by G. Crowfoot (1956). The raised designs are not suitable for textiles which are subject to a lot of wear, such as rugs.

The preference for warp-faced weaves in the Islamic period can be seen in the development of the ikat, an example of which has been found at Quseir al-Qadim (no. 143). It has 3 doubled blocks of mid blue on a natural ground with a natural weft. This type of colouring is typically Yemeni and it is possible that it was imported from that region.

Trade with India is illustrated by a single example of resist-dyed cotton, which has an abstract design of dark blue circles on a pink ground with vermiculated natural areas. According to Pfister (1938: 26) the colouring is unusual; most pieces seem to have had either a red or a blue design rather than a combination of the two. D. King (pers. comm.) has described this design as being typically 14th century.

There are a few examples of weft-faced weaves from the Mamluk loci. Nos. 123 and 124 are simple *kalim* types, but they are not large enough for their use to be identified. There is only one example of true tapestry (where the coloured yarns in the design return before reaching the selvages). This is no. 41, which is illustrated in the 1978 report (Whitcomb and Johnson, 1979), fig. 11.

The single example of a twill from the Mamluk levels is an irregular 2/2 twill with point repeat (no. 258, 62:4). It was woven in light blue and natural flax and is very similar to diamond twills found at Ibrim.

Other similarities between the textiles from Ibrim and Quseir al-Qadim can be seen in the examples of dark blue "veiling" (nos. 83, 208, 264, 265). These are woven in dark blue wool with brocaded bands of double stranded undyed cotton. The designs are all geometric; no. 265 (62:5) is a good example of this type of textile. One example from Quseir al-Qadim is polychrome (no. 208); the ground is blue, but the design is in red, green, and orange wool.

These pieces were classed as veiling after examples from Ibrim, but very few of the Quseir al-Qadim pieces have easily identifiable uses. No. 275 is a gussetted bag in a checked flax; no. 317 is a short sleeve from a tunic (62:6). No. 134 is the remains of a long sleeve, possibly from a child's tunic, which has been well patched, as have many of the examples; none, however, have been darned. An interesting feature of these textiles is the use of a flat ('tatbeet') seam, which is very similar to the standard Run and Fell seam (62:18,19). The only difference is that the 'tatbeet' seam (the word simply means 'flat seam') has not been cut down during construction. Awatif al-Halim has kindly informed me that it is identical to a seam still in use in the Sudan. The introduction of the Run and Fell seam into the Nile Valley appears to have occurred with the Turkish invasions (E. Crowfoot, pers. comm.). A side panel of a silk quilted cap has also been found. Although most of the silk has now disintegrated, the quilt pattern is still recognisable (62:8). The base of the panel is made from two linen diamonds sewn together; rolled cotton (similar to the rolls used in Italian quilting) was then basted onto the linen. Silk was laid on the top and quilted down using natural and blue flax threads. Originally it was sewn to another identical panel, the remains of which can still be seen. There are examples of this type of cap in the Field Museum, Chicago (e.g., No. 173679).

1980 Season

The 1980 textiles have not yet been examined closely, so the following report is only a brief survey of the pieces now in the Oriental Institute, Chicago.

The range of fibres and colours is very similar to those from the previous season; flax, cotton, sheep's wool, camel, goat, basts, and silk are found.

As in the 1978 season, flax tabby checks are predominant with a wide variety of patterns. Many appear to be identical but few actually are. Several pieces have "faded out" areas; this is associated with either the beginning or the end of the cloth piece and has been found on similar textiles at Ibrim.

An interesting example of the use of colour can be seen in a small checked piece in blue and natural (n, d.bl/n, d.bl; zz/zz; 20x10; 1/2 basket) (RN 576). By changing the sequence of colours in both systems--2n, 2bl, 2n, 2bl, 2n, 4bl, 2n, 2bl, etc., a checked effect has been produced.

There is only one example of tapestry; this is a stepped design in light blue, red, and dark blue with a white ground (g/wwww; s(z)/zzzz) (RN 571). The colours are separated by slits which have not been sewn up.

The other examples of woollens also tend to be weft-faced with polychrome bands. Blues, reds, yellow, oranges, and greens have been used frequently, although there are a few examples with purple bands on a yellow ground.

Warp-faced textiles include cotton stripes in dark blue and natural, natural and polychrome "pyjama" cord girths similar to those found in 1978. Heavier warp-faced pieces include examples of matting and carpeting. The largest piece of carpet is 28 x 32 cm. (63:2) and has an inlay (63:1) similar to that used on the girths. It has a stepped geometric design with lines and triangles in blue, red, yellow, and green wool, loosely z-spun (RN 571). There is also a small fragment with a piled design of circles and diamonds in blue, red, and green Sehna/Persian knots. The loop density is 42 per sq. cm.

The examples of dark blue veiling have simpler geometric designs than the pieces found in 1978. One piece of veiling has a long plyed fringe and selvage (65:1) with 2 bands in dark blue and light blue (w/ww; s/ss; 11x11 [2 st]) (RN 577). These bands are in 2/2 twill. Other twills include a naturally coloured fustian (f/c; s/z; 23x17) (RN 571) in a 2/2 herringbone twill and a small 2/2 diamond twill with point repeat (w/w; z/z; n/d.bl; 18x20) (RN 574) (63:3). There is an unusual example of a 1/3 twill with bands of light and dark blue surrounded by broad bands of twill. In order to produce a speckled effect, 2 systems of twill have been used in alternating rows of red and yellow (w/wwww; l.bl/l.bl, d.bl, red, yell; 17x18; 65:1) (RN 571) (63:4).

Non-woven structures are represented by examples of sprang and knitting. The sprang is a simple interlocking form and was probably made as a belt--both selvages are present (c,s,n; 113x13cm.) (RN 572). The knitting is in a coarse stocking stitch and still has a small section of the finishing edge (c; 2x2st; n; 9 stitches per sq.cm.) (RN 577).

Smocking is represented by a single example of a small flax check sewn to a natural ground. (ff/ff; zz/zz; d.bl,n/d.bl,n; 21x34;--c/c; z/z; n/n; 12x18). The stitching is on the reverse side and a honeycomb effect has been produced by double rows of stitching sewn at irregular distances (63:6). Three types of embroidery techniques have been found at Quseir al-Qadim. There is a small example of fine white work with buttonhole stitched eyelets with a surrounding pattern of irregular stem-stitch (c/c,n/n,s/s; emb/t; c,n,z). Cross-stitch and basket stitch have been used on two pieces to produce outlined geometric designs. The third type of embroidery has isolated or band designs worked in satin stitch

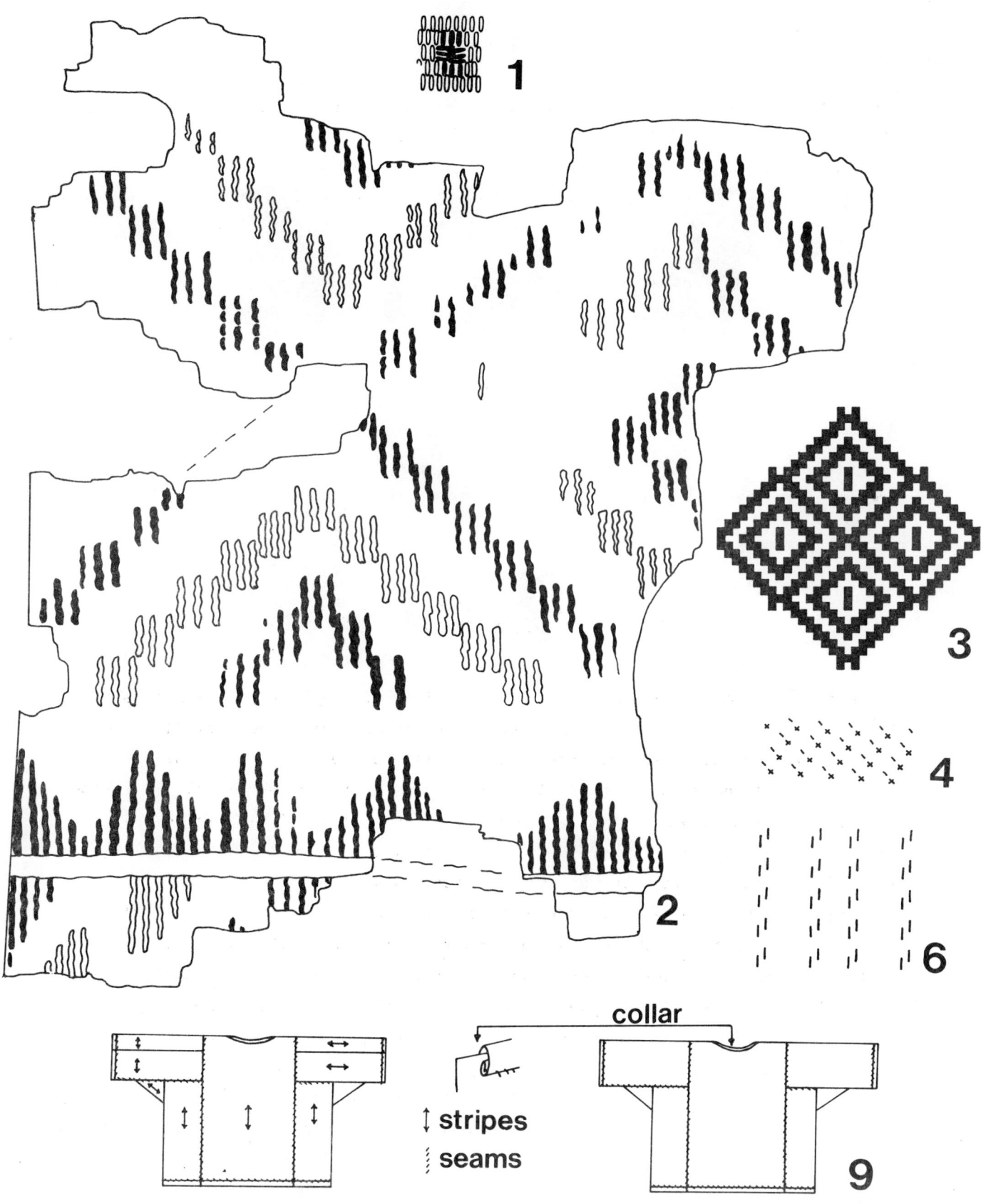

Plate 63: 1980 Textiles

using silk threads (s); again the patterns are geometric, but the effect is more delicate than the outlined designs (64:],b,d,f,h).

Some of the most interesting finds are a group of block resist and block printed textiles (65:g and fig. 20), which are probably of Indian origin. All of them

Figure 20: Block Resist and Block Printed Textiles

have been 'printed' on z-spun natural cotton of various qualities, with a range of counts from 10x12 to 27x23. Technically the block resist dyed textiles are not of a high quality. The outlines are very ill-defined and the colours are patchy. On all the red pieces the dye has faded. There is one example of a blue and red block resist print where the natural ground has been obliterated. The only block printed textile discovered during the 1980 season has a small design of rectangles and rosettes in red on fine cotton (27x23).

There are numerous examples of caps; see fig. 21. All have broad stiffened bands with shaped tops. These tops are usually made from eight triangular sections in natural, check, natural, check, etc., material, padded, lined, and then quilted. The small white work embroidery probably came from the band region of such a cap. There are pieces of coarse rolled cottom used for raised (Italian) quilting used in the silk cap top from the 1978 season.

The only identifiable garment is a child's tunic, made from a poor quality striped linen (z/zz; d.bl,n/d.bl; 17x16) (E18d-7). Although it is badly deteriorated,

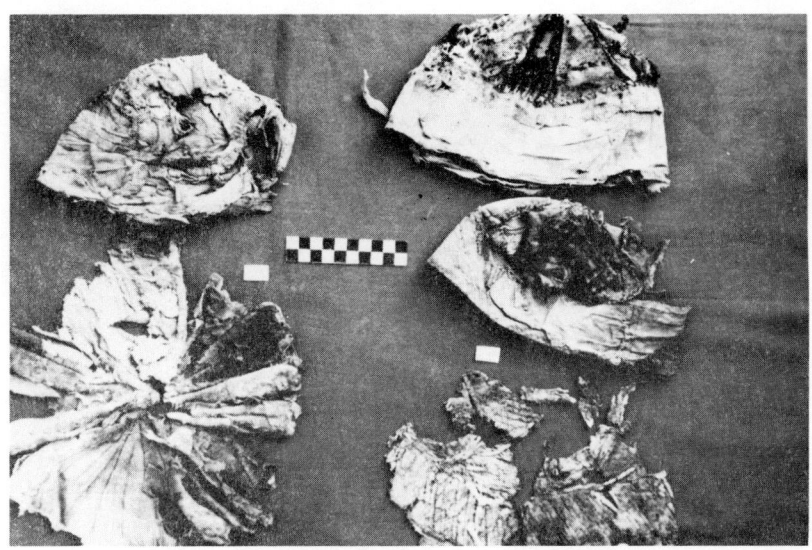

Figure 21: Hats

the construction of the tunic is still recognisable (63:9). All the seams are tatbeet (66:19); the hems are 65:7.

The full description of the 1980 season textiles will be published in the final report; the following catalogue of the 1978 textiles is meant only as a summary; a more comprehensive one of the full three seasons of excavated textiles will be produced when the excavations have been completed.

Bibliography for Textiles

Bergman, I.
    1975   *Late Nubian Textiles, Swedish Joint Expedition*, Vol. 8, Lund

Crowfoot, G. M.
    1956   "The Sudanese Camel Girth," *Kush* 4, pp. 34-38

Pfister, R.
    1938   *Les Toiles Imprimées de Fostat et l'Hindoustan*, Paris

Schoff, W. H., trans.
    1912   *The Periplus of the Erythraean Sea*, New York

Thurman, C. M.
    1979   *Ancient Textiles from Nubia*, Chicago

Whitcomb, D. S., and J. H. Johnson
    1979   *Quseir al-Qadim 1978: Preliminary Report*, Cairo

Wild, J. P.
    1970   *Textile Manufacture in the Northern Roman Provinces*, Cambridge

Plate 64: Embroidery and Batik

    Locus   RN   Description

a E18d-8 593 tan; brown and blue embroidery
b E18c-5 592 tan; embroidered white eyelets
c E18a-14 606 tassel (paper) with red wrapping; white lozenges; green at top and bottom
d E18a-13 589 tan; black embroidery
e J8c-1   594 tan; black printed decoration
f E18d-12 603 tan; purple, blue, and red embroidery
g E18d-14 602 tan; dark blue and red batik
h E19c-10 601 tan; dark blue and red embroidery

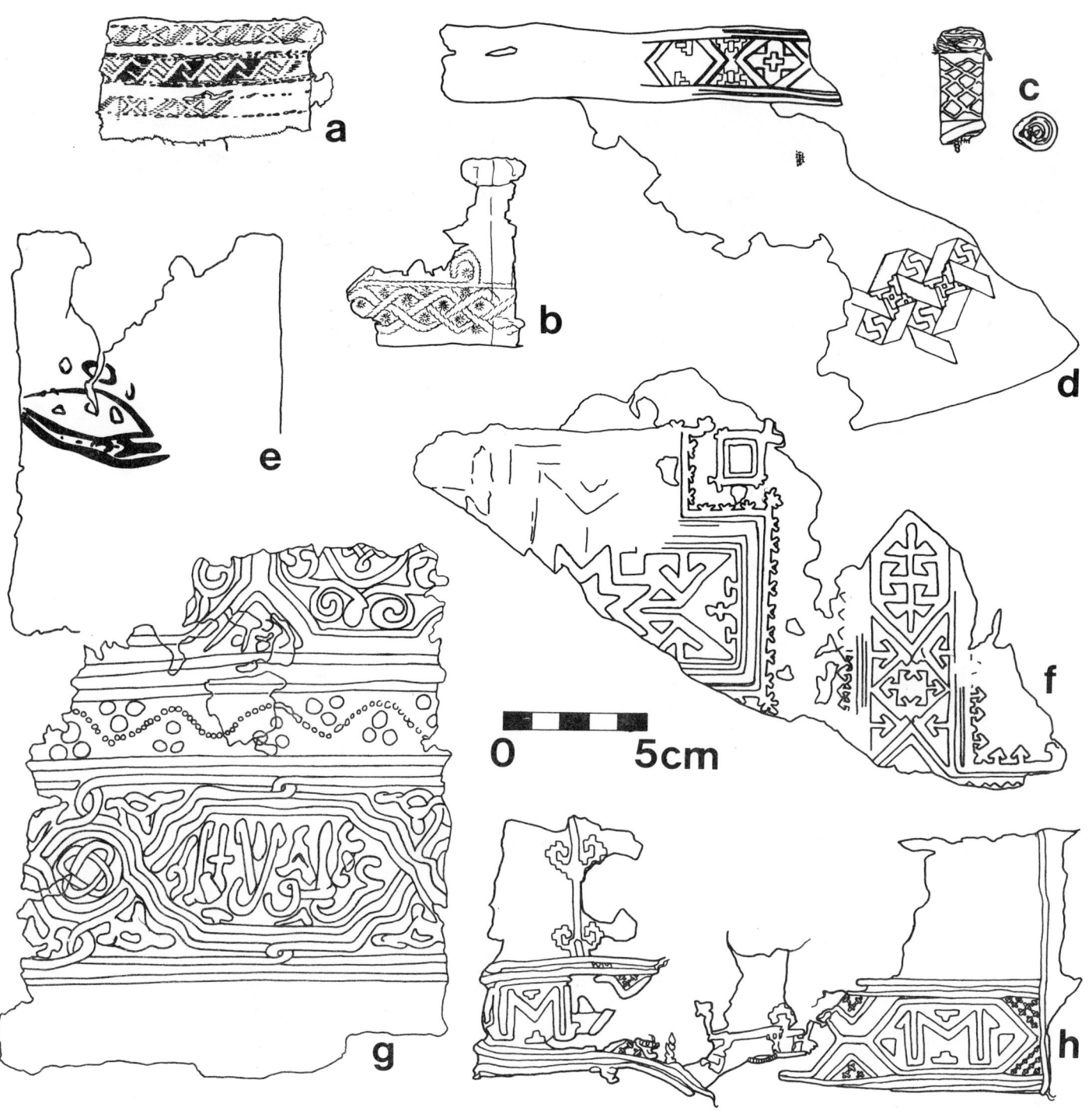

Plate 64: Embroidery and Batik

Catalogue of the 1978 Textiles

The following abbreviations are used:

Fibres		Colours		Others	
b	bast	b	black	st	strands
c	cotton	bl	blue	s/t	sewing thread
ca	camel	br	brown	S-spin	
f	flax	gr	green		
g	goat	n	natural		
m	mohair	or	orange	Z-spin	
s	silk	p	pink		
w	wool	pur	purple		
		y	yellow		
		l	light		
		m	mid		
		d	dark		

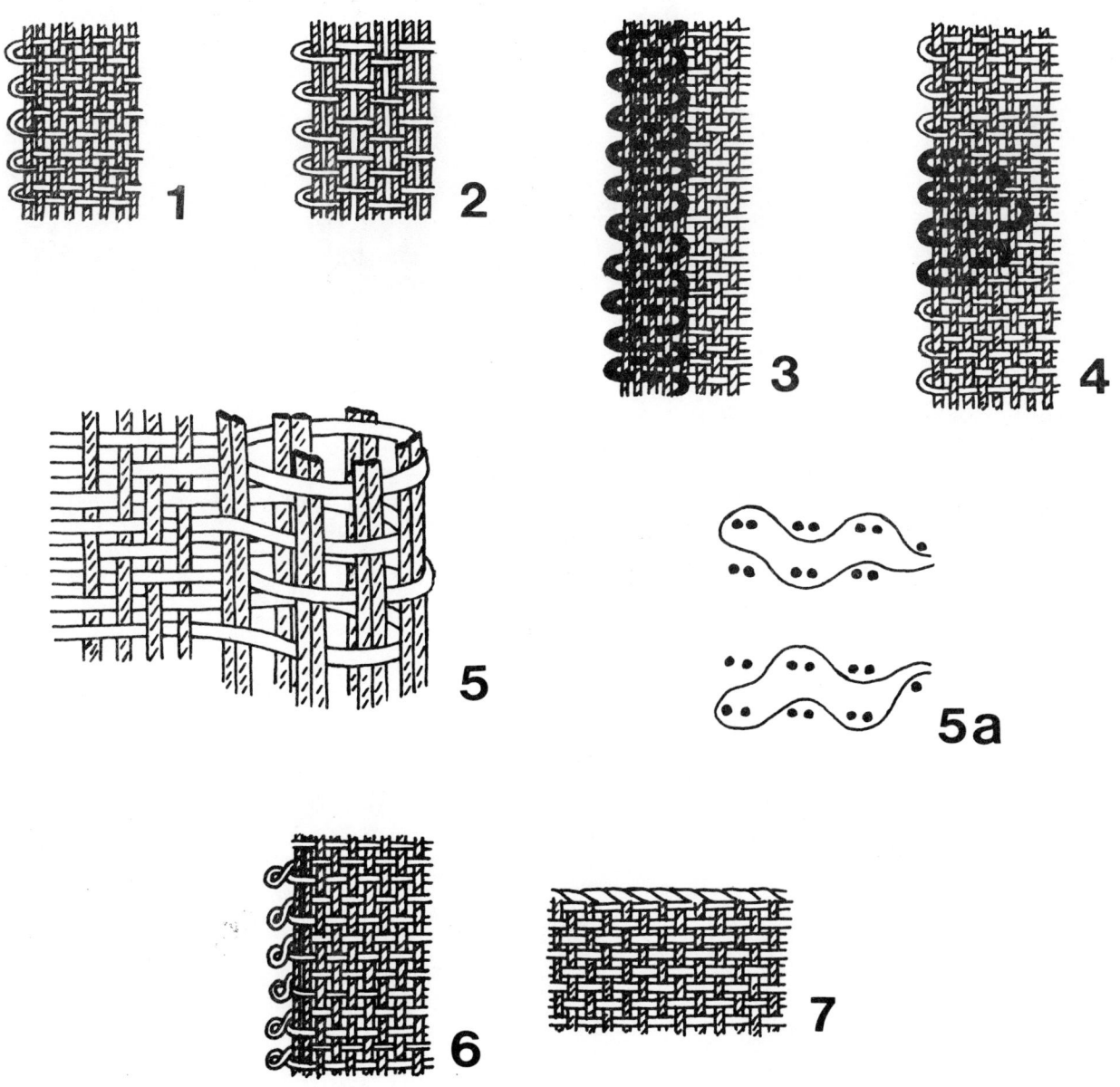

Plate 65: Hems and Edges

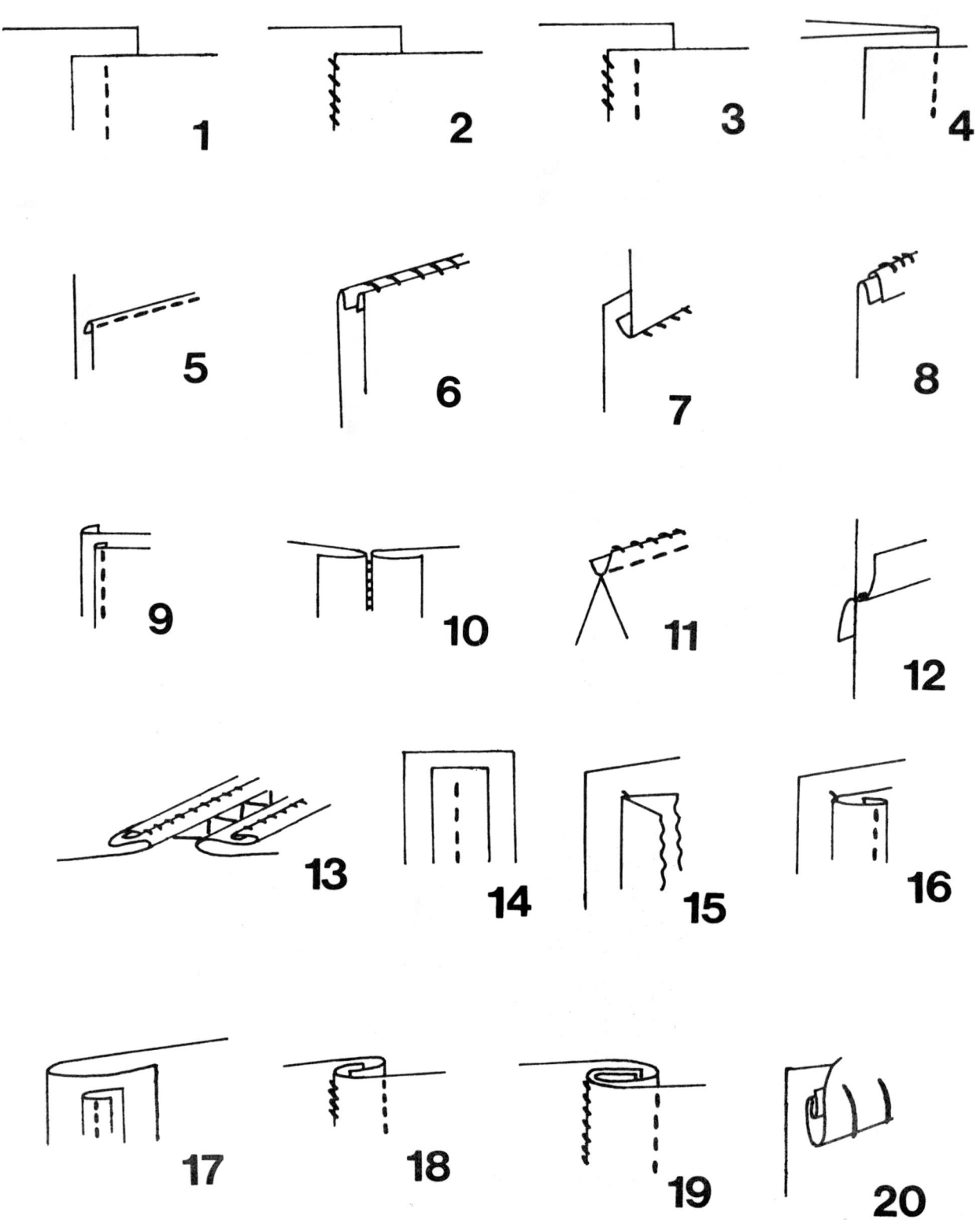

Plate 66: Seams

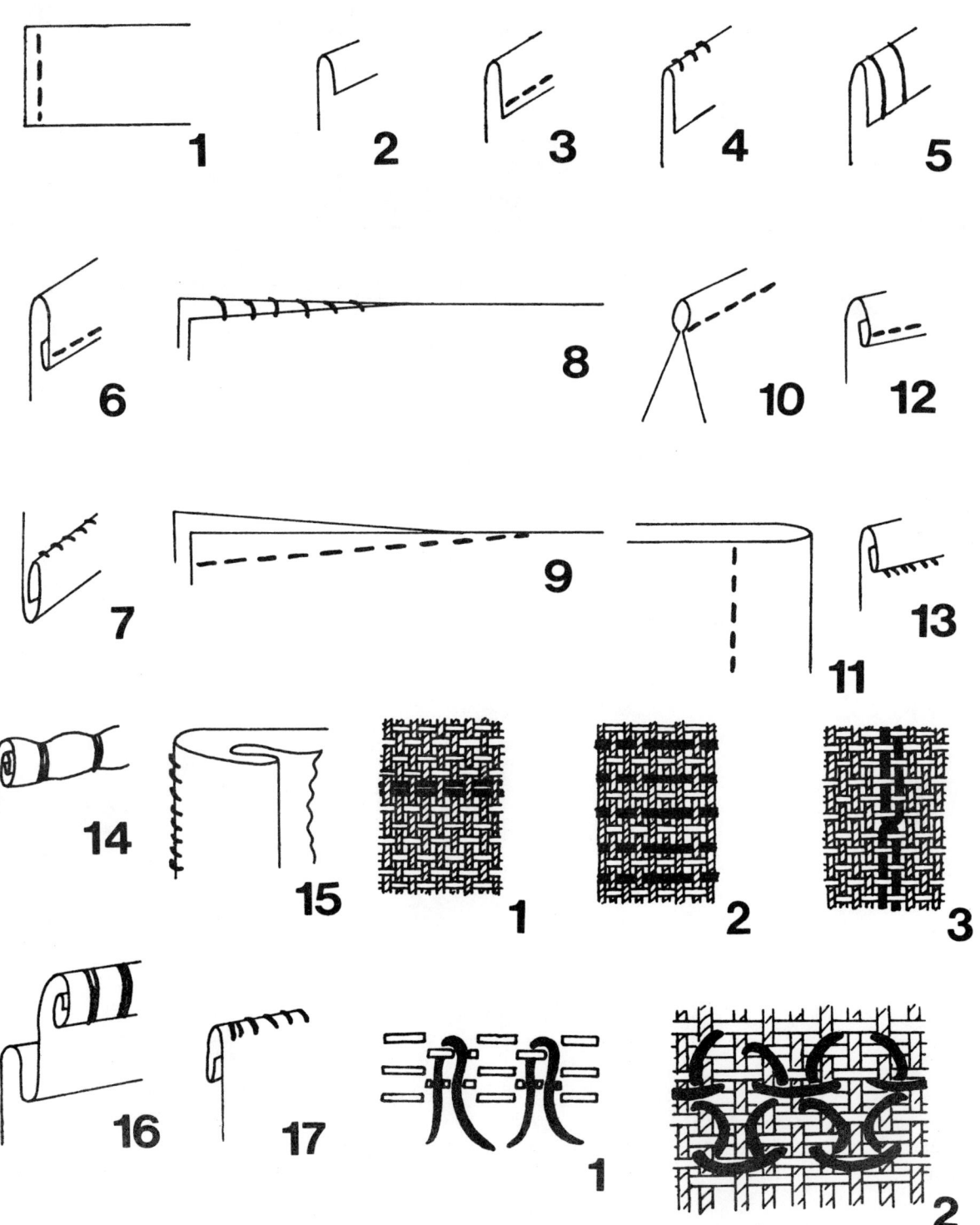

Plate 67: Hems, Darts, etc. (1-17); Faults (18-20); Loops (21-22)

No.	Locus	Fibre	Spin	Tightness	Weave	Count (cm)	Colours	Edges, etc.	Size (cm)	Comment
1	A22d-2 A22d-3	c/c	z/z	m/m	tabby	19x20	n/p,d.bl, n	--	9x10.5 4x1.5 2x4.5	3 fragments of resist dyed cotton pattern of circles and curved lines
2	B4a-1	ff/ff	sz/ss	mm/ll	tabby	11x11	n,d.bl/n, d.bl	--	4.9x7 2.5x2	2 fragments of same material stripes, remains of check on the larger piece
3	B4a-3	w/w	s/s	t/l	tabby	16x16	y/y	67:7	6x9.5	s/t=w.br,s
4	B4a-3	g/gw	z(2)/ss	m/ml	piled	5x17	d.br/d.br y	65:2(3) 67:22	15.5x 5.5	loop density=4/ sq cm
5	B4a-3	c/c	z/z	m/m	tabby	7x7	n/n	65:6	30x9	remains of a starting cord and weft self-bands
6	B4a-4	w/w	s/s	t/l	tabby	15x24	br.red/br. red	--	8.5x6	rippled effect, see 7
7	B4a-4	w/w	s/s	m/l	tabby	16x32	l.gr/l.gr	65:3 67:14 67:18	13x5.5	rippled effect, see 6; s/t=w,n,s
8	B4a-4	w	--	--	felt	--	yellow	--	5x4.5	coarse, circular piece
9	C4c-2	w/www	z/zzz	t/llt	piled	6x23	m.br/m.br loops=d.br l.red	67:18 67:21	18x14	loop density = 5x2cm in rows found with 10, 11, 12
10	C4c-2	w/wwww	s/ssss	m/llll	weft-faced	11x24	n/n,red,gr, l.br	--	12x7	brittle, most of brown bands gone
11	C4c-2	w/ww	s/ss	m/ll	tabby+ weft-bands	14x20	n/n,red	--	1.8x6	red bands on natural ground
12	C4c-2	w/w	z/z	t/t	2/2 twill	8x10	n/n	65:5	8x5.5	circular selvage

No.	Locus	Fibre	Spin	Tightness	Weave	Count (cm)	Colours	Edges, etc.	Size (cm)	Comment
13a	C4c-3	w/ww	s/ss	t/ll	weft-faced	16x19 x26	n/n,d.bl	67:7	2.7x5	2 pieces attached by thread, a has blue band
13b	C4c-3	w/w	s/s	t/l	tabby	16x18	n/n	67:7	4.7x5	
14	C4c-3	g/gg	z/zz (2 ply)	m/lm	tabby	5x5	d.br/n d.br	--	7.5x10	S2 natural was probably put in by hand
15	C4c-4	w/w	s/z	m/l	tabby	13x11	m.gr/m.gr	--	5x3.5	
16	C4c-4	w/ww	s/sz(2)	m/lm	tabby+weft-faced	15x26 7x22+	y/y,d.pur	--	22x8.5	narrow purple band on natural ground
17	C4c-7	w/ww	s/ss	m/ll	tabby+weft-faced	17x19 9x50	y/y,dull pur	--	8x15	2 broad purple bands on natural ground
18	D4b-1	w/w	z/z	t/m	tabby	17x27	d.bl/d.bl	--	9x4	
19	D4b-1	w/wwwww	s/sssss	m/lllll	tabby	13x18	or/or,gr, red,pur,y br,	--	1.7x4.5 1.8x6	2 fragments of shaded band, with central red band
20	D4b-1	w/w	s/s	m/l	tabby	16x13	dull gr/ dull gr	67:7	3.5x3.5 3.2x6	2 fragments same material s/t=w,y,z(2)
21	D4b-1	g/g	z(2)/ s(2st)	m/m	2/1 basket	4x4	d.br/d.br	--	3.5x4	S/t=g,n,z(2)
22	D4b-1	c/c	z/z	m/m	tabby	18x19	dull or/ dull or	65:7	8x11.5	
23	D4b-1	cc/cc	zz/zz	mm/ll	tabby	14x38	n,d.bl/n, d.bl	--	4.5x5 4x4	2 fragments same material check
24	D4b-1	f/f	z/z	m/m	tabby	5x5	n/n	--	9x7.5	nos. 24-36 found wrapped together

No.	Locus	Fibre	Spin	Tightness	Weave	Count (cm)	Colours	Edges, etc.	Size (cm)	Comment
25	D4b-1	f/f	s/s	m/m	weft-faced	3x10	n/n	--	7.7x7.5	
26	D4b-1	f/f	s/s	m/m	2/1 basket	11x5	n/n	2x65:1	9.5x3	"Pyjama" cord
27	D4b-1	f/f	s/s	m/m	2/1 basket	9x5	n/n	65:1	4x1.6	"Pyjama" cord
28	D4b-1	ff/f	ss/s	mm/m	2/1 basket	12x4	n,p/n	2x65:1	44x3.3	"Pyjama" cord
29	D4b-1	c/c	z/z	m/m	tabby	28x28	n/n	--	3.5x5	
30	D4b-1	c/c	z/z	t/t	tabby	17x18	n/n	--	3x9	
31	D4b-1	c/c	z/z	m/m	tabby	9x10	n/n	--	3x6.5	
32	D4b-1	c/c	z/z	m/m	tabby	20x28	n/n	--	11x10	
33	D4b-1	c/c	z/z	l/l	tabby	10x7	n/n	--	7x8.5	
34	D4b-1	c/c	s/s	t/t	tabby	10x10	n/n	--	6x11	
35	D4b-1	c/c	z/z	m/m	2/1 basket	3x10	n/n	--	11x8.5	s/t=f,z(2)
36	D4b-1	?p/p	z/z	l/l	tabby	4x5	n/n	--	4.5x7	brittle
37	F8d-	ff/ff	ss/zs	ml/ml	tabby	22x13	d.bl,n/d.bl,n	65:2(18)	17.6x 3.8	stripes with small checked area
38	F8d-	ff/ff	ss/ss	mm/mm	tabby	13x15	m.bl,n/m.bl,n	67:3,18	15.7x9	check
39a	F8d-	f/f	s/s	m/l	tabby	14x12	n/n	66:19,7	6x36	plain material sewn to striped fustian; s/t= f,n,z(2); f,n,s(2)
39b	F8d-	f/cc	s/zz	m/ll	tabby	14x13	n/n,d.bl	--		see 39a
40	F8d-	f/cc	s/zz	m/ll	tabby	14x12	n/n,d.bl	--	14.5x33	striped fustian see 39b

No.	Locus	Fibre	Spin	Tightness	Weave	Count (cm)	Colours	Edges, etc.	Size (cm)	Comment
41	F8d-1	w/wwww	z/zzzz	m/1111	weft-faced	10x22	y/y,red, d.bl,l.bl	--	12.5x7	design of crosses, stripes and bands see fig., 1978 report
42	F8d-1	fs/f	s-/z	1-/1	tabby	5x19	n,b/n	65:1 67:18	30.5x 7.5	silk selvage stripe
43a	F8d-1	f/f	z/z	m/m	tabby	12x12	n/n	67:7	11.5x 29.5	3 pieces sewn together, s/t= f,n,z(s)
43b	F8d-1	f/ff	s/ss	1/mm	tabby	8x7	n/n,m.bl	66:18(2)		stripes
43c	F8d-1	f/ff	s/ss	1/mm	tabby	8x7	n/n,m.bl			stripes
44a	F8d-1	ff/ff	ss/ss	11/11	tabby	16x-	n,d.bl/n, d.bl	66:14	1.2x 21.5	2 pieces sewn together, stripes and checks, s/t= f,l.bl,s(3)
44b	F8d-1	cc/c	ss/s	mm/t	warp-faced	31x12	d.bl,n/n			
45	F8d-1	f/ff	s/ss	m/11	tabby	14x10	n/n,d.bl	--	10x14	stripes
46a	F8d-2	w/w	s/s	m/1	tabby	13x19	n/n	--	9.5x7	d.bl banded twill sewn to a s/t=w,n,s(2); w,n,z(2)
46b	F8d-2	w/ww	s/ss	m/11	1/2 twill weft-faced	22x31 11x32	n/n,d.bl			
47	F8d-2	g/gg	z/zz (2 ply)	t/tt	tabby	4x4	n/n,d.br	--	6.5x6	brittle
48	F8d-2	fs/ff	s-/sz	1-/11	2/1 basket	-x18	n,d.br/	65:1	34x2	br selvage stripe, knotted at one end

304

No.	Locus	Fibre	Spin	Tightness	Weave	Count (cm)	Colours	Edges, etc.	Size (cm)	Comment
49	F8d-2	ff/ff	sz/ss	ml/ml	tabby	16x18	n,d.bl/ n,d.bl	--	6.8x4	check
50	F8d-2	cc/cc	zz/zz	ll/ll	tabby	15x13	n,d.bl/ n,d.bl	--	3.7x3.5	check
51	F8d-2	cc/cc	zz/zz	ll/ll	tabby	19x21	n,d.bl/ n,d.bl	65:1(6)	5.2x1.4	check
52	F8d-3	cc/ccc	zz/zzz	mm/mmm	tabby	19x15	d.bl,n/ d.bl,p,n	--	8x6	check
53	F8d-4	www/wwww	sss/ssss	mmm/llll	tabby	16x12	red,d.bl, br/red,d.bl br,y	--	8x6	check, y wool inlays
54	F8d-8	w/w	s/s	t/l	1/3 twill	19x15	red/red	--	12x4	1/3 diamond twill with displacement and fault
55	F9c-1	ff/ff	ss/sz	tt/ll	tabby	15x12	m.bl,n/ m.bl,n	--	17.5x16	irregular check shaped 2 pieces sewn together s/t=f,n,z(3)
56	F9c-1	cc/ccc	zz/zzz	mm/mmm	tabby	19x15	d.bl,n/ d.bl,p,n	--	15x7	check
57	F9c-2	ww/w	ss/s	ll/l	tabby	8x8	n,d.bl/n	--	6x5	stripes
58	F9c-2	cc/cc	zz/zz	tt/mm	tabby	20x16	n,p/n,p	65:1(7)	13x9	check, brittle and folded
59	F9c-5	w/w	s/s	t/l	tabby	11x10	n/n	66:19 67:7	6.4x 12.5	3 pieces same material sewn together; s/t= w,z(2)? blood stains
60	F9c-7	g/gg	z/zz	l/ll	tabby	5x5	d.br/d.br n	--	5.5x9	naturally coloured bands

No.	Locus	Fibre	Spin	Tightness	Weave	Count (cm)	Colours	Edges, etc.	Size (cm)	Comment
61	F9c-13	ww/ww	zz/zz	ll/ll	tabby	11x11	n,red/n, red	67:19	4.5x5	check
62	F9c-13	cc/cc	zz/zz	mm/ll	tabby	13x16	d.bl,n/d. bl,n	67:7	9.3x 22.2	check, s/t= f,n,s(2)
63	F9c-14	w/ww	z/zz	m/ll	tabby	11x10	n/n,d.br	--	1.7x5.5 4x7.5	2 fragments same material
64	F9c-14	g/wwww	z/zzzz	t/llll	weft-faced	4x16	d.br/l.gr, y,or,red	--	17x17	polychrome bands found with 63
65	F9c-14	ff/ff	zz/zz	ml/ll	tabby	19x18	n,m.bl/ n,m.bl	--	6.7x3.5	check
66	F9c-14	ff/ff	zz/ss	mm/ll	tabby	16x15	n,d.bl/ n,d.bl	65:2(2)	6x16	check, s/t= d.bl/n,z(2)
67	F9c-14	ff/ff	zz/ss	mm/ll	tabby	14x16	d.bl,n/ d.bl,n	65:2(4)	1.5x 14.3	check
68	F9c-14	ff/f	zs/s	mm/m	tabby	19x14	n,d.bl/n	65:2(18) 65:1	30x2.5	stripes
69	F9c-14	c/cc	z/zz	t/ll	tabby	19x16	l.bl/m.bl, n	--	6.5x12	stripes
70	F9c-14	cc/cc	zz/zz	ll/ll	tabby	16x16	d.bl,n/ d.bl,n	--	13x8.3	check
71	F9c-14	cc/cc	zz/ss	ll/ll	tabby	12x14	d.bl,n/ d.bl,n	67:18	11x2.5	check
72	F9c-14	cc/c	ss/s	mm/m	warp-faced	20x9	d.bl,n/d. bl	--	9x12.5	stripes
73	F10a-1	ww/www	zz/zzzz	lm/lml	tabby	13x12	gr,red/gr red,m.bl	--	3.8x3.8	check
74	F10a-1	fs/fss	z-/z--	m-/m--	tabby	8+x10+	n,m.bl/n, y,d.bl	67:7	11x10	check, silk deteriorated s/t=f,n,z
75	F10a-1	ff/f	zz/z	mm/l	tabby	17x15	n,d.bl/n	65:2(20+)	7x3.7	stripes

No.	Locus	Fibre	Spin	Tightness	Weave	Count (cm)	Colours	Edges, etc.	Size (cm)	Comment
76	F10a-1	f/fff	z/zzz	l/lll	tabby	20x17	d.bl/d.bl, l.bl,n	66:7,19	7.5x6.5	3 pieces same material sewn together stripes; s/t= f,n,bl,s(2)
77	F10a-1	ff/ff	zz/ss	tt/ll	tabby	8x15	d.bl,n/ d.bl,n	--	4.7x8.4	check
78	F10a-1	ff/ff	zz/ss	mm/ll	tabby	10x14	d.bl,n/ d.bl,n	--	15.4x1.8	remains of check
79	F10a-1	ff/ff	zs/sz	ml/mm	tabby	13x10	m.bl,n/ m.bl,n	65:2(20)	6.4x11.5	striped and checked areas
80	F10a-1	ff/ff	zz/ss	tt/ll	tabby	14x17	d.bl,n/ d.bl,n	67:7	16.2x15.5	checks, s/t= f,n,s(2)
81	F10a-1	cc/ccc	zz/zzz	tt/lll	tabby	18x14	m.bl,n/ l.bl,d.bl,n	--	5x11.5	check
82	F10a-1	cc/cc	zz/zz	mm/ll	tabby	20x21	m.bl,n/ m.bl,n	--	6x3.8	check
83	F10a-1	cc/cc	zz/zz	mm/mm	tabby	18x16	d.bl,n/ d.bl,n	--	11x4.8	check
84	F10a-1	cc/c	zz/z	ll/m	tabby	14x12	n,m.b/n	65:2(8) 2(2) 2(5) 1	14.5x7.5	stripes
85	F10a-2	w/wc	s/ss	t/tt	tabby+ brocade	18x-	d.bl/d.bl, n	67:13	22x7	"veiling" with white geometric bands, s/t= w,l.bl,z(2)
86	F10a-2	ff/ff	sz/ss	mm/ll	tabby	13x14	d.bl,n/ d.bl,n	67:18	6x4.5	check
87	F10a-2	f/ff	z/zz	m/ll	tabby	16x17	m.bl/m.bl, n	--	4x5.2	check
88	F10a-2	ff/ff	sz/ss	mm/ll	tabby	14x16	m.bl,n/ l.bl,n	--	1.4x9	check

No.	Locus	Fibre	Spin	Tightness	Weave	Count (cm)	Colours	Edges, etc.	Size (cm)	Comment
89	F10a-2	ff/ff	ss/ss	ll/ll	tabby	14x13	m.bl,n/ m.bl,n	--	2x8.3	remains of check
90	F10a-2	cc/cc	zz/zz	lm/ll	tabby	11x12	n,l.bl/ n,l.bl	--	8x3	check
91	F10a-2	cc/cc	zz/zz	ll/ll	tabby	18x17	n,m.bl/ n,m.bl	--	8.8x6	check
92	F10a-2	cc/ccc	zz/zzz	mm/lll	tabby	28x22	d.bl,n/ d.bl,l.bl,n	--	4.3x9.2	check
93	F10a-2	ccc/ccc	zzz/zzz	mmm/mmm	tabby	19x22	d.bl,p,n/ d.bl,p,n	--	8x5	check
94	K9b-7	c/c	z/z	m/m	tabby	12x13	n/n	66:4	20.4x6	2 pieces sewn together, s/t= c,bl,z(2); c,n,z(2)
95	P7b-2	fff/ff	sss/zz	mmm/ll	tabby	14x14	d.bl,n,l. bl/l.bl,n	65:2(50) 67:19	19x8	check
96	P7b-2	ff/cc	ss/zz	mm/ll	tabby	16x13	n,d.bl/ n,d.bl	--	15x6	fustian, see 97
97	P7b-2	ff/cc	ss/zz	mm/ll	tabby	15x13	n,d.bl/ n,d.bl	--	10.5x9	fustian, check
98	P7b-3	g/gg	s/zs	t/ll	tabby	6x6	l.br/d.br n	65:1 67:18	24x13	natural bands on d.br ground s/t=g,z(2)
99	P7b-3	ff/ff	ss/zz	ll/ll	tabby	17x18	d.bl,n/ d.bl,n	66:10(2) 66:16	10x7	3 pieces same material sewn together, check s/t=2xf,n,z(2) lxf,n,z(3)
100	P7b-3	ff/ff	ss/ss	ll/ll	tabby	13x14	d.bl,n/ d.bl,n	66:19 67:7	15x14	check, s/t= f,n,s
101	P7b-3	cc/c	ss/s	ll/t	warp-faced	50x17	n,d.bl/n	--	19x3.8	natural ground with d.bl stripes

No.	Locus	Fibre	Spin	Tightness	Weave	Count (cm)	Colours	Edges, etc.	Size (cm)	Comment
102	P7b-4	ff/ff	zz/ss	mm/ll	tabby	16x16	m.bl,n/ m.bl,n	--	5.4x2.6	check
103	P7d-2	sf/ssf	-z/--z	-l/--l	tabby	47x23	d.bl,n/ d.bl,red,n	65:2	9x6.1	all warps are double stranded check
104	P7d-2	ff/ff	zz/zz	tt/ll	tabby	32x23	n,d.bl/ n,d.bl	--	11x3	brittle, pleated, check
105	P7d-2	ff/ff	zz/zz	mm/ll	tabby	18x17	n,d.bl/ n,d.bl	65:2(10) 67:2,4	11.5x11	check, s/t= f,n,z(3); f,n,z(2)
106a	P7d-2	c/c	z/z	m/m	tabby	18x18	red/red	66:7,19	5x5.5	2 pieces sewn together, s/t= f,n,s(2)
106b	P7d-2	cc/cc	zz/zz	tt/ll	tabby	30x34	n,d.bl/ n,d.bl			check
107	P7d-2	c/c	z/z	m/l	tabby	20x21	n/n	66:19	20x9	knotted and tied with 2 cords
108	P7d-3	fs/fssc	z-/--z	m-/--l	tabby	13x20	n,b/red, y,m.bl	65:1	13.2x 34	2 pieces tiraz with inscription and rows animals
109	P7d-3	cc/c	zz/z	mm/l	tabby	17x18	d.bl,n/ d.bl	65:2(6) 67:4,18	13x17.2	stripes, s/t= f,n,z(2)
110	P7d-7	ff/cc	ss/zz	mm/ll	tabby	14x10	m.bl,n/ m.bl,n	65:2(40)	11.5x14	fustian, check
111	P8a-2	w/w	s/s	t/l	tabby	9x16	d.bl/d.bl	--	16x4	
112	P8a-2	g/g	s/s	m/l	tabby	8x11	d.br/d.br	67:19	19x19.5	"tenting"
113	P8a-2	f/fff	z/zss	m/ll	tabby	16x17	d.bl/d.bl, l.bl,n	66:19 67:3,18	19x14	check

No.	Locus	Fibre	Spin	Tightness	Weave	Count (cm)	Colours	Edges, etc.	Size (cm)	Comment
114	P8a-2	ff/ff	ss/ss	mm/mm	tabby	13x12	n,d.bl/ n,d.bl	--	10.5x 9.5	check
115	P8a-5	w/wwww	s/ssss	m/llll	weft-faced	7x13	ny/n,d.bl	65:2(2 corded+ 9 doubled)	40x25	stripes
116	P8a-5	ff/fff	ss/sss	ll/lll	tabby	12x13	l.bl,n/d. bl,l.bl,n	67:13	12.8x5	check, s/t= f,n,z(2)
117a	P8a-5	ff/ff	ss/ss	mm/ll	tabby	11x9	n,m.bl/ n,m.bl	66:5,7, 15	17x8	2 pieces sewn together, both checks; s/t= f,n,z(2)
117b	P8a-5	ff/ff	ss/ss	mm/ll	tabby	15x12	n,m.bl/ n,m.bl			
118	P8a-6	ff/ff	zs/ss	ml/ll	tabby	16x14	n,m.bl/ n,m.bl	--	15.5x 3.5	check
119	P8a-6	ff/fff	ss/sss	mm/lll	tabby	20x15	m.bl,n/ m.bl,n	--	18.5x 17.5	check
120a	P8a-7	c/c	z/z	m/m	tabby	13x13	m.bl/m.bl	66:15	25x1.8	2 pieces sewn together, s/t= c,n,z(2)
120b	P8a-7	cc/c	ss/s	ll/t	warp-faced	34x11	d.bl,n/d. bl			stripes
121a	P8a-7	c/c	z/z	m/l	tabby	-x-	m.bl/m.bl	66:14	2.5x 23.4	3 pieces sewn together, 2xb s/t= c,n,z(2) c,bl,z(2)
121b	P8a-7	cc/c	ss/s	mm/t	warp-faced	40x11	d.bl,n/d. bl	66:12		
122	P8a-7	w/ww	s/ss	t/ll	weft-faced	7x23	y/y,red	--	8x9	red bands on yellow ground
123	P8a-9	w/www	z(2)/	t/lll	weft-faced	4x22	br/n,d.bl, d.br,gr	--	16x9	*kalim*, narrow bands br,bl,gr on natural ground

310

No.	Locus	Fibre	Spin	Tightness	Weave	Count (cm)	Colours	Edges, etc.	Size (cm)	Comment
124	P8a-9	w/ww	z(2)/ss	t/mm	weft-faced	4x20	br,n/d. pur,gr	--	10x8.5	kalim, broad bands gr,pur
125	P8a-9	w/ww	s/ss	t/mm	tabby+ brocade	14x16	n/n,d.bl	--	4.4x38	geometric brocade
126	P8a-9	f/f	z/z	m/l	tabby	11x16	m.bl/m.bl	65:1 2x66:19 67:7,18	14x11 7.5x12 5.5x6.8	3 pieces same material sewn together, s/t= f,n,s(2); dyed after weaving
127	P8a-9	ff/ff	zz/zz	mm/ll	tabby	22x18	n,d.bl/ n,d.bl	67:6	9.4x5	check; s/t= f,n,s(2)
128	P8a-9	f/f	s/z	m/m	tabby	19x16	n/n	65:2(5) 66:19	19x9	s/t=f,n,s(2)
129	P8a-9	f/f	s/s	m/m	tabby	16x15	n/n	65:2(2) 1(1) 1(1)	14.3x 10.5	remains of s/t= c,n,z(2)
130	P8a-9	ff/ff	ss/ss	ll/ll	tabby	8x14	d.bl/d.bl n	66:19	11x10	check
131	P8a-9	ff/ff	ss/ss	mm/mm	tabby	12x9	m.bl,n/ m.bl,n	--	7.3x7	check
132	P8a-9	ff/ff	ss/ss	ll/ll	tabby	14x15	n,m.bl/ n,d.bl	--	16x11.5	check
133	P8a-9	c/c	z/z	l/l	tabby	12x12	n/n	--	7.3x7.6	
134	P8a-9	c/c	z/z	m/l	tabby	18x19	n/n	5x66:19 2x66:10	32x19	5 pieces same material sewn together, sleeve s/t=3xc,n,z(2) 2xc,n,s(2);1x c,n,s(3)
135	P8a-9	cc/cc	zz/zz	mm/ll	tabby	12x11	d.bl,n/ d.bl,n	--	10x10.5	check
136	P8a-9	ccc/ccc	zzz/zzz	mmm/lll	tabby	15x16	d.bl,l.bl, n/d.bl,l. bl.,n	--	21x16	check

No.	Locus	Fibre	Spin	Tightness	Weave	Count (cm)	Colours	Edges, etc.	Size (cm)	Comment
137	P8a-9	ccc/c	zzz/z	lll/m	warp-faced	26x16	red,d.bl, n/d.bl	--	18x3.1	broad red and bl stripes with narrow natural stripe between
138	P8b-4	f/f	z/z	m/m	tabby	6x5	n/n	65:1 67:3	9x13.5	s/t=f,n,z
139	P8b-4	f/f	z/z	1/1	tabby	28x29	m.bl/m.bl	--	3.8x4.5	dyed after weaving
140	P8b-4	ff/ff	zz/ss	tt/ll	tabby	14x15	d.bl,n/ d.bl,n	--	13.5x18	check
141	P8b-5	cc/c	ss/s	mm/t	warp-faced	34x10	n,d.bl/ d.bl	65:1	9.5x 11.5	stripes of d.bl and natural heavily sand encrusted
142	P8b-6	w/www	s/sss	t/mmm	tabby	8x6	n/n,m.bl or	65:2(2) 67:18	45x19	bands of blue and red
143	P8b-6	f/f	s/s	m/l	tabby	19x13	n/n,m.bl	--	7x4.5	Ikat
144	P8b-6	cc/cc	zz/zz	mm/mm	tabby	15x15	d.bl,n/ d.bl,n	65:2	15x2.6	most warps are x2, stripes
145	P8b-6	cccc/c	zzzz/z	llll/t	tabby	26x24	m.bl,d.bl, red,n/m.bl	--	6x15.8	most red gone stripes
146	P8b-6	ccc/ccc	zzz/zzz	mmm/mmm	tabby	26x21	m.bl,n/ red,d.bl, m.bl,n	65:2(90)	16.5x8	check
147	P8b-7	ww/ww	zz/zz	ll/ll	2/2 twill	5x5	d.bl,n/ d.bl,n	--	11x7	'Hound's-tooth' twill
148	P8b-7	w/w	s/s	m/l	tabby	6x6	n/n	67:18,20	6x10.5	1 wedge in weave
149	P8b-7	ff/ff	zs/ss	mm/mm	tabby	13x12	m.bl,n/ m.bl,n	--	15.5x 17.2	check
150	P8b-7	cc/cc	zz/zz	mm/mm	tabby	14x18	n,l.bl/ n,l.bl	66:1	29x18.5	irregular check, s/t=c,n,z(3)

312

No.	Locus	Fibre	Spin	Tightness	Weave	Count (cm)	Colours	Edges, etc.	Size (cm)	Comment
151	P8b-7	w/ww	z(2)/ss	t/ll	weft-faced	5x21	y/d.br, red	--	6.3x4.6 8x4	2 pieces same material, broad br and red bands
152	P8b-8	mmm/m	zzz/z	mmm/l	tabby	9x6	d.bl,n d.br/d.br	65:2(3)	7x4	stripes
153	P8b-9	w/w	s/s	m/l	tabby	10x8	gr/gr	--	5x6.8	shallow dye
154	P8b-9	ff/ff	zz/ss	ml/ml	tabby	13x14	d.bl,n/ d.bl,n	--	13.6x16	check
155	P8b-12	ff/f	zz/z	mm/t	warp-faced	35x11	d.bl,n/n	65:1	12x14	blue stripes on natural ground
156	P8b-12	ff/c	ss/z	ll/l	tabby	13x13	n,d.bl/n	--	9.8x4.3	fustian, stripes
157a	P8b-12	c/c	z/z	l/l	tabby	17x16	n/n	--	17x20	6 pieces sewn together with cotton padding between, s/t= c,n,s(2);l.bl,s(2)
157b	P8b-12	c/c	z/z	l/l	tabby	12x9	n/n			
157c	P8b-12	c/c	z/z	l/l	tabby	-x13	m.bl/m.bl			
157d	P8b-12	c/cc	z/zz	m/ll	tabby	12x17	n/n,m.bl			check
157e	P8b-12	c/cc	z/zz	m/ll	tabby	16x16	n/n,m.bl	--		stripe
157f	P8b-12	c/cc	z/zz	m/ll	tabby	17x21	m.bl/m.bl, n	--		stripe
158	P8b-15	w/wwww	s/sssss	t/lllll	weft-faced	6x33	n/d.red,d. bl	--	24x4.5 14.5x15 12x3.5 13x12	4 pieces same material; polychrome bands with decorative strands of 4 ply yarn
159	P8b-15	ff/c	ss/z	ll/l	tabby	11x11	n,l.bl/ d.bl	66:19 67:7	8x8.2	2 pieces same material sewn together; fustian s/t=f,n,s(2); d.bl,z
160	P8b-15	ccc/ccc	zzz/zzz	mmm/mmm	tabby	29x19	d.bl,l.bl, n/d.bl,l. bl,n	66:19 67:4,7, 13	31.7x 4.5	check, s/t=f,n,s(2); f,bl,z(2);f,bl,z(3)

No.	Locus	Fibre	Spin	Tightness	Weave	Count (cm)	Colours	Edges, etc.	Size (cm)	Comment
161	P8b-15	cc/c	ss/s	mm/t	warp-faced	28x12	n,d.bl/ d.bl	--	17.8x8	stripes
162	P8b-16	f/fg	s/ss	t/tt	tabby	2x8	n/n,gr	--	11.5x17	picket-fence pattern
163	P8b-17	ccc/ccc	zzz/zzz	mmm/mmm	tabby	19x17	red,d.bl, n/d.bl,l. bl,n	65:2	17.5x10	red=double stranded, knotted at one end
164a	P8b-18	g/gg	z/zs	m/ll	tabby	4x10	n/d.br,n	--	13x18	2 pieces sewn together, s/t= w,bl,s(2), both stripes
164b	P8b-18	w/ww	s/ss	m/ll	weft-faced	6x18	y/d.red,y	67:18		
165	P8b-18	ff/ff	zz/zz	tt/ll	tabby	13x16	n,d.bl/ n,d.bl	--	8.2x12 9x6.8	2 pieces same material knotted together
166a	8b-18	f/f	z/z	1/1	tabby	15x21	n/n	66:17	7.5x2.8	2 pieces sewn together, s/t= f,n,s(2)
166b	P8b-18	ff/ff	ss/ss	ll/ll	tabby	14x14	n,d.bl/ n,d.bl			check
167	P8b-18	ff/ff	zz/ss	ll/ll	tabby	11x14	d.bl,n/ d.bl,n	--	9.4x8	check
168	P8b-18	ff/ff	zz/ss	ll/ll	tabby	12x13	m.bl,n/ m.bl,n	--	3.7x 16.5	check, s/t= f,n,s(3)
169a	P8b-18	f/fff	z/sss	m/mmm	tabby	14x19	m.bl/m.bl l.bl,n	2x66:19 67:18	14x15	4 pieces sewn together, 3xa, s/t=f,n,z(2) f,n,s(2)
169b	P8b-18	ff/ff	sz/ss	ll/ll	tabby	16x16	m.bl,n/ m.bl,n	66:1		
170	P8b-18	ff/ff	sz/ss	ll/ll	tabby	11x13	d.bl,n/ d.bl,n	--	5x13	check

313

314

No.	Locus	Fibre	Spin	Tightness	Weave	Count (cm)	Colours	Edges, etc.	Size (cm)	Comment
171	P8b-18	ff/ff	sz/ss	ll/ll	tabby	14x11	d.bl,n/ d.bl,n	--	2.9x5.7	check
172	P8b-18	ff/ff	ss/ss	ll/ll	tabby	10x10	n,d.bl/ n,d.bl	65:2(2)	4.5x 14.5	check
173	P8b-18	f/ff	s/ss	l/ll	tabby	13x16	d.bl,n/ d.bl	5x66:5 67:18	14x11.5	3 pieces same material sewn together, s/t= f,n,z(2)
174	P8b-18	cc/cc	zz/zz	ll/ll	tabby	15x17	n,d.bl/ n,d.bl	--	18.5x13	check
175	P8b-18	cc/ccc	zz/zzz	tt/lll	tabby	15x18	d.bl,n/d. bl,l.bl,n	--	12x13.8	check
176	P8b-18	cc/c	zz/z	mm/t	tabby	19x13	red,d.bl/ d.bl	67:18	8x4.6	red=double stranded
177	P8c-2	fs/f	z-/z	l-/-	tabby	24x17	n,d.bl/n	66:19	9x6.5	2 pieces same material sewn together, s/t= f,n,s(2); silk= double stranded stripes
178	P8c-2	f/f	s/s	m/l	tabby	20x18	m.bl/m.bl	66:10 67:3,15	29x16	2 pieces same material sewn together, s/t= f,n,z(2); dyed after weaving
179	P8c-2	f/c	s/z	m/l	tabby	10x12	n/n	67:18	7x6	fustian
180	P8c-2	c/c	z/z	m/m	tabby	20x20	red/red	66:6	5x6	2 pieces same material sewn together, s/t= f,n,s(2), circular
181	P8c-2	ccc/c	sss/s	mmm/t	warp-faced	34x12	d.bl,p,n/ l.bl	66:13 67:18	5x6	'button' in one corner, stripes

No.	Locus	Fibre	Spin	Tightness	Weave	Count (cm)	Colours	Edges, etc.	Size (cm)	Comment
182	P8c-3	fs/fs	z-/z-	m-/m-	tabby	26+x21+	n,d.br/ l.br,n	2x66:19 2x67:14	18x12	5 pieces same material sewn together, s/t= f,n,z(2); f,n,s(2), check
183	P8c-6	w/www	s/sss	t/lll	weft-faced	7x15	y/y,red, d.bl	--	13.2x 3.3	2 bands blue surrounding red
184	P8c-6	w/ww	s/zz	m/ll	tabby	5x6	n/d.br,n	--	6x6	
185	P8c-6	caca/ca cacaca	zz/zzzz	mm/llll	tabby	+8x7	n,d.bl/n d.bl,l.gr d.br	--	47x4.5	check
186a	P8c-6	ff/ff	zz/ss	mm/ll	tabby	17x10	d.bl,n/ d.bl,n	2x66:19	12x9.5	2xa sewn to b both checks s/t=f,n,s(2)
186b	P8c-6	ff/ff	zs/ss	tt/mm	tabby	14x16	n,d.bl/ n,d.bl	--		
187	P8c-6	ff/c	ss/z	ll/l	tabby	16x14	b,m.bl/n	67:7	4.5x5.5	fustian, s/t= f,n,z(2)
188	P8c-6	ccc/ccc	zzz/zzz	mmm/mmm	tabby	27x11	red,d.bl n/red,d. bl,n	--	24x4.5	check
189	P8c-8	fff/f	sss/z	lll/m	tabby	13x13	d.bl,l.bl n/d.bl	67:18	33x8.1	stripes
190	P8c-9	www/www	sss/sss	mmm/mmm	tabby	11x11	red,d.bl, n/red,d. bl,n	--	8x5	check
191a	P8c-10	g/g	z/z	l/l	tabby	4x4	d.br/d.br	--	11x5.6	2 pieces goat material with 4 pieces inside 2xb
191b	P8c-10	w/w	s/s	m/l	tabby	24x23	n/n	65:3		
191c	P8c-10	w/w	s/s	m/m	tabby	14x12	n/n	--	4x4	
191d	P8c-10	w/w	s/s	m/m	tabby	-x-	n/n	--	--	

No.	Locus	Fibre	Spin	Tightness	Weave	Count (cm)	Colours	Edges, etc.	Size (cm)	Comment
192	P8c-10	g/gg	s/zz	m/ll	tabby	4x6	l.br/l.br n	--	12diam.	circular with coarse over-sewing s/t=b,n,z(2)
193	P8c-10	cc/cc	zz/zz	mm/mm	tabby	14x19	d.bl,n/ d.bl,n	--	14x10	mended check s/t=f,n/z(2)
194	P8c-11	w/ww	s/ss	t/ll	weft-faced	8x12	n/n,red	67:18	22x6	broad red band on natural ground
195	P8c-11	fs/fs	zs/zs	ml/ml	tabby	25x23	n,br/n,br	--	16x7.5	check
196	P8c-11	ff/ff	zz/ss	ll/ll	tabby	13x16	n,d.bl/ n,d.bl	67:7	11x1.7	check, s/t= f,n,z(2)
197	P8c-11	ccc/c	sss/s	mmm/t	warp-faced	38x10	n,d.bl, red/n	65:1	3.8x5	stripes, s/t= c,n,s(2)
198	P8c-13	ccc/ccc	zzz/zzz	mmm/mmm	tabby	16x20	d.bl,n, red/d.bl n,red	--	11.2x 6.5	check
199	P8c-13	ff/ff	sz/ss	mm/mm	tabby	13x15	m.bl,n/ m.bl,n	67:7	7.8x7	irregular check s/t=f,n,z
200	P8c-15	cc/cc	zz/zz	tt/tt	tabby	14x23	d.bl,n/ d.bl,n	--	8.5x8	check
201	S11b-2	f/ff	s/ss	m/ll	tabby	8x7	n,d.bl/n	--	5x15	stripes
202	S11b-2	c/cc	z/zz	m/ll	tabby	14x20	n/n,l.bl	67:18	6.2x16	broad natural band with narrow blue bands on either side
203	S11b-2	cc/c	zz/z	ll/m	warp-faced	28x16	red,m.bl/ m.bl	3x67:3	6.5x 13.5	triangular shaped piece
204a	S11b-3	ww/www	ss/zzz (2)	mm/lll	weft-faced	3x12	n,m.br/d. gr,d.red, l.red	66:9,10	15x8	3 pieces sewn together
204b	S11b-3	g/gg	z/zz(2)	l/ll	tabby	3x7	n/n,d.br	65:1		found with 205; s/t=w,n,z(2); g,br,s(2)

No.	Locus	Fibre	Spin	Tightness	Weave	Count (cm)	Colours	Edges, etc.	Size (cm)	Comment
204c	S11b-3	f/f	s/s	t/t	tabby	-x8	n/n	--	--	stripes
205	S11b-3	w/www	s/sss	t/lll	tabby	7x7	n/n,red,m.bl	67:19	10x9	stripes
206a	S11b-3	cc/c	zz/s	ll/m	warp-faced	25x10	n,m.bl/n	66:5,14	6.8x3	3 pieces sewn together, stripes s/t=f,n,s(3)
206b	S11b-3	c/c	z/z	m/l	tabby	-x30	n/n	65:2(2)	--	
206c	S11b-3	c/c	z/z	l/l	tabby	-x16	m.bl/m.bl	--	--	
207	S11b-6	w/www	s/sss	m/lll	tabby	8x13+	y/red,gr n	--	3x3.5 2.5x6	2 pieces same material; broad red bands with green bands on either side
208	S11b-6	w/wcwww	s/sssss	t/ttttt	tabby+ brocade	13x-	d.bl/d.bl n,or,red	65:2(20)	2x6.1	'veiling' with brocade; n,or,red= double stranded
209	S12a-1	w/www	s/sss	m/ttt	weft-faced	5x-	d.bl/d.red d.bl,y	--	2x4	unravelling
210	S12a-1	ff/f	sz/s	ll/l	tabby	13x17	n,d.bl/n	--	10x 19.5	stripes
211	S12a-1	f/ff	z/ss	t/mm	tabby	11x18	n/n,d.bl	--	2.5x3	stripes
212	S12a-1	ff/ff	ss/zz	mm/mm	tabby	12x12	d.bl,n/ d.bl,n	65:1	4x12	check
213	S12a-1	ff/ff	ss/zs	mm/ll	tabby	15x15	d.bl,n/ d.bl,n	--	18.9x8	check
214	S12a-1	cc/c	zz/z	mm/m	tabby	21x9	n,d.bl/ l.bl	66:7 67:18	7x4.5	stripes; s/t= f,n,s(2)
215	S12a-1	cc/c	zz/z	mm/t	warp-faced	21x10	d.bl,n/d. bl	--	6.2x3	stripes
216	S12a-1	cc/c	zz/s	ll/t	warp-faced	35x11	d.bl,n/d. bl	65:1	11x6.5	stripes, folded over and padded with raw cotton

No.	Locus	Fibre	Spin	Tightness	Weave	Count (cm)	Colours	Edges, etc.	Size (cm)	Comment
217	Sl2a-1	cc/c	ss/s	mm/t	warp-faced	22x12	d.bl,n/l.bl	--	5x3	stripes, remains of s/t=c,bl,z(2)
218	Sl2a-3	www/w	sss/s	lll/m	tabby	9x7	y,red,d.bl/y	65:1	3.4x4	broad red, narrow bl then y stripes remains of s/t= b,n,z
219	Sl2a-3	w/ww	s/ss	t/ll	weft-faced	8x18	y/red,d.bl	--	1.8x11	2 red bands surrounded by bl
220	Sl2a-3	w/ww	s/ss	t/tl	warp-faced	8x3	n/n,d.bl	--	4.8x5.7	girth(?), X inlay in bl
221	Sl2a-3	f/fw	s/ss	m/mt	tabby	8x7	n/n,d.bl	66:14	9.5x10	natural band with bl bands on either side; s/t=f,z(2)
222a	Sl2a-3	f/f	z/z	1/1	tabby	10x9	l.bl/l.bl	--	19.5x 3.6	2 pieces sewn together; s/t= f,l.bl,z(2)
222b	Sl2a-3	ff/ff	ss/ss	ll/ll	tabby	13x13	n,l.bl/ n,l.bl	66:12	9.5x1.8	check
223	Sl2a-3	ff/ff	zz/zz	ml/ml	tabby	21x17	d.bl,n/ d.bl,n	--	11x8.5	check
224	Sl2a-3	ff/fff	ss/sss	mm/lll	tabby	11x11	n,d.bl/l.bl,d.bl,n	--	8x5.5	2 pieces quilted together with raw cotton between s/t=f,n,z(2)
225a	Sl2a-3	ff/ff	zz/ss	ll/ll	tabby	14x15	d.bl,n/ d.bl,n	--		
225b	Sl2a-3	c/c	z/z	1/1	tabby	27x30	n/n	67:18	21x8	check
226	Sl2a-3	cc/cc	zz/zz	mm/mm	tabby	14x12	n,d.bl/ n,d.bl	--		
227	Sl2a-3	cc/c	zz/z	ll/m	tabby	12x11	n,l.bl/n	--	7x7.5	stripes
228	Sl2a-3	cc/c	zz/z	mm/t	warp-faced	49+x15	d.bl,n./d.bl	--	1.8x9.4	stripes

No.	Locus	Fibre	Spin	Tightness	Weave	Count (cm)	Colours	Edges, etc.	Size (cm)	Comment
229	S12a-3	cc/c	ss/s	ll/t	warp-faced	44x15	n,d.bl/n	--	11.5x8	stripes
230	S12a-3	cc/c	ss/s	mm/t	warp-faced	39x11	d.bl,n/d.bl	--	8x8.2	stripes
231	S12a-3	cccc/c	ssss/s	llll/m	warp-faced	-x11	d.bl,1.bl n,red/n	--	17x2 2x2.3	2 fragments same material, crumpled up; stripes
232	S12a-4	ww/w	ss/s	ll/m	tabby	10x9	n,m.bl/n	--	2.7x2 2.8x2.5	2 pieces same material, stripes
233a	S12a-4	f/f	z/z	m/l	tabby	21x13	n/n	66:10	11.5x 5.5	3 pieces sewn together; 2xa; s/t=f,n,s(2)
233b	S12a-4	fff/fff	sss/zzz	lll/mmm	tabby	16x15	1.bl,d.bl n/1.bl,d.bl,n	65:2(8)		check
234	S12a-8	fff/fff	sss/sss	lll/lll	tabby	18x18	d.bl,1.bl n/d.bl,l.bl,n	66:3	9x5.2	check; s/t= f,n,s(2)
235	S12c-1	f/cc	s/zz	m/ll	tabby	15x13	n/n,d.bl	--	5x9	fustian, stripes
236	S12c-2	w/ww	s/ss (2 ply)	m/mm	1/2 basket	3x5	n/n,d.br	--	10x13	brown bands on natural ground
237	S12c-2	w/wc	s/ss	t/tm	tabby+ brocade	12x-	d.bl/d.bl n	--	3x9	'veiling' with brocaded band
238	S12c-2	f/f	z/s	1/1	tabby	19x16	n/n	--	9x8.8	cloth tied to 2 wooden sticks; s/t= f,n,z(2);w,n,s(2)
239	S12c-2	f/ff	z/zs	m/ll	tabby	17x15	n/n,m.bl	--	2.5x8	stripes, palm pin
240	S12c-2	ff/ff	zz/ss	ll/ll	tabby	14x18	1.bl,n/l.bl,n	--	6.7x3.4	check
241a	S12c-2	ff/ff	sss/zzz	mmm/lll	tabby	14x13	d.bl,1.bl n/d.bl,l.bl,n	3x66:19	18x13.8	2 plain pieces sewn to check s/t=f,n,z(3)

320

No.	Locus	Fibre	Spin	Tightness	Weave	Count (cm)	Colours	Edges, etc.	Size (cm)	Comment
241b	S12c-2	c/c	s/z	m/m	tabby	17x17	d.bl/d.bl	--		s/t=f,n,z(3);f,bl z(3);bl/n,f,z(3) b=dyed after weaving
242	S12c-2	fff/fff	sss/zzz	lll/mmm	tabby	16x17	l.bl,d.bl n/l.bl,d.bl,n	66:19	9.4x3	check
243	S12c-2	f/fff	z/sss	l/lll	tabby	16x18	n/n,l.bl d.bl	--	6x14	stripes
244	S12c-2	f/ff	s/ss	l/ll	tabby	13x12	n/n,l.bl	--	7.6x7.4	stripes
245	S12c-2	ff/ff	ss/ss	ll/ll	tabby	20x18	n,d.bl/ n,d.bl	--	14.5x 3.7	check, remains of s/t=f,n,s(2)
246	S12c-2	f/ff	s/ss	m/ll	tabby	13x10	n/n,l.bl	67:18	15.5x 10.2	stripes
247	S12c-2	ff/ff	ss/ss	ll/ll	tabby	13x11	n,d.bl/ n,d.bl	--	11x7	check
248	S12c-2	ff/ff	ss/ss	mm/mm	tabby	16x15	n,d.bl/ n,d.bl	67:18	12x2	check
249	S12c-2	fff/fff	sss/sss	lll/lll	tabby	11x12	l.bl,d.bl n/l.bl,d.bl,n	67:19	30x18.5	check, remains of s/t=f,n,z(3)
250	S12c-2	ff/ff	ss/ss	mm/mm	tabby	11x11	n,m.bl/ n,m.bl	65:1	17.5x15	check
251	S12c-2	fff/ff	sss/ss	mmm/mm	tabby	15x13	d.bl,l.bl n/l.bl,n	--	7.7x2.5	check
252	S12c-2	fff/ff	sss/ss	lll/ll	tabby	14x13	d.bl,l.bl n/d.bl,n	3x67:4	21x23.8	check, s/t= f,n,z(3);f,n,s(3)
253	S12c-2	ff/ff	ss/ss	ll/ll	tabby	13x12	m.bl,n/ m.bl,n	65:2(19)	15x3.2	check
254	S12c-2	ff/ff	ss/ss	ll/ll	tabby	16x11	d.bl,n/ d.bl,n	--	13x9	darted, s/t=f,n, z(2); check
255	S12c-2	fff/ff	sss/ss	lll/ll	tabby	12x14	d.bl,l.bl n/d.bl,n	65:1 67:18	2.4x13	check

321

No.	Locus	Fibre	Spin	Tightness	Weave	Count (cm)	Colours	Edges, etc.	Size (cm)	Comment
256	S12c-2	fff/ff	sss/ss	lll/ll	tabby	10x10	l.bl,m.bl n/m.bl,n	--	3x3.4	check
257	S12c-2	cc/cc	ss/ss	ll/ll	tabby	15x12	l.bl,d.bl/ l.bl,d.bl	65:2(1)	14x5.2	check
258	S12c-2	f/f	s/s	m/m	2/2 twill	14x14	l.bl/n	--	5x3	diamond twill
259	S12c-2	ff/cc	ss/zz	mm/ll	tabby	14x13	n,l.bl/ n,l.bl	66:13	10x20.5	2 pieces fustian sewn together s/t=f,n,z;f,bl,s
260	S12c-2	ccc/cc	zzz/zz	lll/ll	tabby	25x32	n,d.bl,l. bl/n,d.bl	67:18	6.5x3.8	check
261a	S12c-3	w/w	s/s	m/m	tabby	6x7	d.br/d.br	--	7.5x7	2 pieces stitched together; s/t= w,n,z(2)
261b	S12c-3	w/ww	s/ss	t/ll	weft-faced	5x9	d.bl/n,d. bl	--		stripes
262	S12c-3	wg/wwww	zz(2)/ z(2)zz s(2)	mm/lllm	warp-faced	9x3	d.br,n/n, d.bl,red, gr	65:1	9x7.5	girth, see 220, 282,289; cross design in red,gr
263	S12c-3	caca/ca caca	zz/zzz	ll/lll	tabby	9x9	n,red/red d.bl,n	--	9x55	check, remains of s/t=b,n,z(2)
264	S12c-3	w/wc	s/ss	t/tt	tabby+ brocade	-x-	d.bl/d.bl n	--	18x2	'veiling' with brocaded band
265	S12c-3	w/wc	s/ss	t/tt	tabby+ brocade	13x12	d.bl/d.bl n	--	19x3	'veiling' with brocaded band
266	S12c-3	fs/fsc	s-/-s-s	1-/1-1	tabby	17x18	n,red/n y,bl	65:1	16x19	red silk selvage stripe, y and bl bands, knotted at one end
267a	S12c-3	f/f	z/z	1/1	tabby	22x21	n/n		26x12	silk cap top quilted with raw cotton; s/t= f,n,s(2);f,bl,s

No.	Locus	Fibre	Spin	Tightness	Weave	Count (cm)	Colours	Edges etc.	Size (cm)	Comment
267b	S12c-3	s/s	-/-	-/-	tabby	-x-	gold/gold			
267c	S12c-3	s/s	-/-	-/-	tabby	-x-	d.br/d.br			
268a	S12c-3	f/f	z/s	1/1	tabby	13x13	n/n	3x66:5 67:3	9x16.4	2 pieces sewn together; s/t=f,n,s(2);f,n,s(3)
268b	S12c-3	f/ff	z/ss	m/lll	tabby	12x16	n/n,m.bl	67:18		check
269	S12c-3	ff/fff	zs/sss	mm/lll	tabby	18x18	n,d.bl/n l.bl,d.bl	--	21x1.7	check, remains of s/t=f,n,z(2)
270	S12c-3	f/ff	s/ss	m/ll	tabby	7x8	n/n,m.bl	67:16,18	22.5x7	stripes
271	S12c-3	ff/ff	ss/ss	mm/ll	tabby	13x10	n,d.bl/ n,d.bl	65:2(24)	9.3x8	blue band with area faded check
272	S12c-3	ff/ff	ss/ss	mm/mm	tabby	15x13	m.bl,n/ m.bl,n	65:2(5)	6.7x8.5	check
273	S12c-3	fff/f	sss/s	lll/m	tabby	13x14	n,l.bl,d. bl/n	--	13x12.5	stripes
274	S12c-3	fff/fff	sss/sss	lll/lll	tabby	13x13	l.bl,d.bl, n/l.bl,d. bl,n	--	21x19	check
275	S12c-3	fff/fff	sss/sss	lll/lll	tabby	13x13	l.bl,d.bl, n/l.bl,d. bl,n	4x66:2 3x66:19	23x12x5	6 pieces same material sewn together in bag s/t=f,n,z(2);f,n,z(3);f,n,s;f,n,s(2)
276	S12c-3	f/ccc	s/zzz	m/lll	tabby	12x17	n/d.bl,l. bl,n	--	15.7x 3.5	fustian, irregular bands
277	S12c-3	f/cc	s/zz	m/ll	tabby	14x15	n/n,d.bl	--	9x15	fustian, see 278 broad bl bands
278	S12c-3	f/cc	s/zz	m/ll	tabby	11x13	n/n,d.bl	--	10x11	fustian, bl bands
279	S12c-3	cc/cc	zz/zz	mm/ll	tabby	14x19	n,d.bl/ n,d.bl	--	7.8x 9.5	check

No.	Locus	Fibre	Spin	Tightness	Weave	Count (cm)	Colours	Edges, etc.	Size (cm)	Comment
280	S12c-3	cc/cc	zz/zz	tt/tt	tabby	15x14	d.bl,n/ d.bl,n	--	10.5x 2.5	check
281	S12c-3	c/ccc	z/zzz	m/mmm	weft-faced	4x44	n/p,d.bl n	--	7x13.4	remains of tabby ground, red and natural bands with 3 rows checked bl bands
282	S12c-4	ww/www www	zz(2)/ z(2)ssz (2)z(2)s	mm/mmm mmm	warp-faced	10x3	n,d.br/n red,d.bl, or,l.bl,gr	65:1	7.5x5	girth, see 220, 262,289,283
283	S12c-4	w/www	s/zzz (2)	m/mmm	warp-faced	11x3	n/n,red, m.bl	--	3x9.3	picket fence pattern; girth, see 220,262,282, 289
284	S12c-4	f/ff	s/ss	m/ll	tabby	7x8	n/n,d.bl	--	11x 17.5	stripes
285	S12c-4	f/ff	s/ss	m/ll	tabby	9x70	n/n,m.bl	--	15x7.3	stripes, looks like fustian
286	S12c-4	cc/cc	zz/zz	mm/mm	tabby	21x18	n,m.bl/ n,m.bl	67:18	19.5x 11.5	check
287a	S12c-4	c/cc	z/zz	m/ll	tabby	16x24	m.bl/br,n	--	7.2x11	2 pieces sewn together with raw cotton padding between, s/t= c,n,s(3), stripes
287b	S12c-4	c/c	z/z	1/1	tabby	8x11	n/n	--		
288	S12c-4	ccc/c	sss/s	111/m	warp-faced	30x13	n,d.bl,p/ n	67:18	8x10	stripes
289	S12c-5	ww/www	zz/zzz	mm/mmm	warp-faced	13x3	n,d.bl/n red,d.bl	--	7.5x4.5	girth, see 220,262 282,283
290a	S12c-5	fff/ff	ss/zs	mm/ll	tabby	15x19	n,d.bl/ n,d.bl	--	11x6.2	2 pieces sewn together with raw cotton padding between; s/t= f,n,z(2);f,bl,z(2)

324

No.	Locus	Fibre	Spin	Tightness	Weave	Count (cm)	Colours	Edges, etc.	Size (cm)	Comment
290b	Sl2c-5	ff/f	zs/z	ll/l	tabby	16x17	d.bl/d.bl,n	2x67:3		
291	Sl2c-5	ff/ff	ss/ss	mm/mm	tabby	13x12	l.bl,n/l.bl,n	--	13x7.5	check
291a	Sl2c-5	fff/ff	sss/ss	lll/ll	tabby	12x13	l.bl,m.bl/n,m.bl	--	7.6x5.6	check, sewn to fustian, s/t= y,w,s;f,n,s(2)
291b	Sl2c-5	f/c	s/z	m/m	tabby	12x10	n/n	--		
293	Sl2c-5	f/cc	s/zz	m/mm	tabby	15x16	n/n,d.bl	--	14.5x3 3x7	2 pieces fustian bands, see 277, 278,294
294	Sl2c-5	f/cc	s/zz	m/mm	tabby	12x15	n/n,d.bl	--	11.2x7	fustian with bl bands, see 277, 278,293
295	Sl2c-5	cc/c	ss/s	mm/t	warp-faced	28x13	d.bl,n/d.bl	--	12.5x 2.5	remains of s/t= c,bl,z(2)
296a	Sl2c-6	w/w	s/s	m/m	tabby	6x12	n/n	66:2 67:3	14x11	2 pieces sewn together; s/t= w,n,s
296b	Sl2c-6	w/ww	s/ss	t/ll	tabby	7x25	d.bl/d.bl,l.bl	--	8x5.5	
297	Sl2c-6	w/www	s/sss	m/lll	tabby	7x13	n/n,red,m.bl	--	8x12	tabby with weft-faced band, remains of s/t= w,n,s(2)
298a	Sl2c-6	w/w	z/z	1/1	tabby	5x9	n/n	--	19x12	mass of fibres and yarns, slipper? pile=z(2); s/t= w,n,s(2);w,bl,s(2)
298b	Sl2c-6	w/wwwww	z(2)/sssss	m/mmmmt	weft-faced	7x16	n/gr,red,bl,or,pur			
298c	Sl2c-6	g/g	z/z	1/1	warp-faced	4x1	br/br			

No.	Locus	Fibre	Spin	Tightness	Weave	Count (cm)	Colours	Edges, etc.	Size (cm)	Comment
299	S12c-6	g/gg	s/ss(2)	m/ll	cord	-	d.br/d.br n	--	20x.6 (diam)	braided cord with coarse g-hair core
300	S12c-6	ff/ff	ss/sz	ll/ll	tabby	17x17	m.bl,n/ m.bl,n	--	8.6x7.2	check
301	S12c-6	ff/f	ss/s	ll/l	tabby	18x23	n,d.bl/n	--	11.8x 6.2	stripes
302	S12c-6	ff/ff	ss/zz	ll/ll	tabby	18x14	m.bl,n/ m.bl,n	--	6.7x1.5	check
303	S12c-6	fff/fff	sss/sss	lll/lll	tabby	14x14	d.bl,n,l. bl/d.bl, n,l.bl	--	9.8x7.9	oval, check
304	S12c-6	c/c	z/z	1/1	tabby	11x12	d.bl/d.bl	--	10x5.4	shaped dyed after weaving
305	S12c-6	ccc/c	sss/s	mmm/t	warp-faced	31x13	d.bl,l.bl n/d.bl	--	3.5x 10.5	stripes
306	S12c-7	ff/ffs	zz/zz-	mm/mm-	weft-faced	26x36 16x53	n/n,m.bl d.br	--	10.5x 1.5	2 bl bands finishing in middle of cloth remains of silk band
307	S12c-7	c/c	z/z	m/m	tabby	33x29	m.bl/m.bl	--	10.5x2	dyed after weaving
308	S12c-8	fff/fff	zzz/zzz	mmm/mmm	tabby	19x18	l.bl,d.bl n/l.bl,d. bl,n	--	6x5.5	2 pieces same material sewn together, s/t= f,n,s(2)
309	S12c-8	ff/c	ss/z	ml/m	tabby	16x15	n,l.bl/n	67:18	16.5x2	fustian, stripes
310	S12c-8	ccc/c	sss/s	mmm/t	tabby	26x10	d.bl,p, red/	65:1 67:18	6.5x 12.5	irregular stripes remains of s/t= c,n,s(2)
311	RN 68f	ff/ff	zz/zz	mm/ll	tabby	25x27	n,d.bl/ n,d.bl	3x66:19	14x13	3 pieces same material sewn together, s/t= f,n,s(2); check

326

No.	Locus	Fibre	Spin	Tightness	Weave	Count (cm)	Colours	Edges, etc.	Size (cm)	Comment
312	--	w/wwww	z/zzzzz	t/mmmmm	weft-faced	9x40	n,red,d.gr,d.bl,d.br,n	--	21x6	2 pieces same material sewn together; s/t= b,z(2); red ground gr,bl,br,n bands
313	--		z(s2-z4)	m	braid	9 strd	y	--	17x2.1	2 pieces knotted together
314	--	f/f	s/s	m/m	warp-faced	9x3	n/n	--	5.2x2.6	
315	--	f/ff	s/ss	l/ll	tabby	13x14	n/n,d.bl	--	7.8x6.7	stripes
316	P8b-18?	fff/fff	sss/zzz	mmm/lll	tabby	21x21	l.bl,d.bl n/l.bl,d.bl,n	--	31.2x 22.3	check
317	--	c/c	z/z	1/1	tabby	12x13	n/n	3x66:19 67:18	39(diam) x15	short sleeve 3 pieces sewn together
318	--	ccc/ccc	zzz/zzz	mmm/lll	tabby	29x23	p,n,d.bl/ p,n,d.bl	65:1 67:18	5.7x 23.4	stripes with start of checked section

CHAPTER 15: SMALL OBJECTS
Janet H. Johnson

Aside from the range of artifacts already discussed in separate chapters, a large number of other objects was discovered during the excavations. This chapter is intended only to make their existence known, not to be a careful study of their place of origin, function, or implications.

One recognizable head from a terra cotta female figurine was found (59:a) as well as fragments from two other figurines. The first is the head of a woman with a high coiffure, above which is what appears to be a tiara bearing vegetable motifs, perhaps indicating a goddess associated with agriculture or fertility. Traces of red, blue, and yellow paint were found on this figurine. The second figurine (59:b) is also a head from a two-sided, molded figurine, but the original surface is badly effaced. Above the head seems to be a three-pointed nimbus, perhaps indicating a deity. The third fragment (59:c) appears to be the hair or top-knot of a female figurine. The well-preserved example was found in the pipeline immediately within or adjacent to the so-called "White Building," on which further work will be done during the third season.

Non-ceramic vessels include faience bowls and tray, basketry, wooden, and stone bowls, and wooden boxes. The faience, which is all Roman, includes cups with a rounded rim and external rounded ridge with low, heavy ring base and spur marks from being stacked in the kiln (68:a,b). The faience vessels found in 1978 had the same characteristic rim and ridge (Whitcomb and Johnson, 1979: 24:e, 26:i, 30:n); similar bases were also found in 1978 (*ibid*.: 20:l, 33:m). A larger version of this cup or bowl with a ring base (68:d) was found on the floor of the small storeroom. The fourth preserved example (68:c) is a wide flat bowl with ring base and sharp carination at the join between base and external ridge. Faience vessels with similar bases were also found in 1978 (*ibid*.: 20:m, 22:j, 30:p). One corner of a flat rectangular tray with scalloped handle was found (68:f); no parallels had been found in 1978. Only one example of incised faience was found during the 1980 season (68:e); no molded examples (such as were found in F10a in 1978 [*ibid*.: 29:i,j,k]) were found.

One Roman period stone vessel is illustrated in 68:n, a rimless, large bowl. A small, rectangular calcite jar was found on the floor of the small storeroom (54:d). Both of the large "steatite" bowls, rimless but with raised ridges at or below the middle of the vessel, are from the eastern, Islamic, area (68:p,q), as is the stone handle fragment (68:o). Note that one of the "steatite" vessels has a mend hole drilled near the rim (68:p). The round bottoms, ridges, and

Plate 68: Faience, Wood, and Stone Vessels

	Locus	RN	Description
a	E6c-1	311	blue frit; tripod marks
b	E7a-11	282	blue frit; tripod marks
c	E6b-48	367	turquoise frit
d	E6b-44	356	blue frit; tripod marks; FN 14
e	E6b-25	367	turquoise frit; blue incised decoration
f	E6c-1	332	green frit
g	E6b-24	366	green frit
h	E area	626	wood; red wash; traces yellow paint
i	E18a-4	248	basketry; raised decoration
j	E18a-10		wood
k	E18a-14	339	wood
l	E18a-14	348	basketry lid
m	E18a-14	348	wooden box; red, black paint; iron and copper repair wires
n	F7a-4	145	stone bowl (alabaster?)
o	E18a-15	147	stone handle
p	E18d-11	144	"steatite"
q	E18a-14	129	"steatite"

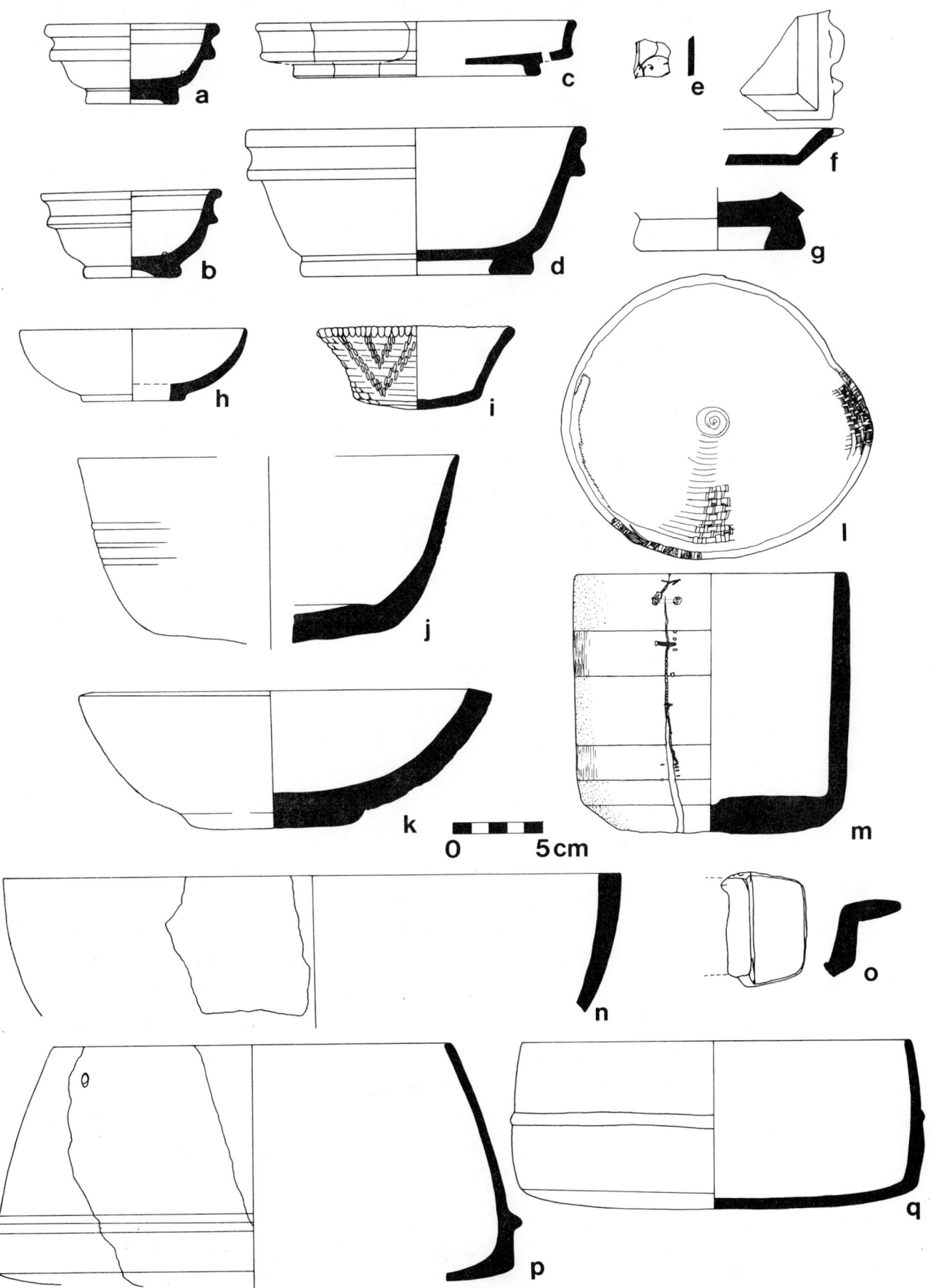

Plate 68: Faience, Wood, and Stone Vessels

incurving sides are similar to several of the chlorite vessels found in the Islamic excavations in 1978 (*ibid.*: 72:j,k). Similar vessels are found in the Islamic period throughout the range of Indian ocean traders.

One small basketry dish with a raised "V" decoration is illustrated in 68:i. A small, deep basketry cup or box is shown in 71:a; fitted lids for similar containers are shown in 71:b,c. Also commonly used as lids are flat coiled disks (similar to those illustrated *ibid.*: fig. 23). The one illustrated in 68:l was carefully finished on the edge and made to serve as lid to the wooden box illustrated below it (68:m). This box was found sitting on a second, similar coiled basketry disk. Many other objects made of basketry (e.g., the brush or wisk broom shown in 71:d), including large baskets very similar to those purchased in Luxor for use by the workmen carrying dirt from the excavations, were also found, as were woven matting of various styles, rope (e.g., 71:q), and loose fiber. These were especially common throughout the eastern, Islamic, area. All the registered basketry from the site (from 1978 and 1980) is being studied by Boyce N. Driskell, who has prepared a typology of the basketry from Qasr Ibrim, in Nubia, and finds many basic similarities between the Islamic basketry from Qasr Ibrim and that from Quseir al-Qadim; see report at end of this chapter.

A large wooden bowl with two handles was found on the floor of the small Roman storeroom (54:e); it is made of a hardwood.[1] Of the 11 Islamic wooden bowls or fragments found during the 1980 season, three are illustrated in pl. 68, two with flat bottoms and gently outcurving sides (h,k), the third deeper with carved horizontal decorative ridges (j). These shapes seem somewhat simpler than the squared or deep, painted wooden bowls found in 1978 (*ibid.*: pl. 71). The smallest of these bowls retains traces of a red wash and yellow painted decoration. A selection of wooden lids for small bowls or cups found in Islamic loci is illustrated in 69:j-m, r. The lids are either rounded or flat on top. Most have a small recessed lidge to fit into the bowl. The example illustrated in 69:l retains traces of black paint on the exterior, 69:m traces of red paint on the exterior. One example, not illustrated, had a red wash applied to the interior. The wooden lid shown in 69:t has a fragment of leather attached to the top, perhaps the remains of a handle. Although red and black painted bands and incising do occur

---

[1] All wood identifications were provided by Regis B. Miller of the Center for Wood Anatomy Research, U. S. Forest Products Laboratory, Madison, Wisconsin.

on bowls not illustrated here, none of the bowls or lids is as elaborately decorated as the pieces found in the earlier Islamic area excavated in 1978 (*ibid.*: fig. 25,26). None of the Islamic bowls or lids found during the 1980 season has been identified as to wood. A fragment of a similar painted wooden bowl found in a Roman locus in the 1978 season (F9c-7, FN 29, RN 563) has been identified as *Tamarix* sp. A Roman period circular lid of bronze attached to a wooden plug, with a bronze handle, is illustrated in 70:t.

One wooden box (68:m) with flat bottom, straight sides, and alternating red and black painted bands was found placed on a basketry coil, with a second such coil as lid (68:l), hidden in a hole under (to the south of) wall A of E18a-14 (see pl. 32; the location of the box is shown as a single circle between two double-circle pot hearths). Above the box were two wooden bowls, including 68:k. A crack along one side of the box has been mended with a wire made of copper or copper alloy. The box contained what would seem to be a woman's toilet articles (see fig. 22), including[2]

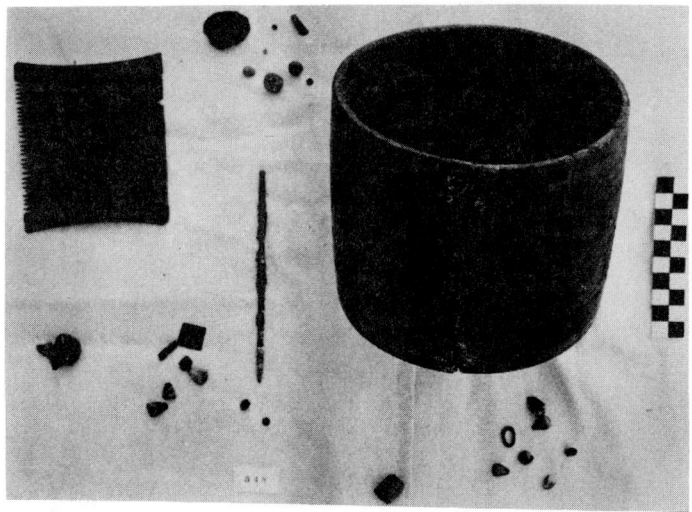

Fig. 22: Islamic Wooden Box with Contents

a) a wooden comb (69:d), 10.8x9.2 cm., complete, but with some teeth and corners slightly worn. The larger teeth measure approximately .2 cm. in width, the

---

[2] The descriptions and identifications are based on those of Catharine Valentour.

finer teeth on the opposite side approximately .1 cm. in width. The only decoration is two sets of three incised lines running the length of the comb and separating the tooth areas from the body. Adhering to the comb were scraps of textile with a blue warp and beige weft.

b) glass beads: one opaque yellow (.3 cm. diameter), one opaque green (.4 cm. diameter), two dark translucent blue (.4 cm. and .5 cm. diameter) perforated seed beads, in good condition; one fragmented large green cylinder bead (maximum diameter 1.3 cm., drill hole .25 cm. in diameter) with three circular decorations of yellow, blue and red; one rectangular bead (maximum length 1.4 cm., width of side .4 cm.) with round drill hole in green with surface degradation on blue and yellow.

c) shell beads: eight cona-shells with apex removed and drilled through, all very worn; one cowry shell with large hole in body.

d) ivory cylinder (chess piece?), 1.7 cm. long, 1.3 cm. maximum diameter. One end is flat with the suggestion of two concentric incised lines around the edge; the other end is slightly rounded with an incised circular line, an incised hole in the center, and two lines coming out of the hole but not touching the circular line around the edge; the body has an encircling incised line near the flat end.

e) stones: two white pebbles, one green stone identified as apatite, one translucent amber colored bead with a circular drill hole identified as agate (both identifications by the Department of Mineralogy, National Museum of Natural History).

f) copper-alloy pin (70:n), 13.3 cm. long and .4 cm. wide at the top of the shaft, heavily encrusted with corrosion and with various organic fibers and cord attached.

g) glass vessels: portion of a neck, cylindrical with a hole in the center (2.7 cm. long, 2.3 cm. wide, maximum diameter of the hole 1.0 cm.), slightly translucent, heavily weathered dark glass with greens, blues, reds, golds; three fragments of a small, flat-bottomed vessel (height 2.1 cm., width 2.0 cm.) of amber colored glass, severly deteriorated and brittle.

h) flat square of bronze, 1.5x1.5 cm., with an incised 5 x 5 magical square which adds up to 65 in every direction. Several of the numbers are difficult to read (a couple involve inversions of numbers). The hand copy and translation given here were provided by David Pingree.

۲۹	۳	۱۱	۲	۲۰
۱۹	۱۰	۲۱	۱۴	۱
۵	۱۷	۱۳	۹	۲۱
۷	۱۲	۱۱	۱۶	۱۹
۵	۲۳	۹	۲۴	۴

```
29   3  11   2  20 = 65
19  10  21  14   1 = 65
 5  17  13   9  21 = 65
 7  12  11  16  19 = 65
 5  23   9  24   4 = 65
65  65  65  65  65
```

i) small oval ring, of lead?, extremely deteriorated, 1.3x.9 cm.

j) flat, rectangular piece of iron, 7.0x1.6 cm., heavily corroded, with blue glass bead, section of wood or root, and bundle of fibers adhering. This was possibly a small knife or tweezers.

k) organic material: cloth bag with numerous dried leaves of family *Lythraceae* (Lawsonia Inermis), i.e., henna (identified by comparison with species from Ceylon and India in the Herbarium of the National Museum of Natural History); a dried seed pod, perhaps an immature dom palm; a large ball of unidentified "dirt-like" material, plus miscellaneous fragments of wood, fiber, textile, insect remains, and seeds.

Similar cosmetic boxes are said still to be part of a woman's trousseau in the Sudan. The careful wire repair of the box (and of other wooden bowls from the site) underlines the value of these possessions whose owners were far from a source where they could replace the object.

Numerous other wooden objects were also found during the excavations. Fifteen wooden combs, all from the Islamic period, were discovered, all with the standard row of wide teeth opposite a row of narrow teeth. In addition to the one complete example from the woman's box of toilet articles (69:d), only one other was complete (69:e), a smaller, undecorated comb the ends of which curve out in an arc, rather than curving in. Most of the pieces were fragmentary, but several bore decoration, usually consisting of patterns of incised circles within incised lines between the rows of teeth and on the end pieces, which are normally incurving (69:a,b). One (69:c) bears an inscription in Arabic on both faces in an elegant cursive script. Only the beginning of the line on the recto is preserved, and only the end of the line on the verso. The inscription is framed by narrow horizontal bands with regularly spaced interior notching. The end which is preserved is decorated with a circle of incised circles and a medallion of incised circles separates the inscription from the end motif. By comparing this comb with other known inscribed combs (Abd al-Raziq, 1972: 406, 407; 1973: 223, 224), one can see that the

Plate 69: Wooden Objects

	Locus	RN	Description
a	E18c-5	215	comb
b	E19c-6	212	comb
c	E18d-13	220	comb
d	E18a-14	348	comb
e	G9a-2	221	comb
f	E18a-10	188	carved panel
g	F18a-1	183	spoon
h	J14a-4	192	clog
i	F18a-1	183	spoon
j	E18c-2		lid
k	F19a-7		lid
l	F19a-4	186	lid; black paint out
m	E18c-11	208	lid; red paint out
n	G8b-2	184	handle; fragment of iron blade
o	E18a-10		handle?
p	E18a-16	187	handle; black and red paint
q	H8c-1	191	toggle
r	G12c-4	199	lid
s	E18a-10		peg
t	E18c-3	200	lid; fragment of leather on top
u	E18a-11	185	tongue depressor
v	G8b-2	209	awl
w	E18a-3	190	awl
x	E18a-3	190	yo yo
y	E18a-11	185	plug
z	E6b-37	189	spatula
aa	E18b-2	338	red; brown paint
bb	F19a-4		hoe

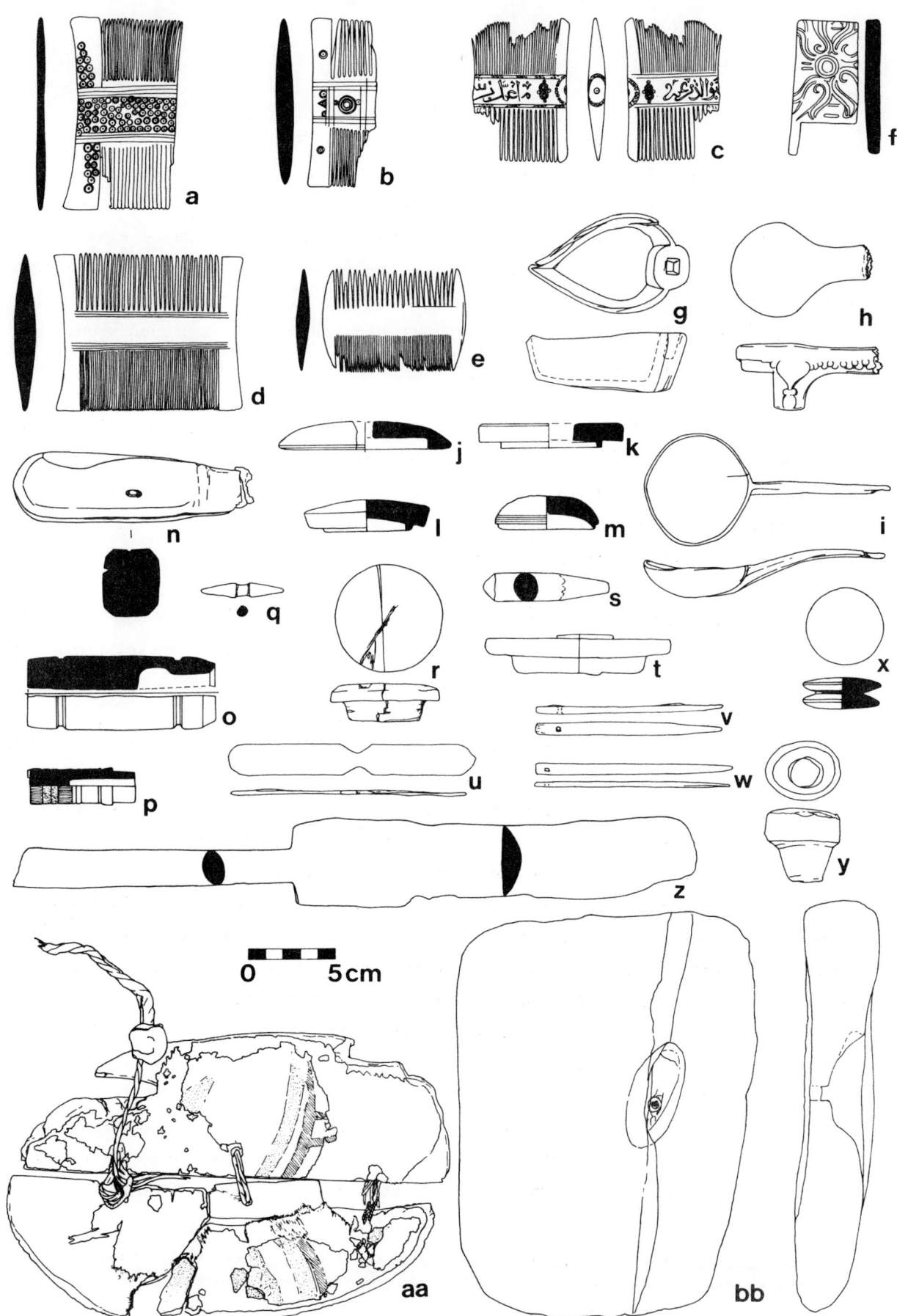

Plate 69: Wooden Objects

incomplete inscription on the recto is the beginning of the formula "This comb is made for...," except that the carver omitted the second *mīm* from the first word.[3] The diacritical points above the first *mīm* and the *shedda* and *fatha* above the second word may have been added for decorative reasons. It has been noted that what follows this opening phrase is usually not a specific name but a general laudatory phrase (*ibid*.) and suggested that such combs may have been produced in some quantity and available from better merchants, in which case the carver may have been more concerned with design than legibility.

The reconstruction of the inscription on the verso is difficult. It is unlikely that the verso is a repeat of the recto; rather, it was probably the completion of the recto or was a completely separate phrase. The diacritical marks and vowel pointing seem to have been placed according to the constraints of design and none of the possible readings fits the range of phrases normally used to complete the recto formula; no convincing reading can be suggested.

The comb found in the wooden box most probably belonged to a woman who lived at Quseir al-Qadim. Although it is possible that some of the fancier combs were being traded through the port, it seems more likely that all were private possessions of residents.

The other small wooden objects also seem to be household utensils rather than trade items. The function of the small carved wooden panel (69:f), which seems originally to have fit into a larger unit, is uncertain, but the use of other objects is clearer. One spoon or ladle is tear-drop shaped with a square notch into which a handle would have been inserted (at right angles to the bowl of the spoon) (69:g); a more standard spoon is illustrated in 69:i. Handles are fairly frequent. Some were carved or painted (69:o,p); one still had part of the original iron blade still attached (69:n). A Roman knife handle made of bone and bronze, also with part of the iron knife blade attached, is illustrated in 70:q.

Various utensils are also illustrated: a toggle (69:q), a peg (69:s), a "tongue depressor" (69:u); needles (69:v,w), a grooved reel or pulley (69:x), a plug (69:y); and a spatula (69:z). The latter is the only one which comes from a Roman locus. The other Roman wooden object illustrated (69:h) looks like a shoe and is here called a "clog." Also from Roman loci came more of the flat wooden rings found in 1978 (Whitcomb and Johnson, 1979: 70:i,k,o,p,s,t). The

---

[3] These comments on the inscribed comb, and many other comments on various wooden objects, are based on the description and research of Mona Megalli.

wood from which one of these rings found during the 1978 season (B4a-4, FN 14, RN 311) was made has been identified as leguminosae. The large wooden block with off-center depression for attaching a handle (69:bb) has been identified as a hoe. A similar piece (E18b-3, RN 205) was identified as being made of fig (*Ficus*). The two flat, painted pieces of wood attached by small rope tied between holes drilled along the straight sides of the two pieces may have served as a hinged lid to a box. Other small fragments of flat, painted wood were also found, but not enough was preserved to determine the original shape or function of the object.

Some wood-carving may have been done on the site, to judge by the amount of wood chips and the occasional unfinished wooden objects found. The needles, spindle whorls, toggle, pulley, etc., may suggest that spinning or weaving were part of the port's domestic activities.

Various types of architectural wood (not illustrated) include stakes, both animal tethers and supports for light structures, from the eastern, Islamic, area; two such stakes have been identified as made of mangrove wood (*Auicennia* sp.). In the Roman villa were found wooden door sills, wall reinforcements, and the trap door and beams to the cellar. The latter have been identified as cedar (*Cedrus* sp.). Two pieces (of 19) of shaped wood, with bitumen on one side, perhaps architectural elements, which were found in 1978 in the Roman area in the far northwestern corner of the site (B4a-2, RN 567) have been identified as teak (*Tectona* grandis). None of these woods is native to Egypt or the Eastern Desert. Cedars are claimed to have been imported into Egypt from early times from the northern Levant (although much of what was imported may actually have been a wood other than cedar); mangrove is known from the East African coast, teak from India. This distribution reflects the trade connections of the port.

There are also many small metal objects; some jewellry was found, including finger rings (70:h,j,k), earrings (70:f,g), bracelets (70:c), buttons (70:d), and pins (70:o). Various other metal rings (70:i,l,m) and pins (70:n), small tools such as fishhooks (70:r), nails, forceps (70:s), the pan for a scale (70:p), and a few decorated pieces of metal (70:a,e) were also discovered.

Also reflecting the daily life of the inhabitants of Quseir al-Qadim are the assorted rope sandals, leather shoes, and leather sandals of which only a sample, all Islamic, is illustrated in pl. 71. Note the one piece of leather worked, by punching holes, in a geometric decoration following the approximate shape of the leather (and of the human foot) (71:j). One of the leather shoes

Plate 70: Metal

	Locus	RN	Description
a	E18d-10	372	tin fitting
b	F19a-4	383	bronze
c	F7a-1	385	bronze bracelet
d	E18d-12	382	silver button
e	G12c-1	491	bronze
f	E18a-13	375	silver earring
g	E18a-10	380	bronze earring
h	G8b-18	373	bronze ring; glass bezel (light blue, red, yellow)
i	G8b-18	373	bronze ring (hollow)
j	E18c-3	381	bronze ring
k	E6b-44	371	bronze ring
l	F7a-2	391	lead ring
m	E6b-36	386	iron ring
n	E18a-14	348	bronze pin
o	G8b-18	373	bronze pin
p	E area	374	bronze pan (for scales)
q	F7a-2	158	bone, bronze fitting, iron blade
r	F7a-6	384	bronze fishhook
s	E18d-12	378	bronze forceps
t	E6b-38	368	bronze lid with wood

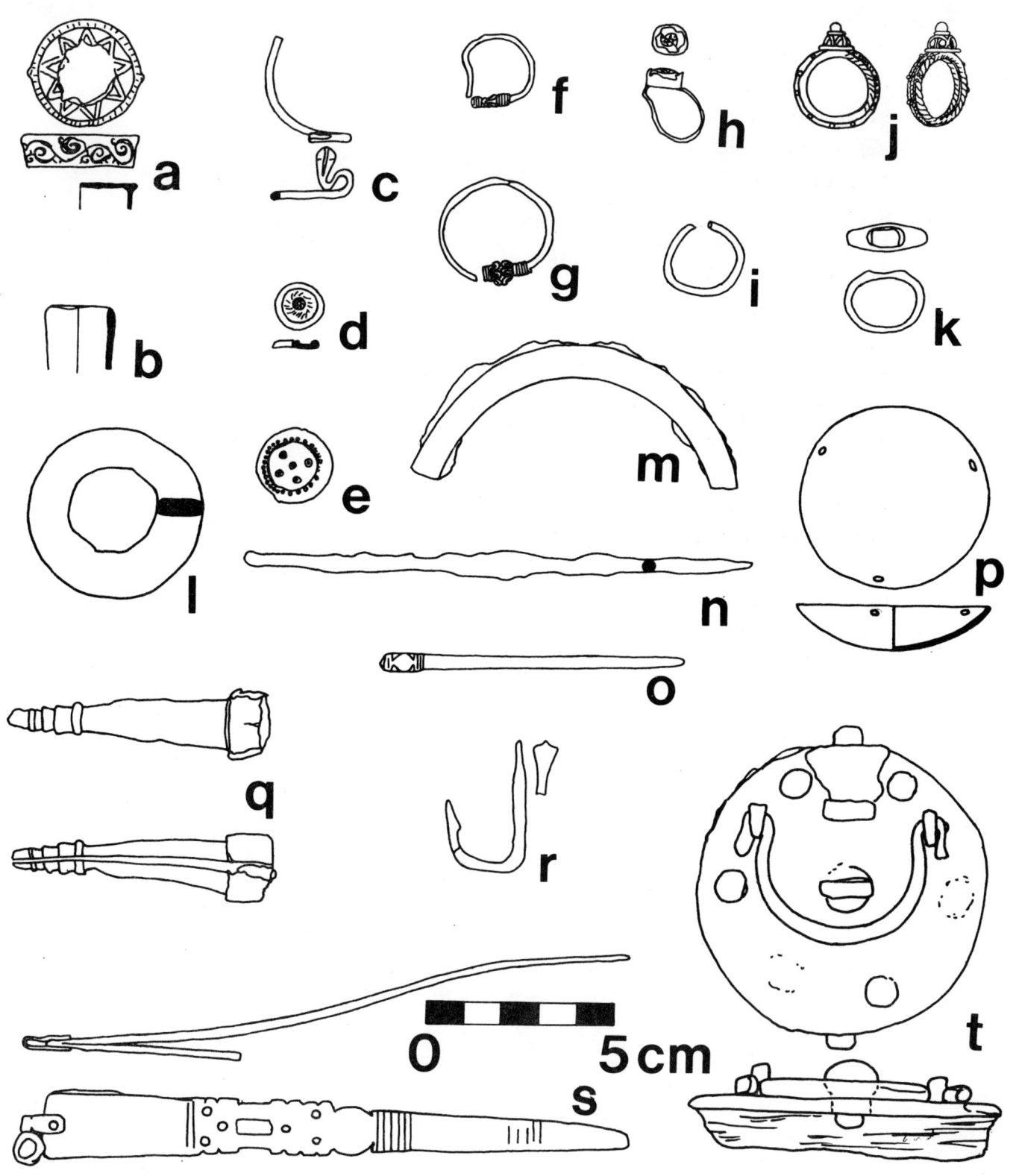

Plate 70: Metal

Plate 71: Shoes, etc.

	Locus	RN	Description
a	E18a-3	250	basketry
b	E18a-4	244	basketry
c	E18d-10	237	basketry
d	E18a-3	249	brush
e	E19c-4	260	leather sheath
f	E18d-5	262	leather sheath
g	G8b-5	259	leather sling
h	F18a-4	266	leather shoe
i	E18d-5	265	leather shoe
j	G8b-5	270	leather sandal, cut decoration
k	E18a-3	267	leather sandal
l	E19c-7	252	leather sandal
m	E19c-9	263	leather sole
n	E19c-9	263	leather sole
o	E18c-3	153	rope sandal
p	G12c-2	152	rope sandal
q	G8b-2		cable

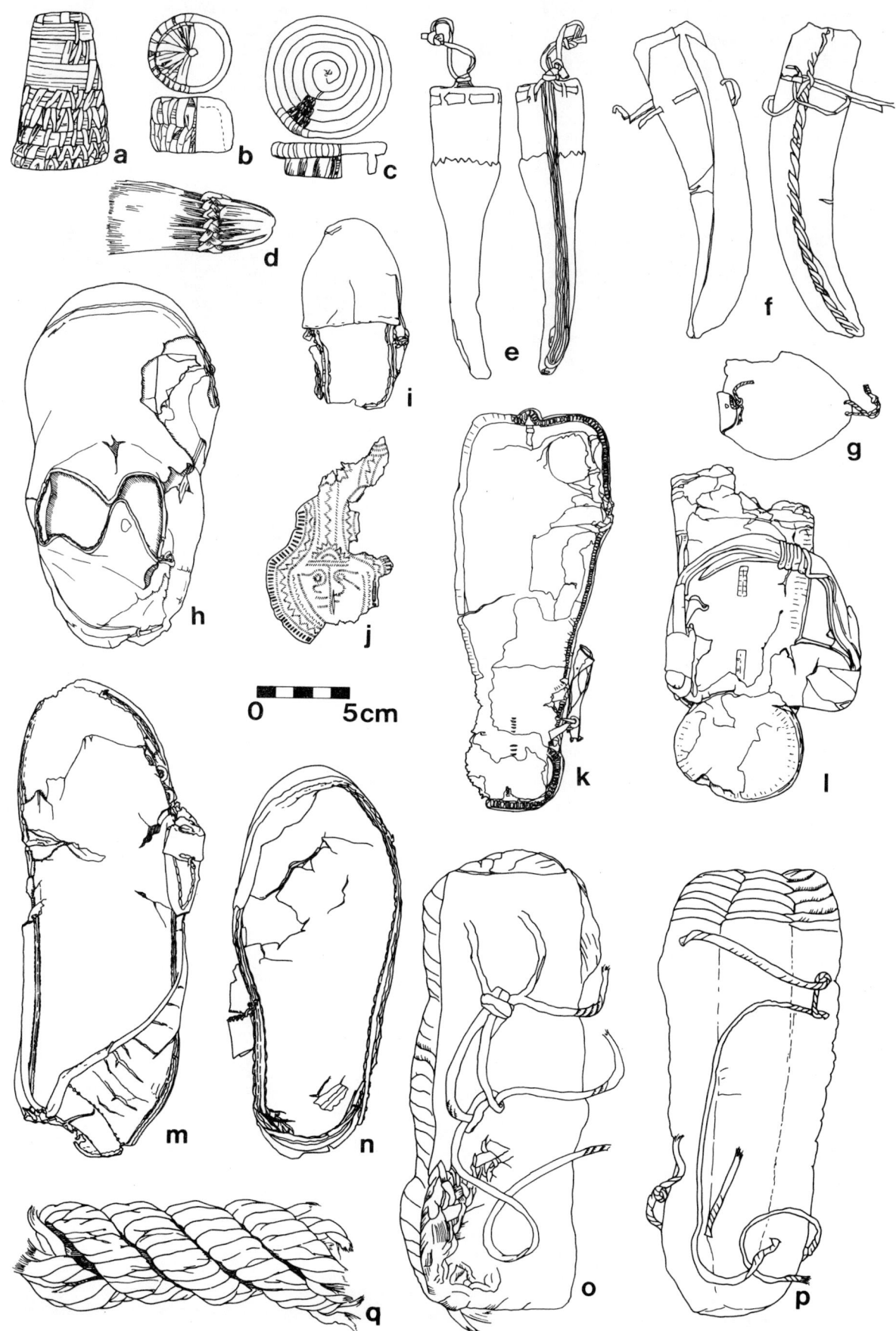

Plate 71: Shoes, etc.

Plate 72: Mills, Incense Burner, and Bir Kareim Uraeus

    Locus   RN   Description

a E18a-14 148 limestone mill (3-notched)

b E18a-16 149 basalt mill

c E18a-6   288 buff; mica and chaff temper; top blackened

d Bir Kareim, central cella, limestone with carved uraeus

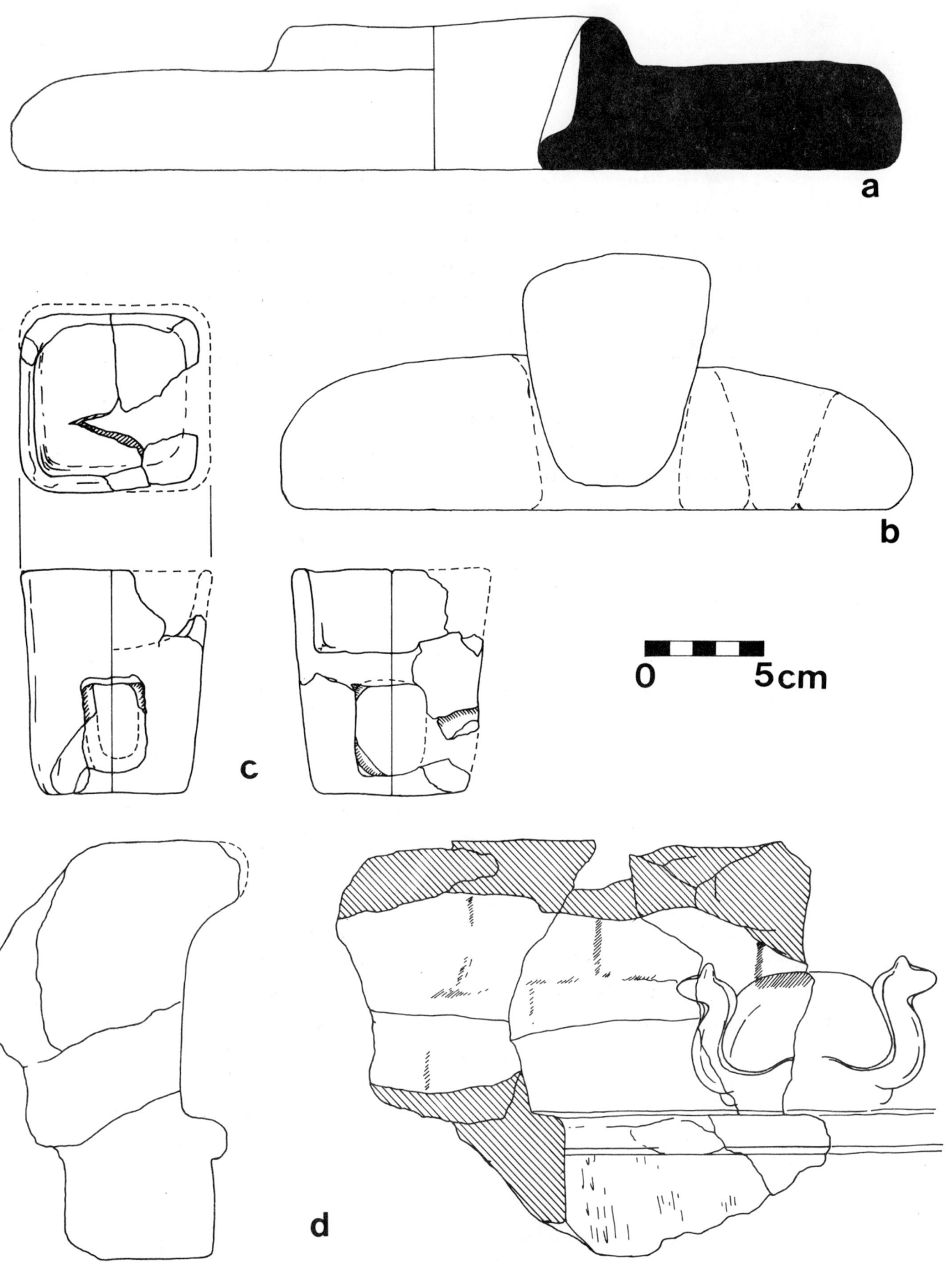

Plate 72: Mills, Incense Burner, and Bir Kareim Uraeus

is that of a small child (71:i). In addition to the leather footwear, leather knife sheaths (71:e,f), a leather sling (71:g), and assorted small pieces of leather were also found. Aside from the textiles discussed in detail in chapter 14, one simple beige piece with black painted or printed decoration (a fish?) (64:e) and one tassel with green at top and bottom and white lozenges on a red wrapping (64:c), which were found in Islamic loci, are illustrated.

The stone grinders found in the Roman villa are illustrated in pl. 54; two Islamic ones found in the eastern area are simple slabs with holes in the center for rubbing (72:a,b). The grinding stone of one (72:b) was also found. Also found in the Islamic area were several small redware incense burners (72:c). All have a flat surface for the charcoal and incense about 1/3 of the way down from the top. The base is hollowed out but the legs join along the bottom. All examples have extensive charcoal and ash remains. The carved limestone with sun-disk and uraeus (72:d) was found in the central cella of the temple at Bir Kareim; see chapter 20.

Basketry (Boyce Driskell)

A small sample of baskets from the 1978 season at Quseir al-Qadim was brought to the Oriental Institute. Preliminary analysis of these specimens is presently ongoing by B. Driskell with the assistance of Melinda Stafford. While the small number of baskets available to the analysts at present is not statistically representative of basketry technology at the site, analysis was initiated to provide some preliminary data on basketry technology and as a comparison to basketry now being systematically analyzed by the author at Qasr Ibrim, a site in the Nile valley some 30 km. north of Abu Simbel. Since we have analyzed less than 50 baskets thus far from Quseir al-Qadim, very few generalizations can be drawn at this time. The few relationships suggested below are very impressionistic.

Four major categories of basketry are represented in the Nile valley. These include plaited, plait connected, coiled, and twined. Plaited basketry, that is, basketry involving continuous unbroken plaiting of fabric to form a finished basket, is rare in the collections. Large plaited mats made of bundles of grass appear to have a long history in the area. However, containers and palm leaf mats of this major type appear to be almost totally restricted to early (Ptolemaic and Roman) deposits. Their rarity and temporal distribution may mean that this is an imported technology. This technology has not been seen in the baskets analyzed from Quseir al-Qadim.

Plait connected basketry forms the bulk of baskets seen in collections thus far. This technology involves weaving of narrow plait strips (usually less than 10 cm. wide) connected to each other at the sides by a running interwoven element or stringer. In mats these strips lie parallel to one another; in containers the single strip curves around and around to form the vessel in the same way as the foundation of coiled containers. This is a spatially and temporally pervasive technology in the Nile valley and its environs and is still today a most prevalent method of basket manufacture. It appears to date at least to the Pharaonic period and probably before. Over one half of the specimens analyzed from Quseir al-Qadim are of this basic type.

Like plait connected basketry, coiled basket technology has a long history in the Nile valley and persists today. Although small bowls and other container shapes are sometimes seen, most baskets are flat or very shallow food covers or platters. Plain, split-stitched specimens are most prevalent in all time periods although various decoratively stitched specimens occur. These decoratively stitched baskets are most prevalent in earlier periods and appear to be rare in later periods. Of six coiled baskets analyzed thus far from Quseir al-Qadim, all were covers or food platters and only one had any decorative stitching. This basket is from a mixed Roman--Islamic locus.

Twined basketry containers are very rare. They appear to be associated with early (Roman) occupation at Qasr Ibrim and may be imports. This is, however, far from clear. Twined mats and loose bags are somewhat more common. At Quseir al-Qadim three mat fragments and four bag fragments have been analyzed. All are from Islamic contexts.

It is clear that basketry from archaeological sites in the Nile valley and adjacent areas, while often an abundant artifact category, has not been analyzed in enough detail to allow culture historians to integrate basketry technology into overall conceptions of social, cultural, and economic history of the area. This is understandable since basketry is not well preserved at many sites and since other, better preserved, artifact categories (such as pottery) are so pervasive and informative. However, basketry, like pottery, offers much potential to the culture historian. A recent analysis of over 1800 specimens from Qasr Ibrim, a site occupied from at least the late Pharaonic period through Ottoman times, suggests significant stylistic and technological changes through time in spite of many surprising indications of long-term stability. More specifically, basic technology remains relatively stable. Detailed attribute analysis indicates much variance in minor technological traits such as center or start technique, splicing technique, selvedge treatment, design configuration, and metric attributes. Considerable variation in form has also been noted. Since a detailed attribute analysis is in the initial stage, no definitive cultural-historical relationships have yet been defined. As our analysis continues we hope to be able to tease out these relationships.

Once we have been able to understand the basic cultural-historical relationships, basketry from an area may well provide an analytical window into several important aspects of culture. First, since some categories of basketry at present, and presumably always in the past, are a cottage industry, certain technological traits may prove to be very localized, thus constituting a micro tradition. When this is the case, basketry analysis may shed light on localized social and economic relationships. This may lead to identification of economic and social units within a particular site as well as between sites. Another important prospect concerns socio-political and socio-economic relationships on a broader scale. Since basketry (at least some important categories) has been used for the duration of Nile valley history as transport containers (augmenting ceramic containers), a detailed understanding of the distribution of basket types may shed additional light on relationships between various areas of the Nile valley and its environs through time. While these are indeed idealistic goals, they are well within the realm of the possible once large samples of baskets from as many sites as possible are analyzed. With the long-range goals in mind, we recently developed a computerized storage and manipulation package which will allow us in the future to handle large volumes of data on baskets from the area.

Bibliography for Small Objects

Abd al-Raziq, A.
    1972   "Les peignes égyptiens dans l'art de l'Islam," *Syria* 49: 399-412
    1973   *La femme au temp des Mamlouks en Egypte*, vol. 5 of Textes Arabes et Etudes Islamiques, Institut Francais d'Archéologie Orientale, Cairo

Whitcomb, D. S., and J. H. Johnson
    1979   *Quseir al-Qadim 1978: Preliminary Report*, Cairo

CHAPTER 16: FAUNA
Patricia Wattenmaker[1]

The patterns of faunal exploitation are being analyzed in relation to their cultural context, with the expectation that faunal analysis can contribute to the investigation of the broad political, social and economic aspects of cultural systems relevant to the overall goals of the Quseir al-Qadim excavations. Under the assumption that periods of expansion and decline at Quseir al-Qadim can in part be linked to the ability or inability of its inhabitants to secure necessary food supplies either locally or from the Nile valley, the fauna are being examined to determine varying degrees of success through time on the part of the inhabitants to establish a reliable faunal resource base. Subsistence remains provide a direct data set with which to determine economic conditions on a local level and are useful indicators of dietary stress. Economic conditions can be inferred from the types of species exploited, the skeletal parts of animals utilized, and the butchering and cooking techniques. Once the dietary conditions have been established for different phases of occupation, such information may prove useful in aiding in an understanding of the factors involved in periods of growth and contraction of the site.

It is also expected that the degree of commitment on the part of central governments to the maintenance of the port will be reflected in the nature of the faunal assemblage. Judging from the barrenness of the region, the port would have been dependent on the Nile valley for most of its food supplies, with the exception of marine resources. It is possible that sheep and goats were purchased in limited quantity from nomadic tribes. Hunting of wild animals such as gazelle and wild birds could have made only a minor dietary contribution. It is hypothesized that periods of decline of central government investment and economic stress will be characterized by an increased reliance on marine resources.

The fauna may also prove useful in investigating the degree of central government involvement in procuring and distributing resources as opposed to individual obtainment and control over subsistence resources. Inferences on the degree of central control over resources can be derived from information such as the degree of spatial uniformity in species exploited and uniformity in the age of slaughter of domestic animals.

---

[1] An earlier version of this report appeared in *Chicago Anthropology Exchange* 13(2) (1980) 62-71.

Field Recovery of Faunal Material

The majority of the deposits were screened in a 0.4 cm. mesh. Samples of dirt from several loci were screened in a fine sieve so that, when these samples are analyzed, it will be possible to estimate the nature and quantity of fauna that was lost through the 0.4 cm. screen.

Both identifiable and unidentifiable bone recovered in the field was collected; material was not presorted by excavators. Consequently, it will be possible to examine patterns of bone fragmentation and their cultural implications.

Preliminary Results

To date, a small sample of the mammal bones has been analyzed. Due to a lack of comparative material in the field, none of the non-mammalian bones have yet been processed.

A total of 2,095 bones have been analyzed; 1,031 were identifiable to element (e.g., mandible) and at least family. The identifiable bones have been analyzed for 33 characteristics using the computer code "Bonesort II" (Redding, Zeder, and McArdle, 1978: 135). Measurements of identifiable bones were taken following Driesch (1976).

1,066 bones were unidentifiable as to family or element. These bones were separated into size category of animal (e.g., medium), class and element. Bones in each category (e.g., medium mammal femur) were counted and weighed.

From the Roman deposits 197 bones were identifiable and 504 were unidentifiable. 834 bones from the Islamic period were identifiable and 562 were not identifiable. The preservation of fauna from the Islamic period is excellent and is reflected in the relatively small number of bones which were not identifiable.

There was a significantly lower density of faunal remains in the Roman period than in the Islamic period, and the sample of bone from the Roman occupation is relatively small. The reason for this difference in density is not clear and is probably due to a number of factors. It is in part a result of different recovery strategies since many more Islamic than Roman deposits were screened. However, even the screened Roman deposits yielded few bones. Islamic remains were better preserved and the differing post-depositional conditions are partially responsible for the difference in bone density between the two periods. Hard-pan formation in the Roman area of the site caused the destruction or loss of some bone. However, even in the Roman deposits where there was no hard-pan, there was little bone. Among other possible contributing factors are a lesser role of fauna in the diet in the Roman period or, more likely, differences between the two periods in practices of disposal of meal remains. Finally, it is possible that differences in the functional nature of the loci excavated for each period contributed to the differences in faunal sample sizes.

Roman Occupation

From the Roman period one element was identified as *Equus* sp. (most likely *Equus asinus*), 18 elements belonged to *Sus scrofa*, six to *Camelus dromedarius*, 144 to *Ovis-Capra*, five to *Ovis aries*, 14 to *Capra hircus*, and nine to *Bos* sp. All species represented, with the probable exception of *Equus* sp., had clearly been used as food sources, as indicated by the presence of butchering marks on bones.

No elements of pig useful in distinguishing wild from domestic individuals were recovered. However, all elements useful in age determination were from individuals less than two years old, which suggests a degree of control over the age of slaughter that would be expected if the population being slaughtered was domestic. In addition, wild pigs are not found in the region.

The non-mammalian finds included a large number of fish bones; fish undoubtedly played a major dietary role. The only fish identified was *Scarus* sp. (parrotfish), and this was the best represented genus of fish.

A small number of bird bones was found. Most of these were *Gallus domesticus* (chicken), but a few belonged to a small member of the family Phasianidae, perhaps *Alectoris barbara* (Barbary partridge).

Islamic Occupation

Bones from the Islamic occupation have been separated into two categories: those from trench G8b and G9a and those from the eastern area of the site. G8b and G9a are believed to be earlier than the Islamic deposits of the eastern area.

From the earlier Islamic occupation 51 elements were assigned to *Camelus dromedarius*, 273 to *Ovis-Capra*, 16 to *Ovis aries*, nine to *Capra hircus*, and seven to *Bos* sp. All species were exploited as food sources.

The sample size of caprines from the late Islamic phase was adequate for determining the kill-off pattern. The fusion data indicate that some caprines were slaughtered as early as their first year and that most did not survive beyond three years of age (see Table 1). This is the pattern that would be expected if animals were raised primarily for meat.

Bone	Age of Fusion	Raw Fusion Data	Percent Fused
scapula	6-8 months	3 unfused, 5 fused	62.5
proximal radius distal humerus	10 months	1 unfused, 8 fused	88.8
first phalanx second phalanx	13-16 months	9 unfused, 19 fused	67.8
distal tibia	21 months	4 unfused, 7 fused	63.6
metacarpal metatarsal	18-28 months	9 unfused, 7 fused	43.7
proximal femur calcaneum distal radius	30-36 months	6 unfused, 2 fused	25.0
proximal tibia distal femur proximal humerus	36-42 months	15 unfused, 8 fused	34.7

Table 1: Percentage of Late Islamic Caprine Bones Fused

One carapace of a sea turtle and a small number of fish bones were also recovered.

From the later Islamic phase, three elements belonged to *Equus* sp., three to *Camelus dromedarius*, three to *Ovis-Capra-Gazella*, 431 to *Ovis-Capra*, five to *Ovis aries*, and 25 to *Capra hircus*. There is evidence that all species but *Equus* sp. made a dietary contribution.

A very large quantity of fish bones, mostly *Scarus* sp. and *Sparidae* (porgy), was recovered from the eastern area. It is certain that fish played a major, if not primary, dietary role in this period. The fish remains included a large quantity of heads and tails of dried fish, found elsewhere on the site only in small quantity. In addition, a large number of artifacts used in fishing, such as fishnets and line or net sinkers, was recovered from deposits in the eastern area. It is suggested that fish processing took place in this area of the site. An analysis of the spatial distribution of skeletal parts of fish, to be conducted at a later date, may yield more conclusive information on fish processing. The possibility of seasonal occupation during the Islamic period has been considered by the staff. An emphasis on fishing might be expected if the population were relatively mobile, since inhabitants would not be tied to herds. One of the motives for fish processing may have been the stockpiling of food resources for trade expeditions.

A large number of sea turtle bones and a few bird bones were removed from this period. One turtle bone was identified as *Chelonia mydas*.

Conclusions

Throughout the occupation of Quseir al-Qadim, the strategy of faunal exploitation was basically consistent. There was a heavy reliance on marine resources, especially fish, which was expected since marine fauna was the primary locally available food resource. Caprines, which were either purchased from nomads, raised locally, or brought in from the Nile valley, were also of major importance throughout the occupation of the site. Camel, cattle, and wild and domestic birds played a supplementary role in the diet.

Although the sample size is small and some conclusions are likely to change when a larger body of material is analyzed, there are some differences between periods which have been noted. Pig, presumably imported from the Nile valley, was found only in Roman deposits and its absence in Mamluk deposits is due to the Islamic injunction against pork. The faunal assemblage of the earlier Islamic period stands out as different from the other two in a few respects. Discrepancies between findings from the Roman and earlier Islamic phases may be an artifact of cultural and perhaps environmental factors. However, architectural and artifactual evidence suggest that differences in faunal exploitation between the early and late Islamic phases may be a function of wealth.

One index of wealth of the community and degree of central government involvement might be the proportion of fauna which was obtained locally as opposed to imported species. One means of determining whether a species was imported would be if meat were brought to the site after the animals had been slaughtered, and only meat bearing bones of the species were present at the site. However, for all species identified, elements of the skeleton generally discarded in butchering were recovered at the site. This indicates that if animals were imported they were brought in on the hoof and subsequently slaughtered. Age-curves may be useful in determining whether animals had been imported. If only immature individuals of a species are represented, it can be inferred that a breeding population was not present at the site, and that the species was necessarily imported.

It will be assumed for the purposes of this analysis, on the basis of knowledge of herding practices and environmental conditions of the region today, that marine resources and goat would have been obtained locally, and that pig, cattle, and sheep would have been imported. The statistically significant higher proportion of sheep to goat in the earlier Islamic deposits compared with the later Islamic deposits is interpreted as consistent with other findings that indicate the earlier

Islamic period was one of comparative wealth; see table 2. The relatively high percentage of camel in the earlier Islamic period is not presently believed to be significant since most of the bones seem to have come from a single individual.

	Ovis aries	Capra hircus
Early Islamic	16 (64%)	9 (36%)
Late Islamic	5 (17%)	25 (83%)
		55

Table 2: Proportion of Sheep to Goat

(Chi-square value [with continuity correction for one degree of freedom]= 11.01, $p < .001$)

A second striking difference between the two Islamic periods was the comparatively lower density of fish in the earlier period. Although this difference may prove to be simply an artifact of the economic importance of fish in the eastern area, and may be unrelated to subsistence practices, it does seem to support the hypothesis that fishing would be more important when other resources could not be as easily afforded.

	Roman # bones	%	Islamic # bones	%	Later Islamic # bones	%
Equus sp. (horse)	1	.51	--	--	3	.6
Sus scrofa (pig)	18	9.1	--	--	--	--
Camelus dromedarius (camel)	6	3.1	51	14.3	3	.6
Ovis-Capra-Gazella (sheep-goat-gazelle)	--	--	--	--	3	.6
Ovis aries	5	2.5	16	4.5	5	1.
Capra hircus	14	7.1	9	2.5	25	5.2
Ovis-Capra	144	73.1	273	76.7	431	90.2
Bos sp. (cattle)	9	4.6	7	2.	8	1.7

Bibliography for Fauna

Driesch, A. von den
    1976   *A Guide to the Measurement of Animal Bones from Archeological Sites*, Peabody Museum Bulletin 1, Cambridge

Redding, R., M. Zeder, and J. McArdle
    1978   "'Bonesort II'--A System for the Computer Processing of Identifiable Faunal Material," in *Approaches to Faunal Analysis in the Middle East*, ed. by R. H. Meadow and M. A. Zeder, Peabody Museum Bulletin 2, Cambridge

Whitcomb, D. S., and J. H. Johnson
    1979   *Quseir al-Qadim 1978: Preliminary Report*, Cairo

CHAPTER 17: PLANT REMAINS
Wilma Wetterstrom

The site of Quseir al-Qadim presents a unique opportunity for studying the economic plants and diet of a Roman and Islamic period community. Here under the arid conditions of the Red Sea coast, a large quantity of plant remains, representing food, fodder, fuel, and construction material, has been moderately well preserved. In addition, the arid setting has placed a unique "control" on the collection; only those plants carried in by the inhabitants are likely to be represented here, while "background noise"--plants deposited by natural factors--is almost certainly absent. A study of this unique collection of plant materials was begun in 1980 with the goal of trying to determine the nature of the diet and the plant economy. The preliminary results of this work offer some insights into the ways in which Quseir al-Qadim's inhabitants satisfied their needs in a desert setting.

Plant Collection Procedures

The author joined the 1980 Quseir expedition during the excavations to develop methods for recovering a reliable and representative sample of plant remains. Quseir al-Qadim posed several obstacles: In the Mamluk component plant remains were exceptionally abundant and well-preserved, while in the Roman section they were sparse and badly damaged by salt deposits. In addition, the most efficient method for extracting plant remains, flotation or water separation, could not be used on most of the materials. The bulk of the plant remains were desiccated and because of their density sank to the bottom of the flotation tub along with the sediments, rather than floating on the surface. As a result, most of the plant materials had to be recovered through fine-sieving and hand-sorting, a slow procedure which severely limited the amount of material that could be processed.

After a period of experimentation, the following recovery and sampling procedures were used at Quseir al-Qadim: Samples of sediment were routinely collected for fine-sieving from most areas within the Roman and Mamluk areas of the site. One or two sacks of sediment, each averaging 9 liters, were collected from middens, courtyards, rooms, and test pits. When possible the entire contents of ash lenses and hearth was collected. Unfortunately, no equipment was available in the field for weighing these large samples.

Most of the sediment samples were fine-sieved through a strainer with a mesh of about 1 mm. The fine fraction that passed through the sieve was scanned for small seeds and other identifiable parts but none were found. The large fraction was spread on a photographic tray and systematically sorted by the author in the field. Wood, seeds, seed-like structures, such as grains, seed fragments, and other identifiable plant parts, as well as bone, were picked out and later shipped to the United States for analysis.

Most ash lenses and other charred samples were processed by flotation since the light, porous burned plant remains floated readily and could easily be separated from the sediments in water. The samples were poured into a bucket of sea water, stirred, and allowed to settle. After several minutes, the flotate was decanted onto a cloth set over a strainer. Once drained, the cloth was gently removed, folded over, and set on newspapers to dry. Later the sample was packed for shipment to the United States. The heavy fraction was poured into the strainer, swirled in sea water until free of silts, and saved for bone analysis.

In addition to these recovery procedures, large, visible plant remains were routinely collected by hand during excavation.

Laboratory Procedures

At Massachusetts Institute of Technology, the flotation samples and partially-sorted sieved samples were fully sorted with the aid of a binocular microscope using magnifications of 7 to 10 X. Specimens were taxonomically identified by careful comparison of morphological features with modern reference collections. Most identifications were based on the author's own reference collection, which Dr. Loutfy Boulos of the National Research Center in Cairo kindly identified. In addition, the collections of the Cairo University Herbarium and the Agriculture Museum, Dokki, Cairo, were also consulted.

After identification, the materials were counted and tabulated. The large specimens, hand-picked by excavators, were also examined, identified, and tabulated.

Results

Tables 3, 4, and 5 list the materials which have been analyzed thus far. All of the Roman samples collected in 1980 were analyzed, yielding over 200 seeds and seed-like structures. Only 11 of the Mamluk flotation and fine-sieved samples have been examined thus far, but because of the wealth of materials in this portion of the site, they produced over 6000 seeds and seed-like structures. In addition, over 3000 large items were recovered by excavators. A large quantity of wood and charcoal was also collected but has not yet been analyzed.

The Quseir al-Qadim plant remains included:

Cereals: Barley, 6-rowed, hulled
          Wheat, free-threshing
          Sorghum

Locus of Sample	Barley Rachis	Barley Grains	Wheat Rachis	Wheat Grains	Fava Beans	Chickpeas	Lentils	Bitter Vetch Beans	Safflower Achenes	Olive Stones	Grape Pips	Date Kernels	Christ's Thorn Fruit stone	Egyptian Plum Fruit stone	Watermelon Seeds	Coriander Seeds	Pepper Peppercorns	Other
E6a-1 fill												1f				3		
E6b-4 fill	1	2c																
E6b-24 sediment under oil jars		3c							1	1cf								
E6b-24 sediment under mill stone										2cf						1cf		
E6b-24 test pit											2					1		
E6b-43 hearth		1c																
E6b-46 test pit					1c					1f	2	1fc	1c			3		unknowns
E6b-44 fill		5c		1c									6fc					
E6b-54 ash lens		4c																unknowns
E6c-3 fill		1c																
E7a-10 fill		1c								2f	2		1f	1+1f				unknowns
E7c-6 fill														1f				1 Zilla seed
E7a-5 fill							2c											

357

Locus of Sample	Barley Grains	Barley Rachis	Wheat Grains	Wheat Rachis	Fava Beans	Chickpeas	Lentils	Bitter Vetch Beans	Safflower Achenes	Olive Stones	Grape Pips	Date Kernels	Christ's Thorn Fruit stone	Egyptian Plum Fruit stone	Watermelon Seeds	Coriander Seeds	Pepper Peppercorns	Other
E7a-7 ash lens	1c										1			1				
G8a-3 ash lens	3d	4c																1 zilla seed
G8a-8 ash lens	3			1														
G8b-3 midden	22	13	154	6			8	34	1+f	2+f	2+f	2+f		1	1	2		unknowns, Flax capsule f
G8b-6 midden	21	18	140	3										1				unknowns
G8b-8 fill	4c	8c																
G8b-13 ashy soil from pot emplacement											1c							
G8b-8 ash pit									1c			5c			1d 1c			
G9a-1 soil from burned area																		
G12c-1 fill	4		1c															
G12c-9 fill	1c	1c	3c	1c														
J8a-1 fill	6d	1c	3d	2c	1f	1		1c	1							4f		unknowns

Locus of Sample	Barley Grains / Rachis	Wheat Grains / Rachis	Fava Beans	Chickpeas	Lentils	Bitter Vetch Beans	Safflower Achenes	Olive Stones	Grape Pips	Date Kernels	Christ's Thorn Fruit stone	Egyptian Plum Fruit stone	Watermelon Seeds	Coriander Seeds	Pepper Peppercorns	Other
J8c-13 fill	1c									24						unknown

Note: All materials are desiccated unless otherwise indicated
c = carbonized   d = desiccated (used only where there might be ambiguity)

Table 3: Plant Remains from Fine-Sieve and Flotation Samples--Roman Quseir al-Qadim

Locus of Sample	Barley Grains	Barley Rachis	Wheat Grains	Wheat Rachis	Sorghum Grains	Sorghum Spikelets	Fava Beans	Chickpeas	Lentils	Bitter Vetch Beans	Safflower Achenes	Fenugreek Beans	Grape Pips	Date Kernels	Christ's Thorn Fruit stone	Watermelon Seeds	Coriander Seeds	Pepper Peppercorns	Zilla Seeds	Other
E18a-4 fill	2	9	1d 2c	9	17	1							1	21+f			1f		1f	unknown
E18a-14 ash lens	10		6		1	1								35						unknown
E18a-4, SW fill	91d 4c	6	19d 3c	18	33	9					3f		2	58		2f	2f	1	8+f	unknowns
E18a-14, SW fill	71	8	57d 2c	52	108	49						2	2	11		5f	2f	1	4+f	unknowns
E18a-15 ash from pot hearth	60d 1998c	9	46d 1334c	24	2	12c	1f		1c			1	1+f	16+f	1c	6f	1f	1		3 Acacia f unknowns
E18b-4 fill outside room	9		4		12	1						4	1	12			1f	1		
E18d-6 fill	219d 2c	34	257d 9c	100	64	20	17f				1+f	5	1				5f	1	11d 4c	
F19a-4 pot hearth	2d 66c		2d 53c		2d 15c	3							1d 2c	3c 1d		1f		7c	1+f	unknowns 2 Flax seeds
E19, SE fill	226	41	54d 4c	46	25d 1c	390 1c	2+f	5d 1c	1			18	1	83		2+f	22f	12	14+f	1 Garlic clove f 1 Acacia pod f unknowns
E19c-3, NW fill	238	15	40	104	12	27	1f				1+f		1	37		1f	1+f	1	9	1 Garlic clove f

Note: All materials are desiccated unless otherwise indicated
c = carbonized   d = desiccated (used only where there might be ambiguity)

Table 4: Plant Remains from Fine-Sieve and Flotation Samples--Islamic Quseir al-Qadim

Locus of Sample	Olive Stone	Date Kernel	Dom Fruit	Christ's Thorn Stone	Peach Stone	Egyptian Plum Stone	Walnut Shell fragment	Hazelnut Shell fragment	Pine Nut Shell fragment	Coconut Shell fragment	Other
Roman											
E6a-1	1		2			1					
E6a-2	1		2								1 Pine cone bract
E6b							1				
G8a-4	4	2	2				1				
G8a-7	2	11		1			1	1	1		2 Pine cone bract 1 Almond? shell f
G8b-1		4									1 Balanites? stone
G8b-3	19	27	1				1	1	1		1 Almond? shell f
G8b-5		3	3				1	4			
G8b-6	1					1			1		
G9a-1		26			4		2				Unknown
G12c-5	1										
H8a-1		23	1					1			
H8c-1		6	1					2	1		
H8c-2		2									1 Pine cone bract
J8c-1								1			
Islamic											
E18a-4		101									
E18a-14		794	1								
E18a-15		318	1								
E18a-16		153	2								
E18b-4		91	1								
E18c-1		6	1								
E18c-2		570								1	
E18c-3		413	1								
E18d-1		476									
E18d-4		21								1	
E18d-5		47									2 Almond? shell f

Locus of Sample	Olive Stone	Date Kernel	Dom Fruit	Christ's Thorn Stone	Peach Stone	Egyptian Plum Stone	Walnut Shell fragment	Hazelnut Shell fragment	Pine nut Shell fragment	Coconut Shell fragment	Other
E18d-6		11									
E18d-7		8									
E18d-10		8								1	
E18d-11		29									
E18d-12		9									
E18d-13		90									
E18d-14		9								1	
E19a-2		76			1						
E19c-3		32	1								
E19c-4		36	1								
E19c-5		14									
E19c-6		33	8								1 Almond? shell f
E19c-7		27	1							1	
E19c-8		11	1								
F19a-2		4									
F19a-6			2								

Note: all materials are desiccated

f is fragment

Table 5: Plant Remains Recovered by Hand During the Excavations

Pulses: Fava beans
Chickpeas
Lentils
Fenugreek
Bitter Vetch

Oil Plants: Safflower
Olive
Flax

Fruits:
: Grape
  Dom palm
  Date
  Christ's thorn
  Egyptian plum
  Peach
  Coconut

Seeds:
: Watermelon

Seasonings:
: Coriander
  Garlic
  Pepper

Nuts:
: Pine nut
  Hazelnut
  English walnut

Wild plants:
: Zilla
  Acacia

In addition, a number of seed types have not yet been identified. The items listed above are described in detail below.

Barley

Hulled barley (*Hordeum vulgare*), a major cereal of Egypt since Neolithic times, is used today primarily to feed livestock and brew beer. Egyptians also use barley to make *subia*, a nonalcoholic beverage, and *bouza*, an alcoholic drink, as well as to make bread, either alone or with other cereals (Täckholm, Täckholm, and Drar, 1941: 284). In both Roman and Islamic Quseir al-Qadim, hulled, six-rowed barley grains were the most abundant plant type. The grains are spindle-shaped with a blunt apex and a pointed tip that is either straight or slightly curved. The latter, a characteristic of 6-rowed barley, is a feature of the two grains that grow on the lateral or side positions of the three-grained spikelet. The grain in the center position, in contrast, is straight. The desiccated grains, still encased in their hulls, are 7.0 to 12 mm. in length and range from exceptionally well-preserved specimens that look new except for their color, which is much darker than fresh material, to partially decomposed grains in which most of the endosperm is gone. Carbonized grains, also abundant, exhibit the same features as the desiccated material, but are smaller and have lost their hulls as a result of burning.

Like the grains, the small quantity of rachis or spike stem fragments found at Quseir al-Qadim range from well-preserved material, still retaining hairs, to badly damaged specimens. These flattened stem fragments, consisting of one or several internodes still attached, are narrow at the base, flaring at the top where the grains were attached. Nearly all are clearly of the 6-rowed type; that is, each internode appears to have accomodated three grains. The exceptions are several narrow internodes that appear to have held only a single grain, a feature of two-rowed barley, suggesting that some of the barley may have been of this type. However, 6-rowed barley sometimes produces only one fertile grain in a spikelet.

The "fresh-looking" grains and rachis segments in the Islamic occupation raise the possibility that some of the material might be intrusive and of more recent origin than the Mamluk period. Indeed, rodent dung was common in these areas of the site suggesting that mice might have deposited grains sometime after Quseir al-Qadim was abandoned. However, the assemblage of recent-looking grains was no different from the rest of the plant collection in any other respect. In addition, it is possible for grains and spikelets to retain a surprisingly "fresh" appearance when preservation is good. Jackson, for example, noted that the barley he examined from Neolithic granaries in the Fayyum, dating from around 4500 B.C., were in a "perfect state of preservation....(E)xcept for the barley having a curious mahogany tinge and being very light and brittle, it might have been harvested yesterday" (Caton-Thompson and Gardner, 1934: 48).

Wheat

Several species of wheat (*Triticum* spp.) have been major cereals in Egypt since Neolithic times. Emmer (*T. dicoccum*), a husked wheat, predominated through Pharaonic times, but was displaced during the Graeco-Roman era by the free-threshing wheats, bread wheat (*T. aestivum*) and hard or macaroni wheat (*T. durum*) (Täckholm, Täckholm, and Drar, 1941: 237, 241, 245). The latter wheats are cultivated today in Egypt for bread and pasta, while the straw, *tibn*, is an important fodder.

The Quseir al-Qadim wheats, which follow barley in abundance, are free-threshing and may be hard or bread wheat. The desiccated Islamic period grains, which are generally well-preserved, most closely resemble hard wheat, but because bread wheat exhibits so much variability some of the grains might belong to this group as well. The grains are long, the majority greater than 7.0 mm., with almost parallel flanks and rounded or pointed ends. The ventral surface is flat with a narrow furrow, while the dorsal surface is rounded with the maximum height at a point behind the scutellum, the embryo area. The flanks are perpendicular to the ventral surface, sloping in toward the dorsal surface, creating a rounded-triangular cross-section. The best preserved grains still retain their epidermal hairs and some could be mistaken for modern materials if it were not for their darkened, dull surface which ranges from a light to very dark brown.

Portions of the rachis were preserved as well in desiccated form and clearly indicate a free-threshing wheat. That is, the glumes and grains have separated cleanly from the spike, leaving a bare stem of connected internode segments. Rachises of bread wheat and hard wheat are very similar and often difficult to distinguish in archaeological materials (van Zeist, 1976: 36) but several spikelet fragments show features diagnostic of the latter. The glumes have a distinctive keel that runs from the tip to the base of each grain, a feature of *T. durum* (Renfrew, 1973: 53). In addition, the few terminal spikelets recovered were positioned perpendicular to the axis of the spike, another hard wheat characteristic (*ibid.*)

The Roman grains, including charred and desiccated specimens, and rachis fragments, closely resemble the Islamic materials but are not nearly as well preserved. Both collections require further study before a positive identification to species can be made.

Sorghum

An important cereal in Africa, sorghum (*Sorghum bicolor*) is cultivated in Egypt today primarily for fodder but has also been used with wheat and barley in making bread (Darby, et al., 1977: 494). A late introduction, sorghum was apparently not grown in Egypt until Roman or Byzantine times (*ibid.*)

The Quseir al-Qadim sorghums, all from the Islamic occupation, are predominantly desiccated grains, rounded with a pointed embryo, somewhat flattened on the dorsal and ventral surfaces, ranging from 3.6 to 5.1 mm. in length, 2.5 to 4.5 mm. in width, and 1.8 to 2.8 mm. in thickness. The colors range from dull beige to reddish brown. The sorghum remains also include spikelet fragments consisting primarily of the tough glumes, which vary from a dull beige to brown. Like the other cereals, some of these are exceptionally well-preserved. Both the glumes and the grains closely resemble the modern durra race cultivated in the Nile valley today.

Fava Beans

Cultivated as a winter crop in Egypt, the fava or broad bean (*Vicia faba*) is a staple of the Egyptian diet along with wheat bread. It apparently was introduced or became popular during Graeco-Roman times since the earliest reliably-dated archaeological specimens are from sites of this period. The fava bean was one of the major foods of the ancient Romans, who celebrated it at their Fabaria feast, and also used it to heal contusions and burns (Meyer, 1980: 408). It was the most abundant plant food recovered in the remains of three communities destroyed by Mt. Vesuvius in A.D. 79 (*ibid.*).

The Quseir al-Qadim specimens, from both Roman and Islamic occupations, consist primarily of desiccated seed coat fragments with a dull dark brown or purple color. Several specimens exhibit an oval hilum approximately 5 to 6 mm. long. The one complete bean found here is 12 mm. x 9.3 mm. x 7.6 mm., glossy, reddish-brown, flattened and oval angular.

Chickpeas

The chickpea (*Cicer arietinum*), known in Egypt since the Middle Kingdom (Darby, et al., 1977: 685) is popular today as a seasoned puree and as a dry, roasted bean eaten as a snack. The Quseir al-Qadim chickpeas, representing both Roman and Islamic occupations, consist mainly of desiccated seed coat fragments, identified on the basis of the diagnostic "beak." The few whole specimens measuring 5.5--5.7 mm. x 7.1--8.1 mm. x 4.9--5.9 mm., are globular with two flattened faces which come to a point forming the "beak." The surfaces are wrinkled and vary from a buff splotched with salt deposits to a dark reddish brown.

Lentils

A popular food in Egypt today, the lentil (*Lens culinaris*) has been cultivated here since the Predynastic (*ibid.*: 687). Raised as a winter crop, it is prepared primarily in soups. The Quseir al-Qadim specimens, most of which are from the Roman occupation, include charred and desiccated beans. The latter, poorly preserved with badly damaged seed coats, are lenticular, 2.9 to 4.7 mm. in diameter, and similar to the small-seeded variety cultivated in Egypt today. The colors, which have probably been affected by salt deposits, are buff and black.

Fenugreek

Fenugreek (*Trigonella foenum-graecum*), called *helba* in Arabic, is cultivated in the Nile valley today for its highly aromatic seeds. Ground, these are added to bread dough as a flavoring (*ibid.*: 802) and mixed with water for a medicinal beverage. In India they are also used as fodder and in curry powder (Renfrew, 1973: 188). Although fenugreek seeds were reported at a Neolithic site in Egypt (*ibid.*), there is no archaeolgoical evidence of them until much later periods.

The Quseir al-Qadim specimens, all from the Islamic occupation, are flattened-cylindrical with flat ends and a distinctive groove along one side of the seed between the radicle and the cotyledons. Ranging from 4.1 mm. to 11.0 mm. in length, they are a dull greyish brown to dark brown and slightly mottled.

Bitter Vetch

Bitter vetch (*Vicia ervilia*), a legume, is cultivated today throughout the Middle East where the seeds and plants are fed to livestock (Duke, 1981: 275) and the beans are sometimes used as famine foods (Zohary and Hopf, 1973: 893). The bitter principle, a cyanogenetic glycoside, which imparts an unpleasant taste to the beans, is toxic to pigs, horses, and poultry, but ruminants and humans are highly resistant to it (Meyer, 1980: 409). Weedy varieties of the plant often invade cultivated fields and as a result the beans are sometimes found in grain harvests (Zohary and Hopf, 1973: 893). Bitter vetch seeds have been found at Predynastic sites in Upper Egypt where they were probably field weeds (Wetterstrom, in press). Both the Roman site of Karanis in Egypt (Wetterstrom, unpublished data) and Pompeii (Meyer, 1980: 409) produced large quantitites of bitter vetch beans suggesting that they were used as fodder during Roman times.

The Quseir al-Qadim materials, all from the Roman occupation, include several charred specimens and some 30 desiccated, poorly-preserved beans. Among the latter, the whole beans, measuring 2.1--4.5 mm. x 3.1--3.9 mm. x 3.1--4.9 mm., are compressed-globose with four more or less triangular faces. Most have lost the seed coat but the hypocotyl can still be seen on most of them. The color of the seed coats is a dingy, dull brown while the bare beans are a rich reddish-brown.

Safflower

The safflower (*Carthamus tinctorius*), a European thistle with orange flowers and square, white glossy fruits, is cultivated for the oil found in the seeds and the red and yellow dyes obtained from the flowers (Tackholm, 1961: 33). Since at least Graeco-Roman times, ancient Egyptians used the safflower for oil and for burial garlands (Darby, et al., 1975: 805).

Specimens of safflower achenes and shell fragments were found in both Roman and Islamic Quseir al-Qadim. Dull, beige or brown, the desiccated fruits vary from 7.8 to 9.3 mm. in length and 3.2 to 4.6 mm. in width. They are oblong angular and flattened with a rounded apex and a triangular or diamond-shaped cross-section.

Olive

Primarily a Mediterranean tree, the olive (*Olea europaea*) is cultivated today in Egypt in the Fayyum, along the west Mediterranean coast (Täckholm, 1961: 28) and in Siwa Oasis (Darby, et al., 1977: 718). Both olive oil and fruits were consumed in ancient Egypt but archaeological finds are scarce until Roman times (*ibid.*: 720, 285). The olive was apparently cultivated in the Fayyum since at least late Pharaonic times, but most of the oil was probably imported from Syria and Palestine (Täckholm, 1961: 28).

The Quseir al-Qadim olive specimens, all from the Roman occupation, are desiccated spindle-shaped stones, rounded in cross-section, with pointed ends and irregular furrows that run the length of the stone. The complete specimens range from about 15 to 25 mm. in length.

Grape

Grape vines (*Vitis vinifera*) have been cultivated in Egypt at least since early Pharaonic times for table fruit, wine, and raisins (Darby, et al., 1977: 712-13, 715). Quseir al-Qadim grape pip specimens, from both Roman and Islamic occupations, are pyriform with an oval "shield" in the center of the dorsal surface, two length-wise depressions on the ventral surface, and a long stalk. The desiccated specimens range from 4.6 to 7.4 mm. in length, 2.5 to 4.5 mm. in width, and 1.9 to 3.2 mm. in thickness.

Dom Palm

The dom (*Hyphaene thebaica*), a fan-palm of Upper Egypt, produces large, glossy, chestnut-brown fruits which are collected for their tough, sugary mesocarp (Täckholm, 1961: 9). This fibrous material with a ginger flavor is eaten raw after being soaked in water or prepared as a syrup (Darby, et al., 1977: 730). The hard stone inside the fruit, a vegetable ivory, is used in making buttons, rings, beads, and other objects (*ibid.*). The fruits have been used in Egypt since at least Neolithic times (Täckholm and Drar, 1950: 282).

Dom fruits, common in both Roman and Islamic Quseir al-Qadim, ranged from complete, untouched specimens with glossy brown surfaces to spent fruits from which most of the mesocarp had been removed. The complete specimens were large, irregularly globular, with a longitudinal keel or ridge along one side, and ranged between 40 to 50 mm. in length and 32 to 43 mm. in width. Some of the specimens had been sawed open, apparently to extract the ivory.

Date Palm

Cultivated throughout Egypt since Pharaonic times, the date palm (*Phoenix dactylifera*) is one of the country's most valuable trees; virtually every part is utilized. The fruit is eaten fresh or dried and used to distill a strong liquor; unripe or low quality fruits are fed to animals. The vegetative parts of the tree are used as construction material and in making bags, ropes, mats, and baskets (El-Hadidi and Boulos, 1979: 83).

Evidence of dates, abundant in both Roman and Islamic areas of Quseir al-Qadim, consisted of desiccated and charred fruit kernels and perianth fragments. The kernels, cylindrical with a round cross-section and a deep longitudinal furrow, range widely in shape and size, from short, squat stones, about 15 mm. long, with rounded ends, to long narrow stones, up to 30 mm. in length, with pointed ends. Such variation could indicate that the fruits came from a number of locations, which is very likely since nearly all of them must have been imported. Indeed, some of the stones even match the descriptions of modern local varieties in Brown and Bohgot's (1938) classic monograph on the date. However, more study is required before any significance can be attached to the wide range of variation in the Quseir al-Qadim date kernels. With the kernels alone it is difficult to identify varieties, and, in addition, date fruits can vary widely in size on even a single branch (*ibid.*: 46).

Christ's Thorn

The Christ's thorn (*Ziziphus spina-Christi*) is cultivated throughout Egypt today primarily for shade, but also grows wild in the southern part of the country. The small apple-like fruit, popular in the countryside today (El-Hadidi and Boulos, 1979: 129), has been enjoyed since at least Predynastic times (Täckholm, 1961: 25).

The charred and desiccated fruit stones and fragments, found in Roman and Islamic Quseir al-Qadim, are globular with a pattern of raised diamond-like bumps on the outer surface. The two complete specimens, both charred, are 8.9 x 7.1 mm. and 8.1 x 6.7 mm.

Egyptian Plum

An important fruit tree during Pharaonic times, the Egyptian plum (*Cordia myxa*) is cultivated today in the Mediterranean region of Egypt and the Oases for its fruit. The latter, an orange drupe with a sweet, somewhat astringent taste, is used today primarily for bird-lime but in the past it was eaten in cakes and as a fruit, was taken as medicine, and was fermented as wine (*ibid.*: 29). The fruit stones, strung as beads, have also been found in burials from the Graeco-Roman period (*ibid.*: 30).

The Quseir al-Qadim specimens, all from the Roman occupation, are charred or desiccated fruit stones and fragments. The complete specimens, measuring 10.1--13.1 mm. x 7.5--10.0 mm., are ellipsoid, flattened, and edentate at both ends with a slightly wrinkled surface and a sharp keel along the length of the stone. Two of the stones have been cut or drilled on the ends, suggesting that they may have been strung as beads. The color of the desiccated specimens is a dull grey to brown.

Peach

A native of China, the peach (*Prunus persica*) was apparently introduced to Egypt during Graeco-Roman times; archaeological examples are known from Roman and Coptic sites (*ibid.*: 15-16). The peach stone specimens from Roman and Islamic Quseir al-Qadim, all desiccated fragments, are ovate flattened and deeply wrinkled with a dull grey color.

Coconut

The coconut palm (*Cocos nucifera*) is cultivated in tropical regions, especially Southeast Asia, for the flesh, milk, and oil from its fruit. Several specimens found in the Islamic deposits of Quseir al-Qadim appear to be fragments of the hard stone that surrounds the coconut's flesh. The fragments, dark brown, very hard, and approximately 2.5 to 3.0 mm. thick, have apparently been cut, while the surface has been scraped. The largest piece, a bowl-shaped fragment, is approximately 80 mm. in diameter, which is probably only a little less than the maximum diameter of the complete stone.

Watermelon

Several varieties of watermelon (*Citrullus colocynthus*) have been grown in Egypt since Pharaonic times for fruit and seeds. The sweet watermelon is raised in the summer for its delicious red fruit, while an inedible variety is both cultivated in Egypt and imported from the Sudan for its seeds. The latter are roasted and sold by street vendors as a snack called *libb*.

The Quseir al-Qadim specimens, most of which are desiccated seeds and come from Islamic deposits, are ovate, flattened, rounded at one end, tapering at the other. The margins are rounded except at the narrow end where two short notches run from the tip along the sides on both dorsal and ventral surfaces. The dimensions of the seeds, 12.6--14.1 mm. in length and 7.4 to 8.2 mm. in width, are slightly larger than modern specimens of *libb*, which rarely exceed 11 to 12 mm. in length, and closer to the sweet watermelon seed which is over 12 or 13 mm. However, nearly all the specimens are a dull beige or brown similar to fresh *libb*. Of course, the salt deposits and time may have dulled the color.

The Roman specimens, from an ash lens, are charred and embedded in burned fruit. Since *libb* seeds separate from the stringy fruit at maturity, these may be immature fruits or sweet watermelons.

Flax

Flax (*Linum usitatissimum*), important in Egypt since Neolithic times, is cultivated today for the oily linseeds and for the stem fibers from which linen is made (Renfrew, 1973: 124). According to Pliny, the Roman also mixed parched flax seeds with barley and coriander for porridge (*ibid.*). The two charred flax seeds, found in a pot hearth in the Islamic deposits, are flattened and elliptical with a "beak" at the narrow end where the testa projects to the side. Both well preserved, their dimensions are 4.8 x 1.7 mm. and 4.0 x 1.6 mm. In a Roman midden, desiccated fragments of a linen capsule were also found. These are well preserved, dark brown, almost paper-thin, and covered with fine, longitudinal striations.

Coriander

Cultivated in the Nile valley and sometimes occuring wild, coriander (*Coriandrum sativum*) is a major seasoning in Egyptian cuisine. The fruit, a cremocarp, is dried and used whole or ground (Brouk, 1975: 297). The earliest archaeological examples in Egypt date from the 18th Dynasty (Darby, et al., 1977: 798) and are known from Graeco-Roman sites as well.

The Quseir al-Qadim specimens, from both Roman and Islamic areas of the site, are globular, 4.2--4.9 mm. x 2.6--3.7 mm., and most have split into two hemispheres or mericarps. The surface is covered with alternating wavy and straight longitudinal ribs (Brouk, 1975: 297).

Pepper

One of the most common household seasonings, pepper (*Piper nigrum*) is the fruit of a tropical perennial vine cultivated in Southeast Asia. The whole, unripe drupes, peppercorns, are ground for black pepper, while white pepper is derived from ripe or nearly ripe fruits stripped of the outer covering (*ibid.*: 316-17). Known in Egypt since the Graeco-Roman period, pepper was imported from India via Red Sea ports (Darby, et al. 1977: 804) such as Quseir al-Qadim.

The Quseir al-Qadim peppercorns, most of which come from the Islamic deposits, are complete charred or desiccated drupes. The latter, ranging from 3.5--10.2 mm. x 3.3--4.7 mm., are globular and covered with a reticulate pattern of ridges, which have been partially worn away on some specimens. The color ranges from dull greyish brown to almost black.

Garlic

Cultivated in Egypt today, a special Egyptian variety of garlic (*Allium sativum*) (Girgis, 1924-5: 47) has been known here since Pharaonic times (Brouk, 1975: 302). An essential seasoning in Egyptian cuisine, garlic is also valued for its medicinal properties (Darby, et al., 1977: 657). The garlic from Islamic Quseir al-Qadim consists of fragments of the membranous scales from the "clove" which are brittle and discolored but well preserved.

Pine

The stone pine (*Pinus pinea*), indigenous to the northern Mediterranean coast, bears a flavorful nut popular in the Middle East (Meyer, 1980: 419). It is known from Egyptian sites of the Roman period but was probably imported (Darby, et al., 1977: 735).

Roman Quseir al-Qadim produced desiccated pine cone bracts and pine nut shells. The latter are thin-walled fragments, approximately 1.0 to 1.5 mm. thick, with a curvature indicating an oblong nut, rounded or squared at one end with a squarish cross-section. Both inner and outer surfaces are smooth with a dark reddish-brown color. The bracts, or cone fragments, some of which are still attached to the center of the cone, are flattened, diamond shaped, with a raised diamond at the apex of the bract.

Hazelnut

The hazelnut or filbert (*Coryllus avellana*), indigenous to Europe (Meyer, 1980: 407), has a small, flavorful nut that is imported to Egypt but has never been cultivated here (Darby, et al., 1977: 752). The Quseir al-Qadim hazelnut fragments, all from the Roman occupation, consist of desiccated dull reddish-brown pieces of shell or endocarp, approximately 1.5 to 2.0 mm. thick, with smooth inner and outer surfaces. The most complete specimens are globular or ovate nuts ranging from approximately 12 to 21 mm. in length and 15 to 21 mm. in width. Several specimens bear a diagnostic hilum scar.

Walnut

The English or Persian walnut (*Juglans regia*), cultivated primarily in the United States and Europe for its fruit, was introduced to Egypt during the period of the Ptolemies and today a few scattered trees are found in the country (Darby, et al., 1977: 753). The Quseir al-Qadim walnut specimens, all dating from the Roman occupation, consist of desiccated or charred endocarp fragments. A reddish-brown color, each of the fragments is thin-walled, averaging about 1.5 mm. in thickness, shows a slight curvature and bears irregular grooves. The inner surface has an irregular pattern of ridges.

Zilla

One of the few wild plants found at Quseir al-Qadim, zilla (*Zilla spinosa*) is a spiny desert shrub, common throughout the Eastern Desert (Täckholm, 1974: 197). Most grazing animals cannot tolerate its dense spines, but camels feed on it (Bailey and Danin, 1981: 148). The globular seeds with pointed bases were abundant at Roman and Islamic Quseir al-Qadim. The desiccated specimens, flattened on the sides with distinctive longitudinal ridges, vary from 4.44 to 6.8 mm. in length and 3.2 to 9.9 mm. in width.

Acacia

The acacia (*Acacia nilotica*), one of Egypt's most common trees, is an important source of fuel and building material. The foliage, green pods, and seeds are valuable fodder for livestock (El Hadidi and Boulos, 1979: 8). The pods and bark, rich in tanin, are used to tan leather (Duke, 1981: 9), while the flowers and pods are esteemed for their medicinal properties in Egyptian folk medicine (Osborn, 1968: 173).

The Quseir al-Qadim specimens, all from the Islamic occupation, include a desiccated pod fragment and several desiccated and charred seeds. The latter are flattened, ellipsoid, with an ellipse etched on the dorsal surface. The desiccated specimens range from 5.2 to 7.3 mm. in length and 4.0 to 5.6 mm. in width.

Discussion and Conclusions

Lying between a salt sea and an arid desert, the village of Quseir al-Qadim was poorly situated for satisfying the inhabitants's needs for food, fuel, fodder, and construction material. The bulk of the resources clearly had to be imported although some plants might have been collected or even raised locally. The wadis, flowing from the Red Sea hills into the Red Sea, probably abounded in tamarisk and rushes, both of which are common today, tolerate saline conditions, and offer fuel and building material. After winter rains in the Red Sea hills, weedy annuals probably sprang up in the wadis and low areas, providing some grazing for animals. Inland, the wadis probably offered acacias, palms, and other vegetation.

At the ancient village some palms and possibly Christ's thorn trees may have been planted, as they have been in the modern village. A few small kitchen gardens might have been tended as well, but with the scarce water supply, their numbers must have been very small.

Indeed, the archaeological record reflects an economy almost entirely dependent on imports. The middens contained no field weeds or the large quantities of chaff that are so abundant in the archaeological remains of agricultural villages. The grains and associated debris at Quseir are as clean as the grains found in markets today; a few rachis fragments are scattered here and there among the grains. In addition, nearly all of the remaining plants are foods that could have been dried, shipped, and stored for long periods, such as raisins, dates, *libb* seeds, nuts, beans, coriander, and pepper. Moreover, it appears that the plants were stored in order to last for many months. The grains, fenugreek, safflower, and coriander were all stored whole and apparently ground or pressed as needed. In this form they would have had the longest "shelf life." Likewise, flax was apparently transported in its fruit capsules, at least during the Roman period, and later pressed for oil or cooked in porridge. During Roman times, pine nuts were even imported in their cones.

On the basis of historic records, one would suspect that the staples were the grains along with the legumes. The archaeological record certainly suggests that this was the case at Quseir al-Qadim, but because of differential preservation the quantitative plant data has to be viewed with caution. In addition, some of the grains are clearly traces of animal fodder rather than the remnants of human meals.

Safflower, and possibly olives, was apparently used for cooking oil; while coriander and pepper seasoned the meals. The latter are almost certainly abundant in the Islamic deposits because of Quseir al-Qadim's role as a port. Dried fruits and nuts probably provided variety in the diet, while some perishable items, such as greens, may have been eaten but failed to leave any traces in the archaeological record.

Yet, even with added greens, these plant foods combined with sheep and goat meat and fish were probably a monotonous diet, short on the trace elements and vitamins that are usually obtained from fresh fruits and vegetables. As a result, the permanent residents of Quseir al-Qadim may have paid for their life at this port with a variety of deficiency diseases not seen among the Nile valley inhabitants.

Quseir al-Qadim's inhabitants and the traders and pilgrims who crossed the Eastern Desert were faced with a special challenge in trying to feed their pack animals and livestock destined for butchering. Some grazing was probably found in the wadis, as suggested above, but large shares of fodder came from wheat and barley and probably bitter vetch. Most of the charred barley and wheat grains in an Islamic pot hearth came from camel dung which had been used as fuel. The dung specimens which had not yet disintegrated were packed with grains. These might have come primarily from inferior crops since they subjectively appeared smaller than other charred grains from the site. However, this cannot be verified until the grains are measured and statistically analyzed.

Although sorghum is an important animal feed today, it was apparently not used as fodder at Quseir al-Qadim; at least, no sorghum was found in the animal dung examined. Wild plants, such as acacia and zilla, probably provided some grazing while the animals travelled.

Animal dung, as indicated above, supplied some of Quseir al-Qadim's fuel, with camel excrement providing a substantial share of it during the Islamic period. The Roman inhabitants apparently used some sheep and goat dung but the hearths that were tested were filled almost entirely with charcoal, which has not yet been identified. Perhaps vegetation was slightly more abundant during the Roman occupation. Local scrub vegetation, such as zilla, was almost certainly used as kindling.

During both occupations, the inhabitants faced similar problems in satisfying their needs and seem to have solved them in similar fashion. The apparent differences between the two periods are surprisingly few, but they reflect some major economic changes. Throughout both periods, the staples of the Nile valley, grains and legumes, supplied the bulk of the diet. By the Mamluk period, sorghum had apparently become popular and may have been used with wheat and barley in breads and porridges. Condiments and treats of the Mediterranean world, including olives, pine nuts, hazelnuts, and walnuts, which were common at other Egyptian Graeco-Roman sites were imported to Quseir al-Qadim as well. They probably did not make a significant contribution to the diet, but they may have been symbolically important in establishing the community as a Roman settlement. Moreover, they probably indicate the presence of Roman administrators, if not a Roman populace. By the Mamluk period, the condiments and treats are primarily products of the Nile valley. The few "exotics," such as pepper and coconut, reflect Quseir al-Qadim's role in the trade with Southeast Asia.

This preliminary survey of Quseir al-Qadim's plant remains indicates that the collection can yield a wealth of information about the inhabitant's diet and can offer insights into their subsistence practices, economy, and environment. Work planned for the future will explore each of these areas further by examining the materials that have not yet been analyzed, including the wood and charcoal, and items to be excavated in 1982, and through more detailed studies of the plant remains.

Bibliography for Plant Remains

Bailey, C., and A. Danin
    1981   "Bedouin Plant Utilization in Sinai and the Negev," *Economic Botany* 35 (2): 145-62

Brouk, B.
    1975   *Plants Consumed by Man*

Brown, T. W., and M. Bohgot
    1938   "Date Palm in Egypt," Ministry of Agriculture, Egypt, Booklet No. 24

Caton-Thompson, G., and E. W. Gardner
    1934   *The Desert Fayum*

Darby, W., P. Ghalioungui, and L. Grivetti
    1977   *Food: The Gift of Osiris*

Duke, J.
    1981   *Handbook of Legumes of World Economic Importance*

El Hadidi, N. B., and L. Boulos
    1979   *Street Trees of Cairo*

Girgis, A.
    1924-25   "Garlic Cultivation in Nigeita," *Agricultural Journal of Egypt* New Series: pp. 47-50

Meyer, F. G.
    1980   "Carbonized Food Plants of Pompeii, Herculaneum, and the Villa at Torre Annunziata," *Economic Botany* 34 (4): 401-37

Osborn, D. J.
    1968   "Notes on Medicinal and Other Uses of Plants in Egypt," *Economic Botany* 22: 165-77

Renfrew, J. M.
 1973 *Paleoethnobotany*

Täckholm, V.
 1961 "Botanical Identification of the Plants Found at the Monastery of Phoebammon," in *Le Monastere de Phoebammon dans le Thebaide Tombe III. Publications de la Société d'Archéologie Copte. Rapport de Fouille.* pp. 1-38
 1974 *Student's Flora of Egypt*

Täckholm, V., and M. Drar
 1950 *Flora of Egypt*, vol. 2

Täckholm, V., G. Täckholm, and M. Drar
 1941 *Flora of Egypt*, vol. 1

van Zeist, W.
 1976 "On Macroscopic Traces of Food Plants in Southwestern Asia (with some reference to pollen data)," *Philosophical Transactions of the Royal Society, London Bulletin* 275: 25-41

Wetterstrom, W.
 in press "Paleoethnobotanical Studies at Predynastic Sites in the Nagada-Khattara Region," in *Predynastic Studies in the Nagada-Khattara Region of Upper Egypt,* F. A. Hassan, ed.

Zohary, D., and M. Hopf
 1973 "Domestication of Pulses in the Old World," *Science* 182 (4115): 887-94

CHAPTER 18: MARINE INVERTEBRATES
David S. Reese

During the course of excavations at the Roman and Ayyubid-Mamluk Islamic Red Sea harbor site of Quseir al-Qadim over 1000 marine invertebrates (shells, sea urchins and coral) were uncovered. Most of these were made available to the author for analysis in Cambridge, England, and New York, except for a sample retained in Egypt by the Egyptian Museum.

The material discussed here is grouped into two broad periods, Roman and Islamic, to see if there are any general differences in marine invertebrate utilization between the two cultures. The final report will include both the 1982 material and material still in Egypt and will deal with the finer phasing and horizontal distribution of the marine invertebrates.

The list below records the species found in both Roman (25 deposits) and Islamic (16) deposits. The species are listed in order of frequency. [The figures in brackets are the percentage of the entire Roman or Islamic shell population the given species provides.]

Roman	Islamic	% Islamic	Species
121/4 [60]	22/3 shell/opercula [10]	17	*Turbo chrysostomus* Linnaeus, 1758 (Turban shell) *Turbo argyrostomus* Linnaeus, 1758 (Silver-mouthed turban, Turban shell)
6 [3]	45 [18.5]	88	*Nerita* spp. (Nerite shell)
2 [1]	16 [6.5]		*Cypraea* spp. (various species) (Cowries)
1 [.5]	13 [5]	89	*Cypraea tigris* Linnaeus, 1758 (Tiger cowrie)
1 [.5]	5 [2]		*Cypraea* (=*Monetaria*) *moneta* Linnaeus, 1758 (Money cowrie)
16 [7.5]	13 [5]	45	*Lambis truncata sebae* (Kiener, 1843) (Giant spider conch, Scorpion shell)
2 [1]	26 [10.5]	93	*Cerithium caeruleum* Sowerby, 1855 (small Cerith, Horn shell)
10 [5]	12 [5]	55	+*Tridacna squamosa* Lamarck, 1819 (Scaly or Fluted clam, Squamose giant clam) +*Tridacna maxima* (Röding, 1798) (Giant clam)
7 [3]	12 [5]	63	+*Pinctada margaritifera* (Linnaeus, 1758) (Black lip pearl oyster)
4 [2]	11 [4.5]	73	*Conus* spp. (various species) (Cone shell)

Roman	Islamic	% Islamic	Species
4 [2]	9 [4]	69	*Strombus gibberulus albus* (Morch, 1850) (Humped conch, Stromb)
1 [.5]	8 [3]	89	+*Chama* sp. (Jewel shell, Hoof shell)
4 [2]	4 [1.5]	50	*Tectus dentatus* (Forskal, 1775) (Top shell)
3 [1.5]	4 [1.5]	57	*Vasum turbinellus* (Linnaeus, 1758) (Vase shell)
1 [.5]	4 [1.5]	80	+*Anadara* (Gray, 1847) sp. (Ark shell)
2 [1]	1 [.5]		*Tonna* sp. (Tun shell, Cask shell)
1 [.5]	2 [1]		*Terebra* spp. (Auger shell)
1 [.5]	1 [.5]		*Nerita undata* Linnaeus, 1758 (large Nerite shell)
1 [.5]	1 [.5]		*Heterocentrotus mamillatus* (Linnaeus, 1758)
16	31		Others
208	243		
451			

gastropod
+bivalve (counts are of individuals, not valves)
*echinoid or sea urchin

Most of the *Turbo* shells and their calcareous opercula or "cat's eyes," 83%, come from Roman deposits [where they form 60% of the Roman shells while forming only 10% of Islamic shells] and are likely to be food remains. In fact, two of the Islamic *Turbo* shells are water-worn and were collected dead on the beach while all the Roman shells are "fresh." Some of these shells (and also *Cerithium*) are presently being analyzed by oxygen-isotope analysis (using a mass spectrometer) to determine season of collection; this work is being done through the kindness of Dr. N. J. Shackleton of the Sub-department of Quaternary Research at the University of Cambridge.

The majority of the *Nerita* spp. shells (88%) come from Islamic deposits [where they form 18.5% of the Islamic shells while forming only 3% of the Roman shells]. Of the six shells from five Roman deposits only one has a man-made hole for stringing; it comes from the test along the baulk and probably from land fill under the Roman villa (E6a-14, RN 346). There are 45 shells from six Islamic deposits, 28 of which are holed: 17 (11 holed) from E18d-12 (RN 346), 13 (8 holed) from E18d-13, 8 (6 holed) from E18d-14, 1 burnt and holed from E18d-15 and 5 (2 holed) from E18d-16.

The vast majority of all cowries (89%) come from Islamic deposits [where they account for 14% of Islamic shells while accounting for only 2% of Roman shells] and of special note are 10 very fresh *Cypraea tigris* Tiger cowries from a room with ash, sand and other organic debris (F19a-4, FN 4, RN 347).

Two of the Roman *Lambis* Spider conchs have been cut open horizontal to the axis of the shell, probably to remove the meat or to turn the shell into a vessel, or both. These shells grow very large; the largest in the collection is 184 mm. long. *Lambis* meat is today eaten in Sri Lanka and the Ellice Islands in the Central Pacific, either raw or roasted, and in some areas is considered an aphrodisiac. In Egypt it is eaten dried; it is called surumbak. One piece was found during the 1980 excavations (E18a-3, RN 275) (Whitcomb, pers. comm.).

Ninety-three percent (93%) of all *Cerithium caeruleum* come from Islamic deposits [where they account for 10.5% of the Islamic shells while accounting for only 1% of Roman shells] and many of these were collected already dead. *Tridacna* valves are evenly distributed between the periods and include small fragments to valves 225 mm. long and both water-worn and fresh shells. The fresh shells might be evidence for food; this meat is today eaten by the South Sea islanders and Malayans, and is sometimes dried.

Pinctada is slightly more common in the Islamic deposits and may have been eaten or collected for its pearls and Mother-of-pearl nacre. Carefully carved Chinese *Pinctada* are today commonly sold in Europe and America.

Conus are also more common in the Islamic and some have holes at the apex and might have been strung. One Islamic *Anadara* valve has marine growth inside and must have been collected already dead. Two *Terebra* shells have been cored by carnivorous gastropods and so were also collected dead.

A number of shells are found in Roman but not Islamic deposits, including 3 *Cerithium erythraeonense* Lamarck, 1822 (large Cerith or Horn shell), 2 *Charonia tritonis* Linnaeus, 1758 (Triton or Trumpet shell), 2 *Strombus fasciatus* Born, 1778 (True conch, Stromb), 2 *Olivia* sp. (Olive shell), 1 chiton and six other shells of five species.

Roman deposits of large size include 42 shells from the brown fill (possibly land fill) containing many sherds in the "anteroom" (E6b-30), including 35 *Turbo* (83% of deposit), 1 *Tectus* and the only 2 *Drupa* (Drupe) and 1 *Natica* (Moon or

Necklace shell) from the site. A surface layer with sand and caliche, brown fill and lots of sherds (E6a-9, RN 343) produced 32 shells including 26 *Turbo* (81%), 1 *Nerita*, 1 *Lambis*, 2 *Strombus*, 1 of the 2 *Strombus fasciatus* and 1 of the 2 *Olivia*.

One Roman deposit (E6b-49, RN 347), the hard yellow caliche and soft brown soil extending down to the floor of the storeroom, produced a 224 mm. long *Charonia* Trumpet shell (Pot A, FN 5) and also a *Tonna* Tun shell (under Pot H and Shell, FN 6) which is 107 mm. long. The only other *Charonia* shell, also Roman, comes from D6d-7 (RN 344), the lower fill in the cellar.

There are 31 shells from Islamic deposits not found in Roman levels, including 13 *Patella* (Limpets), 11 *Mytilus* (Mussels), 1 *Cypraea* (=*Monetaria*) *annulus* Linnaeus, 1758 (Money cowrie, Gold ringer) and 6 other shells of 5 species.

From the Islamic surface of E18d-12 (RN 346, over donkey dung) come 42 shells, including 4 *Turbo* (10%), 17 *Nerita* (40%; 11 holed), 6 cowries (14%), 1 *Lambis*, 4 *Cerithium* (10%), 2 *Conus*, 1 *Strombus*, 3 water-worn *Chama* and 5 *Mytilus* (12%). From below this stratum of dung and in a brown pebbly soil (E18d-13, RN 346) come 70 shells, including 2 *Turbo* shells and 1 operculum (4%), 13 *Nerita* (19%; 8 holed), 8 cowries (11%), 1 *Lambis*, 18 *Cerithium* (26%), 2 *Tridacna* (192 and 235 mm. long), 3 *Conus*, 3 *Strombus*, 2 *Anadara*, 4 *Patella* and 2 *Mytilus*. The *Lambis*, *Cerithium*, *Conus* and most of the cowries were collected dead.

A nearby open area with dark-brown fine soil and much organic material (E18d-14, RN 346) produced 23 shells, including 8 *Nerita* (35%; 6 holed), 4 cowries (17%) including the only *Cypraea annulus*, 1 *Lambis*, 1 *Tridacna*, 1 *Pinctada*, 1 *Tonna*, 1 *Terebra*, 2 *Patella*, 1 *Mytilus* and no *Turbo*. Outside the walls, the heavy organic trash with dark-brown soil, some ash and stakes set upright (E18d-18, RN 343) produced 30 shells, including 4 *Turbo* shells and 2 opercula (20%), 5 *Nerita* (17%; 2 holed), 1 cowrie, 2 *Lambis*, 2 *Cerithium*, 2 *Tridacna* (water-worn and 105 mm. and 164+ mm. long), 1 *Pinctada*, 2 *Conus*, 1 *Strombus*, 1 water-worn *Chama*, 1 *Patella* and 1 *Mytilus*.

There are three deposits and 19 shells from "possibly mixed" deposits which include 13 *Turbo*, 1 cowrie, 2 *Lambis*, 1 *Tridacna*, 1 *Tectus* and 1 *Vasum*. There are also five "mixed" deposits producing 468 shells. Most of these (429) come from the mixed surface debris of G8b-3 (RN 345), which includes 58 *Turbo* and 5 operculum, 297 small gastropods, 3 *Nerita* (1 holed), 32 *Cerithium*, 4 *Tridacna*, 1 *Anadara*, 1 *Cerithium erythraeonense*, 1 *Strombus fasciatus*, 3 *Mytilus*, 2 coral species, 2 sea urchin species, etc.

It seems that *Turbo* and possibly *Lambis* were food sources but only in the Roman period. A larger number of the Islamic shells are definite beach specimens than in the Roman deposits. *Tridacna* is found in both periods and might have been eaten or used as a vessel, as also possible for the cut-open *Lambis*, the Roman *Triton* and *Tonna*. The holed *Nerita* (almost all Islamic) and holed *Conus* were probably used as ornaments. The cowries (mainly Islamic) are obviously of some special significance, particularly the 10 Tiger cowries found in a cache, although they are not holed or otherwise modified.

All of the shells so far found at Quseir al-Qadim come from the Indo-Pacific province of marine fauna and flora. This area includes the Red Sea, the eastern shores of Africa, the Arabian Gulf, Indian Ocean and most of the Pacific Ocean, including the northern half of Australia and the southern half of Japan, and extends as far east as Hawaii. There are no Mediterranean shells in the collection and the shells are all most likely to have come from the local beach.

Red Sea/Indo-Pacific shells are certainly items of trade, and this is particularly evident when they are found outside of their natural environment. A few examples of this "trade" can be noted here. One *Cypraea moneta* with an open dorsum comes from Neolithic Suberde in southern Turkey (personal analysis), an unmodified shell comes from Late Chalcolithic Zambujal in Portugal (von den Driesch and Boessneck, 1976: Table 2, p. 104, pl. 8, #33) and *C. moneta* shells are known from Archaic Greek tombs at Salamis in eastern Cyprus (Demetropoulos, 1970: 301, 302, fig. 2).

A *Cypraea tigris* is known from a prehistoric pit-dwelling at St. Mary Bourne in Hants, Hampshire, England (Tomlin, 1912) and at least 2 *Cypraea pantherina* Lightfoot, 1786 (Panther cowrie) are known from various Saxon women's graves in Kent, England. From Pompeii in southern Italy come the Indo-Pacific *Conus textile* Linnaeus, 1758 (Textile cone), *Cypraea erosa*, *Cypraea pantherina*, *Cypraecassis rufa* Linnaeus, 1758 (Bull-mouth helmet shell) and *Pinctada margaritifera* (Damon, 1867; Tiberi, 1879). *Cypraea tigris* are also known from a 4th century B.C. cinerary urn and an 11th century (of the modern era) deposit at Otranto near Lecce in southern Italy (personal analysis) and from a 5th century (of the modern era) deposit at Carthage in Tunisia (personal analysis).

It is possible that some of the above shells, particularly those from Saxon England, Italy, and Tunisia, came from one of the Egyptian or Arabian Red Sea ports of which Quseir al-Qadim is a prime example.

Bibliography for Marine Invertebrates

Damon, R.
    1867   "Notes on a collection of Recent shells discovered among the ruins of Pompeii preserved in the Museo Barbonico at Naples," *Geological Magazine* 4 (7): 293ff.

Demetropoulos, A.
    1970   "Marine Molluscs, Land Snails, etc.," App. VI in V. Karageorghis, *Excavations in the Necropolis of Salamis*, Nicosia; pp. 299-305

Tiberi, N.
    1879   "Le conchiglie Pompeiane," *Bull. Soc. malac. Ital.* 5: 139ff.

Tomlin, J. R. le B.
    1912   "A Prehistoric *Cypraea tigris* L. in Hants," *Journal of Conchology* 13: 251-52

von den Driesch, A., and J. Boessneck
    1976   "Die Fauna vom Castro do Zambujal," in *Studien über frühe Tierknochenfunde von der Iberischen Halbinsel*, Munich, pp. 4-129

CHAPTER 19: CONSERVATION
Catharine Valentour

During the 1980 field season at Quseir al-Qadim, field conservation procedures were established for all objects removed from the site during excavation. A field laboratory was maintained and all objects were submitted to preliminary examination and subsequent treatment as required by individual artifacts. The quantity of material recovered limited most treatments to basic cleaning and stabilization for purposes of registration and transport. Outlines for treatment of objects by material were devised and objects which required more specialized attention were treated as such and documented.

All variety of materials were represented in the finds from Quseir al-Qadim. The climate of Quseir is arid, with high soil salinity due in part to the proximity of the sea as well as the regional rate of moisture evaporation exceeding the rate of precipitation in this desert environment. The environmental conditions and the lack of biological activity are responsible for the excellent state of preservation of much of the material, especially the organic remains. On the other hand, the metals, particularly the iron and copper alloys, showed extensive deterioration due to the corrosive effects of the soluble salts in the soil.

In preparation for the field season, the report on conservation for the 1978 season submitted by the conservator, Richard Jaeschke, was an invaluable guide for anticipating the nature of the material preservation. I have adopted many of Jaeschke's procedures which proved equally successful during the 1980 season.

As stated, all materials recovered from the site passed through the conservation laboratory except for the unworked faunal, floral, and mollusk remains, which were handled by specialists in those respective disciplines.

All conservation treatment implemented at Quseir al-Qadim were reversible procedures intended to provide stabilization of the artifacts until further, more extensive treatment could be undertaken in a complete conservation laboratory facility. It should be noted that there was no distilled water available at Quseir. The tap water used for washing was reclaimed sea water which retained a high chloride content. Therefore, any washing or soaking procedures did not effectively eliminate the presence of soluble salts in the artifacts. In providing a general summary of conservation procedures, the artifacts are discussed in view of their material composition.

Inorganic Materials

Stone

Worked stone artifacts, which included grinding stones and some bowl fragments, were in a good state of preservation. Although there was undoubtedly a high concentration of soluble salts, there was no recrystallization on the surfaces of these objects after excavation. All the stone objects were washed to remove surface dirt and light encrustations. One alabaster juglet with red surface pigment was not washed but was cleaned of loose surface dirt mechanically with a soft bristle brush.

Plaster

A large number of plaster amphora plugs were recovered, some of which had remains of red pigment. These were cleaned by light brushing under running tap water to loosen surface dirt. The plugs were allowed to dry completely before handling due to the softening action of the water on plaster.

Glass

Large amounts of glass fragments were excavated, particularly from the areas of Islamic occupation. The glass was generally in excellent condition exhibiting very little "onion-skinning" or iridescence. In all cases, the glass was washed using tap water and bristle brushes to remove surface dirt. The specimens were allowed to dry thoroughly before bagging.

Shell

The few objects of worked shell, primarily beads, were cleaned either by dry brushing or in some instances with cotton swabs and water. There were no preservation problems except with the fragments of ostrich shell which had a tendency to separate in layers.

Ceramics

As expected, the largest amount of material recovered was ceramic. All unpainted ceramics were treated in a similar manner, except the ostraca. All diagnostic sherds, partial and whole vessels were soaked in water and brushed with a stiff bristle brush to remove surface dirt and minimize soluble salts which had crystallized on the surface. In spite of the salinity of the tap water, in all cases the disfiguring surface crystals were successfully removed. After complete drying, partial or complete reconstruction of vessels and sherds was accomplished with Jade 403 and Jade 454 PVA emulsions. No attempt was made to deal with the extremely friable, salt degraded ceramics which required complete desalinization before possible impregnation. In these cases, surface dirt was removed by dry brushing. Ceramics which had remains of surface paint were also dry brushed to remove dirt accumulation.

For the ostraca, soaking of the sherds was avoided when possible since the inks were usually water soluble. The areas around the inscriptions were cleaned with cotton swabs and water. When surface salts obscured the inscriptions, the ink was coated with Acryloid B-72 in acetone and soaked to remove soluble salts. After drying, the temporary coating was removed with acetone.

Restoration of ceramics was limited to the joining of fragments where diagnostic information could be gained. In some cases, mended vessels were taken apart after drawing and photography to facilitate transport.

Metals

The range of metals represented in the finds from Quseir al-Qadim included silver, copper, lead and iron alloys. The treatment of metals was severely restricted to mechanical cleaning of surface dirt to delineate design elements on such items as rings and pins. This was accomplished with stiff bristle brushes, glass bristle brushes and scalpels.

The iron pieces were primarily nails and spikes which were kept dry but not treated. The same was true for the copper alloy nails and fragments. The few lead objects were brushed of surface dirt and kept dry.

Generally, the copper alloy coins were in poor condition due to the reaction of the copper with chloride compounds in the soil. Extremely thick layers of basic cupric chlorides and copper carbonates characterized many of the coins causing large cracks and actual "bursting" of the coins themselves. It was desirable to clean as many coins as possible in the field for identification purposes. Cleaning was usually begun by mechanical removal of loose encrustations and corrosion layers. If they were determined to be structurally sound and potentially identifiable, the coins were then placed in a 30% solution of formic acid to gradually strip away corrosion layers. For the Islamic coins, this method proved very satisfactory. The coins were rinsed with water, allowed to dry thoroughly and were coated with microcrystalline wax before further handling.

The Roman coins showed more extensive deterioration and the stripping process was more tedious and less successful. Due to the lack of distilled water, there was no possibility of chloride removal by soaking for any of the coins. Diagnostic coins were cleaned as much as possible, rinsed in water, dried, and coated with microcrystalline wax as well. Coins which did not prove retrievable in the field using the formic acid method were kept dry in storage, anticipating further laboratory treatment at a later date.

Organic Materials

The preservation of the organic material was very good due to the absence of biological activity in the arid environment. Most conservation problems were related to the dessication which had occurred.

Paper and Papyrus

The paper and papyrus, when removed from the ground, required flattening and some cleaning of dirt and salt encrustations. Most of all, fragments were inscribed with black ink which proved to be water soluble. After preliminary cleaning with a soft brush, the fragments were subjected to high humidity for a relatively short time (one half hour on the average) and then unfolded and dried between blotters under weights. Thymol was added to the water in the humidity chamber to prevent biological growth. After complete drying, the fragments were again lightly brushed to remove any loose surface dirt. All fragments were stored flat between blotters.

Textiles

After initial sorting, all the cloth was routinely soaked in water to remove soil. The cloth was then air-dried. Pieces of particular interest such as embroidery and identifiable articles of clothing were carefully rinsed in water baths and then dried on blotters after aligning fibers. A large number of hats were washed in this manner and then dried on forms to restore their original shape. All textiles were structurally very sound. The fibers were flexible and easily shaped after rinsing.

Wood

Objects made of wood were divided into groups of sample materials, architectural fragments and wooden objects. The samples were left as they came out of the ground and stored in polyethylene bags. The architectural fragments were cleaned of superficial dirt and encrustations and then bagged as well. Wooden objects were usually cleaned with cotton swabs and water which removed surface dirt and dissolved surface salt crystals. In some cases painted wood fragments needed consolidation of the paint layers. Microcrystalline wax was used to tack down the flaking paint. Extremely friable wood was impregnated when absolutely necessary for the lifting of these objects in the field. A 10% solution of Acryloid B-72 in xylene was brushed on the surface until no further penetration occurred in order to provide the necessary structural support and adhesion for moving the objects.

Bone and Ivory

Objects of worked bone and ivory required only light brushing to remove surface dirt.

Fibers and Leathers

Objects of fiber and leather were extremely dessicated but showed no evidence of biological decay. In most cases, dry brushing was sufficient to reveal details of design and manufacture. Cleaning with water-dampened swabs on some leather objects was necessary to reveal "tooling" designs which also made it possible to reshape some sandals and shoes.

Miscellaneous

There were some objects of organic and inorganic materials which could not be categorized using these general headings, including clumps of hair, geological samples, surumbak, etc. Again, light brushing was sufficient to remove surface dirt.

During the excavation, molds were made of the terra sigillata stamps and the coins. A latex liquid was used for the terra sigillata stamps and Coltene "President" Impression Compound (a polysiloxane material) was used for the coins. A latex impression was taken of fiber and wood architectural elements in the field to provide an illustration of roof construction in the Roman occupation area.

After conservation, all objects were stored in polyethylene bags and were accompanied by a record card describing field information and conservation reports particular to each object. After registration, drawing and photography, the objects were packed according to material and fragility for transport to Cairo.

CHAPTER 20: BIR KAREIM
Donald Whitcomb

The site of Bir Kareim was first surveyed and reported by Prickett (1979: 300-4). Following Prickett's analysis, it was recognized that this site holds a potential importance for the understanding of Quseir al-Qadim. Based on the ceramics (Prickett, 1979: pl. 86-87), the contemporaneity of Bir Kareim with the Roman occupation at Quseir al-Qadim poses certain questions concerning the interaction of the port with this mining encampment and hydreuma. The wells of Bir Kareim are one of the most likely sources for fresh water for the port during Roman times, although perhaps not the only one. It is difficult to determine whether this vital commodity for the completely waterless port was the prime factor for the settlement at Bir Kareim or whether, on the other hand, the mining operations, which would have influenced the long term economic development of the port, provided the original impulse. The exploitation of mineral resources, outlined in detail by Prickett (1979: 265-70), may have represented for the Roman port an economic function equal to, or greater than, the maritime trade. A third aspect of the settlement at Bir Kareim is its situation on a route parallel to and south of the Wadi Hammamat connecting the Nile valley with the coast (via the Wadi Qash; see Pricket, 1979: 304). This connecting route may represent an important alternative to the Wadi Hammamat route, should it be well-watered the full length. (The 1982 season will begin the survey of this route along the Wadi Qash.)

The second season at Quseir al-Qadim had intended to map Bir Kareim carefully and to begin limited excavations there. Unfortunately, the excavations at the ancient port combined with the inaccessibility of Bir Kareim (the heavy winter rains, which provided such a boon for our botanist, had wiped away the roads leading inland) limited the work here to a brief visit. The importance of the site for the understanding of Quseir al-Qadim justifies including this information which, although still superficial in detail, may prove of some significance in the comparison of such mining sites in the eastern desert.

The flooding of the wadis, which wiped out the roads and inhibited our access, was also a factor in the organization of the settlement at Bir Kareim. The surviving architectural remains are ranged along the edges of the wadi away from the *sail* or flood bed. On the southern side of the wadi, building complexes are nestled around small outcrops (*qurns*), presumably for protection against flooding or as defense; see pl. 73 and fig. 23. It was in one of these outcrops (51d) that a small mine shaft was found (Prickett, 1979: fig. 33). The southern building

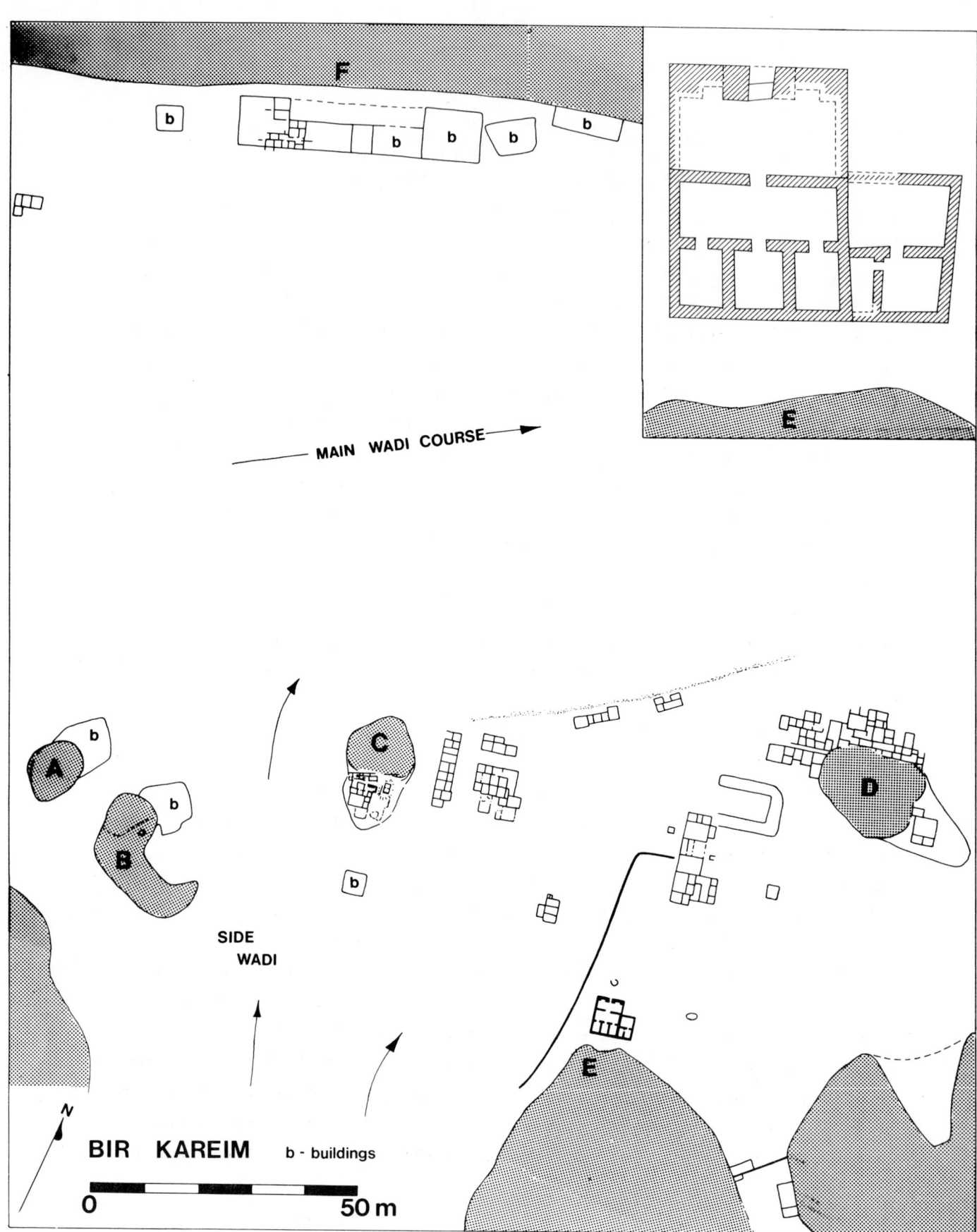

Plate 73: Bir Kareim

complexes were separated from one another by the mouth of a tributary wadi which, while small, still necessitated some channelling to avoid the buildings.

Fig. 23: Looking South at Houses Built up against *Qurn* in Area A, Bir Kareim

The building complexes associated with the outcrops on the south side of the wadi make use of the sheer sides of the stone and of natural boulders for walls. All walling is made of local stone originally set with a mud mortar. The complex on the south slope and top of area C (see pl. 73) is typical: Rectangular rooms vary from small storerooms to larger living areas. Passages climbing up the rock lead to more rooms and two small guard rooms(?) at the summit. The architectural remains on the slopes of areas A and B are similar (they were not drawn). East of hillock C is a building complex composed of rows of rectangular rooms separated by a broad street, oriented north-south, and a second street perpendicular to this. The impression is a barracks-like area, as one might expect in a workmen's village planned by a governmental authority. The precise relationship of these rooms, as elsewhere on the site, is difficult to determine due to the tumbled nature of the debris. Also, it is possible that further units existed to the south which have been covered with sediment from the tributary wadi. Two isolated complexes of four or five rooms were situated south and southeast of area C. Between hillocks C and D are rooms arranged along the present bank of the floodbed; these buildings differ from the orientation of most of the other southern buildings in departing from an almost exact orientation with the cardinal compass points.

The easternmost hillock is area D, which is composed of a similar set of buildings nestled around the slopes of the outcrop. The majority are on the north and west sides, exhibiting the same orientation as those of area C and with one narrow street or alley running east-west. South of these buildings is a large open area where a rectangular basin has been excavated and the earth piled on its sloping sides; while the orientation of this basin coincides with that of the structures around it, the excavation is somewhat similar to disturbances at the hydreuma of Nakheil (QRS-16, Prickett, 1979: 305-10) by modern Italian engineers.

South of the basin is a row of buildings along a north-south axis; these front a long narrow terrace which leads toward the temple (area E; QRS-51b). It is tempting to see this terrace as a ramp or processional way before the temple, as Prickett has suggested. Unfortunately, the section cut by the wadi on the western edge of the terrace shows no sign of artificial construction, so this suggestion must remain open to question. Within the wadi opposite the terrace are the disturbed remnants of a building (QRS-51c).

The temple at Bir Kareim was first identified by Prickett (1979: 301). The building is constructed of angular stone, undressed and set in a mud mortar; but, unlike the other buildings, a purple-red stone was used exclusively in this building. The temple itself has two courts and three cellas against the rear wall; see pl. 73. The front wall of the first court seems to have been constructed as four pilasters with possible curtain walls between them. The entrance rises two or three steps to the first court, with curtain walls on either side. The second court is marked by a thin wall; bonding of this wall strongly suggests that the first court is a later addition.

The second court is a long, transverse room giving access through three doors to the cellas of the temple. The central cella was cleared of some of the fallen stone. The rear wall had a bench running its length. Several small fragments of carved stone were found and subsequently joined to form part of an uraeus and sun disk; see pl. 72. This would have surmounted the naos of this cella. On the east side of the temple were three rooms, presumably priests' or servants' quarters. They were built of a lighter, pinkish stone. See fig. 24.

The temple, situated near a prominent talus of the mountain, is modest, but served as a focus for this community of miners, the two major concentrations of settlement flanking the ground before it. Opposite the temple and building complexes, along the northern bank of the wadi, were remains of further buildings (F).

Most notable among these was a series of rooms flanking two large enclosed courts, suggesting a possible stable area. The small interconnected rooms on either side suggest storage facilities, the whole perhaps functioning as a *khan* or way-station.

Fig. 24: Temple at Bir Kareim, Looking North from behind Temple with Cellas in Foreground, Priests' Quarters(?) to Right

The investigation of Bir Kareim is far from complete and the above outline is intended as a preliminary sketch. This site as an example of Roman mining operations in the eastern desert invites comparisons with the well known, and much larger, facilities at Mons Claudianus and Mons Porphyrites (Murray, 1925). This aspect, as well as its importance to the functioning of the Roman port at Quseir al-Qadim and its connections with the Nile valley, will be explored during the coming season.

Bibliography for Bir Kareim

Prickett, M.
  1979   "Quseir Regional Survey," in D. Whitcomb and J. H. Johnson, *Quseir al-Qadim 1978: Preliminary Report*, Cairo, pp. 257-352

Murray, G. W.
  1925   "The Roman Roads and Stations in the Eastern Desert of Egypt," *JEA* 11: 138-50

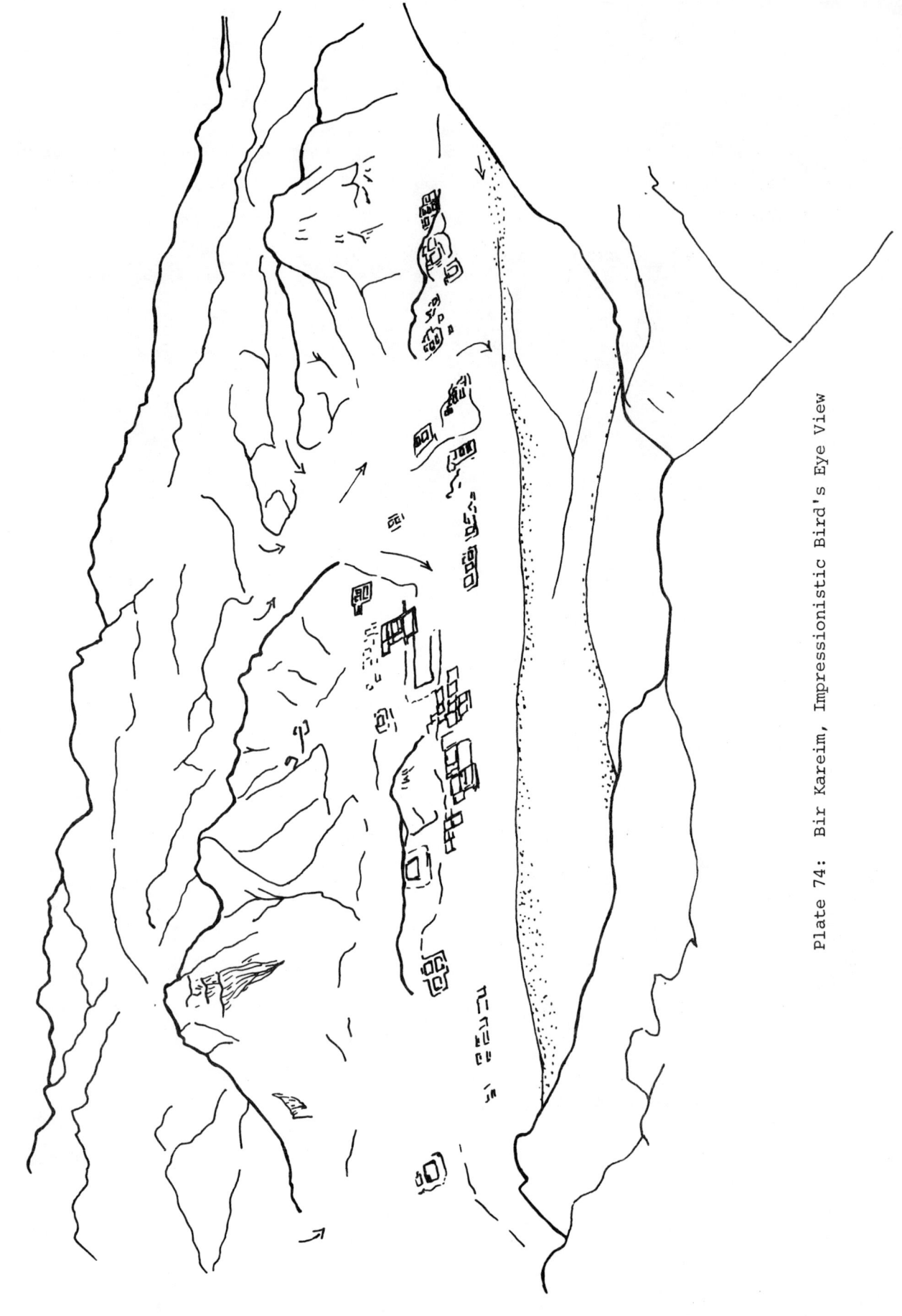

Plate 74: Bir Kareim, Impressionistic Bird's Eye View

CHAPTER 21:
NOTES ON SOME OF THE OLD MOSQUES IN QUSEIR
Haini el-Zeini
Introduction

An investigation into the history of the oldest mosques in Quseir revealed some interesting features about them which are quite distinct from the usually modest mosques in the villages in the Nile valley. There are, however, many points of similarity in the architectural features of these old mosques in Quseir and the old mosques (*masjids*) often found in the towns on either side of the Red Sea. These *masjids* are usually square, measuring approximately 4.5x4.5 m., and contain the burial of a Sheikh. The domes of the mosques contain two rows of protruding bricks, probably for decorative purposes.

Reverence for religious people by both Muslims and Christians has been the rule in Egypt. It is practically impossible to find any village or small town in Egypt without at least one Sheikh's tomb. Coptic churches dedicated to early Christian saints are not uncommon, particularly in Upper Egypt. But what struck the writer as a particularly unusual feature in Quseir is the fact that the oldest and most revered *masjids* were those of non-Egyptian Sheikhs. This is very unusual outside of Cairo where, after the growth of al-Azhar, many learned *ulemas* from all over the Arab and Muslim world came to settle (Petry, 1980).

The six most important mosques in Quseir bore the names of Sheikhs from six different countries: Sheikh el-Zilaii was from Somalia, Sheikh el-Farran was from Saudi Arabia, Sheikh Abd el-Ghaffar was a Yemeni, Sheikhs Abdullah el-Hindi and Abd el-Qadr el-Jilani were Indians, Sheikh Mohammed el-Fassi came from Fez, Morocco, and Sheikh el-Tikruni (originally el-Tikruri) came from Tikrur, the West African kingdom of which Timbuktu was the capital.

Unfortunately, the city council of Quseir does not contain any documentation concerning the history of these mosques. The scanty information obtained from the Department of *Waqf*'s in the Governorate of the Red Sea in Hurghada confirmed the data supplied by long talks with five elderly men in Quseir.[1] Agreement among the five on descriptions and dates, as well as historical background, lends credence to their accounts.

---

[1] The five men are Sheikh Mohammed Saleh, Mohammed Ahmed (Abu Ntifa), Mohammed Sibak, Hassan el-Tuty, and Mobarak Khalil. Their ages, calculated in relation to the revolt of General Ahmed Orabi against Khedive Tewfik, which culminated in the British occupation of Egypt in 1882, vary between 85 and 103 years.

The western entrance to the mosque bears a wooden lintel bearing the Koranic[1] inscription سلام عليكم بما صبرتم فنعم عقبى الدار ۱۱۲٦
It is dated 1126 *Hijri* (1714), either the date of the burial of Sheikh el-Farran or the date of the erection of this doorway. The inscription is bounded on each end by the decoration shown in fig. 25, which the writer has not seen in any other Egyptian mosque. On the wall, just above the wooden lintel, there are two square

Fig. 25: Decoration of Door Lintel of Mosque of Sheikh el-Farran

depressions approximately 60x50 cm. in which a decorative motif, including, perhaps, verses from the Koran, were originally embedded.

The minaret, still in a fairly good state of preservation, is approximately 10 m. high. It is hexagonal in shape and probably built of wattle and daub around a central nucleus which is actually a supporting column having the shape of an irregular half circle. The diameter of the minaret is approximately 2.5 m.; the minaret is serviced from inside by a rather steep spiral staircase of irregular steps. The height of the wooden steps varies between 20 and 30 cm. The lower courses are made of palm tree trunks while the upper courses are made of another wood, probably acacia. The wooden pieces are embedded both in the central column, which is approximately 90 cm. in diameter, and in the wall of the minaret itself. Both the steps and the minaret are covered with a layer of gypsum or plaster or a mixture of sand and slaked lime. Both are painted white.

The minaret has three light holes measuring 90x150 cm., two on the eastern side and one on the western side. These three light holes admit enough daylight to enable the *muezzin* to climb to the balcony of the minaret. The narrow balcony itself is made of wood. The upper part of the minaret towering over the *muezzin*'s balcony is unusual. Although it follows the hexagonal pattern of the lower part of the minaret, yet its sides are hollow, perhaps for decorative purposes or in order to reduce the weight of the upper half of the minaret.

The family of Sheikh el-Farran is now in Saudi Arabia; they are helping finance renovations and enlargements to this mosque.

---

[1] Sura 13, Verse 24; Peace be with you for you have been patient; your reward will be good in the Other House.

El-Zilaii Mosque

All five informants agreed that the Zilaii mosque was the oldest and most frequented *masjid* in Quseir until the middle of the last century. Very little remains of this originally very large mosque which was rectangular in shape, measuring approximately 40x60 m. The minaret has disappeared as well as most of the mud brick walls with the exception of part of the eastern wall where the *qibla* is still visible. The *qibla* still includes two large limestone blocks evidently taken from an older building or temple. The writer was told that when excavation was done early in this century, column bases were found and a few inscribed blocks were "taken away." It is said that this mosque was built on the ruins of a Roman temple. A large concrete house has recently been built in the western part of the *masjid*; the Antiquities Inspectorate in Qena has ordered that no further building be erected on the site pending further investigation.

The full name of the Sheikh was Zilaii Ibn Ahmed. His name is that of Zilah (Zilai), a small old port north of Berbera in Somalia. Both these towns were under Egyptian occupation during Mamluk times and also during the early reign of the Mohammed Aly dynasty. It is said of Sheikh Zilaii that he came from a long line of Somalis that lived in Quseir for a long time. No trace of the family could be found in any official document, but the elderly informants confirmed that their grandfathers used to tell them the mosque was already very old when they were in their boyhood (18th century).

El-Farran Mosque

Sheikh el-Farran was a patron saint to Muslim sailors all over the Red Sea. Before a ship set sail, the crew members would pray in his mosque asking for a safe voyage; prayers were also offered immediately on arrival at the port of Quseir. Since ships usually made the voyage either in pairs or in a small flotilla of several ships, for reasons of safety and mutual assistance in case of trouble or navigational difficulties, often the outgoing crews would all perform their prayers together in the mosque. Likewise, often there would be a collective prayer as a token of thanksgiving for the crews of incoming ships.

Of the originally very large mosque there remains only the minaret and part of the courtyard not exceeding 8x12 m. There used to be stepping stones inside the sea over which one could walk to the mosque from the southern side. This would confirm the tradition that the original area of the mosque actually extended to the tongue of dry land now occupied by the condenser station of the phosphate company.

Abd el-Ghaffar Mosque

This mosque is the only one among the six oldest mosques that still occupies a prominent and conspicuous place in modern Quseir. It faces the fort on the eastern side of the main road of the town. No prayers are currently held in this mosque, whose large courtyard is now used solely as a sort of town hall for funerary ceremonies. Of all the old mosques of Quseir, Sheikh Abd el-Ghaffar's was the only one chosen by any of the Governors of (the fort of) Quseir as their burial place, perhaps because of its closeness to the Quseir fort. Sheikh Abd el-Ghaffar was of Yemeni origin. He must have settled in Quseir well before the reign of Mohammed Aly. The tomb itself does not contain any indication of the date of his burial. While trying to find any inscriptions or stelae fixed to the tomb to indicate the date of death, as is customary in Muslim burials, the writer found, reclining against the tomb itself and hidden by the covering *kisswa* (curtain or covering cloth), two marble stelae written in Arabic and a piece of marble with decoration, probably part of a larger decorative motif in stone covering either a fountain or a reception hall. On the eastern wall of the mosque there was a third stela, in Turkish, also made of marble and fixed to what looked like a raised floor or platform stretching from the eastern to the western wall of the mosque. It was said that this raised floor used to have a marble fountain. Beside the Turkish stela, and also fixed to the ground, was a fourth, smaller marble stela whose surface was regularly hacked off beyond recognition.

Each Arabic stela memorializes a follower of Hussein Agha, Governor of (the fort of) Quseir, who died within about one month of one another in 1257 *Hijri* (1841), during the rule of Ibrahim Pasha, son of Mohammed Aly. The first stela (fig. 26) can be translated as follows:

> He (the Lord God) is the Creater, the Everlasting One
> This is the tomb of the forgiven Mohammed
> son of Hasan Jawūsh
> Follower of Husein Aghā
> Governor of the town of Quseir
> Died on the 22nd of Rabi^c the Second 1257.
> [Say a] prayer for his soul!

The last line is in Turkish. The top of the second stela (fig. 27) is missing; the preserved portion can be translated as follows:

> son of Rustum Effendi
> Follower of Husein Aghā
> Governor of the town of Quseir
> 19th of Rabi^c the First 1257.
> [Say a] prayer for his soul!

As with the first stela, the last line of this stela is in Turkish.

Fig. 26: Stela Found in Abd el-Ghaffar Mosque

Fig. 27: Stela Found in Abd el-Ghaffar Mosque

The deaths of the two followers of Hussein Agha, Governor of Quseir, within such a short period of time suggests violent deaths, perhaps resulting from an attack by Wahabi pirates, or an epidemic, but such suggestions must remain speculation in the absence of any written documents.

There is no date on the third stela, which is written in Turkish; see fig. 28. It may be translated as follows (translation by R. L. Chambers):

God is Eternal.
[Say a] prayer for the soul of the late (and pardoned)
el-Haj Ahmet Agha, the father of Mahmud Efendi of Istanbul
(who is) still Governor of (the fort) of Quseir!

$$
\begin{array}{c}
\text{هو الباقى} \\
\text{حالا قصير محافظ} \\
\text{استانه عليه لى محمود} \\
\text{أفندى ينك بدرلرى} \\
\text{مرحوم و مغفور} \\
\text{الحاج أحمد أغانك} \\
\text{روحيجون فاتحه}
\end{array}
$$

Fig. 28: Text of the Third Stela Found in the Mosque of Abd el-Ghaffar

The decorative plate of marble found near the Arabic stelae is actually composed of two pieces which fit into one another. Like the inscriptions on the stelae, the decorations are in raised relief; they are formed of decorative foliage and plant buds. The motif of the decoration resembles those found in Qasr el-Gawhara, the palace of Mohammed Aly in the Citadel in Cairo. Further examination is needed.

Where did the marble of the stelae and the decorative piece come from? The marble has a greenish tinge. The inscriptions are made by the expert hand of a skilled artisan. Were the marbles carved in Quseir? It seems more likely that the pieces were worked in Cairo, or elsewhere in the Nile valley, and brought to Quseir.

Abdullah el-Hindi Mosque

Like most of the other mosques in the town, this is a very modest shrine of approximately 4.5x4.5 m. It stands to the north of Quseir's secondary school. The contents of this shrine and the shape of the *maqam* make it a very unusual tomb. The walls are decorated in paintings of unusual motifs which appear to be neither Egyptian nor Arabic. The northern wall is painted in colored squares and trees drawn in a rather sketchy hand. Hanging on the eastern wall is a small model of a wooden boat about 60 cm. long by 15 cm. high. The hull is painted in black and white. Hanging beside the boat is the dried front part of a sawfish; the saw itself is about 180 cm. long. The tomb, covered by a wooden scaffolding to support the *kisswa*, is of a very unusual design. The woodwork on the eastern part of the tomb is of non-Egyptian design. There is an enormous candle of an elongated conical shape supported by an iron tripod just fitting into its bottom. The candle is about 60 cm. in length, about 10 cm. in diameter at the bottom and 8 cm. at the top; it is of a dark yellowish color, suggesting that it could be made of yellow beeswax. An incense burner, a candle stand, a broken pilgrim flask, and a rectangular pottery vessel shaped like a modern mini-jerrycan complete the extraordinary outfit found in this unusual shrine.

Among the paintings on the western wall are two sketchy stars similar to painted or cast bronze ones seen by the writer in some temples in northern India and Nepal. On the northwestern corner of the wall, facing north, is an inscription written in a hardly legible handwriting (see fig. 29), which can be translated as follows:

> This is the shrine of Sheikh Abdullah the Indian. May God have mercy on him. On the 10th of JA [Jumāda] 1260 [1844] Monday.

Fig. 29: Corner of the Mosque of Sheikh Abdullah el-Hindi

Until very recently, Indian or Pakistani Muslims used to visit this shrine as well as the other Indian shrine, that of Sheikh Abd el-Qadr el-Jilani, which is on the seashore near the mosque of Sheikh el-Farran. This shrine of Sheikh Abd el-Qadr el-Jilani is very simple, bearing no inscrption indicating the date of his burial. His descendants who still live in Quseir have confirmed his Indian origin. The adjacent shrine to the south bears the inscription: "This is the tomb of Sidi Abu el-Hassan el-Shazly." Sidi Abu el-Hassan el-Shazly, one of the most popular Sufis in all the Arab world, is known to be buried in Wadi Hemeithra, in the eastern desert almost 250 km. to the southwest of Quseir. His mosque is visited by thousands of his followers every year, especially at *Kourban Bairam*. Is the Quseir shrine a cenotaph? Although such a tradition is common among Shiite sects, it is entirely unknown to the Sunnis, and the attribution of the Quseir tomb must remain dubious.

El-Fassy Mosque

This is a very modest, out-of-the-way shrine topped, like the others, by a dome decorated by two lines of protruding bricks whose purpose is possibly decorative. The shrine contains a very simple burial; it has been rebuilt in recent times by a family named el-Ghazali who claim to be direct descendants of this Sheikh. The name is very frequently mispronounced el-Farsi "the Persian." The head of the family told the writer that el-Fassy was of Moroccan origin and born in the well-known town of Fass not very far from Meknas in the Maghreb. The wooden door lintel of the old shrine is kept by the family in Abnud, about 15 km. south of Qena. It apparently contains the date of the burial, said to be in Mamluk times.

El-Tikruni Mosque

Very few indeed are the remains of this once very important shrine. The name of the Sheikh would originally have been el-Tikrury. He is said to have been a Sudanese, but he must have come from the well-known kingdom of Tikrur, a flourishing and advanced West African civilization. The capital of the Kingdom of Tikrur was Timbuktu, which flourished from the 16th into the 18th century, before European colonization. Timbuktu was the largest city south of the Sahara and was the capital of a vast kingdom that included the republics of Mali, Niger, and parts of other West African states situated on the western and southwestern frontiers of the present Republic of Sudan.

In these areas Islam had penetrated as a result of Arab merchants and missionaries, not through armed conquest. In the western part of Cairo there is a section still named Boulaq el-Dakrur, originally Boulaq el-Tikrur. It is reputed to have been the resting place of Tikruri pilgrims following the long and strenuous journey across the African Sahara before setting out on the final leg of their trip to Mecca. The people of Quseir still feast for Sheikh el-Tikruri (or el-Tikruni) on the first day of *Kourban Bairam*.

Conclusions

The writer is quite aware of the shortcomings of data not related to written or official documents. However, great care has been taken to screen irrelevant data and the exaggerated traditional stories told about "Men of God." Only the information upon which all the informants unanimously agreed has been accepted. The inscriptions, dates, and contents of the mosques combined with the verbal tradition handed down by these informants show clearly that Quseir was an important town of a rather cosmopolitan character in which many non-Egyptians of Muslim faith could settle. The shrines belonging to people from West Africa, the Maghreb, and Somalia may reflect the insecurity of the northern pilgrim route across Sinai and North Arabia down to Mecca. Under good conditions, and with the favorable and usually prevailing northwestern wind, one can sail from Quseir to Saudi Arabia in less than 12 hours. Many pilgrims apparently preferred this route to the land one (and see the inscription left by one pilgrim on a rock face near Quseir al-Qadim in 755 *Hijri* [1354], Whitcomb and Johnson, 1979: 249).

The presence of the Saudi, Yemeni, and Indian Sheikhs may reflect Quseir's role in international trade. The old informant who had been a sailor can remember when grain was shipped through Quseir to Saudi Arabia and the ships came back loaded with camels, dry dates, and a wild desert weed that was used, after drying, to make baskets. From Somalia ships brought incense, chewing gum, ginger, and cardamom. From Sudanese ports like Suwaken and Port Sudan, ships came back with habaque (a dried yellowish date), dom, sesame, peanuts, and, occasionally, Abu Amari (a special type of tobacco probably coming from Rhodesia). Nutmeg and clover were brought occasionally from Zanzibar.

Thus, like Quseir al-Qadim, where remnants of an old, active trade have been found, New Quseir remained a somewhat cosmopolitan town despite its small size until the opening of the Suez Canal and the growth of Suez as the major Egyptian port on the Red Sea.

Bibliography for Old Mosques

Petry, C.
   1980   "Geographic Origins of Academicians in Cairo during the Fifteenth Century," and "Geographic Origins of Religious Functionaries in Cairo during the Fifteenth Century," *JESHO* 23: 119-41, 240-64

Whitcomb, D., and J. H. Johnson
   1979   *Quseir al-Qadim 1978: Preliminary Report*, Cairo